Prose Merlin

Middle English Texts

General Editor

Russell A. Peck
University of Rochester

Associate Editor

Alan Lupack
University of Rochester

Advisory Board

Rita Copeland
University of Minnesota

Thomas G. Hahn
University of Rochester

Lisa Kiser
Ohio State University

Thomas Seiler
Western Michigan University

R. A. Shoaf
University of Florida

Bonnie Wheeler
Southern Methodist University

The Middle English Texts Series is designed for classroom use. Its goal is to make available to teachers and students texts which occupy an important place in the literary and cultural canon but which have not been readily available in student editions. The series does not include those authors such as Chaucer, Langland, or Malory, whose English works are normally in print in good student editions. The focus is, instead, upon Middle English literature adjacent to those authors that teachers need in compiling the syllabuses they wish to teach. The editions maintain the linguistic integrity of the original work but within the parameters of modern reading conventions. The texts are printed in the modern alphabet and follow the practices of modern capitalization and punctuation. Manuscript abbreviations are expanded, and *u/v* and *j/i* spellings are regularized according to modern orthography. Hard words, difficult phrases, and unusual idioms are glossed on the page, either in the right margin or at the foot of the page. Textual and explanatory notes appear at the end of the text. The editions include short introductions on the history of the work, its merits and points of topical interest, and also include briefly annotated bibliographies.

Prose Merlin

Edited by
John Conlee

Published for TEAMS
(The Consortium for the Teaching of the Middle Ages)
in Association with the University of Rochester

by

Medieval Institute Publications

WESTERN MICHIGAN UNIVERSITY

Kalamazoo, Michigan – 1998

Library of Congress Cataloging-in-Publication Data

Merlin (Prose romance)
  Prose Merlin / edited by John Conlee.
       p.   cm. -- (Middle English texts)
  Includes bibliographical references.
  ISBN 1-58044-015-0 (pbk. : alk. paper)
  1. Merlin (Legendary character)--Romances.   2. Arthurian romances.
3. Romances, English.   I. Conlee, John W.   II. Title.   III. Series:
Middle English texts (Kalamazoo, Mich.)
PR2062.A2C66 1998
823' .2--dc21

                                                                    98-39779
                                                                        CIP

ISBN 1-58044-015-0

Printed in the United States of America

Cover design by Elizabeth King

Contents

Preface

I wish to thank Professor Russell A. Peck for his patience and his generous assistance during the lengthy period in which this volume was being completed. I would also like to thank Jennifer Church for all her assistance in preparing the volume for publication; Angela Gibson for her checking of my manuscript against the Cambridge source; Mara Amster for her proofreading of the manuscript; and Alan Lupack for his careful reading and learned commentary on my manuscript. The staff at the Cambridge University Library was helpful during the time that I was consulting the manuscript; I thank them for permission to use Cambridge University MS Ff.3.11 as my base text. I would also like to thank Stanley Kustesky (the king of eye-slip), who performed the initial and laborious task of typing the unedited text onto computer disks. At Kalamazoo, Thomas Seiler and Juleen Eichinger gave the camera-ready copy its careful perusal before publication. Finally, I wish to thank the National Endowment for the Humanities for its generous support of the Middle English Texts Series.

Prose Merlin

Introduction

The Middle English *Prose Merlin* survives in a single manuscript text, Cambridge University Library MS Ff.3.11. This late medieval Arthurian work was written, scholars believe, near the middle of the fifteenth century, not long before Thomas Malory was composing his *Morte D'Arthur*. Because it pre-dates Malory's work, the Middle English *Prose Merlin* is considered the earliest piece of Arthurian literature written in English prose. In contrast to Malory's work, however, which draws upon a wide variety of sources and combines them in a unique fashion, the Middle English *Prose Merlin* offers a straightforward and fairly accurate translation into English of a single source, the Merlin section of the Old French Vulgate Cycle, an interconnected set of Arthurian works composed during the first half of the thirteenth century. One of the real values of the Middle English *Prose Merlin* is that it gives students of medieval Arthurian literature access, though at one remove, to this important Old French work. But the value of the *Prose Merlin* goes far beyond that, for the work is a treasure trove of Arthurian characters, incidents, and motifs — many of which are found nowhere else in Arthurian literature. Perhaps its greatest potential value for students of English medieval literature, however, lies in the dramatic literary counterpoint the Middle English *Prose Merlin* provides to Thomas Malory's *Morte D'Arthur*. A careful examination of these two nearly contemporaneous texts, in their relationships to each other, can do much to illuminate each of them.

The *Prose Merlin*: An Overview

The Middle English *Prose Merlin* is, first and foremost, the history of Merlin. Just as Malory's *Morte D'Arthur* begins with the events leading up to Arthur's birth and concludes with those occurring shortly after his death, the *Prose Merlin* does much the same for the figure of Merlin, providing its readers with a complete account of Merlin's life.

1

Introduction

The initial episode in the *Prose Merlin* describes the events surrounding Merlin's birth, and the final episode, occurring after Merlin has said farewell to those dearest to him, provides a clear indication of the fate he must endure henceforth — a kind of living death.

In addition to presenting a full account of the life of Merlin, the *Prose Merlin* also presents a detailed account of the initial phase in the evolution of Arthurian civilization, a phase which may be called the Rise of Arthur. This is the segment of the Arthurian story that extends from Arthur's birth through his coronation and marriage and the pacification of Britain. It describes at great length the several threats to the land the young king must address — particularly the baronial revolt and the Saxon invasion — before peace and stability can be returned to Britain. This early phase in the larger story also includes Arthur's courtship of Gonnore (Gwenyvere) and their subsequent marriage, Merlin's intense emotional involvement with his protégé Nimiane (Nyneve), as well as several events contributing to the initial development of a code of knightly conduct. In this last matter Gawain (Gawayne) and his brothers and cousins — a group known collectively as the Young Squires — figure prominently. This important early phase in the larger narrative concludes shortly after Merlin's departure, with the implication that Merlin has fulfilled his function and Arthur must now proceed without his mentor's guiding hand.

In its larger structure, scholars believe, the *Prose Merlin* consists of two principal sections. The first, which begins with the story of Merlin's birth and continues through Arthur's coronation — the first five sections in this volume — is probably derived from the Old French poem *Merlin* by the late twelfth-century writer Robert de Boron. The remainder of the *Prose Merlin* is thought to be based on a lengthy sequel to Robert's poem that was written during the first half of the thirteenth century, when a Merlin section was needed to complete the overall design of the Old French Vulgate Cycle. This sequel section of the *Prose Merlin* accomplishes several things: it fleshes out the story of Arthur's rise to his apogee; it describes the manner in which many important characters first became a part of the story; it lays the groundwork for many later events in the Vulgate Cycle, most importantly those having to do with the Holy Grail; and it provides a smooth transition into the next major phase in the larger story which will focus on the figure of Lancelot.

These two sections of the *Prose Merlin* are merged without fanfare, however, and there is little in the Middle English text to indicate that a structural division even exists. And yet as one moves from the Robert de Boron section to the so-called Sequel, it becomes clear that the basic approach to the handling of the narrative has been altered. In the Robert de Boron section the narrative is relatively simple, straightforward, and single-stranded; in the Sequel it becomes far more digressive and diffuse, and more importantly, it becomes multi-stranded. The Sequel clearly manifests the interlacing pattern — that of pursuing one strand of the narrative for a few pages, then a second strand, and then a third, before returning to the first — that typifies the works belonging to the Vulgate Cycle.

The Robert de Boron Section

The Robert de Boron section of the *Prose Merlin* opens dramatically upon a council of devils. Dismayed and aggrieved by Christ's Harrowing of Hell, an event in which the Old Testament patriarchs have been freed from Satan's bondage, the fiends of hell seek a means by which to undo the work of Christ. The plan they hit upon is to create their own demonic agent — a kind of antichrist — who will go into the world and do their bidding in the cosmic struggle between good and evil. This plan is put into effect, and such a being is soon fathered upon a virtuous woman by one of the fiends. But their scheme goes awry, in part because of the advice the woman receives from her religious advisor, a holy man named Blase (Blaise), in part because of the purity of her own heart. And thus it comes about that the special powers with which the fiends have endowed the child — who is christened Merlin, after the woman's father — will be used for benevolent ends rather than malevolent ones. And yet, although Merlin has been snatched from the service of Satan and entered into the service of God, reminders of his demonic origins persist through-out the work, most obviously in Merlin's impish sense of humor and his childish delight in playing pranks.

The second episode in the Robert de Boron section relates the story of Vortiger (Vortigern) and his ill-fated tower. This episode provides the boy Merlin, now aged seven, with ample opportunities to display his astonishing prophetic powers. When the tyrant Vortiger — who has usurped the British throne and who now lives in fear of the rightful heirs, Pendragon and Uther — attempts to build himself a great tower, his efforts prove futile for the tower continually collapses. Vortiger's sages claim the foundations will not hold unless they are sprinkled with the blood of a fatherless boy; the fatherless Merlin is soon discovered and brought before the tyrant. The boy saves himself by revealing what Vortiger's sages can not, the true reason for the tower's collapse, which is the shaking of the foundation caused by a pair of red and white dragons who struggle in a pool buried beneath the tower. That struggle, the youthful prophet tells them, signifies the struggle

3

which will soon be taking place between Vortiger and the brothers Pendragon and Uther. (This is in contrast to other works, where the fighting dragons are said to be emblematic of the conflict that is going to occur between the Saxons and the Britons.) The pool is drained and Vortiger's tower is completed, only to become the site of Vortiger's fiery death, which Merlin had also predicted.

After Vortiger's death, Merlin assists Pendragon, who is now the British king, and his brother Uther in their struggles against the invading Saxons. Just as Merlin has foreseen, a great battle is fought near Salisbury in which Pendragon meets his death. Uther then ascends the throne and adopts the name "Uterpendragon" to honor his brother, and Merlin erects the great stone ring (Stonehenge) on Salisbury Plain as a memorial to the fallen Britons. With Uther now firmly established as Britain's king, Merlin advises him on the creation of the Round Table — one of the most significant events in the *Prose Merlin*. The table he will construct, Merlin tells Uther, is a replica of the table of the Grail that was first fashioned by Joseph of Arimathea, which was itself a replica of the table used at the Last Supper. Together, the three tables represent the Holy Trinity. Moreover, the Round Table that Merlin creates for Uther's knights comes to represent a bonding between the ideals of worldly chivalry and the transcendant spiritual mysteries represented by the Holy Grail.

In the fourth episode of the Robert de Boron section, King Uther becomes enamored with Ygerne, the wife of the Duke of Tintagel, and he soon begins waging a civil war against his Cornish liegeman. With the aid of Merlin's shape-shifting abilities Uther, in the likeness of the Duke, sleeps with Ygerne at the castle of Tintagel, and Arthur is conceived. Following the Duke's death in battle, Uther and Ygerne are wed, thus ensuring Arthur's legitimacy; and after Arthur is born, he is given into the foster care of Antor (Ector), who raises him as his own son. Great emphasis is placed throughout this episode on Ygerne's virtue and on her fidelity to her husband. She is shown to be entirely blameless in Arthur's having been conceived out of wedlock, and much the same thing occurs later in the *Prose Merlin* in the episode concerning the begetting of Mordred, when the wife of King Lot is similarly exonerated from any moral wrong-doing. (Perhaps we are meant to see a "trinity" of virtuous women in the three somewhat parallel episodes involving the conceptions of Merlin, Arthur, and Mordred.)

The final episode in the Robert de Boron section relates the famous story in which Arthur draws the sword from the stone, thus proving that he is Britain's king by divine election. The recalcitrant barons force Arthur to perform the feat repeatedly at every high feast from New Year's to Pentecost, but eventually they capitulate — at least for the time being — and the episode culminates in Arthur's coronation. This episode should seem very familiar to most readers since the version of the "Sword in the Stone" story told here closely resembles the account contained in Malory's *Morte D'Arthur*. Although Malory's rendition of these events is more abbreviated, the two versions accord with each other in almost every significant detail — which is rarely the case for this pair of contrastive works.

The Sequel Section

Following Arthur's coronation, the narrative tapestry becomes far more complex. Numerous plot lines are introduced, as well as a huge cast of characters. Also, medieval warfare becomes very much at the center of things in this section of the *Prose Merlin*, with the narrative focusing on five distinctive sets of military conflicts: Arthur's civil war against his rebellious barons; Britain's war against the invading Saxons; the war King Rion wages against King Leodegan; the war in France that Claudas de la deserte wages against King Ban and King Bors; and finally, Arthur's European campaign against the Romans. The text includes a great many extended descriptions of battles which, it must be said, are not likely to have much appeal for most modern readers. For the purposes of this volume, therefore, much of this material has been summarized. But military events vital to the larger story have been retained, along with enough battle description to capture the flavor of this central feature of the work.

The most important wars in the *Prose Merlin* are those involving the rebellious barons and the invading Saxons. The least important is Arthur's European campaign, which seems to receive a rather half-hearted treatment and which is greatly inferior to accounts such as those found in Geoffrey of Monmouth's *The History of the Kings of Britain* or the Middle English *Alliterative Morte Arthure*. It does preserve a spirited description of Arthur's fight with the Giant of St. Michael's Mount, however, and it also contains the curious though extraneous episode in which Arthur fights the gigantic devil cat of Losane. The war in France, which occurs late in the work and which is mostly summarized in this volume, is important in demonstrating Arthur's commitment to repaying King Ban and King Bors for supporting him in his struggle against the barons. The war between King Rion and King Leodegan provides the opportunity for Arthur to meet and fall in love with Gonnore and for the re-introduction into the story of the Uther's Round Table, which had

5

been placed in Leodegan's care after Uther's death.

The two vitally important conflicts in the *Prose Merlin*, though, are Arthur's struggle with his unruly barons and Britain's war against the Saxons, both of which threaten to destroy Arthurian society before it has had a chance to take root. Following Arthur's coronation the Eleven Kings, a large group of Britain's most powerful barons, renew their refusal to accept Arthur as their liege lord. Assembling a huge military force, they rise against him and his loyal supporters, intending to remove Arthur from the throne. This civil war reaches its climax in the Battle of Bredigan Forest — the first of the many lengthy battle descriptions in the *Prose Merlin*. Merlin plays a major role in the battle, both as military strategist and as a direct participant in the action. Merlin also arranges for Arthur's secret rendezvous with the French forces led by King Ban and King Bors, who become Arthur's close friends and allies. With the help of Ban and Bors, to say nothing of Merlin's special powers, Arthur's outnumbered army inflicts a humiliating defeat upon the rebels. In the meantime, the Saxons have entered Britain in vast numbers and are overrunning the rebel barons' own homelands. Many of the barons now regret having opposed Arthur. It is not until much later, however, that they actually become reconciled with the king, an accord that comes about through the brave deeds of young Gawain (Gawayne), whose noble instincts have led him to side with Arthur against his own father.

Gawain is by far the most impressive figure among the many young heroes who are first introduced in the *Prose Merlin*. He is the leader of a group of noble youths who become known as the Young Squires, a group that includes Gawain's brothers Agravain, Gaheriet (Gaheris), and Gaheris (Gareth); his cousins, including Ewain (Uwayne), Galashin, and Dodinell; and others, including a daring young knight from Constantinople named Sagremor. All of these "children" (i.e., youths) leave their homes to seek out Arthur, whom they wish to serve and by whom they wish to be knighted. They perform many illustrious deeds against the Saxons, and at one point Gawain achieves a daring rescue of his mother and baby brother Mordred from their Saxon kidnappers. With his mother and baby brother now under his protection, Gawain uses them as leverage in persuading his father King Lot, one of the leaders of the rebels, to make peace with Arthur and swear allegiance to him. By the end of the *Prose Merlin*, Gawain has emerged as the pre-eminent young knight in Arthur's court. The final episode in the *Prose Merlin* focuses on Gawain and his partially successful quest to find Merlin, and it provides an explanation — one very different from that provided by Malory — for the great courtesy with which Gawain treats women from that time on.

Prose Merlin

One of the intriguing things about the *Prose Merlin* is the way in which it provides explanations for details and motifs commonly encountered in other Arthurian works. Numerous examples of this characteristic occur throughout the *Prose Merlin*, such as the explanation it offers for Kay's habit of rude speaking and for Arthur's tolerance of it; the explanation it offers for the great enmity that develops between Morgan le Fay and Queen Gonnore; and the explanation it offers for why Arthur will not eat on important feast days until a special adventure has presented itself. Also explained is how Gawain comes into possession of his wonderful horse Gringolet, and how Gawain comes to be the possessor of Arthur's sword Calibourne (Excalibur).

The *Prose Merlin*[1] not only attempts to explain how things came about, but it also attempts to explain *away* some aspects of the narrative that are potentially unsavory. The account of the begetting of Mordred — in which all parties are exonerated from any serious wrong-doing, in stark contrast to Malory's account — is an especially good example of this; the writer states explicitly that his intention is to set the record straight about the matter, since many people seem to have erroneous notions about what actually happened. Indeed, a strong element of Christian morality permeates the *Prose Merlin*, normally working to shield characters from criticism or censure, especially the women characters, and the work reflects a very generous view of almost every well-known Arthurian figure. That includes several major characters — e.g., Gawain, Gonnore, and King Lot — whose weaknesses and flaws are much more openly revealed in Malory's work. While a few characters in the *Prose Merlin* remain ambiguous and enigmatic — Nimiane is perhaps the best example — none of the familiar Arthurian characters is seriously vilified. The closest the work ever comes to doing that is with Agravain and Morgan le Fay, whose hot tempers and vengeful, malicious natures are briefly glimpsed.

The great triumvirate of heroic figures in the *Prose Merlin*, clearly, is comprised of Merlin, Arthur, and Gawain. Merlin is the central unifying figure in the entire work, virtually ever-present and constantly moving about between the various sets of characters; he is frequently involved in prompting the actions of the other characters, orchestrating events, and heading off catastrophic situations, and he himself participates in events to a degree rarely, if ever, encountered elsewhere in Arthurian literature. In contrast to Malory, where

---

[1] Given the fact that the Middle English *Prose Merlin* is a close translation of the Old French Vulgate version, when I speak of the *Prose Merlin* here and elsewhere in the Introduction, the remarks apply both to the ME and OF texts.

7

Merlin operates primarily behind the scenes, here Merlin is a character of great vitality who does not hesitate to ride in front of Arthur's troops as they go into battle, personally carrying Arthur's fire-spewing-dragon battle standard, an emblem (and weapon) of Merlin's own devising.

Arthur, of course, performs many heroic deeds throughout the work, several of which have already been mentioned, such as his defeat of the Giant of St. Michael's Mount and his killing of the devil cat of Losane. Arthur's most glorious deed in the *Prose Merlin*, though, is his great triumph over King Rion in single-combat. Arthur's victory means, among other things, that his beard will not be used to complete the trimming of King Rion's beard-lined mantle; but its greater significance is that the last external threat to Britain has been extinguished, and Arthur has succeeded in bringing peace to the land of Britain, which he now firmly controls. But it also signals another significant change, for as Arthur completes his final heroic deeds in the *Prose Merlin*, his active role is nearing its end, and Arthur is about to assume a more passive and regal role, as the focus shifts toward the adventures of the more youthful figures of Arthur's court, young knights such as Sir Gawain — and before long, Sir Lancelot — who will be the main figures in the dazzling array of knightly adventures that lie ahead.

The Old French Vulgate Cycle

After the appearance in the second quarter of the twelfth century of Geoffrey of Monmouth's great Latin work *The History of the Kings of Britain*, the work which contained the first full-scale account of King Arthur's life, Arthurian literature experienced a remarkable burgeoning in popularity throughout western Europe. By the early thirteenth century, an ever-expanding number of Arthurian lays, romances, and chronicle accounts were being recorded in a great many vernacular literatures, and a highly diverse body of new materials, drawn from various literary sources and from folklore, had been brought into association with King Arthur and his court. Among the most significant additions to the Arthur story were narratives concerning the Holy Grail and tales involving the famous lovers Tristan and Isolde. By the early decades of the thirteenth century, Arthurian literature had evolved to such a point that Geoffrey's original account had long since been swallowed up in a sprawling and fairly amorphous body of narrative materials. It was perhaps for this reason that during the first half of the thirteenth century certain writers in

France undertook an ambitious project designed to bring order and coherence to Arthurian literature by culling and sorting these materials and arranging them into a single sustained narrative sequence. What emerged from this project was the monumental set of Old French prose works generally known as the Vulgate Cycle.

The Vulgate Cycle — which has also been called "The Pseudo-Map Cycle" and the "Lancelot-Grail Cycle" — is an expansive set of interconnected narratives that traces the Arthurian story in chronological order from its beginning, in apostolic times, to its end, which occurs in the aftermath of Arthur's death. The Vulgate Cycle was probably written during a twenty- to thirty-year period, from around 1210 until perhaps the middle of the 1230s. Scholars believe that the long section dealing with Lancelot was probably the first part of the Vulgate Cycle to be written. That section led logically and directly into a section concerning the quest for the Holy Grail, which led in turn into a section dealing with the events surrounding Arthur's death. Those three parts having been completed, the writers then turned their attention to the very beginnings of the story, first writing the section that deals with the earliest history of the Grail, its initial guardians, and how it came to Britain; and then writing the Merlin section, which filled in the last remaining segment of the larger narrative sequence. When it was finished, then, the completed Cycle contained five major sections: 1) *The History of the Grail*; 2) *Merlin*; 3) *Lancelot*; 4) *The Quest for the Holy Grail*; and 5) *The Death of Arthur*.

At the time the Vulgate Cycle was being composed, the romances of the late twelfth-century writer Chrétien de Troyes had already become extremely popular and influential. But the Vulgate Cycle reflected two important attributes that set it apart from Chrétien and the writers influenced by him. For the sequence of works in the Vulgate Cycle were presented as being *historical* works, not romances, and at their center they possessed a serious *religious* purpose. They also convey a strong sense of the importance of preserving and recording all of the deeds and adventures surrounding their religious center — primarily, matters pertaining to the Holy Grail. This is done initially through Merlin's reporting of all the events to his mentor Blase, who has the responsibility of recording them for posterity. Religious prophecies and miracles are interspersed throughout the parts of the Vulgate Cycle, most of which are directly or indirectly concerned with the story of the Holy Grail. Thus in the works of the Vulgate Cycle a great effort is made to bestow upon the events of the Arthur story a fundamentally religious purpose, and also to suggest that the ultimate achievement of Arthurian society, for which only a few would be worthy, is the attainment of a transcendent spirituality.

9

Introduction

Before concluding these remarks on the Old French Vulgate Cycle, it is important to mention two other thirteenth-century prose works that are closely associated with it. One of them is the prose work commonly known as the *Prose Tristan*, which was probably written as a sequel to the Vulgate Cycle. The importance of the *Prose Tristan* for students of English medieval literature stems from the fact this work provided the principal source for the Tristan material found in Malory's *Morte D'Arthur*. While this work has no special pertinence for the *Prose Merlin* and no bearing on the question of the relationship between Malory's *Morte D'Arthur* and the *Prose Merlin*, another thirteenth-century prose work that is closely connected to the Vulgate Cycle certainly does. This is the work known as the *Suite du Merlin*.

In the overview of the *Prose Merlin* presented above, it was pointed out that the *Prose Merlin* contains two major sections, a Robert de Boron section and a Sequel section. The *Suite du Merlin*, like the Sequel section of the *Prose Merlin*, is a continuation of the Robert de Boron material, but its contents differ substantially from the material contained in the *Prose Merlin*. In order to distinguish between them, these two works are often called the historical continuation (the *Prose Merlin* Sequel) and the romantic continuation (the *Suite du Merlin*). (The *Suite du Merlin* has also been called the "Huth Merlin" because it is contained in British Library Addit. MS 38117, which is known as the Huth MS.) The narrative contents of the *Suite du Merlin*, though, may seem rather familiar to students of Arthurian literature, since this is the work that Malory drew upon for the first major section in the *Morte D'Arthur* — the section titled "The Tale of King Arthur" in the Vinaver edition of Malory (*Works*, pp. 3–110). Malory handled this material very freely — condensing it, rearranging it, and sometimes altering it — but all in all, the ground covered in the two works is much the same. Both Malory and the *Suite du Merlin* not only describe Arthur's war with the rebels and his later marriage, but they also include the tragic tale of Balin, the triple quests of Gawain, Tor, and Pellynore, Morgan's plots against Arthur, and the triple adventures of Gawain, Ewain, and Marhaus — none of which occurs in the *Prose Merlin*. The *Suite du Merlin* is only preserved in a few manuscripts, two of which are the Huth MS of the British Library and Cambridge University Library Addit. MS 7071.

Prose Merlin

The *Prose Merlin* and Thomas Malory's *Morte D'Arthur*

The Middle English *Prose Merlin* and Thomas Malory's *Morte D'Arthur* have much in common: both are lengthy Arthurian works in prose, both were written in England near the middle of the fifteenth century, and both are derived in part (Malory) or in full (the *Prose Merlin*) from thirteenth-century French sources. And, while Malory's work presents a "romance-biography" of the life of King Arthur, the *Prose Merlin* does the same for the life of Merlin. The two works also contain a few very similar episodes within their larger narratives, such as their depictions of the episode in which Arthur removes the sword from the stone. But despite the existence of such similarities, the two works are in fact extremely different. The *Prose Merlin* is much more narrowly focused than Malory's work, being concerned only with the initial phase in the evolution of Arthurian society; at the same time, it is far more diffuse and detailed, and treats this phase of the story in a very drawn-out fashion. Malory's *Morte D'Arthur* is much broader in the overall design of its narrative, and yet his tendency throughout is to simplify, reduce, and disentangle the narrative threads of his sources. Thus it is not surprising that the *Prose Merlin*'s depiction of the rise of Arthur is roughly six times longer than the equivalent section in Malory's *Morte D'Arthur*.

But as striking as the differences between the two works are in regard to their structures and the presention of their narratives, the differences in their thematic concerns and tonal qualities are even more striking. One of Malory's chief concerns throughout the *Morte D'Arthur*, for example, is with human frailty and human fallibility. As a result, his work carries strong tragic overtones and is imbued with an overriding sense of pessimism. In the playing out of the larger story, almost all of Malory's characters are morally compromised by their choices and actions. There are extreme examples of this — e.g., Morgan, Margawse, and Gawayne — but even the characters Malory most admires — Arthur, Merlin, and Lancelot — prove unable to exert much control over their actions or their hearts. Only Malory's trio of Grail Knights (Galahad, Percivale, and Bors) and Gawayne's brother Gareth remain essentially untainted by the darker undercurrents of human nature that surface in his other characters.

The *Prose Merlin*, on the other hand, is brimming with optimism, and the intention of this work is to portray Arthur and his fledgling court in the most favorable possible light. While Arthur's external enemies — the Saxons, the Romans, and King Rion — are portrayed as being out-and-out villains, the British never are, not even the rebellious barons;

although they are seriously misguided for much of the narrative, they eventually see the error of their ways, are forgiven, and are welcomed back into the fold. Perhaps a telling example of this fundamental difference between the *Prose Merlin* and Malory's *Morte D'Arthur* may be seen in the way each of them depicts King Lot, Gawain's father. In the *Prose Merlin* King Lot, even though he strenuously opposes Arthur's kingship, is consistently portrayed as a courageous and noble figure. He is also a loving husband and father, and he is a man who, when he realizes his mistakes, tries to atone for them. Malory's King Lot, however, is shown to be jealous and brooding and malicious. He nurses a personal hatred for Arthur (which is not entirely undeserved), and he and Arthur never reconcile. In contrast to what occurs in the *Prose Merlin*, in Malory King Lot is slain in battle before the rebellion has been put down; and his influence on events does not end there, for Lot's death drives a wedge between two factions of Arthur's knights and contributes directly to several vengeful deeds that occur later in the story.

There are many aspects of the *Prose Merlin* and Malory's *Morte D'Arthur* that are worth considering in relation to each other — the contrasting roles played in the works by Merlin, their treatments of the relationship between Arthur and Gonnore, their treatment of the relationship between Merlin and Nimiane, to list only a few of particular significance. But this is not the place to do that, and so we leave such undertakings to students of Arthurian literature who might wish to pursue them on their own.

Manuscripts

The Middle English *Prose Merlin* is recorded in Cambridge University Library MS Ff.3.11. The text in the Cambridge MS is nearly complete, and is flawed only by the lack of its final three MS leaves; a summary of the missing material has been provided here, based upon an analogous Old French text. No other significant Middle English texts of the work survive, although MS Rawlinson D.913 of the Bodleian Library in Oxford preserves a small fragment of the work on a single MS page (fol. 43). Bodleian Library MS Ashmole 802, which dates to the second half of the sixteenth century, contains a prose rendition of the opening section of the *Merlin*, but this material, which is probably the work of Simon Forman, M. D., has no direct relationship to either of the Middle English texts.

Prose Merlin

A Note on the Text

Modern conventions for punctuation and capitalization have been followed throughout this edition of the *Prose Merlin*. The paragraph divisions contained in this text result from editorial decision, though they often coincide with divisions in the MS text indicated by small capital letters; however, the MS divisions are usually much longer than would be normal for modern paragraphs, and at times, too, they also seem rather idiosyncratic. The MS text does not contain many contractions or abbreviations, but the few it does contain have been silently expanded. The MS text does contain a great many instances of Roman numerals; for the convenience of modern readers, those numerals have been written as words. In several places I have supplied words to clarify the sense of the text. The author often omits the subject within a series of clauses. In some instances words have been left out or are obliterated by blemishes in the MS. All such additions or emendations are set off by brackets. If I have emended a word that is found in the MS, that emendation is cited in the notes.

The MS spelling of words has been preserved, and spelling has not been normalized; the only the exception to this is in the case of words containing *u/v*, where modern conventions have been followed; for example, the name *Vter* in the MS has been printed as *Uter*. In the few cases where archaic letters occur, they have been modernized; e.g., "thorn" is printed as *th*. Word division and spacing have also been modernized in some instances; for example, the word *togethir* is printed as a single word, as in modern English, not as two words as it appears in the MS. Also, hyphens have occasionally been inserted into words to make them more immediately understandable: the syllabic final -*e*, I have marked -*é*; to indicate the long vowel of the second-person familiar pronoun, I have transcribed *thee* where the MS has *the*.

Emendations have been made sparingly and only when it appears obvious that there is an uncorrected error in the MS text; in all such instances, the actual MS readings are recorded in the Textual Notes. Words or phrases contained in square brackets in the text have been editorially supplied. This occurs when the words in the MS were indecipherable; and it also occurs in some sentences where a verb or pronoun is required to make the sentence grammatically complete according to modern usage. This has been done only to make the text more immediately understandable to modern readers.

Introduction

Select Bibliography

Manuscripts

Cambridge University Library MS Ff.3.11. [This nearly complete text provides the basis for this edition.]

Bodleian Library MS Rawlinson D. 913. [This MS contains only a very small fragment of the Middle English *Prose Merlin*, found on a single MS leaf (fol. 43).]

Editions

Wheatley, Henry B., ed. *Merlin, or the Early History of Arthur: A Prose Romance.* EETS o.s. 10, 12, 36, 112. London: K. Paul, Trench, Trübner & Co., 1865–98.

Cranmer-Byng, Lancelot, ed. *Selections from the Prose Merlin.* London: Sedgwick & Jackson, 1930.

Studies and Related Materials

Ackerman, Robert W. "Arthur's Wild Man Knight." *Romance Philology* 9 (1955–56), 115–19.

Bogdanow, Fanni. "The *Suite du Merlin* and the Post-Vulgate *Roman Du Graal.*" In *Arthurian Romance in the Middle Ages: A Collaborative History.* Ed. Roger Sherman Loomis. London: Oxford University Press, 1959. Pp. 325–35.

Boron, Robert de. Fragment of *Merlin* poem. In *Le Roman de l'Estoire dou Graal.* Ed. William A. Nitze. Paris: H. Champion, 1927. Appendix, pp. 126–30.

Burns, E. Jane. *Arthurian Fictions: Rereading the Vulgate Cycle.* Columbus: Ohio State University, 1985.

Prose Merlin

Carman, J. Neale. *A Study of the Pseudo-Map Cycle of Arthurian Romance, to Investigate Its Historico-Geographic Background and to Provide a Hypothesis as to Its Fabrication.* Lawrence: The University Press of Kansas, 1973.

Dean, Chistopher. *A Study of Merlin in English Literature from the Middle Ages to the Present: The Devil's Son.* Lewiston: Edwin Mellen Press, 1992.

Frappier, Jean. "The Vulgate Cycle." In *Arthurian Romance in the Middle Ages: A Collaborative History.* Ed. Roger Sherman Loomis. London: Oxford University Press, 1959. Pp. 295–318.

Kibler, William W., ed. *The Lancelot-Grail Cycle: Text and Transformations.* Austin: University of Texas Press, 1994.

Kölbing, E., ed. *Arthour and Merlin nach der Auchinleck-Hs, nebst zwei Beilagen.* Altenglische Bibliothek, IV. Leipzig: O. R. Reisland, 1890.

Lacy, Norris J., ed. *The Arthurian Encyclopedia.* New York: Garland Publishing, Inc., 1991. Pp. 373–74; 496–99.

———, ed. *Lancelot-Grail: The Old French Arthurian Vulgate Cycle and Post-Vulgate in Translation.* Trans. Lacy *et al.* 5 vols. New York: Garland, 1993–96.

Le Gentil, Pierre. "The Work of Robert de Boron and the *Didot Perceval.*" In *Arthurian Romance in the Middle Ages: A Collaborative History.* Ed. Roger Sherman Loomis. London: Oxford University Press, 1959. Pp. 251–62.

MacDonald, Aileen Ann. *The Figure of Merlin in the Thirteenth-Century French Romance.* Lewiston: Mellen Press, 1990

Micha, Alexander. "La Guerre contre les Romains dans la vulgate du *Merlin.*" *Romania* 72 (1951), 310–23.

———. "Les Sources de la *Vulgate* du *Merlin.*" *Le Moyen Âge* 58 (1952), 299–345.

————. "The Vulgate *Merlin*." In *Arthurian Romance in the Middle Ages: A Collaborative History*. Ed. Roger Sherman Loomis. London: Oxford University Press, 1959. Pp. 319–24.

————, ed. *Lancelot: Roman en prose du XIIIe siècle*. 9 vols. Geneva: Droz, 1978–83.

————, ed. *Merlin: Roman du XIIIe siècle*. Geneva: Droz, 1979.

Newstead, Helaine. "The Prose Merlin." In *A Manual of the Writings in Middle English*. Vol. I: *Romances*. Ed. J. Burke Severs. New Haven, Connecticut: The Connecticut Academy of Arts and Sciences, 1967. P. 49.

Sommer, H. Oskar, ed. *The Vulgate Version of the Arthurian Romances*. 7 vols. Washington D.C.: Carnegie Institute, 1908–16.

Works Cited

Alliterative Morte Arthure. In *King Arthur's Death: The Middle English Stanzaic Morte Arthur and Alliterative Morte Arthure*. Ed. Larry D. Benson. Rev. Edward E. Foster. Kalamazoo: Medieval Institute Publications, 1994.

Chrétien de Troyes. *Arthurian Romances*. Ed. and trans. William W. Kibler. London: Penguin Books, 1991.

Didot Perceval. Ed. William Roach. Philadelphia: University of Pennsylvania Press, 1941.

Geoffrey of Monmouth. *The History of the Kings of Britain*. Ed. and trans. Lewis Thorpe. London: Penguin Books, 1966.

————. *The Vita Merlini*. Ed. and trans. John J. Parry. University of Illinois Studies in English 10, no. 3. Urbana: University of Illinois Press, 1925.

Gildas. *The Ruin of Britain and Other Documents*. Ed. and trans. Michael Winterbottom. London: Phillimore & Co., 1977.

Layamon. *Brut*. Ed. G. L. Brook and R. F. Leslie. EETS o.s. 250, 277. London: Oxford University Press, 1963, 1978.

Lovelich, Herry, skinner and citizen of London. *Merlin: A Middle-English Metrical Version of a French Romance*. Ed. Ernst A. Kock. 3 vols. EETS e.s. 93, 112; o.s. 185. London: Oxford University Press, 1904–32.

Mabinogion. Ed. and trans. Jeffrey Gantz. London: Penguin Books, 1976.

Malory, Sir Thomas. *Malory: Works*. Ed. Eugene Vinaver. Second ed. London: Oxford University Press, 1971.

Nennius. *Historia Brittonum*. In *Nennius's "History of the Britons", together with "The Annals of the Britons" and "Court Pedigrees of Hywel the Good", also "The Story of the Loss of Britain."* Ed. and trans. A. W. Wade-Evans. London: Society for Promoting Christian Knowledge, 1938.

Of Arthour and of Merlin. Ed. Macrae-Gibson, O. D. EETS o.s. 268, 279. Oxford: Oxford University Press, 1973, 1979.

Perlesvaus. Ed. and trans. Nigel Bryant. Cambridge: Brewer, 1978.

Sir Gawain and the Green Knight. Ed. J. R. R. Tolkien and E. V. Gordon. London: Oxford University Press, 1960.

Thorpe, see Geoffrey of Monmouth.

Vinaver, see Malory.

Völsunga Saga. Trans. William Morris. Ed. Robert W. Gutman. New York: Collier Books, 1962.

Wace. *Le Roman de Rou de Wace.* Ed. Anthony J. Holden. Publications de la société des ancient textes français. 3 vols. Paris: A. J. Picard, 1970.

Whiting, Bartlett Jere. *Proverbs, Sentences, and Proverbial Phrases from English Writings mainly before 1500.* Cambridge, Mass.: The Belknap Press of Harvard University Press, 1968.

[The Birth of Merlin]

Full wrothe and angry was the Devell, whan that oure Lorde hadde ben in helle and had take oute Adam and Eve and other at his plesier. And whan the fendes sien that, they hadden right grete feer and gret merveile. Thei assembleden togedir and seiden: "What is he this thus us supprisith and distroyeth, in so moche that oure strengthes ne nought ellis that we have may nought withholde hym, nor again hym stonde in no diffence but that he doth all that hym lyketh? We ne trowed not that eny man myght be bore of woman but that he sholde ben oures; and he that thus us distroyeth, how is he born in whom we knewe non erthely delyte?"

Than ansuerde anothir fende and seide, "He this hath distroyed, that which we wende sholde have be mooste oure availe. Remembre ye not how the prophetes seiden how that God shulde come into erthe for to save the synners of Adam and Eve, and we yeden bysily aboute theym that so seiden, and dide them moste turment of eny othir pepill; and it semed by their semblant that it greved hem but litill or nought, but they comforted hem that weren synners, and seide that oon sholde come which sholde delyver hem out of tharldome and disese?

"So longe have thei spoken of hym that now is he comen and hath taken from us tham that non othir ne myght us bereve. Ye knoweth well that he maketh hem to ben waisshen in a water in the name of the Fader, Sone, and Holy Goste; and after that have we no powre upon them but yef they do turne agein to us by theire evell werkis. In this wise hath He putt down oure power, and yet moreover, for [He] hath his mynystres lefte in erthe that dayly hem saveth from us, thowh they have don never so many of oure werkes, yef they will repent and forsake their

---

2 plesier, pleasure. **3 sien**, saw (had seen). **4 What . . . this**, Who . . . that. **5 ne nought**, nor anything; **nought**, not. **6 ne trowed not**, did not believe. **10 wende**, thought; **be**, been. **12 yeden**, went. **13 semblant**, appearance. **15 tharldome**, servitude; **disese**, suffering. **17 tham**, those (them); **bereve**, deprive. **19 yef**, if. **21 mynystres**, ministers; **thowh**, even though. **22 never so many**, i.e., very many; **werkes**, i.e., sins.

myslyvinge, and do as they teche hem that ben for the grete love He hadde to man and gret tendirnesse, whan for to save man He wolde come down in to erthe to be
25   born of a woman. And we yede and assaied Hym in alle the maners that we cowden, and when we hadde [assaied] Hym, and we dyd that [synne] nought fynde in Hym; yet wolde He dye for to save man, ful moche lovede He man, when He [wolde] suffer so grete peyne for to have hym agein, and to take hym from oure power. Thanne moche oughte we for to laboure with grete besynesse to gete agayn
30   that He hath us beraffte in soche wyse, that they may not repente ne speke with hem that myght gete hem pardon, and turne hem agayn from oure power."

In this maner the fendes helden a gret conseill and seide that tho that hadde greved hem moste that were they that tolde tydinges of His comyng in to erthe: "And they have don us gret damage and hynderyng, and the more they tolde of
35   His comyng, the more we dide hem anger and disese; and as us semeth, He hasted Hym the rather to come for to delyver them from our daunger. [But] how myght we have a man of oure kynde that myght speke and have oure connynge and [maystrie] worke, and have the knowleche as we have of things that be don and seide, and of thynges that be past, and that he myght be in erthe conversant with
40   these other? For witeth it wele that soche on myght moche helpe us to begile His pepill, like as the prophetes begiled us and tolden that we trowe never myght have ben. In the same wise sholde soche oon telle alle thynges that were don and saide, both of that is passed and of thynges that is to come, and be that sholde He be bileved of moche peple." Than thei ansuerde alle, and seiden that wele hadde he
45   sped that soche a man myght gete, for he sholde be long beleved of all thinges that he seide.

Than ansuerde anothir fende and seide, "I have power for to sowe seede in woman and make her conceyve, and I have oon that doth all that ever I wille." And thus undirtoke he this enterprise, to gete a man that sholde do their werkes
50   after their alle entente. Full grete foles were thei whan they wende that oure Lorde sholde have no knowynge of their ordenaunce and engine. Thus they departed

25 yede, went; **assaied**, tested. **30 beraffte**, taken away. **31 hem¹**, them; **gete**, place; **hem²**, themselves; **hem³**, themselves. **32 tho**, those. **33 that were they**, were those. **36 Hym**, Himself; **rather**, quicker. **38 [maystrie]**, mastery (power). **40 on**, one. **41 trowe**, believe. **42 soche oon**, such a one. **43 be that**, by that means. **45 gete**, beget. **50 wende**, thought. **51 engine**, plan.

from this conseille and were assented to this conclusion; and this feende that toke this enterprise ne taried not, but in al the haste that he myght, he come theras this woman was that wrought all his wille.

[**Summary**. *The woman over whom the fiend has such power is married to a rich man, and they have a son and three daughters. To achieve his end, the fiend makes the rich man's animals die, strangles the man's son, and causes the wife to commit suicide. Grief-stricken, the rich man dies, whereupon the fiend sets about to corrupt the daughters. One of them commits fornication, for which she is executed, and another becomes a prostitute. But the eldest daughter withstands the fiend's tempting and seeks a holy hermit's advice. Fols. 1v (line 9)–3r (line 4).*]

55   And when the elder mayden sye that hir suster was thus gon, she yede anoon to the holy man that hadde taught hir the right creaunce, full hevy and pensif, makynge grete doell and sorow. And when this gode man sye her so pensif, he hadde grete pitee and seyde to hir, "Blesse thee and comaunde thee to God, for I se thee gretly affraied." And she ansuerde, "I have grete cause, for I have loste my suster, that is
60   become a comyn woman."

And when the gode man herde this he was gretly astonyd and seide, "The feende is full besy abowte yow, which will not cesse till he have disseyved thee, but God be thyn helpe." "A sir," quod she, "how may I kepe me from his disceytis? For ther is no thynge that I have so grete feire of as that he sholde have over me eny
65   power." Quod the holy man, "Yef thow wilte do after my counsell, he shall never disceyve thee." "Certeyn," quod she, "I will gladly do your counsell."

"Than," quod he, "belevest thow not in the Fadir, Sone, and Holy Goste, and that these thre persones be oon God in Trynité, and that God com down in to erthe, and becom man for the redempcion of mannes sowle, of hem that in Hym
70   stadfastly beleve, and kepe His comaundmentis?" And she seide, "Right as ye sey, I beleve. And so, veryly, I pray to God be my socoure and helpe." "Now then," quod he, "I pray thee and comaunde that thow kepe thee fro fallynge into grete ire or wrath, for in that the feende repairethe moste, bothe in man and woman,

55 sye, saw; **yede,** went. **56 creaunce,** beliefs. **57 doell,** grief (dole). **60 comyn woman,** prostitute. **64 feire,** fear. **65 Yef,** If. **73 repairethe,** resorts.

21

namly, when they be in grete ire and comberauncis. That thow haste yelde thee in

75 the graces of oure Lord and alle seyntis; and at alle tymes [when] thow goist to
bedde or arysist, blisse thee in the name of the Fader, Sone, and Holy Goste, and
make upon thee in the name of the crosse, on the whiche He suffred His passion to
bye us fro the peynes of helle. And yef thow do thus, thow shalt have no drede of
the feendes power. And where that thow slepest on nyght, loke that thow have

80 lyght, for the devell hatyth all clerenesse and lyght, and gladly will not com there."

Thus taught the holy man the mayden, which hadde grete drede of the develes
engynes. And so she returned hom ageyn to her house, full stabill in the feith, and
full humble to God, and to the pore peple which comen unto hir and seiden:
"Trewly, it is no wonder though ye be gretely affraied of the turment that is falle

85 of youre fader, and of youre moder, and youre broder and sustres, that thus be
myscheved; but now taketh gode counsell and be of gode comfort, for ye ar right
ryche and have grete herytage. Wherfore every worthy man will be glad to have
yow." And she ansuerde ageyne and seide, "Oure Lorde kepe me in His servyse,
as He knoweth it is grete nede."

90 Thus endured she wele two yere, that the feende myght never begyle her, ne
never myght make her do evell werke. And he sye wele that he ne cowde not make
her lese that the holy man hadde hir lerned, lesse than she were made wroth. Than
made he hir suster come on a Saterday, at even, to do hir more turment and anger,
to loke yef he might gete hir in that manere. And when hir suster com, it was fer

95 withynne nyght, and she brought with her a grete hepe of harlotys. And when she
sye her suster so com, she was angry and seide unto here, "Feire suster," quod
she, "as longe as ye caste yow to lede soche lyf, ye ought not to come in this place,
for ye make me have grete blame, wherof I have lityll nede."

And she ansuerde ageyne, as a woman that the feende was withynne, and seyde

100 that she wolde yet do worse, and seide that she was more evell than she, and bar
hir on honde that she loved the holy man paramours, and yef it were knowen the
trouth, that she [was] worthy to be distroid. And when her suster herde this, she
griped her be the shulders and put hir owt at the dore. And the tother, to avenge

74 comberauncis, troubles; **thee**, yourself. **76 arysist**, arise. **78 bye**, redeem. **82 engynes**,
devices. **86 myscheved**, harmed. **91 cowde**, could. **92 lese that**, lose what; **lerned**, taught;
lesse than, unless. **95 grete hepe**, large group. **100–01 bar hir on honde**, claimed falsely.
101 paramours, as a lover. **103 tother**, other.

105 hir, made the harlotys that come with her to kache hir suster and bete hir right evellé. So with grete peyne she aschaped fro them and fledde into hir chamber and shet her dore and barred hit from her and the harlottis that were come with her.

And she abode in her chamber alone, and leyde her down on her bedde all clothed and wepte tendirly for sorowe. And when the devell sye that she was 110 angry and sole by herself, and that it was derke, he was gladde. And she remembred the myschef of hir fader and moder and brother and susters, and sore wepte when she hadde thought on all parteis. And so ther was grete sorowe and grete ire at hir herte. And when the feende sye that she hadde foryete that the holy man hadde taught her, he thought that she stode owte of Goddes grace, and of her maister. 115 "And now myght I well put oure man in hir."

And this feende that hadde power to make woman conceyve was all redy and lay by hir while she was slepynge.

And when she hadde concayved she awaked, and in her wakyng she thought on the holy man, and therwith she blissed here and seide, "Seynt Mary, what is me 120 befalle, for I am disceyved sith I leyde me here. Now gracyouse Lady, pray unto [thi dere] sone that He have mercy upon me, and diffende my body fro turment of the enmy." And than she [aros, and sought aboute] after hym that sholde have done that dede, for she wende to have founde hym [therynne, and she ran to the] dore and fonde it shet in the same maner as she hadde barred it herself. And than 125 she sought over all in her [chamber], but nought cowde she fynde. Than she demed that it was the enmy that so hadde her begiled; and than she made full grete sorowe and cryde moche upon oure Lord, prayinge Hym that He wolde not suffer her to be shamed here in this worlde.

And anoon as it was day, the feende ledde away this othir suster, for she hadde 130 fully espleyted his purpos. And when they were alle passed, she com owte of hir chamber sorowfull and pensif and called after her servaunt, and anoon sente after two women. And when they were come, anoon she wente to hir confessour. And the gode man sye her comynge; he seide, "Thow hast som grete nede, for I se thee gretely affraied." And she answerde, "I ought wele to be affrayed, for it betyde to

105 aschaped, escaped. **113 foryete that**, forgotten what. **118 concayved**, conceived. **119 here**, herself. **119–20 is me befalle**, has befallen me. **125 over all**, everywhere. **130 espleyted**, completed.

135   me that never fill to [eny] woman saf oonly to me. And therfore I come to seche
youre counseill, for I have herde yow saye that ther was nevere creature that dede
so grete offence that yef he were confessed and repentant, that he wolde resceyve
penance for his trespasse, that he sholde anoon have foryevenesse. Sir, I have
synned, and wete ye wele I am disceyved be the devell."

140   Than she tolde how hire suster com to hir howse, and all, gynnynge and ende,
as ye have herde, and how she fill on slepe [on her] bedde, and hir dore shette and
barred, and how hir grete [sorowe made hir] foryete to blisse hir. And quod she,
"When I awoke, I fonde me diffoulde and my maidenhede loste. Sir, I sought
thourgh my chamber and fonde my dor shet, ne I cowde fynde no lyvinge creature

145   that eny suche [thynge myght] have don to me. For in [this] wyse I have sinned,
wherfore I crye God mercy, and yow, and that I may have soche penance that I
lese not the lif everlastynge."

    The holy man lestned well to all hir confession, but he yaf no grete credence to
that she seide, for he herde never before of no soche thynge. And therfore he

150   seyde unto hir, quod he, "Thow art full of the devell. How sholde I absoyle thee or
enjoyne thee penance for thynges which I wene thow lyest veryly, for never was
ther woman that loste her maydenhede but she wiste by whom and how; or at the
leste, that she myght fele the man that dyde the dede. And thow woldiste make me
bileve this merveyle that thow seyest in this wyse is thee befalle!" And she

155   ansuerde, "So, verily, God be my socoure in my moste nede, as I have seide trouth."

    The holy man seide, "Yef it be so as thow haste seyde unto me, it shall verily be
knowe bothe to thee and to me withynne shorte tyme. Thow haste broken the
obedyence that I comaunded thee; therfore I charge thee in penaunce that alle the
Saterdayes while thow lyvest that thow ete no mete but ones on the day. And as

160   touchynge the lecherye that thow hast tolde — wherof I can not leve thee — thow
oughtest to have penaunce all thy lyftyme, yef thow wil take soche as I shall the
enjoyne." And she answerde, "Ye can not charge me with noon but I will gladly
performe it."

    Than seyde the holy man, "Thou comest to have counseill of Holy Church, and

165   to the mercy of oure Lorde Jhesu Criste, that bought us with His precyouse blode

---

135 fill, fell; **seche**, seek. **140 all . . . ende**, from beginning to end. **142 hir³**, herself. **144
ne**, nor; **no**, any. **149 that**, what. **150 absoyle**, absolve. **151 enjoyne thee**, assign you;
lyest veryly, truly lie. **160 leve**, believe. **161 yef**, if. **162 noon**, anything.

and with His bitter deth. And [thow] haste very repentaunce of herte, like as thow seyest with thy mouth, and forsakeste all lechery and synne, saf oonly that fill in thi slepynge, fro the whiche no creature may kepe hym clene."

And she graunted hym, with that he wolde be hir plegge before God that she
170 sholde be saved, and that she were not dampned for that synne. She toke hir soche penaunce as he enjoyned her with gode will, sore wepynge as she that was very repentante. And this gode man assoiled hir and yaf hir his blissynge, and sette hir ageyne in the love of God in his beste manere; and brought her to the haly water and made her to drynke in the name of the Fader, Sone, and Holy Goste; and caste
175 of the same water upon her and badde hir to thynke wele on that he hadde charged her with. "And alle tymes, when thow haste eny nede, come to me ageyn." And than he betaught hir to God. And so he put in her penaunce alle her gode dedes and almesse and prayers that she sholde do.

And so returned this damsell in to her howse, and ledde full holy lyf. And when
180 the devell sye that he hadde loste her in soche manere that he wiste not what she dede ne what she seyde, he was wroth and angry.

Thus longe she abode that the seed myght no lenger ben hidde whiche she hadde in hir body, so that her wombe gan to waxen grete, that the peple aperceyved wele that she was with chylde. And they that were hyr frendes axeden hir be whom it
185 was. And she ansuerde, so God be hir helpe, she wiste not be whom it was. Quod they, "How may this be? Have ye than hadde so many men that ye knowe not who is the fader?" And she ansuerde, "God lete me have delyveraunce yef ever man, my witynge, hadde to do with me in soche maner." And they that this herden blessed them for merveyle, and seyde that it myght never be so, neythir of hir ne
190 of noon other — "but that ye hope to excuse hym so that hath don the dede. But truly, grete pité it is of you, for as soone as the juges knowe therof, ye moste be deed."

When she herde this she was sore abaisshed and seyde, "So veryly God make my soule safe, as I sawe hym never that hath don me this, ne never I hym knewe."
195 And the women that her herde speke helde her for a foole and untrewe, and clatered

---

166 very, true. **167 that fill**, what befell. **169 with that**, so that. **171 enjoyned**, ordered. **172 assoiled**, absolved. **177 betaught**, committed. **182 abode**, abided. **184 be**, by. **186 than**, therefore (then). **188 my witynge**, with my knowledge. **190 but that**, because. **191 moste**, must. **193 abaisshed**, disconcerted. **195 clatered**, chattered.

it aboute, and seyden certeynly that hir bewté was foulé spente, seth it was loste in soche manere. And when she herde this, she remembred on hir confessour, and com to hym, and tolde as the wymen hadden seide. The gode man sye that she was grete with quyk childe, and merveiled gretly, and axed hir yef she hadde wele 200 holden hir penaunce. "Sir," quod she, "ye, withoute fayle."

Quod he, "Befill yowe never this merveyle saf ones?" "Certes, sir," quod she, "never before ne after." And when the gode man herde this, he merveyled strongeleche, and sette the oure and the nyght in writynge, like as she hadde tolde hym, and seide, "Be ye right syker, when this chelde shal be born, I shall well 205 knowe yef ye have made eny gabbynge, and I have very trust in God that yef it be as ye have seide, ye shall not be deed therfore. But ye may wele have grete feer, for as soone as the juges knowe therof, they well make yow to be take for covetyse of youre londes and herytage, and do justice upon yow. But when ye be taken, sende me worde, and I shall come to helpe yow and comforte in all that I may. 210 And wite well that God shall helpe yow, yef ye be soche as ye sey." And then he seide, "Goth hom to youre howse and have no drede. And loke ye, be of gode counfort and good lyvynge, for that ledith man and woman to gode endynge."

And so she departed and come to hir owne house and ledde holyly hir lif, till the juges made hir to be taken and brought hir before them. And anon as she was 215 arested, she lete sende after the gode ermyte that hadde alwey ben her counfort. And he cam in all the haste that he myght. And when he was comen, he fonde that the juges hedde brought hir byfore them. The justyces clepid hym to hem, and told hym the ansuere that she hadde seide hem, [that] she hadde never knowynge of mannes company. "And trowe ye," quod thei, "that eny woman myght have 220 childe withoute mannes company?"

The gode man ansuerid and seide, "I shell not sey all that I thynke, but thus moche I sey unto yow: yef ye will do my counsell, ye shall not put hir to jugement while she is with childe, till that she be deliverd, for the childe hath no deth deserved." The juges seiden, "We shall do as ye counsele."

225 Quod the holy ermyte, "Yef ye do by my counsele, ye shall put hir in a stronge tour in gode warde, wher she shall have no power over hirself; and with hir ye

196 bewté, beauty; **seth,** since. **199 quyk,** living. **203 strongeleche,** greatly; **oure,** hour. **204 syker,** certain. **205 gabbynge,** falsehood. **207 well,** will. **210 wite,** know. **217 clepid,** called; **hem,** them. **221 shell,** shall. **226 in gode warde,** under guard.

shall put two women for to helpe hir at hir delyveraunce when tyme is, in soche maner that thei may not come oute no more. And thus shell she be lefte till she have chelde, and let hir aftar be kepte tyll she be stronge to goo by herself. And

230   then yef ye se none other thyng be her than ye se now, than do the justice as ye seme right. Thus shall ye do now be my rede, and yef ye do othirwise, I may no more." And even as the good man devised, they dede.

And so she was shet in a stronge tour, and with her two women, the wiseste that they knewe of soche mysteré, and made hem a wyndowe to hale upe that hem

235   ought to have. When this was don, the gode man spake to hem benethe on the grounde withoute, and seyde to the damsell, "When thow haste childe," quod he, "make it to be baptiseth as soone as thow mayste. And when thow shalte be brought oute ageyn to jugement, lete me have wetynge."

In this wyse abode they stille in the tour a grete while, til that she was delyvered

240   of a sone, as God wolde. And when he was born it hadde the engyne and the witt of a feende, after the kynde of hym that begate hym. But the devell wrought so folily that our Lorde toke it to His owne use, be the very repentaunce of the modir, that hir put in the mercy and ordenaunce of God and holicherche, and hilde wele the doctryne of His mynystres. And therfore, oure Lorde wolde not lese that shulde

245   be His. And ther the devell was disseyved of his purpos, that he hadde ordeyned that childe to have his art and witte to knowe alle thynges don and seide, bothe that were paste and that were to come. And oure Lorde, that alle thynges knoweth, [when He] sye the repentaunce of the moder and that it was not her will that was so befellen, He wolde have hym on His parte; nevertheles, He yaf hym fre choys

250   to do what he wolde, for yef he wolde he myght yelde God His parte, unto the fende his also.

Thus was this childe born, of whom the wemen were sore afeerde, for they sye hym more roughe than other childeren that they had seyn. And so they shewed [it] to the moder, and when she it sough, she sayned her and sayd, "This childe maketh

255   me to have grete feer." Quod the wemen, "So doth it to us." Quoth the moder,

---

229 chelde, child. **231 rede**, advice. **234 mysteré**, matters; **hale upe**, haul up. **238 have wetynge**, know. **240 engyne**, cunning. **241 kynde**, nature. **242 folily**, foolishly; **be**, by; **modir**, mother. **243 hir put**, placed herself. **244 lese that**, lose what. **249 parte**, side. **253 more roughe**, hairier. **254 sough**, saw; **sayned her**, crossed herself.

"Lete it be let don owte at the wyndowe that it may be baptysed." And they dyd
soo.

"What shalbe his name?" "I will," quod she, "that it have name after my fader."
Then they let it down by a corde owte at the wyndowe of the tour, and cherged
260 hem that weren benethe that it shulde be baptysed and named after the gode man
that was fader of the modre; and so it was. And so was it cristened Merlyn, and
was delyvered to the women upe to the wyndowe to the moder, and ther was none
othir women that durste norishe it but the moder, for it was so grysly to syght, and
therfore was the moder suffred to norishe it tell it was ten monthes of age. And
265 than it semed two yere age or more. And whan it was twelve monthes of age the
wemen seide to the modre, "Dame, we will no lenger be here in this case from
oure frendes. We will gone owte, for we have be here longe tyme."

Then quod she, "As sone as ye departe from hens shall I be brought to jugement."
Quod they, "We may no more be hereynne, and therfore we ne may no more do
270 therto." Then she wepte and cryde hem mercy, praynge hem to abyde a while, and
they graunted hir. And as they lened lokynge oute at the wyndowe theras she
were sore wepynge, [she] toke the child in her armes sayinge, "Feyre sone, for
youre sake shall I suffir the deth, and I have it not deserved. For ther is noon, saf
oonly God, that knowith the trowthe. And I may not be byleved, wherfore I most
275 with grete wronge be put to deth."

And as she made this lamentacion, the chelde gan to beholde hir and seyde,
"Moder," quod he, "be not dismayed, for ye shull never be juged to deth for my
cause." And when the moder herde this ansuere, she aferid that as she sodenly
made a sprynge, the childe fill oute of hir arme and cryde. The wemen that were
280 at the wyndowe wenden that she hadde ben aboute to kylle the childe, and sodeynly
axed hir, "Whi made the childe this shrike? Wilt thow slen it?" And she ansuerde,
"I thought it never, but it was for a merveyle that it seide unto me." Quod she, "It
seyde I sholde never be deed for hym." Than quod thei, "We shull heire hym sey
othir thynges."

285 Than they toke the childe and cherishid it, prayinge [it] to speke to hem. But
for ought they cowde do, thei myght gete of hym no mo wordes, till on a tyme the

256 don, down. **258 will**, wish. **263 durste**, dared to. **268 hens**, hence. **278 aferid that
as**, was so startled that. **280 wenden**, thought. **281 shrike**, shriek. **283 heire**, hear. **285
cherishid**, embraced. **286 cowde**, could; **mo**, more.

modir seyde to the wemen, quod she, "Manace me and sey I shalbe brente," for fayn wolde she that the wemen herde it speke. The wemen seyde to the moder, "Truly, it is grete damage and pité that youre fayre body shalbe brent for so foule

290 a creature. Better it were that he hadde never be born."

"Certes," quod he, "falsly ye lyen, and that hath my moder made yow to sey." And when they herde this they were sore abaisshed and seiden, "Certes, this is no childe, but it is a devell who myght this have knowen that he hath seide." Than they axed hym many demaundes, but he wolde speke no more, saf he seide, "Let

295 me be, and beth in pes, for ye ben more synfull than is my moder." And when they hadde herde this they hadden grete merveyle and seide, "This may not be kepte counseill, ne it ought not to be, and therfore we will telle it to the peple benethe withoute forth."

Tho wente they unto the wyndowe and clepeden to the peple and tolde them

300 this merveyle of the childe, insomoche that these tydinges com to the juges; and thei hadde therof grete merveile, and seide it was tyme to do justice upon the moder. Thei sente to the bailé that withynne forty dayes she sholde be brought before them to have her jugement. When the moder of Merlyn knewe that hir day was come, she hadde grete feer and sente worde to the gode hermyte, hir confessour.

305 Thus she abode eight dayes or more, till the tyme com that she sholde be brent. Whan she remembred hir on hir deth she made grete lamentacion for grete drede. The childe wente aboute in the tour and sye his moder wepynge, and he lowgh and was mery. The wemen that this beheilde seide, "Thow thynkest full lityll on thi moders grete sorowe, that this weke for thee shall be brente."

310 To this worde ansuerde the childe, "Feire moder, be not afeirde, for while I leve shall noon be so hardy to putt yow to deth, saf oonly God that is Almyghty." When the wemen herde this they seiden, "This childe shall ben a wise man and a wonderfull."

And when the day com that was sette, the wemen were taken oute of the tour,

315 and she bar hir sone in hir armes. The juges were come and toke the two women in counseill, and axed yef it were trewe that the childe hadde seyde soche wordes. And they seiden like as they hadden herde. And the juges seiden he moste be

287 Manace, Threaten. **288 fayn wolde she,** much she desired. **291 lyen,** lie. **294 demaundes,** questions. **299 Tho,** Then; **clepeden,** called. **300 insomoche,** with the result. **302 bailé,** bailiff. **307 lowgh,** laughed. **309 weke,** week.

connynge of moche thynge, yef he shulde save his moder. And the gode hermyte
was come to conforte the moder. And oon of [the] juges seide to hir, "Dame,
320 make yow redy, for ye moste suffir this martire of deth." And she ansuerde, prayinge
she myght speke with hir confessour; and they yaf hir lycence. And they entred
into a chamber and lefte hir childe withoute, and the peple aresoned it with many
questyons, but he yaf noon ansuere.

The moder spake with hir confessour, pitosly wepynge. And when she hadde
325 seyde all that she wolde, the gode man axed yef hir childe spake, and she seyde,
"Ye." "Certes," quod the gode man, "therof shall come merveiles."

Than thei come oute before the juges. The damsell was in hir smok, with a
mantill abouten hir, and fonde hir son withoute the chamber, and toke him in her
armes and stod still. And the juges examyned hyr: "Who was the fader of the
330 childe?" And she ansuerde, "I knowe well I go to my deth, and so God have
mercy and pyté on my soule, as I never knewe the fader, ne never hym saugh, ne
never erthely man hadde I of knowleche, wherthourgh I sholde have childe." The
juges seide, "We may never bileve that this be trewe that thow seiste."

Than the juges drough hem apart and cleped these othir wemen and seide,
335 "Dames, befill it ever to yow or to eny othir woman that ye herde of speke, that
myght have childe withowte carnall knowynge of man?" And those seyde,
"Withoute manes feliship myght no woman have chylde." Than the juge turned to
this damesell and tolde how those wemen hadde seide: "and, therfore, it is grete
reson that we do justice upon yow."

340 Then Merlyn sprong oute of his mother's armes angrye, and seide to the juge,
"It is not right that she be deed, for she hath it not deserved. And yef other shulde
be don justice upon all tho that don avouterye besyde ther housbands, many there
were werthy to be brent. And as touchynge this that is putte on my moder, she is
nothynge gilty. Freinde of that gode man yef ye charge hym to say the trouthe."

345 Then the juges examyned the gode hermyte yef it were so, and he seide "Ye,"
as by his wetynge; and he told hem how she was begiled in her slepe, and that
"she never sedd him that dide the deed, ne I never hym sygh, wherfore al that
aperteyneth to God I take upon me for hir. Nevertheles, I herde never of no soche

318 **connynge**, knowledgable. **320 martire**, torment. **322 aresoned**, addressed. **327 smok**,
smock. **332 wherthourgh**, by which means. **334 drough**, drew. **342 avouterye besyde**,
adultery against. **344 Freinde**, Ask. **346 wetynge**, knowing. **347 sedd**, saw; **sygh**, saw.

merveyle, safe only of this."

350 Than seide the child, "Ye have the houre and the tyme writen that I was ynne conceyved, and therby may you knowe yef my mother sey troath." The gode man ansuerde, "Thow seist soth, ne I wot not how thow myght knowe this." Than were the women cleped which tolde the hour of the childes berthe, and so was the gode mannes writyng fonde trewe. And the juge seide, "For al that, she sholde not go

355 quyte."

Than wrathed the childe and seide, "I know better my fader than thou doste thyn, and thy moder wiste beter whom is thy fader than my moder knoheth mynne." Than wrathed the juge and seide, "Yef thow censt ought say of my moder, sey on." Quoth the child, "I cowde sey so moche be thy moder that she hath beter deserved

360 the deth then hath my moder therfore, yef that thove me. Leet my moder be in pese that natht knoweth of that thow puttest on hir in thy inngendure."

Tho gan the juge to be right wrath and seyd, "Yef thow canste do so, then haste reserwed thy moder fro brennynge, but wyt thow well, yef thow canste not prewe this upon hir, I shall brenne bothe thee and thy moder togedere." "That shall never

365 be while I lyfe," quoth Merlyn, "that thow shall have no powre overene my moder." This was Merlyne's pletere for his moder.

[***Summary***. *Merlin tells the judge that he knows his own father better than the judge knows his. Angered by the implications of Merlin's assertion, the judge summons his own mother, and in a private chamber asks her if her husband is really his father. She assures him that he is; but when Merlin offers a detailed account of the judge's having been fathered by a parson, the astonished mother admits that this is so. Fols. 6v (line 1)–7r (line 20).*]

Than [Merlin] toke the juge apart and said, "Thi moder will anoon go telle hym that thee bygat all that I have seide, and when he hereth this, he will fle for feer of thee. And the devell, whom he hath ever servid, shalle lede hym to a water ther to

370 drowne hymself. And so mayste thow prove that I knowe thynges that be to come." "Yef this be so," quod the juge, "never shall I mystrowe thee."

355 quyte, free. **357 knoheth**, knows. **358 censt ought**, can anything. **359 be**, about. **360 thove**, allow. **361 inngendure**, engendering. **362 wrath**, angry. **363 reserwed**, saved. **366 pletere**, pleading. **371 Yef**, If; **mystrowe**, disbelieve.

Thus departed this counsell and come before the peple, and the juge seide well he hadde delyvered his moder fro brennynge be gode reson: "And be it well knowe to yow alle that never was seyen so wyse a man." And they ansuerde, "Blessed be oure Lorde that she is quyt fro the deth."

375

Thus delyverid Merlyn his moder, and [he] abode with the juge. And the juge sent thre men with his moder to witte yef it were trewe that the childe hadde seyde. And anoon as the juges moder was com hom, she tolde the person the merveyle that she hadde herde. And when [he] herde that, he was so astonyed that he kowde ansuere no worde, supposynge that anoon as the juge were come, he wolde sle hym. And so he spedde hym oute of the town till he com to a ryver, and seyde to hymself that better it were ther to drowne hymself than the juge sholde hym shamfully do hym to deth before the peple. Thus ledde hym the devell that he hadde served, that he hadde lepte into the ryver and drowned hymself. And that saw they that were sent with the lady.

380

385

And when they were returned, they told the juge, and hadde grete merveyle, and seyde unto Merlyn this thynge. And Merlyn lowgh. "I pray thee," quod he, "tellith to Blase, my moder's confessour." The juge tolde the gode man the merveyle that was befalle of the person. Than wente Merlyn and his moder and Blase and the juge whereas they liked.

390

This Blase was a nobill clerk and subtile, and herde Merlyn speke sotilly as of his age, as he that was but two yere olde and an half, and he merveylede gretely whereof his grete wytte myght come. And he assaide Merlyn in many maners. And Merlyn seyde, "The more thow assayest me, the more shalt thow fynde. But do and beleve that I shall sey, and I shall lyghtly teche thee to have the love of Jhesu Cryste and the lyf everlastynge."

395

Blase ansuerde, "I have herde thee sey, and I leve well that thow art the sone of the devell. Wherfore I doute thee sore, lest thow me disceyve and begyle." "Hit is a custome," quod Merlyn, "that alle shrewed hertys gon in alle their afferes, as well the evell as the gode, even as thow hast herde me sey that I was conceyved of the devell. So haste thow herde me sey that God hath yove me mynde to knowe thynges that be to come. And wyte thow well that it is Godes will that I sholde knowe it, for He wolde that the devell sholde lese his part in me. But I have not

400

---

375 quyt, reprieved. **378 person**, parson. **387 lowgh**, laughed. **393 assaide**, tested. **395 that**, what. **399 shrewed**, sinful. **401 yove**, given.

loste the knowynge of here engynes, but I holde of hem that I ought to conne. But
405   they ne shole therby take profyte, for they have fro henesforth loste ther travayle,
for they put me in so digne a vessell, the whiche ne ought not to be theirs. But yef
they hadden putt me in an evell woman, I sholde have hadde no power to have
knowen what God hadde i-be. Therfore, leve that I sey unto thee. And I shall telle
thee soche thynges that thow woldest trowe no creature myght sey unto thee. And
410   therfore make a boke, and alle tho thate this boke shul se sholde the rather kepe
hem from synne."

Blase ansuerde and seide, "The boke I will gladly make, but I conjure thee in
the name of the Fader, Sone, and Holy Goste that thow have no power me to
begyle, ne to make me do soche thynge that God sholde with [me] be displesed."
415   "Alle these thynges," quod Merlyn, "ne mowe thee hynder in body ne in sowle,
for never shall I make thee do thynge that shal be ageyn the volenté of oure Lord
Jhesu Cryste." "Than sey what thow wilt, and fro hensforth I will do it gladly."
Quod he, "Gete ynke and parchemyn and all that longeth to writynge, and than I
will telle thee."

420   Blase sought all that hym mystered to write with, and when he was all redy,
Merlyn began to telle the lovynge of Jhesus Criste, and of Joseph Abaramathie,
like as thei hadden ben of the slayn; and of Pieron, and of othir felowes like as
they weren departed; and the fynyshment of Joseph and of alle other. And after he
tolde hym that whan alle thise thynges were don, how the develles toke theire
425   counseile of that they hadde loste their power that they were wonte to have over
man and woman. And how the prophetes hadden hyndred here purpos, and how
they were acorded to purchase a man that sholde have their witte and mynde to
disceyve the peple. "And thow hast herde be my moder, and also be other, the
travayle that they hadden to begete me. But through theire foly they alle loste their
430   travayle."

Thus devised Merlyn this boke and made Blase to write it, which hadde therof
so grete merveile that he wolde not telle it to no persone, and alwey hym thought
that his tales weren gode, and therfore he herkened hem gladly. In the menetyme

404 here engynes, their deceits; **holde of hem**, retain of them; **conne**, know. **405 shole**,
shall. **406 digne**, worthy. **408 i-be**, been; **leve**, believe. **410 tho**, those. **411 hem**, themselves. **415 ne mowe thee hynder**, can not hinder you. **416 volenté**, desires. **420 mystered**,
needed. **423 fynyshment**, ending. **426 here**, their.

that they entended aboute this mater, come Merlyn to Blase and seyde, "Thow
435   moste have grete traveyle aboute the makynge, and so shall I have moche more."
And Blase axed, "How?" Merlyn seyde, "I shall be sente after to seche oute of the
weste, and they that shull come to seche me have graunted their lorde that they
shull me sle. But whan thei come and here me speke, they shull have no will me
to sle. And I shall go with hem. And thow shalt go into that partyes where they be
440   that have the Holy Vessell. And ever hereafter shall thy boke gladly be herde.
And he that will know the lyf of kynges whiche were in the Grete Bretayne before that Cristendom come, beholde The Story of Bretons, that is a boke that
Maister Martyn traunslated oute of Latyn. But heire resteth this matere."

434 **entended aboute**, attended to. **436 to seche**, to be sought. **439 partyes**, districts. **442
Bretons**, Britons (i.e., the British, not the Bretons).

34

[Vortiger's Tower]

[*Summary*. *The story now concerns Constance, King of the Britons, and his sons Moyne, Pendragon, and Uther; and the treacherous deeds of Vortiger, Constance's steward.*

After a long reign, King Constance dies and is succeeded by his son Moyne. The heathen Danes take this opportunity to invade Britain. Because King Moyne is unable to repulse them, the people begin to turn against him. The barons want Vortiger to become king, but he says that he will not do this as long as Moyne is alive, a remark that leads some of his followers to murder the king. Vortiger feigns anger at Moyne's murder but accepts the throne. Mistrusting Vortiger, Constance's two remaining sons flee to Benoye in Gaul. Vortiger executes Moyne's killers, angering their friends and causing them to rebel; Vortiger drives the rebels out of the kingdom.

Now the people realize that Vortiger is a vicious tyrant. They rise against him, and Vortiger requests help from the Danes. Vortiger marries the daughter of Aungier, the Danish leader. Fearing his own people and fearing the surviving sons of Constance, Vortiger begins building a mountain stronghold. But when his tower reaches a certain height, the walls tumble down. Vortiger's wisemen cannot explain this marvel, but seven of them tell Vortiger he must find a seven-year-old boy born without an earthly father. The boy's blood, they say, will strengthen the tower's foundations. Search parties are sent out to find such a boy. They are instructed to kill him and bring back his blood. Fols. 8r (line 10)–10r (line 15).]

Thus thei reden in oon company, alle four, till on a day that thei passeden thourgh a feelde beside a town wherein were grete plenté of children that therin were pleyinge. And Merlyn, that knewe well that these four com to inquere after hym, drough hym towarde oon of the richest of the company, for that he wiste hym moste fell and hasty. He hente his staf and yaf this childe a grete buffet. And anoon, this othir began to crye and wape and to myssey Merlyn, and reproved hym with a lowde voyce, and cleped hym mysbegeten wrecche and faderles.

5

1 **reden**, rode. 5 **fell**, cruel; **hente**, seized; **yaf**, gave. 6 **wape**, weep; **myssey**, revile. 7 **cleped**, called; **wrecche**, wretch.

When these messagers herden this, thei com toward the childe that was wepynge
and axed hym whiche was he that hadde smyten hym. And he hem ansuerde, "It is
10 the sone of a woman whiche never knewe who hym begat, ne never man cowde
telle of his fader."

And when Merlyn herde this, he com ageyn them laughinge and seide, "I am
he that ye seche, and he that ye be sworn ye sholden sle, and brynge my blode to
Kynge Vortiger." And [whan] thei herden hym thus sey, thei were sore a-merveyled
15 and axeden hym, "Who hath tolde thee this?" Quod he, "I wiste it er ye were
sworn." Quod thei, "Than moste thow come with us." "Nay," quod he, "I doute
that ye will me sle." And yet he knewe well that thei hadde therto no talant, but he
seide that for to preve hem better.

Quod Merlyn, "Yef ye will graunte me that ye shull not do me disese, I will go
20 with yow, and also telle why the tour may not stonde." And when thei herde that,
thei were more abaissed than before. "Truly," quod thei, "this childe is merveilouse,
and grete pité it were hym to sle." And eche of hem seyde that hem were better to
be forsworn than to sle this childe.

Than seide Merlyn, "Ye shull come herberewe theras is my moder, for I may
25 not go with yow withoute takynge leve of here, and also of a gode man which is in
the same place." Thei seide, "We will go where that thow wilte."

Thus brought Merlyn the messagers of the kynge to his moder place, and when
Merlyn come into the house, he comaunded that thei sholde have gode chere.
When thei were alyght, he brought hem before Blase and seide, "Se hem here that
30 I tolde sholde come to seche me to sle." And [he] seide to them, "I pray yow that
ye sey the trouthe before this gode man, why that ye beth sente, and wite ye well
yef ye gabbe enythynge, I know it wele inough." And thei ansuerde, "We will no
lesynge make."

Quod Merlyn to Blase, "Maister, understonde well what thei sey." Quod the
35 massanger: "We be with Kynge Vortiger, whiche hath begonne to make a stronge
toure. And when the werke of this tour is thre or four fadom of height, it may not
holde, but synketh in an hour all that is wrought in thre monthis. Wherefore the
kynge is angry and wroth, and he dide sende after clerkes to knowe the cause that

12 **ageyn**, towards. 15 **wiste**, knew. 16 **moste**, must. 18 **preve hem**, test them. 19 **disese**,
injury. 21 **abaissed**, abashed. 23 **be forsworn**, break their promise. 24 **herberewe**, lodge.
29 **alyght**, dismounted. 32 **gabbe**, lie. 33 **lesynge**, falsehood. 36 **fadom**, fathom.

his werke may not holde."

40 "Ye," quod Merlin, "but noon of the clerkes ne cowde se the cause that letted the werke to holde. But thei sien how I was born and how that I myght hem distroie, and so thei dide acorde that I sholde be slayn and seide that the kynges werke sholde stonde yef he myght have the blode of the childe born withoute fader. And when Vortiger herde this, he heilde this a grete merveile, and trowed

45 that that the clerkes seiden [was] trewe. And the clerkes charged the kynge that in no maner he sholde not se me alyve; but as sone as I were founde, that I sholde withoute respite be slain, and my blode to be brought to be putte with the morter in the foundement of the tour, and by that thei seiden it sholde holde. Vortiger, by their techynge, toke twelve messagers and made alle twelve to swere that thei

50 sholde me sle and bringe with hem my blode. And of these twelve be heer four whiche, when ye were met, passeden thourgh the feild where childern were bourdinge, and I, that knewe ye come me for to seche, smote oon of my felowes, for I wiste well he wolde sey of me the werste that he knewe in his anger. And therfore I it dide, that this gode man shulde fynde me trewe of that I hadde seide.

55 Now, maister," quod Merlin to Blase, "axe hem yef it be so as I sey."

"Truly," seide Blase, "it were grete pité hym to sle, for yef he lyve he shal be right wise." "Certes," seide evereche of the messagers, "I hadde lever be disherited than he hadde resceyved deth thourgh me, and he hymself seth that he knoweth all thynge, wote yef therto we have talent or noon."

60 Than thei cleped in ageyn Merlyn, that was gon oute at dore. And Blase seid to hym how thei badde hym axe yef he wiste that thei hadden talent hym to sle. And Merlyn lowgh and seide, "I wote well now thei be nothynge in will therto." Quod thei, "Wilt thow go with us?" And Merlin seide, "Ye, with gode will, yef ye will promyse me truly to brynge me before the kynge, and that ye ne suffer noon other

65 to do me harme ne disese, er I have with hym spoken." And thei hym graunted.

Than seide Blase, "I se well that thow wilt now leve me. What wilt thow that I shalle do of this werke that I have begonne?" "That shalle I telle thee," quod Merlin. "Thow woste well that oure Lord hath yove me so moche witte and

---

40 letted, prevented. **44–45 trowed that that,** believed that which. **48 foundement,** foundation. **50 heer,** here. **52 bourdinge,** playing. **57 evereche,** every one; **lever,** rather. **59 wote,** knows; **talent,** intentions [to slay him]. **68 yove,** given.

70 memorye that he that wende to be siker of me hath failed of his purpos, and I
moste go in to that contré fro whiche these be come to fecche me. And ther shalle
I be the beste beleved man that ever was, sef all only God that is Almyghty. And
thow shalt come thider to make an ende of the werke. But thow ne shalt not come
with me, but by thy self, and axe after a londe that is cleped Northumbirlonde.
And that contré is full of grete forestis and full wylde to them of the selve contré.
75 Ther thow shalt abide, and I shall come to thee and telle thee all the mater that
longeth to thi werke. And moche is thy travayle, and thow shalt have gode leyser;
and as longe as the worlde dureth shall thi boke gladly ben herde. And wite thow
well that my grete traveill shall not be byfore this kynges courte. This kynge, to
whom all my grete traveill shall be, and the traveile of Grete Breteyne, his name
80 shal be Arthur. Thow shalt go thider, as I have told thee, and I shall often come to
thee and brynge soche tidinges as thow shalt put in thi boke. And wite it well,
peple shul be glad ever to heiren it. For shul but fewe thinges be don but in no
place, but therin shal be a partye. And thi boke shal be cleped while the worlde
endureth the *Boke of the Seynt Graal*."

85 Thus spake Merlyn with his maister, and taught hym how he sholde do. He
ycleped hym "maister" for that he was maister to his moder. When the gode man
herde Merlin thus speke, he was glad and seide, "What thow wilte comaunde me,
I am redy to do it."

Thus Merlyn made hym redy to go and seide to the messengers, "I will go take
90 leve of my moder." Tho he brought hem theras was his moder and seide, "Feire
moder, heire ben come men of fer contrees for to seche me, and I will go by youre
leve. For me hoveth to yelde thee to Jhesu Criste, of that He hath yove me power.
And that I may not do but I go thider as thei shullen lede me. And Blase, youre
maister, also shall go, and moste we bothe departe fro yow at this tyme."

95 "Feire sone," quod she, "to God I comaunde yow, for I knowe not yef it were
wisdome to witholde yow or noon. But yef it were youre plesier, I wolde that
Blase sholde abide." "Dame," quod he, "it may in no wise ben." Thus toke Merlyn
leve of his moder and wente with the massengers; and on the tother side Blase

69 **wende**, thought; **siker**, certain. 71 **sef**, except. 74 **selve**, same. 76 **moche**, great; **travayle**,
toil; **leyser**, leisure. 86 **ycleped**, called; **maister**, religious instructor. 90 **Tho**, Then. 91
fer, distant. 92 **me hoveth**, it behooves me. 95 **comaunde**, commend. 96 **witholde**, re-
strain.

departed and yede in to Northumberlond, ther Merlin had him comaunded.

100   And the massagiers rode forth till thei come thourgh a town in whiche was a market. And when thei were passed thorugh thei overtoke a carl that hadde bought a payre of stronge shone, and also stronge lether to clowte hem with. And when Merlyn sye the carle, he began to laughe. The messagiers axed hym wherfore he lough. "I laugh," quod he, "at this cherl that hath bought hym so stronge shoone,
105 and also clowte lether, and I telle yow certeynly that he shal be dead before he com fully to his howse."

    And when thei herde that, thei heilde it a grete merveile and seide thei wolde wyte yef that were trewe. Than two of them sewed hym, and other two abode with Merlyn. They hadde not folowed the cherl half a myle that thei fonde hym deed in
110 myddell of the wey, and his shone aboute his nekke. Than thei returned and overtoke hir felowes and tolde hem the merveyle that thei hadde seien.

    "Forsothe," quod thei, "grete foles were the clerkes that so wise a man wolde have slayn." "In faith," quod the oon, "I sholde suffer grete myschef er he had eny harm." And so thei seiden all four that Merlyn ne herde it not. And when thei were
115 come to Merlyn, he thanked hem of that they hadde seide, and that [thei] wolden hym so moche gode. And thei were gretly abasshed and seiden, "We may nought sey ne do but this childe knowes it."

    Thus thei riden forth her journeis till thei come withinne Vortigers power. And as thei passed thourgh a town, they saugh a deed childe on a beere born to chirche
120 to be beried. And after the corse was made grete doel and wepynge. And when Merlyn saugh the wepynge and sye the preste and the clerkes wente synginge before, he gan to laugh and seide to his felowes, "I se a merveile." And thei axed, "What?" Quod Merlyn, "Ye se that gode man that maketh this grete sorowe?" And thei seide, "Ye." "And se ye not the preeste that singeth al before?" Quod
125 thei, "We se hym well." "Forsothe," quod Merlin, "he ought to make the sorowe that the tother gode man maketh, for wethet it well that the childe is the prestes sone. And the other man wepeth and hath more cause to laugh." Quod thei, "How may we knowe that it be so?" "Goth to the moder and axe whi she doth wepe. And she will sey for her sone that is deed. And ye shall sey, it is not hir sone but the

99 yede, went. **101 carl**, churl, peasant. **102 shone**, shoes; **clowte**, mend. **108 wyte**, know; **sewed**, pursued. **116 abasshed**, amazed. **118 her**, their. **119 beere**, bier. **123 Ye se**, Do you see. **126 wethet**, know.

130 prestes sone that so hye singeth. And than shall ye heere what she will sey."

The massagers wente to the woman and toke her in counseill and seide as Merlyn hadde hem taught. And when the woman herde hem so say, she was abaisshed, and seide, "Seres, for Godes love, mercy! I se wele I may not to yow lye, thowgh I wolde, for that ye sey is trewe. But I beseche yow, telle it not my housbonde, for

135 than he wolde me sle." And when thei hadde herde this merveile, thei turned and overtoke her felishep and seiden as thei herde.

And than thei reden forth till they come a journey fro thens ther Vortiger was. Than seide two of the messagers to Merlin, "We shall go before to the kynge and telle hym that we have founden. Now yeve us counseile how thow wilte we shall

140 sey, for I trowe he will blame us that we have not thee slayn."

"Sirs," quod Merlyn, "Sey as I shall telle yow, and ye shal be well excused. Ye shull go to Vortiger and sey that ye have me founden, and sey I shall telle hym truly the cause whi his tour may not stonde. With this condicion: that the clerkes have the same juyse that thei hadde ordeyned for me. And also sey hym I can telle

145 hym why the clerkes wolde have me deed. And when ye have seide thus, doth hardely that he yow comaundeth."

With that the messagers departed and come to Vortiger. And when he sye them he was gladde, and axed anoon how they hadde spedde. "Sir," seide thei, "in the beste wise that we may." Than thei cleped the kynge in counseile and tolde how

150 thei hadde found Merlyn. And also they seide, yef he hymself ne wolde, thei sholde him never have founden.

"Of whiche Merlin," seide the kynge, "speke ye? Sholde ye not have sought the fadirles childe and have brought me the blode of hym?" "Sir," thei seide, "that same is Merlin that we of speke to yow. And wetith it wele that he is the wisest

155 man and the beste devynour that is, saf only God. And sir," seide thei, "right as ye made us to swere to do youre comaundement, all that was don and seide he cowde wele telle us at oure firste metynge. And he tolde us also that the clerkes ne knewe not the cause why that youre tour may not stonde. But he shall telle yow apertly. And many other grete merveiles hath he us shewed be the wey, and hath us sente

160 for to wite yef ye will with hym speke. And yef ye will we shull sle hym, for two

136 **her felishep,** their company. 137 **reden,** rode. 144 **juyse,** justice. 146 **hardely,** boldly. 150 **ne wolde,** had not wished. 154 **wetith,** know. 155 **devynour,** diviner. 158 **apertly,** openly. 160 **will²,** wish.

of oure felowes beth thereas he is."

"Yef ye," quod the kynge, "will take upon youre lyves that he shall telle me whi my toure fallith, I will not that he be deed." "We will undertake it," quod thei. "Than go fecche hym," quod the kynge.

165   The messagers yede their wey and the kynge rode after hem. When Merlin saugh the messagers he seide to them, "Ye have plegged me upon youre lyves that I shall have no drede of deth." And thei ansuerde, "Thou seiste trewe, for [we] hadde lever a be in grete aventure than thow sholdest dye, and that oon moste us nedes do." "I shall waraunte yow," quod Merlin, "of that ye have undertake."

170   Thus thei rode forth till thei mette with the kynge, and anoon Merlin hym salued and seide, "Sir kynge, lete me speke with yow in counseile." Than the kynge drough apart and called hem that he hadde brought with hym.

"Sir," quod Merlyn, "thow haste do seche me for thi toure that may not stonde and comaundeste me to sle, be counseile of thy clerkes that seide the toure sholde
175   holde by vertu of my blode. Thei have not seide the trouth. But yef thow wilte graunte me to do to hem the same that thei wolde do to me, I will telle the cause whi it falleth, and also I shall teche thee how thow shalt make it to stonde and endure."

And Vortiger ansuerde, "Yef thow do as thow seiest, I will do with hem as
180   thow wilte." "Than," quod Merlin, "go we thideras this toure is in makynge, and make the clerkes be brought theder, and I shall axe hem whi the toure doth falle, and so mayst thow hier ther ansuere." Than thei wente to the place ther the toure sholde be made, and the clerkes were sente fore and come before the kynge.

And whan thei were come, Merlyn made oon to axe of hem whi that that toure
185   fill; and thei ansuerde, "We knowe no cause whi it fill, but we can telle what shall make it for to holde." And then seide the kynge, "Ye tolde me a merveillouse thynge, that I sholde do seche a childe born withouten fader, and I wote not how he myght be founden."

Than spake Merlyn and seide to the clerkes, "Sirs, ye holde the kynge a fole,
190   that thus make hym seche a man that is born withouten fader, and ye no do it nothynge for his profite. But ye dide it for this, that ye fonde in youre sorte that ye

161 **thereas**, where. 168 **lever a be**, rather have been; **aventure**, uncertainty. 169 **waraunte**, protect. 170 **salued**, hailed. 173 **do seche me**, saught me. 174 **sle**, be slain. 180 **thideras**, where. 189 **fole**, fool. 191 **fonde**, found; **sorte**, divinations.

shulde be deed thourgh hym, and for drede therof have ye do the kynge to understonde that I sholde be slayn, and my blode be putte in the foundement of the toure, and that sholde make it to laste and holde. Thus ye thought to sle hym

195   be the whiche ye sholde be brought to the deth as be youre sorte."

When thei herde the childe telle hem that thei supposid no creature hadde knowen, thei weren abasshed and wiste wele that thei sholde deye. Than Merlin seide to the kynge, "Now may ye knowe whi these clerkes wolde have me slayn: nought for to holde youre toure but for theire sorte seyde thei sholde dye for me.

200   Now axe hem yef this be true, for thei sholde not be so hardy before me to make yow no lesynge."

"Seith he trewe?" quod the kynge. "Sir," seide the clerkes, "ye, truly. But we merveile wherby he myght this knowe. Wherfore we beseke yow graunte us to live, that we may see that he shewe the trowth whi the toure fallith, and yef he can

205   telle the remedye." "Certes," quod Merlyn, "have ye no drede to dye before ye se the cause that the toure doth falle, and that the werke may not laste."

"Sir kynge," quod Merlin, "understonde, and I shall telle thee. Under this erthe is a grete water, and under that water be two dragons that see no sight. So is that oon reade and that other white. And above them is two grete flat stones, and when

210   thei fele that the werke peyseth hevy upon them, they turne hem, and the water maketh so grete bruyt that all that is made aboven it moste nede falle. Now lete loke yef this be trewe or no. And yef it be founde that this be [the] cause that the werke stondeth not, lete my plegges be quyte, and the clerkes in blame, that of all this ne knewe nothinge."

215   "Certes," quod Vortiger, "yef this be as thow seist, than art thow the wisest man of the worlde. Now telle me how this erthe may be hadde awey." And Merlin seide, "In cartes and on mennes nekkes."

Anoon the kynge made come laboreres, and Merlin comaunded that the clerkes sholde be wele kepte. And so wrought the laboreres that thei hadde awey the

220   erthe, and fonde the water, and dede it to laden oute, and lete the kynge wite how thei hadden don. The kynge come thider gladly and brought with hym Merlin. When he com thider, he beheilde the water that was grete, and cleped two of his counsellers and seide, "This childe is right wise that knewe this to ben heere, and

192 do, caused. **200 make**, tell. **201 lesynge**, lie. **209 reade**, red. **210 fele**, feel; **peyseth**, weighs (presses). **211 bruyt**, turmoil. **213 plegges be quyte**, pledges be fully paid.

42

yet seith that ther ben two dragons under, and I will knowe the soth, whatsoever it
225 coste."

Than the kynge cleped Merlyn and seide, "How shall we have this water awey?"
Quod Merlyn, "Lete make goteres into the diches." Than were the diches made,
and the water to renne oute. And Merlyn come to Vortiger and seide, "As soone
as these dragons felen togeder, thei will fighten strongely, and that oon shall sle
230 that other. Therfore, send after alle the gode men of thi londe to se the bataile, for
it hath grete significacion."

Than sente Vortiger after alle the worthy men of his londe, clergie and other.
And when thei were alle comen, Vortiger tolde hem the merveiles that Merlin
hadde shewde and of the two dragons how thei shulde fight. Than seide oon to
235 another, "It is gode to be seen." And they axed the kynge yef he knewe whiche
sholde have the better. And the kynge seide he hadde not yet tolde.

Whan the water was all voided, thei saugh the two stones that were upon the
two dragons. The kynge axed how thei myght be hadde awey, and Merlyn seide,
"Full wele, for they will never meve till eche of hem fele other, and than shull thei
240 fight till that oon muste dye." The kynge axed, "Whiche shall have the victorie?"

"In the fightynge," quod Merlyn, "is grete signifiance whiche I may not telle,
but gladly I will telle thee before three worthi men." Than Vortiger cleped thre
men that he moste truste inne, and Merlyn axed, "Be these thre men wele of thi
counseile?" And he ansuewerde, "Ye." "Than may I telle before them that thou
245 demandest. I do thee to wete," quod he, "that the white shall sle the reade. But
first shall he have grete peyne, and in that he shall sle hym is grete tokenynge to
hym that can it understonde. But I will sey no more till the bataile is at an ende."

Then yede the peple to oon of the stones and leften it up and founde the white
dragon. When the peple saugh hym so grete and hidouse thei hadde grete drede.
250 Than wente thei to the tother ston and drough it awey; and than thei were more
aferde than before, for it was moche greter and semed more feirce. And as Vortiger
semed, he moste overcome that other. And Merlin seide to the kynge, "Now lete
my plegges be quyte." "So be thei," seide the kynge.

Tho spronge up the two dragons and foughten togeder with teeth and feet, and

227 **goteres**, gutters, drains. 229 **felen togeder**, collide. 245 **do thee to wete**, want you to
know. 246 **tokenynge**, meaning. 252 **semed**, thought. 253 **plegges be quyte**, promises be
kept. 254 **Tho**, Then.

255   never herde ye of so stronge bataile betwene two bestes, ne so crewell fight. And so thei foughten to mydday, and the peple semed that the reade sholde overcome the white, till that the white threwe so moche fiere and flame that he brente up the reade, and so was he deed. Than the white leide hym down to reste for werynesse, and ne lived after but thre dayes. And thei that this syen seyde that never so grete

260   merveile hadde be seyn beforn.

And Merlin seide to the kynge, "Now mayste thow make thi toure as grete and large as thow wilte, for it shall no more falle." Than comaunded Vortiger the werkemen to make up the toure the strengest that myght be devised. And often axed Vortiger of Merlyn the significance of the two dragons. And he seid, "It was

265   the tokenynge of thinges that were don and also of thinges that were to come, and yef thow wilte ensure me that thow shalt do me noon harme heere in audience of this peple, ne suffer noon other to do me harme in thy reame, I will telle the significacion." And Vortiger made hym soche suerté as he wolde.

Quod Merlin, "Bringe hethir thy counsell and the clerkes that sorted of this

270   toure." The kynge dide as he comaunded. When thei were come, Merlyn spake to the clerkes and seide, "Ye were foles in youre art, that wolde not aquite yow as trewe men; and therfore ye be worthi to have as ye have deserved. And ye sawgh wele how I was bore. And he that shewed yow that made yow semblance that ye sholde be deed for me; and that dide he for sorowe that he hadde loste me, and

275   therfore he wolde that ye hadde me putte to deth. But I have soche a goode Lorde that He shall me deffende yef it be His plesier, and I shall make hym a lyer, for ye shull never for me be deed, yef ye will me graunte to do that I shall yow sey."

And when they herde hym sey that thei sholde be respited fro deth, thei were gladde and seiden, "What that thow comaundest we shall do it, for we se well that

280   thow arte the wisest man that liveth." Quod Merlin, "Ye shull swere never to entermete of that arte, and I will that ye be confessed and take youre penaunce so that youre soules be not dampned." And thei hym thankeden and seide thei sholde don his comaundement. Thus delyvered Merlin the clerkes whiche made hym to be sought for to be putte to deth.

256 the peple semed, it seemed to the people; **reade**, red. **257 brente**, burned. **267 reame**, realm. **268 suerté**, promise. **269 sorted**, made divinations. **273 made yow semblance**, showed you. **274 for**, because of. **278 respited**, saved. **281 entermete**, practice; **will**, wish. **283 delyvered**, saved.

44

285 Vortiger com to hym and seide, "Telle me the significaunce of the two dragons." "The reade dragon," quod Merlin, "betokeneth thee, and the white dragon
signifieth the sones of Constance." When Vortiger herde this, he was ashamed.
And Merlin seide, "Yef thow wilte, I will sey more, with that thow conne me no
magré."

290 Vortiger seide, "Here ne is no man but of my privé counsell. And therfore I will
thow telle me all the trouthe." "I tolde thee," quod Merlin, "that the reade signifieth
thee, and I shall telle thee how the children of Constance were yonge and tender,
after the deth of their fader. And yef thow were soche as thow oughteste to have
ben, thow sholdeste have kepte hem and yeven hem counseile ageins alle erthly

295 men. And well thow knowest that thow haste their heritage wrongfully; for when
thow knewest the peple loved thee, thow drowest thee abakke for to helpe them in
their nedes. And when eny of the londe complayneth to thee for the kynges inno-
cence, and seiden thei wolden thow sholde take upon thee to be kynge to defende
the reame fro their enmyes, thow ansueredest covertly, and seidest thow myghtest

300 not while Kynge Moyne was livinge. And thei that thow seidest this to undirstoden
wele that thow woldest have hym deed. And therfore thei slowen their kynge. But
thei leften two brethern, the whiche fledde into straunge londe for drede of thee.
And so were thow made kynge, and yet thow holdest their heritage with wronge.
And when thei hadden kylde the Kynge Moyne, thei come before thee. Thow

305 madest hem to be distrowied, to shewe semblaunce as thow hadde forthought the
kynges deth."

 Vortiger undirstode wele that Merlyn hym tolde and wist wele that he tolde
hym the trouth, and seide, "I se well that thow art oon of the wisest men of the
worlde. Wherfore, I pray thee to yeve me counseill in this cas, and also telle me

310 on what deth I shall dye."

 Quod he, "Yef I telle thee that I wil not sey the betokenyng of the two dragons.
I do thee to wite that the reade dragon signifieth thee; in that he was so grete and
hidouse, betokeneth thee and thy grete power. And the white dragon betokeneth
the two childeren that be fledde for drede of thee. And that thei foughten so longe

315 togeder, betokeneth that thow haste so longe kepte their herytage with wronge.
And that the white dragon brente the redde dragon betokeneth that the two brethern

288 with, provided that. **288–89 conne me no magré,** bear me no grudge. **304 kylde,**
killed. **305 shewe semblaunce,** make it seem. **312 do thee to wite,** caused you to know.

shull brenne thee with theire power. And therfore I ne trowe not that this toure shal be thy warante, but that thow shalt dye by hem."

320   When Vortiger undirstode this, he gan to wrathe and axed hym, "Where ben these children?" Quod Merlyn, "Thei be in the see, with grete strengthe of peple, and come into heir londe to take vengaunce on thee. For thei seyn thow dedist their brother to be slain. And wite it wele that thei shall aryve withinne thre monthes withoute eny faile."

318 warante, protection. **320 see**, sea. **321 heir**, their; **dedist**, caused.

[Vortiger's Demise; The Battle of Salisbury; and The Death of Pendragon]

*[**Summary**. Vortiger leads his forces to Winchester to face the sons of Constance, and Merlin goes to Blase, who records what Merlin tells him in his book. When Pendragon and Uther arrive with their army, most of the people desert Vortiger and hold with the brothers. Vortiger retreats to his tower, pursued by the brothers. They set fire to the tower, killing Vortiger and his followers.*

Pendragon, having been made king, wages war against the Danish invaders. Hearing of the wondrous boy Merlin, Pendragon sends for him. Merlin amazes the messengers, who fear they have spoken with the devil. Pendragon goes himself to see Merlin, leaving Uther in command. Merlin also amazes Pendragon with his prophetic and shape-shifting abilities. Merlin informs Pendragon that Uther has just slain Aungier, the leader of the Danes. Pendragon asks Merlin to return with him, and Merlin says he will come in eleven days. Merlin then goes to see Blase.

On the eleventh day Merlin appears at court, disguised as a messenger from Uther's mistress. When Merlin reveals who he really is, the brothers are delighted. They promise to follow Merlin's advice, and Merlin says he will come whenever they want him. Pendragon asks Merlin how to defeat the Danes. Merlin says to offer them safe-conduct if they will leave Britain. Ulfin and other knights carry the message to the Danes, who attempt to bargain; Merlin refuses to negotiate. The Danes finally agree, and they leave Britain.

An envious baron tries to trick Merlin into making erroneous predictions. Merlin predicts that the man will die by a combination of breaking his neck, hanging, and drowning. This comes about when the baron is thrown from his horse while crossing a bridge. The people say that anyone who disbelieves Merlin is a fool; they begin recording his prophecies in a book. Fols. 13v (line 33)–18r (line 10).]

Than began Merlin to speke so mystily, wherof the *Boke of Prophesyes* is made. And after come Merlin to the kynge and to Uter his brother and seide to hem pitously, "I love moche yow and youre wurship. Have ye no mynde of the sarazins that ye drive oute of the londe after the deth of Aungis?" And thei seide, "Yesse,

1 **mystily**, obscurely. 3 **mynde of**, concern with. 4 **drive**, drove.

47

5 full wele. But why sey ye?" Quod Merlin, "I sey for this: that they sey thei shull never fenisshe till thei have avengid the deth of Aungis. And thei have assembled a grete power, and wele to conquere this londe be force."

When the kinge and his brother herde this, thei merveiled gretly and axed of Merlin, "Have thei so grete power to holde party ageyn oures?" And he ansuerde
10 ageyn, "Every man that ye have defensable, they have tweyne. Therfore, but ye be wisely ruled, ye shull be distroied and lese youre reame." Quod the kynge, "We wil be ruled be youre counseile." And than he axed, "When trowe ye that they shull come?" And Merlin seide, "The eleventh day of Juyne; and noon ne shall this knowe saf ye two; and I deffende yow to speke therof, but do as I shall
15 yow counseile. Sende after alle youre peple and make hem the grettest joye and feste that ye may, and comaunde hem to be the laste day of Juyn on the playn of Salisburye."

Than seide the kynge, "Shall we suffer hem to aryve withoute deffence?" And Merlyn seide, "Ye, yef ye will do my counseile; and suffer hem to come as fer as
20 ye may fro theire arivage. And so shall ye kepe hem two dayes, and thei shull have grete dissese for lakke of water. And the thirde day ye shull with hem fighten. And yef ye do thus, ye shull have the victorye."

Than seide the two brethern, "I pray yow telle us yef eny of us shall dye in that bataile." And Merlin ansuerde, "Ther is nothynge that hath begynnynge but it
25 moste have endynge. Ne no man ought to be dismayed of deth, to resceyve it as he oweth to do. And therfore I will that ye bringe the hiest reliques that ye have, and ye shull bothe swere to do as I shall sey yow, for yowre profite and youre worship; and than shall I boldely telle yow how ye shul be governed."

And thei swore as Merlin dide devise. And when they were sworn, Merlin seide
30 unto hem, "Ye have sworne that in this bataile ye shull be gode men and true, agein God and youreself. Ne noon may be trewe to hymself but he first be trewe to God. And loke ye be trewly confessed for that ye shull fight ageyn yowre enmyes. And after, have no doute to overcome theym, for thei have no bileve in the Trinité. And wite ye wele that seth Cristendom come first into this ile, was never so grete
35 bataile, ne never shall in youre tyme. And also, knoweth wele that ther oon of yow two moste nede passe in this bataile. Therfore eche man ordeyne for his

6 **fenisshe**, desist. 7 **wele**, wish. 14 **deffende**, forbid. 20 **arivage**, landing place. 21 **dissese**, discomfort. 31 **agein**, between. 34 **seth**, since.

moste worship that he can, ageins that he cometh before his Lorde. And [knoweth] that oon of yow moste go to Hym. And therfore goth in soche wise that ye may have His love when ye come to His presence."

40 Thus ended the counseile of Merlyn. And the two brethern understode what he hadde seyde, and sente after alle the estates of theire londe. And when thei weren alle come, thei yaf hem grete yeftes. And the kynge hem praide to make hem garnysshed of theire armes and of horse; and also the laste weke of Juyn to be redy, in the entré of the playnes of Salisbury, upon the river of Tamyse, to diffende

45 the reame. And thus it lefte till the day that was somowned. And the two brethern ageyn their burghes and townes made gode ordenaunce, as Merlin dide hem counseile.

And at Pentecoste thei heilde courte upon the rivere, and ther were many riche festes. Ther thei were so longe till thei herden that the Danoyse weren arived.

50 Than the kynge sente to prelates of the Churche that every man of the oste sholde be confessed, and every man to foryeven other and be in charité and clene lyf.

Than seide Pendragon to Merlin that tydinges were come: the Sarazins weren arived. And Merlin seide it was trewe. Than the kynge axed what was his counseile to do. And Merlin seide, "Ye shall tomorowe sende thedir that oon half of youre

55 peple; and when they be come from their arivage, than go betwene hem and the aryvage. And youre peple shulde holde hem so shorte that ther ne shall be noon of hem but thei wolde fayn be theras they come fro. And thus shull ye do two dayes. And the thirde day, whan ye se a dragon all reade fleynge up in the ayre, than boldly fight with hem, for ye shall have the vyctorye."

60 At this counseile were no mo but Pendragon and Uter. And when thei hadde herde this thei were gladde. And than seide Merlin, "I will go; and be ye right sure of this that I have yow seide. And thenke to be gode men and gode knyghtes."

Thus thei departed, and Uter made redy his felishep to go betwene hem and the ryver. And Merlyn come to hym and seide, "Thenke to do wele, and have no

65 drede, for thow shalt not dye in this bataile." When Uter herde this, he was gladde in herte. Than Merlin went to his maister Blase in Northumbirlonde and tolde hym many thinges that he wrote in his boke.

Uter and his peple rode till thei come betwene the Danes and theire shippes,

41 estates, social classes. **43 garnysshed**, prepared. **44 entré**, entry. **45 somowned**, named. **46 ordenaunce**, plan. **50 oste**, host.

70 and kept hem two dayes that thei myght never ryde. The thirde day the kynge come so nygh that that oon myght se that other. Whan the sarazins saugh the two hostes, thei were gretly dismayed, and sye wele that thei myght not repaire to their shippes withoute grete bataile.

Than shewde the sign in the ayre that Merlin hadde seide, and than the Danes hadden grete drede. And the kynge seide to his peple, "Now upon hem in all that 75 we may." And whan Uter saugh the kynges bataile, and the Danes assembled, he sette upon hem as vigorously or more. In that bataile was grete mortalité on bothe parties, but the hethen peple hadde moche the werse.

And ther Pendragon did merveloise knyghthode amonge his enmyes, and so dide Uter, but I may not telle alle their well dedis. But Pendragon was ther deed, 80 and many another gode baron, wherof was grete pité and losse to the Cristen partye. And as the boke witnessith, Uter venquysshed the bataile, and ther ne ascaped noon of the sarazins but that thei weren deed or taken.

And thus ended the bataile of Salisbury wheras Pendragon was deed. And so all the londe [was] lefte hoill to Uter his brother. He made geder alle the Cristen that 85 weren deed, and made hem to be beried in a place bi themself, and areised his brothers tombe moche hier than eny of the tother, and lete write upon eche beryinge place his name that lay under. But on his brother wolde he nought write, for he seide who that them beheilde myght wele undirstonde that he was chief lorde.

Than Uter wente to Logres and alle the prelates of the Cherche, and ther was he 90 sacred and crowned. And thus was Uter kynge of the londe after the deth of his brother Pendragon. And the quynsynne after that, Merlyn come to courte, and grete was the joye the kynge made to hym. And than seide Merlyn to Uter, "I will that thow have surnonn of thi brother name. And for love of the dragon that appered in the ayre, make a dragon of goolde of the same semblaunce."

95 And the kynge dide do make this dragon in all the haste he myght, like to the dragon that sewde in the ayre. Than he lete sette it on a shafte instede of a baner, and lete it be born before hym in every bataile at alle tymes when he sholde fight. And thus was ever after he cleped Uterpendragon. And Merlyn abode with hym longe tyme after, till on a day that Merlyn hym axed, "Ne shall thow do no more

70 sarazins, heathens. **71 sye**, saw. **75 bataile**, army. **79 well**, gallant. **84 hoill**, wholely. **90 sacred**, consecrated. **91 quynsynne**, fifteenth day. **93 surnonn**, surname. **96 sewde**, showed. **99 Ne shall thow**, Will you not.

100　　to the place in the playn of Salesbury wheras thy brother is buried?"

And the kynge ansuerde, "What wilt thow that I do, for I will do even as thow wilte devise?" Quod Merlin, "I will that thow ordeyne ther soche a thinge as shall endure to the worldes end." And the kynge seide, "Telle me in what wise, and I will do it with gode will." Than quod Merlin, "Sende after the grete stones that

105　　ben in Irlonde, and make hem to be brought in thy shippes, and I shall go to shewe them whiche I will have that thei shull brynge."

Than Uterpendragon sente vesselles grete plenté, and Merlin hem shewde the stones that were grete and longe, and seide, "Lo, these ben the stones whiche ye ben come fore." And when they hem saugh, they it helden for a grete merveile,

110　　and seide it was a thynge impossible to charge, they were of soche gretnesse and wight. And in their vessellis they seiden sholde they not come, yef God wolde. And so thei returned to the kynge and tolde the merveile, and the kynge than seide, "Suffer till Merlyn come."

And when Merlyn was come, the kynge hym tolde like as his men hadden seide,

115　　and Merlin seide, "Sith it is so that they may not hem hider bringe, I shall aquyte me of my promyse." And than Merlin made by crafte of his arte to bringe the stones that weren in Irlonde to the playn of Salesbury. And the kynge and moche peple wente to se the merveile. And when thei saugh the grete stones, thei seiden that all the worlde ne myght not hem remeve. And Merlin badde they sholde be

120　　dressed upright for thei sholde seme feyrer so than liggynge. And the kynge seide that myght no man do, saf only God. Than seide Merlyn, "Let me worthen therwith, and I shall aquyte me of the covenaunt that I made." And so all the labour [was] lefte to Merlyn. And he dressed [hem] as thei ben yet over the beryinge place of Pendragon, and ben yet cleped the Stonehenges.

125　　And than come Merlin to Uterpendragon, and hym served longe tyme and moche hym loved. And so on a tyme he toke the kynge in counseile and seide, "Sir, I moste discure to yow the hiest counseile that ye herde ever, and that thinge that I shall of speke shall be right straunge. And I requyre yow that ye it not discure to no man lyvynge." And the kynge graunted his requeste.

130　　　Than seide Merlin, "I will that ye wite that the knowinge that I have cometh be

110 charge, carry. **111 wight**, weight. **113 Suffer**, Wait. **115 aquyte**, fulfill. **120 liggynge**, lying. **121 worthen**, go. **123 dressed [hem]**, arranged them. **127 discure**, disclose. **130 knowinge**, wisdom.

the enmy by nature, and oure Lorde that is almyghty above alle thynge hath yove me witte and memorye to knowe grete partye of thynges that be to come. And by this sovereyn vertu, the enmye hath me lorn that with the plesaunce of God they shull never have power over me at her volunté. And sir, now ye knowe fro whens

135   I have this power. And I will telle yow a thinge that God will that thow shalt do. And whan ye knowe what it is, loke ye performe it to His plesier. Sir, ye ought well to knowe that God come in to erthe to save mankynde, and also, as ye well knowe, He made a soper, and seide to Hys apposteles, 'Oon of yow shall me betrayen.' Sir, many povertees and grete suffraites suffred oure Lorde her in erthe

140   for oure sake, and many shames that the Jues Hym diden. And after that, He suffred bitter deth for us upon the Crosse, and a knyght axed His body when He was deed upon the seide Crosse. And it was graunted hym of Pilate in lower of his servyse.

"Sir, it fill after that, this knyght whiche hadde taken oure Lorde down of the Crosse, that he was in a waste contree full of diserte, and moche of his lynage.

145   And sir, upon hem fill a grete famyne and hunger, and thei complayned to the knyght that was thier maister. And he prayde oure Lorde to shewe His mercy to hem, and to shewe some demonstraunce that they myght be conforted of their grete disese. And oure Lorde hym comaunded to make a table, in the name of that table at the whiche He was sette in the house of Symond leprouse, and bad hym

150   take the vessell whiche that he hadde and sette it upon the table; and cover the table with white cloth, and also the vessell, all save the parte toward hym. Sir, this vessell was brought to this seide knyght by oure Lorde Jhesu Criste whyle he was in prison forty wynter, hym for to comforte. And, sir, by this holy vessell were departed the company of gode and evell. And also at this table was ever a voyde

155   place that betokeneth the place of Judas theras he satte at the soper, whiche he lefte whan [he] herde that oure Lorde seide that worde for hym, whan He seyde that he that ete with Hym sholde Hym betrayen. Thus lefte Judas the place voyde till that oure Lorde set ther another that hight Matheu. This Matheu was sette in that place to fille up the nombre of twelve apostles.

160   "Sir, this place that was voyde at the table of Joseph betokeneth the place that

131 enmy by nature, i.e., fiend; **yove**, gave. **133 lorn**, lost. **134 her volunté**, their desire. **139 suffraites**, hardships. **140 Jues**, Jews. **142 seide**, this same; **lower of**, reward for. **144 diserte**, desolation. **148 disese**, suffering. **154 departed**, divided; **voyde**, empty. **158 hight**, was called.

Matheu fulfilde, and sir, thus be these two tables convenable. And thus hath oure Lorde filled the werke of man. And sir, the peple that were therat cleped this vessell that thei hadden in so grete grace the Graal. And yef ye do my counseile, ye shall stablisshe the thirde table in the name of the Trinité. And I behote yow,

165 yef ye do this, therby shall come to yow grete honour and grete profite of youre soule. And also, it shal be a thynge that moste shall be spoken of thourgh the worlde."

Thus seide Merlyn to Uterpendragon, wherof he was well plesed. And [he] seide to Merlin, "I will that oure Lordes wille be performed in all that is in me, in

170 all thynge that be to His wille. And all I putte in youre ordenaunce." And than was Merlyn gladde, and seide, "Sir, loke where ye plese beste that it be sette."

"Certes," quod the kynge, "whereas thow wilte, and theras thow trowest it be moste oure Lordes wille." And Merlyn seide, "It shall be at Cardoll, in Walys, and make ther thy feest at Pentecoste. And array thee to make gode chere and to

175 yeve grete yeftes. And I shall go before and make the table, and whan thow arte come, I shall setten them that owen therat to sitten."

---

161 convenable, alike. **164 behote**, promise. **170 ordenaunce**, control. **176 owen**, ought.

[Uther and Ygerne]

All as Merlyn devised dide the kynge, and warned thourgh all his reame to be at Cardoell in Walys at the Pentecoste. And thus he lete crye thourgh all his reame, and Merlyn dide ordeyne all that longed to the table. The weke afore Witsontyde come the kynge to Cardoell. And whan he was come, he axed Merlin how he hadde spedde, and he seide, "Wele." Quod the kynge, "What men shull ye chese to sitte at this table?" And Merlyn seide, "Ye shull se tomorou that ye wende never to seen, that I shall chese fyfty of the beste knyghtes of this londe. And whan thei be ones sette, thei will have no grete desire to returne into their contrees. And thus ye may knowe whiche were gode men and worthy, whan ye se the signifiaunce of the voyde place."

Thus Merlyn on the Witsonday chese fifty knyghtes and comaunded hem to be sette at that table to mete; and thei so diden with gode chere. And Merlyn, that full of stronge arte was, yede hem aboute, and cleped the kynge as they weren sette, and shewed hym the voyde place. And many othir it syen, but they ne knewe not the tokenynge, ne why it was voyde.

When Merlyn hadde don all thus, he badde the kynge that he sholde go sitte; and thus thei diden, alle eight dayes. And the kynge yaf grete yeftes to lordes and to ladyes and to dameseles. And when they departed, the kynge come to the fyfty knyghtes and axed how hem lyked. And thei seyde, "Sir, we have no talent to remeve fro hens, and therof we have merveile what it maketh, for we be entred as brethern; and therfore we will never departe till deth us departe." When the kynge herde hem thus sey, he hadde grete merveile and comaunded hem to be served and kepte as his owne body. And thus departed the grete prese.

5

10

15

20

1 warned thourgh, announced throughout. **3 dide ordeyne**, arranged; **longed to**, concerned. **5 spedde**, fared (prospered); **chese**, choose. **6 that**, what; **wende**, thought. **8 ones**, once. **10 voyde**, empty. **12 mete**, dine. **13 yede**, went; **cleped**, named them to; **sette**, seated. **15 tokenynge**, meaning. **17 yaf**, gave. **19 hem lyked**, they felt; **talent**, desire. **23 prese**, company.

And than the kynge come to Merlyn and seide, "Truly, thow seidest me soth
25   that oure Lorde wolde that this table sholde be stablisshed; but I wolde praye thee
to telle me yef thow knowe who shall fulfille the place that is voyde." And Merlyn
ansuerde, "Wite thow right wele that it shall not be in thy tyme, ne he that shall
acomplesshen it is not yet begeten. But it shall be in the kynges tyme that shall
come next after thee; ne he that shall hym engendere shall not knowe that he shall
30   hym engendere; and he that shall acomplysshe that sete must also complysshe the
voyde place at the table that Joseph made. And I pray yow therfore that ever
hensforth that ye hoilde alle youre grete festes in this town." "Certes," quod the
kynge, "I will gladly." And than seide Merlyn, "Sir, I moste go, and of longe
tyme ye shull not se me ageyn." And the kynge hym axed whider he sholde go.
35   Quod he, "Shall ye not be here at alle tymes when I holde my grete courte?" And
Merlyn seyde, "No."

Than departed the kynge. And Merlyn yede to Blase and told hym the
stablisshement of this table and many other thynges. And thus abode Merlyn thre
yere that he come not to courte. They that loved not Merlyn but by semblaunce
40   come to the kynge on a day as he was at Cardoell, and axeden hym of his voide
place and why ther was not sette some worthy man that the table myght be full.
And the kynge seide, "Merlin tolde me a grete merveile, that seide noon myght it
acomplisshe in my tyme, ne yet ne ys he born that shall engendre hym that shall it
complesshen." And thei lough therat as they that weren full of envye, and seide,
45   "Sir, trowe ye that ther shal be better peple after youre tyme than beth now, and
that ther ne be now as gode men in youre londe as thei shull be?" "Truly," seide
the kynge, "I wote never." And thei seide, "Ye do not wele but ye assaye."
"Certes," quod the kynge, "I will it not assaie, for I doute that Merlin wolde be
wroth."
50   And than they ansuerde, "Yef ye wele yeve us leve, we will assaye it, and for
to preve the grete lesynge." And the kynge seide, "Ne were the drede I have of
the wrath of Merlyn, ther is nothynge that I desire so moche to assayen." And
they seide, "Yef Merlyn be livynge and he knowe that we will it assayen, he will
come without faile er eny man shall it assayen; but suffre that we may it assaien
55   at Pentecoste." And the kynge hem graunted, wherfore they weren gladde. Thus

28 begeten, begotten. **39 semblaunce**, appearance. **47 assaye**, try it. **48 doute**, fear. **51
lesynge**, falsehood; **Ne were**, If it were not for.

55

it lefte till at Witsontyde that the kynge hadde do warne all his barons to be at his feste at Cardoell. And Merlyn, that all thys wiste wele, tolde unto Blase the evell thoughtes that they hadden that hadde take this enprise, and seide he wolde not go till he knewe who sholde assaye to preve that place, for he hadde lever have it

60   preve by a shrewe than a gode man. Thus suffred Merlyn to the quynsyne of Pentecoste.

     Uterpendragon the kynge come to Cardoel and brought with hym grete plenté of peple. And thei that were come for to assaie the place made it to be seide that Merlyn was deed, and that he was founden in a wildernesse madde, and cherles

65   hym kylde. And so moche peple spake therof that the kynge hymself it leved, and more for that he was so longe awey than for eny thinge elles; and namely he wende in no wyse he wolde not have suffred that eny man sholde have assaide the voyde place yef he were lyvynge.

     Thus was the kynge on Witson-even at Cardoel, and axed of hem that sholde it

70   assaie whiche of hem sholde it do. And he that all this hadde ordeyned seide, "Sir, I will that ye wete that ther shall noon assaie it but I." Than he com to the table whereas the fifty knyghtes weren sette and seide, "I am come to sitte with yow and for to holde yow company." And they ansuerde no worde but full mekely behelde what he wolde do. And the kynge and grete partye of the barons weren

75   ther assembled. This [man] sette hym down in the voyde place; and anoon as he was sette, he sanke down as it hadde be leed, so that noon wiste where he was become. Than the kynge comaunded alle the other gode men to aryse, and they so diden. And than anoon began so grete a noyse and sorowfull crye that all the court was trowbled. And the kynge hymself was gretely abaisshed.

80   Thus they abiden to the quynsyne after Pentecoste that Merlin come to courte. And whan the kynge wiste of hys comynge, he was right joyfull, and wente hym ageins to mete with hym. And anoon whan Merlyn saugh the kynge, he seide he had evell spedde to suffre eny man to sytte in that place. "Trewly," seide the kynge, "I was disceyved thourgh here wordes." "In feith," seide Merlyn, "it falleth

85   often to hem that wolden begile that thei [be] begiled hemself; and that maist

---

59 lever, rather. **60 shrewe**, rascal; **quynsyne**, fifteen-day period. **64 madde**, insane; **cherles**, ruffians. **65 moche**, many; **leved**, believed. **69 Witson-even**, Whitsunday Eve. **70 ordeyned**, devised. **75 anoon as**, as soon as. **76 leed**, [molten] lead. **80 quynsyne**, fifteenth day. **83 evell spedde**, done wrongly.

thow wele preven be this." After the kynge axed yef he wiste where he was becomen that set hym in the sege. And Merlin ansuerde, "Therof no force is for to enquere, ne nought it sholde avayle for to wite, but thenke on them that in the other places sitten, and to mayntene that thow haste begonne; and alle thy festes and alle thy

90   courtes, come holde hem heir in this town for to wurship this table, for thow knowest by the assay that thow haste seyen that it is of grete dignité. And now I go; now loke thow do as thow haste seyde."

And thus departed the kynge. And Merlin comaunded the kynge to beilde feire howsynge where he sholde ever after holde his courte and his hye festes. Than the

95   kynge lete it be knowen thourgh his reame that alle high festes, as Pasch and Pentecoste and Yole and Halowmesse, sholde be holden at Cardoel. And ageyn the Feste of Yole he somowned alle his barons in soche maner that everich of hem shulde brynge with hem their wyves and doughtres and her neces or susteres. And the knyghtes so diden alle. I may not telle yow alle tho that ther weren, sef of hem

100   that the tale reherses, oon after another.

Ther was the Duke of Tintagel and Ygrine his wif; and hir the kynge loved gretly, but therof he made no semblaunce, saf that often he beheilde her more than another, insomoche that hirself it perceyved and knewe that the kynge behelde her often. And whan she it perceyved, she eschewed to come in his presence, for

105   she was right a gode lady and full of grete bewté and right trewe ageins hir lorde. And the kynge for her love, and for he sigh she hadde taken hede of his lokynges, he sente juwelles to every lady that was at the feste. And to Ygerne he sente as he trowed sholde beste hir plese. And she knewe and sigh wele that he hadde sente to alle other ladies, and therfore she durste not refuse hirs but receyved hem, and

110   thought wele in her herte that the kynge ne hadde not yeven to other ladyes but for she sholde not refusen hirs.

Thus hilde the kynge that feeste, that yet is withouten wif, and was so supprised with the love of Ygerne that he wiste not how to do. And thus departed the court. But firste the kynge praide alle the barons to be at Cardoel at Pasch, and so he

86 be, by. **87 sege**, seat; **no force is**, is no point. **88 ne nought**, nor anything. **89 that**, what. **90 wurship**, honor. **93 beilde**, build. **94 howsynge**, housing. **95 as Pasch**, such as Easter. **96 Yole**, Yule; **Halowmesse**, Allhallows; **ageyn**, before. **97 everich**, each. **99 sef of**, except for. **105 ageins**, to. **106 sigh**, saw. **108 trowed**, believed. **112 hilde**, held; **that²**, who. **114 praide**, requested; **Pasch**, Easter.

115   prayed alle the ladies, and thei graunted to be ther.

Whan the Duke of Tintagel departed fro courte, the kynge hym conveyed and gretly hym honoured at theyr departynge; and whan he hadde hym a while conveied, he toke leve and yede thourgh the courte in his othir necessitees, till that the tyme of Pasch. And than gan to assemble alle the barons and alle the

120   ladyes at Cardoel. And grete was the joye that the kynge made till it come to the mete tyme, that the kynge made the Duke of Tintagel to be set before hymself and also his wif Ygerne, so that Ygerne ne myght not eschewe but to receve his yeftes, so that she it aparceyved verily that the kynge hir loved, wherof she was right hevy, but ne she mot it suffer. Thus was this feeste holden in grete joye. And the

125   kynge hem prayde to come at alle tymes whan he hem comaunded; and thei seiden so thei wolden as to theire sovereyn lorde. And thus departed the courte.

And so endured the kynge in grete mysese for love of Ygerne. And at laste he complayned hymself to tweyne that he moche trusted, of grete angwysshe that he suffred for the love of Ygerne; and they seiden, "What will ye that we shull do?"

130   Quod the kynge, "I wolde have youre counseile how I myght have her company." And they seide, "Yef ye go in to the courte theras she is, the peple shull it aperceyve, and so myght ye be in blame." And he seyde, "What counseile yeve ye me thanne?" "The beste counseile," seid thei, "that we se therinne is that ye somowne a grete courte to be at Cardoel and that ye make hem all to wite that it shall holde to the

135   quynsine, and that eche come araide to abide fifteen dayes, and everiche man to brynge with hym his wif. And thus may ye have longe the company of Ygerne and have grete counfort of youre love." And the kynge was plesed wele with her counseile, and sente to alle the barons to be at Pentecoste at Cardoel, and every baron to brynge with hym his wif. And as the kynge hem comaunded thei diden.

140   And at that feeste the kynge bar crowne and yaf grete yeftes to alle astates, as hym semed beste sittynge.

Gretly was the kynge at that feeste, and joyfull and mery. And he spake to oon of his counseile to whom he hadde moste truste of eny other, and his name was Ulfyn. And the kynge hym tolde of the grete peyne that he was inne for the love

---

116 conveyed, attended. **121 mete,** dinner. **122 eschewe,** avoid. **123 aparceyved,** realized. **127 mysese,** discomfort. **128 tweyne,** two. **131 theras,** where. **133 somowne,** summon. **134 holde to,** be held until. **135 quynsine,** fifteenth day; **araide,** prepared. **140 astates,** estates. **141 beste sittynge,** appropriate. **142 Gretly,** Exuberant.

145   of Ygerne, that so hym constrayned that he myght nother ete ne slepe ne go ne ride, and that he wende verily to dye whan he was oute of her sight, and that he myght not longe lyve but he hadde other counseile of her love. And Ulfyn seide, "Sir, it is a wonder thynge that for the delyte of a woman ye wene to dye. And I am but a pore man, and yef I loved a woman so strongly as ye, I sholde not wene

150   therfore to dyen. Who herde ever speke of eny woman, yef she were wele requereth, but ye sholde have of her youre volunté; with that to yeve her gret yeftis and juwels and to hem that ben abouten hir. I ne herde never speke of woman that cowde hir diffende ageyn this; and thow that arte a kynge, dismayest thee so of feynt herte!" And the kynge seide, "Ulfyn, thow seyst right wele, and thow knowest

155   wele what longeth to soche mystere. I pray thee helpe me in all maners that thow can or may, and take of my cofres what thow wilte, to yeve to alle that ben hir abouten, and speke so to hir as thow knowest is for my spede." Quod Ulfin, "Be of gode counfort, for I shall do all my power."

    And thus undirtoke Ulfin to helpe the kynge. And so all the fifteen dayes hilde

160   the kynge grete feste, and every day hadde the duke in his company and yaf hym a grete juwell, and also to his compers. And Ulfyn spake with Ygerne and tolde hir many thinges that he myght, as he trowed beste her plese; and many tymes he brought her a preciouse juwell. But Ygerne wolde noon, till on a tyme that Ygerne hilde Ulfyn in counseile and seide, "Ulfyn, wherefore that ye wolde me yeve alle

165   these juwelles and these riche yeftes?" And Ulfin seide, "Madame, for youre grete wisdome and your grete beauté and faire contenaunce I may noght yeve yow, for all erthely gode is yours and alle the londe of Logres and alle the mennes bodyes at your plesier to do your volenté." And she ansuerde, "How?" "How?" quod he; "for ye have the herte of hym to whom alle moste obbeye." Quod she, "Whos

170   herte is that ye of speken?" And Ulfin seide, "Of the kynge."

    And she lifte up hir hande and hir sayned and seide, "A, mercy God, shold eny kynge be traytour so as he maketh semblaunce to myn husbonde of love and so shamefully wolde me diffoule? Ulfin, now be right well ware that thow never speke to me more of these wordes, for wite thow wele I shall telle my lorde; and

145 ne, nor. **148 wonder**, wondrous. **151 volunté**, desire. **153 dismayest thee so**, do you despair. **155 longeth to soche mystere**, concerns such matters. **157 spede**, success. **161 compers**, companions. **163 wolde noon**, would [have] none. **164 hilde**, kept; **wherefore**, why [is it]. **168 volenté**, wishes. **171 hir sayned**, crossed herself.

175   yef he it knowe, thow moste dye." And Ulfyn ansuerde, "That were to me grete wurship, yef I sholde dye for my lord; ne never lady that refused a kynge in soche wyse as do ye, that loveth yow more than eny other thynge. And I trowe ye do but jape. But for Goddes love, haveth pité of the kynge that is youre lorde, and also upon youreself, for yef ye have no mercy of this thynge, witeth wele that therof

180   may come grete harme; ne ye ne youre lorde may not yow diffende ageyn the kynges wille." And Ygerne ansuerde, wepynge, "I shall therfore me right wele diffende, for I will never come in place wheras he may me seen."

    And so departed Ygerne. And Ulfin come to the kynge and tolde hym like as she hadde seide. And the kynge seyde so sholde a gode lady ansuere, for ther was

185   never gode lady that lightly wolde be overcome; and therfore he ne cessed not of prayinge.

    And on the eleventh jour of Pentecoste the kynge satte at mete and with hym the Duke of Tintagel. And the kynge hadde a riche cowpe of goolde; and Ulfyn kneled before the kynge and seide, "Sir, sende this cuppe to Ygerne, and praye the duke

190   to bidde hir to take it and drynke for your love." And the kynge cleped the duke and badde hym sende that cuppe to Ygerne, his wif, and sende hir worde to drynke for his love. And the duke ansuerde as he that thought noon evell and seyde, "Sir, gramercy." The duke cleped a knyght of his owne that he loved well; "Bretel, take this cuppe and bere to thy lady, and sey her that she drynke for the kynges love."

195   And Bretel cam in to the chamber where Ygerne sat at mete amonge othir ladyes and kneled before hir and seide, "Madam, the kynge sente yow this cuppe, and my lorde comaundeth that ye sholde it take and also to drynke for the kynges sake."

    Whan the lady undirstode these wordes, she wax all reade for shame, but she durste not refuse the comaundement of hir lorde but toke the cuppe and dranke

200   and wolde have sente it ageyn be the same knyght. And he seide, "My lorde sente yow worde ye sholde it kepe, for so the kynge hym prayde." When she sye that, she sigh wele that nedes she muste kepe the cuppe. And Bretell com agein and thanked the kynge on Ygernes behalfe, that therof hadde seide no worde. And glad was the kynge that she hadde resceyved his yefte. And Ulfin wente into the

176 wurship, honor. **178 jape**, jest. **180 ne ye ne**, neither you nor. **181 me**, myself. **182 diffende**, protect. **187 jour**, day. **188 cowpe**, cup. **192 noon evell**, no evil. **193 gramercy**, great thanks; **cleped**, called. **195 mete**, dinner. **198 wax**, turned; **reade**, red. **200 be**, by. **202 sigh**, saw.

205 chamber to se what semblaunce she made, and he fonde hir pensif and angry. And whan she saugh Ulfin, she cleped hym to hir for the bourdes weren up, and seide, "Ulfyn, thourgh grete treson thy lorde hath here sente me a cuppe, but therby shall he gete litill wurschip er tomorow day, for I will telle my lorde of the treson that ye betwene yow two have purposed." And Ulfyn ansuerde, "Bewar therof, that it

210 yow never passe." And she seide, "Mysaventure have that it kepeth eny counseile." With that departed Ulfyn from hir. And be than the kynge hadde waisshe, and was right mery and gladde, and toke the duke be the hande and seide, "Gowe, se these ladyes." Than they yede to the chamber wheras Ygerne hadde eten; and she knewe wele that he come for noon othir cause but for hir. And so she suffred all

215 the day till the nyght, and than she wente hom to hir loigynge. And when the duke come, he fonde hir wepynge and makynge grete sorowe; wherfore he was right hevy, and toke hir in his armes, as he that moche hir loved, and axed whi she made soche sorowe. "Trewly," quod she, "ther [is] nothynge that I will kepe from yowr counseile, for ther is nothynge that I love so moche as yow. The kynge, that is my

220 lorde and yowr, seith that he loveth me. And alle these courtes that ye se hym holde, and alle these ladyes that he sendith fore, it is nought elles but for me, and that ye sholde brynge me with yow. And these othir tymes I parceyved it wele inough, and I me kepte both fro hym and from his yeftes. And so hiderto I have me wele deffended that I have nought taken of his. And now have ye made me to take

225 a cuppe, and sente me that I sholde drynke for his love. And therfore I wolde I were deed, for I may never have reste for hym and Ulfyn hys counseiller. And now I have tolde yow all as it is, I knowe wele that therof muste come more anger, wherfore I beseke yow, as I ought to do my lorde, that ye brynge me to Tintagel, for I will no lenger abide in this town."

230 Whan the duke, that moche loved his wif, herde this, he was als wroth as eny man myght be. Than he sente after his men thourgh the town, and when they were come, he seide to hem prevely, "Make yow redy for to ride in all haste, so that no man of the town it wyte; and axe not the cause why till I telle yow." And thus the

205 semblaunce, appearance. 206 bourdes weren up, tables were put away. 210 Mysaventure, Ill luck; counseile, secret. 211 be than, by then. 212 Gowe, se, Let us go see. 214 suffred, waited. 215 loigynge, lodging. 225 wolde, wish. 228 beseke, beseech. 230 als, as.

duke and his knyghtes lepe to horse and rode home to his contré, and ledde with
235   hym his wyf.

On the morowe whan the kynge wiste the Duke was thus igon, he was hevy and
sorowfull for that he hadde ledde awey Ygerne. And [he] sente after his counseile
and shewde hem the shame and the dispite the duke hadde hym don. And they
seide they merveyled ther gretly, and that [the Duke] hadde don grete folye. Thus
240   seide they that wiste not why he was gon. And the kynge seide, "As ye have sen
alle, I have do to hym more wurship than to eny othir." And they seiden it was
soth; "wherfore we gretly merveyle why he hath don so grete outerage." And the
kynge seide, "Yef it be youre rede, I will sende after hym that he come ageyn and
amende this forfet, and that in the same wise as he is gon that he come agein, for
245   that me semeth is right." And the counseile therto assented.

On this massage was sente two worthy men fro the kynge, and rode till they
come to Tintagell, and ther they fonde the duke and tolde hym their message as
they weren charged. Whan the duke herde that in the same forme he moste come
ageyn, he undirstode wele he sholde bringe with hym Ygerne. And than he seide
250   to the messagers, "I ne will not come at his courte, for he hath so don to me and to
myne that I owe hym neyther to truste ne to love." And thus departed the messagers
withouten other ansuere.

And than the duke sente after alle the worthy men of his counseile and seide
hem the cause why he was come fro Cardoel, and the untrouthe and the shame that
255   the kynge hadde hym purposed. And they therof merveileden gretly, and seide
that sholde never betyden, with Goddes grace, and wele oughten he to have shame
that this shame hath purposed to his liege man. Thanne seide the duke, "I pray
yow and requyre be the feith that ye me owen, that ye helpe me to diffende my
londe yef he me assawte with werre." And thei ansuerde that so wolde they do to
260   put alle ther lyves and godes in jepardye. Thus the duke counseiled with his men.

And the messagers come to Cardoel and fonde the kynge and his barons, and
tolde as the duke hadde yeve hem ansuere; and they seiden alle, thei merveiled of
the duke that was wonte to be so wise a man and so had him ruled. The kynge
praide his barons and hem requyred as his liege men that thei wolde hym helpe to
265   redresse that forfet and avenge the shame that he hadde hym don. And they seiden

---

236 wiste, knew. **238 dispite,** insult. **242 outerage,** insult. **243 rede,** advice. **244 forfet,**
offence. **248 forme,** manner. **256 betyden,** happen. **259 assawte,** assault. **260 godes,** goods.

that they myght not that refusen; but thei seiden yef it were hys plesier to sende, knowynge that he hym diffied forty dayes before, er he hym assailed. And the kynge seide that wolde he do; but the kynge hem praide that at the ende of forty dayes they be redy assembled ther he hem assigned, arayed for to osteye.

270 The kynge sente his messagers for to diffie the Duke of Tintagel. And when the duke herde that he hym diffied at the ende of forty dayes, he seide he sholde hym diffende yef he myght. And than he sente to his peple and shewde hem the diffiaunce of the kynge, prayinge hem to helpe hym in that grete mister. And they seide thei sholde hym helpe with all their power. And than the duke counseiled

275 with his peple and seide, "I have but two castelles that agein the kynge may holde." But the tweyne wolde he holde as longe as he hadde lyf. And he devised to leve his wif at Tintagel, and with hir ten knyghtes, for he knewe that castell hadde no doute of no man; and hymself wente to another castell that was of lesse strengthe, and it stuffed in the beste wise that he myght, and seide that he myght not his

280 other londes agein hym diffende.

The messagers that hadde the duke diffied come to the kynge and seide how the duke wolde hym diffende. Thanne the kynge sente to somowne his barons and his peple, and made hem alle to assemble in the duke's londe in a grete medowe upon a rivere. Whan the barons were assembled, the kynge to hem rehersed the grete

285 dispyte of brekynge of his courte, and the barons seiden it was reson that the forfet were redressed. Thus the kynge lefte in the duke's londes, and tok his castelles and his townes and distroyed all the contré. And than the kynge herde seyd that Ygerne was at Tintagel and the duke in another castell; and than the kynge axed of his counseile whiche castell he sholde firste assaile. And the barons yaf hym

290 counseile firste to assaile the duke, and therto the kynge graunted. And so thei rode to the castell that the duke was ynne; and than the kynge seide to Ulfin, "What may I do whan I ne may not se Ygerne?" And Ulfin seide, "The thinges that a man may not have, he muste nede suffer; and therfore ye must put to grete besynesse to take the duke, for after that ye shall well to purpose bringe the

295 remenaunt."

267 diffied, challenged. **269 ther**, where; **arayed**, prepared; **osteye**, make war. **275 agein**, against. **278 doute of no man**, fear of anyone. **279 stuffed**, provisioned. **282 somowne**, summon. **285 dispyte**, insult; **reson**, reasonable. **286 forfet**, insult; **lefte in**, occupied. **294 besynesse**, effort.

Prose Merlin

Many assaute made the kynge at the castell, but he cowde it in no wise gete, wherfore he was full of sorowe and right irouse. And on the tother side he was sore distreined with the love of Ygerne, that on a tyme as he was in his pavilyon he gan to wepe. Whanne his peple saugh hym wepe they weren hevy, and hem
300 withdrowen and leften hym alone. And whan Ulfin it wiste therof, he come anoon and axed the kynge why he wepte. And the kynge seide, "Thow knowest wele wherfore, for thow woste wele that I dye full of love of Ygerne, for I have loste bothe mete and drynke and all reste that a man ought to have." And whan Ulfyn this undirstode he seide, "Ye be of ful febill herte whan ye thynke to dye for oon
305 sole woman; but I shall sey yow gode counseile." "What is that?" seide the kynge. "That ye wolde sende to seche Merlin that he myght come to yow; and it myght noon otherwise be but that he sholde yeve yow some gode counseile that sholde yow profite. And ye shull hym yeve what he will desire."

And than seide the kynge, "Ther is no thynge that is possible to a man but that
310 he can it do; but I wote wele Merlin of my distresse knoweth, and so I am in drede that he be wroth for the voide place of the table that I suffred to be assaide. And longe tyme it is passed sethe he was in place whereas I myght hym se. And also, I trowe he is not well plesed that I love the wif of my liege man; but trewly, I may not do therto ne I ne may not therfro me deffende. But I have well in mynde that
315 he badde I sholde not sende hym for to seche." And Ulfin ansuerde, "I am in certeyn of oon thynge, that he farith well and is in hele. Yef he love yow as he was wonte to do, he knoweth what distresse that ye beth ynne, and it shall not be longe er ye here of hym tydynges." Thus Ulfyn counforted the kynge and counseiled hym to sende for his meyné to hym, and that sholde cause hym to foryete a grete
320 partie of his sorowe. And the kynge seyde so he wolde do; but his love myght he, ne his sorow, in no maner wise forgete. Thus the kynge peyned to conforte hymself and his peple, and made the castell to be assailed. But take it they myght not in no wise.

And on a day, as Ulfin rode thourgh the oste, he mette with a man that he nothinge

297 **irouse,** angry; **on the tother side,** at the same time. 298 **sore distreined,** sorely upset; **that,** so that. 299 **hevy,** sad. 303 **reste,** sleep. 304–05 **oon sole,** one single. 311 **suffred,** allowed. 312 **sethe,** since. 314 **do therto,** do anything about it; **ne[1],** nor. 316 **hele,** health. 319 **meyné,** retinue. 320 **partie,** portion. 321 **ne,** nor; **maner wise,** fashion. 324 **oste,** host.

325   kenned. And he seide, "Ulfin, I wolde fain speke with thee." And thanne they
yede oute of the hoste, the man on his fete and Ulfyn on horsebak. And Ulfin light
down on foote to speke with this man, and hym axed what he was. And he seide,
"I am an olde man, as thow maist se, and som tyme in my yowthe I was holden
wise; and now of moche thinge that I sey, men sein that I dote. But I sey to yow in
330   counseile that I was at Tintagel not longe sithe, and ther I was aqueynted with a
gode man that tolde me that youre kynge loveth the duke's wif, and that is the
cause that the kynge distroyeth his contré, for that he brought his wif fro Cardoel.
And yef ye and the kynge will wele quyte my nede, I shall make yow aqueynte
with a gode man that shall make yow speke with Ygerne, and that shall wele
335   counseile the kynge of his desir."

When Ulfyn herde this man so say, he merveled who that hym sholde have
tolde, and prayde hym that he wolde teche hym to that man that cowde counseile
the kynge of his desires. And the olde man seide, "I will first here what rewarde
the kinge will yeve." Quod Ulfyn, "Where shall I yow fynde when I have spoke
340   with the kynge?" The olde man seide, "Ye shull finde me or my messager betwene
this and the hoste." And so he hym comaunded to God, and bad hym come on the
morowe, and hym wolde telle soche tydinges as sholde hym plese.

And Ulfin com to the kynge as hastely as he myght and told how the olde man
hadde seide. And whan the kynge hadde herde these wordes, he lowgh and made
345   feire semblaunce and seide to Ulfin, "Knowest thow ought the man that thow
spake with?" And he ansuerde, "It is a man right olde and feble." And the kynge
seide, "Whan shull ye mete efte togeder?" And Ulfyn seide, "In the morowe, for
he badde me wite of yow what he shulde have to rewarde." And the kynge seide,
"Lede me thider as thow shalt mete with hym." And Ulfin seide, "With gode will."
350   "And yef thow speke with hym withoute me, profer hym what he will desire of
myn." Thus thei leften till on the morowe; but that nyght was the kynge merier
than he hadde ben eny tyme before.

The morowe after masse the kynge and Ulfyn rode forth as Ulfin wolde hym
guyde; and as thei issued oute of the hoste, thei sye a crepell that semed blinde.
355   And as thei passed forth by hym, he cried with an high voyce, "Sir kynge, so God

---

324–25 nothinge kenned, knew not at all. **333 quyte**, satisfy. **335 counseile**, satisfy (provide for). **338 here**, hear. **344 lowgh**, laughed. **345 ought**, at all. **347 efte**, again. **354 crepell**, cripple.

acomplesshe thyn hertys desire of that thow desirest moste to have, so yeve me
som thynge that I may conne thee thanke fore." And the kynge beheilde Ulfyn and
seide lawghynge, "Ulfyn, do that I shall comaunde thee for my grete profite and
for my love and for to compleisshe my grete desire." And Ulfyn seide, "Ther is

360   nothinge that I desire so moche as for to do that myght acomplisshe youre desire."
And the kynge seide, "Hast thow nought herde what the crepell axed, that I sholde
remembre the thinge that I beste loved in this worlde, and that I am moste
desiraunte? Go and sette thee adown by hym and sey that I have sente thee to
hym, and ther is nothinge in this worlde that I have in possession but that I wolde

365   come to yeve it hym, yef I durste come to se hym."

And Ulfin, withoute eny grucchynge, yede and yaf hymself to the crepill, and
sette hym down by hym. And whan the crepill felte Ulfyn, he axed what he was
and what he was come for to seche. And he ansuerde, "The kynge hath sente me
to yow, and that I sholde ever be youres." And whan the crepill that herde, he

370   lowgh and seide to Ulfyn, "The kynge is sone perceyvinge, and me knoweth better than do ye. I will that thow wite that the olde man that thow spake with yesterday sente me to thee; but I will not telle thee what he seyde. Go to the kynge and
sey he wolde do a grete thynge for to have his desire, and that I sende hym worde
that sone he is parceyvinge, and he shall spede the better." And Ulfin seide, "I dar

375   nought aske what ye ben." "Aske the kynge," quod the crepill, "and he shall telle
thee wele inough." And Ulfyn lepe on horse and priked after the kynge.

And whan the kynge saugh hym come, he drough aside and seide, "Ulfyn, is it
that thow art come after me? Ne have I not yove thee to the crepill?" Quod Ulfin,
"He seith that ye be sone aperceyvaunte of hym, and that ye sholde telle me what

380   he is, for he wolde not telle me, but seide ye sholde telle wele inough." Than seide
the kynge, "Wost thow what olde man that was that spake with thee yesterday?
That same is this that thow haste seyn a crepill." And Ulfyn seide, "May this be
true, that oo man may hymself thus desfigure? And what is he than that thus hym
disfigureth?" And the kynge ansuerde, "Knowe it verily it is Merlin that thus hym

---

357 **conne**, give. 366 **grucchynge**, complaining. 370 **sone perceyvinge**, quick to under-
stand. 371 **will**, wish. 375 **what ye ben**, who you are. 376 **priked**, hastened (galloped,
pranced). 378 **yove**, sent. 379 **aperceyvaunte of hym**, aware of who he is. 383 **oo**, one;
than, then. 384 **hym**, himself.

385   kepeth fro yow. And whan he will, he will make yow wele to knowe that it is
thus."

Thus they passed forth thourgh the feilde. And Merlin come in his right
semblaunce into the kynges teynte, and asked where was the kynge. And a
messanger come to the kynge and seide Merlin was come. And than was the kynge
390   so gladde that he myght not ansuere, but in all haste returned and cleped Ulfyn
and seide, "Now shalt thow knowe yef it be so as I have seide, for Merlyn is
comen, and I knowe wele that he doth not seke me for nought." And than seide
Ulfyn, "Now shall it be sene yef ever he were ought wroth, and yef ye can other
do well or sey to his plesir of alle thinges; for ther is no man that may yow helpe
395   so wele to have the love of Ygerne." And the kynge seide, "Thow seiste soth, and
ther is no thynge that he doth comaunde me but I shall it gladly performe."

Thus thei rode till thei come to the teynte whereas thei fonde Merlin. And the
kynge hym made grete joye and mery chere, and ran hym agein with armes spred
abrode and hym halsed, and seide he was the man in all the worlde that was moste
400   to hym welcome. And than he seide, "Wherto sholde I me complayne unto yow,
for as ye it knowe as myself, and ther was never man that I longed so sore after;
and I pray yow and requyre, telle me of that ye knowe my herte desireth so." And
Merlin seide, "Of that ye me asken, I shall not speke withoute Ulfyn." Than made
the kynge to clepe after Ulfin, and droughen hem aside in counseile. Than seide
405   the kynge to Merlyn, "I have tolde Ulfin of that ye comaunded, and that ye were
the olde man that he sigh yesterday, and also the crepill this day." And Ulfyn
beheilde hym strongely and seide, "May this be trewe that the kynge seith?" And
Merlin seide, "Ye, it is trewe withouten faile; and as sone as I saugh he sente thee
to me, I wiste well he hadde me perceyved." And than Ulfyn seide to the kynge,
410   "Sir, now sholde ye speke of youre gref, and not wepe whan ye ben soill."

And the kynge seide, "I wote not what to sey ne preyen. He knoweth well my
corage, and I may not make hym no lesynge, but he it knowe as wele as I. But I
pray hym hertely to helpe me to have the love of Ygerne, and he ne shall devise
nothinge that is to me possible but that I shall it gladly don." And Merlin seide,
415   "Yef ye will graunte me that I shall aske, I shall purchace yow hir love and make

390 **cleped**, called. 393 **ought wroth**, at all angry; **other**, either. 398 **agein**, toward. 399
halsed, embraced. 406 **sigh**, saw. 407 **strongely**, probingly. 409 **perceyved**, recognized.
410 **soill**, alone. 412 **corage**, desire; **lesynge**, lie. 415 **purchace**, obtain.

67

yow to ly in here chamber and in hir bedde, bothe naked." And [whan] Ulfyn that
herde, he lough and seide, "Now shall I se what a mannes herte is worth!" And the
kynge seide to Merlin, "Ye can not aske me nothinge that be founden in this worlde
but I sholde it yow yeven." And Merlin ansuerde, "How may I hereof be sure, but

420   yef ye be sworn, and also lete Ulfyn swere, that I shall have that I aske on the
morn that ye have leye with Ygerne, and don with hir your beste?" And the kynge
seide that wolde he do with gode will. And Merlin asked Ulfyn yef he wolde
swere, and Ulfyn seide, "That me forthinketh, for I was never yet sworn in no
tyme."

425   When Merlin herde that worde he lough and seide, "Whan youre othes be made,
I shall telle yow how it shall be." Than the kynge made be brought the hiest
seintewaries that he hadde and the best relikes, and theron they dide swere as
Merlin dide hem devyse, and thei seiden thei sholde it feithfully holde withouten
fraude or mal engyn. After the kynge swore Ulfyn, and thus hath Merlin take their

430   othes. And than seide the kynge, "Merlin, now I requere yow sone to helpe myn
hertes desire, as the man of all the worlde that moste therafter longeth to have it
complisshed."

And than seide Merlyn, "Ye muste be wisely demened, for she is a trewe lady
and full wise, and trewe to God and to hir lorde. But now shall ye se what power

435   I have hir to begile, for I shall make yow semblaunce of the duke so wele that ther
is no man that yow doth sen but he shall wene it be the duke. And [there are] two
knyghtes that ben moste privy with hym that noon ne knoweth so moche of his
counseile, not Ygerne hersilf; and that oon hight Bretell and that other Jordan.
And I shall have the semblaunce of Bretel and Ulfin shall be like Jordan, and so

440   shall I make hem to open the gates of the castell, and we shall alle thre ly withinne.
But full erly on the morow we moste gon oute, for er we departe thens we shall
here straunge tidinges. And therfore aray youre oste and your barons and comaunde
hem to make gode wacche to diffende hemself, and that noon of hem ne go towarde
the castell till that ye be come ageyn. And be well ware that ye telle no creature

445   wheder that ye shall go."

416 here, her. **418 be founden**, exists. **423 me forthinketh**, I regret. **426–27 hiest
seintewaries**, most holy relics. **429 mal engyn**, evil purpose, deceit. **433 demened**, conducted. **435 semblaunce**, appearance. **436 wene**, think. **437 privy**, trusted. **438 hight**, is
called. **440 ly**, lodge. **445 wheder**, where.

Uther and Ygerne

And Uterpendragon dide as Merlin hadde devised, and anoon com agein and seide that he was redy, and Merlin seide how he was also redy: "Ther is not ellis but to spede us forward." And so thei wenten forth alle thre till thei com ner at Tintagell; and than seide Merlyn to the kynge, "Abyde ye here, and I and Ulfyn

450 shall go this wey." And than eche drough aside by hymself; and whan thei were dissevered and Merlin hadde don his art, he toke an herbe and brought it to the kynge and seide, "Frote youre visage with this herbe, and youre handes." And the kynge toke the herbe and rubbid his handes and his visage and his feet; and anoon as he hadde thus idon, he hadde aperteliche the semblaunce of the Duke. And than

455 seide Merlyn, "Have ye eny mynde that ever ye saugh Jordan?" And the kynge seide, "Ye, I knowe hym wele." And Merlyn com to Ulfyn and transfigured hym to the semblaunce of Jurdan, and than sente hym to the kynge. And whan the kynge saugh Ulfyn, he hym blissed and seide, "Mercy God! How may eny man make oon man so like another?" And than he seide to Ulfyn, "How semeth thee be

460 me?" And Ulfyn seide, "I knowe yow nought but for the duke." And the kynge seide he was verily like unto Jurdan. And as thei stoden so, thei beheilde Merlyn, and thei semed verily it was Bretel. And thus thei speken togeder and taried till it was nyght. And in the evenynge thei come to the castell gate.

And Merlyn, that wele resembled to Bretel, cleped the porter. And the peple

465 com to the gate and saugh apertly the duke, as hem semed. And thei seide, "Open — lo, here the Duke!" And thei thought it was Bretel and Jurdan. And whan thei weren entred, Bretel diffended that no man in the place sholde not wite that the duke was comen. Inowe ther were that yede to telle the duchesse. And Merlyn toke the kynge in counseile and seide that he sholde contene hymself myrily. And

470 anoon alle thre thei come before the chambir where Ygerne that yet was in her bedde; and in all haste that thei myght, thei mad their lorde redy.

And so he yede to bedde to Ygerne. And that nyght he gat upon hir the gode kynge that after was cleped Arthur. The lady made grete joye of the kynge, for she wende verily it hadde ben the duke hir lorde, that she loved moche with a trewe

475 herte. Thus thei lay togeder till on the morowe.

451 dissevered, separated. **452 Frote**, Rub; **visage**, face. **455 mynde**, recollection. **459–60 semeth thee be me**, do I look to you. **462 semed**, thought. **464 cleped**, called. **465 apertly**, clearly; **hem semed**, it seemed to them. **467 diffended**, ordered; **not wite**, know. **468 Inowe**, Enough. **469 contene**, enjoy. **472 gat**, begat.

In the dawenynge, the tidinges com into the town that the duke was dede, and also his stewarde itake. And than thei com full previly in; and when these other tweyn that tho were arisen herde these tidynges, thei ran theras their lorde lay and seide, "Aryse up and go to youre castell, for ther be soche tydinges come hider

480   that oure peple wene that ye be deed." And he lepe up and seide, "It is no merveyle though they wene so; for I yede oute of the castell that no man knewe therof no worde." Anoon he toke leve of Ygerne, and hir kiste, seynynge hem alle at her departynge. And thus they departed oute of the castell in all the haste they myght, that never oon ne knewe but it was the duke.

485   And whan they weren oute, thei weren right gladde. And Merlyn seide to the kynge, "Sir, I have kept wele the covenaunte. Now loke thow kepe as wele myne." And the kynge seide, "Ye sey trewe, for ye have don me the beste servise that ever man dide to another; and therfore youre covenauntes shall I well holde." And Merlyn seide, "I hem aske now and will that they be holden." And the kynge

490   seide, "I am redy hem to performe." And than seide Merlyn, "I will that thow knowe that thow haste engendred an heyre male on Ygerne, and that hast thow me yoven. And therfore I shall write the houre and the day in the whiche it is begeten, and so shalt thow knowe yef I sey soth." Quod the kynge, "As thow hast seide, I have sworn; and I yeve it thee with gode will."

495   Thus they rode till they come to a rivere, and ther Merlyn did hem waisshen, and than hadde thei semblaunce as that thei hadden before. And than the kynge rode forth as faste as he myght; and as sone as he was come, his barons and his peple gedered aboute hym. And he hem asked how the duke was deed. And thei hym tolden: "The day when ye were departed, the oste was stille and koye; and

500   therby the duke undirststode that ye were not in the oste, and dide his peple to arme and come upon us, and dide us grete damage er we myghten ben armed. The cry arose and the noyse, and oure meynee hem arayde and set on hem, and drof hem ageyn, even before the yate. And ther the duke abode and dide many maistries in armes. And ther was his horse slayn and the duke overthrowe. And ther was he

505   deed amonge oure peple on foote that hym nought knewen. And we driven the

482 **seynynge hem**, blessing them. 486 **covenaunte**, bargain. 488 **covenauntes**, promises. 490–91 **will that thow knowe**, want you to know. 491 **an heyre male**, a male heir. 492 **yoven**, given. 496 **semblaunce**, appearance. 499 **koye**, quiet (coy). 502 **meynee**, company. 503 **maistries**, great deeds.

Uther and Ygerne

remenaunt in at the yates, that sympilly hem deffended whan they hadde loste their lorde." And the kynge seide that he was right sory for the deth of the duke.

*[**Summary**. After the death of the Duke of Tintagel, the barons harbor no ill feelings toward King Uther, who acts generously toward the duke's kindred. Merlin reminds Uther of his bargain concerning the child, suggesting that Ygerne would be ashamed to raise the child herself. Uther makes peace with Ygerne and restores her lands. The council of barons suggests that the king and the duchess should marry, and Uther is happy to accept their advice if Ygerne assents. She does, and their wedding occurs on the twentieth day after Arthur was conceived. Also on that day Ygerne's daughters are wed to King Lot and King Ventres. Morgan, the illegitimate daughter of the duke, is sent to school in a religious house where she learns the art of astronomy; as a result she becomes known as Morgan le Fay.*

Ygerne, now noticeably pregnant, tells Uther what happened on the night Arthur was conceived. Uther never reveals that he was the man who visited her, but he asks her to give him the child and she agrees. Merlin arranges for the child to be raised by a good man named Antor. Ygerne weeps and grieves when the child is taken away. Antor's wife nurses the child herself, and her own son is turned over to a wet-nurse. Antor is not told the child's identity, but he has the child baptized and names him Arthur.

While Uther is stricken with gout, the invading Danes defeat Uther's army. Merlin tells Uther he must lead his army against the Danes while being carried on a litter; he also tells him that he will not live long after the Danes are defeated, and that he must give away his worldly goods for his soul's sake. Uther asks about the child, and Merlin assures him the child is flourishing. The king leads his army against the Danes and defeats them, and then he does many alms deeds. As Uther lies on his death bed, Merlin whispers to him that his son Arthur will be the next king and that he shall complete the Round Table that Uther had begun. Uther hopes that Arthur will pray for his soul; then he dies. Uther is buried with honor, but he leaves the kingdom without an heir. Fol. 26r (line 18)–31v (line 13).]

506 sympilly, weakly.

[Arthur and the Sword in the Stone]

Whan he was come before hem they seide, "Merlyn, we knowe well thow art
wise and haste alwey loved wele the kynges of this reame. And thow knowest
wele that this londe is lefte withouten heir, and a londe withoute a lorde availeth
litill. Therfore we pray thee and requere to helpe us to chese soche a man as
myght the reame governe to the profite of the peple and savacion of Holy Cherche."

And Merlin seide, "I am no soche man that owe to entermete of soche counseile,
ne that I sholde chese a man to be a governoure. But yef ye acorde to myn awarde
I shall telle yow; and yef I sey not wele, acordeth not therto." And thei seide,
"Alle to the welfare and profite of us alle oure Lorde sende grace!" And Merlin
seide, "I have moche loved this reame and the peple therinne, and yef I wolde
telle yow whom ye sholde make youre kynge, I ought wele to be beleved, and it
were right. Bot oon faire aventure is yow befallen, yef ye will it knowen. The
kynge is now deed sithe Martinmasse, and fro hens to Yoole is but litill space.
And yef ye leve my counseile, I shall yeve yow gode and trewe, bothe ageyn God
and the worlde." And thei seiden alle at ones, "Sey what thow wilte, and we shall
it holden."

And he seide, "Ye knowe wele that now cometh the feste that oure Lorde was
inne ibore, and He is Lorde of alle lordes. And I will undirtake, yef ye and alle the
peple comynyally pray to oure Lorde for His grete pité for to sende yow a rightfull
governour, as He though His grete humylité at this feste cleped Yoole liste to be
born of a virgyn, and Kynge of alle kynges, that He at this feste chese yow soche

---

1 **hem**, them (i.e., the barons). **3 availeth**, thrives. **4 chese**, choose. **6 no soche man**, not
the right man; **owe**, ought; **entermete of**, be involved in. **7 acorde**, agree; **awarde**, advice. **8 yef**, if. **12 faire aventure**, good fortune. **13 is now deed sithe Martinmasse**, has
now been dead since November 11; **Yoole**, Yule, Christmas. **14 leve**, believe; **ageyn**,
towards. **18 will undirtake**, suggest that. **19 comynyally**, together. **20 as**, just as; **liste**,
chose.

a man to be youre kynge and lorde, that the peple may rule and governe to His plesir; and that He shew soche demonstraunce that the peple may se and knowe that it is be His eleccion, and that he that so is chosen be kynge withoute eny other

25 eleccion. And wite ye well, yef ye thus do, ye shull se the eleccion of oure Lorde Jhesu Criste." Than they ansuerde alle with oon assent and seide, "We acorde with this counseile, and ther is noon erthly man but that he ought therto acorde."

Than thei praide alle bisshopis and archebisshopes to comaunde thourgh all the cherches that the peple to praye as ye have herde. And alle the lordes were sworne

30 oon to another to holde the awarde of Holy Cherche, in that God wolde hem shewen. In this maner be thei acorded to the counseile of Merlin. And Merlyn toke leve of hem, and thei hym praide to be with hem at Cristemasse, to se yef it were soth or no that he hadde hem taught. And Merlyn seide, "I shall not be ther, for ye shull not se me till the elecccion be made." Thus wente Merlin to Blase and tolde hym

35 alle these thinges.

Than alle the worthy men of the reame of Logres, thei come unto Logres at the Yole. Thus was this thinge don and abiden to the Yole. And Antor, that hadde this childe norisshed till he was a moche man of fifteen yere of age, he hadde hym trewly norisshed so that he was faire and moche; and he hadde never soken other

40 mylke but of his wif, and his sone he hadde made to be norysshed of another woman. Ne Antor wiste not whether he loved better, ne he cleped hym never but his sone; and he wende verily that he hadde ben his fader. At Halowmasse Antor made hys sone knyght, and at Yoole he come to Logres, as did the other knyghtes of the londe, and brought with hym his two sones.

45 On Yoole Even was assembled alle the clergie of the reame, and alle the barouns that weren of valoure and wele hadde don as Merlin hadde seide. And whan they were alle come, thei ledde alle symple lif and honeste. Thus thei abode all the Yoole Even and weren at messe at mydnyght, and made mekely theire orisouns to oure Lorde, that He of His grace sende hem soche a man that myght profitably

50 meyntene hem and the Cristen feith.

Thus they abode the messe of the day, and so ther were many that seide thei

---

23 **demonstraunce**, demonstration. 24 **eleccion**, choice. 38 **norisshed**, raised; **moche**, grown. 39 **moche**, large. 41 **wiste not whether**, knew not which. 42 **he²**, i.e., Arthur. 45 **Yoole Even**, Christmas Eve. 47 **symple**, plain. 48 **orisouns**, prayers. 51 **abode**, awaited.

were foles that trowed oure Lorde wolde put his entente to chesinge of her kynge. And as thei were in this talkynge, thei rounge to messe of the day, and so thei yede to servise. Whan thei were alle assembled, ther was oon of the holiest men of the londe araied to singe the messe. But er he yede to messe, he spake to the peple and seide, "Ye be assembled for thre thinges for youre profite, and I shall say yow which thei be: first of all, for the savacion of youre soules; and for the wurship of God; and the myracle and high vertu that He thys day shall shewe amonge us, yef it be His plesir to yeve us a kynge and chiefteyn that may save and mayntene Holy Cherche, that is the sustenaunce of alle trewe Cristen peple. We be come to chese oon of us; we be not so wise to knowe who is moste profitable of alle this peple. And for that we ne knowe, we owe to praye to the Kynge of kynges that is Jhesu Criste oure Saveoure, that He shewe us verry tokenynge to His pleasaunce, as He was bore on this day. So every man praye in the beste wise he can."

And thus they did as the gode man hem counseiled. And he yede forth to masse, and he com to the gospell and that thei hadden offred. Some of the peple yede oute of the cherche where ther was a voyde place. And whan they com oute of the cherche, thei sawgh it gan dawe and clere, and saugh before the cherche dore a grete ston foure square, and ne knewe of what ston it was — but some seide it was marble. And above, in the myddill place of this ston, ther stode a styth of iren that was largely half a fote of height. And thourgh this stithi was a swerde ficchid into the ston.

When thei sye this that firste weren come oute of the chirche, thei hadde gret merveile and yede agein into the chirche and tolde the archebisshop. And whan the gode man that sange masse herde this, he toke haly water and caste upon the stith. And the archebisshop lowted to the swerde and sawgh letteres of golde in the stiel. And he redde the letteres that seiden, "Who taketh this swerde out of this ston sholde be kynge by the eleccion of Jhesu Criste." And when he hadde redde this letteres, he seide to the peple what it ment.

Than was the ston delivered to ten worthi men to kepe, and to two clerkes.

---

52 trowed, believed; **her,** their. **55 araied,** ready; **er,** before. **61–62 profitable,** qualified. **62 owe,** ought. **63 verry tokenynge,** true sign. **64 as,** because. **67 and that,** after. **68 voyde place,** open space. **69 dawe,** to dawn; **clere,** brighten. **71 styth,** anvil. **72 ficchid,** fixed. **77 lowted to,** bent over. **80 this,** these. **81 delivered,** assigned; **kepe,** guard.

Than thei seiden that oure Lorde hadde hem shewed feire myracle, and yeden agein into the mynistre to heir oute the masse and to yelde oure Lorde graces. And thei songen "*Te Deum Laudamus.*" And whan the gode man was come to the

85   awter, he turned to the peple and seide, "Feire lordes, now may ye se that some of yow be goode men, when thourgh youre prayers and orisouns oure Lorde hath shewde this grete myracle. Wherfore I praye and reqire yow above alle vertues in this erthe, for highnesse ne erthly richesse that God hath yoven in this worlde, that noon be agein this eleccion that God hath us shewde the demonstraunce. And the

90   surpluys He shall us shewen at His volunté."

Thanne the gode man sange forth the masse. And whan it was fynisshed they assembled aboute the ston, bothe oon and other who that myght take oute this swerde firste. And than thei seiden and acorded alle that thei sholde assaien it as the mynistres of Holy Cherche wolde assigne. To this ther was grete discorde

95   amonge the higheste men and moste puyssaunt. And thei that hadde force seide they wolden asseyen firste. So ther were many wordes that ought not to be rehersed.

The archebisshop spake that alle myght heren and seide, "Sirs, ye ne be not so wise ne so wele avised men as I wende. And I will wele that ye alle wite that oure Lorde hath oon ichosen, but I knowe not whom. And thus moche may I say to

100   yow, that gentilnesse ne richesse shall have no power agein the wille of Jhesu Criste, but truste so moche in Hym that yef he that is therto chosen were yet unbore, it shall never be taken oute of the ston till he come that it is ordeyned the honour."

Than acorded alle the noble men and wise, and seide that he hadde seide soth. And the wise men and the high barouns toke their counseile and acorded to stonde

105   the ordenaunce of the archebisshop, and [thei] com agein and seiden heringe alle the peple. And than made the bisshop grete joye and dide wepe for pité and seide, "This humylité that is in youre hertes is of God. And I will that ye knowe after myn entente shall be to the volunté of God and profite of Cristen feith, so that I shall have no blame yef God will." This parlament was before high messe of the

110   assay of the swerde, till that high messe was saide.

Than seide the archebisshop to the peple and shewde hem the gret myracle that

---

83 mynistre, minster. **84 *Te Deum Laudamus***, see note. **85 awter**, alter. **88 highnesse**, high rank. **90 surpluys**, remainder; **volunté**, desire. **95 puyssaunt**, powerful; **force**, power. **98 wende**, thought; **wite**, know. **100 gentilnesse**, nobility; **richesse**, wealthy. **104–05 stonde the ordenaunce**, follow the plan. **105 heringe**, in the hearing of. **107 is of**, comes from.

God hadde don for hem at this eleccion: "And whan oure Lorde sette justice in erthe, He sette it in the styth and in the swerde. And the justice over the lay peple ought to be the swerde, for the swerde at the begynynge was take to thre orderes
115 to diffende Holy Cherche and mayntene rightwisnesse. And oure Lorde hath now made eleccion be the swerde. And wite it wele, alle that this have seen and beholde, to whom He will the justice yeve. And lete no man be to hasty for to assaye, for it shall never be drawen oute for richesse ne for pride. Ne the poure peple be not displesed though the lordes and the high astates assaye before, for it is right and
120 reson that the lordes assaien firste. For ther ne is noon of yow but he ought to have his kynge and his lorde the beste and moste worthy man that he kowthe knowe be his reson."

Thus thei acorded to the archebisshop with gode herte and withouten evyll will, that he sholde chese hem that he wolde to assaye firste. Thus thei graunted
125 alle to holde hym for hir kynge to whom God wolde shewe his grace. Thanne the archebisshop chese oute one hundred fifty of the hiest and moste worthi lordes and made hem go to the assaie. And whan they hadde alle assayed, than he commaunded alle other to assaye. And than they assayden alle they, oon after another, that assaye wolde. But ther was noon that myght it taken oute. And so it
130 was comaunded to be kept with ten noble men, and thei were charged to take goode hede who com to assaien, and yef eny ther were that myght drawen out of the ston.

Thus was the swerde assaied alle the eight dayes, and alle the barouns were at high messe. And the archebisshop hem preched and shewde as hym semed beste.
135 And than he seide, "I tolde yow wele that all be leysere myght he come that was ferthest fro the assaye of this swerde. Now may ye verily knowe that never noon, saf he that oure Lorde will, ne shall it not oute take." And than thei seiden alle that thei wolde not out of the town till thei westen to whom God wolde graunte that honoure.
140 In that maner thei abiden oute the messe, and after thei wente to their hosteles to mete. And after mete, as they were used that tyme, yede the barouns and the

113 **styth**, anvil. 114 **take**, entrusted. 118 **poure**, poor. 120 **reson**, proper. 121 **kowthe**, could. 129 **assaye wolde**, wished to try. 130 **kept with**, guarded by. 135 **all be leysere**, all by leisure, i.e., later on. 137 **will**, wishes. 138 **westen**, knew. 141 **mete**[1], dine; **mete**[2], dining.

knyghtes to boorde in a feire pleyn, and the ten men that were ordeyned to kepe this swerde yede also to se this bourdise. And when the knyghtes hadde turneyd awhile, thei toke their sheldes to their squeres so that the peple of the town yede to

145   arme them. And Antor hadde made his eldeste sone knyght at the Halowtide before Yoole. And whan the medlé was begunne, Kay called his brother Arthur and seide, "Go faste to oure oste and fecche my swerde."

And Arthur was goode and servisable and seide, "With gode will." And than [he] smote the hors with the spores and rode forth to his ostell for to fecche his

150   brothers swerde, or ellis some other, yef he myght eny fynde. And he fonde noon, for the hostesse hadde sette it in hir chambir. And so he turned to hem agein. And whan he saugh he myght noon fynde, he gan to wepe for grete anger. And as he come before the mynster ther the ston was, he saugh the swerde whiche he hadde never assaide, and thought, yef he myght it gete, to bere it to his brother.

155   And as he com therby on horse bakke, he hente the swerde be the hiltes and drough it oute, and covered it with his lappe. And his brother that abode after withoute the towne saugh hym come, and rode agein hym and asked his swerde. And Arthur seide he myght not have it, "but I have brought heere another," and drough it oute from undyr his cote and toke it to his brother. And anoon as Kay

160   saugh this swerde, he knewe it wele that it was the swerde of the ston and thought he wolde be kynge, and seide he wolde seche his fader till he fonde hym; and than he seide, "Sire, I shall be kynge. Lo, here is the swerde of the ston."

Whan the fader it saugh, he hadde merveile how he it gatt. And he seide he toke it oute of the ston. Whan Antor herde that he leved it not but seide he dide lye.

165   Than thei yede to the mynster ther the ston was, and the tother squyre after. Whan Antor sigh the ston and the swerde not therynne he seide, "Feire sone, how hadde ye this swerde? Loke ye do not lye; and thow do lye, I shall it knowe wele and never shall I thee love."

And he ansuerde as he that was sore ashamed, "I shall yow lye no lesynge, for

170   my brother Arthur it me brought whan I badde hym to go fecche myn. But I wote never how he it hadde."

142 **boorde**, play; **pleyn**, field. 143 **this bourdise**, these games; **turneyd**, tourneyed. 144 **toke**, gave. 146 **medlé**, melee. 147 **oste**, hostel. 149 **spores**, spurs. 155 **hente**, seized. 156 **lappe**, surcoat; **abode after**, waited. 159 **cote**, coat; **anoon as**, as soon as. 164 **leved**, believed. 165 **ther**, where; **the tother squyre**, i.e., Arthur. 167 **and**[1], if.

Whan Antor herde this he seide, "Sone, yeve it me, for ye have therto no ryght."
And Kay it delivered to his fader. And he loked behynde hym and saugh Arthur
and cleped hym and seide, "Come hider, faire sone, and take this swerde and put
175   it theras ye it toke." And he toke the swerde and put it in the stith, and it heilde as
wele or better than it dide before. And Antor comaunded his sone Kay to take it
oute. And he assaied, but it wolde not be. Than Antor cleped hem bothe and seide
to Kay, "I wiste well that thow haddest not take the swerde oute."

Thanne he toke Arthur in his armes and seide, "Feire dere sone, yef I myght
180   purchase that ye be kynge, what gode sholde I have therfore?" "Fader," quod he,
"I may nother have that honour ne noon other goode but that ye be therof lorde, as
my lorde and my fader." And he seide, "Sir, youre fader I am as in norture, but
certes, I dide yow never engender, ne I wot never who dide yow engender."

Whan Arthur saugh that Antor hym denyed to ben hys fader, he wepte tendirly
185   and hadde grete doel and seide, "Feire sir, how sholde I have this dignité or eny
other whan I have failed to have a fader?" "A fader muste ye nede have. But feire
dere sir, yef oure Lorde will that ye have this grace and I helpe yow it to purchase,
telle me what I shall be the better." And Arthur seide, "Sir, so as ye will youreself."

Thanne Antor tolde hym what bounté he hadde hym don, and how he hadde
190   hym norisshed, and how he put awey his sone Kay and made hym to be norisshed
of a straunge woman. "Wherefore ye owe to yeve my sone and me guerdon, for
ther was never man more tenderly norisshed than I have yow. Wherefore I praye
yow, yef God yeve yow this grace and I may helpe yow therto, that ye guerdon me
and my sone." And Arthur seide, "I pray yow that ye denye not me to be my fader,
195   for than I sholde not wite whether that I sholde go. And yef ye may helpe to
purchase this grace, and God will that I have it, ye can nothinge sey ne comaunde
but I shall it do."

And Antor seide, "I shall not aske thi londe; but thus moche I will praye yow,
that yef ye be kynge, that ye make my sone Kay youre stywarde in soche maner
200   that for no forfet that he do to yow, ne to man of youre londe, that he lese not hys

---

180 purchase, arrange; **gode**, benefit. **181 nother**, neither. **183 certes**, indeed; **ne I wot
never**, nor do I know. **187 purchase**, obtain. **188 what**, how; **so as**, just as; **will**, desire.
189 bounté, kindnesses. **191 owe**, ought; **guerdon**, reward. **195 wite whether**, know where.
199 stywarde, steward. **200 forfet**, offence; **lese**, lose.

office. And yef he be fool or fell or vilenis, ye owe better to suffre hym than eny other. And therfore I praye yow to graunte hym that I yow demaunde." And Arthur seide he wolde it do with gode will. And than he ledde hym to the auter and swore that he sholde this trewly performe. And whan he hadde sworne, he com before

205   the mynster; and the turnement was ended, and the barouns com to hire evesonge.

Than Antor cleped alle his frendes and com to the archebisshop and seide, "Sir, lo, here is a childe of myn that is no knyght, that prayeth me that I wolde helpe that he myght assay the aventure of the swerde, and that it plese yow to clepe the barouns." And so he did, and thei assembled aboute the ston. Than Antor bad

210   Arthur take oute the swerde and delyvere it to the archebisshop. And Arthur toke the swerde be the hiltes and withoute more taryinge yaf it to the archebisshop. And anoon he toke Arthur in his armes and seide, *"Te Deum Laudamus,"* and so brought hym into the mynster.

And the barouns and high men that this hadde seyn and herde were angry and

215   sorowfull for this, and seiden it myght not be that soche a symple man of so lowe degré sholde be lorde of hem alle. Therwith was the archebisshop displesed and seide, "Sirs, oure Lorde knoweth beste what every man is." And Antor and his frendes abode by Arthur, and alle the comen peple. And alle the barouns were ageyn them and ageyn Arthur.

220   And thanne seide the archebisshop wordes of grete hardynesse: "I do yow to wite thaugh alle thei that ben in the worlde wolde be agein this eleccion, and oure Lorde will that this man be kynge, he shall be it withouten faile. And I shall shewe yow how and what affiaunce I have in oure Lorde Jhesu Criste. Now, feire brother Arthur, go put the swerde ageyn in the same place that ye toke it fro."

225   And Arthur put the swerde ageyn in the selve place, and it hilde as faste as byfore. And than seide the archebisshop, "So feire eleccion was never sene. Now go ye riche barouns and lordes and assay yef ye may take oute the swerde." Than yede alle for to assaye, but noon it myght remeve fro the place that it was inne. Than seide the archebisshop, "Grete folye do ye that be ageyn oure Lordes wille

230   — for now ye se well how it is." And thei seide, "Sir, we ne be not agein oure

---

201 fool, foolish; **fell**, cruel; **owe better**, ought more. **208 and**, if. **212** *Te Deum Laudamus*, We praise thee, O Lord. **218 abode by**, stood by. **220 hardynesse**, boldness. **221 and**, if. **222 will**, wishes. **223 affiaunce**, trust. **225 selve**, same.

Lordes wille, but it ys grevouse thinge to us to have a garcion to be lorde over us alle." And the archebisshop seide, "He that hath hym chosyn knoweth beste what he is."

Thanne the barouns praide the bisshop to lete the swerde be stille in the ston tille Candelmesse; and by that tyme, men of ferther contrees myght come to assaye the aventure. And the archebisshop hem graunted. Than come oute of every contree and asseyde, who that wolde. And whan they hadden assaied, the archebisshop seide, "Arthur, yef it be pleser to oure Lorde Jhesu Criste that thow be kynge, go forth and brynge that swerde." And Arthur yede to the swerde and toke it oute as lyghtly as nothinge hadde it holden. Whan the prelates and the comen peple saugh this, thei gunne to wepe for joye and pité and seiden, "Sirs, is ther yet eny man that seith agein this eleccion?" And the barouns seide, "Syr, we pray yow that the swerde be suffred yet in the ston to Passh, but eny man come by that terme that may take it thens; and ellis we will obbey to this. And yef ye will not suffre so longe tyme, every man do the beste he may."

And the archebisshop seide, "Yef so be he abide to Passh, and noon other come that may parforme this aventure, wele ye than obbey yow to this eleccion?" And thei seide alle, "Ye." Thanne the archebisshop seide to Arthur, "Sette the swerde agein in the ston, for yef God will, thow shalt not faile of the dignité that he hath thee promysed." And Arthur did as he comaunded. And ther was ordeyned to kepe the ston ten men and five clerkes; and in this maner thei bode to Pasch.

And the archebisshop that hadde take Arthur in warde seide, "Wite ye right well ye shall be kynge and lorde of this peple. Now loke that ye be a gode man, and fro hensforth cheseth soche men as shull be of youre counseile and officers for youre housolde, even as ye were now kynge, for so ye shall be with the helpe of God."

And Arthur seide, "I put me holly in God and in Holy Cherche and in youre gode counseile. Therfore chese ye as ye seme be moste to the plesaunce of Jhesu Criste. And I praye yow clepe to yow my lorde my fader." Than the archebisshop cleped Antor and shewde hym the ansuere of Arthur. Thanne chose they soche

235

240

245

250

255

260

231 garcion, boy. **234 be stille**, remain. **238 be pleser**, pleases. **241 gunne**, began. **243 Passh**, Easter; **but**, unless; **terme**, time. **244 thens**, thence; **ellis**, then; **obbey**, agree; **And yef**, Or if; **suffre**, wait. **250 ordeyned**, assigned. **251 kepe**, guard. **252 in warde**, in his care. **258 seme**, think.

counsellers as thei wolde; and be counseile of the archebisshop and certein of the barouns, Kay was made stiwarde. And of alle othir thinges thei abode to Pasch, and than thei assembled at Logres.

265 Whan thei were alle assembled on the Ester Even, the archebisshop drough hem alle to his paleis and rehersed hem the grete wisdom and the gode condiciouns that he fonde in Arthur. And the barouns seide, "We will not be agein Godes ordenaunce; but it is unto us a mervelouse thynge that so yonge a man, and of so base lyngnage, sholde be lorde and governour of us alle." The archebisshop seide, "Ye do not as Cristen men thus to be agein Cristes eleccion." And they seide, "We

270 be not ther agein; but ye have seyn his condiciouns, and we ne have not don so. And therfore we praye yow to suffre us to knowe his condiciouns and the manere of hys governaunce that he will ben of hereafter." The archebisshop seide, "Will ye thus delaye his coronacioun?" And they seide, "We wolde that his sacringe and coronacion be respite to Penticoste. Thus we alle pray and requere." And the

275 archebisshop it graunted.

Thus departed alle the counseile. And on the morowe whan high messe was seide, Arthur yede to the swerde and toke it oute as lightly as he hadde don before. Than thei seiden alle that thei wolde have hym to their lorde and governoure, and thei praide hym to sette ther the swerde agein. And Arthur ansuerde to the barouns

280 full debonerly and seide he wolde do their requeste, or eny thinge that thei wolde of hym desire. Thanne they ledde hym into the mynster to speke with hym and to assaye his condiciouns and seide, "Sir, we se well that God will that ye be oure kynge and lorde over us, wherfore we will do to yow oure homage and of yow holde oure honoures. And we beseke yow to respite youre sacringe into Pentecoste,

285 ne therfore shull ye nothynge be inteript but that ye shull be oure lorde and oure kynge. But to this we praye yow to seye us what is your volunté."

Quod Arthur, "Of that ye sey ye will do to me youre homages and holde youre honoures of me, I may it not receyve, ne I ne ought not to do so, for I may not to yow ne to noon other yeve noon honoures till I have receyved myn. And ther ye

290 sey ye will that I be lorde of yow and of the reame, that may not be byfore that I be sacred and receyved the honoure of the empere. But the respite that ye desire I it

265 **condiciouns**, personal conduct. 268 **lyngnage**, linage. 273 **sacringe**, consecration. 274 **respite**, delayed. 280 **debonerly**, courteously. 282 **will**, desires. 283 **of**, from. 284 **respite**, delay. 286 **volunté**, desire. 289 **ther**, where.

graunte yow with gode will, for I will not be sacred, ne nothinge that therto aperteneth, ne I may not withouten Godes will and youre volunté."

Thanne seide the barouns amonge hemselfe, "Yef this childe live, he shall be
295 right wise; and wele he hath us ansuerde." And than thei seide, "Sir, us semeth with youre advice that ye be crowned and sacred at Pentecoste, and by that terme we shull obbey to yow at the comaundement of this archebisshop." Thanne thei made be brought juellis and alle othir richesse and yaf it to hym to se whedir he wolde be covetouse and cacchynge. And whan he hadde alle these yeftes resceyved,
300 the booke seith he departed it: to knyghtes, the stedes and coursers and fresshe robes; and to hem that were joly and envoisies, he yaf the juwellis; and to hem that were averouse, golde and silver; and to sadde wise men, he yaf soche thinge as hym thought sholde hem plese. And with hem he heilde companye and enquered in the contré what myght hem beste plese.

305 Thus departed he the yeftes that were yoven hym, for to knowe of what condicion that he wolde be of. And whan thei sawgh hym thus demened, ther was noon but that hym gretly preysed in theire hertes, and seide that he sholde be of high renon, and that thei cowde not in hym espie no poynte of covetise. But as sone as he hadde the grete avers, he besette hem in soche manere that every man seide that
310 noon cowde have do better, everych astate and degré. Thus thei assaide Arthur and nought cowde fynde in hym but high vertu and grete discrecion.

And so thei abiden to the Witsontide, and than alle the baronage assembled at Logres. And ther thei assaide agein at the swerde alle that assaie wolde, but never was ther founde man that it myght remeve fro the ston. And the archebisshop
315 hadde ordeyned redy the crowne and septre and all that longed to the sacringe. On Witson Even, be comen counseile of alle the barouns, the archebisshop made Arthur knyght. Alle that nyght dide he wake in the chief mynster till on the morowe day. And whan it was day, alle the baronye come to the mynster. The archebisshop seide, "Sirs, lo, here is the man that God hath chosen to be youre kynge, like as ye
320 have seyn and knowe. And lo, here is the crowne and the vestementis rioall, ordeyned by youre avys and alle the comen assent. And yef ther be eny of yow

299 **cacchynge**, greedy. **300 departed**, divided. **301 envoisies**, lively. **302 averouse**, avaricious; **sadde**, serious. **306 demened**, behaved. **309 avers**, properties; **besette**, assigned. **310 assaide**, tested. **311 nought**, nothing. **312 Witsontide**, i.e., Pentecost. **315 longed**, pertained. **316 be comen**, by common.

that to this eleccion will not assent, lete hym now sey."

And they ansuerde and seide, "We acorde that in Godes name he be sacred and anoynted with this, that yef ther be eny of us that he be with displesed of that we
325 have be ageyn his coronacion, that he pardon us alle into this day." And therwith thei kneled alle at ones to Arthur, askynge hym mercy. And Arthur for pité gan wepe and seide to hem, "That Lorde whiche hath graunted me to have this honoure mote yow pardon; and as moche as is in me, I make yow quyte." And therwith thei risen up and toke hym bytwene their armes and ledde hym to the vestymentis
330 rioall. And whan he was araied, the archebisshop was redy to synge masse and seide to Arthur, "Now go fecche the swerde wherewith ye shull kepe justice, to deffende Holy Cherche, and mayntene right and the Cristin feith to youre power."

And so they yede in procession to the ston. Thanne seide the archebisshop to Arthur, "Yef thow wilt swere to God and to oure Lady Seint Marye and to oure
335 Modir Holy Cherche and to Seint Petir and to Alle Seyntes, to save and to hold throuth and pees in the londe, and to thy power kepe trewe justice, com forth and take this swerde wherby God hath made the eleccion upon thee."

Whan Arthur herde this, of pité he gan wepe, and so dide many other. And he seide, "As verily as God is Lorde over alle thynge, so He of His grete mercy
340 graunte me grace and power this to mayntene like as ye have rehersed, and I have it well undirstonde." And than he sette hym on his knees, holdinge up his hondes, and than toke oute the suerde lightly withoute grevaunce, and so bar it upright. And thei ledde hym to the auter, and ther he leide the swerde. And than thei hym sacred and anoynted and dide that longed to a kynge. And after all the servise was
345 ended, thei yede oute of the mynstir and come by the place theras was the ston. And no man cowde knowe where it was become. Thus was Arthur chosen to kynge, and heilde the reame of Logres longe in pees.

324 of that, because. **328 mote**, must; **quyte**, forgiven. **331 wherewith**, with which. **333 yede**, rode. **342 lightly**, easily.

[The Barons' Revolt]

[Summary. In August Arthur convenes his royal court at the city of Carlion, with all the barons in attendance. Arthur honors the barons and offers them gifts; but the barons insult Arthur, refuse his gifts, and order him to leave the country or be killed. Eluding them, Arthur takes refuge in the fortress of Carlion. After fifteen days Merlin arrives on the scene and announces his support for Arthur. He tells the barons that Arthur is not Antor's son but is actually Uterpendragon's son, and Ulfin verifies Merlin's account of Arthur's birth. But the barons, continuing their opposition to Arthur, declare that no bastard will ever be their king; they prepare themselves for battle. Arthur has only a few knights on his side, but the townspeople offer their support. Merlin then confronts the assembled barons. Fols. 35v (line 27)–37v (line 16).]

And as thei spake thus, com Merlin to hem and seide, "Sirs, what is that ye purpose to do? Y do yow to wite ye will gete yourself the werse and shull lese theron more than ye shull wynne; for God will shewe soche wreche that ye shull be full rebuked and foule shamed, the moste quyente of yow alle. For ye beth
5   agein hym with wronge of the eleccion that the archebisshop hath made, like as ye have seyn."

"Now hath the enchauntor well spoken!" seide the barouns, and begonne for to jape oon to another. And whan Merlin saugh thei made japes of his wordes, he returned anoon agein to Kynge Arthur and bad hym he sholde nothinge be dismaied,
10   for he sholde not drede hem alle; for he wolde hym helpe so that the moste hardy of hem in the oste, er it were nyght, sholde wiesshe to be at home in his owne contree. Than Arthur toke Merlyn and ledde hym aparte, and the archebisshop and Antor and Kay and Ulfyn and Bretell; these seven were prevely in counseile.

And than seide Arthur to Merlin: "Dere frende Merlin, I have herde say that ye
15   loved well my fader Uterpendragon as longe as he was lyvinge; and therfore I

---

2 do yow to wite, want you to know. **3 wreche,** vengeance. **4 foule,** foully; **quyente,** cunning. **8 jape,** mock.

praye yow, for the love of God and for norture, that ye will me counseile in this matere, as ye knowe well these barouns do me grete wronge. And I wolde fayn and it plesed yow to be with me as ye were with my fader; and knowe it for trouthe that I shall never do thinge that ought yow to displese to my power; and ye
20 have me holpen in my yowthe and in my tendirnesse, and therfore I praye yow helpe to mayntene and to strengthe me to kepe my londe; for by yow and by my fader the archebisshop, and Antor that hath me norisshed, am I come to this that I am atte. And therfore, at the reverense of God, have pité of me and of the mene peple that alle shull be distroied but God sette remedye."

25 "Now dismaye yow nothinge, sir," seide Merlin, "for ye shull not have no fere of hem. But as soone as ye be deliverid of these barouns that beth here now come for to assaile yow, do that I shall yow rede and counseile. This is the trouthe, that the Knyghtes of the Round Table that was stablisshed and founded in the tyme of Uterpendragon youre fader — on whos soule God have mercy — thei be gon to
30 sojourne to their owne contrees, for the grete untrouthe that thei syen in this reame. This is in the reame of Kynge Leodegan of Tamalide, that is an olde man and his wif is deed, and of alle his childeren is lefte but oon doughter, to whom the reame shall falle after his deth. And the Kynge Leodegan hath grete werre agein the Kynge Ryon, that is kynge of the londe of geauntes and of the londe of pastures,
35 wherin dar noon inhabite for diverse aventures and merveiles that ther fallith bothe day and nyght.

"This Kynge Rion of whom I speke is right myghty of londe and of peple, and full of high prowesse, and is right a crewell man. And he hath conquered by force twenty kynges crowned, fro whom he hath taken alle their berdes by force and in
40 dispite, and sette hem in a mantell whiche he maketh every day a knyght to holde afore hym atte mete at alle tymes whan he holdeth courte rioall; and he hath sworn that he shall never finysshe till he have conquereth thirty kynges. This kynge werreth upon Leodegan and in his londe doth grete damage. This Leodegan marcheth to thy reame, and yef he lese his londe, thow shalt lese thyn after. And

16 for norture, for instruction. **17 fayn,** be glad. **18 and[1]**, if. **20 tendirnesse,** inexperience. **21 mayntene,** support. **23 mene,** common. **24 but,** unless. **26 deliverid of,** freed from. **27 rede,** advise. **30 untrouthe,** dishonor. **33 werre,** war. **34 geauntes,** giants. **39 berdes,** beards. **39–40 in dispite,** as an insult. **40 mantell,** mantle, cloak. **43 werreth,** makes war. **44 marcheth to,** borders on.

45 undirstonde well that he sholde have loste his londe longe er this tyme, ne were the Knyghtes of the Rounde Table that mayntened his werre, for he is now in grete age. And therfore I rede that thow go and serve hym a while, the Kynge Leodegan, and he shall yeve thee his doughter to be thy wif, to whom the reame longeth after his deth. And she is right feire and yonge, and the wisest lady of the

50 worlde of so yonge age. And of thy londe have thow no doute, for eche of these barouns that now werreth upon thee, thei shull have so moche to do that litill shull thei forfete in thy londe, but passinge thourgh the playn contrees.

"But er thow go, do garnysshe thy forteresses of every citee and every castell with vitayle and men and stuffe of other artrye. And the archebisshop shall a-

55 curse alle tho that in thy londe eny thinge forfete agein thee or in thy contree. And the archebisshop hymself shall shewe the cursynge in sight of alle the barouns that now ben here, and comaunde alle the clergie to do the same in heringe of hem alle. And soone after ye shall se soche thinges, by the helpe of God, that the proudest of hem shall be affraide. And wite ye well that I will be redy with yow in

60 every grete nede. And whan I crye to yow, 'Now upon hem,' set forth boldely and smyte in amonge hem, and wite it verily that thei shull be so abaisshed that litill thei shall yow disese, but alle thei shull be fayn to fle as discounfite." "Sire," seide the kynge, "gramercy." And than thei departed.

And the archebisshop wente upon the walles on high, and the Kynge Arthur

65 dide his peple make hem redy; and [thei] lepe on horse and in that manerwise thei abide longe tyme. And Merlin made to Kynge Arthur a baner wherein was grete significacion, for therin was a dragon which he made sette on a spere, and be semblaunce he caste oute of his mouth fire and flame. And he hadde a grete taile and a longe. This dragon no man cowde wite where Merlin it hadde, and it was

70 merveilouse light and mevable. And whan it was set on a launce thei beheilde it for grete merveile. Than toke the kynge the dragon and yaf it to Kay his stiwarde, in soche forwarde that he be chef banerer of the reame of Logres ever while his lif doth dure.

45 **ne were**, if it were not for. **48 yeve**, give. **49 longeth**, will belong. **50 doute**, worry. **52 forfete**, injure; **but**, except; **playn contrees**, open countryside. **53 garnysshe**, provision. **54 vitayle**, food; **artrye**, weapons. **61 wite**, know; **abaisshed**, surprised. **62 disese**, harm; **discounfite**, defeated. **69 it hadde**, got it from. **72 forwarde**, agreement.

The Barons' Revolt

Thus arraied thys mayné the Kynge Arthur, and abode in soche maner on horsbak
before the yate before the paleis. And the barouns made picche her teynte and
pavelouns thourgh the medowes that were large and faire. And whan the
archebisshop that saugh, he asked what thei were come to seche so armed. And
thei seide that thei were come to take the maister toure, which thei wolde no man
sholde be inne but by hem.

Than the archebisshop yaf the scentence full dolerouse, and cursed of God and
with all his power alle tho that in the londe dide eny forfet, or were agein the
Kynge Arthur. And the barons seide that for eny cursinge, thei wolde not cesse
till thei hadde dryve the kynge oute of the londe. And yef thei myght hym take,
thei lete hym knowe that he sholde not escape withoute the deth. And whanne
Merlin undirstode their bobaunce, he caste his enchauntement so that alle their
logges and pavilouns were alle on fire aflame. And thei therof were so abaisshed
that hem thought longe er thei myght gete oute into the medowes fro the fyre. But
er thei myght come ther thei caught grete harme, and foule were thei skorched
with the fier. Merlin ran to the kynge and seide, "Sir, now hastely upon them!"

And thei spronge oute at the yate as moche as theire horse myght renne, the
speres on their asseles, theire sheldes before her bristes. And thei were so abaisshed
and affraide that the moste hardy of hem wolde fain have be thens, for thei wende
not that ther hadde be so moche peple withinne. For thei withoute were sodenly
many of hem born down with speres, and moche peple slain; for thei were so
astoned with the hete of the fier that theire deffence was but symple. Ther was
grete slaughter of men and horse. Ther dide Arthur merveillouse dedes of armes
that gretly he was beholden, bothe on that oon part and on the tother. He overthrewe
knyghtes, bothe horse and man, with stroke of spere and of swerde. And therto
hadde the princes and barouns grete envye, and assembled hem togeder, and seide
that it were grete shame yef he so escaped. And thei were noble knyghtes and
hardy, and full of high prowesse, and many of hem carnell frendes.

74 mayné, army. **78 wolde,** wished. **80 yaf,** gave; **dolerouse,** grievous. **81 forfet,** damage.
82 for, despite. **83 yef,** if. **85 bobaunce,** proud boasts. **86 logges,** lodges, tents. **90 moche,**
fast; **horse,** i.e., horses. **91 on their asseles,** under their armpits; **bristes,** breasts. **92 be
thens,** been thence. **92–93 wende not,** had not thought. **95 astoned with,** overcome by;
symple, meager. **97 gretly,** widely; **beholden,** observed. **100 yef,** if. **101 carnell frendes,**
blood-relatives.

Than seyde Kynge Ventres of Garlot that he wolde hem delyvere in short tyme, for yef Arthur oonly were deed, the werre of the remenaunt were soone fynysshed. "Goth on," seide the othir prynces, "and yef ye have myster we shall yow socoure."

105 Therwith departed the Kynge Ventres and his company, that was a moche man of body, and a gode knyght and yonge, of prime barbe. And he was mervelouse stronge, and he helde a shorte grete-growen spere, sharp grounden, and rode agein Arthur.

Whan Arthur saugh hym come, he dressed agein hym his horse hede, and griped

110 a grete aisshen spere, the heede sharp trenchaunt of stiell, than smote the horse with the spores that it ran so faste and so briaunt that alle hadden merveile that it behelden. And he afficched hym so in the sturopes that the horse bakke bente; and [thei] smote togeder so hetely upon the sheldes that thei preced thourgh. The Kynge Ventres brake his spere upon Kynge Arthur, and Arthur smot hym agein so sore

115 that he bar hym over the horse crompe, and his legges upright, that the erthe rebounded; but he hadde noon other hurte. And whan the Kynge Loth of Orkanye saugh the Kynge Ventres overthrowen, he was wroth and sorowfull, for thei were bothe cosin germains, and also thei hadde wedded two sustres.

Than smote he the horse with spores agein Arthur, that yet hadde he his spere

120 hoill. And whan he saugh the comynge of Kynge Loth, he come agein with grete hardinesse, as he that of hym hadde no dowte. And [thei] mette togeder on the sheldis so that the horse ne myght not passe ferther till the tymbres were broken. And on the passinge forth thei hurtelid togeder so fiercely with sheldes and with her beyes and her helmes that the Kynge Loth was so astonyed that he fley over

125 his horse crowpe.

Than aroos grete noyse and cry on the oon part and the tother. Ther began a grete stoure and merveillouse. The knyghtes that were with Kynge Ventres peyned hem sore to socoure their lorde, and so dide the knyghtes of Kynge Loth. And Arthur's knyghtes peyned hem sore to helpe Arthur, and to take and holde these

104 **myster**, need; **socoure**, aid. 105 **moche**, large. 106 **prime barbe**, first beard. 107 **grete-growen**, thick. 109 **dressed agein**, directed towards. 111 **briaunt**, well. 112 **afficched**, affixed. 113 **hetely**, heartily; **preced**, pierced. 115 **crompe**, flanks. 115–16 **rebounded**, shook. 118 **cosin germains**, first cousins. 120 **hoill**, whole. 121 **dowte**, fear. 122 **tymbres**, spears. 123 **hurtelid**, rushed. 124 **beyes**, mail; **astonyed**, overcome. 125 **crowpe**, haunches. 127 **stoure**, battle.

130   other two kynges. And so began the medlé on bothe parteis crewell and fellenouse.
But with grete peyne were these two kynges rescowed and horsed agein.

Whan Arthur was releved, he drowgh his swerde oute of skabrek, whiche was
so cler and bright shynynge, as thei semed that it behelden, that it glistred as it
hadde be the brightnesse of twenty tapres brennynge. And it was the same swerde
135   that he toke oute of the ston; and the letteres that were write on the swerde seide
that the right name was cleped Escaliboure, whiche is a name in Ebrewe that is to
sey in Englissh, "kyttynge iren, tymber, and steill." And the letteres seide trewe,
as ye shall heeren hereafter.

Whan the Kynge Arthur hadde drawen oute his swerde, he smote into the prese
140   theras he saugh thikkeste, and smote a knyght on the sholder so that he made it
discendir from the body. The stroke was grete and the swerde trenchaunt, so that
he slyt asonder the sadell and the chyne of the horse, that bothe the knyght and the
horse fill on an hepe. And than he smote aboute hym grete strokes, bothe on the
lefte syde and on the right side, and made so grete occision aboute hym that all
145   that it syen helde it grete merveile, and ne durst not abide his strokes, but made
wey and voided place for drede of his swerde and of his fell strokes.

Whan the seven kynges saugh the damage and the grete losse that they hadde
thourgh hym, thei were wroth and right sorowfull, and seyde eche to other, "Now
let us alle sette on hym attones and bere hym down to the erthe, for elles may we
150   nothynge conquere." And to this thei acorded. Than thei henten speres grete and
rude, and ronnen agein hym with as grete ranndon as their horse myght hem bere,
and smyten hym on the shelde and on the haubrek; but [it] is so stronge and sure
that no mayle ne perced. But thei bar to hym so harde that Arthur was throwe to
erthe, bothe he and his horse on oon hepe.

155   And whan Kay and Antor and Ulfin and Bretell and other of Arthur's frendes
syen this, Antor hasted hym to Kynge Carados and met hym so hedylyche with a

---

130 medlé, melee; **fellenouse**, fierce. **131 peyne**, effort. **132 skabrek**, scabbard. **133 semed**,
thought. **134 tapres brennynge**, burning torches. **136 Ebrewe**, Hebrew. **137 kyttynge**,
cutting. **139 prese**, crowd. **141 discendir**, fall. **142 chyne**, spine. **144 occision**, slaying.
146 fell, fierce. **149 attones**, all at once; **for elles**, or else. **150 henten**, took. **151 ranndon**,
force. **152 haubrek**, hawberk, mail shirt. **153 no mayle ne perced**, the mail was not pierced;
bar to hym, rushed against him. **156 hedylyche**, headlong.

grete spere that bothe the tymbir and stelen heede shewed thourgh his shuldre, and threwe bothe hym and his horse to the erthe, and [he] lay longe in swowne. And Ulfin and Kynge Ventres of Garlot mette so sore togeder that ether bar other to the grounde, and the horse upon hem. And the Kynge Ydiers and Bretell brake their spers that oon upon the tother, withoute more harme doynge.

And alle the tother barouns abode upon the Kynge Arthur that yet lay at the erthe all stonyed, and thei smote on his helme grete strokes and pesaunt, so that thei made hym moche more astonyd. And whan Kay saugh that the kynge was at so grete myschef, he griped his swerde and come ther the kynge was overthrowen, and smote the Kynge Loth upon the helme that he made hym stoupe on the arson of his sadell, and leyde on hym so grete strokes that Loth all astonyed fill to the grounde. Than come thei to the rescowe, bothe on the oon and on the tother.

Ther was grete bataile and stronge stour and grete slaughter, bothe of men and horse. And so peyned thei that were with Kynge Arthur that thei have hym re-mounted on his horse. But firste hadde thei grete payne and traveile and grete losse, for the meene peple of the town were come oute with all wepen that thei myght have deffensable. And the cry and the noyse rose thourgh all the contré, so that alle the commons hasted thider all that myghten, and seiden that thei wolden alle be deed on the same grounde er that Kyng Arthur hadde eny greef, as longe as thei myghten hym deffende. Than they smyten in amonge the preesse of the seven kynges that many they dide sle and wounde, and so put hem to flight whether they wolde or noon. And so thei yede discounfit. But thei seiden thei sholde never have gladnesse till they were venged, and that they wolde not take of Arthur but his heed.

The Kynge Arthur, that was full wrothe, and Kay hem chased fercely before alle other. And so fill it that Arthur overtoke Kynge Ydiers and wende to smyte hym on the helme, but the horse bar hym to faste, so that the stroke descended on the horse and slyt hym even asondre behynde the sadill; and Ydiers and his horse blusshet to the erthe, wherefore his men were gretely affraied leste he hadde be

157 **tymbir**, wood; **stelen heede**, steel head. 162 **abode upon**, surrounded. 163 **stonyed**, stunned; **pesaunt**, heavy. 164 **astonyd**, stunned. 166 **stoupe**, stoop, droop; **arson**, bow. 169 **stour**, fighting. 172 **meene**, common. 178 **wolde or noon**, wished to or not; **yede discounfit**, departed in defeat. 179 **not**, nothing. 180 **heed**, head. 182 **fill it**, it happened. 184 **even asondre**, in two. 185 **blusshet**, fell.

slain, and returned hym to rescowe. Ther began the stour grete and merveillouse, for that oon part peyned to withholde and to take Kynge Ydiers, and on the tother syde thei peyned hym to rescowe; and so was ther do more damage and harme than hadde be all the day before. For ther was neyther horse ne man that myght endure agein the swerde of Arthur that was cleped Calibourne, that was all blody of brain and blode so that his armes were so steyned that nought was sein but all reade.

Nevertheles, so peyned Ydiers men that they have hym remounted on horsebak; and so ben thei departed discounfited, and the chase lasted longe tyme. And so the seven kynges losten inough, for of all the harneys that thei hade brought thider, thei hadde not with hem the valew of two pence, that all ne was brente with the fier that Merlin made discende amonge theire tentes and pavelouns, saf only the vessels of golde and silver and the money.

186 **stour**, battle. 191 **steyned**, stained. 192 **reade**, red. 195 **harneys**, equipment. 196 **valew**, value; **brente**, burned.

[The Grand Tournament at Logres]

[Summary. After defeating the seven kings, Arthur assembles a huge army, provisions his cities and castles, and goes to his chief city of Logres where he knights many men. For Arthur's benefit, Merlin rehearses much of the recent history of Britain. He tells Arthur about Blase, the hermit who helped Merlin and his mother; about Vortiger and his tower; about Uterpendragon's great love for Ygerne; about Ygerne's daughters and their husbands; and about the five sons of King Lot, revealing that Arthur himself fathered the last one. Merlin also tells Arthur about two kings in Little Britain named Ban and Bors, whose help he should seek. Then Merlin says that he must go to the forest but will return when Arthur needs him.

Arthur sends Ulfin and Bretell to Little Britain to request the help of Kings Ban and Bors, who are at war with the villainous Claudas de la deserte. Ulfin and Bretell meet Elein, the young wife of King Ban, and they have a fierce encounter with several of Claudas's knights. At last they find King Ban and King Bors and convey Arthur's message. The kings agree to postpone their own concerns and help Arthur. They travel to Logres, where Arthur greets them warmly. Fols. 40r (line 18)–44r (line 33).]

Than these lordes entred into the citee of Logres, began the caroles and the daunces of the ladies and damsels and the turnementes of yonge bachelers, that all the day dured till the nyght. And the town was thourgh hanged with clothes of silke, and it was feire wedir and clere, for it hadde not yet nothir reyned ne snowed ne frosen, but was as stille as aboute August. And the stretes were strowed with small grasse, and incense and myrre in fires in the stretes thikke. And in the wyndowes [were] many lightes, and so swote savoured thourgh the cytee that fer men shulde fele the odour.

5

1 **Than**, When. 2 **bachelers**, young knight-aspirants. 3 **thourgh**, completely. 4 **wedir**, weather; **nothir reyned ne**, neither rained nor. 5 **strowed**, strewn. 7 **swote**, sweet. 7–8 **fer men**, men far off. 8 **fele the odour**, smell the fragrance.

Thus come the lordes togeder into the maister mynster, and whereas the procession hem abode and receyved hem fro fer with humble reverence. That day
songe the archebisshop masse; and whan it was ended, they yede up into the grete
paleyse whereas the mete was arraide with all the coriouse ordenaunce that myght
be don. And the thre kynges were sette togeder at oon table, and the archebisshop
and Antor that hadde norischid Arthur. And Kay served at tables as was reson,
and two yonge knyghtes of grete prowesse and were sones to two casteleins —
that oon was cleped Lucas the Boteler, and that other Gifflet, the sone of Doo of
Cardoell, which hadde be maister forester to Uterpendragon. And thei served with
the stiwarde, and with Ulfin and Bretell, that wele cowde hem enforme so that thei
were well served and richely.

After mete was the quyntayne reysed, and therat bourded the yonge bachelers.
And after they begonne a turnemente, and departed hem in two partyes, and were
well on eyther syde seven hundred and three hundred of the reme of Benoyk, that
kepte hem togeder in oon partye. And whan the turnemente was assembled redy
to smyte togeder, the Kynge Ban and the Kynge Boors and her brother that was a
mervilouse clerke of astronomye — noon in that tyme [was] so expert saf Merlin
— these were lenynge oute at wyndowes, and Arthur and the archebisshop with
hem, and Antor that thei wolde not leve, behelden the turnement on bothe partees;
and [they] saugh the signes, and the stedes to neye and crye and to praunce under
knyghtes and bacheleres, that the hilles and the medowes resouned all abowte.

And whan thei were so nygh assembled, than departed oute of the renge a knyght
that was cleped Gifflet, the sone of Do of Cardoell, that satte upon a grey stede
that merveilously was swyfte. And on that other part com agein hym a knyght of
Benoyk that was cleped Ladynas, and he was of grete renoun; and he sette agein
Gifflet as faste as the stedes myght renne, theire sheldes aboute their nekkes,
gripynge the speres. And thei smote togeder in the sheldes so grete strokes that

9 **maister mynster**, main cathedral; **whereas**, there. 10 **abode**, waited. 11 **songe**, sung;
yede, went. 12 **mete**, food; **coriouse ordenaunce**, elaborate arrangement. 13 **and**, along
with. 14 **norischid**, raised; **reson**, fitting. 15 **and**[1], along with; **and were**, who were;
casteleins, castle constables. 17 **whiche hadde be**, who had been. 18 **cowde hem**, could
them. 20 **quyntayne reysed**, tilting-board raised; **bourded**, sported. 21 **departed hem**,
divided themselves. 22 **well**, at least. 24 **her**, their. 27 **leve**, leave behind. 28 **signes**,
banners; **neye**, neigh. 30 **oute of**, out onto; **renge**, range, field.

bothe brake theire speres, for bothe were they gode knyghtes and covetouse to gete worship. And they mette so togeder with helmes and sheldes so fiersly that they semede the yen fill from theire hedes. So eche bar other to the erthe, and theire horse aboven hem, and bothe lay longe in sowowne that thei semed deed.

40 And every man seide that thei saugh never so crewell incountre betwene two kynghtes. With that they renged hem on that oon part and on that other for the rescewe of the two knyghtes.

At the metynge of this turnement was sein many justinges that gladly were beholden; and some ther were that threw other to the erthe, and some that brake

45 theire shaftes withoute fallynge to grounde. Whan the speres were broken, thei drough oute swerdes and began the turney grete and huge. And ther was oon knyght that dide many maystries of arms with his body, of whom was moche spoken and preysed thourgh the contree; and [he] was cleped Lucas the Boteler and [was] cosin germain to Gifflet that hadde the grete encountir. This Lucas smote down

50 knyghtes and horse and began soche dedis of armes that noon myght his strokes endure. He arached helmes fro hedes and sheldes fro nekkes, and began to do so well that it was merveile hym to beholde. And the thre kynges preysed him moche, and so dide many other.

Grete was the turnement in the medowes by Logres upon the Ryver of Temse,

55 and longe it endured that noon ne wiste who sholde have the better. For on bothe sides were many worthi men, and longe it was er the two were releved that hadden the grete encountre. And whan thei were horsed, thei smeten into the turnemente, and tho gan Gifflet to do soche dedes of armes that he and Lucas the Botiller, that thei gate place upon hem of Benoyk and put hem fer bakke in the playn feilde.

60 And than com hem to helpe the three hundred knyghtes of Benoyk that yet ne hadde no stroke smyten, and on that othir syde come also three hundred all fressh. And so eche ran to other. Ther was grete stour and merveillouse and harde strokes smyten, and whan the speres were broken, thei leyde honde to swerdes and began the chaple so stronge and dured longe tyme. Ther men myght se many feire

36 **covetouse**, desirous. 38 **semede**, looked [as if]; **yen fill**, eyes fell. 41 **With that**, Then; **renged hem**, formed themselves. 46 **drough**, drew. 49 **cosin germain**, first cousin. 51 **arached helmes**, knocked off helmets. 54 **Temse**, Thames. 55 **noon ne wiste**, no one knew. 56 **er**, before. 57 **smeten**, charged. 58 **tho gan**, then began. 59 **thei gate place**, they gained the advantage; **playn**, open. 62 **stour**, fighting. 64 **chaple**, engagement.

65   chevalries don on bothe parties, for ther were many yonge bachelers that dide right wele. But above alle other Gifflet the sone of Do of Cardoell and Lucas the Botiller, these tweyn were preised of prowesse above alle other.

Whan the turnemente hadde longe indured and they were somdell wery for traveyle, than lept Kay the Stywarde oute of his enbusshement that yet hadde no
70   stroke smyten, he and other five felowes that were well horsed, and theire shildes aboute her nekkes, theire launces in their hondes; and whan thei aproched the renges, thei smote in amonge hem as faucouns amonge starlinges, and bar the firste that thei mette to grounde. And when theire speres were broke, thei drough oute swerdes and begonne to do soche maistryes and dedes of armes that Kay
75   hadde the prys and the wurship of the turnemente on that oon part, and on that other part Gifflet and Lucas the Boteller. And the beste after hem was Marke de la Roche, and Guynas le Bleys, and Drias de la Foreste Savage, and Belyas the Amerouse of Maydens Castell, and Blyos de la Casse, and Madyens le Crespes, and Flaundryns le Blanke, and Grassien the Castelein, and Placidas le Gays. These
80   dide so well whan thei come to the turnement that noon myght agein hem endure.

But after that the felowes of the reame of Benoyk dide so well that they made all the turnement resorte bak to theire firste place, for the felisship of the table of Logres were gon oute for to chaunge helmes that weren tohewen and rente. And whan thei saugh theire party turned to disconfiture, thei hem hasted and henten
85   speres and come into the turnemente as faste the horse myght hem bere, and smote in amonge the grettest presse. And Kay cam before alle his felowes as he that was desirouse to shewe his knyghthode, and griped a grete-growen spere. And he was a merveillouse gode knyght yef he ne hadde not be so full of wordes; for his evell speche made hym to be hatid of amonge his felowes and also of straungers that
90   herden of hym speke, that after refuseden to go in his felisshep to seche aventures in the reame of Logres; that after endured longe tyme, as this boke shall reherse hereafterwarde.

This tecche hadde Kay take in his norice that he dide of sowke, for he hadde it

---

65 **chevalries**, noble deeds. 68 **somdell**, somewhat. 69 **enbusshement**, hiding place. 75 **hadde the prys**, received the most honor. 82 **for**, because. 83 **tohewen and rente**, hacked and torn. 84 **disconfiture**, defeat; **hasted**, hurried; **henten**, grabbed. 86 **presse**, crowd. 87 **grete-growen**, thick. 93 **tecche**, fault; **in**, from; **norice**, nurse; **sowke**, suck.

95

nothynge of norture of his modere, for his moder was right a gode lady and wise and trewe. But of what Kay seide, his felowes that knewe his costomes ne rought never; but he was full of myrthe and japes in his speche, for [he] seide it for noon evyll will of no man, and therat lough thei gladly that knewe his maners. And on the othir syde, he was oon of the beste felowes and myriest that myght be founde.

100

Whan he was come to the turnement, as ye have herde, he mette with Lydonas that wele hadde do all the day. And moche he and his felowes peyned to dryve hem of Logres oute of the feilde. And so thei were nygh at disconfiture. And whan Kay saugh this he was sory and wroth. Than he smote into the presse and mette Lydonas in the shelde so sore that he perced thourghoute, and the spere poynte stynte at the haubrek. And he shof so harde that he caste hym to the

105

grounde upright. And with the same course he smote Grascien of Trebes that he overthrewe hym and his horse. Than he leyde honde to his swerde and cride "Clarence," the signe of Kynge Arthur. And they beheilde hym and saugh the socour that he brought, for they wende they hadde all loste. Than they returned and begonne to do so well that they hadde not do so well all the day before.

110

This justynge that Kay hadde don saugh well the Kynge Arthur and the Kynge Ban and the Kynge Boors his brother; and they preysed moche Kay and seide he was wight and delyver, and thei beheilde hym gladly. And whan Lucas the Botyller saugh Kay hadde don so well, he smote the horse the spores into the grettest presse and smote Blios so harde that he fill to the grounde and the spere fly on peses.

115

Than he pulde oute hys swerde and spronge in amonge hem and began to yeve grete strokes and to do so well that moche he was preysed; and so began the turnement newe to enforse for the rescewe of theire felowes.

Than com Gifflet freschely armed, his spere in fewtre, as faste as his horse myght hym bere, and saugh Blioberes and two of hys felowes that leyde on Kay

120

the Stiwarde with here swerdes, and heilde hym so short that he hadde grete nede of helpe, for thei were thre and he was but alone. And also they were thre the beste of all the turnement. And Placidas hadde hitte Kay on the helme that he

---

94 of norture, from the nursing. **95 rought,** cared. **96 japes,** jokes. **97–98 on the othir syde,** in addition. **101 nygh at disconfiture,** close to defeat. **104 stynte,** stopped. **105 upright,** on his back. **108 wende,** thought. **110 saugh,** saw. **112 wight and delyver,** swift and agile. **114 fly on,** flew into. **117 enforse for,** achieve. **118 fewtre,** its spear-rest. **119 leyde on,** attacked. **122 that,** so that.

lened on his sadill bowe. And whan Gifflet sye this he forthought it sore, and he
smote Blioberis so harde that he fill to the erthe, bothe he and his horse, and the
125   spere fly on peces; and [he] leide honde to his swerde and smote Placidas on the
helme that he bowed over the arson of his sadell, and after leyde on hym so grete
strokes that he was so astooned that he fill to the erthe upright. And Kay hym
dressed, that grete nede hadde of that socoure, and after he beheilde and knew that
it was Gyfflet that so hadde hym delyvered, and thought to quyte hym that bountee
130   yef he myght. And so he dide withynne short tyme, as ye shall heren heirafter; and
for that thei felishiped first togeder, and woned well togeder longe tyme after of
grete love, alle the dayes of her lyf.

        Whan Gifflet hadde delyvred Kay, as ye have herde, he loked aboute hym and
saugh Jeroas, that moche hadde greved in that stour. Than he griped his swerde
135   and ran upon hym for ire and yaf soche a stroke that the fire fley oute, and therwith he kytte a pece of his helme; and but the swerde hadde swarved, he hadde
ben deed for evermore. The stroke descended upon the lifte sholder that he fill to
the erthe all blody. Than arose the noyse and the crye, for well wende thei that
this syen that he hadde be deed withoute recover. Than come his felowes to the
140   rescowe, and on that other parte com the felowes of Kay the Stywarde.

        Than began the medlé grete and hidouse, that many were wounded and
overthrowen er that other was rescowed and sette on horse. And the fyve felowes
that were before rehersed, whan thei saugh the medlé so begonne, thei smot so
five of the first that thei metten that thei blushit to the erthe. Than thei smyten in
145   amonge hem and began to do so well that alle hadde merveile how they myght it
suffre or endure.

        Ther began agayn the turnement on bothe partyes, and well thei dide in armes
on that oon part and that other, till it drough towarde evenesonge, that the thre
kynges descended from the paleise and com into the place whereas was the
150   turnement, and saugh that thei heilde hem even like, that noon ne wiste wele whiche

123 sye, saw; **forthought it sore**, regretted it greatly. **126 arson**, bow. **127 astooned**,
stunned; **upright**, on his back. **127–28 hym dressed**, observed him. **129 quyte**, repay.
131 for that, as a result; **felishiped**, became friends; **woned will**, were bound well. **134
moche**, many; **greved**, injured; **stour**, battle. **136 kytte**, cut; **but**, if; **hadde swarved**, had
[not] swerved. **137 lifte**, left. **139 syen**, saw. **141 medlé**, melee. **144 blushit**, fell. **150
heilde hem even like**, performed very evenly; **noon ne wiste wele**, no one knew clearly.

hadde the better.

Than com the thre kynges and hem departed and seide it was tyme to cesse, for it was to late eny more to turney. And so were they departed, and eche yede to his ostell to resten, for therto hadde thei nede and gret myster, for many were ther hurte. And the kynges yede to here evesonge, and than thei yede to soper, and after begonne the carolles and to speke of the turnemente, and asked oon of another how hem semed of whom that hadde don beste. And thei seide that the Kynge Ban hadde fifteen knyghtes that hadde don alther beste more than eny other; and on that other part were eight that hadde don merveiles in armes, and gretly hadde they traveylled and peyned, and moche were thei to alowe. Thus heilde they here tales longe, and alwey they yaf the loos and the pris to Kay the Stiward and to Lucas the Boteller and to Gifflet the sone of Do. These were the thre that beste hadde don, and oft tymes justed and in every nede were redy.

Whan the tables were up, arisen the thre kynges and the archebisshop and Antor and Guynebans, that was brother to the two kynges. Than thei yede into a chamber that was besyde the halle, towarde the gardyn up the River of Temse, and with hem yede tweyne that ne ought not to be foryeten — that was Ulfin and Bretell. And so thei pleide and spake togeder of many thinges.

Than [King Arthur] beheilde Ulfin and Bretell, and than he gan to laugh, for he bethought hym on the wordes that Merlin hadde hym tolde, whan thei were gon on his message, how thei were assailed in the deserte of seven knyghtes, and how thei dide hem deliver. Than the kynge cleped hem bothe and comaunded hem be the feith that thei hym oughten, that thei sholde hym telle all the trouthe, how thei hadde spedde in theire message. Whan thei herde the kynge thus speke, that oon loked on the tother and begonne to smyle. And Bretell ansuerde the kynge, that thought well he it knewe thourgh Merlin, and seide, "Sir, wherto sholde we telle you oure spede in oure jurney, for as wele ye do it knowe as we oureself, thourgh hym that hath it tolde, and therfore it were but speche loste."

Than seide the Kynge Ban, "Who is that that hath hym this tolde?" "Certein,

152 departed, separated. **154 ostell**, hostel; **myster**, necessity. **157 semed**, thought. **158 alther beste**, best of all. **160 alowe**, praise. **161 here tales**, their discussion; **loos**, honor; **pris**, praise. **163 nede**, situation. **164 tables were up**, dinner was over. **166 Temse**, Thames. **171 of**, by. **172 cleped**, called; **be**, by. **173 oughten**, owed. **178 speche loste**, wasted words.

180 sir, the wisest man of the worlde." "And where is he?" quod Ban, "and what is his name?" "Sir," quod Bretell, "it is Merlin, and he resteth in my chamber hereynne, and by his counseile hath my lorde sente after yow." "Sir," quod Kynge Ban, "lete hym come hider, for we have moche disired hym for to see, for the merveiles that we have herde of hym spoken."

185 And Arthur seide that so wolde he do with gode will. And than he sente Ulfin for hym, and therwith anoon entred Merlin into the chamber agein Ulfin and seide "returne"; and so thei wente before the kynge and asked wherefore he hadde sente hym to seche. And the Kynge Ban blissed hym for the merveile that he hadde, how he myght knowe these thingis, and Merlin seide, "Therof no forse,

190 for hereafter ye shull wite inough."

Than he began to telle a party of his lif; and than com forth Guynebande the clerke and opposed hym of dyverse thynges, for he was a profounde clerke. And Merlyn hym ansuerde to alle the questiouns that he asked, the very trouthe as it was; and so indured longe the disputacion betwene hem tweyne. And at laste Merlin

195 seide that all for nought he traveylede, "For," quod he, "the more thow sechest, the more shalt thow fynde." And than seide Merlin to hem that were aboute hym that he hadde never founde no clerke that ever hadde spoke to hym of so high clergie — ne not Blase that was so holy a man — ne cowde not so moche enquere. Wherto sholde I make yow longe tale? But longe thei spake togeder so that the

200 toon was well aqueynted with that other, and well thei loved togeder.

And whan the disputaciouns were don, Merlin com to the two kynges that were his brethern and seide, "Lordynges, ye be worthi men and of high renoun, and also ye beth right feithfull and trewe. And lo, here the Kynge Arthur that ought to be youre lorde, and of hym sholde ye holde youre londes and do hym homage.

205 And he ought to helpe yow and to socoure agein alle men, yef ye have nede." And thei seide, "Merlin, now telle us how he was chosen to be kynge, and wherfore, and yef Antor knowe whether he be the sone of Uterpendragon." And Merlin seide, "Ye, withoute faile." Than he tolde hem alle the thinges like as was befalle, so that the archebisshop and Ulfin it recorded.

210 "Merlin," quod the Kynge Ban, "we will that thow make us sure of oon thinge

186 **agein**, toward. 187 **returne**, come with me. 189 **no forse**, have no concern. 191 **party**, portion. 198 **clergie**, learning; **ne not**, not even; **ne cowde not**, nor could. 200 **toon**, one. 205 **agein**, against. 208 **was befalle**, occurred.

that we shall aske, for so moche we knowe in yow that ye will not to us sey no lesynge for all the londe that longeth to the crowne." "A ha!" quod Merlin, "ye desire to have me sworn that it be trewe that I sey." And thei begonne to laugh and seide that ther nas noon so wise as was he in no reame. And Merlin seide, "I

215 graunte youre requeste and youre desire." And so thei toke respite till on the morn.

Thus ended theire parlament, and [they] departed and yede to bedde; and the thre kynges and the archebishop lay in oon chamber, for they wolde not departe on sondre. And moche Guynebande aqueynted hym with Merlin, that taught hym many grete maistries and many feire pleyes. And Guynebande well hem undirstode,

220 as he that was wise and a grete clerke, so that he wrought somme of the craftes ofte in the Bloy Breteyne that longe tyme after endured, and as it shall hereafter reherse.

Whan these thre kynges weren abedde and at her ese that nyght, the storye seith that they lay till on the morn that thei ronge to messe right erly, for it was a litill

225 afore Halowmesse. Than com Merlin and awoke hem, and opened the two wyndowes towarde the gardyn, for he wolde that thei hadde lyght therynne. And they hem clothed and arayed and yede to the mynster, and the archebisshop sange the messe. And than Merlin dide swere before the kynges that Arthur was the sone of Uterpendragon, and that he was begeten on the Quene Ygerne that nyght

230 that the Duke was slayn, and that he was the moste rightfull heire that the londe myght holde.

After that swore Ulfin that, so God hym helpe and alle seyntes, that it was trewe all as Merlin hadde rehersed. Whan the two kynges hadde take the oth of these two, anoon thei dide to Kynge Arthur their homage full debonerly as was right;

235 and the kynge hem receyved with gode herte and sympilliche with wepynge, and than thei kiste with gode herte for grete love. And than was the joye more than before. And than thei yede up into the halle to mete, and thei were served as high men ought to be. And after mete, Arthur and Merlin wente togeder to counseile, and the two kynges that were brethern, and Ulfin and Bretell and Kay the Stywarde.

240 Thanne seide Merlyn, "Feire lordynges, ye be alle worthy men and trewe, and I

212 lesynge, falsehood. **214 reame**, realm. **219 maistries**, marvels; **pleyes**, skills. **220 wrought**, worked. **221 Bloy Breteyne**, Little Britain (Brittany). **222 reherse**, be told. **223 her ese**, their ease. **224 messe**, mass. **232 seyntes**, saints. **234 debonerly**, courteously. **235 sympilliche**, humbly.

knowe yow alle as wele or beter than ye do youreself. And lo, here youre lorde the Kynge Arthur that is right a worthi man, and a gode knyght shall he be of his honde. And ye knowe well that grete wronge that is do to hym by his barouns of his londe, that will not resceyve hym for their lorde ne do to hym homage as thei

245 ought to do of right, but besy hem to greve hym with all her power. And therfore I pray yow do as I shall yow counsell, and knowe it well that it shall be the beste counseile that I may yow yeve."

And they seide thei wolde do like as he wolde devise, and he [hem] thanked debonerly. And than he seide, "Lordynges, se here the kynge that hath no wif; and

250 I knowe a mayden that is kynges doughter and quenes and of right high lynage, and also she is right feire and of grete valour that no lady ne may have more. And that is the doughter of Kynge Leodegan of Carmelide, that is now an olde man and hath no mo children but this doughter, whos name is Gonnore, to whom the londe moste falle after his discesse. And he hath grete werre agein the Kynge

255 Rion that is of the lynage of geauntes, and he is right riche and right puyssaunt, and yef it happe that he conquere the reame of Carmelide that marcheth to the reame of Logres that is Arthures, wite it well that Arthur ne shall not longe kepe his londe in pees. And alle the dayes of his lif he shall have werre on alle partees.

"And ne were the Knyghtes of the Rounde Table, that deffende the reame of

260 Kynge Leodegan agein the geauntes, thei sholde have all his londe wasted and distroied. And therfore I counseile yow that ye take with yow certein of youre peple and go with Arthur and abide with the Kynge Leodegan a yere or two, till that ye be with hym well aqueynted. And ye shull but litill while be ther but he shall love yow better than theym that with hym now [be] ther. And knowe it wele

265 that he shall profer Arthur his doughter to be his wif, and therby shall he have his reame all quyte. Ne never after that the geauntes knowe that he hath her wedded shull they not be so hardy to abyde in the contré ne nygh it by a journey."

245 **besy hem**, busy themselves. 254 **discesse**, death; **werre agein**, war against. 255 **geauntes**, giants; **puyssaunt**, powerful. 256 **marcheth to**, borders on. 258 **partees**, sides. 259 **ne were**, if it were not for. 263 **but**, until. 266 **quyte**, saved. 267 **journey**, a day's travel.

[The Battle of Bredigan Forest]

[**Summary**. Merlin assures King Ban that assisting Arthur against the rebelling barons will work to Ban's advantage in Benoyk later, and Merlin predicts that Ban will win control of that realm. Ban agrees to help, summons his forces, and sends them off to rendezvous with Arthur at Bredigan Forest. Meanwhile, the barons swear vengeance against Arthur and recruit several new allies. A brief digression follows, on Brutus's founding of Britain and on the origin of the placenames Logres, Bloy Bretaigne, and Cornwaile. Then Merlin and the army from Little Britain arrive at Bredigan, joining forces with Arthur. Merlin tells Arthur that he must win the support of the people with gifts, and Merlin amazes Arthur and his friends by telling them that a great treasure lies buried in the ground beneath them. Then Arthur's troops, and those of Ban and Bors, are deployed in companies and prepare for the battle. While this is going on, the Danes invade the barons' lands in the north of Britain. Fols. 47v (line 21)–51v (line 10).]

The boke seith that while Kynge Arthur and Kynge Ban of Benoyk and Kynge Boors of Gannes ordeyned her batailes in this wise as ye have herde, that nyght the eleven kynges ne toke noon hede to sette no wacche in thayr hoste, but wente to their bedde and slepte as thei that nothynge knewe that her enmyes were so
5   nygh. But oon feire fortune thei hadde, that alle the eleven kynges lay in the kynges teynte that was cleped Roy de Cent Chivaliers, and thei ne wende not to have no dred of no man. And as thei thus were slepynge, befill that Kynge Looth was in a ferfull dreme, for hym semed that he saugh so grete a wynde arise that it caste down howses and stepelis of chirches, and after that ther come a thounder so
10   grete and merveilously sharpe that hym thought all the worlde trembled for fere and drede; and after that com a water so sharply that drof down the howsynge

---

2 ordeyned her batailes, deployed their troops; **wise**, fashion. **3 ne toke noon hede**, did not bother. **5 feire fortune**, bit of good luck. **6 ne wende not**, did not expect. **11 a water**, i.e., a flood; **drof down**, destroyed; **howsynge**, buildings.

and a grete parte of the peple, and hym semed how hymself was in grete pereile to drowne.

15 And as the Kynge Loth was in this affray, he dede awake and hym blissed and was sore abaisshed of this dreme that he was in; and [he] aroos and apareiled hym and yede to his felowes and hem dide awake and tolde hem his avision. And thei asked hym fro whiche part com the water; and he seide from the foreste com all the rage and the tempeste, as hym semed. And thei seide thei knewe verily that thei sholde hastely have bataile, and that merveillouse. And therwith thei arisen

20 and awoke alle the knyghtes therynne, and comaunded hem to serche all the contré environ that thei were not supprised of no peple. And thei armed hem right wele, and lepte on ther horses and rode serchynge the contrey. And the eleven kynges hem armed and araide in the beste maner that thei cowden.

And than Merlin began to haste Arthurs peple, that well knewe the governaunce

25 of the tother party; and thei com so faste on that thei toke noon hede till thei were even fallen on hem that the contrey serched. And whan thei saugh hem armed, thei hadde grete drede and asked Merlin that mette with hem formeste what peple thei were. And Merlin seide it was the Kynge Arthur that was come to chalange his londe agein alle hem that therwith wolde be greved.

30 Whan thei herde these wordes, thei turned bakke and smote the horse with spores; and whan thei come into the hoste thei cryde, "Treson, treson. Now as armes, lordes, gentill knyghtes, for ther was never so grete nede; for lo! here cometh Arthur even at youre teyntes." And thei ronne to here armes, that yet were in her beddys, and hadde no leyser hem to clothe; and that was yet a fair happe for hem

35 that her horses were redy sadellyd. But yet for all that thei myght hem hasten, thise other were upon hem er thei myght be half araied of her harneyse.

---

12 hym semed, he thought. **14 affray,** state of fright; **hym blissed,** crossed himself. **16 yede,** went; **hem dide awake,** awakened them. **17 fro whiche part,** from what direction. **19 hastely,** soon. **20–21 contré environ,** surrounding country. **21 that,** so that; **were not,** would not be. **23 araide,** prepared; **cowden,** could. **24 governaunce,** actions. **25 toke noon hede,** i.e., did not stop. **25–26 were even fallen on hem,** encountered them. **26 thei,** i.e., the scouts of the eleven kings. **28 chalange,** i.e., protect. **29 agein,** against. **30 spores,** spurs. **31 as armes,** to arms. **33 even at,** near to. **34 a fair happe,** lucky. **36 araied of her harneyse,** ready with their equipment.

And therwith hem fill a grete encomberaunce that Merlin sente hem soche a wynde and tempeste that her tentes fill upon their hedes; and amonge hem was soche a truble that unethe myght eny of hem se other ne heren. And that was a

40   thynge that gretly hem distrubled in her armynge, and therynne thei caught grete damage, for Arthurs peple smote in amonge hem and overthrowe and slowgh all that thei myght areche. But the eleven kynges were departed and desevered, and yeden oute into the playn feldes withoute the tentes, and made blowe a trompe high and clere. And that was don for that all theire men sholde drawe towarde

45   hem.

And thei dide so, as many as myght aschape fro hem that of hem hadde no pyté, for ther was of hem so many slayn in that grete myschef that of the thirde parte thei were well delyvered; and therto thei saugh hem of so grete puyssaunce that thei turned to flight towarde her baner whereas thei herde the trompe sowne, for

50   the kynges were stynted at the entré of the forest by a river, and ther assembled alle her peple that thei myght have. And so thei encresed litill and litill, till thei were 20,000 that fledde, some heere and some there, that ne myght not come to here baner but with harde peyne. And so were thei sory and wroth for theire grete damage and losse, and sore thei compleyned their grete annoye. And 10,000 [were]

55   lefte liggynge in the felde, what dede and wounded, that no power hadde hem to diffende ne for to greve noon other.

Whan the Kynge Arthur saugh that all the herbegage was to hym belefte, than he com to Merlin and asked hym how he sholde do. Quod Merlin, "I will telle yow what ye shall do. Ye shall go here before to the passage at the forde whereas be

60   gadered 20,000 men, and ye shall fight with hem and make hem entende to yow. And the Kynge Ban and his brother shull go abowte and come on the tothir syde of hem and come on hem fro the foreste. And thei shull so be astoned that in hem shall be but litill defence."

Than thei departed the toon fro the tother. And the kynge yede thedir as the

---

37 fill, befell; **encomberaunce**, difficulty; **that**, because. **39 unethe**, scarcely; **ne heren**, nor hear. **41 slowgh**, slew. **42 areche**, reach; **departed**, separated. **43 playn**, open; **withoute**, beyond; **trompe**, trumpet. **46 aschape**, escape. **48 well delyvered**, i.e., destroyed; **puyssaunce**, might. **49 sowne**, sound. **50 stynted**, stationed. **57 herbegage**, i.e., encampment. **58 how**, what. **60 entende**, submit. **62 astoned**, surprised. **64 toon**, one; **yede**, went.

65   barouns were abidynge, that ne wende to have no drede of noon other saf of hym. And of hym thei ne drede but litill, for thei trowed hem wele to diffende agein gretter peple than ther was with hym. And the Kynge Ban torned towarde the foreste, and Arthur rode with his company till he com theras the eleven kynges were togeder assembled.

70   Whan thei come to the passage of the forde, ther sholde ye have seyn speres perce thourgh sheldes and many knyghtes liggynge in the water, so that the water was all reade of blode. And Kay heilde so the pas with the baner and payned that his company gate over. And whan the eleven kynges saugh so small a peple, hem thourgh preced and rushed, for thei were but 4,000, and thei were more than 20,000;

75   thei hadde therof grete dispite and shame, and diffended hem apertly.

> *[**Summary**. A fierce battle ensues in which Ulfin and Bretell and Kay and Gifflet do bold deeds. When the barons begin to get the upperhand, Arthur enters the fray and does many marvels, including unhorsing the King de Cent Chevaliers and rescuing Kay and Gifflet. Fols. 52v (line 6)–54r (line 8).]*

Whan the Kynge Arthur saugh this nede, he turned that wey as wroth as a lyon and leide aboute hym on bothe sides and slow all that he raught with a full stroke, so that thei voyded hys strokes and made hym rome. And Kay and Gifflet pressed to the kynges, that moche hem hadde greved and with hem sore foughten. And on

80   the tother side faught Bretell and Ulfin and Antor with the Duke Escam of Cambenyk and ageyn Tradilyvaunt and agein Clarion of Northumberlonde and agein Carados that was a noble kynght; so thei made hem to blenche thider as Kynge Arthur faught, that dide merveilouse prowesse of werre. Ther thei stynte, that oon agein the tother, for ther was the maister baner. And ne hadde be the

85   Kynge Arthur hymself, alle thei hadden be discounfited, for these kynges were odde noble knyghtes, and more peple be the toon half than on Arthurs syde; and

---

65 ne wende, did not expect. **66 trowed hem wele to diffende**, believed themselves capable of defending. **68 theras**, where. **73 gate**, crossed; **small**, few. **74 thei**, i.e., Arthur's men. **75 dispite**, insult; **apertly**, boldly. **77 leide**, struck; **slow**, slew; **raught**, struck. **78 voyded**, retreated from; **rome**, room. **78–79 pressed to**, attacked. **81 ageyn**, against. **82 blenche**, move. **83 stynte**, stood. **84 ne hadde be**, had it not been for. **85 hadden be discounfited**, would have been defeated. **86 odde**, brave.

therfore it myght no longe endure withoute grete damage.

Than com upon hem the Kynge Ban and the Kynge Boors from the foreste, where thei wende to have no drede of no man lyvinge. And whan thei were come and thei hem sye, thei yaf ascry that all the foreste and river resounde; and thei saugh well that the losse and the damage moste nede falle upon hem. Thanne the princes and the barouns drowen apart togeder in the medowes and devised among hemself what thinge that thei myght do.

*[**Summary**. The barons devise a strategy enabling them to address the separate attacks of Arthur's forces and those of Ban and Bors. The heavy fighting that follows is fairly even until King Ban begins to do impressive deeds. When several of the rebels set upon Ban together, Arthur comes to his aid. Fols. 54r (line 24)–55v (line 34).]*

Than fill it that the Kynge Arthur fonde the Kynge Ban on fote in myddell of the presse, his swerde in his fiste, that hym deffended so vigerously that noon ne durst hym aproche. And he was a moche knyght and a stronge out of mesure. And he lepe upon hem thourgh the presse; and whan he neyghed ner thei made hym wey, for so thei douted his strokes that ther was noon so hardy that durst hem abyde. Therwith com the Kynge Arthur brekynge the presse, gripynge his swerde all besoyled with blode of men and of horse, for he dide many merveilles of armes with his body. And whan he saugh the Kynge Ban at so grete myschef, he wax wode for ire. Than he rode to a knyght that [was] richely horsed, and Arthur lifte up the swerde and smote hym thourgh the helme soche a stroke that he slyt hym to the teth, and he fill to grounde. Than he toke the horse be the reynes and ledde it to Kynge Ban and seide, "Frende, lepe on lightly, for in evell tyme ben oure enmyes entred; anoon shall ye se hem forsake the felde."

Whan the Kynge Ban was horsed be the helpe of Kynge Arthur, he was gladde of that hadde hym founden. And than thei two smyten in amonge her enmyes. And whan the tother perceyved the grete damage that the Kynge Arthur and the

89 **thei²**, i.e., the barons. 90 **sye**, saw; **yaf ascry**, gave a shout. 95 **presse**, throng. 95–96 **noon ne durst**, no one dared. 96 **moche**, large. 97 **neyghed ner**, came near. 98 **douted**, feared. 99 **brekynge the presse**, breaking through the crowd. 101 **myschef**, trouble. 101–02 **wax wode for ire**, became enraged. 106 **anoon**, soon.

110   Kynge Ban hem dide her peple that were so loste and discounfited, and that thei hadde loste all talent of wele doyng and turned the bakkes. And thei hem chased to the wode; but ther were many slayn and defouled. So were thei distreyned betwene the wode and the river. Ther thei stalled and abode, and knewe well yef thei hadde be in the playn thei hadde be in pereyle of deth. Than the Kynge Loot and the

115   Kynge Ventres and the Kynge de C. Chivalers and the Kynge Carados and the Kynge Urien and the Kynge Ydiers and the Kynge Brangore and the Kynge of Northumbirlonde helde hem togeder. Whan Marganors hem seide and badde hem suffre and abide while thei myght, for to socour theire peple: "for yef thei be thus disconfite, oure peple shull be all loste and distroied."

120   Thus chased hem the Kynge Arthur and the Kynge Ban before alle other till thei come to a grete water and a depe, whereas thei that fledde hadde made a brigge of tymber and of plankes. And thei passed over the water after the tother, and so enchased hem the Kynge Arthur and the Kynge Boors that thei come to that brigge that was so made and wolde passe over after hem. And than com Merlin and seide,

125   "Kynge Arthur, what wilt thow do? Haste thow overcome thyn enmyes? Go into thi londe and lede with thee thy frendes that thow haste brought with thee, and hem serve and worschipe at theire pleiser, for I moste go into the wode for to my distynee aboute Blase, that right moche is my frende."

    Anoon he departed from Arthur and entred into the forest and fonde Blase, that

130   longe after hym hadde desired. And than he asked hym where he hadde so longe abiden. And Merlin tolde hym how he hadde be aboute the Kynge Arthur for to counseile hym. And Blase seide he dide but foly to abide so moche abowte hym, saf only for to counseile the crowne royall. Than Merlyn tolde hym alle thynges that were falle to the Kynge Arthur seth he departed fro hym, and how he yede for

135   to fecche socour in the Litill Breteyne. And than he tolde hym how the hethen peple were entred into the londes of the barouns and how thei werred. And Blase wrote alle these thinges that Merlin hym tolde and sette hem in his boke, and

110 discounfited, defeated. **111 talent**, desire. **112 defouled**, slaughtered; **distreyned**, trapped. **113 yef**, that if. **117 Whan**, Then; **Marganors**, the King de Cent Chevaliers's steward; **seide**, addressed. **117–18 badde hem suffre**, told them to persevere. **119 disconfite**, defeated. **124 wolde**, wished to. **125 what wilt thow do**, what do you wish to do; **Haste thow**, Have you. **131 be aboute**, been with. **134 were falle to**, had happened to; **seth**, since; **yede**, went. **136 werred**, fought.

therby have we the knowleche therof. But now leveth the tale to speke of Merlyn
and of Blase, and speketh of Kynge Arthur and of the twey other kynges that ben
140   in his company.

Now seith the boke whan that Kynge Arthur hadde discounfited hys enmyes
and the eleven kynges and a duke, by the counseile of Merlin that was gon to
Blase his maister in Northumberlonde, than he returned gladde and joyfull of that
oure Lorde hath yove hym the victorye of hys enmyes. Than he com to the logges
145   wherof the walles layn at the erthe, as Merlin hadde beten hem down. Than thei
leged and pight teyntes and pavilouns and hem rested, and lete the hoste be
wacched. And Leonces and Pharien hadde the governaunce of the wacche, and
Gifflet and Lucas the Botiller. Pharien and Leonces kepte towarde the wode, and
Gifflet and Lucas towarde the medowes, and alle the tother lay and rested hem till
150   day. And than thei ete and dranke grete plenté, for thei hadde inough of vitaile.

In this manere rested the hoste till in the morowe, till the Kynge Arthur made
be leide on an hepe all the wynynge and the richesse that ther was geten. And
whan thei hadde herde messe, thei com agein theras the tresour was leide togeder.
And the thre kynges it departed aboute to soche as hem semed was for to do, to on
155   lesse and to another more, after that the persones were of astate or degre. And so
thei departed to pore knyghtes and squeres that never after were pore, insomoche
that thei kepte not to hemself the valew of a peny.

And after thei departed stedes and palfreyes and clothes of silk, and yaf all
while ther was ought to departe, and sente agein alle knyghtes and squyres and
160   sergeauntes and other meyné, saf forty that sholde go with hem into Carmelide.
Thus yede Pharien and Grassien and Leonces, lorde of Paerne, and ledde with
hem her peple for to kepe her londe and her contrey, that the Kynge Claudas ne
dede hem no stade. Whan these barouns were come into theire contrey, thei

138 **therby**, thus. 141 **discounfited**, defeated. 143 **of that**, because. 144 **yove**, gave.
146 **leged**, lodged; **pight**, pitched. 147 **wacched**, guarded. 150 **vitaile**, food. 152 **on an
hepe**, in a pile; **wynynge**, winnings; **richesse**, valuable things. 153 **theras**, where. 154
departed aboute, distributed; **as hem . . . do**, as they thought fitting; **on**, one. 155 **after
that**, according to. 157 **hemself**, themselves. 158 **departed**, bestowed; **stedes**, steeds,
warhorses; **palfreyes**, fine riding horses. 159 **ought**, anything; **sente agein**, sent away.
160 **meyné**, retainers. 161 **yede**, went. 162 **that**, so that. 162–63 **ne dede hem no stade**,
did not harm them.

boughten londes and rentes, wherwith thei leved after in grete honour with the
165   aver that was departed that made hem after riche.

And the Kynge Arthur lefte in his contrey the two kynges with hym, as ye have
herde. So thei sojourned at Bredigan that was in the marche of Breteyne the Grete
and in the marche of Carmelide. And ther thei abode Merlin that sholde come to
hem thider. And on the morow whan Arthur sholde departe his peple, and that he
170   hadde made hem grete feste and grete joye at Bredigan and the kynges hadde
dyned, they yed up into the loges that were upon the ryver for to se the medowes
and the gardynes.

And as thei behelden, they saugh come a grete karl thourgh the medowes by the
ryver with a bowe in his honde and his arowes under his girdell. And in the brooke
175   were wylde gees that hem dide bathe as theire kynde is to do. The karll drough his
bowe, and with a bolte smote oon in the nekke that it brake in sondre. Then he
shette anothir bolte and slowgh a malarde. Than he toke hem and henge hem be
the nekkes at his girdell, and yede towarde the loges whereas the thre kynges
were lenynge and hadde well seen the shotte of the karll. And whan he com nygh
180   the loges, he shette another bolte and whowped to the Kynge Arthur.

And whan the karll com nere, the kynge asked yef he wolde selle the briddes.
And the cherll seyde, "Ye, with gode will." Quod the kynge, "How wilt thow
yeve hem?" And he ansuerde no worde. And the cherll hadde on grete boysteis
shone of netes leder and was clothed in cote and hoode of rosset, and he was
185   girde with a thonge of blakke shepes skyn. And he was grete and longe and blakke
and rowe rympled. The cherll also seemed to be crewell and fell, and seide to the
kynge, "I ne knowe nought of the kynge that loveth tresoure and is regrater and a

164 **rentes**, properties. 165 **aver**, wealth. 166 **lefte**, kept. 167 **in the marche**, on the
border. 168 **abode**, waited until. 169 **and that**, after. 171 **yed**, went. 173 **grete karl**, huge
rustic. 174 **girdell**, belt. 175 **gees**, geese; **kynde**, nature; **drough**, drew. 177 **shette**,
shot; **slowgh**, slew. 178 **yede**, went. 180 **whowped**, cried out. 181 **yef**, if. 182–83 **How
wilt thow yeve hem**, What do you want for them. 183 **cherll**, churl. 183–84 **boysteis
shone**, rough shoes. 184 **nete's leder**, cow's leather; **rosset**, russet (homespun cloth).
185 **grete**, large; **longe**, tall; **blakke**, dark (from the sun). 186 **rowe rympled**, rough-
bearded, shaggy, unkempt; **fell**, fierce. 187 **I ne knowe nought of the kynge**, i.e., I have
never heard of a king. 187–88 **regrater and a wyssher**, i.e., one having a monopoly on
goods.

wyssher, that dar not make a pore man riche that myght hym do gode servyse."
Quod the cherll, "I yeve yow these briddes, and yet have I no more than ye se.

190 And ye have not the herte for to yeve the thirde parte of youre gode that in the
erthe doth rote er ye have it uptaken, and that is nether youre profite ne worship."

Whan these kynges herde the wordes of the karll, thei beheelde the oon the
tother; and than thei seiden, "What devell! Who hath tolde this cherll?" Than the
Kynge Ban cleped the karll and asked hym what he seide; and the karll ne ansuerde

195 no worde but bad the Kynge Arthur to do take the briddes and than he wolde gon
hys weye. "Now by thy faith," quod Kynge Ban, "telle me who hath tolde thee
that the Kynge Arthur hath tresour in the erthe." Quod the cherll, "A wylde man
tolde me that is cleped Merlin. And also he tolde me that he sholde this day come
to yow for to speke with yow."

200 In the tyme that thei spake thus togeder, come Ulfin oute of a chamber and
come thider as the kynge spake to Merlin. "Go forth thy wey," quod the kynge;
"how may I thee trowe that thow haste spoke with Merlin?" Quod he, "Yef ye
will, leve me; and yef ye ne will, leve ne nought. For I ne leve yow nought, and so
be we quyte." And whan the cherll hadde seide thus, and after Ulfin a while hadde

205 listened, and than he began to smyle and wiste wele it was Merlin. And whan
Merlin saugh Ulfin he seide, "Sir stiwarde, take these briddes and do dight hem
for youre kynges soper, that hath not the hardynesse to make a man riche that
myght hym well guerdon, and to hym that this day hath spoke with the man that
hath hym tolde of the grete richesse unther the erthe."

210 Than began Ulfin to lawgh right harde and seide, "Sir, yef it plese yow, come
with me here above, for I wolde speke with yow of many thynges." And he seide
he wolde go with gode will. And the kynge beheilde Ulfin and saugh hym laugh
hertely, and than he required hym to telle why he dide laugh so sore. And he seide

188 that dar not, that would not. **190 gode**, wealth. **191 that is nether . . . worship**, that
works neither to your profit nor to your honor. **192–93 beheelde the oon the tother**,
they stared at each other. **193 What devell**, What the devil. **194 cleped**, called. **195 bad**,
asked. **198 sholde**, should. **202 trowe**, believe. **202–03 Yef ye . . . leve ne nought**, If you
wish to, believe me; and if you do not wish to, then do not believe me. **203–04 For I ne
leve . . . so be we quyte**, For I do not believe you at all, and so we are even. **205 wiste**,
knew. **206 dight hem**, prepared them. **207 hardynesse**, courage. **208 guerdon**, reward.
210 yef, if.

that he sholde wyte another tyme.

215 Than yede the cherll, so araide as he was, and mette with Kay the Stiward and seide, "Holde here, sir seneschall, now may ye plume; and as gladly mote the kynge hem ete as I it hym yeve."

With that com Bretell, and hadde wele herde that Merlin hadde seide and also that Ulfin hadde seyde to hym, that better semed a cherll than eny that was in the

220 worlde. And whan he hadde herde hem awhile speke, he perceyved that it was Merlin and began to lawgh undir his mantell right harde. And the kynge herde hym and badde hym telle the cause why that he lowgh. And he tolde he wolde telle hym yef the carll wolde assente. And the cherll than began to laugh lowde and seide to Ulfin, "Tell on, for I will that thow do so."

225 Than seide Ulfin to the Kynge, "Sir, ne knowe ye not youre frende Merlin and ne sholde not he come to speke with yow today?" And the kynge seide, "Yesse. Wherefore sey ye?" "Sir," quod Ulfin, "I sey for that ye knowe hym not so wele as I wolde that ye dide. For ye se somme two tymes or thre, and yet ye ne knowe hym not, and therof I merveyle." Whan the kynge undirstode Ulfyn, he was gretly

230 dismayed that he wiste not what for to ansuere. "Certes," quod Ulfin, "ye have seyn hym many tymes, and that I knowe well." Than seide the kynge, "Telle me, what is this cherll?" "Sir," quod Ulfin, "sholde ye ought knowe Merlin yef ye myght hym se?" "Yee, trewly," seide the kynge, "right wele." "Thanne beholde this worthi man, and loke yef ye have ever hym seyn."

235 And the kynge hym behelde and seide that he hadde hym never seyn beforn. "Trewly," quod Ulfin, "he may sey that evell hath he besette his servise on yow. For it is Merlin that so moche hath don for yow and loved so moche and holpen of all that he myght do or sey agein alle tho that upon yow do werre." And whan the Kynge Arthur undirstode this, he blissed hym for merveile. And also the two kynges

240 were sore amerveiled and seide, "How may this be Merlin? Is it thus? Never dide we se yow in soche habite." And he seide that myght well be so.

214 wyte, know. **215 araide**, dressed. **216 plume**, pluck; **mote**, might. **217 yeve**, give. **218 and hadde**, who had; **that**, what. **221 mantell**, cloak. **225 ne knowe ye not**, do not you know. **225–26 and ne sholde not he**, i.e., and that he intends to. **227 for that**, because. **228 wolde**, wished. **232 what**, who. **236 evell**, poorly (evilly); **besette**, given; **on**, to. **238 agein**, against; **tho**, those. **239 blissed hym**, crossed himself. **241 habite**, clothing.

"Sirs," seide Ulfin, "dismaye yow not, for he shall shewe yow the same semblaunce that ye saugh hym in firste." And thei seide that thei wolde that fayn se. "Now," quod Ulfin, "come with me into this chamber, for I wolde speke with

245   yow." And thei com in. And than seide Ulfin, "Sirs, no merveile nought of Merlins dedes, for he shall shewe yow semblaunces inowe. And at alle tymes whan he will, he chaungeth hym by forse of his art whereof he is full. And Gynebans the clerk it witnesseth wele. And wyte ye well that ye shall hym se yet many tymes that ye shull not knowe that it is he. And for that he chaungeth hym so ofte he is

250   dowted of many a man, for ther is many oon in this londe that full gladly wolde se hym deed. Now lete us go in this chamber, and ye shull se hym in the same semblance that ye saugh hym firste whan he aqueynted hym with yow."

And whan thei come agein, they fonde Merlin in the halle in the same semblaunce that thei hadde seyn hym in firste. Than thei ronne to hym and embraced hym and

255   made hym grete joye, as thei that hym loved with gode herte. Than thei satte and japed and pleyde with hym alle togeder, and of the shetynge that thei hadde seyn, and of the wordes that he hadde seide to the kynge. And than seide Arthur, "Merlin, now I knowe that ye love me, whan with so gode chere that ye have yove me these fowles, and that I sholde ete hem for youre love." And Merlin began to

260   laugh. Thus thei abode in joye and solace till the Lenton.

And so it fill that by the love of Merlin Arthur aqueynted hym with a mayden, the feyrest that myght be founden. This mayden was cleped Lysanor and was doughter to the Eirll Sevain that was deed; and [she] was heyr of the Castell of Campercorentyn. This maide was come to do homage to the Kynge Arthur, and

265   with here other barouns that dide homage as soone as he hadde conquerid these eleven kynges. For thei douted that he sholde bereve hem of her londes, and also thei thought that thei myght no better lorde have than hym. And some ther were that come with gode will, and some for drede of more losse.

And this mayden that was feire com to Bredigan whereas the kynge sojourned,

270   and was at hoste with a riche burgeys. And so be the helpe of Merlin he spake

243 semblaunce, appearance; **fayn,** happily. **245 no merveile nought,** do not marvel at. **246 inowe,** enough; i.e., aplenty. **247 will,** wishes; **forse,** the power. **248 wyte,** know. **249 for that,** because. **250 dowted of,** feared by. **254 ronne,** ran. **256 japed,** joked; **shetynge,** shooting. **258 yove,** given. **260 abode,** continued; **the Lenton,** the time of Lent. **266 douted,** feared; **bereve hem of her,** deprive them of their. **270 at hoste,** lodged.

with her previly and lay with her anyght; and that nyght upon her was begeten Hoot, that after was a full noble knyght and was also a felowe of the Rounde Table. This Hoot was of right high prowesse, as ye shull heren hereafter.

And at myd-Lenten the kynge toke leve of the damsell, and he and the other two
275   kynges toke their wey into Tamelide, hymself the fowrtithe. But of hem now ne speketh not the tale no more now at this tyme, but returneth to speke of the eleven kynges that were disconfited, and telleth where thei be com and whider thei yeden.

274 myd-Lenten, the middle of Lent. **275 fowrtithe,** the fortieth man [in the company]. **277 disconfited,** defeated; **yeden,** went.

[The Young Squires]

Now seith the story that full of sorowe and hevynesse were the barouns of theire disconfiture and losse, and [thei] riden forth playnynge and regretinge theire grete damage; ne thei ne ete ne dronke of all that nyght, and no more ne hadde thei don of all the day before, for the bataile hadde endured all the day. And it was full
5   colde weder and grete froste, and therfore thei were at more disese for hunger and for grete colde.

Than thei com to a citee that was cleped Sorhant and was a town of the Kynge Uriens. And a nevew of the kynges resceyved them with grete joye, and his name was cleped Bandemagu. Ther thei rested and esed hem in the town as thei that
10   therto hadde grete nede, for many of hem were hurt and wounded that abode stille till thei were heled. But thei were not ther thre dayes whan the messagers of Cornewaile and of Orcanye com to hem and tolde hem the losse and the distruxion of the sarazins that dide thourgh ther londes and were at a sege before the Castell Vandeberes, and hadde filde the londe full of here peple, and seide how thei sholde
15   never be remeved ne driven oute of the londe. And whan the lordes [herde] these tidynges, ther ne was noon of hem but their fleishe trymbled for this aventure that was hem befallen, for well thei knewe that thei were distroyed; and than thei wepte full tenderly.

[Summary. King Brangore summons the rebel leaders to a consultation and tells them they can expect no help from others in addressing the Saxon invasion. The kings decide to garrison several of their cities and to defend those strongholds against the Saxons. One of the strongholds is King Ydiers's city of Nauntes, and a second one is King Ventres's city of Wydesande. Fols. 58v (line 9)–60r (line 34).]

2 disconfiture, defeat; **playnynge and regretinge,** lamenting. **3 ne thei . . . dronke of,** they neither ate nor drank. **3–4 no more . . . don of,** i.e., nor had they eaten. **5 more disese,** great discomfort. **12 Orcanye,** Orkney. **12–13 distruxion of,** destruction caused by. **13 dide,** i.e., moved.

114

[Kynge Ventres] hadde a sone be his wyf, a yonge bacheler of sixteen yere of
age, that was of merveilouse grete bewté. And the wif of Kynge Ventres was
suster to Kynge Arthur on his moder side, Ygerne, that was wif to Uterpendragon,
and wif also to Hoel, Duke of Tintagell, that begat Basyne, the wif of Kynge
Ventres. And upon this Basyne begate he his sone that was so gode a knyght and
hardy, as ye shall here herafter, and how he was oon of the two hundred fifty
Knyghtes of the Rounde Table and oon of the moste preysed; and his right name
was Galashyn, the Duke of Clarence, that the Kynge Arthur hym yaf after he
hadde wedded his wif Gonnore.

This Galashene of whom I speke, whan that [he] herde tidinges how the Kynge
Ventres his fader hadde foughten with Kynge Arthur his oncle, and he herde the
grete prowesse and the grete debonertee that was in hym, he com to hys moder
Basyne and seide, "Feire moder, ne were not ye doughter to Duke Hoel of Tintagell
and to the Quene Ygerne that after was wif to Uterpendragon, that begat, as I
herde sey, thys kynge that is cleped be his right name Arthur, that is so noble and
worthi a knyght that eleven princes hath disconfited with so small a peple as he
hadde, as I have herde sey? I pray yow, telle me the trowthe yef ye can how it is,
for I may not trowe that he sholde be of soche herte as is recorded of hym but yef
he were sone unto Uterpendragon, that in hys tyme was oon of the beste knyghtes
of the worlde."

Whan the moder undirstode here sone that so here aresoned, hir yen begonne
to water that the teers wette her chekes and hir chyn; and [she] seide, sighynge
and wepinge as she that was hevy and tender for her brother that hir sone
remembred, "Feire sone," quod she, "knowe this truly that he is youre uncle and
my brother, and cosin to youre fader on the modir side of Uterpendragon, as I
have herde my moder sey many tymes whan she here complayned prively in her
chamber for her sone, that the Kynge Uterpendragon made it to be delyvered to a
cherll as soone as it was borne; and how all the matere hath sethe be discovered
of Antor that hym hath norisshed before the barouns to whom that Merlin tolde
the trouthe; and how that Ulfin dide witnesse this thinge for trewe, that so wele

19 **bacheler**, knight-aspirant. 20 **bewté**, beauty. 24 **here**, hear. 30 **debonertee**, courtesy.
31 **ne were not ye**, were you not. 34 **disconfited**, defeated. 36 **trowe**, believe; **soche
herte**, such courage; **but yef**, unless. 39 **yen**, eyes. 46–47 **sethe be discovered of**, since
been revealed by. 48 **that[2]**, who (i.e., Ulfin).

was trusted of Uterpendragon, and how he ordeyned the mariage of my moder
50   and the kynge. But the barouns of this londe ne will not knowe hym for her lorde;
and oure Lorde that is so mercyfull hath hym chosen thourgh His high myracle
that He hath shewed many sithes." And than she tolde hym of the ston and of the
swerde and alle the aventure as it was befallen.

And whan Galashene undirstode his moder, he prayed God that thei sholde
55   never wele spede that hym were ageyns. "And," quod he, "God lete me never dye
till that he hath made me knyght. Ha! Now God yeve me grace to do so moche
that he may me girthe with my swerde; and I shall never departe fro hym while I
may lyve, yef he will me withholde aboute hym." With that he departed from his
moder and yede into a chamber and began to stodye how he myght spede to go to
60   the Kynge Arthur. Than he bethought hym to sende a messenger to Gaweyn, the
sone of Kynge Loot, his cosin, and sende hym worde that he sholde come to
speke with hym at Newewerke in Brochelonde as pryvely as he myght, and that
he be there the thirde day after Phasche withoute eny faile. Than Galashene com
oute of the chamber and gat hym a messenger and sente to his cosin Gaweyn. But
65   now resteth the tale of the message of Galashene and speke of the kynges, how
thei departed fro Shorhant and wheder thei wente, and telleth of the aventres that
to hem befillen.

Now seith the boke that after that Kynge Ventres of Garlot was departed fro the
citee of Sorhant and the other barouns also, as ye have herde, that than the Kynge
70   Loot wente to the citee of Gale with three thousand knyghtes and fightynge men,
of hem that were lefte in the bataile where thei hadde be discounfited. And whan
he com thider the cetizenis made of hym grete joye, for gretly thei were affraied
of the Saisnes that eche day rode and ronne thourgh the contrey and toke prayes
and putte fire in townes and vilages all abowte as thei wente and dide grete dam-
75   age. And whan the kynge was come thider, he sente and somowned all the peple
that he myght, bothe fer and nygh, of sowdiers; and withinne a monethe he hadde
assembled mo than eight thousand on horse and on fote alle defensable, withoute
hem of the citee, whereof were four thousand for to kepe the citee.

52 **sithes**, times. 55 **wele spede**, succeed. 58 **withholde**, keep. 59 **spede**, manage. 62
pryvely, secretly. 63 **Phasche**, Easter. 69 **than**, then. 73 **Saisnes**, Saxons; **prayes**, livestock. 76 **sowdiers**, soldiers. 77–78 **withoute hem**, not including those.

And he kepte right wele the citee and the contré environ that noon that entred
80   ne myght but litill it mysdo. And ofte tymes he faught with the Saisnes whan that
he herde telle that thei come to forrey; and ther wan the pore bacheleres that therto hadde grete myster. And ther the Kynge Loot ne toke never thinge fro hem that
thei dide wynne, but frely yaf hem all, and therthourgh encresed his grete loos
that the peple hym yaf. And therfore com to hym moo than three thousand men
85   for the grete bounté that thei herde of hym speke, whiche ne wolde never have
hym seyn but for the high renoun that was of hym spoken, and that he was manly
and wise and full of largesse; and therof shewed wele his sones after hym, but
oon yet more than another, after the gode lynage that thei were come of, and I
shall telle yow how.

90   This is trouthe that the wife of Kynge Lotte was suster to Kynge Arthur by his
moder side, in the same manere as was the wif of Kynge Ventres. And of the wif
of Kynge Loot com Gawein and Agravayn and Gaheret and Gaheries. These four
were sones to Kynge Loot. And of hir also com Mordred that was the yonghest,
that the Kynge Arthur begat. And I will telle yow in what manere, for so moche is
95   the storye, the more clere that I make yow to undirstonde in what wise he was
begeten of the kynge, for moche peple it preyse the lesse that knowe not the
trouthe.

Hit befill in the tyme that the barouns of the reame of Logres were assembled at
Cardoell in Walys for to chese a kynge after the deth of Uterpendragon. And the
100   Kynge Loot brought thider his wif, and so dide many another baroun. Hit fill so
that the Kynge Loot was loigged in a faire halle, he and his meyné. And in the
same loigynge was Antor and his sone Kay and Arthur, in the pryvieste wise that
he myght. And whan the kynge knewe that he was a knyght, he made hym sitte at
his table, and Kay that was a yonge knyght.

105   And the Kynge Lotte hadde do made a cowche in a chamber where he and his
wif lay. And Antor lay in myddell of the same chamber, and Kay and Arthur hadde

---

79 kepte, protected; **contré environ**, surrounding countryside. **80 mysdo**, harm. **81
forrey**, forage; **wan**, won. **82 myster**, need. **83 loos**, praise. **85 bounté**, goodness. **87
largesse**, generosity. **88 oon**, one (i.e., Gawain). **94 moche**, important. **95 more clere
that I make yow**, more clearly must I make you. **96 moche**, many. **101 loigged**, lodged;
meyné, retinue. **103 he²**, i.e., Antor. **105 do made a cowche**, made a couch (i.e., a bed).

made her bedde atte the chamber dore of Kynge Loot in a corner, like as a squyre sholde ly. Arthur was a feire yonge squyer, and he toke grete hede of the lady and of hem that were abouten hire. And he saugh that she was feire and full of grete
110 bewté, and in his herte he covetted her gretly and loved. But the lady ne knewe it not, ne toke therof noon heede, for she was of grete bounté and right trewe to hir lorde.

Hit fill that the barouns hadde take a counseile for to speke togeder at the Blak Crosse. And whi it was cleped the Blake Crosse ye shall here herafter, and the
115 names of the Knyghtes of the Rounde Table, but yet the tyme is not come to speke therof more. At this crosse the barouns toke a day for to assemble erly on a morowe. And so it fill that on the nyght before that the Kynge Loot sholde go to this counseile, and he comaunded that previly his horse were sadeled aboute mydnyght and his armes were alle redy. And thei dide all his comaundement so
120 secretly that noon it perceyved, ne not the lady herself. Thus aroos the kynge aboute mydnyght, that his [wif] it ne wyste ne aperceyved it nought. And he wente to the parlement to the Blake Crosse, and the lady lefte alone in the chamber in her bedde.

And Arthur, that of all this toke gode kepe, sawgh well how the kynge was gon.
125 And he aroos as stilliche as he myght and yede to bedde to the lady, and lay turnynge and wendynge that noon other thynge durste do, leste the lady sholde hym aperceyve. And hit fill so that the lady awoke and turned hir toward hym, and toke hym in her armes as a woman slepynge that wende verely it hadde ben her lorde. And that nyght was begete Mordred, as ye have herde. And whan he hadde
130 don his delite with the quene, anoon after she fill on slepe. And Arthur aroos sleyly that he was not aperceyved till on the morowe, that he hymself it tolde at the dyner whan he served her at table knelynge.

And so it happed that the lady seide, "Sir squyre, arise up, for longe inough have ye be knelynge." And he ansuerde softly and seide that he ne myght never
135 deserve the bountees that she hadde hym don. And she hym asked what bounté it

108 toke grete hede of, observed closely. **109 saugh**, saw. **110 covetted**, desired. **111 bounté**, goodness. **116 toke**, i.e., planned. **120 ne not**, i.e., not even. **121 wyste**, knew. **124 kepe**, notice. **125 stilliche**, quietly; **yede**, went. **126 turnynge and wendynge**, tossing and turning; **noon**, no; **durste**, dared. **130 anoon**, soon. **131 that²**, i.e., when; **it tolde**, i.e., told it to her. **135 bountees**, goodness.

was that she hadde hym don. And he ansuerde he wolde not in no wise telle it here, but yef she hym ensured that she sholde hym not discover to no persone, ne purchase hym no blame ne harme. And she seide that it sholde not hir greve, and ensured hym with gode will, as she that of this thynge ne toke noon kepe. And

140 than he tolde hir how he hadde leyn by her that nyght; and than hadde the lady grete shame and wax all rody, but noon ne knewe the cause. And than the lady lefte her mete utterly.

And thus lay Arthur by his suster, the wif of Kynge Loot; but never after it fill her no more. And so the lady undirstode that she was grete by hym; and the childe

145 that she hadde at that tyme was of hym withoute faile. And whan the childe was born, and also the tidynges spredde abrode that he was the sone of Uterpendragon, she loved hym so moche in her herte that no man myght it telle; but she durst make no semblant for the Kynge Loot hir lorde. And she was sory for the werre that was betwene hym and the barons of the reame.

150 Upon a day Gawein com fro huntynge, and [he was] clothed comly in a robe that was warme as a robe for the wynter, and ledde in honde a leeshe of grehoundes and ledde also two brace folowinge hym. And it becom hym full wele all thynge that he dide. And he also was of the feirest makynge that eny man myght be as of his stature. But the tale ne of hym deviseth no more here saf only of a tecche that

155 he hadde, that whan he aroos that he hadde the force and myght of the beste knyght that myght be founde; and whan he com to the houre of pryme he doubled, and at the houre of tierce also. And whan it come to mydday, he com agein to his firste strength that he hadde at the houre of tierce; and whan it come to the houre of noone he doubled, and alle houres of the nyght. And in the morowe he com

160 agein to his firste force. This was the custome of Gawein.

Whan Gawein entred the halle, as ye herde, his moder lay in a chamber by a chymney whereynne was a grete fiere, and she was right pensif for her brother

137 **but yef**, unless; **ensured**, promised; **discover**, reveal. 139 **ne toke noon kepe**, had little concern. 141 **wax all rody**, blushed. 142 **lefte her mete utterly**, left her food untouched. 143–44 **it fill her**, it befell her. 144 **grete**, pregnant. 146 **also**, as; **he**, i.e., Arthur. 148 **for**[1], because of; **werre**, war. 149 **hym**, i.e., Arthur. 151 **leeshe**, a set of three. 152 **brace**, pairs. 154 **tecche**, characteristic. 155 **whan he aroos**, i.e., in the very early morning; **force**, strength. 156 **pryme**, 9 a.m. 157 **tierce**, 12 a.m.; **mydday**, 3 p.m. 159 **noone**, 6 p.m.

the Kynge Arthur, and for the barouns that were departed fro hym in evyll will,
and of the grete mortalité of peple that was come by the foly of the barouns of the
165 londe, and also of the Saisnes that were entred into the londe, wherfore thei were
in aventure to be distroide. And ther was she sore dismayed.

And whan the lady saugh Gawein, that was so feire a yonge squyer and moche
of his age, and thought it tyme for hym to be a knyght. And than she began to
wepe, and that hevied moche Gaweine, and [he] asked wherefore that she dide
170 wepe; and she ansuerde and seide, "Feire sone, that I have grete cause, for I se
yow and youre bretheren that spende youre tyme in foly, that fro hensforth ye
oughten to be knyghtes and bere armes; and ye sholde be at the court of Kynge
Arthur, for he is youre oncle and is the beste knyght of the worlde, as it is seide;
and ye sholde hym serve and purchase the pees betwene hym and youre fader.
175 For it is grete damage of the evell will betwene hem and the other barouns of the
londe that sholde hym love and serve, but for their pride thei deyne not hym to
knowe for her lorde. And wele it sheweth that it displeseth oure Lorde, for more
have thei loste than wonne in here stryf. And on the tother side, the Saisnes be
entred into the londe that us will distroye but yef God us helpe. And ne we ne shull
180 no helpe have of hym that sholde hem alle enchace oute of this londe that is the
Kynge Arthur. And therfore ar ye moche to blame and youre bretheren, for now
sholde ye bere armes and seche to acorde of youre oncle and of youre fader by
what wey thei myght be made frendes; and ye do nought elles every day but hunte
after the hare thourgh the feldes and so lese ye youre tyme; and therfore me
185 semeth ye ought to have blame."

Whan Gawein undirstode his moder he seide, "Moder, sey ye for trouthe that
this Arthur that now is kynge, that he be youre brother and myn oncle?" "Feire
sone," seide she, "ne doute yow nought, for youre oncle is he trewly." And than
she tolde hym, fro the begynynge to the ende, all how it was. And whan Gawein
190 hadde all undirstonde he seide full debonerly, "Feire moder, ne be not therfore so

163 **evyll will**, enmity. 164 **mortalité**, slaughter; **by**, because of. 166 **aventure to be**, in
danger of being; **ther**, therefor. 167–68 **moche of**, large for. 169 **hevied**, grieved. 171
foly, frivolous things. 174 **purchase**, obtain; **pees**, peace. 176 **deyne**, deign. 178 **here**,
their. 179–80 **ne we ne shull no helpe have**, nor shall we have any help. 182 **acorde of**,
make peace between. 183 **nought elles**, nothing else. 184 **lese**, waste. 184–85 **me semeth**,
it seems to me. 188 **ne doute yow nought**, doubt it not at all. 190 **debonerly**, courteously.

pensif, for be the feith that I owe onto yow, I shall never be girde with swerde ne
bere helme on myn hede till that the Kynge Arthur make me knyght, yef in me be
so moche valoure that he will me adubbe; and we will go to courte for to feeche
oure armes and helpe to mayntene his lordship agein alle tho that hym will greve
195 or anoye."

"Feire sone," than seide the lady, "for me shull ye never be letted, for grete
gladnesse sholde it be to me yef oure Lorde wolde graunte that ye myght do so
moche that youre fader and youre oncle were gode frendes, for than sholde I have
gladnesse at myn herte, and I ought wele above alle other." "Dame," quod Gawein,
200 "cesseth now at this tyme, for wete it well, by I ones oute of my fader house, I
will never returne ne entre therynne agayn till that my fader and myn oncle be
acorded, though that I sholde do right moche agein my fader will." "Feire sone,"
seide the moder, "God graunte yow grace this to performe."

In the tyme that Gawein and his moder spake thus togeder, com in Agravayn
205 and Gaheret and Gaheries and com before theire moder, that heilde stille her talkynge
with Gawein. And than seide Agravain to Gawein, "Ye be more to blame than eny
other, for ye be oure eldeste brother, and ye ought to lede us forth, and that we
sholde be knyghtes and serve hym that all the worlde of speketh that aboute hym
repeire. And we ne do but as musardes, and ne awayte nought elles but when we
210 shall be take as a bridde in a nette. For the Saisnes be but a journé hens, that all the
contré robbe and distroye. Ne we ne have not peple to chase hem hens but by the
prowesse of the Kynge Arthur. But lete us take oure armes of hym and helpe to
defende his londe agein his enmyes. For that is the beste that I can se, for here ne
may we nought gete. And therfore, better it were for us to do some prowesse in
215 his servise, yef we myght be of soche valoure, than here to be take to prison as
cowardes and lese oure tyme of oure ages." And whan Gawein undirstode the
speche of his brother, he hadde of hym hertely joye and moche he hym preysed
and ansuerde that so wolde he do. "And therfore, in haste lete us apareile us, for
we will meve hens withynne fourteen dayes."

191 **pensif**, sad. 194 **tho**, those. 196 **letted**, held back. 200 **wete**, know; **by**, be. 202
agein, against. 205 **heilde stille**, continued. 209 **repeire**, abide; **musardes**, dullards,
idlers; **ne awayte nought elles**, await nothing else. 210 **take**, caught; **bridde**, bird; **a
journé hens**, a day's journey away. 214 **nought gete**, nothing achieve; **prowesse**, valor-
ous deeds. 216 **lese . . . ages**, i.e., waste our youth. 218 **apareile us**, prepare ourselves.

220 And whan the moder saugh that hadde this undertaken, she was full of joye and
thanked God hertely. And to hem she seide, "Dismay yow nought of nothynge,
for I shall ordeyne yow horse and harneys." And therof were thei gladde and
merye. But now here resteth the tale of the moder and of the childeren, and speketh
how the kynges departed fro Sorhant, that be yet sorowfull and wroth for theire
225 discounfiture and losse, and also for the Saisnes that be entred into her londes and
contrees.

[***Summary***. *Just as King Ventres and King Lot had done previously, other rebel
kings — Clarion of Northumberland, the King de Cent Chevaliers, Tradylyvans of
North Wales, and Brangore of South Wales — return to their chief cities and prepare
them for war with the Saxons. Fols. 63r (line 6)–63v (line 13).]*

This Kynge Brangore hadde a gentill lady to his wif that was doughter to Kynge
Adryan, the emperour of Constantynenoble, that was myghty and riche. And he
hadde no mo childeren by his wif but two doughteres, whereof the Kynge Brangore
230 hadde oon and the tother was in Costantynnoble. In that tyme ther was a riche
lorde and a myghty that was Kynge of Blagne and of Hungré; but he deyde withinne
five yere after he was wedded and lefte a sone, the feirest creature of man that
was formed. And this childe dide wex moche and semly and right wise and hardy.
And at that day that Kynge Brangore was departed fro Sorhant, he was so well
235 waxen that he was able to be a knyght. And his right name was Segramore. This
Segramore that I of speke dide afterwarde many high prowesse in the reame of
Logres, whereof the tale shall declare yow hereafter, and I shall tell yow how it
fill.

Renomee, that thurgh all the worlde renneth, yede so thourgh every londe so
240 that every contrey spake of the Kynge Arthur and of his grete largesse. And so his
renoun spredde thourgh every contré so that in Costantynnoble it was in every
mannes mouthe, so that Segramore herde therof speke, and was but fifteen yere
of age and was oon of the feirest men of the worlde, and of large stature and beste
shapen of alle membres, and therto hardy and wise. And whan he herde tidynges

221 hem, them (i.e., her sons); **Dismay**, Worry. **222 ordeyne yow**, arrange for you. **227
gentill**, noble. **230 hadde oon**, i.e., married one. **231 deyde**, died. **233 moche**, large. **236
high prowesse**, great deeds. **239 Renomee**, Renown; **yede**, went. **240 largesse**, generosity.

245 of the Kynge Arthur, he desired gretly to se the day and the houre that he myght
be made knyght of hys honde, and seide often to hem that were of his counseile
that whoso myght take ordere of chivalrye moste in evry wise be a gode knyght.
And whan his grauntsire, the Kynge Adrian, that tho was livynge, counseiled hym
to take the ordere of knyghthode, for he was the next heire male to the empere
250 after his deth. And he hym ansuerde that he wolde never be knyght till that Arthur,
the kynge of Grete Breteyne, hadde made hym a knyght with his owne hondes.
And so hereof spake thei day be day till that the Kynge Adrian appareiled Segramore
and sente hym to the Grete Breteyne richely arayed. But now cesseth of hym to
speke more at this tyme, and turneth to telle how these other kynges departed fro
255 Sorhant.

[**Summary**. *Three more of the rebels — King Carados, King Aguysans of Scotland,
and Duke Escam — also return to their chief cities and prepare for the Saxons. Fols.
64r (line 5)–64v (line 4).]*

Thus departet the eleven barouns fro Sorhant. And the Kynge Urien leffte in his
citee and sente thourgh every londe and contrey aboute; and sowdiours [cam] so
that he hadde togeder nine thousand, withoute the peple of the citee wherof were
wele six thousand; and the sege was thens but a journé.

260 And so thei fought togeder many tymes, and loste and wonne as is the fortune
of werre. And thus this stryfe lastid longe tyme, so that the contrey was wasted
and made pore so sore that in five yere therin was nought to gete. And in the
contrey they lived by nought elles saf by that oon myght take of another bytwene
the Cristen men and the Saisnes, but yef eny ship by aventure arived at eny port in
265 the londe. In this manere were thei sustened that otherwise ne laboured not, but
werred that oon agein that other right harde. And the Saisnes ronne thourgh the
londe of Kynge Arthur and thereinne dide grete damage, for ther was noon that
hem dide lette, till that by aventure, as God wolde, he sente feire yonge squires

246 of², by. **247 whoso**, whoever; **moste in evry wise**, must in every respect. **248 tho**,
then. **252 appareiled**, readied. **256 leffte**, remained. **258 withoute**, without counting.
258–59 were wele, were at least. **259 sege**, i.e., invading Saxons; **journé**, a day's
journey. **260 thei**, the barons and the Saxons. **262 so sore**, so severely; **nought to gete**,
nothing left. **263 nought elles saf by that**, no other means except by what. **264 but yef**,
unless; **by aventure**, by chance. **268 lette**, hinder.

270

and gentill it to socoure. And I shall telle yow what thei were that so longe kepte the londes of Kynge Arthur till that he com ageyn oute of the londe of Tamelide, so that the Saisnes loste more, and the barouns that were his enmyes, than dide Arthur. And now returneth the tale agein to Galashyn, the sone of Kynge Ventres.

[**Summary**. *Galashin, the son of King Ventres, sends a message to Gawain, urging Gawain and his brothers to meet him at Newerk. When the cousins are assembled together, Galashin asks Gawain what he intends to do. Gawain says he will seek the most worthy knight of the world — King Arthur — against whom their fathers and the other barons are making war "with great wrong." The cousins agree to summon as many knights and squires as they can find, and to go to Logres and place themselves at King Arthur's disposal. Fols. 64v (line 34)–65r (line 34).]*

[The Deeds of the Young Squires]

Now seith the boke that aboute the entré of May, in the tyme whan these briddes
syngith with clier voys and all thynge rejoyseth, and than these wodes and medowes
beth florished grene, and these medowes full of newe tendir erbys and entermedled
with dyverse colours that swote be of odoures, and these amerouse yonge lusty
5 peple rejoyse because of the lusty seson, it befill that Gawein and Agravayn and
Gaheret and Gaheries and Galashyn, and thei that become in here companye, ben
risen erly for the heete that dide hem grete anoye on the day, as they that wolde
ride in the cole of the mornynge that was feire and stille and a softe weder. And
thei were yonge and tender to suffre grete travayle, and thei were wele armed and
10 hadde on hattes of stile as squyres used in tho dayes, and theire swerdes hangynge
at the pomell of theire sadeles before; for the contrey was not sure for the Saisnes
that rode and ronne thourgh the contrey for vitaile and for to robbe and distrye
the londe that was so plenteuouse and riche er the mysbelevynge peple were
entred, wherof was grete pité that so goode a londe sholde be distroyed for synne
15 and for myslyvinge, as God hath ofte sithes chastysed diverse remes.

The thirde daye that thise childeren rode togeder, lyke as that ye have herde,
thei mette the Kynge Leodobron and the Kynge Segagan and the Kynge Mandalet
and the Kynge Sernagut of the londe of Yroys, that hadde the contré aboute Logres
brent and wasted, and ledde with hem grete plenté of vitaile, so that the hoste for
20 longe tyme was refresshed of brede and wyne and of flessh. For thei hadde so
piled and robbed thourgh the contrey and the portes where the shippes were aryved,
and the marchaundise was so grete, that five hundred someres were charged, and

1 **entré**, beginning. 2 **than**, when. 3 **erbys**, plants; **entermedled**, mixed. 4 **swote**, sweet;
lusty, lively. 7 **for**, because of. 9 **travayle**, hardship. 11 **sure for**, safe because of; **Saisnes**,
Saxons. 12 **vitaile**, food. 13 **er**, before; **mysbelevynge peple**, the pagan Saxons. 15 **ofte
sithes**, many times. 16 **childeren**, youths. 19 **brent**, burned. 21 **piled**, pillaged. 22
someres, pack horses; **charged**, loaded.

twenty-five cartes and seven carres; and the cariage and the multitude of peple was so grete that the duste arose so huge that unnethe oon myght knowe another;

25 and also the fiere and the smoke so grete in the contrey that half a journey aboute men myght knowe what peple ther were. And whan thise childeren approched to this chyvachie, and herde the playntes and the cryes that the mene peple made for the Saisnes that hem so distroyed, that were well ten thousand of horsemen, withoute the putaile that ronne up and down and robbed the peple and brente the vilages as

30 thei passed thourgh the contrey.

Whan the childeren saugh this doloure and this sorowe, thei asked of hem that passed by that thei saugh so affraied, where that Kynge Arthur was. And they seyde he was gon into Tamalide at myd-Lenton, and hadde wele garnysshed alle the forteresses of his londe that noon ne myght not gretly forfete. And thei were so

35 doilfull that the sarazins so distroied the londe, as ye have herde. And whan the childeren herde that the kynge was not in the contrey, thei seide thei wolde [deffende] the londe and the contrey for her oncle, and also the pray that the Saisnes ledden, and that thei wolde kepe the londe and it deffende till here oncle were come home. And whan the peple of the contrey herde hem speke thus, thei asked

40 of hem what thei were that so wolde deffende the londe of Kynge Arthur as thei seiden. And thei lete hem beknowen what thei were. And whan the peple knewe what the childeren weren, thei hadde grete joye, for by hem thei trowed that the Kynge Arthur sholde be lorde of all the reame of Logres. And the love of the fadres he sholde have thourgh the childeren that ther were come with thise five

45 cosins and with other that were ryche mennes sones, as castelleins and vavasours of the londe, that after were of grete prowesse in the house of Kynge Arthur, and of soche as were moste preysed.

And as soone as the childeren saugh the grete damage, theire hertis begonne to ryse and [they] cried, "As armes, gentill squyers, for now shall it be sene how is

23 carres, wagons; **cariage**, baggage train. **24 unnethe**, scarcely. **25 journey**, a day's travel. **27 chyvachie**, foraging expedition; **playntes**, complaints; **mene**, ordinary. **28 withoute**, not counting. **29 putaile**, rabble. **33 garnysshed**, provisioned. **34 forfete**, harm. **34–35 so doilfull**, very sorrowful. **37 pray**, livestock. **38 kepe**, guard. **40 what**, who. **41 beknowen what**, know who. **42 trowed**, believed. **45 castelleins and vavasours**, i.e., protectors and overseers. **49 As**, To; **how**, who.

126

50   goode and hardy and worthy to bere armes, for we be in oure heritages; and therfore we sholde deffende oure right agein these mysbelevynge peple that thus this londe robbed and wasted." Hastely ronne these squyers to armes and lepen to horse and hem renged and distreyned as the knyghtes hem taughten, whereof were twenty-four that were noble men and right gode knyghtes and trewe. And

55   whan the peple of the contré saugh that thei hadde socoure, ther com to hem more than five hundred, what on horse and on fote. And than thei yede togeder as starlynges, and mette first the cariage and the vitaile that the Sasines ledden towarde the hoste, and were moo than three thousand with the cariage.

      And as the storye seith, it was passed myd-day and was right hote weder, and

60   the duste arose so thikke that scantly a man myght se fro hymself the caste of a stone. And as soone as that the childeren saugh theire enmyes, thei lete theire horse renne; and [thei] overthrew and slowgh alle that thei ateyned that ther ne ascaped oon ne other. That day Gawein slowgh many a Sarazin of the Saxouns, more than eny of his felowes, so that he was all blody, bothe he and his horse.

65   And he heilde an axe in his honde, and he was so crewell and fiers that whom he araught a full stroke, neded hym no salve. And his other bretheren dide also right wele, so that noon of hem ne durste abide of hem a stroke. And Galashyn was all day with Gawein that merveilously dide wele, for ther myght noon endure his strokes that he ne smote of arme or legge or heede or other membre. But above

70   alle othir, it was merveile to se the martire that Gawein made, for agein his strokys ne myght not endure iren ne style ne no mannys body, were he never so myghty ne stronge.

      And so the childeren smyten up and down aboute hem that of three thousand that ledde the pray towarde the hoste, ne ascaped not thirty. And ten of hem that

75   ascaped returned unto her chivachie that were comynge after with seven thou-

---

50 in oure heritages, i.e., in lands belonging to our kin. **51 oure right**, i.e., what is rightfully ours. **52 ronne**, ran. **53 hem renged and distreyned**, i.e., arranged and ordered themselves. **55 socoure**, help. **56 what**, counting those; **yede**, went. **57 cariage**, baggage train. **60 scantly**, scarcely. **62 ateyned**, reached. **62–63 ne ascaped oon ne other**, neither escaped one or another. **63 slowgh**, slew. **66 araught**, struck. **67 ne durste abide**, were able to withstand. **69 of**, off. **70 martire**, slaughter; **agein**, against. **71 style**, steel. **73 that**, so that. **74 pray**, livestock. **75 chivachie**, foraging party.

sand. But thei were not wele armed, for thei hadde made it to be trussed for the
grete hete that hem greved. And whan the ten that fledden com into the hoste, thei
cryed that all was deed that were lefte with the cariage. Whan thei herde that all
was loste, thei ronne to theire armes, alle they that eny hadden, and hem armed in
80   the beste wise that thei myght. And the thirde part of hem ne myght not come to
their armoure, for theire squyers were gon before with the cariage that the childeren
hadde wonne, and let it be ledde to Logres, and lete it be condited by men of the
same contrey that ther were dwellynge and weren fallen into theire company; and
after thei pursude the Saisnes, that fledden into the tyme that thei were fallen in
85   amonge the rerewarde.

Ther than was fierce bataile and stronge stoure and harde and crewell that
merveille it was to have seyn. Ther Gawein slowe the Kynge Noas of Iselonde,
for he smote hym with an axe with bothe hondis that he cleft hym to the briste
bon. And Galashyn smote so the Kynge Sarnagut with a swerde trenchaunt that he
90   made his heede fle into the feilde. And Agravayn, that was plonged into the presse,
smote on bothe sides hym aboute and began yeve so grete strokes that sore thei
hym douted. And Gaheries hadde chased Gynebande the length of a bowe draught
from his felowes, for that he hadde smyte down his brother Gaheret with a spere,
but he hadde noon other harm; and therfore wende well Gaheries he hadde be
95   slayn, and therfore he pursude upon hym with swerde drawen as fiercely as a
wilde boor.

Whan Guynebans saugh Gaheries so fiercely come, he turned to flight for he ne
durste not abide for the grete merveilouse occision that he hadde seyn hym do.
And withoute faile he was of merveilouse prowesse, for as the story rehersith, it
100   failed but litill that he was even like of bounté to Gawein his brother whan he com
to his right age and was knyght. And whan Gaheries saugh the Sarazin thus fleynge,
he swore be God that he sholde never cesse ne leve hym, for playn ne wode, till he
were avenged of his brotheres deth. And so he hym chased as faste as his horse

76 **trussed**, packed away. 78 **cariage**, baggage train. 80 **wise**, manner; **come to**, get at.
82 **condited**, conducted. 84 **after**, afterwards; **into**, until. 85 **rerewarde**, rear guard. 86
stoure, fighting. 87 **slowe**, slew. 88–89 **briste bon**, breast bone. 89 **trenchaunt**, sharp.
90 **plonged**, plunged; **presse**, crowd. 91 **yeve so**, to give such; **sore**, greatly. 92 **douted**,
fear; **draught**, shot. 94 **wende**, thought; **he**[2], i.e., Gaheret; **be**, been. 98 **occision**, killing.
100 **bounté**, ability. 102 **be**, by; **wode**, wood.

myght hym bere till he hadde lefte his felowes behynde the space of an arblaste.
105 And so he hym overtoke amonge the meyné of Guynebans that com redy to fight,
and gladde were they of the pray that thei hadde so ledde.

When Gaheries hadde overtake Guynebans, he stroke hym so sore upon the
helme that he kutte awey a quarter, that he made hym to stope; and the swerde
swarved betwene the shelde and the nekke and kyutte the gyge of the shelde with
110 all the arme, so that he dide it falle into the felde. And whan this kynge saugh
hymself so dismembred, he fill in swowne. And than Gaheries was gladde of the
vengaunce of his brother and turned his horse hede. But the Saisnes that this stroke
hadde sein ne concented not to lete hym passe. And than thei hem renged by
hundredes and by thowsandes, and closed hym in on alle partyes, and smote upon
115 hym with theire speres at ones, and overthrewe hym and his horse. And whan the
tymbir of theire speres were broken, he lepe upon his feet vigerousely, as he that
hadde inough of breth and myght that ther nas noon so hardy that durste put to
hys honde hym to take; and [they] launched at hym fro fer speres and swerdes
and knyves, that thei made hym falle on his knees two tymes or thre. But so
120 myght he not longe endure but that he sholde have be take or deed.

Than a squyer that saugh hym chase so the hethyn kynge com cryinge and
betynge his hondes togeder and rendinge his heer to Gawein that hadde remounted
Gaheret upon another horse, that hadde smeten down the Kynge Sernage fro. Than
the squyer cried, "Ha, Gawein! Where aboute arte thow? For thow hast loste thy
125 brother Gaheries but thow hym socoure delyverly. For he chased a Saisne that he
hath overtake in this derke valey, and hath hym smetyn down; but the sarasins
have besette hym on alle partyes and have hym overthrowen, and slayn his horse,
and made hym falle upon his kne I wote not how often. And yef ye hym thus lese,
it is grete doel and grete damage."

130 When Gawein undirstode hym that made soche doel for his brother, he seide,
"Ha! Seinte Marie Virgin and Moder to Jhesu Criste, ne suffre not that I lese my

104 **arblaste**, cross-bow shot. 105 **meyné**, retinue. 106 **pray**, animals. 108 **stope**, bend
over. 109 **kyutte**, cut; **gyge**, handle. 109–10 **with all**, along with. 110 **dide**, made. 111
swowne, swoon. 113 **ne concented not**, were not willing; **hem renged**, arranged themselves. 114 **partyes**, sides. 116 **tymbir**, wooden shafts. 117 **durste**, dared. 118 **fro fer**,
from afar. 122 **rendinge**, tearing; **heer**, hair. 123 **that**, i.e., Gawain. 125 **but**, unless;
socoure delyverly, help quickly. 128 **wote**, know; **yef**, if. 129 **doel**, sorrow.

brother, for than myn herte shall never be gladde. And yef I hym thus lese, shall ther never shelde hange aboute my nekke." Than he asked of the squyer whiche wey it was. And he shewde hym the valey be the wodeside. And he cryed to his

135 felowes with high voys, "Now shall it be sein who that shall me sewe."

"Feire cosin," quod Galashyn, "whider will ye go in so grete haste shall noon abide from yow; and therfore set forth smartly, for I drede leste we tarye to longe." Than the childeren hem renged and priked as faste as quarelles of arblast; and [Gawein] perced the presse with his gode horse and heilde an axe in bothe

140 handes wherewith he made soche martire and soche slaughter that thei fly from hym on alle partyes. And it lasted the space of a myle aboute of the peple that thei hadde leide to grounde. And thei sought up and down till thei founde Gaheries, that was lyggynge at erthe upright. And thei hadde pulled of his hatte of stiell and his coyf of mayle for to smyte of his heed, but thei thought to have take hym quyk

145 and lede hym to Bernage, the Kynge of Saxon. Than thei fillen upon hym at ones and wolde bynde hys hondes behynde hys bakke.

Than com Gawein prikinge, gripynge a spere, and sprange in amonge hem so full of ire and maltelent for that he sawgh his brother so vileinliche araide that ny he yede oute of witte. And than he leide aboute hym so grym strokes and rude that

150 noon durste hym abide but disparbled abrode fro hym as from a wode lyon in rage. Whan that thei that heilde his brother saugh the merveile that he dide, thei ne durste not abide ne holde his brother no lenger but yef thei wolde have receyved the deth, but turned to flight and made hym wey. Whan Gaheries saugh his brother Gawein, he lepte upon his feet and sette on his heed his hatte delyverly, and hente

155 agein his swerde and appareilede hym to diffende. And Agravayn hym brought an horse and seide, "Brother, now lepe up lightly, for grete foly have ye do to go so fer oute of oure company, for full nygh hadde ye more loste than wonne." Whan

---

135 **sein**, seen; **sewe**, follow. 136 **Feire**, Fair; **whider will ye go**, wherever you wish to go. 136–37 **shall noon abide**, no one will depart. 138 **hem renged**, arranged themselves; **priked**, rode; **quarelles**, bolts; **arblast**, cross-bow. 140 **martire**, torment; **fly**, flew. 141 **partyes**, sides. 143 **lyggynge at erthe upright**, lying on the ground face up. 144 **coyf**, hood; **take**, capture; **quyk**, alive. 148 **maltelent**, wrath; **vileinliche araide**, shamefully arrayed. 149 **yede**, went; **rude**, furious. 150 **noon durste**, no one dared; **disparbled**, dispersed; **wode lyon**, crazed lion. 152 **but yef**, unless. 154 **delyverly**, swiftly; **hente**, seized. 155 **appareilede**, prepared. 156 **do**, done. 157 **full nygh**, very nearly.

Gaheries saugh hymself hooll and sounde and that he was agein ihorsed and delyvered, he was right gladde.

160   Than the bretheren drough hem togeder to relied her peple. And the Saisnes blewe hornes and trumpes and armed hem and assembled hem thourgh all the contrey, and ordeyned theire batailes. But now cesseth awhile to speke of thise childeren and of the Saisnes, and speke of the men of the contrey that ledde the pray that the childeren hadde conquered, and the cariage, to the cité of Logres.

165   Here seith the storye that full gladde were the peple of the contrey of the wynnynge that the childeren hadde geten; and [they] wente joyfull and mery with the vitaile for thei were but two Scottissh myle fro the town, and therfore thei peyned hem faste to come to the cité saf, for well thei knewe that the Saisnes were to moche peple to fight ageyn the childeren and her feliship. And therfore thei

170 douted that the pray sholde be rescued and take agein be strength, and therfor thei hasted to come tymely to saf garde. And whan thei that kepte the cité saugh come the riche pray, thei asked how it was geten. And thei tolde how Gawein, the Kynges sone Loot, and his bretheren and Galashin, the Kynges sone Ventres, that is cosin to Gawein, be come to helpe the Kynge Arthur and have lefte theire londes

175 and theire contrey; and [they] sey thei will never faile the Kynge Arthur while that thei be lyvinge, "For thei be come with twenty-seven felowes, and mette with thre thousande forayoures that this pray ledden, and foughten with hem till thei have hem alle slayn and discounfited, and sesed us with the pray to brynge to this citee saf. And therfore open the yates and receyve it in, and after we shull returne

180 hem for to socoure, for grete pité it were yef thei were deed or taken in so tendre age, for thei ben of high valoure and grete worthynesse."

     Whan the cetezeins undirstode these wordes of the childeren that were come in soche manere, anoon after thei opened the gates and receyved hem into the citee. And after thei seiden that a parte of hem sholde go helpe the childeren. Thanne

185 thei lete blowe an horn in the maister toure, and than ronne to armes thourgh the

159 **delyvered**, rescued. **160 relied her**, rally their. **162 ordeyned**, arranged. **164 pray**, livestock; **conquered**, i.e., recovered; **cariage**, baggage train. **168 peyned hem**, took pains. **169 to moche**, too many; **her feliship**, their companions. **170 douted**, feared; **pray**, animals. **176 mette with**, encountered. **177 forayoures**, foragers. **178 discounfited**, defeated; **sesed us with**, i.e., have given to us. **180 socoure**, aid; **yef**, if. **182 cetezeins**, citizens. **183 anoon**, soon. **184 seiden**, said; **parte**, portion. **185 toure**, tower.

town. Anoon they were armed with grete spede and issed oute at the maister gate, and than abode the Castelein of Cardoell, that was a noble man and a trewe. And whan he was come, he fonde oute of the town seven thousand; and than he seide, "Sirs, it were no wisdom to leve the town ungarnysshed of peple, for we knowe

190 not what shall falle ne what peple we shall mete." And than thei ansuerde that he seide well, ne thei wolde not go but soche as he wolde have. Than he toke oute five thousand, and two thousande he lefte for to kepe the town that it were not supprised.

Than thei rode forth and renged close that wey whereas the childeren foughten

195 full sore, for the Saisnes were no mo than seven thousand in a flote. And as soone as thei hem saugh, thei ne douted nothinge so small a peple that were so ynge. And ther was of hem but twenty-four knyghtes, and five squyers and twenty that were not yet adubbed, and three hundred men what on horsebak and of fotemen of peple of the contrei that were falle to hem; and [they] seide thei wolde rather be

200 deed than thei wolde forsake her companye.

But Madelans and Guynehan hadde departed her men in two partyes, and eche was four thousande, for alle the Saisnes were assembled to hem two. Than com Guynehan first with a grete spere, for he was myghty and stronge and moche oute of mesure and therto right hardy; and [he] ran upon hem so fiercely as he hymself

205 alone all wolde have confounded. And Gawein, that was before his felowes, heilde an ax trenchaunt and com agein hym fiercely. And Guynehan, that com formest, ran agein hym and smote Gawein so harde with his spere that it fley all to peces, for the haubreke was so stronge of dubble maile and the squyer so full of prowesse that he ne meved not for the stroke, but yaf Gynehans soche a stroke with his ax

210 upon the helme that he bente over his horse croupe. And the stroke of the ax glenched and smote the horse bakke asonder that thei fill to grounde bothe upon oon heepe.

186 **Anoon**, Soon; **issed**, issued. 187 **abode**, they awaited. 189 **ungarnysshed of**, unprotected by. 191 **but soche**, unless. 192 **that**, so that. 194 **renged**, followed. 195 **flote**, group. 196 **thei hem saugh**, the Saxons saw them; **douted**, feared; **ynge**, young. 198 **adubbed**, knighted; **what**, including those. 201 **departed**, divided; **partyes**, groups. 203–04 **moche oute of mesure**, immensely large. 204 **as**, as if. 206 **agein**, against; **formest**, foremost. 208 **haubreke**, mail shirt; **the squyer**, i.e., Gawain. 209 **yaf**, gave. 210 **croupe**, hind quarters. 211 **glenched**, glanced.

The Deeds of the Young Squires

Whan the Saisnes saugh that stroke, thei shodered aboute hym, for thei wende that the Kynge Guynehan hadde ben deed; and than thei pressed faste to the rescowe. And Gawein smote amonge hem, and thei smote hym with theire speres and slow his horse under hym. And he lept lightly upon his feet and yaf so grete strokes that noon durste hym aproche. Than com the socours on bothe sides and ther began the bataile abowte Gawein, fell and longe lastinge, for the Saisnes coveyted to remounte Gynehans and for to take Gawein, and his felowes so hym defended that it was merveile for to beholden.

Whan Gawein saugh that thei desired so hym to take and holde, he griped hys axe and com to a Saisne that hadde made Agravayn to stoupe in his sadill, and moche he hym payned for to smyten of the heed. And whan Gawein saugh this, he wax ny wode for ire. Than he threste thourgh the presse to that Saisne, and for to yeve hym a gret stroke he reysed his ax. And the Saisne saugh he myght not voyde the stroke and caste his shelde ther ageins; and Gawein hym hitte so harde that he slytte the shelde in two partyes; and the stroke descended on the lifte shulder so grete that he slyt hym to the girdill, and than he fill to grounde. Than Gawein sesed the stede and lepte into the sadill, and than he cryed to his felowes, "Now shewe youre hardynesse, that these sarazins not us ascape, and that nother wode ne playn hem shall warante, for ye shall se my strokes and my prowesse double."

Than he smote the stede and rode in amonge hem and made of hem soche martire that thei lay upon hepes in the feilde, as hey in a medowe. But for all that, the Saisnes have horsed Guynehans. And whan he was remounted amonge the Saisnes, he hente a stronge spere and a rude and com to Agravayn, that hadde his nevewe slayn before hys iyen. And he hitte Agravayn with his spere so sore that it preced two folde thurgh his haubreke, and therto he shof theron so harde that Agravayn fill to the erthe, bothe he and his horse on an hepe.

Whan Gaheries and Galashin saugh Agravayn falle, thei hadde grete drede that

213 **shodered**, crowded; **wende**, thought. 217 **socours on**, aid from. 218 **fell**, terrible. 219 **coveyted**, desired. 222 **stoupe**, slump. 223 **moche**, greatly; **of**, off. 224 **wax ny wode for ire**, grew crazed with anger; **threste**, broke; **presse**, throng. 228 **girdill**, belt. 229 **sesed**, seized. 230–31 **nother wode ne playn hem shall warante**, neither wood nor plain shall protect them. 232 **stede**, steed; **martire**, slaughter. 233 **hepes**, heaps; **as hey**, like hay; **medowe**, meadow. 235 **hente**, grabbed; **rude**, rough. 236 **iyen**, eyes. 237 **two folde**, i.e., very far.

240   he were slayn. And Galashin come formest and smote Guynehans with his swerde
upon the helme that he made hym enclyne on his sadill bowe; and Gaheries smote
hym with his swerde upon the arme that it fly into the feilde; and Gaheriet smote
hym betwene the nekke and the shulders as he was stopynge, that he made the
heed fle into the playn; and Galashin with his fote spurned his body to grounde
245   and laught the steede and ledde it to Agravayn that sore hym deffended on fote.
And whan Agravayn hadde the horse, he lepte up as soone as he myght; and than
began the meddelynge amonge hem full crewell and fell. But of Gawein knewe
thei no tidynges, for he was so depe in amonge the Saisnes that it was no light
thynge hym for to fynde.

250   Whan the Saisnes sawgh the Kynge Gynehans deed, thei were so amasid that
thei wiste not what to do, but turned to flight upon the bataile of Kynge Madelen
that was theire chief lorde, and there recovered thei that fledde. And Gawein, that
hadde gon here and there, that nothynge cowde here of his bretheryn and wiste
not whether thei were discounfited or noon, he hovid stille till he saugh his felowes
255   comynge, and whan that he knewe it were thei, he was gladde. And thei renged
hem aboute Gawein, for of hym thei hadde be in grete feere, and Madalen rode
with grete plenté of peple, and were six thousand; and it ne myght not longe
endure but that Gawein sholde have ben loste, whereof it hadde ben grete damage
and harme to all the londe of Logres, but as the socoure com oute of the citee,
260   and were five thousand men of armes. Whan the childeren saugh the socour that
com oute of Logres and the baner that Doo of Cardoell brought, the men of
contrey that were with the childeren badde hem be of gode counforte, for "Loo!
Heere cometh the citee of Logres yow for to helpe and to socoure."

    Whan the childeren undirstode that thei of Logres were come hem for to helpe,
265   thei were gladde and joyfull. Than thei refresshed theire horse and girde hem
newe agein and lepten up and hem renged, and after rode streyte and close. And

---

241 enclyne on, slump over. **242 fly**, flew. **245 laught**, took; **sore hym**, with difficulty
himself. **247 meddelynge amonge**, fighting about. **248 light**, easy. **250 amasid**, stunned.
251 bataile, company. **252 recovered thei that**, were rescued those who. **253 cowde
here of**, could hear about; **wiste**, knew. **254 discounfited**, defeated; **noon**, not; **hovid
stille**, waited. **255–56 renged hem aboute**, arranged themselves around. **256 be**, been;
and, for. **259 but as the socoure com**, if not for the aid that came. **262 badde hem**, told
them to. **265 refresshed**, readied; **girde**, saddled. **266 streyte**, tight.

the Saisnes com hem ageins full irouse and crewell for the deth of Guynehans. Than thei braste theire speres in theire counterynge upon sheldes and helmes, and began a bataile full fell and merveillouse whiche myght not be withoute grete losse

270 on bothe partyes. Than com in amonge hem the socour that com oute of Logres as faste as theire horse myght renne, and ther sholde ye have herde grete crasinge of speres. And than thei drowgh oute swerdes and begonne ther a stronge bataile and mortall, for ther was shedde so moche blode that it ran like stremes doun the valey.

275 Full grete was the stour and the medlé in the playnes before Logres of the childeren and the socoure that com oute of Logres, and of the Saisnes; and [it] dured all the day till it was nyght. Ther dide Gawein soche merveiles in armes that wondirfully was he beholden of hem of Logres, for he smote down men and horse and slow so many that noon ne durste hym no stroke abide. Than fill it that

280 he mette with the Kynge Madelen that hadde overthrowe Doo of Cardoell, that was the captein of Logres, and heilde hym be the helme at the erthe, and peyned sore hys heede of to smyten. And therwith com Gawein; but ther tho was grete stoure and hidouse, for that oon part bisied for the rescew and the tother hym for to sle or withholde. But the kynge ther myght thei not take, for he hadde so grete

285 plenté of peple. And therwith Gawein smote so grete strokes amonge hem that he made hem alle to dissever. And it fill so that Madalen com in his wey, and he smote hym so with bothe hondes with his axe upon the helme that he slitte hym to the brayn, and he fell ded to the erthe.

Whan the Saisnes saugh the Kynge Madalen deed, thei were so mased that they

290 turned to flight, oon here and another there, and toke the wey to Valdesbires ther the sege lay. Than aroos the duste and the powder so grete that unnethe oon myght knowe another, ne noon ne abode his felowe. But there were many overthrowen in that chase, for as soone as Doo was remounted, he hem chased vigerously. But the childeren were ever to foren, that made soche martirdom upon

---

267 irouse, wrathful. **268 braste**, burst. **269 fell**, fierce. **271 crasinge**, crashing. **275 stour**, battle; **medlé**, melee. **277 dured**, lasted. **278 beholden**, regarded. **279 Than fill it**, Then it happened. **282 of**, off; **tho**, then. **283 stoure**, battle; **oon part bisied**, one side worked. **285 so**, such. **286 dissever**, disperse. **289 mased**, startled. **290 ther**, where. **291 sege**, siege; **unnethe**, scarcely. **292 ne noon ne abode**, nor could one wait for. **294 to foren**, before [the others]; **martirdom**, slaughter.

295   the Saisnes that fyve myle lay the wey full of hem that were wounded and caste to grounde. And though the helpe of God and of hem that come oute of the citee, thei slough of hem so many that of twelve thousand ne ascaped not thre thousande that ne were deed or wounded. And thus were the Saisnes discounfited, and the chase endured till nyght. Than thei turned gladde and joyfull to the citee, whereas

300   thei founde merveilouse richesse that thei hadde rescued fro the Saisnes of that thei hadde robbed and piled thourgh the londe and the contrey, whiche was all ledde into the cité of Logres.

      Whan the childeren were alle come to Logres, the citee made of hem grete joye whan thei hem knewe. Than thei brought before theym all the riche prise that thei

305   hadde geten and seide unto Gawein that thei heilde for the chief lorde that he sholde it departe at his voluntee. And he ansuerde that he wolde therof medle in no manere before Doo of Cardoel; "For," he seide, "he can it beter departe and yeve than can I, for he knoweth beste the pore and the suffretouse; and therfore do his volunté." Whan the citezins herde Gawein thus speke, thei hym comended and

310   preysed moche and seide he myght not faile to be a worthy man. And thei hym loved hertely above alle thynge and preised the grete gentilnesse that thei in hym founden.

      Thus restede the childeren and sojournede in the citee of Logres, that the Saisnes ne dide hem no forfete. But now cesseth the story of the childeren at this tyme that

315   ne speketh a gret while, and returneth to Kynge Arthur and Kynge Ban and Kynge Boors and her companye that be gon into the reame of Tamelide for to serve the Kynge Leodogan.

---

296 thourgh, through. **297 ascaped**, escaped. **298 discounfited**, defeated. **301 piled**, pillaged. **304 prise**, goods. **305 heilde for**, held to be. **306 departe at his voluntee**, distribute it as he saw fit. **306–07 medle in no manere**, not involve himself. **307 yeve**, give. **308 suffretouse**, needy. **308–09 do his volunté**, follow his wishes. **314 forfete**, harm. **314–15 that ne speketh**, i.e., will not speak of them.

[Arthur at Tamelide]

Right here seith the Frensch Booke that whan the Kynge Arthur was departed fro Bredigan, he and the Kynge Ban of Benoyk and the Kynge Boors of Gannes his brother, that thei rode so her journés till thei com to Tamelide and after to Toraise, whereas the Kynge Leodogan sojourned upon the Pasche Even. And whan thei entred into the citee, Merlin rode with hym upon a grete stede, as he that wolde not hym leven in no manere.

Than thei com to the paleise and fonde the Kynge Leodogan gretly affraied, for the Kynge Ryon was entred his londe upon hym with fifteen kynges crowned and hadde hym discounfited and dryven oute of the feilde. And thei were loigged at a seige before a citee cleped Nablaise, that was a grete town and a riche and plenteuouse of alle goodes. Of this thynge was the Kynge Leodogan gretly abaisshed and dismayed, for his enmyes hadde brought upon hym soche a grete puyssaunce of peple, and he ne kowde no counseile how he myght his londe deffende agein the Kynge Ryon, for he hadde not peple in his reame sufficient to areyse hem fro the sege ne to chase hem oute of his reame; and so therof he counseilled with his kynghtes that were with hym belefte and asked of hem counseile and her advys.

In the while that Kynge Leodogan toke thus his counseile of his knyghtes, entred in the Kynge Arthur and his companye into the paleise and com before the Kynge Leodogan, holdynge eche othir be the honde, two and two togeder. And the storye seith that with Arthur were forty, and hymself and Merlin made forty-two; and thei weren alle right wele clothed and richely arrayed, and alle yonge bacheleres at pryme barbe, excepte the two kynges that yede before that somdell were in age,

---

3 her, their. **4 whereas**, where; **sojourned upon**, abided until; **Pasche Even**, Easter Eve. **6 leven**, depart from. **7 paleise**, palace; **fonde**, found. **9 discounfited**, defeated. **11 abaisshed**, upset. **12 puyssaunce**, force. **13 kowde**, knew; **agein**, against. **14 areyse hem**, free themselves. **16 belefte**, remaining. **22 at pryme barbe**, in early manhood; **yede**, went; **somdell**, somewhat more.

and thei were feire knyghtes and semely. And thei were beholden of grete and
smale of alle that were therinne, for thei were of freissh aray and riche atire. And
25   whan thei com before the Kynge Leodogan, anoon he aroos and yede hem ageins,
for hym semed thei weren high men and of grete astate.

    Than spake the Kynge Ban first and salued the Kynge Leodogan as soone as he
myght; and the kynge seide thei were welcome yef thei come for goode. "Certes,
sir," seide he, "for noon evell ne be we not entred into youre reame, but we be
30   come to serve yow with this condicion — that ye desire not to knowe oure names
into the tyme that we lete yow wyte of oure volunté. And but it plese yow in this
maner, we commaunde yow to God that He yow deffende from all evell and disese,
for we shulde fynde inowe that us will resceyve in soche forme as we yow
demaunde; but we have herde sey that ye withholde alle the sowdioures that to
35   yow will come. Now sey us youre pleysier."

    Than ansuerde the Kynge Leodogan that he wolde avise hym by his counseile
and besekynge hem therwith not to be displesed; and thei ansuerde agein to be at
his leiser. Than cleped the Kynge Leodogan the Knyghtes of the Rounde Table
and asked how hem semed of that the knyghtes hym demaunded, and what was
40   her counseile. And thei ansuerde that to withholde hem myght he have no damage, for thei semede to be of grete worthynesse; "And resceyve hem in Goddes
name, and pray hem as soone as thei may to sey what thei be and to make hem to
be knowen."

    Than departed the kynge fro the counseile and com into the halle where the
45   barouns hym abiden. And than he seide to hem, "Feire lordynges, me merveileth
gretly of that ye have me requered, that ye will not that noon knowe what ye be ne
what be youre names, and of soche thynge herde I never speke. But by youre
semblaunce ye seme alle worthi men, and therfore I will in no wise withsey that

25 yede hem ageins, approached them. **26 hym semed,** he thought. **27 salued,** greeted.
29 noon evell ne, no evil purpose. **31 into,** until; **wyte,** know; **volunté,** own volition; **but,**
if. **32 disese,** suffering. **33 inowe,** enough; **in soche forme,** on such terms. **34 withholde,**
support; **sowdioures,** soldiers. **35 sey,** tell; **pleysier,** desires. **37 besekynge,** urged. **37–
38 be at his leiser,** do his bidding. **38 cleped,** called. **39 how hem semed,** what they
thought; **demaunded,** asked. **40 her counseile,** their advice; **withholde hem,** retain them.
41 worthynesse, worthiness. **46 will,** wish; **noon,** anyone; **what ye be,** who you are; **ne,**
nor. **48 semblaunce,** appearance; **withsey,** deny; **that,** what.

ye requere; and be ye right welcome, and I yow withholde as my lordes and
50 felowes in soche forme that ye shull me ensure to helpe me feithfully and trewly
while that ye be in my companye. But thus moche I will yow hertely prayen, that
as soone as ye godely mayen, ye will lete me wite what ye be. And I shall telle yow
wherfore, for ye may be soche that I sholde have shame that I have yow not
served as ye ought for to be, for paraventure ye be of higher astate than am I."
55 And thei ansuerde that he ne sholde to hem do nothynge but thei wolde it gladly
take in gré. And the Kynge Ban hym graunted for to telle her names as soone as
tyme requered; and than thei made theire suerté to the Kynge Leodogan hym trewely
for to serve.

Than thei departed from the kynge and wente into the town for to take the beste
60 loiggynge that thei myght knowe. And Merlin hem ledde to the house of a vavasour
that was right a gode man and a yonge bacheler; and the herberowe was right
godely and esy, and the wif was right a noble woman and a feire and goode to God
and to the worlde. The lorde of the house was a worthy man and of gode livynge,
and his name was Blaires and his wif Leonell. And whan thei com before the place,
65 Blaires lepe oute hem agenis and seide thei were welcome, and thei hym thankeden.
Anon thei lighten and yede up into the halle that was right feire and wel beseyn,
and the yomen dight her horses well at ese.

Thus thei sojourned in the town eight dayes full, and nothinge dide but ete and
dranke and made hem mery and wente to the courte even and morowe whan thei
70 wolden. And the Kynge Leodogan hem served and wurshiped in all that he myght,
and yet he will more whan he knoweth what thei be; he will not holde his travayle
nothinge loste. And moreover, the Kynge Leodogan somowned his peple thourghoute
his reame, alle tho that armes myght bere, that at the Ascencion thei sholde be at
Toraise, redy armed hemself to deffende in bataile agein theire enmyes. And alle
75 tho that ne wolde not com, he lete hem well wite that thei sholde have as streyte

---

49 withholde, retain. **51 thus moche**, this much. **52 godely mayen**, are able; **wite**, know.
54 paraventure, perhaps. **56 take in gré**, accept; **graunted for**, agreed. **57 suerté**,
pledge. **60 loiggynge**, lodging; **vavasour**, lesser nobleman. **61 herberowe**, lodging. **62
esy**, pleasant. **65 lepe**, rushed; **hem agenis**, to them. **66 lighten**, alighted; **yede**, went.
67 yomen dight, yeomen put. **70 wurshiped**, honored. **71 holde**, think. **71–72 travayle
nothinge loste**, efforts were wasted. **72 somowned**, summoned. **73 tho**, those. **75 wite**,
know; **streyte**, strict.

justice as longed to thevis and traytoures. And also the Kynge Leodogan sente after hys frendes and sowdiours over all where he myght hem gete for golde or silver, and ther com so grete plenté of oon and other that thei were assembled on the Ascencion Even in the medowes undir Toraise and loigged in teyntes and pavilouns, forty thousand what on horse bakke and on fote, withoute hem that were in the town, whereof ther were six thousand; but the story seith that in tho dayes fyve hundred was cleped a thousande.

In the tyme that Kynge Leodogan hadde somowned so his peple, it befill on a Tewisday at even, in the entreynge of May, that the Kynge Ryolent and the Kynge Phariouns of Irelonde and the Kynge Senygres and the Kynge Serans were departed fro the hoste with fifteen thousande men of armes, and ran thourgh the contrey for vitaile whereof thei hadde grete nede. And it befill that thei com wastynge the contrey toward Torayse, where the Kynge Leodogan of Tamelide sojourned and abode his peple that he hadde sente after.

Than herde the kynge the noyse of hem that gadered togeder the pray and robbed the londe and the contrey aboute Torayse. And thei of the town hem perceyved, and than thei closed the gates; and the knyghtes that were withynne at sojourne ronne to theire armes and lepe to theire horse and assembled hem togeder withynne the yates. Than were alle the Knyghtes of the Rounde Table armed, and the governaunce of hem hadde Hervy the Rivell and Males ly Bruns; and thei were two hundred and fifty that alle were noble gode knyghtes and trewe, and were so worthi in armes that under sonne men myght fynde noon better. These were alle in a wynge by hemself, for thei wolde not be medled amonge noon other. And on the tother side the knyghtes and the peple of the citee arayed hem, and thei were four thousand, and of these hadde the stiward the governaunce hem to lede that was cleped Cleodalis.

This Cleodalis was wonte to bere the chief baner of the kynge, but ever after that the Knyghtes of the Rounde Table were come, Hervy the Rivell it bar; but he

---

76 **longed to thevis,** deserved thieves. 77 **sowdiours,** soldiers. 80 **what on,** counting those; **withoute hem,** excluding those. 84 **entreynge,** beginning. 87 **vitaile,** food. 89 **abode,** awaited. 90 **pray,** livestock. 92 **at sojourne,** at their ease. 97 **sonne,** the sun. 98 **medled amonge noon,** mixed with any. 99 **arayed hem,** prepared themselves. 102 **was wonte to bere,** used to carry. 103 **he,** i.e., Cleodalis.

bar a smal ganfanon of two smale losenges of goules and the feelde of golde and
105 crownes of ynde; and the grete baner that Hervy bar was of four losenges full of
crownes of golde. Whan thei were well armed, thei renged hem before the portes
and abode the comaundement of the kynge. And whan the kynge was armed, he
lepe on a grete stede of greet bounté and rode to the baner that Hervy bar. And
ther he hoved stille till thei saugh come the sarazins, and [thei] were mo than
110 seven thousande on horsebak.

And on the tothir side was Arthur well armed and alle his companye, and thei
were alle richely horsed. And Merlin bar that day the baner, and he comaunded
hem alle that as dere as thei heilden her owen bodies, that thei sholde sue that
baner all that day in what place that it yede. And thei seide alle that thei so wolden.
115 Than thei set forth her wey thourgh the town, so fresch and richely armed that no
peple myght be better, and thei were forty-one withoute Merlin that bar the baner,
soche oon that for a grete merveile was beholden of oon and other that day; for he
bar a dragon that was not right grete and the taile was a fadome and an half of
lengthe tortue, and he hadde a wide throte that the tongue semed braulinge ever,
120 and it semed sparkles of fier that sprongen up into the heire of his throte.

With that com the geauntes and the sarazins and smote theire speres upon the
yates of the town, and after turned down the medowes, for thei fonde no man that
yaf hem ansuere, and gadered togeder alle the prayes of bestes that were in the
medowes. And Merlin eschuwed alle that were in the stretes of the town and rode
125 thourgh hem even to the yates with his meyné, and seide than to the porter, "Lete
oute, for it is tyme." And the porter seide thei sholde not oute of the yates till the
kynge hadde comaunded. "What!" seide Merlin, "makeste thow daunger of that I
have as grete power as thow?" Than Merlin caught the flayle of the yate and
plukked it to hym, and yede oute as lightly as it hadde not have ben lokked, and

104 ganfanon, standard; **losenges of goules,** diamond-shapes in red; **feelde,** field (background). **105 ynde,** blue. **106 renged hem,** stationed themselves; **portes,** gates. **107 abode,** awaited. **108 bounté,** excellence. **109 hoved stille,** waited quietly. **113 dere,** dearly; **sue,** follow. **114 what,** whatever; **yede,** went. **117 soche oon,** such a one. **118 right grete,** very large; **fadome,** fathom (6 feet). **119 tortue,** entwined; **braulinge,** fluttering. **120 heire of,** air from. **121 With that,** Then. **123 prayes of bestes,** group of animals. **124 eschuwed,** avoided. **127 makeste thow daunger of,** i.e., do you doubt. **128 flayle,** bar.

130 than departed oute, magré how he grucchid.

      Whan these forty-two felowes weren oute of the towne, than the gate was as close as it hadde never ben opened at that tyme. And of that merveile blissid the Kynge Ban and the Kynge Boors his brother and alle the tother. And Merlin priked faste his horse till he overtoke a grete company of sarazins that were two thousande 135 or mo that ledde grete plenté of beestes. And Merlin frusht amonge hem with his banere and his companye with hym, and leyde on sore strokes and in her metynge overthrew alle that thei countred. And in lesse than an hour thei hadde hem so slayn and chased that thei toke the pray and ledde it to the yates of the town. But thei hadde gon but a while whan thei saugh four kynges com with fifteen thousande 140 men of armes that ledde so grete cariage of robbery that thei hadde piled thourgh the contrey, and were towarde the see. Whan Merlin hem saugh he seide to his felowes, "Suweth me!" and thei so diden. And it fill so that anoon as Merlin hadde caste a charme, there rose soche a wynde and storme so grete that the powder and the duste arose with the wynde and smote in the visages of the geauntes and sarazins 145 that oon myght not right wele knowe another.

      And anoon as the forty-two felowes were in amonge hem, thei slowe and overthrewe so many that it was wonder to thinke. And than comaunded the Kynge Leodogan to open the yates; than issed oute first the stiwarde Cleodales formeste with four thousand men of armes, and fonde the yate close whereas thei yssed 150 oute, that foughten agein fifteen thousand men so harde that it was merveille. Than com Cleodalis with his banere and smote in amonge the presse right hidously. Ther sholde ye have herde grete brekinge of speres and grete noyse of swerdes upon helmes and upon sheldes, that the sownde was herde into the citee clerly. Ther was grete defoulinge of men and horse, but ther the forty-two felowes shewed 155 merveiles with her bodies.

      Whan these four kynges saugh that these were amonge hem medelinge, thei departed her peple in tweyne and left eight thousand fightinge stille; and seven

130 **magré**, despite; **grucchid**, complained. **131–32 as close as**, as closed as if. **132 blissid**, crossed themselves. **133 priked**, rode. **135 frusht**, rushed. **138 pray**, group of animals. **140 so grete cariage**, a large baggage train; **piled**, pillaged. **142 Suweth**, Follow; **fill so**, happened; **anoon as**, as soon as. **143 charme**, spell. **144 visages**, faces. **148 issed**, issued. **153 into**, inside. **156 medelinge**, fighting. **157 departed**, divided.

thousand rode agein the banere of Kynge Leodogan that thei saugh come oute of the town. And the ton rode agein the tother full fiercely; and whan thei neighed
160 nygh, thei lowed ther speres and yaf togeder so grete strokes upon sheldes that thei perced haubrekes and dismailed, and many ther were throwen to grounde sore bledynge with stroke of speres. And many ther were that passed thourgh withoute fallinge. Whan the speres were broken, thei leide honde to swerdes and begonne the bataile grete and merveilouse. But ther sholde ye have seyn the
165 Knyghtes of the Rounde Table do wondres, and thei were but two hundred and fifty, and thei that were fightinge with hem were seven thousand; and so were the Knyghtes of the Rounde Table at gret myschief, for thei behoved to disparble, whethir thei wolde or noon, and voyde the place. But thei heilde hem togeder so close and streite that noon myght hem perce ne entyr in amonge hem.
170 Whan the Kynge Riolent and the Kynge Placiens saugh that so litill a peple withstode so grete a power as thei were, thei hadde therof grete merveile and grete dispyte. Than thei cried theire ensigne and swore that never oon of hem sholde ascape. Than thei yaf hem a grete shoure and a felonouse, for at that shofte thei overthrewe mo than forty, and moche thei hem peyned hem to diffoule and to
175 maymen; but her felowes were upon hem arrestynge, and hem deffended from theire enmyes with her swerdes with all theire myght.
And than it fill that the Kynge Leodogan was throwen fro his horse full lothly, and thei token hym with strengthe and ledde hym toward prison with moo than five hundred, into the hoste of Kynge Rion of Irlonde; and thei hym ledde full
180 fiercely, for thei wende wele that alle here werre hadde be fynysshed. And so thei ledde the Kynge Leodogan in all the haste that thei myght. And whan the Kynge Leodogan saugh hym so mysfallen and that his enmyes hadde hym taken, he sowowned often tymes and made grete sorowe. And thei that hym ledden spedden hem so faste that thei were fro the town two myle.

158 agein, against. **159 ton**, one; **tother**, other. **159–60 neighed nygh**, drew near. **161 dismailed**, pierced mail. **167 at gret myschief**, in great trouble; **behoved**, were forced; **disparble**, retreat. **168 wolde or noon**, wished to or not; **voyde**, leave. **169 streite**, tight. **170 litill**, few. **172 dispyte**, anger; **ensigne**, battle-cry. **173 shoure**, rush; **shofte**, push. **174 diffoule**, injure. **175 maymen**, maim; **felowes**, i.e., opponents; **arrestynge**, i.e., fighting back. **177 lothly**, badly. **180 wende**, thought; **alle here werre**, all their fighting. **183 sowowned**, swooned.

185   Full grete was the noyse of the seven thousand and the two hundred fifty
Knyghtes of the Rounde Table that were full hevy and wroth for the kynge that
thei hadde loste; and than [thei] seide amonge hem and assured togeder, seth it
was com therto and that thei saugh all sholde be loste, that thei wolde avenge her
shame and deth as longe as they myght lyven. Than thei sette her bakkes eche to

190   other, and hem deffended merveilously and [made] soche slaughter of men and
horse aboute hem withoute remevynge oute of place; and so moche peyne and
traveile thei suffred that thei that were at the wyndowes of the palise that saugh
the merveile wepte for pité. And Gonnore, the doughter of Kynge Leodogan, whan
she saugh her fader ledde amonge his enmyes, she made so gret sorowe that nygh

195   she slowe hirself for doell. But now lete us cesse to speke of hem till tyme cometh
agein and speke of the Kynge Arthur and his felowes, how that thei have spedde
in the bataile agein the seven thousande with the stiwarde Cleodalis of Tamelide.

    Now seith the storie that stronge and crewell was the stour theras the bateile
was, whereas the forty-two felowes and the four thousand that were with Cleodalis

200   the stiwarde that foughten agein the seven thousand sarazins. And many ther were
slayn that lay grennynge on the grounde. And whan thei hadde longe tyme fought
togeder, Merlin rode a grete walop oute of the bataile and cried to his felowes that
thei sholde sue hym; and thei so dide in grete haste and rode as faste as the horse
myght hem bere, till that thei were passed all theire peple. And than thei encresed

205   her pas gretter and rode towarde the siege the right wey theras the geauntes and
the sarazins were, till that thei come in a valey that was right depe; and ther thei
overtoke the five hundred sarasins that ledde the Kynge Leodogan. And as soone
as Merlin hym saugh he cried, "Now, lordinges, upon hem! For ye be bytrayed
and deed yef eny of hem ascape!"

210   Than thei drive in amonge hem as tempest of thunder and kilde and slough all
that thei raught a right stroke in her comynge; and ther ne was noon of the forty-
one but he slowe or maymed whom that he mette. Ther sholde ye have seyn soche
martirdom and soche slaughter of men and of horse that noon ne myght ascape, so
were thei supprised and astonyed, saf oonly fyve that ascaped, fleinge thei rought

194 **nygh**, nearly. **195 slowe**, slew; **doell**, grief. **198 stour**, fighting; **theras**, where. **201
grennynge**, grinning. **202 walop**, gallop. **203 sue**, follow. **205 pas**, pace; **theras**, where.
210 drive, drove; **slough**, slew. **211 raught**, struck. **213 martirdom**, death. **214 rought**,
cared.

215   never what wey.

Thus have thei rescowed the Kynge Leodogan. And whan the kynge saugh the grete martire and the occision that so fewe peple hadde don agein so many, he merveyled gretly what thei myght be. Than he beheilde and knewe it was the dragon that Merlyn bar. Than knewe he wele that it were the sowdiours that he

220   hadde withholden, and than he thanked God of the socoure that He hadde hym sente. Than com Merlin to hym, and than he rested. Whan [he] saugh the Kynge Leodogan bounden, he alight, and so dide Bretell. And [thei] hym unbounden, and right his armoure, and sethen made hym to lepe on a steede that was stronge and swyfht. And the kynge hem thonkeden hertely of the servise thei hadde hym don.

225   Than cried Merlin, "Gentill kynghtes, what tarye ye heere so longe? Suweth me!" Than he rode a grete raundon towarde the town where the Knyghtes of the Rounde Table were at gret myschief, that of two hundred and fifty ne were but twenty on horsebak, but deffended hem on fote as wilde bores. And Merlin bar the baner before and rode as faste as he myght, and his felowes also that theire

230   horses swetten. And the dragon that Merlin bar caste oute gret flames of fiere that it sparkeled up in the ayre, that thei upon the walles of the town saugh the clernesse of the light half a myle longe.

Whan thei of the citee saugh the kynge that was her lorde and saugh it were the forty-two felowes and with hem the Kynge Leodogan that thei hadde rescued, thei

235   hadde grete joye. And whan Gonnore this saugh, she spronge for joye and merveiled what the kynghtes were that com in that company. And thei com as faste as thunder so harde amonge her enmyes, and in her comynge ech threwe oone to grounde. And as soone as the forty-two felowes were smyten in amonge hem, ther began a grete bataile and soche slaughter of men and horse that the maiden that was lenynge

240   oute at the wyndowes of the paleise herde the grete strokes.

Ther yaf the Kynge Ban of Benoyk many strokes with Corchense, his gode swerde; for whom he arafte a full stroke, ther waranted hym neither shelde ne

217 martire, slaughter; **occision**, killing. **218 beheilde**, looked. **219 sowdiours**, soldiers. **220 withholden**, retained; **socoure**, aid. **221 rested**, stopped. **223 right**, readied; **sethen**, then. **225 what**, why; **Suweth**, Follow. **226 raundon**, pace. **227 at gret myschief**, in great danger. **231 that**, so that; **clernesse**, brightnesse. **232 longe**, away. **235 spronge**, jumped. **235–36 merveiled what**, wondered who. **241 yaf**, gave. **242 whom**, whomever; **arafte**, struck; **waranted**, protected.

haubreke ne noon armure that he kutte all thourghoute at oon stroke. And many
sithes he smote bothe horse and man to grounde at a stroke, and so dide hys
245   brother, the Kynge Boors of Gannes. And the sarazins hem beheilde for grete
merveile that thei saugh hem do. And the Kynge Arthur dide soche merveiles with
Calibourne, his gode swerde, for ther agein myght noon armure endure were it
never so stronge, for what he araught was at his endynge forever.

    Grete was the bataile before the towne of Toraise theras the two hundred fifty
250   Knyghtes of the Rounde Table and the forty-two felowes [foughten] agein the
sarazins; but thei have so foughten that of the seven thousand beth lefte but five
thousand; wherfore thei beth sory and wroth for this Kynge Canlent that thei have
loste. And than fill it so that the Kynge Ban mette with Kynge Clarion that was
the moste man of the hoste of alle the geauntes. And the storye seith that the
255   Kynge Ban was a moche knyght of body and a stronge, and coragous and hardy.
The kynge heilde Corchense, his gode suerde, and smote the Kynge Clarion so
sore upon the helme that he slit it dowon to the eere; the stroke fill upon the lifte
shulder that he slitte hym to the girdell. And the Kynge Boors so smote Sarmedon
the ganfanouer that he kutte of the arme with all the sheilde, and the baner fill to
260   the erthe. This stroke saugh the Kynge Leodogan and seide, "Now be there no
knyghtes but these that so well conne helpe at nede."

    And whan the geauntes saugh theire lord deed and her baner fallen, thei turned
to flight, oon here, another there. And than com oute of the town knyghtes and
sergeauntes two thousande and begonne the chase upon hem that turned to flight.
265   But Merlin turned not that wey as thei fledde, but wente to the bataile theras
Cleodalis faught fercely with four thousand men agein eight thousand. Whan Merlin
com to the bataile, he fonde Cleodalis was on fote fightinge and heilde yet the
baner upright, and his men aboute hym renged, that well hym deffended as worthy men. But thei were at grete myscheif and in poynte to have hadde grete losse
270   in short tyme, whan Merlin com drivinge amonge hem with his dragon and his
forty-one felowes, of whiche ye have herde that in her comynge ferde as tempeste;

244 sithes, times. **248 what**, who; **araught**, struck. **249 theras**, where. **254 moste**,
largest. **255 moche**, large. **257 eere**, ear; **lifte**, left. **258 girdell**, belt. **259 ganfanouer**,
standard-bearer; **of**, off; **with all**, along with. **261 conne**, can. **265 theras**, where. **268
renged**, arranged. **269 in poynte**, about. **271 ferde**, moved.

and therto thei were alle so well horsed that no men myght be better, and the Kynge Leodogan was ever with hem that in no wise wolde hem leten. And whan these forty-two felowes were in amonge the geauntes, ther was soche marteleise and soche noise as so many carpenteres in a wode.

Ther was stronge stour and fell and dolerouse, for ther sholde ye have sein knyghtes and sergeauntes falle as thikke as it hadde be reyn. Ther sholde ye se stedes and horse renne maisterles, their reynes trailynge undir fote, wherof the sadeles were all blody of knyghtes that therynne hadde be slayn. Ther sholde ye have herde soche bruyt and soche noyse and cry that it was merveile and grete doel to here. Ther dide the forty-two felowes so well that it was spoken of longe tyme after her deth in that contrey. And the storye seith thei mangled and slow so many that by the traces oon myght have sued half a day every wey of the deed bodies and horse that thei hadde wounded, as thei that nought ne cessed ne rested. And therfore me semeth reson to reherse the names of tho worthi men.

The first was Kynge Ban of Benoyk, and the seconde was Kynge Boors of Gannes, and the thirde was Kynge Arthur, and the forthe was Antor, the fifth was Ulfin, the sixth was Bretell, the seventh was Kay, the eighth Lucas the Botiller, the ninth was Gifflet, the tenth Maret de la Roche, the eleventh Drias de la Forest Savage, the twelfth Belias de Amerous of Maydons Castell, the thirteenth Flaundryns le Bret, the fourteenth Ladynas de Benoyk, the fifteenth Amoret le Brun, the sixteenth Anticolas le Rous, the seventeenth Blois del Casset, the eighteenth Blioberis, the nineteenth Canade, the twentieth Meliadus le Bloys, the twenty-first Aladan the Crespes, the twenty-second Placidas ly Gays, the twenty-third Leonpadys of the Playn, the twenty-fourth Jerohas Lenches, the twenty-fifth Christofer de la Roche Byse, the twenty-sixth Ayglin de Vaus, the twenty-seventh Calogrevaunt, the twenty-eight Aguysale de Desirouse, the twenty-ninth Agresiaux the nevew of the Wise Lady of the Foreste Withoute Returne, the thirtieth Chalis the Orpheyn, the thirty-first Grires de Lambal, the thirty-second Kehedin de Belly, the thirty-third Meranges de Porlenges, the thirty-fourth Gosnayus Cadrus, the thirty-fifth Clarias of Gaule, the thirty-sixth the Lays Hardy, the thirty-seventh Amadius the Proude, the thirty-eighth Osenayn Cors Hardy, the thirty-ninth

273 leten, leave. **274 marteleise**, hammering. **276 stour**, fighting; **fell**, cruel. **278 renne maisterles**, run riderless. **280 bruyt**, sounds. **281 doel**, grief; **here**, hear. **283 traces**, remains; **sued**, followed. **284 nought ne**, neither; **ne**, nor. **285 tho**, those.

Galescowde, the fortieth Gales, the forty-first Bleoris the sone of Kynge Boors, the forty-second was Merlin; and the forty-third was the Kynge Leodogan, that in
305   no wise wolde hem leve.

These forty-three worthi knyghtes wente to the rescew of Cleodalis, the Stiwarde of Tamelide, that was a noble knyght and right trewe and full of grete hardynesse; and well it shewde that for noon unkyndenesse that the Kynge Leodogan hadde don agein hym, he wolde hym not forsake ne leve hym in his myscheif in no nede
310   that he was in; but therynne he dide moche more than many other wolde have don, and I shall sey yow the cause why.

This was the troweth, that the Kynge Leodogan hadde a wif, a lady of grete bewté and of high lynage; and whan he hadde brought here into Tamelide out of her fader londe after that he hadde her wedded, this lady brought with hire a
315   mayden that was of grete bewté. This maiden loved the stiward so moche that on a day he asked hir of the Kynge Leodogan for to have her to his wif, that many a day hadde hym served; and the Kynge hym graunted for his gode servise. And whan thei were maried and she satte at the table amonge other ladyes and she was richely arayed, the kynge liked moche hir bewté; and soche a fantasie fill in his
320   herte that he cowde not it remeve, and he hym covered in the beste maner that he cowde; and she was withoute faile oon of the feirest of the worlde. Till it fill on a Feste of Seint John that the kynge sente Cleodalis upon a journey agein the Saisnes that upon hym werred that tyme, and the lady that was lefte with the quene for companye that moche her lovid with grete love.

325   Hit fill on a nyght that the Kynge Leodogan lay by the quene, and that nyght upon hir he begat a doughter that was cleped Gonnore whan she was baptised, the whiche after was of merveilouse bewté and the wif of Kynge Arthur. And this lady that was wif to Kynge Leodogan was a goode lady and holy of livinge and hadde an usage to arise on nyghtes and go to chirche to sey Matyns and to heere
330   all servyse to messe. That nyght that the quene hadde conceyved Gonnore her doughter, she yede to Matyns and com by the stiwardes wif and fonde her slepynge

305 leve, leave. **308 for noon unkyndenesse**, i.e., for despite whatever unkindness. **309 ne leve**, nor leave; **myscheif**, troubles. **312 troweth**, truth. **320 cowde**, could. **321 faile**, doubt; **Till it fill**, It happened. **322 agein**, against. **325 Hit fill**, It befell. **326 cleped**, called. **327 bewté**, beauty. **329 an usage**, a habit. **330 servyse to messe**, the services until mass. **331 yede**, went.

and wolde not her awake; but wente and lefte her lyinge aslepe, and wente forth alone to the cherche that was faste by, with hir sawter in her hande. And the kynge, that longe hadde desired to speke with that lady, arose as soone as the

335 quene was gon, and dide oute the taperes that were brennynge and than wente to ly by the stiwardes wif. And whan the lady felte oon lyinge by her, she asked what he was, all affraied; and than he ansuerde how it was he, and bad hir be stille, and seide yef she made eny noyse she sholde be deed. The lady her deffended inowgh as with speche, but she durste not crye ne make no noyse; but litill availed her

340 defense for the kynge by hir lay; and on hir he gat a doughter, the same nyght that he hadde geten Gonnore on his wif.

And whan the quene was delyvered, ther was founde upon the childes reynes a litill crosse like a crowne for a kynge; and as soone as the quene was delyvered, the stiwardes wif began to traveyle, and hadde a doughter of feire bewté, and

345 [she] was so like the quene's doughter that oon cowde not knowe oon from another but by the crosse upon her reynes. And eche of hem hight Gonnere in bapteme; and [thei] were norrisshed and brought up togeder till that the quene was deed. And the kynge yet was not keled of the love of the stiwarde's wif, and he her toke and shet her in a castell, for he wolde not the stiwarde sholde speke with hir.

350 In soche maner he heilde her more that five yere, till that the stiwarde's frendes spake unto hym; and he seide he wolde not faile the kynge while he hadde werre, and yet the same tyme that Kynge Arthur com for to serve, he hir heilde in the selve maner; and yet for all this the stiwarde never feyned to serve. But now lete us retourne to speke of the stiwarde ther he is fightynge on fote amonge the

355 gyauntes, for all betyme we shull speke of the twey Gonnores whan the mater fallith therto.

[Summary. A lengthy battle against King Rion's forces ensues. Both Arthur's group of Forty-two Knights and the Knights of the Round Table do many valiant deeds,

333 sawter, psalter. **335 dide**, put; **brennynge**, burning. **336 what**, who. **338 deffended**, resisted. **341 geten**, begotten. **342 reynes**, loins. **344 traveyle**, be in labor. **345 oon cowde**, one could. **346 reynes**, loins; **hight**, was named; **bapteme**, baptism. **348 keled**, cooled. **349 shet**, shut. **350 heilde**, held. **351 he**[1], i.e., the steward. **353 never feyned**, i.e., was always glad. **354 ther**, where. **355 all betyme**, in time; **twey**, two. **355–56 mater fallith**, story turns.

including rescuing Cleodalis the steward from the enemy's grasp. Merlin remains in the thick of the battle with his dragon banner; and while the ladies of Tamelide look on, Arthur wields his sword Calibourne with great success. King Rion's troops are finally put to flight, but Rion vows he will not leave the land until King Leodegan has been captured. Fols. 73v (line 34)–77v (line 10).]

Now seith the booke that gladde and joyfull were thei of the town of Toraise for the discounfiture of the Saisnes that were chased of so small a peple, for thei were at the bygynnynge but six thousand and three hundred, and the Saisnes were more than fifteen thousand; and [thei] were discounfited be the counseile of Merlin that moche hem helped, and by the Knyghtes of the Rounde Table, and also of the forty-two sowdioures. And as the booke seith, whan thei hadde chased the Saisnes unto nyght, that than thei returned to Toraise gladde and mery, and fonde the kynge in the town that his men hadde remounted and sette on horse. And whan he knewe that the sowdiours com, he wente hem ageins and made of hem the grettest joye that eny man myght, and fonde Antor and Gifflet and Kay and Lucas the Botiller and alle the other felowes hool and sounde, of whom thei hadden had grete drede that thei hadden be deed or elles taken. And ther was founde grete wynnynge, and the kynge made it to be take and presented to the sowdiours that he hadde withholden. And he seide he myght it no better employe for thei hadde it all wonne. "And myself," seide the Kynge Leodogan, "have thei rescued fro deth and fro prison."

And whan thei saugh the grete worschip that the kynge hem dide, thei thanked hym hertely and seide that thei wolde it not, for in tyme comynge thei [wolde] resceve his yeftes and take of hym other fee. And the kynge seide seth thei wolde it not resceyve that thei sholde it departe and yeve theras thei wolden. Than com Merlin to the thre kynges and bad hem take it. And thei it token and yaf it theras Merlin hem assigned, that thei ne lefte not to hemself the valewe of a peny. And thei that it hadden, thanked and preised moche the sowdiours, alle tho that hem

360

365

370

375

358 **discounfiture**, defeat; **small**, few. 360 **discounfited**, undone. 361 **of²**, by. 362 **sowdioures**, soldiers. 363 **fonde**, found. 365 **hem ageins**, to meet them. 367 **hool**, whole. 368 **wynnynge**, booty. 370 **withholden**, retained. 373 **worschip**, honor. 374 **wolde**, wished. 375 **yeftes**, gifts; **seth**, since. 376 **departe**, distribute; **yeve**, give. 379 **hadden**, received; **tho**, those.

380   knewen, and also thei [that] knewen hem nothynge. And that so moche were thei beloved in the contrey for her largesse be the counseile of Merlin that nought was spoken of in the contrey but of the sowdiours. And the Kynge Arthur yaf so moche to his ooste and to his wif of horse and palfreyes and robes that alle ther lyves after were thei riche.

385   Whan the Kynge Arthur hadde departed the richesse that was wonne of the Saisnes, thei entred into the town; and the Kynge Leodogan wolde not suffre hem in no wise to alight but at his paleise with hym, ne never after wolde he lete hem be oute of his companye, and with the Knyghtes of the Rounde Table. And whan thei were unarmed, the Kynge made his doughter to aray hem in riche robes and

390   made her take warme water in basyns of silver and bare to the thre kynges and hem serve. But Arthur wolde not take her servyse till that the Kynge Leodogan and Merlin comaunded hym and made hym to take it. And the maiden hersilf wosh his visage and his nekke and dried it full softely with a towaile, and than after to the tother twey kynges.

395   And the tother Gonnore that was of the stiwarde's wif and the other maydenes served the othere knyghtes; and whan the kynge's doughter hadde served the thre kynges, than she served hir fader. And whan thei were waisch, the maiden put on ech of hem a mantell aboute her nekkes. And the Kynge Arthur was right feire, and the maiden hym beheilde moche, and he her. And she seide softely to herself

400   that well were that maiden that so feire a knyght wolde requere hir of love, and namely so gode a knyght as is this. And well ought she to be shamed ever after that hym denyed.

    Anoon were the tables set, and whan the mete was redy thei satte alle the knyghtes therynne; but the Knyghtes of the Rounde Table seten with the sowdiours

405   at table be hemself. And the Kynge Ban and the Kynge Boors sette the Kynge Arthur betwene hem two and dide hym grete honour as affiered to so high a man. And therof toke the Kynge Leodogan goode hede, that by hem satte side by syde at the heede of the table, and thought well in his corage that by the honour and the reverence that thei to hym bar that he was lorde over alle, and merveiled sore

---

380 nothynge, not at all. **381 largesse be**, generosity by; **nought**, nothing. **383 ooste**, host (i.e., Blaires). **385 departed**, distributed. **387 alight**, stay. **390 bare**, carry. **404 the sowdiours**, i.e., Arthur's forty knights. **406 affiered**, belonged. **409 hym**, i.e., Arthur.

410   what he myght be, and grete desire he hadde for to knowe the trowthe what he
was, and thought in his herte that, "And it were plesynge to God that he hadde my
doughter spoused, for trewly I can not thynke that so high prowesse myght be
shewed in soche a childe but yef he were come of right high lynage; other elles I
trowe that it be som spirituell man that God hath me sente for to deffende this
415   reame, nought for me but for Cristynté and Holy Cherche to mayntene." And therto he seide ne yede he not oute of this towne withoute leve of the porter.

At this soper the Kynge Leodogan satte stille in a grete stodye, and lasted longe;
and it fill in his mynde how that he hym rescued in the depe valay with the forty-
one felowes agein five hundred knyghtes that ledde hym to prison, and remembrede
420   alle the prowesses that he hadde sein hym do; and so sadly he sat in that thought
that alle thei were troubled and lefte theire mete. Of this was war Hervy de Ryvel
and was therfore sory in his herte, and aroos and yede to hym full wroth to the
heede of the table and seide, "Sir, I saugh never yow so mystake youreself, ne
never I saugh yow so abaisshed, for ye ought well to make joye to these worthi
425   men; and ye thenke as that ye were in a dreme, and I merveile moche of youre
grete wisdome where it is become."

Than the kynge yaf a grete sigh and loked on Hervy and seide, "Hervy, frende,
I thought upon the moste worthi man of the worlde, fro the whiche I myght not me
withdrawe; and yef thow knewe what my thought were, thow woldest not me
430   blame." And he seide, "Sir, it may well be so; but now at this tyme cesseth till
eftesones, for this is no place now therto, but maketh joye to these barouns and
disporte yow, for ye have at this tyme to moche yow mystaken save youre honoure."
"Gramercy, feire frende," seide the Kynge, "I knowe well that I have mysdon."
Then Hervy yede and sat down by his felowes. And the kynge tho spake to the
435   barouns merily.

And the maiden that was the doughter of Kynge Leodogan served Arthur upon
her kne of wyne with hir fader cuppe. And Arthur hir beheilde full debonerly, and
[it] plesed hym wele that he saugh hir so nygh, for she was the feirest lady that

410 **what**[1], who. 411 **And**, If. 412 **spoused**, wedded. 413 **but yef**, unless; **other elles**, or
else. 415 **nought**, not. 418 **fill in his mynde**, came to mind. 420 **prowesses**, deeds. 421
war, aware. 422 **yede**, went; **wroth**, angry. 423 **heede**, head. 424 **saugh**, saw; **abaisshed**,
reserved. 425 **thenke**, appear; **that**, though. 430–31 **cesseth till eftesones**, cease until
later on. 434 **yede**, went; **tho**, then. 437 **debonerly**, courteously. 438 **nygh**, near.

was in all Breteigne in that tyme. And the mayden was fayre and hadde on hir

440　heede a riche chapelet of precious stones, and her visage fressh and wele colowred, so entermedled white and redde so naturally that it neded nother more ne lesse; and her shulderes streyghte and even and merveylously well shapen of body, for she was sklender aboute the flankes and the haunche lowe and comly well sittynge, and of alle fetures the feirest shapen that myght be founde in eny londe; and yef

445　she hadde grete bewté therto, she hadde as moche bounté of valour, of curtesie, and nurture.

Whan Arthur saugh this mayden that hadde so grete bewté, he beheilde her with a gladde chere, and saugh her pappes smale and rounde as two smale appelis that were harde; and her flessh whitter than snowe and was not to fatte ne to

450　sklendir; and he coveyted her gretly in his herte that he waxe all pensif, and lefte his mete and turned his chere another wey, for he wolde not the two kynges ne noon other hym aperceyved. Than the mayden profered hym the cuppe and seide, "Sir, drynke, and displese yow not though I clepe yow not be youre name; and be ye not abaisshed at youre sopere, for at armes ye do not faile at no nede, and well

455　it shewed this day where ye were beholden of five thousand that nothynge yow dide knowe but by sight."

And he turned and seide, "Feire lady, with goode will, and gramercy of youre servyse. And God graunte me power that I may yow this guerdon yelde." "Sir," seide she, "ye have quyte it double more than I may deserve, for ye have rescued

460　my lorde my fader, ye and youre companye, that was amonge so many of his enmyes that ledde hym to prison." And he satte stille withoute ansuere. "And," quod the lady, "was ther moche more, for here before the yates at the brigge-foote ye shewed well sembelant that it yow greved, and that ye were sory for his anoye theras he was unhorsed amonge his enmyes and his horse under hym slayn. For

465　ye slow hym that hym dide overthrowe, and ye youreself were in aventure of deth hym to rescuen, and so wele ye dide that thei were fayn to leve the feelde."

440 visage, face. **441 entermedled,** mingled; **nother,** neither. **444 fetures,** features; **yef,** if. **445 bounté,** goodness. **448 pappes,** breasts; **appelis,** apples. **450 pensif,** melancholy. **451 chere,** face; **wolde not,** did not want. **451–52 ne noon,** nor any. **452 aperceyved,** observed. **453 clepe,** call. **454 abaisshed at,** frightened by. **455 were beholden,** sustained. **458 guerdon yelde,** debt repay. **459 quyte,** repaid. **463 sembelant,** the appearance; **greved,** saddened. **465 aventure,** danger. **466 fayn,** glad.

Thus spake the doughter of Kynge Leodogan to Arthur, but he spake no worde agein but toke the cuppe and dranke with goode will and after comaunded the mayden to arise, for to longe hadde she kneled; but the kynge her fader ne wolde

470 not. Thus were thei served right highly of alle thynges that man myght devise. And whan the clothes sholde be taken up, the Kynge Ban seide to Kynge Leodogan that satte nexte by hys side, "Sir," seide the Kynge Ban, "I have grete merveile of yow that be so wise and worthy a man that have not maried youre doughter to som high prynce that myght yow helpe in youre werres, for she is now wele woxen

475 and therto right wise; and as me semeth, ye have no mo heyres to whom youre londe shall descende after youre deth; and therfore ye sholde here before have her sette to some noble prynce."

"Certes, sir," seide Leodogan, "I have be letted by the werre that me sore hath greved and longe dured, for it is seven yere passed that the Kynge Rion of

480 Denmarke and of Irelonde ne cessed never upon me to werre; ne never seth com ther no man in this londe to whom I ought hir to yeve. But so helpe me God, yef I myght fynde a yonge bacheler that were a worthi man of armes that myght wele endure peyne and travayle to meyntene my werre, to hym wolde I yeve my doughter yef he wolde her take, and alle my londe after my desesse, that never shall I spare

485 for high lynage ne grete richesse of lordeschip. And that it plesed oure Lorde Jhesu that it myght ben he that I thynke now in my mynde, and trewly than sholde she be maried withynne these thre dayes unto a feire yonge bacheler that is full of high prowesse; and trewly, I suppose in my corage that he be of hiher astate than am I." And Merlin beheilde the Kynge Boors and began to smyle and made hym a

490 signe that it was seide for the Kynge Arthur; and withoute faile, for hym was it seide.

Than begonne thei to speke of many thynges and turned her tales other weyes, for more wolde thei not speke therof at that tyme. That perceyvede well the Kynge Leodogan that thei heilde no cure to maytene that tale, and therwith he yaf

495 a sore sigh, for fayn he wolde that oon hadde hym more therof aresoned. And so

469–70 ne wolde not, did not wish [her to]. **471 clothes,** table cloth. **474 werres,** wars; **wele woxen,** well grown. **475 heyres,** heirs. **476 here before,** before now. **478 letted,** prevented; **werre,** war. **480 seth,** since. **481 yeve,** give; **yef,** if. **484 desesse,** death. **488 corage,** heart. **494 cure,** desire. **495 fayn he wolde,** gladly he wished; **aresoned,** discussed.

he heilde his pees and herkened yef he myght eny thynge aperceyve in eny manere what thei were and of what londe, and saugh the joye and the honoure that the worthi men made to Arthur; and that was a thynge that brought hym more mysese, and so moche the worthy men of the Rounde Table more than the forty felowes that were of her companye, that alle that it saugh hadde therof merveile and weren abasshed. But above alle, hym coveyted the kynge's doughter; and right hertely she hym loved and mused hereon so moche that she was sore troubeled, and fayn wolde she have hym to be her lorde and make above alle tho that ever she hadde seyn before.

And the storyes seyn that she was the wisest lady of all the Bloy Breteyne, and the feirest and the beste beloved that ever was in the londe or in the contrey, saf only Helayn that was withouten pere, that was the doughter of Kynge Pelles of Lytenoys of the Castell of Corbenyk, that was nece to the Kynge Pesceor and of the seke kynges wounded, wherof the name of the ton was cleped Alain de Lille in Lytenoys. This Kynge Alain was seke of the woundes of the spere vengeresse, wherof he was cleped Mehaignyes, for he was wounded thourgh bothe thyghes with that spere; and his right name was Kynge Alain, and the Kynge Pellynor was his brother germayn; and this maiden of whom I speke was theire nece and doughter to Kynge Pelles, brother to these two kynges that I have yow named.

*[**Summary**. After dinner, Merlin tells Arthur, Ban, and Bors what has been happening in Logres during their absence, particularly extolling the deeds of the Young Squires in defending Arthur's land against the Saxons. During this same time that Arthur has been helping Leodegan and the Young Squires have been protecting Logres, the rebel kings have been fighting the Saxons in their own homelands. Another group of Young Squires — including Sagremor, the nephew of the emperor of Constantinople; Ewain of the White Hands and his half-brother Ewain Avoutres, sons of King Uriens; Dodinell the Savage, son of King Belynans of South Wales; and Kay Destranx and Kehedin — having heard of the deeds of Gawain and his brothers, set off toward Logres to meet the other Squires and to be knighted by Arthur. Fols. 79v (line 16)– 90r (line 11).]*

496 pees, peace; **herkened yef**, watched if; **aperceyve**, learn. **497 what[1]**, who. **498 hym**, i.e., Arthur; **mysese**, discomfort. **501 abasshed**, surprised; **hym coveyted**, he desired; **hertely**, truly. **502 fayn**, gladly. **503 make**, husband; **tho**, those. **509 seke**, sick; **ton**, one; **cleped**, called. **510 vengeresse**, vengeful. **511 cleped**, called. **513 nece**, niece.

[Merlin and the Young Squires]

Full grete was the joye that thei ledde in the town of Toraise for the victorie and the wynnynge that thei hadde upon theire enmyes; and thei abode theire peple that assembled every day on every part. And the Kynge Arthur ther was full richely served and honoured of the Kynge Leodogan and of his doughter, that moche her peyned be the comaundement of hir fader.

And upon a day as the Kynge Arthur was moche worshiped and in grete ese, than Merlin com and toke the thre kynges apart and seide, "Sirs, I moste go into the reame of Logres, for ther is now grete nede of counseyle and of helpe, nought for that the londe hath eny pereile, but that it shall well be deffended from evell doers. And I do yow to wite that the princes and the barouns beth moche greved with the Saisnes that to many have in her londes; and thei have beseged two citees though her pride, wherof that oon is Vandesberes and the tother is Clarence. And ther be assembled the peple of moo than forty dyverse regiouns, and yet thei encrece every day more and more."

And than he hem tolde how that the Saisnes were departed, and how that oo parte yede upon the Kynge of Cornewaile, and the tother upon the Kynge Loot, and the thirde upon the Kynge Clarion and the Duke Escam. And after that he tolde hem alle the tidinges and alle the batailes and all the trouble that hadde i-be, and all the discounfitures betwene the Saisnes and Cristin kynges, and the grete parliament that the Saisnes heilden for to asege the two townes; and how Ewein the Grete and Ewein the Avoutres were departed fro Kynge Urien her fader; and how Dodinell the Savage and Kay Destranx and Kehedin Lebeus com on the tother

1 **ledde**, experienced. **2 abode**, waited upon. **4 of**, by. **5 be**, by. **6 ese**, ease. **7 moste**, must. **8–9 nought for that**, not because. **9 pereile**, peril. **10 do yow to wite**, want you to know; **beth**, are. **11 to many**, too many [invaders]. **12 her**, their. **13 moo**, more. **15 departed**, divided; **oo**, one. **16 yede upon**, went against. **18 hadde i-be**, had occurred. **19 discounfitures**, fierce encounters. **20 asege**, besiege.

side toward Logres to abide ther with Gawein, and seide how thei wolde never be cleped knyghtis unto the tyme that the Kynge Arthur hem girde with her swerdes.

25   "And I do yow to wete that thei may not endure but thei have other counseile than her owne, for the Saisnes be so spredde aboute thourgh the londe that thei shull be take but thei have better counseile than hemself. And that is the cause that I will go. And loke that ye be mery and well at ese and resteth yow, that ye go nothir hider ne thider till that ye se me. And I shall not longe tarye."

30   "Ha, feire frende," seide the Kynge Ban, "ne abide not longe, for than sholde we alle be deed and distroied; yef ye us now forsake, we myght sey that ye hadde us alle betraied." "How is that, feire lordes? Have ye doute that I sholde not come agein? Now bewar that never ye it thinke, for than have ye loste my love." "Sir," seide the Kynge Ban, "I thenke it for noon evell that I have to yow, but for to have

35 your companye that I so moche love." "Now lete it be," quod Merlin, "for ye shull me have here agein with yow er than ye have bataile in this reame. And therfore I yow comaunde to God, for I may here no lenger tarien." And with that he departed so sodeynly thens that thei knewe not where he was become.

    And than he com the same nyght to Blase his maister in Northumbirlonde, that

40 grete joye hym made whan he hym saugh, as he that loved moche his companye. And Merlin tolde hym alle these aventures that were befallen in the reme of Tamelide seth that he departed; and after that he tolde hym alle thinges that were fallen to the kynges of the reame of Grete Bretaigne, that nought he lefte untolde. And he wrote in hys booke worde for worde like as he hym tolde; and by hym

45 have we the knowinge therof into this tyme. And whan he hadde alle these thinges writen, thanne he tolde hym for what nede he hadde lefte the thre kynges in the reame of Tamelide. And the same nyght that Merlin spake thus with Blase was Orienx and his meyné logged upon the river of Humbir, enteringe into the londe. But now resteth the processe of Merlin and of Blase a while, and of the Saisnes,

50 and speketh of Seigramor that is departed fro Costantynnoble with thre hundred felowes for to be made knyghtes of Kynge Arthurs honde.

24 cleped, called. **25 do yow to wete,** want you to know; **but,** unless. **27 be take but,** be defeated unless. **29 nothir hider ne thider,** neither here nor there, i. e., nowhere. **31 yef,** if. **34 noon evell,** no ill will. **36 er than,** before. **37 comaunde,** commend. **38 thens,** thence. **39 than,** then. **42 seth,** since. **42–43 were fallen to,** had befallen. **48 meyné,** army; **logged,** encamped.

Now seith the booke of Blase that so hath Seigramor hym spedde seth that he departed fro the riche citee of Costantynnoble, that he com to the port of Hucent, that thei arived at the port of Dover. And whan thei were alle come to the londe,

55 thei were right gladde, and trussed theire harneys and lepe on theire horse and toke theire wey toward Kamelot, and journeyed so as thei that knewe not the weyes ne fonde not of whom to aske after the Kynge Arthur, and fonde also the contrey brent and wasted as the Saisnes hadde passeth thourgh. And the childeren ne wiste no worde till sodeinly thei blusshed upon a grete parté of Saisnes that

60 Orienx hadde dessevered on a companye; and [thei] were twenty thousand and wente robbinge aboute Norhant that noon hem ne letted of the pray that theire peple hadde gadered.

Whan these childeren aproched the Saisnes withynne a myle, thei mette with peple of the contrey that fledde to the wode for drede, for in the londe was grete

65 sorow and desese in tho dayes. Whan the childeren hem mette, thei asked what hem eiled; and thei hem tolde that thei fledde for the Saisnes that all the contré distroied. And than Seigramor asked, "Where is the Kynge Arthur?" And thei ansuered that he was gon into the reame of Tamelide. "And who is than in this londe?" quod Seigramor. Than seide the men of the contrey that the sones of

70 Kynge Loot of Orcanye, that were nevewes of Kynge Arthur, were come for to serve for to take theire armes of Kynge Arthur. "And where ben thei?" quod Seigramor. "At Camelot," seide thei. "But for Goddes love, feire gentill knyghtes, ne go not ferther, for than shull ye alle be slain and distroied."

"Now," quod Seigramor, "telle us what wey stondeth Camelot." "Trewly," seiden

75 thei, "ye be right well in the wey, yef it ne were for these false sarazins that here be comynge; and therfore fleeth, or ye be alle deed." "How fer is it hens to Camelot?" quod Seigramor. "Sir, it is six mile unto a plain that dureth wele two myle fro thens."

Whan Seigramor undirstode that he hadde but eight myle, he cried to his felowes

---

52 seth, since. **54 that**, [and then] that. **55 trussed theire harneys**, readied their gear. **56 so as thei**, just like those. **57 fonde not of whom**, found no one. **58 brent**, burned. **59 ne wiste no worde**, knew nothing; **blusshed**, came. **60 dessevered on**, separated into. **61 noon hem ne letted of the pray**, no one stopped them from taking the booty. **63 childeren**, young warriors. **65 tho**, those. **66 eiled**, ailed. **68 than**, then. **74 what wey stondeth**, which way is. **75 right well**, perfectly. **77 dureth wele**, i.e., stretches for.

80   and seide, "Gentill squyers, now as armes, for now shall be sein who is noble and
worthi; and loke that thise mysbelevinge Saisnes that thus distroieth the Cristin
feith ne bere nought awey of youres be force but it be dere solde; for yef we may
passe hem thourgh and gete betwene hem and Camelot, we shull than come thider
be strengthe of oure horse yef we have grete mystere."

85   Than alight the squyers and hem armed. Ther sholde ye have sein hem do on
fressh newe hauberkes, bright shynynge as fin silveir; and thei hadden hattes of
fin steill above their coiffes of iren upon their heedes. And than thei lefte theire
palfreyes and lepe upon stedes covered in maile that thei hadde ther, so goode and
so feire that no man neded to seche better in no londe. And than thei hem renged

90   clos on a sop as starlinges, and rode forth toward the Saisnes that saugh hem
comynge. But now a litill resteth of hem and speke of Merlyn that was in
Northumberlonde with Blase.

Whan Merlin hadde tolde to Blase alle the merveiles of the londe as thei were
fallen seth he departed from hym, in the morowe erly he com before the town of

95   Camelot. And he com in the semblaunce of an olde man and hadde on a russet
cote, torne and all thredebare; and he was moche and longe and courbed and brode
sholdered and leene for age, and the heer of his heede entermedled white and
broun, and longe berde, and bar a grete staff on his nekke, and drof gret foyson of
beestes before hym.

100   And whan he com before the town, he began to make grete sorow and cried
high and cleer that thei withynne upon the walles myght wele it here how he yede,
seyinge, "Ha! Lorde God! How grete pité is it that so feire children shull thus be
slayn and alle tohewen with wronge and grete synne! A-Ha! Kynge Arthur! Goode
sir, whiche frendes thow shalt lese this day that moche thee sholden helpe, yef

105   thei myght lyve, thi londe to mayntene! Ha! Seigramor! Gentill squyer, fre and
deboneir, that thow shalt thus suffre angwissh of deth! Now oure Lorde God yow

80 as armes, to arms. **82 bere nought,** take nothing; **be,** by; **dere solde,** dearly bought.
83 hem thourgh, through them. **84 be,** by; **mystere,** skill. **85 do on,** put on. **87 coiffes,**
hoods of mail. **89 seche,** seek. **89–90 renged clos,** gathered closely. **90 on a sop as
starlinges,** as starlings on a piece of bread. **93–94 were fallen seth,** had occurred
since. **96 cote,** coat; **moche,** tall; **courbed,** bent over. **97 entermedled,** mixed. **98–99 drof
gret foyson of beestes,** drove a great many beasts. **101 here,** hear; **yede,** went. **104
whiche,** what; **lese,** lose.

socoure and helpe that ye be not slain; and yef that ye be ded, He have the sowle of yow that it be never turmentid in the peynes of Helle, as He is a very God and man full of mercy and grace, and also to save and helpe yowre felowes in the manere that thus dispitousely shull be martired for defaute of socoure."

110

These wordes that the carl seide undirstode well Gawein and his bretheren that were upon the walles of the towne. And [thei] were alleredy armed and beheilde the fier and the smoke of the Saisnes as thei brente the contrey aboute, for he was come to Camelot for to kepe the town as soone as thei wiste the Saisnes were entred the contrey, and were gon upon the walles to see yef the Saisnes come for to assaile the town. And Gawein hadde wele herde and undirstonde the wordes that the karll hadde seide. Than Gawein hym cleped with an high voyse and seide, "Man! Man! Com hedir and speke with me and tell us what thow aylest and whi thow makest this sorow; and telle us who is that that thow goist thus regratynge and bemonynge."

115

120

And the carll leide to the deef ere and smote his staff on the grounde as he hadde ben oute of his mynde for grete sorow that he hadde at his herte. And than he lenyd hym upon his staff and began to make grete sorowe. And whan he hadde thus hym longe waymented, he drof agein his bestes as though he wolde have fledde to the forest. And than he seide agein with an high voyce, "A-Haa! Chivalrie of Logres, where art thow become? For withynne these eight dayes men seide ther was come into this contrey all the socoure of the worlde, and I herde sey that the nevewes of Kynge Arthur sholde defende this contrey. Certeys, evell it sheweth whan he suffreth to be slain the merveile of the worlde."

125

Whan that Gawein undirstode these wordes, he was right angwisshouse for to knowe whi the carll hadde this seide and whi he so waymented, and cleped hym agein with a lowde voyce thre or foure tymes and seide, "Howe, karll, howe! Speke to me and telle me what thow eilest."

130

107 **sowle**, soul. 108 **very**, true. 109 **man**, one. 110 **dispitousely**, pitifully; **martired**, put to death; **defaute**, lack. 111 **carl**, rustic fellow. 113 **he**, i.e., Gawain. 114 **kepe**, protect; **wiste**, knew. 117 **karll**, rustic; **cleped**, called; **high**, loud. 118 **hedir**, here; **thow aylest**, troubles you. 119 **regratynge**, lamenting. 121 **leide**, put his hand; **as**, as if. 124 **waymented**, lamented; **bestes**, animals. 128 **Certeys**, Surely. 130 **angwisshouse**, anxious. 131 **waymented**, lamented. 132 **Howe**, Stop.

And ever he turned the heed in travers and made semblant as he hadde hym not
135   herde. And Gawein hym cleped eftesoones, and than he lefte up his heed that was
lothly and rivelid and loked on high to hym with oon eye open and another clos,
and grennynge with his teth as a man that loked agein the sonne, and ansuered,
"What wilt thow?"

Quod Gawein, "Come a litill nerre and speke with me." And he drough ner till
140   he com undir the walles of the town upon the diche and seide, "Now maist thow
sey what thow wilt, but sey hastely, for my bestes gon." "I will," quod Gawein,
"that thow telle whi that thow wepest, and what he is that thow hast thus regreted,
and whi thow hast so blamed the chyvalrie of this contrey." "Yef thow wilt graunte
me that thow shalt do thi power to delyver hym, I will telle thee." "I thee graunte,"
145   quod Gawein, "as I am trewe squyer that I shall therto do all my myght that I have
in the worlde."

And whan the karll herde that Gawein was so desirouse for to wite whi he was
come thider, he seide to Gawein, "Feire sir, what be ye?" "My name," quod he,
"is Gawein, the nevew of Kynge Arthur." "Treuly, I have grete pitee of a companye
150   of yonge gentilmen that beth high mennes sones that beth fightinge at the ende of
this launde ayen the Saisnes, that never so fewe men contened so longe agein so
moche peple, for thei [be] but thre hundred that fighten agein thre thousande."
"And what be thei," quod Gawein, "and what go thei for to seche?"

Quod the karll, "Thei sey that the lorde of hem is cleped Seigramor, the nevew
155   of the emperour of Costantinnoble, that is come into this contrey for to take his
armes of the Kynge Arthur. Now have I seide all that I knowe; but I knowe it well
that ye will not hym socoure, and so I have loste my laboure, for I knowe well
that ye have not the herte ne the hardynesse for to go thider. Netherdeles, yef ye
go thider and ye may hym socoure, ye may yow avaunte that ye have wonne a
160   feire emprise and a riche."

Whan Gawein undirstode the wordes of the karll that so hym cleped cowarde,

---

134 in travers, the other way; **as**, as if. **135 eftesoones**, again; **lefte**, raised. **136 lothly**,
ugly; **rivelid**, shriveled. **138 wilt thow**, do you want. **139 nerre**, nearer. **140 diche**, dry
moat. **141 will**, wish. **142 whi that**, why; **what**, who; **regreted**, lamented. **143 graunte**,
promise. **144 delyver**, rescue. **147 wite**, know. **148 what**, who. **151 ayen**, against;
contened, fought. **153 what be thei**, who are they. **158 ne**, nor; **Netherdeles**, Nevertheless. **159 avaunte**, boast. **160 emprise**, enterprise.

he was ashamed and cried, "Now to horse, gentill knyghtes and gentill felowes, and sue me, for I go!" And as sone as he hadde seide that worde, he lepe to horse and alle his felowes after, and rode oute of the town in all haste; and whan thei

165   were alle oute, thei were four thousand what oon what other. And Gawein com all before and come to the karll and seide, "Lepe upon this horse and lede us ther these childeren fighten." And the karll dide his comaundement that for noon other thinge was come theder, and rode formest theras thei were fightynge.

     And whan thei neyhed nygh, thei founde the childeren fightinge merveilously

170   and hadde slain of the Saisnes moo than seven hundred; but ther were so many of hem that thei myght not longe endure. And ther dide Seigramoor the grettest prowesse that eny man saugh ever, for he heilde an axe with bothe hondes and was before his felowes upon a stede that was swyfte and right stronge; for whan thei gan hym assaile, he smote in amonge hem so harde and so depe that he was

175   loste as it hadde be in a see from the sight of his felowes. And the Saisnes hym enclosed on alle sides, and Seigramor, that heilde the ax that was sharp igrounde, thought to perce thourgh to his felowes. He smote so grete strokes on bothe sides that he slowgh all that he raught a full stroke, and thei fledde on every side from hym that knewen his strokes; and noon was so hardy that durst hym abyde but

180   launched to hym sharpe grounde speres and gleyves and other wepnes.

     But thus myght thei not longe endure that thei ne sholde have be deed or elles taken but as Gawein com with his companye, for Orienx peyned hym moche hem for to take, that was a noble knyght and a sure. And he sette upon the childeren and kepte hem in so short and streite that noon myght passe, and foughten so felly

185   that the childeren were waxen feble for lakke of breth; and yef it ne hadde be for Seigramor only, ther hadde noon of hem ascaped. But his defence was so grete all aboute hym that merveile it was how he myght it endure; but in the ende availed litill the well-doynge of hym or eny other, ne hadde Gawein come soone with his

163 **sue**, follow. 165 **what oon what other**, all told. 166 **ther**, where. 167 **childeren**, youths. 168 **thinge**, i.e., purpose; **formest**, in front; **theras**, to where. 169 **neyhed nygh**, came near. 171 **hem**, them (Saxons). 172 **prowesse**, deeds. 175 **as**, as if; **be**, been; **see**, sea. 177 **perce thourgh**, break through; **so**, such. 178 **raught**, struck. 179 **durst**, dared. 180 **launched to**, hurled at; **gleyves**, lances. 181 **that**, unless. 182 **but as**, except that. 184 **kepte hem**, held them; **short and streite**, tightly together; **noon**, none; **felly**, fiercely. 188 **ne hadde**, had not.

companye of yonge bachelers.

190   And as Gawein com to the stronge stour, the childeren were in gret mischief; and than he and his felowes spronge upon hem so sharply that at the first shofte thei threw of hem to grounde mo than two thousande. And of that was Orienx sorowfull, for never hadde he sein so fewe peple so well hem contene. And he heilde a stronge spere and the heed sharp igrounde, and rode into the renge formest,

195 and seide he wolde be avenged on hem that hadde hym wratthed. And Gawein hadde so smyten aboute hym on every side that he fonde the childeren full wery for travaile; and [he] saugh Seigramor that was afore in the fronte and hielde an axe in bothe handes wherwith he smote grete strokes out of mesure. And he was moche and semly and therto the beste shapen chielde to have sought thourgh eny

200 reame; and whom that he araught was hitte so harde that it warant neither iren ne stiell ne noon armour that he ne smot thourgh owther arme or sholder or thigh or other member, and shewde merveiles all aboute.

    And whan Gawein saugh all this, he asked of the olde man that was by hym what he was. And he seide it was Segramor, the nevew of the emperour of

205 Costantinnoble. "But helpe hym delyverly, for it is grete myster." Than Gawein renged his companye and lete renne at hem so fiercely that in her comynge thei threwe to grounde of the Saisnes grete plenté, deed and wounded thourgh with sharpe wepenes. Grete was the bataile agein Orienx of the chylderen, but at grete myschief thei were, for on Gaweins side were but four thousand and thre hundred

210 that Seigramor hadde brought; and of the Saisnes were twenty thousand, withoute hem that ronne thourgh the contrey that brente and robbed, of whiche were forty thousand. Whan that Orienx saugh that so small a peple withstode hym so felly, he hadde therof grete dispite and cried to his men and swor that in evell tyme sholde eny ascape he caught; and [he] com drivinge agein Agravain that oon of his nevewes

215 hadde slain before his iyen.

    And whan Orienx saugh that, he spored his steede and smote Agravain upon

---

190 stour, battle; **mischief**, danger. **191 shofte**, thrust. **193 contene**, fight. **194 renge**, field. **195 wratthed**, angered. **196 fonde**, found. **199 moche**, large. **200 araught**, struck; **warant**, protected. **204 what**, who. **205 delyverly**, quickly; **myster**, need. **206 renged**, grouped; **lete renne**, charged. **208 agein**, against; **of**, by. **210–11 withoute hem**, not counting those. **211 brente**, burned. **212 saugh**, saw; **felly**, fiercely. **215 iyen**, eyes.

the shelde that he perced through the plites of his haubreke undir the side, that the
spere hede shewed on the tother side; and he shof theron so sore that he bar hym
from his horse to the grounde. Whan Gawein saugh his brother falle, he hadde

220 grete drede leste that he hadde be deed; and he heilde a trenchant axe and come to
the Saisne that hadde him unhorsed and wende to smyte hym upon the helme. But
whan Orienx saugh the stroke come, he it douted and covered hym with his shielde;
and Gawein hym smote that the axe bente and slit the sheilde in two, the stroke
was [so] grete; and Orienx spored his horse forth. The stroke descended upon

225 the helme and kut the cercle and a quarter of the helme and the mayle of the
haubreke behynde and the horse chyne asonder, that he blusht to the grounde.
And Gaheries smote so Solunant thourgh the heed with an axe that ded he drof to
the erthe; and Gaheret smote Vabibre thourgh the helme that he slit hym to the
teth; and Galashin smote Pinadoos that the heed fley into the feilde.

230 Whan the Saisnes saugh Orienx lye at the grounde, thei hadde grete drede that
he hadde be deed, and shof aĺle to the rescewe ther aboute hym environ, and bar
hym oute of the presse into the feilde. But he was stonyed of the stroke that he
myght not stonde on his feet ne meve no membre that he hadde; and therto he
made so lothly chere and so hidouse semblant that alle wende he hadde ben deed,

235 and made amonge hem grete doell and wepynge that all the bataile lefte.

And the childeren have Agravain taken up ther he was fallen and set hym on
horse. And the karll that hadde brought thider Gawein hadde chaunged his forme
to another and hadde take the semblance of a knyght armed, and than com to
Gawein and to his other bretheren and seide, "Feire lordes, yef ye do be my

240 counseile, lete us take the wey now right towarde Camelot while these Saisnes
entende to make this sorowe."

Whan Gawein undirstode these wordes, he wiste wele his counseile was wise
and withoute trecherie. And [he] com anoon to Seigramore and seide he was right
welcome and his companye; and he agein hym salvde as deboner and curteys.

217 **plites**, folds. 221 **Saisne**, Saxon; **wende**, intended. 222 **douted**, feared. 225 **cercle**,
helmet band. 226 **chyne**, backbone; **he**, i.e., Orienx; **blusht**, fell. 227 **drof**, fell. 229 **heed**
fley, head flew. 230 **at**, on. 231 **environ**, around. 232 **presse**, fray; **stonyed of**, stunned
from. 233 **ne meve no membre**, nor move any limb. 234 **lothly chere**, terrible looks; **so**
hidouse semblant, such a hideous appearance; **wende**, thought. 235 **doell**, mourning.
239 **yef**, if; **be**, by. 242 **wiste**, knew. 244 **salvde**, greeted; **deboner**, gracious.

245 And than he seid, "Ha! Seigramor, feire frende, it is tyme now that we go and lede with us the peple that is us belefte, for inough have we wonne seth that saf and sounde we repeyre." Than Seigramor asked what he was that so spake unto hym. And he seide, "My name is Gawein, the nevew of Kynge Arthur, and the sone of Kynge Loot of Orcanye; and [we] kepe the londes of myn oncle, I and my bretheren, 250 till he be come from Tamelide. And we be come hider for not elles but yow for to helpe and to socoure, for in the morowe it was tolde how ye were assailed of the Saisnes right sore."

Than com forth the knyght that hadde spoke to Gawein and cried, "A! Gawein, feire sir, what abide ye that ye come not forth youre wey? Se not ye that all the 255 worle of peple cometh upon us, wherefore we may not ascape yef ye abide?" Whan Gawein herde hym so haste to garison, he beheilde and saugh come so grete plenté of Saisnes and so grete foison that all the feilde was covered. And thei were alle armed and com rydinge fiercely and made soche noyse and soche mur-mur that a myle of lengthe it myght have ben herde. And whan that Gawein saugh 260 the Saisnes come in soche maner he seide to Seigramor, "Sir, and hit plese yow, go we hens." And he hym ansuerde and seide, "With goode will." And thei than rode forth toward Camelot clos togeder and streite that ye myght have caste a glove over her hedes covered undir steill.

And the Saisnes yet entended to Orienx, makynge doell and sorowe. But with-265 ynne a while aroos the Saisne fro disturdison, and saugh hem aboute hym made grete sorowe and hevynesse. Than he asked a newe helme and sheilde and spere, for he was of grete herte and a goode knyght and hardy as of his age. And he swore yef he myght with hym that yaf hym that acooley whereof he hadde so leyen in swowne at erthe, he sholde it hym wele aquyte. And than he lepe to horse 270 that was stronge and swyfte rennynge, and rode that wey as he wende to have hem founden; but thei were go thens a myle. Whan Orienx saugh hem gon in this maner, he cried his ensigne and seide, "Now after hem!" And than he swore that noon of hem sholde ascape.

246 seth that, since. **247 repeyre**, abide; **what**, who. **250 not elles**, no reason. **254 what abide ye**, why do you tarry. **255 worle**, tumult. **257 so grete foison**, so many. **260 and hit**, if it. **261 go we hens**, [let us] go hence. **262 streite**, tightly. **264 entended**, attended. **265 disturdison**, [his] distress. **268 acooley**, blow. **269 aquyte**, pay back. **270 wende**, thought. **271 were go thens**, had gone hence. **272 ensigne**, flag-bearer.

165

275 Than pressed forth the Saisnes hastely alle that myght, that oon ne abode not another; and the shoute and the noyse aroos so grete that wonder it was to here, and the duste and the powder aroos so thikke that the clier air was troubled; and thei com drivinge on so faste that thei nyghed nygh to atteyne the Cristin.

And than the knyght that hadde yeve Gawein this counseile saugh hem come so faste, he hasted sore Gawein and alle the tother for to go faste, and spake unto

280 hem that thei rode a gretter paas; but er thei com to the town of Camelot thei were sore hasted. But the noble Gawein and Agravain and Gaheret and Gaheries and Galaishin and Seigramor were the laste, and sente in theire felowes and her peple and her harneys before, as the heirde driveth his bestes to pasture, and therwhile thei suffred the Saisnes to breke theire speres. And whan thei saugh eny of her

285 felowes over charged, thei hem delyvered at her power as thei that were of high prowesse. And thei dide so well that ther nas Saisne so hardy that durste that wey go wheras as thei were, ne of hem abide a stroke.

Than com Orienx with the grete baner and hadde a grete spere whereof the heed is sharp and trenchaunt. And [he] saugh hym that hadde hym smyte to grounde

290 and knewe hym full well, and swoor by his god that he wolde be avenged. Than he spored his horse fiercely; and the chielde saugh hym come, but he made semblaunt as therof he rought litill. And whan he com even at the metynge, Gawein lefte the wey and lete hym passe forth that his horse cowde not restreyne. And Gawein, that was wight and delyver, returned his horse upon hym and smote hym

295 upon the heed with bothe hondes, but it was with the flat for the haste that he hadde hym tosmyte, so that he wiste not how he it heilde. And the stroke was so grete and hevy that the fier sparkeled up in the aire, and astoned hym so sore that he fill flat to the erthe.

And Seigramor smote Driant the Rede thurgh the sholder so harde that it dis-

300 severed fro the body. And Galaishin smote so Placidas that his heed he hym be-

274 **oon ne abode not**, one did not wait for. 277 **nyghed nygh to atteyne**, nearly reached; **Cristin**, Christians. 278 **than**, when; **yeve**, given. 279 **hasted sore**, urged; **tother**, others. 280 **gretter paas**, faster pace. 280–81 **were sore hasted**, had to hurry. 283 **harneys**, gear; **heirde**, herdsman. 285 **over charged**, knocked down. 286 **nas**, was not any; **durste**, dared. 287 **wheras as**, where; **ne**, nor. 291 **chielde**, youth (knight). 292 **rought litill**, cared little. 293 **restreyne**, stop. 294 **wight and delyver**, quick and agile. 295 **flat**, i.e., the side of the ax. 296 **wiste**, knew; **heilde**, held. 297 **astoned**, stunned.

rafte. And Agravain and Gaheret and Gaheries hadde eche of hem caught a short
spere, the iren sharp and trenchaunt, and that oon smote Gynebant and the tother
Taurus and the thridde smote Fannell, that eche bar his to the erthe from theyre
horse all blody; and with the same cours thei smote thre other. And Gawein and
305   Galaishin and Seigramor rested upon Orienx, for thei wolde hym have take yef
thei myght. But the Saisnes ne wolde it not suffre, but assembled so thikke aboute
tho thre felowes that thei hadde many grete strokes taken and yeven. And thei thre
were noble and worthi and slough of hem so many that her armes and her brestes
were alle blody, and also their horse heer; and so thei hem stered that noon was so
310   hardy to abyde of hem eny stroke.

    Whan the thre felowes saugh thei moste nede forsake Orienx and saugh a worlde
of peple that upon hem com drivinge, thei ronne upon Orienx and hym diffouled
with theire horse feet till he was all tobrosed. And whan he was all tobrosed and
hym diffouled at her lust saf thei have hym not slain, than thei rode after her
315   felowes that be that tyme myght be nygh Camelot, for never seth thei remeved
were thei not enchased but wente forth delyverly. And whan the thre felowes
saugh her men were withynne the town, thei were gladde and mery; and than thei
rode a softe paas.

    And the Saisnes abode aboute her lorde that was caste down and so diffouled
320   under horse feet; whereof he was so sorowfull whan he aroos from disturdison
that thei be so ascaped, that nygh he was wode for wratthe and ire, and swor yef
he myght hem gete in his bailly that he sholde do hem be flain all quyk and drawen
asondre with horse. "Sir," seide his men, "a full fell pawtener is he that twies this
day thus hath yow smyten to grounde." "Ye," quod Orienx, "but yef I may have
325   bailly over his body, he shall so be deffouled that ther ne shall nothinge in the
worlde hym warantise."

    And thei hadde so riden that thei com before Camelot, whereas thei abode stille,

300–01 berafte, cut off. **301 caught,** grabbed. **304 cours,** charge. **305 rested upon,** set
upon; **have take,** capture. **306 suffre,** allow. **307 tho,** those. **308 slough,** slew. **309
stered,** conducted. **312 diffouled,** trampled. **313 tobrosed,** bruised. **314 saf,** except. **315
be,** by; **seth,** since; **remeved,** departed. **316 delyverly,** freely. **318 a softe paas,** an easy
pace. **320 disturdison,** his distress. **321 wode,** crazed. **322 bailly,** custody; **do hem be
flain all quyk,** have them skinned alive. **323 full fell pawtener,** terrible fellow. **325
bailly,** custody. **326 warantise,** protect.

and asked oon of another where the other thre were become. But ther was noon that ought cowde sey. Whan Agravain and Gaheret and Gaheries undirstode how

330 that Gawein her brother, and her cosin, and the nevew of the emperoure were loste, thei turned bakke and seide thei wolde not reste till thei hadde hem founden, and comaunded her felowes not to remeve till thei saugh hem com agein; and than alle thre rode agein a walop as thei hadde com. But thei hadde but litill while riden whan thei mette the karll that satte upon the steede that Gawein hadde hym yoven,

335 the same that hadde brought tidinges of Seigramor. And whan he mette these three bretheren, he asked whider thei wente; and thei seide thei sought Gawein her brother and her cosin Galaishin and the nevew of the emperour, for thei wiste not where thei were becomen.

"Full evell," seide he, "have ye yow demened, and well sheweth the worthi and

340 noble where thei ben, and loo heere where thei come. But whom it displese, thei owe to come yow no thonke of her lyves, for ye lefte hem foulé as cowardes; and well it sheweth theras thei abode for to socour these other that now ben saf at garison. And thei have doon many feire chivalries and yoven many grete strokes that thei ought to be comended and preised of all the worlde that therof heren

345 speke, and to holde yow for soche as ye be. And wele have ye it shewed theras ye lefte youre felowes at soche nede, and thei ne lefte yow never for deth ne for lif. And every gentillman that therof hereth speke ought yow to blame be right and reson and have yow ever suspect in every nede. And wite it well, it shall turne yow to repress." With that the cherll departed, that lenger with hem ne wolde

350 talke.

And thei passeden forth all shamefest and mate and sory of the wordes the karll hadde spoken. But thei nadde but litill wey riden whan thei mette the thre felowes that were so araied that it semed by her armes that thei were come from felon place. And whan thei mette togeder thei made grete joye. Than Gawein asked

355 tidinges of her other felowes where thei were, and thei seide that thei hem lefte before the yates of Camelot where thei abide. Than thei rode forth togeder, gladde

332 remeve, move. **333 walop,** gallop. **334 yoven,** given. **339 evell,** poorly; **demened,** conducted yourselves. **341 come yow,** i.e., give you; **foulé,** foully. **343 chivalries,** fine deeds; **yoven,** given. **344 that**[1], so that. **345 theras,** when. **349 repress,** disgrace. **351 shamefest,** ashamed; **mate,** dejected. **352 nadde,** had not. **353 felon,** a horrible. **356 yates,** gates.

and mery for her newe feliship that be come hem to helpe, and of that thei have hem thus rescewed, and he and his companye hooll and sounde.

But er thei hade a while riden togeder, thei mette the cherles horse sore affraied that com fleynge, and saugh the arson of the sadell all blody. And whan these felowes that he hadde reprovid saugh the horse, that oon beheilde the tother and begonne to laugh. Of that toke hede Gawein and Galashin and asked whi thei lowghen, and thei stynte for to tellen; and thei hem conjured another tyme right harde for to tellen the trouthe. And Gaheries tolde hym alle the wordes that the cherll hadde hem seide. And whan that thei it herde, thei merveiled what it myght be; and than com Gawein to the horse that fledde and toke hym by the bridell and saugh that all the arson was blody, and wend that the karll hadde be slayn.

Than he asked of Agravain and of the tother yef thei mette eny of the Saisnes seth thei departed fro Camelot. And thei seide how thei mette neyther man ne woman seth thei departed from theire men, saf the cherll that satte upon that horse. Quod Gawein, "I trowe he be slayn or wounded sore, or paraventure he is fallen whereso it be to grounde; and therfore lete us hym seche till we may hym fynde. And yef he be alyve, lete us bere hym to Camelot, for it were synne to suffre hym to dye for defaute here in the feilde." And than thei sought up and down in the feilde and amonge the busshes, but yet thei myght have sought hym into this tyme, for he was come into her hoste in the semblaunce of a knave on foote with a tronchon of a spere in his honde.

And whan Gawein saugh he myght not be founde, thei repeired to Kamelot and fonde her felowes hem abydynge at the brigge foot, that thei were of hem joyfull whan thei saugh hem hooll and sounde. And than thei entred into the town and drough up the brigge and shette the yates, and than wente upon the walles for to loke yef the Saisnes come toward the town it for to assaile. But thei therto hadde no talent, for thei desired not ther so longe to sojourne till thei hadde it taken, for it was right stronge.

And the childeren hem unarmed and wente to theire loggyngis, and hem esed of all thinge that to mannys body belongeth. And grete joye and feste thei made of

358 hooll, whole. **360 arson**, bow. **363 stynte for**, refused; **conjured**, begged. **365 what it**, who he. **367 wend**, thought. **369 seth**, since. **370 saf**, except for. **371 trowe**, believe; **paraventure**, perhaps. **372 seche**, seek. **373 yef**, if. **374 for defaute**, by default. **376 knave**, youth. **381 drough**, drew; **yates**, gates. **383 talent**, desire.

Seigramor whan thei hym knewen. And whan he hadde hem tolde wherfore he
was come fro Costantinnoble to Kynge Arthur to take of hym his armes, and than
was he moche worshiped and moche preised of oon and other, and seiden that he
390   was of grete herte and hardy, for thei hadde hym sein in bataile, and he was of
merveilouse bounté. And moche reverence and worship dide hym the noble
gentilmen therinne, and disported and pleide and beheilde Seigramor that was moche
and semly and well furnysshed of membres.

    And thus thei lyven in disporte and joye thre dayes, that nothinge thei ne herde
395   on noo part but that the Saisnes wente into the Northumberlonde and into the
londe of the Duke Escam of Cambenyk, that ther foughten sore bataile at the
strayte of the Roche Magot agein the peple of Orienx upon the river of Savarne.

[**Summary**. *The narrative then offers a lengthy description of the struggles of King
Clarion and Duke Escam against King Orienx and the Saxon invaders, before returning to describe the deeds of the Young Squires, led by Gawain, against the Saxons
who have been ravaging the lands of King Ydiers near the Castle of Arondell. Merlin,
in the guise of a yeoman, bears a letter to Gawain, urging him to come to the aid of his
cousin Ewain, the son of King Uriens, who is sorely beset by the Saxons. Gawain and
the other Squires rescue Ewain and his companions, who are joyfully added to their
group. Fighting together, the Young Squires perform gloriously against the Saxons.
The Saxons retreat, and the Squires ride toward the Castle of Arondell, which they
discover is besieged by yet another group of Saxons. They force the Saxons to lift the
siege, and they are welcomed joyfully by those within the castle. The story then shifts
to King Lot, Gawain's father, against whom the Saxons have been waging a fierce
campaign. Fols. 95r (line 17)–103v (line 29).]*

387 **wherfore**, why. 389 **of oon and other**, by everyone. 391 **bounté**, ability. 392 **moche**,
large. 397 **agein**, against.

[Gawain's Rescue of his Mother]

Whan the kynge saugh how the Saisnes wasted his londe and distroied and
hadde slain so moche of his peple that he myght not but kepe hym in stronge
place, and than he was full of sorowe and of hevynesse and cursed the hour and
the day that he was at werre with Kynge Arthur, "For by hym have I loste alle my
5   childeren." And on that other side his citee was all wasted, and he ne loked but
after the hour to be take withynne, for the walles were broke down in many
places; and [he] saugh also how the Kynge Arans was loged all aboute hym, and
he hadde no peple in his companye that myght eny while hym withstonde, yef the
Kynge Arans wolde eny while sojourne. But he desired it not gretly, but aboode
10   after his men that the contrey wasted and distroied all environ.

Whan the Kynge Loot saugh hymself in soche aventure, he toke counseile what
was beste to do, and his counseile in the ende was this, that at the firste cokke
crowinge he sholde lepe to his horse — he, and his wif, and his litill sone that was
but two yere of age — and lede hem to Glocedon, and sholde have with hym five
15   hundre men well armed; and that other part sholde abide stille that yet were six
thousande of noble men and hardy. And thei hym promyseden that thei sholde
kepe well the citee while there life myght endure.

At mydnyght, the kynge and his companye toke theire horse and his litill sone
Mordered, that the Kynge Arthur hadde begeten in soche manere as ye have herde
20   devised; and a squyer hym bar in a litill cradell hym before upon his horse nekke;
and [thei] rode oute by a fause posterne of the citee toward the gardins and entred

---

1 **the kynge**, i.e., King Lot; **saugh**, saw. 3 **and than**, then. **5–6 ne loked but after**, could
only await. **6 take withynne**, captured. **7 loged**, encamped. **8 he**, i.e., King Lot. **9 wolde
eny while sojourne**, i.e., would continue the siege; **he**, i.e., King Arans. **9–10 aboode
after**, accompanied. **10 all environ**, all about. **11 soche aventure**, such straits. **14 hem**,
them. **19 begeten**, begotten. **20 bar**, carried. **21 fause posterne**, rear entrance.

into a lane, and rode all nyght and all day till noone, that nevere hadde distrubinge. But than was the Kynge Loot sore aflayed, for thei mette Taurus, with thre thou-sand Saisnes that repaired from Arondell, that condited the pray to the Kynge

25 Arans.

And as soone as thei knewe the Kynge Loot, thei ronne upon hym with grete hete, and ther a while was stronge stour; and full nobly dide the Kynge Loot and the five hundred that were in his companye; but of well doynge was litill myster, for soone were thei discounfited and chased oute of the feilde, and his wif also

30 itake. Than the squyer fledde towarde Arondell as faste as the horse myght hym bere. But now cesseth a litill of Kynge Loot and returne to Gawein.

Full gladde and mery were Gawein and his felowes at Arondell that nyght, that whan thei were knowen togeder of the squyres that thei hadde rescuwed. And as thei were in this joye and in this feeste, com a knyght right well armed upon a

35 grete steede all forswette — and his shilde all todaisht and hewen with strokes that he hadde resceyved of swerdes above and benethe, and his coverynge cote all torente, and his hauberke torn and broken in many places. And he com before Arondell a grete walop, gripynge his launce; and whan he com before the castell yate he stynte, and saugh the squyres above on the walles that grete joye made

40 oon to another. And anoon he gan to crie yef therynne were eny squyer that were so hardy that durste hym suewen thider as he wolde go, be soche a condicion that he sholde have no drede of no man but of his owne corse.

Whan Gawein it undirstode, he asked what wey he wolde go. Quod the knyght, "What art thow that spekest to me?" "My name," quod he, "is Gawein, the sone of

45 Kynge Loot." "Than shall I telle yow," quod he, "for the aventure aperteneth to yow more than to eny other. And certes," seide the knyght, "into the entré of this foreste is the prowesse that I of speke. But ye have not that prowesse ne the hardynesse that ye dar me sue; and yet is it oon of the moste honourable aventure

22 that, i.e., and. **23 sore aflayed**, greatly alarmed. **24 condited**, carried; **pray**, booty. **27 hete**, heat; **stour**, battle. **28 myster**, value. **29 discounfited**, defeated. **30 itake**, cap-tured. **32–33 that whan**, when. **33 were knowen togeder of**, became acquainted with. **35 all forswette**, i.e., in a great hurry; **todaisht**, smashed to pieces. **38 walop**, gallop. **39 yate**, gate; **stynte**, stopped. **40 yef**, if. **41 durste hym suewen**, dared follow him; **be**, by. **44 What**, Who. **45 aperteneth**, belongs. **46 entré**, first section. **47 prowesse**[1], adven-ture; **ne**, nor. **48 me sue**, follow me; **aventure**, adventures.

in this worlde, and that ye sholde moste be preised yef ye myght it acheve. But ye
50 have nother the herte ne the hardynesse that ye durst thider come. And wite it
well, but ye will come, I will go sooll be myself."

Whan Gawein undirstode hym that so cleped hym cowarde, he was shamefaste
and seide that though he sholde dye, he wolde hym companye. And he began for
to go, that full well knewe his corage. And Gawein cleped hym agein and cried,
55 "Sir knyght, lo! me here all redy to go with yow — but that ye shull me ensure
that for noon evell ye make me it for to do, and that ye shull me helpe at youre
power agein alle tho that will me mysdo."

Whan he herde these wordes, he abode and began to smyle as it were in scorne,
and seide as for that sholde he not lette, but that he wolde make hym the assuraunce.
60 And Gawein asked his armes and armed hym wightly anoon; and he aboode, that
gretly hym hasted. And the felowes of Gawein com to hym and seide, "Sir, what
thinke ye to do? Ne goth not withouten us, for we wote never whether it be for
goode or for evell." And Gawein seide that he wolde well that thei wente with
hym, yef the knyght wolde assente. "And we shull hym aske," seide Galashin.
65 Than ran Seigramor to the knyght and asked, "Sir knyght, and it plese yow, ther
ben somme hereynne that fayn wolde go with yow in companye, and theire feliship
shall yow nought empeire; and therfore thei yow preyen by me that ye will hem
graunte to holde with yow companye." And the knyght hem ansuerde, and seide
he wolde it well; and well it hym plesed that alle wente that go wolde, "For the
70 aventure is soche that noon shall faile to fynde his aventure that ther cometh"; and
than Seigramor was gladde. And anoon thei armed hem therynne with grete spede
till thei were seven thousand, that mo thei wolde not lede; but tho were of the
beste and of theym that were beste horsed. And whan thei com oute of the castell,
Gawein toke the assuraunce of the knyght that for noon evell he com not hym for
75 to seche.

49 and that, and; **yef,** if. **50 nother . . . ne,** neither . . . nor. **51 but,** unless; **sooll be,** alone
by. **52 cleped,** called. **53 he³,** i.e., Merlin. **54 that,** a man who; **his,** i.e., Gawain's. **55 but
that,** if. **57 agein,** against; **tho,** those. **58 as,** as if. **59 lette,** refuse. **60 asked,** called for;
wightly, quickly; **aboode,** waited; **that,** the man who. **61 hasted,** prompted. **63 wolde
well,** much desired. **64 yef,** if. **65 and²,** if. **66 fayn,** happily. **67 nought empeire,** not harm.
69 go wolde, wished to go. **70 aventure¹,** undertaking; **aventure²,** excitement. **72 mo,**
more; **lede,** take; **tho,** those. **74 noon evell,** no evil purpose. **75 seche,** seek.

173

Than thei wente ridinge all the day and all the nyght till it com to the dawenynge; and than thei herde at the ende of a launde a grete crye and a grete noyse of peple; and as hem semed, ther were many. And than thei mette a squyer that fledde upon a grete horse that bar a chielde before hym in a cradell. And whan Gawein hym

80 mette, he asked hym with whom he was and whi he fledde so faste. And he hem beheilde and saugh that thei were Cristin and seide, "I am with the Kynge Loot that the Saisnes han discounfited at the ende of this launde towarde that wode; for he was goynge toward Gloceden and ledde with hym his wif, and now thei have hir taken and chased hym oute of the feilde. And I am thus fleynge, as ye

85 seen, with this childe that is hers; for never shall I it lete till I have sette it in soche place that it shall not have drede of the Saisnes that into this contrey ben entred. And for the love of God, ne go ye no ferther, feire lordes, for ye shull fynde ther so grete plenté of Saisnes that ye ne may hem endure."

"Certeis," seide Gawein, "but I shall telle thee what thow shalt do. Thow shalt

90 go reste thee here in this wode till thow se what shall falle of this bataile; and after, yef I may ascape, I will thee bringe theras thow ne childe shull have no drede of noon evell that no man shall yow do." And [he] praide hym so that he hym graunted.

With that thei departed that oon from that other, and the knyght wente forth

95 that moche dide Gawein for to haste, and badde hym sue faste withoute lettinge, and therwith he rode faste before. And whan Gawein saugh he wente, he spored his horse after, and so dide his felowes also. And [thei] rode faste till thei were paste the foreste, and saugh the chase that even tho was begonne after the Kynge Loot, that fledde to Glocedon with the peple that was hym belefte of the bataile.

100 And on that other side Gawein beheilde in the myddill of the medowe and saugh a lady of grete bewté, ne hadde be the doell and the sorowe that she made and the

---

77 **herde**, heard; **launde**, meadow. 78 **hem semed**, it seemed to them. 79 **chielde**, child. 81 **saugh**, saw. 82 **han discounfited**, have defeated. 85 **lete**, stop. 89 **Certeis**, Indeed. 90 **falle of**, happen in. 91 **theras thow ne childe**, where [neither] you nor the child. 92 **praide**, urged. 93 **graunted**, assented. 94 **the knyght**, i.e., Merlin. 95 **sue**, follow; **lettinge**, stopping. 96 **faste before**, quickly in front; **saugh**, saw. 98 **tho**, then. 99 **was hym belefte**, remained to him. 100 **beheilde in the myddill**, looked toward the middle. 101 **ne hadde be the doell**, were it not for the grief.

myschief that she was ynne. And she was all dischevelee in her heer, and Taurus hir heilde be the tresses and drough hir after his horse; and hir robe that she was in clad was so grete that for combraunce she myght not arise; and she braied and

105 cride with an high voyse, "Seint Marie, Blissed Lady and Moder of God, helpe me and socour!"

And whan she cried and cleped Oure Lady Seint Marie, Taurus smote hir with his honde armed right sore that she fill down to the erthe even as she hadde be deed. And whan he hadde sette hire upon his horse, she fill agein down to the

110 erthe as a woman that was hurte, and cried and braide right lowde and seide that she wolde fayne be deed. And he agein sette hir upon horse, and she fill down agein to grounde and seide as longe as she myght lyve, sholde he never lede thens for no power that he hadde. And whan he saugh that he myght not hir maistrie, he hente hir be the tresses and drough hir towarde the horse trailinge, and smote hir

115 so that she was all covered in blode, what from mouthe and nose. And so he hath hir trayned and drawen, that the lady myght no lenger crye ne brayen; she was so hoorse and so brethles that on hire feet myght she not stonde ne sustene.

And whan the knyght saugh the lady so evell besein, he seide to Gawein, "Now, Gawein, knowest thow not that lady yonder? And yef ever ye hir loved dayes of

120 youre lyf, thinke hir to rescowen and to avengen." And as soone as Gawein saugh, he knewe hire wele; than he was so full of angwissh that ner he yede oute of his witte; ne he wende never to have sein the hour to have come therto. Than he smote the horse with sopores all that he myght, and hielde a grete shorte spere, the heed right sharp and trenchaunt. And mydday was somdell passed and the

125 sonne right high, and Gawein cried to Taurus, "Leff the lady, traitour fitz a putain! In evell tyme hast thow her so dolerous mette, for never in thi liff didest thow foly

---

102 myschief, plight; **dischevelee**, dishevelled; **heer**, hair. **103 be**, by; **drough**, drew. **104 grete**, long; **combraunce**, the hindrance; **braied**, screamed. **108 honde armed right sore**, armored hand very painfully; **fill**, fell; **even as**, as if; **be**, been. **110 braide**, screamed; **lowde**, loudly. **111 fayne**, gladly. **112 lede thens**, lead [her] thence. **113 maistrie**, control. **114 hente**, grabbed; **drough**, drew. **116 trayned**, dragged; **brayen**, shout. **117 hoorse**, hoarse. **118 evell besein**, evilly treated. **119 yef**, if. **121 ner**, nearly. **122 ne he wende never**, he never expected. **123 sopores**, spurs. **124 somdell**, somewhat. **125 Leff**, Leave; **fitz a putain**, son of a whore. **126 dolerous mette**, unfortunately met.

175

that thow shalt bye so dere."

And whan Taurus saugh hym come that so gretly to hym cried and menaced, he lete the lady falle, and righted his armes and toke a grete spere and a rude, and
130 lete renne his horse agein hym. And Gawein and he smote togeder as harde as theire armes myght dure, and Taurus brake his spere; and Gawein smote hym so rudely thourgh shelde and hauberke that the spere heede shewde thourgh his chyne an arme lengthe, and he blussht so harde to grounde that his nekke brake asonder.

And Gaheret and Gaheries and Agravain alight down, and oon smote of his
135 heed, and another thriste hym thourgh with his swerde, and the thirde smote of bothe his armes, for it was not inough to hem that Gawein hadde don, but made of hym smale peces. And these other smote in amonge the Saisnes and made of hem soche martirdom and soche occision that thei slough mo than ten thousand er thei leften. And Gawein slough so many that he was all wete in blode and brayn that
140 his armes dropped down as he hadde be wete in a flode.

And whan that the Saisnes saugh the grete occision that upon turned, thei fledden alle that myght thourgh wode and thourgh playn. And Gawein repeired thideras he saugh hys moder ly, and alight on foote, and toke hir in his armes and fonde hir even as deed. And he wepte sore that the teeris ronne down from his iyen as
145 thikke as water hadde be throwen in his visage, and cried and wrange his handes and made soche doell and sorowe that alle his felowes were therwith anoyed, and hadden therof grete pité, that ther nas noon but wepte water with his iyen. And whan the bretheren of Gawein com thider, ther began the doell and sorowe so grete that noon erthly man myght devise noon gretter.

150 Whan the lady undirstode the brayes and the cries that the bretheren made aboute hir, she opened hir iyen and saugh hir sone Gawein that hir heilde in his armes, and knewe hym wele anoon; and [she] lifte up hir handes joynynge towarde hevene, and thanked oure Lorde of that socoure that He hadde hir sente. Than she spake as she myght and seide, "Feire sone Gawein, be stille and wepe no more, for I have

127 **bye so dere**, pay for so dearly. 128 **menaced**, threatened. 132 **rudely**, fiercely; **chyne**, back. 133 **blussht**, fell. 134 **of**, off. 138 **martirdom**, slaughter; **occision**, slaying; **mo**, more; **er**, before. 141 **occision**, slaughter; **that upon turned**, that had come upon them. 142 **repeired thideras**, returned to where. 144 **even as**, as if. **iyen**; eyes. 146 **anoyed**, sad. 147 **nas noon**, was not one; **iyen**, eyes. 149 **noon**[1], no; **noon**[2], any. 150 **brayes**, shouts. 151 **iyen**, eyes. 152 **anoon**, immediately; **joynynge**, clasped together.

155 not the harme that I sholde dye fore, but hurte I am right sore."

And than she asked hym where his bretheren were, and anoon thei com before hir makynge grete doell. And whan she hem saugh she thanked oure Lorde; and in a while aftere anoon she seide, "Haalas! My sone Mordred have I loste, and my lorde youre fader, that this day hath suffred grete peyne me for to rescewen and

160 socour; for whan he hadde alle loste his men, I saugh hym fight longe agein five hundred men, and abode while oon myght have gon half a myle of grounde upon his feet. And therfore I have grete drede that he be wounded to the deth, for I saugh hem launche at hym knyves and gavelokkes and dartes soche foison as it hadde reyned from hevene. Ne never wolde he voide the place ne me forsake till

165 I hym conjured, for that he loved beste in the worlde, that he wolde gon his wey; and than he dide, so sorowfull that no man myght more."

"Dame," quod Gawein, "of Mordred my brother I can telle yow tidinges, for the squyer that it bar hath hym kept wisely, and us abydeth in this foreste; but of the kynge my fader I can not sey."

170 Whan the lady undirstode that, it hevied her herte and [she] swowned in Gaweins armes; and he her kiste and wepte right sore. And whan she com agein from swownynge, she yaf a sore sigh, and with that the coloure com agein into her visage. And than she asked Gawein watir to waisshe hir face that was all soilede with blode; and oon it brought in an hatte of stiele, and than she wossh hir visage

175 as softely as she myght. And than thei ordeyned hir a litier upon two palfrayes, and leide her therynne fresch gras and erbes plenté and clothes, and than leide her therynne softely, and than gadered the prayes that thei hadde wonne of the Saisnes, and wente forth to Arondell a goode spede.

And thei hadde but litill while riden whan the squyer com before hem with the

180 childe. And than was Gawein gladde, and rode forth with the childe till thei com to Arondell, whereas thei sojourned eight dayes full till the lady was hooll. And than thei departed from thens and wente to Logres, the chief citee of the Kynge Arthur, alle the company togeder. But two hundre squyers thei lefte at Arondell to

---

155 dye fore, die from. **158 Haalas**, Alas. **161 abode**, stand firm. **163 hem**, them; **gavelokkes**, spears; **soche foison**, so many. **164 reyned**, rained; **voide**, leave. **165 hym conjured**, begged him; **that¹**, the one. **168 it**, i.e., Mordred's cradle; **abydeth**, awaits. **172 yaf**, gave. **175 softely**, gently; **litier**, litter. **177 prayes**, spoils. **181 hooll**, healthy.

kepe the castell, and ledde with hem the lady and hir litill sone.

185   And the foure bretheren swore that never sholde the Kynge Loot her fader have agein theire moder till that he hadde acorded with Kynge Arthur theire uncle. Of this thinge that thei seide was the lady gladde. And so thei spedde theire journeyes till thei com to Logres, where thei were receyved with grete honoure and reverence. And Doo of Cardoell made to hem grete joye and feeste, and so dide alle the

190   citee. But whan thei parceyved the lady, thei made moche more joye, and hir dide as grete worship as myght be don to eny lady of the worlde. And every man was gladde of the aventure that God hadde hem sente.

    And than made Gawein to enquere and serche yef eny man knewe the knyght that hadde hem ledde to socour his moder; but noon cowde telle of hym no tidinge.

195   And so the tidinges ronne up and down that Doo of Cardoell it wiste, that was a noble knyght and a sure and a wise, and thought well in his herte who this knyght myght be. And than he com to Gawein and seide, "Sir, knewe ye never that man that brought yow firste tydinges of Seigramor and also of Ewein youre cosin?" "I never hym knewe ne saugh before," quod Gawein.

200   "Nor hym," quod Doo, "that taught yow where was youre moder, ne knowe ye no hym?" "No, truly," quod Gawein.

    Than thought Doo anoon what he was, and gan to smylen. And Gawein merveiled moche why he dide aske, and than he hym conjured be the feith that he ought to the Kynge Arthur his lorde, and praied hym dierly also to telle hym whi he asked

205   hym that demaunde and wherfore he lowgh. And than he seide, "Gawein, Gawein, so moche ye have me conjured that I shall telle yow whi. But be well ware that ye lete no man knowe of nothinge that I sey unto yow."

    And Gawein seide, "Nay," for hym were lever to have his tonge drawen oute. "Knowe it verily," quod Doo, "that he that alle these tidinges hath brought, it is

210   Merlin, that is the beste devynour that is in all the worlde or evere was."

    "How, sir," quod Gawein, "speke ye of that Merlin that was so well beloved of Uterpendragon, that was begeten of the devell upon a woman?" "Of that same," seide Doo, "speke I withoute faile." "A! God mercy!" seide Gawein, "how myght

---

184 ledde with hem, took with them. **190 parceyved**, recognized. **193 yef**, if. **194 noon cowde**, no one could. **195 wiste**, knew. **202 what**, who. **203 hym conjured**, requested him; **be**, by; **ought**, owes. **204 dierly**, dearly. **205 demaunde**, question; **wherfore**, why; **lowgh**, laughed. **206 conjured**, beseeched; **ware**, careful.

this be or bifalle that I have seyn hym in so many maner formes, for I have seyn
215   hym in thre semblaunces." "Wite it well," quod Doo, "how that ever ye have hym
seyn, it is he verily, for he is so full of stronge art that he hym chaungeth into as
many semblaunces as he will."

Than Gawein hym blissed for the merveile that he therof hadde, and seide that
he wolde with hym be aqueynteth yef it hym plesed, "For I wote well now that he
220   us loveth, whan that he entermeteth hym of oure deedes." "Knowe it well," quod
Doo, "yef it plese hym ye shall it wite, for we may nothinge do ne sey but he it
wite."

Thus abode the squyres at Logres, gladde and myrry of that oure Lorde hadde
hem assembled togeder. And thei kepte the contrey aboute that the Saisnes ever
225   more loste than wonne. But now leveth the tale of hem and speketh of the knyght
that ledde Gawein for to socour his moder.

218 hym blissed, blessed himself. **219 yef**, if. **220 entermeteth hym of**, involves himself
in. **222 wite**, know.

[Merlin and Nimiane]

Now seith the storye that whan Gawein and his felowes were medled with the
meyné of Taurus, and this knyght saugh that Gawein hadde his moder rescowed,
he departed awey so sodeynly that no man wiste where that he be com, and
wente into Northumbirlonde to Blaase his maister and tolde hym alle these aventures

5   that hadde be don in the reame of Logres. And Blase of hym was joyfull and
gladde, and wrote these thinges that he hym tolde; and by hys booke have we yet
the knowynge of the seide aventures.

And whan he hadde be ther as longe as hym liked, he seide he wolde go into the
reame of Benoyk, for soone elles myght the Kynge Ban and the Kynge Boors

10   have grete damage while thei ben with Arthur in Tamelide; and that were dedly
synne, for thei ben full noble men and trewe. For the Kynge Claudas de la Desert
hath don homage to the Kynge of Gaule, and he hath promysed hym to helpe and
to mayntene; and on that other side, this Claudas hath so purchased that he hath be
at Rome; and he and the Kynge of Gaule have take theire londes to the emperoure

15   be soche covenaunt that the Emperour Julius shall sende hym socour and wolde
sese the two remes of Benoyk and Gannes.

And thei assemble and somowne on alle partees, and now be meved the
Romaynes with an huge peple; and theire lorde and governoure is Pounce and
Antony, tweyne of the counseillours of Rome that be two grete lordes and myghty.

20   And also on that other part cometh for love of hem Frolle, a Duke of Almayne,
that is right a grete lorde of londe and of richesse and of frendes, and is cosin
germain to Antony and to Pounce. And ech of these bringeth twenty thousande at

1 **were medled with**, were involved with. **2 meyné**, army; **saugh**, saw. **3 wiste**, knew. **5**
reame, realm. **9 soone elles**, otherwise. **13 on that other side**, furthermore; **purchased**,
arranged. **15 be**, by. **16 sese**, seize; **remes**, realms. **17 somowne**, summon; **partees**,
sides; **be meved**, are on the move. **20 on that other part**, in addition; **hem**, them. **21–22**
cosin germain, first cousin.

his baner; and thise of the reame of Benoyk ne knowen it nought, and so sholde thei alle be distroide er thei token hede or were therof war.

25   Whan Blase this undirstode, he began to wepe and seide to Merlin, "For the love of God, have pitee of Cristin peple that thei be not distroied." And he seide while that he myght lyve he wolde hem helpe with all his counseile. "And yet," quod Merlin, "it is the londe that I ought moste for to hate, for in that londe is the wolf that the lupart shall bynde with cercles that shall nother be of iren, ne steile,

30   ne tree, ne golde, ne silver, ne lede, ne nothinge of the erthe, ne of the water, ne herbe; and [he] shall be so streite bounde that he shall not meve."

    "A! God mercy!" quod Blase. "Merlin, what is that ye sey? Is not the leopart more of strength than is the wolf, and more he is to doute?" "Yesse, truly," quod Merlin. "How may the wolf than have power over the leopart?" quod Blase. "Ye

35   shull no more knowe," quod Merlin. "But thus moche I will telle yow, that this prophesie shall falle upon me, and I wote well I may me not kepe therfro."

    And Blase hym sayned for the merveile; and than he began to aske and seide, "Merlin, now telle me this. Yef ye go now into Benoyk, what shall falle of this londe that the Saisnes thus go distroyinge?"

40   "Of this ne care yow nought," quod Merlin, "for Arthur shall never justise his barouns till that thei be well scowred; and knowe it well, thei shall be driven oute in short tyme. And on that othir side, ne were for the merveillouse leopart that shall come oute of the reame of Benoyk that shall be so grete and so fiers that alle other beestes shall surmounte, bothe of this contrey and of the Bloy Bretaigne.

45   And of hym shall come the grete lyon to whom alle beestes shull enclyne and for whos look the hevene shall open. I wolde not go ne come ther as longe as I myght me holde thens, but I shull synne dedly yef I sholde do agein the ordenaunce of God; wherefore He hath me yove soche witte and discrescion as I have, for to helpe acomplissh the aventures of the Seynt Graall that shall be acomplisshed and

50   made an ende in the tyme of Kynge Arthur. But enquere now no ferther, for thow

23 **thise**, i.e., the people. 24 **er**, before; **war**, aware. 26 **that**, so that. 29 **lupart**, leopard; **cercles**, circles; **ne steile**, nor steel. 30 **tree**, wood; **lede**, lead. 31 **streite**, tightly. 33 **doute**, fear. 34 **than**, then. 36 **wote**, know. 37 **hym sayned**, crossed himself. 38 **Yef**, If; **falle of**, happen to. 40 **justise**, i.e., control. 41 **scowred**, cleansed; **thei**, i.e., the Saxons. 44 **surmounte**, surpass; **Bloy Bretaigne**, Brittany. 45 **enclyne**, bow down. 47 **yef**, if; **do agein**, work against. 48 **yove**, given.

shalt it [wete] in tyme comynge what this may be, and youreself shull it se at youre yie er ye be deed."

Whan Blase herde Merlin thus covertly speke, he thought longe on these wordes; but ever be putte hem in writinge as he hadde hem seide.

[**Summary**. *Merlin goes to Benoyk. There he advises Leonces to prepare for the invasion by the Roman forces, and he tells Leonces what defensive tactics to employ. He also predicts that there will be a great battle before Trebes on the Feast of St. John. Fols. 107r (line 24)–108r (line 7).]*

55   Than eche departed from other, and as soone as Merlin was departed fro Leonces, he wente to se a maiden of grete bewté; and [she] was right yonge, and was in a maner that was right feire and delitable and right riche, in a valee under a mounteyne rounde side, beside to the Forest of Briok that was full delitable and feire for to hunte at hertes and at hyndes and bukke and doo and wilde swyn.

60   This mayden of whom I speke was the doughter of a vavasor of right high lynage, and his name was cleped Dionas. And many tymes Diane com to speke with hym, that was the goddesse, and was with hym many dayes, for he was hir godsone. And whan she departed, she yaf hym a yefte that plesed hym wele. "Dionas," quod Diane, "I graunte thee, and so doth the god of the see and of the
65   sterres shull ordeyne, that the firste childe that thow shalt have female shall be so moche coveyted of the wisest man that ever was erthly or shall be after my deth, whiche in the tyme of Kynge Vortiger of the Bloy Mountayne shall begynne for to regne, that he shall hir teche the moste parte of his witte and connynge by force of nygremauncye in soche manere that he shall be so desirouse after the tyme that
70   he hath hir seyn that he shall have no power to do nothinge agein hir volunté. And alle thinges that she enquereth, he shall hir teche."

Thus yaf Diane to Dionas hir yefte, and whan Dionas was grete, he was right a

---

51 wete, know. **51–52 at youre yie**, with your eyes. **52 er**, before; **deed**, dead. **57 maner**, manor. **58 beside to**, near. **60 vavasor**, a lesser noble. **61 Diane**, the goddess Diana. **63 godsone**, godson; **yaf**, gave; **yefte**, gift. **64 see**, sea. **66 coveyted of**, desired by. **68 witte and connynge**, knowledge and skills. **68–69 by force of nygremauncye**, by the power of necromancy. **70 volunté**, wishes. **71 enquereth**, asks about. **72 yaf**, gave; **yefte**, gift; **was grete**, i.e., was a grown man.

feire knyght and a goode, of high prowesse of body, and he was moche and longe, and longe tyme served a Duke of Burgoyne that to hym yaf his nyece to ben his wif, that was right a feire maiden and a wise.

This Dionas loved moche the deduyt of the wode and the river while that he was yonge; and the Duke of Burgoyne hadde a parte in the Foreste of Brioke so that was his the halvendell all quyte; and that other half was the Kynge Ban. Whan the Duke hadde maried his nyece, he yaf to Dionas his part of this foreste and londe that he hadde aboute grete plenté. And whan Dionas wente it for to se, it plesed hym wele, and he lete make a maner to repeire to, that was right feire and riche by the Vyvier. And whan it was made, he com thider to be ther for the deduyt of the wode and the river that was nygh.

And ther aboode Dionas longe tyme, and repeired ofte to the court of Kynge Ban, [and] hym served with nine knyghtes. And in his servise he yede at many a grete nede agein the Kynge Claudas, to whom he dide many a grete damage, till that the Kynge Ban and the Kynge Boors hadden hym in grete love, for thei knewe hym so noble a knyght and so trewe. And the Kynge Ban to hym graunted his parte of this foreste in heritage to hym and to his heyres, and londe and rentys grete foyson. And the Kynge Boors yaf hym also a town and men and londe, for the grete trouthe that he saugh in hym. And he was so graciouse that alle tho that aboute hym repeyred loved hym above all thinge.

Thus dwelled Dionas in that londe longe tyme, till that he gat upon his wif a doughter of excellent bewté, and hir name was cleped Nimiane. And it is a name of Ebrewe that seith in Frensch, "ment neu ferai"; that is to sey in English, "I shall not lye." And this turned upon Merlin, as ye shall here herafter.

This mayden wax till she was twelve yere of age, whan Merlin com to speke with Leonces of Paerne. And Merlin spedde hym so that he com to the Foreste of Brioke, and than he toke a semblaunce of a feire yonge squyre and drowgh hym down to a welle, whereof the springes were feire and the water clere and the

73 **moche and longe**, large and tall. 76 **deduyt**, pleasure. 77 **hadde a parte in**, owned a section of. 77–78 **so that**, that. 78 **halvendell all quyte**, an even half [of the forest]. 79 **yaf**, gave. 81 **maner**, manor; **repeire to**, stay at. 82 **Vyvier**, the name of a river? 83 **deduyt**, pleasure. 85 **yede**, went. 86 **agein**, against. 89 **parte**, portion; **heyres**, heirs. 90 **foyson**, plenty. 91 **saugh**, saw; **tho**, those who. 92 **repeyred**, lived. 94 **cleped**, called. 95 **Ebrewe**, Hebrew; **seith**, means.

gravell so feire that it semed of fyn silver. To this fountayn ofte tyme com Nimiane for to disporte; and the same day that Merlin com thider was she come. And whan Merlin hir saugh, he behilde hir moche and avised hir well er he spake eny worde, and thought that a moche fole were he yef he slepte so in his synne to lese his

105 witte and his connynge for to have the deduyt of a mayden, and hymself shamed, and God to lese and displese.

And whan he hadde longe thought, he hir salued. And she ansuerde wisely and seide, "That lorde that alle thoughtes knoweth, sende hym soche volunté and soche corage that hym be to profite, and hym not greve ne noon other; and the same

110 welthe and the same honour hym sende as he wolde to other." And when Merlin herde the maide thus speke, he sett hym down upon the brinke of the welle and asked hir what she was. And she seide she was of this contrey, the doughter of a vavasour, a grete gentilman that was at a manoir therynne.

"And what be ye, feire swete frende?" quod she. "Damesell," quod Merlin, "I

115 am a squyer traveillinge that go for to seche my maister that was wonte me for to teche; and moche he is for to preise." "And what maister is that?" seide the maiden. "Certes," quod he, "he taught me so moche that I cowde here reyse a castell; and I cowde make withoute peple grete plenté that it sholde assaile, and withynne also peple that it sholde defende. And yet I sholde do mo maistries, for I cowde go

120 upon this water and not wete my feet; and also I cowde make a river whereas never hadde be water."

"Certes," seide the maiden, "these be queynte craftes, and fayn wolde I that I cowde do soche disportes." "Certes," seide the squyer, "yet can I mo delitable pleyes for to rejoise every high astate more than these ben, for noon can devise

125 nothinge but that I shall it do and make it to endure as longe as I will."

"Certes," seide the maiden, "yef it were to yow no gref, I wolde se somme pleyes by covenaunt that I sholde ever be youre love." "Certes," seide Merlin, "ye

103 **saugh,** saw; **moche,** greatly; **avised,** studied; **er,** before. 104 **moche fole,** great fool; **yef,** if; **slepte,** slipped; **lese,** lose. 105 **deduyt,** delight. 106 **lese,** lose. 107 **salued,** greeted. 108 **volunté,** wishes. 109 **corage,** desires. 112 **what,** who. 113 **vavasour,** a member of the gentry. 116 **moche,** much. 117 **cowde,** could; **reyse,** raise. 118 **withoute,** on the outside. 119 **mo maistries,** marvels; **go,** walk. 122 **queynte,** rare; **fayn wolde,** happily would. 123–24 **mo delitable pleyes,** more delightful marvels. 124 **noon,** no one. 125 **will,** wish. 126 **yef,** if; **gref,** grief. 127 **pleyes,** wonders; **by covenaunt,** with the agreement.

seme to me so pleasaunt and deboneir that for youre love I shall shewe yow a party of my pleyes, by covenaunt that youre love shall be myn, for other thinge
130 will I not aske."

And she hym graunted, that noon evell ne thought. And Merlin turned hym apart and made a cerne with a yerde in myddell of the launde; and than [he] returned to the maiden and satte agein down by the fountayn. And anoon the mayden beheilde and saugh come oute of the Foreste of Briogne ladyes and knyghtes and
135 maydons and squyres, eche holdinge other by the hondes; and [thei] com singinge and made the grettest joye that ever was seyn in eny londe. And before the maiden com jogelours and tymbres and tabours, and [thei] com before the cerne that Merlin hadde made. And whan thei were withynne, thei begonne the caroles and the daunces so grete and so merveilouse that oon myght not sey the fourthe parte of
140 the joye that ther was made. And for that the launde was so grete, Merlin lete rere a vergier whereynne was all maner of fruyt and alle maner of flowres that yaf so grete swetnesse of flavour that merveile it were for to telle. And the maiden that all this hadde seyn was abaisshed of the merveile that she saugh, and was so at ese that sche ne atended to nothinge but to beholde and entende what songe thei seiden,
145 saf that thei seiden in refreite of hir songe, "Vraiement, comencent amours en joye et fynissent en dolours."

In this maner dured the joye and feste from mydday to evenesonge, that oon myght here the noyse from fer, for it was right high and clere and plesaunt to heren, and it semed to be of moche peple. And oute of the castell com Dionas and
150 man and wif grete plenté, and beheilde and saugh the feire orcharde and the daunces and the caroles so feire and so grete, that never hadde thei seyn soche in theire lives. And thei merveilled gretly of the orcharde that thei saugh ther so feire ther noon was before; and on that other side thei merveiled whens alle these ladyes and

129 party, portion. **131 that . . . thought,** who suspected no mischief. **132 cerne,** circle; **yerde,** stick; **myddell,** middle; **launde,** meadow. **133 anoon,** soon. **137 jogelours,** jugglers; **tymbres,** tumblers; **tabours,** i.e., musicians; **cerne,** circle. **140 for that,** because; **rere,** rear (i.e., rise up). **141 vergier,** garden; **yaf,** gave. **143 abaisshed of,** astonished by. **144 entende,** study; **seiden,** said (i.e., sang). **145 saf,** except; **in refreite,** in the refrain; **hir,** their. **145–46 Vraiement . . . dolours,** Truly, love begins in joy and ends in sorrows. **148 here,** hear. **149 heren,** hear. **150 man and wif,** i.e., men and women. **152 ther²,** where.

155 the knyghtes were come so wele apareiled of robes and juewelles. And whan the caroles hadde longe dured, the ladyes and the maydenys satte down upon the grene herbes and fressh floures; and the squyres set up a quyntayne in myddes of the medowes, and wente to bourde a party of the yonge knyghtes; and on that other parte bourded the yonge squyres with sheldes, oon agein another, that never ne lefte till evesonge tyme.

160 And than com Merlin to the mayden and toke hir be the hande and seide, "Damesell, how seme ye?" "Feire swete frende," seide the mayden, "ye have don so moche that I am all yours." "Damesell," quod he, "now holde my covenaunt." "Certes," seide the mayden, "so shall I with goode chere." "Also," quod Merlin, "be ye eny clerk, and I shall teche yow so many merveilles that never woman 165 cowde so many."

Quod the maiden, "How knowe ye that I am a clerke?" "Damesell," quod Merlin, "I knowe it well, for my maister hath me so well taught that I knowe alle thinges that oon doth." "Certes," seide the mayden, "that is the moste connynge that ever I herde and moste myster were therof in many places; and that I wolde 170 faynest lerne. And of thinges that be to come, knowe ye ought?" "Certes," quod he, "swete love, yee, a grete part." "God mercy!" quod the mayden, "what go ye than sechinge?" "Truly," quod Merlin, "of that ye moste yet abide, yef it be youre plesier."

And while the mayden and Merlin helde this parlement, assembled agein the 175 maidenes and the ladyes, and wente daunsinge and bourdinge toward the foreste fro whens thei were come fyrste. And whan thei were nygh, thei entred in so sodaynly that oon ne wiste where thei were become. But the orcharde abode stille ther longe tyme, for the maiden that swetly therof hym praide, and was cleped ther by name the Repeire of Joye and of Feeste. And whan Merlin and the maiden 180 hadde be longe togeder, Merlin seyde at the laste, "Feire maiden, I go, for I have

155 **dured**, lasted. 156 **quyntayne**, tilting board; **in myddes**, in the middle. 157 **bourde**, sport with. 158 **bourded**, sported. 161 **how seme ye**, i.e., what do you think. 164 **be ye eny clerk**, i.e., if you are a scholar. 165 **cowde**, knew. 169 **moste myster**, greatest wonder. 170 **faynest**, most happily. 172 **of**, for; **abide**, wait; **yef**, if. 173 **plesier**, pleasure. 174 **parlement**, conversation. 175 **bourdinge**, playing. 176 **fro whens**, from whence. 177 **oon ne wiste**, one did not know. 178 **cleped**, named. 179 **Repeire**, The Abode; **Feeste**, Mirth.

moche to do in other place than here."

"How," quod the maiden, "feire frende, shull ye not teche me firste some of youre pleyes?" "Damesell," quod Merlin, "ne haste yow not sore, for ye shull know inowe all in tyme, for I moste have therto grete leyser and grete sojour, and

185 on that other side I have yet no suerté of youre love." "Sir," quod she, "what suerté wolde ye aske? Devise ye, and I shall it make."

"I will," quod Merlin, "that ye me ensure that youre love shall be myn, and ye also for to do my plesier of what I will." And the maiden her bethought a litill, and than she seide, "Sir," quod she, "with goode will, by soche forwarde that after

190 that ye have me taught all the thinges that I shall yow aske and that I can hem werke."

And Merlin seide that so it plesed hym well. Than he asured the maiden to holde covenaunt like as she hadde devised, and he toke hir sureté. Than he taught hir ther a pley that she wrought after many tymes, for he taught hir to do come a

195 grete river over all theras her liked, and to abide as longe as she wolde, and of other games inowe, whereof she wrote the wordes in perchemyn soche as he hir devised; and she it cowde full well bringe to ende. And whan he hadde abiden ther till evesonge tyme, he comaunded hir to God and she hym. But er he departed, the maiden hym asked whan he sholde come agein. And he seide on Seint Johnes

200 Even; and thus departed that oon fro that other.

And Merlin wente to Tamelide, where the kynges made hym grete joye whan that thei hym saugh. But now awhile we moste cesse here, and speke of the message that the Kynge de Cent Chivaliers sente to speke with the princes by the counseile of the kynge cleped Tradilyvaunt of North Wales.

183 pleyes, marvels; **ne haste yow not sore**, do not be in a hurry. **184 inowe**, enough; **moste**, must; **sojour**, time to stay. **186 suerté**, pledge. **187 will**, wish. **189 by soche forwarde**, with such agreement. **190 hem**, them. **193 sureté**, pledge. **194 pley**, marvel; **wrought**, worked; **to do come**, to make appear. **196 inowe**, enough; **perchemyn**, parchment. **197 cowde**, could. **199–200 Seint Johnes Even**, St. John's Eve. **202 saugh**, saw; **cesse**, cease.

[Arthur and Gonnore; and The Battle against King Rion]

*[**Summary**. The rebel barons meet at Leicester and commiserate over the damage done to their lands by the Saxons; King Lot laments the loss of his wife and children. The King de Cent Chevaliers urges them to join forces and engage the Saxons as a united army. They assemble their forces and camp beside the Severn River.*

Meanwhile Merlin arrives at the city of Toraise in Tamelide; he tells Arthur, Ban, and Bors how they must assist Leodogan in his forthcoming battle with King Rion. Merlin also makes several prophecies, including one about the engendering of "the gret leopart" (i.e., Lancelot). Fols. 109v (line 23)–111v (line 7).]

Than spake Merlin to the kynge and seide, "Sir, dismay yow nothinge, for be the feith that I owe unto yow, er that the Kynge Rion from yow ascape, he wolde have ben in hys contré all naked by the condicion that it hadde coste hym the beste citee that he hath. Ne ye be not at soche myschef but that ye have sixty thousande men at armes and moo. But I shall telle yow what ye shall do: sendeth ten of youre beste men for to serche the contrey that ther be neither asspie ne ribaude but anoon he be taken and brought before yow and put in prison, so that youre enmyes may nothinge knowe of youre ordenaunce. And than devise youre wardes and youre bateilles, and loke that ye make ten withoute mo; and in eche of hem ye shall putte ten thousande men. And than meveth on Monday two houres before day, and goth all esely oon after another withoute sore traveile and that we be ther on Wednysday at even.

"And I do yow to wite that on Thursday, a litill before day, we shall hem fynde all slepinge, for into the hoste is come grete plenté of flessh and of wyne and of

---

1 the kynge, i.e., Leodegan. **2 er**, before; **ascape**, escapes. **3 all naked**, i.e., vulnerable; **by the condicion**, with the result. **4 at soche myschef**, in such a plight; **but that**, because. **6–7 asspie ne ribaude**, spy nor robber. **8 ordenaunce**, plans; **devise**, arrange. **9 wardes**, companies; **bateilles**, divisions. **10 hem**, them. **11 esely**, slowly; **and**, so. **13 wite**, know. **14 flessh**, meat.

15   corne and other vitaile grete foyson; and thei drinke and ete ech day and trouble so theire braynes that thei sette litill wacche in theire hoste. But towarde the playnes thei have hemself closed with cartes and chariettes, that litill or nought oon may hem mysdo on that side. And therfore we moste werke wisely, for I knowe a place whereas thei take litill hede, and that wey ye shull hem alle fynde aslepe. And

20   therfore, yef God will, we shull somwhat have hem at oure wille, and we shull so chastice hem at this envay that thei shull have litill corage eny more in this londe to werrye."

Whan the Kynge Leodogan herde Merlin thus speke, he merveiled what he myght be. And he beheilde hym ententefly that he loked on noon other, and after

25   that he beheilde his felowes, that were stille and koy, that seiden not o worde but beheilde hym that spake. And whan he hadden hem beholden a longe while, he yaf a grete sighe and that was right sore. And [he] thought well in his corage that thei were right high men and gretter of astate than he cowde thinke. And aboute his herte com so grete errour that it wete all his visage with teeres of his yien, that

30   com from the herte that unethe myght he sowne oute o worde. And he fill down at her feet as half deed, and cride hem mercy so as he myght, that for the love of God thei sholde of hym have pitee and of his londe. "For I wote well," quod he, "and also myn herte telleth me, that I shall all lese yef God and ye be not my warant."

Whan that the Kynge Arthur saugh hym at erthe before hym knelinge, he hadde

35   therof grete pité, and so hadde the other kynges, and caught hym in her armes and reised hym up and assured hym of all that thei myght. And than thei wente to sitte down alle five togeder as goode felowes and trewe; and than began Merlin his reson and seide to the Kynge Leodogan, "Sir sire, ye wolde fayn wite what we ben and of what peple and of what lynage." And he seide ther was nothinge that

40   he desired so moche to knowe.

15 vitaile, food; **foyson,** amounts. **16 wacche in,** guard on; **playnes,** fields. **17 closed,** blocked off; **charietts,** wagons; **oon,** one. **18 hem mysdo,** harm them. **19 whereas,** where. **20 yef,** if; **will,** wishes. **21 envay,** assault; **corage,** desire. **22 werrye,** make war. **23 what,** who. **24 beheilde,** studied. **25 koy,** quiet; **o,** one. **27 yaf,** gave; **corage,** heart. **28 right,** very; **cowde thinke,** realized. **29 errour,** emotion; **teeres,** tears; **yien,** eyes. **30 unethe,** scarcely; **sowne oute o,** say one. **31 her,** their. **33 all lese yef,** everything lose if; **warant,** protection. **34 at erthe,** on the ground. **38 reson,** explanation; **fayn wite,** happily know. **38–39 what we ben,** who we are.

"I shall telle yow," quod Merlin, "firste for what we be come to seche. Lo, here a yonge lorde that is a goode knyght, as ye knowe well inough; and wite ye well in trouthe, whatsoever he be, he is a man of higher lynage and of londe and frendes than ye be, and yet ye be a kynge crowned. And he hath no wif, and therfore we come through londes to seche aventures till that we may fynde some high prince that his doughter wolde yeve hym in mariage."

"A! Lorde mercy!" quod the Kynge Leodogan. "What go ye ferther than sechinge? I have a doughter that is holden oon of the feirest of the worlde and the wiseste and oon of the beste lerned, and for defaute of goode lynage ne of goode londe ought she not to be refused. And yef it be youre plesier, I yeve hir yow to be youre wif. And I have no mo heires to whom my londe moste falle after my discesse." And Merlin ansuerde that he hir not sholde refuse never, yef God will; and thanked hym the foure felowes right hertely.

Than the kynge hymself wente to fecche his doughter, and made hir to be appareiled in the richest wise, and ledde hir be the honde into the chambre where-as the foure felowes dide abide. And after hem com grete route of knyghtes wherof therynne were grete plenté; and ther also were alle the companye of the Rounde Table, and the forty that the storye hath rehersed, and many other of high astate that were come into the hoste for to socoure the Kynge Leodogan.

And whan the kynge and his doughter entred thourgh the chambre that was feire and grete, the foure felowes com hem ageyns. And spake the Kynge Leodogan that he myght wele ben herde and seide, "Gentill sir, cometh forth — for I can not yet yow namen — and resceive here my doughter to be youre wif, that is so feire and courteise and therto right wise, with all the honour that to hir appendeth after my deth. For to a worthier than yow may I not hir yeve, and that knowe well alle these worthi men hereynne."

And Arthur stode forth and seide, "Sir, gramercy." And the Kynge Leodogan delyvered hir to hym by the right honde. And that oon graunted to that other full debonerly; and the kynge hem blissed with his right honde, and the Bisshop of Toraise was sent fore. And than was the joye grete therynne that never before

45

50

55

60

65

70

43 whatsoever he be, whoever he is. **46 yeve,** give. **47 What,** Why. **48 holden,** considered. **49 defaute,** lack. **50 yef,** if; **yeve,** give. **51 mo,** more. **52 discesse,** death. **54 fecche,** fetch. **55 be,** by. **56 route,** company. **61 hem ageyns,** to meet them. **64 therto,** also. **65 yeve,** give. **67 stode,** stepped. **69 debonerly,** courteously.

was ther seyn gretter.

And than com Merlin and spake to the kynge heringe alle that were therynne, "Sir, ye wolde gladly knowe what we be and to whom ye have yoven youre doughter." And the kynge that it so moche desired that yet wende it not to have knowen, seide certeynly, that gladly wolde he wite yef it were hir plesier.

"Now knoweth wele," quod Merlin, "and alle tho that it will heren, that ye have yoven youre doughter to Arthur, the Kynge of Bretaigne, the sone of Kynge Uterpendragon; and thei owe hym homage, bothe ye and alle the barouns of this reame. Now let hem don it, alle tho that will hym honour. And after shall we go the gladlyer and the more wightly to turneyen agein these sarazins that this londe do werryen and wolde take and distroien; but it shall be otherwise than thei wene. And also I do yow to undirstonde that these two noble men ben bretheren and also kynges crowned, and that oon is cleped the Kynge Ban of Benoyk, and that other the Kynge Boore of Gannes, and [thei] be comen of the heighest lynage that eny man knoweth. And alle these other felowes beth the sones of erles and barouns and castelleynes."

Whan the Kynge Leodogan and the other felowes undirstode that this was the Kynge Arthur, thei weren so gladde that never hadde thei so grete joye beforn. And the two kynges com first before hym and dide hym homage, and after the Kynge Leodogan and alle the other barouns; and thei made the feste of the mariage so riall that never in that londe was seyn soche. But over alle other was the Quene Gonnore gladde of hir newe lorde.

And that nyght Merlin lete hymself be knowen of the Knyghtes of the Rounde Table withoute eny moo. And whan the Kynge Leodogan hym knewe, he seide that God in this worlde hadde sente hym goode eure that to so noble and worthi man hadde hym yove the love and aqueyntance. "And from hensforth, gode Lorde God, do with me Thy wille, seth my londe and my doughter is be sette in so noble wise to the worthiest of the worlde." Thus seide the Kynge Leodogan; and than after thei yede to bedde for to reste. And on the morowe the kynge sente the

---

72 **heringe**, in the hearing of. 73 **yoven**, given. 75 **wite**, know. 76 **tho**, those. 77 **yoven**, given. 80 **wightly**, swiftly. 81 **werryen**, war upon. 82 **do**, want. 83 **oon**, one; **cleped**, called. 86 **castelleynes**, constables. 91 **riall**, royal; **over alle other**, beyond all others. 94 **withoute eny moo**, but to no one else. 95 **eure**, fortune. 96 **yove**, given. 97 **seth**, since. 99 **yede**, went.

100   knyghtes into tho parties as Merlin hym taught whereas the peple of Kynge Rion sholde assemble, and than devised his wardes of his bataile whereof were ten.

    In the firste warde, whereas the dragon was, was the Kynge Arthur and the Kynge Ban and the Kynge Boors and her forty felowes; and so were the Knyghtes of the Rounde Table and so many of other that thei were seven thousand men right
105   well armed. And the seconde warde ledde Guyomar, the kynges cosin, with seven thousand men of armes. The thridde warde ledde Elunadas, a yonge lorde that was nevew to the Wise Lady of the Foreste Saunz Retour. The fourthe bataile ledde Blios, the lorde of Cloadas, a merveillouse castell, and were with hym seven thousand men of armes and horse of prise. The fifth warde ledde Aridolus, a knyght of
110   grete renoun, and weren also seven thousand men. The sixte bataile ledde Belcys le Loys, that was inough riche and puyssaunt, and hadde with hym also seven thousand men of armes well horsed. The seventh bataile ledde Ydiers of the londe of Norwey, to whom the feire aventure fell in the courte of Kynge Arthur of the five ringes that he drough oute of the deed knyghtes honde that asked vengaunce,
115   that never knyght that was in that court myght have, as the tale shall yow declare hereafter; and he hadde in hys companye seven thousand, and he was a noble knyght and an hardy. The eighth bateile ledde Landons, the nevew of the stiward of Tamelide, that was a full noble knyght of his honde; and he ledde seven thousand in his companye soche as he hadde brought. The ninth bateile ledde Groinge
120   Poire Mole, that was a noble knyght of his body, but he hadde no gretter nose than a cat; this chese oute seven thousand in whom he trusted. And the tenth bataile ledde the Kynge Leodogan and his stiwarde Cleodalis, that right wele cowde hym helpe; and were in her companye ten thousand, what oon and other, that wolde not fle for lif ne lym.

125   Whan these batailes were dissevered that oon from that other and renged by hemself, thei devised whan thei shulde meve. And thus thei acorded that on the morowe after Pentecoste thei shulde move at the firste cok crowynge. And than thei rested all day and on the morn, for on the Witsonday the Kynge Leodogan

---

100 **tho parties,** those companies; **whereas,** where. 101 **wardes,** divisions; **bataile,** army. 109 **prise,** great value. 111 **puyssaunt,** powerful. 114 **drough,** drew. 121 **this chese oute,** i.e., he chose. 123 **what oon and other,** all told. 124 **lif ne lym,** life nor limb. 125 **dissevered,** separated. 126 **acorded,** agreed. 128 **the Witsonday,** Whitsunday.

helde court roiall for love of the barouns that ther were assembled.

130   And the thre kynges and Merlin satte togeder at the hede of the deyse; and before hem satte the two Gonnores that were wonder like, saf a litill that oon was heigher and fressher coloured, and that was Arthurs wif; and the better tonge she hadde, for she was of all the worlde the feirest speker and the beste, and also she hadde more heer than the tother Gonnore. But of alle other thinges thei resembled
135 so like that unethe myght oon knowe that oon from that other. And after satte the felowes that Arthur hadde brought with the Knyghtes of the Rounde Table for chierté and gret love, for so wolde Merlin and Gynebans the Clerke. And whan thei hadde eten, thei wente to bedde; but litill while thei lay, for thei roos at mydnyght.

140   Whan the armes of Kynge Arthur were brought, Gonnore hym helped for to arme right wele and feire, as she that right wele cowde her therof entermete; and hirself girde hym with his swerde. And whan the kynge was all armed saf his helme, she toke the spores and sette hem on bothe knelinge. And Merlin, that all this behilde, began to laughe and shewde to the two kynges how Gonnore hir
145 entermeted and peyned hym to serve. And hir preised moche the twey kynges. But in the fin, she hadde a riche guerdon whan she loste the kynge hir lorde by mysaventure and by Bertelaux the traitour, as the book shall reherse hereafter.

    And while Merlin beheilde the maiden that served hir lorde, he lough and seide to the kynge as he that cowde all goode and full well cowde jape in myrthe and
150 game, "Sir sire, never were ye so verily a newe knyght as ye be now, and ther ne faileth bot o thinge that ye were alle a newe knyght. And well may ye sey whan ye departe hens that a maiden that is a kynges doughter and quenes hath made yow a newe knyght." "Sir," seide the kynge, "sey what thinge that is and my lady shall it do, but yef it be to grete a thinge or that she sholde therby have shame."

---

130 deyse, dais. **131 hem,** them; **wonder like,** wondrously alike; **saf,** except that. **132 heigher,** taller. **135 unethe,** scarcely; **oon,** one. **137 chierté,** affection; **wolde,** desired. **141 right wele cowde her therof entermete,** i.e., very much wished to be involved. **142 saf,** safe. **144 shewde to,** showed. **144–45 hir entermeted,** involved herself. **145 peyned hym to serve,** took pains to serve him. **146 fin,** end; **guerdon,** reward. **147 mysaventure,** ill fortune. **148 lough,** laughed. **149 the kynge,** i.e., Arthur; **jape,** joke. **151 sey,** say. **152 hens,** hence. **154 but yef,** unless; **to grete,** too hard.

155   "Certes, sire," seide the maiden full wisely, as she that [was] full well lerned, "in nothinge that I do to yow may I have no shame ne vilonye, for I knowe yow so noble and worthy and also curteyse that ye wolde me not requere nothinge that to vilonye shulde turne for the beste castell that ye have." "Lady," seide Merlin, "ye sey wisely. Never for nothinge that I have seide shall ye have no reprof ne that

160   sholde turne yow to no shame."

    "What is it, than?" seide the kynge. "I pray yow telle me."

    "Sir," seide Merlin, "hit is the baisyers, yef to the lady it plese." "Certes," seide the kynge, "and for that shall I not leve to be a newe made knyght." "No," quod the maiden, "as for that shall I yow not lese, but that ye shull be myn and I yowrs.

165   And why sholde ye therof me preyen, for also well it pleseth me as it doth to yow."

    Whan the kynge herde hir thus sey, he began to laugh. Than the kynge toke hir in armes and kissed hir swetly, as yonge peple that full well togeder loved. And than were the horse apareiled and brought forth. And Gonnore yaf hir lorde an

170   helme of merveillouse bountee, and he sette it on his heed; and than ech comaunded other to God. And rode forth eche warde after other, the ganfanouns folden and the speres lowe, and rode a softe pas as Merlin hym guyded, as he that wele knewe alle the passages. And the ten knyghtes that were gon before hadde taken mo than ten pantoneres that alle weren espies of the Kynge Rion, and bounde hem and

175   sette hem in prison, and kepte so well the passages that thei herde no tidinges.

    And so well spedde hym Merlin that the firste warde dide condite that thei come the Wednysday at nyght after the mydnyght into the hoste of Kynge Rion. And the nyght was right clere and stille, but the moone shone a litill trouble. And thei slepte strongeliche in the hoste for the tyme that relented, for on the day was

180   right grete hete in the hoste, and therto thei hadden dronken inough. And Merlin sette in betwene the wode and the river, and comaunded that no man presse into

159 **no reprof ne**, no blame. 162 **baisyers**, kisses; **yef**, if. 163 **leve**, fail. 164 **lese**, fail; **but that**, so that. 165 **preyen**, ask; **also well**, just as much. 169 **apareiled**, readied; **yaf**, gave. 170 **bountee**, strength. 170–71 **comaunded other**, commended the other. 171 **ganfanouns folden**, standards furled. 172 **a softe pas**, at a slow pace; **guyded**, directed. 173 **passages**, backroads. 174 **pantoneres**, spies. 175 **kepte**, watched. 176 **dide condite**, conducted. 178 **trouble**, darkly. 179 **strongeliche**, deeply; **relented**, remained. 180 **hete**, heat. 181 **sette in**, placed them; **presse into**, attack.

the hoste till that thei herde an horne blowe. And as the wardes passeden over oon after another, Merlin abode hem alle and made hem close togeder. And than wente Merlin to the baner and toke an horne and blewe it so lowde that all the foreste

185 and the river resownnded, that a man myght heere the horne well half a myle.

Than Merlin cried, "Lady Seint Marie, praye to oure Lorde God, thi blissed Sone, that He now be oure helpe. Now sette on manly," quod he, "gentill knyghtes, for now shall it be sein who is noble and worthi; for I do yow to wete that ye be alle at the deth or at the lif, and noon ne hath no heede but he hit now deffende."

190 And whan thei herde the horne, anoon thei slaked theire reynes and spored theire horse and smote into the hoste with grete ravyne. And ther ye sholde have sein tentes and pavilouns reverse to the grounde, for Merlin by crafte made soche a trobellion arise that ther lefte nother tente ne pavilon stondinge, but fellen upon theire heedes that lay withynne. And thei smyten into the hoste on alle parties, and

195 slowgh and maymed what thei myght areche, for ther was made of hem grete slaughter er thei were aparceyved in the hoste what peple thei were, till that thei herde the brayes and the dolerouse cries as thei weren slain and mangeled of hem that of hir deth hadde no pitee.

Than comaunded the heigh lordes to theire squyres to make theire horse redy

200 thourgh the hoste, and thei so dide; and than thei ronne to armes hastely, and peyned hem harde to be smartly armed and soone. And as soone as thei myght be armed, thei assembled at the tente of Kynge Rion, and blowen hornes and trumpes right harde. And the Cristin hadde so hurled amonge hem up and down that mo than thre thousande thei hadde so araied that never repeired thens, and [thei]

205 chase the remenaunt to Kynge Rions tente ther thei made hir gaderinge; and ther thei stalled, for thei were moche peple and stronge. And than armed hem thei that were not armed, and tho apered the feire day and cleire. And than the wardes drowen up and appereilled hem in ordre, and eche gadered his peple aboute hym; and ther thei reised theire baners alofte that flekered in the wynde. And the bright

183 **abode**, awaited. 188 **do yow to wete**, want you to know. 190 **slaked**, loosened. 191 **ravyne**, rage. 192 **reverse**, fall. 193 **trobellion**, wind; **nother**, neither. 194 **parties**, sides. 195 **slowgh**, slew; **what**, whoever; **areche**, find. 196 **were aparceyved**, realized. 197 **brayes**, shouts. 203 **Cristin**, Christians. 204 **araied**, stood. 207 **tho apered**, then appeared. 208 **drowen up**, were drawn up; **appereilled hem**, arranged. 209 **flekered**, flapped.

210   sonne smote upon the bright armurs that it glistered so bright that merveile was to
beholden.

Whan the Kynge Rion saugh the damage that thei hadde hym don, he was nygh
wode for ire, and satte upon a grete horse that was wonder stronge and swight,
and hadde an ax hanginge at his sadill before that was grete and hevy of harde
215   stiell, and rode up and down, devisinge who sholde go before and who sholde go
behynde. And than he cleped Solynas, a knyght of grete prowesse and right hardy
that was his nevew, and seide, "Solinas, thow shalt lede the first bataile with an
hundred thousande men of armes of soche peple as ye will; and thow shalt go and
avenge my shame and youre harmes." And he seide he wolde well, so that he
220   wolde deserve of hym no blame.

Than departed he that was wight and hardy and merveillouse stronge. And as
soone as Merlin saugh hym come, he rode hym ageins with the dragon, and he
hym disfigured in soche manere that no man saugh who it bar saf the thre kynges.
Whan Merlin saugh that he com nygh, he seide to the Kynge Arthur, "Arthur,"
225   quod he, "now shall it be sene how well ye shull do, and loke that the kisse that
youre love yow yaf be to somme solde so dere that ever after therof be spoken."
And he ansuerde agein and seide that in hym sholde be no feyntise; and no more
he ne seide. And than approched that oon bataile to that other right nygh, and than
thei leide theire speres in fewtre and mette togeder with trenchaunt heedes upon
230   the sheldes that ech hurte other and wounded and bar to the grounde. Ther dide
the Kynge Arthur a pointe that moche was beholden.

Whan Arthur saugh bothe parties so nygh approche, he smote the horse with
the spores agein Jonap, a grete geaunt and merveillous stronge. And he saugh
hym so come, he douted hym but litill, for he semed agein hym but a chielde. Thei
235   com faste and rudely, and Arthur was smyte with Jonappes spere in the shelde so
rudely that the shafte passed thourgh his lifte flanke an arme lengthe; and Arthur
smote hym agein so sore that thourgh shelde and sholdre he shof the trenchaunt

210 **glistered**, glistened; **bright**, brightly. **212–13 nygh wode for ire**, nearly mad with
rage. **213 swight**, swift. **216 cleped**, called. **219 wolde well**, would. **221 wight**, able. **222
hym ageins**, toward him. **223 hym disfigured**, disguised himself; **it bar saf**, the dragon
carried except. **226 yaf**, gave. **227 feyntise**, cowardice. **229 in fewtre**, in their holders.
233 And, And when; **he**, i.e., Jonap. **234 douted**, feared. **235 smyte**, smitten. **236 rudely**,
strongly; **lifte**, left.

spere; but the sarazin was so proude and of so grete strength that he made no
semblaunt of no grevaunce. But [thei] hurteled togeder so rudely with theire bodyes
240 and with the myght of theire horse that eche bar other to erthe, and the horse upon
theire bodyes; and ther thei lay a longe while sore astonyed that the ton cowde
telle no tidinges of the tother. Than ronne to the rescowse on bothe two sides; ther
was many a grete spere crased and stronge stour of swerdes upon helmes and
sheldes. Ther loste the geauntes more than the Cristin, but nevertheles, thei
245 traveyled so on bothe parties that bothe were thei releved and sette on horse; and
than began the stoure stronge and merveillouse. Ther dide the Knyghtes of the
Rounde Table wondres, and the Forty Felowes, for agein hem myght endure noon
harneys ne no kynge ne warde ne sheltron, were it never so clos.

[**Summary**. *A great and lengthy battle ensues between the Christians and King
Rion's army. A young knight named Nascien performs deeds of great valor, and the
writer notes that later on Nascien becomes a hermit and is the person who records the
events of the Grail story, which he writes in a book that is "anexed to the booke that
Blase wrote." During the battle Merlin rebukes Arthur for having done little, and
shortly thereafter, Arthur spies King Rion among the throng and pursues him relent-
lessly. Fols. 114v (line 13)–119r (line 14).*]

So longe Arthur enchased the Kynge Rion that he hym atteyned in a depe valey
250 betwene a litill wode and a medowe at a passage of a litill brooke that com rennynge
of two welle sprynges of a mountayne; and the sonne was so lowe that for the
mounteynes and the wode hit was all derke. And ther overtoke Arthur the Kynge
Rion, and than he cried, "Turne thee, cowarde geaunte, or thow shalt dye fleynge,
for thow seist well ther is no moo here but thow and I."
255 And whan the geaunte undirstode the kynge that so hym maneced, he helde
therof grete dispite, for he saugh that he semed ageyn hym but a childe. Than he
returned toward hym with his betell in his honde, and put his targe hym beforn

241 **astonyed**, stunned; **ton**, one. 242 **tother**, other. 243 **crased**, shattered; **stour**, clash.
245 **traveyled**, labored; **parties**, sides. 246 **stoure**, battle. 247–48 **noon harneys**, no
weapons. 248 **warde**, troop; **sheltron**, company. 249 **he**, i.e., Arthur; **atteyned in**,
reached. 254 **moo**, more. 255 **maneced**, challenged. 256 **dispite**, insult; **saugh**, saw.
257 **betell**, club, hammer; **targe**, shield.

that was of the bon of an olyfaunte; and the Kynge Arthur helde a shorte spere
with a longe trenchaunt heede of sharp grounde steill. And [thei] ronne togeder
260 wroth and maletalentif that oon agein that other, and that oon desiraunt of pris and
honour, and that other covetouse to avenge hys shame and his harme. The Kynge
Arthur com faste for he was meved from fer, and Rion hym abode with his betill
in his honde; and Arthur hym smote so sore with this spere thourgh the shelde,
though it were never so harde, that the stiell passed through two plites of the
265 hauberke on the lifte side, that the blode lepe oute grete foyson that all the shafte
was covered in blode. But for no myght that he cowde shove myght he not make
hym to remeve his sadill; and the spere splyndered in peces.

And whan the geaunte felte hymselfe wounded, he gnasshed his teth and rolled
his iyen that were grete swollen for ire and malentelent that he hadde; and he lifte
270 up his betill of brasse as he that was merveillouse grete and stronge above alle tho
that eny man knewe in tho dayes; and as the boke seith, he was fourteen foote of
lengthe, and half a palme betwene his browes, and was grete and lene and full of
veynes and senewes, and was also so grym a figure that he was dredefull for to
beholde.

275 Whan Arthur saugh the geaunte lifte up his malle, he douted the stroke and ran
to hym so rudely with the body of his horse that he bar to the erthe bothe Rion and
his horse. But soone was he upon his foote, but first was Arthur garnysshed of his
armes er the geaunt were reised; for Arthur was also fallen to grounde with the
frayinge that thei hurteled togeder. And Arthur was wight and lifly, and yet hadde
280 he not but twenty yere of age; and the Kynge Rion hadde moo than forty-two
largely, and was grete and hevy by the thirde part more than he. And as soone as
thei were up, thei ronne ther togeder; and Arthur griped Calibourne, his goode
swerde that he pulde oute of the ston, wherwith that day he hadde yove many a
stroke. And as soone as he hadde it drawen oute, hit yaf so grete light as it hadde
285 ben a grete bronde of fire, and covered hym with his shelde and raught a stroke to

258 **bon**, bone; **olyfaunte**, elephant. 260 **maletalentif**, angrily; **pris**, praise. 261
covetouse, desiring. 262 **betill**, club. 264 **plites**, layers. 265 **lifte**, left; **foyson**, quantity.
267 **remeve**, budge from. 269 **iyen**, eyes; **malentelent**, hatred. 270 **betill**, club; **tho**,
those. 275 **malle**, mallet; **douted**, feared. 276 **rudely**, strongly. 278 **were reised**, got up.
279 **wight**, agile; **lifly**, lively. 281 **largely**, at least. 283 **yove**, given. 284 **hit yaf**, it gave.
285 **raught**, dealt.

the geaunte er he were covered upon the heede. And whan he saugh the stroke comynge, he caste the shelde ther agein, for sore he dredde the stroke of the swerde that he saugh so bright shynynge, for he knewe it was of right grete bountee.

290 And the Kynge Arthur smote so in the malle that he helde before hym in bothe hondes that he kutte the helve asonder faste by the hede, and yet was it bounde with iren. The stroke was grete and rudely smyten and discended upon the corner of his shelde that he slitte it to the bokill; and with the plukkynge of his swerde agein to hym, he made the Kynge Rion for to stomble, that was sory for his
295 brasen malle that he hadde so loste. And than he leide honde to his swerde that was oon of the beste of the worlde, for as the booke seith, it was som tyme Hercules, that ledde Jason into the Ile of Colchos for to fecche the flees of goolde; and with that swerde dide Hercules sle many a geaunte in that londe where Jason ledde Medea that so moche hym loved; but after, he hir failled, whereas Hercules
300 hir dide helpe by his grete debonertee. And the booke seith that Vlcan iforged that swerde in the tyme of Adrastus, the Kynge of Greece, that many a day hadde in his tresour. This same swerde hadde Tideus, the sone of the Duke of Calcedoyne, that day that he dide the message to Ethiocles for Polemyte; and in his comynge homwarde with the same swerde he slowgh fifty at an hill. And after wente this
305 swerde fro hande to hande and from heir to heir that now hath it the Kynge Rion that com of the lynage of Hercules that was so noble and hardy.

Whan the Kynge Rion saugh his malle smyten asonder, he drough this swerde that was of so grete bountee; and as soone as it was oute of the skawberke, it caste so grete claretee that it semed a flame of fire; and the name of this swerde was
310 Marmyadoise. And whan Arthur saugh the swerde that so flambed, he preised it moche in his herte and drough hym a litill up, hit to beholde, and coveyted it right sore, and thought that in goode houre were he born that it myght conquere. And whan the Kynge Rion saugh hym stonde so stille, he withstode and hym aresoned as ye shull here.

315 "Sir knyght," quod he, "I wote never what thow art, but thow haste do grete

291 helve, handle; **by**, near. **292 rudely smyten**, strongly struck. **293 bokill**, buckle. **295 brasen malle**, brass hammer. **297 flees**, fleece. **299 failled**, betrayed. **300 debonertee**, courtesy. **307 saugh**, saw; **malle**, mallet; **drough**, drew. **309 claretee**, brightness. **314 here**, hear. **315 wote never what**, never knew who; **do**, done.

hardynesse that me durste sue or chace alone withoute companye; and for the prowesse that I se in thee, I shall do thee grete curtesie that I dide never to no man. Yeve me that swerde and thyn armes and telle me thy name; and after thow shalt go quyte, for I have grete pité for to sle thee for that thow semest so yonge."

320   Whan Arthur undirstode the wordes of the Kynge Rion, he hadde therof grete dispite, and ansuerde hym felly. "How wenest to take me so lightly, that I sholde yelde me recreaunt for that thow art so grete and so stronge! But ley down that swerde and tho armes and putte thee in my mercy, to do with thee my plesier outerly, for I thee assure but the deth."

325   At these wordes lowgh the geaunte and turned the heede in traverse and asked hym what he was and what was his name, and conjured hym by his creaunce to sey the trouthe. And Arthur seide he wolde telle hym by covenaunt what he were; and he hym graunted. "Now knowe thow well," quod he, "that my name is Arthur of Bretaigne, the sone of Uterpendragon, that am come to chalenge this reame that

330 is myn all quyte, for the Kynge Leodogan hath yove me hys doughter to my wif, and me have don homage alle the high barouns of this reame, and also he hymself. Now telle me what thow art, and what is thy name, for I have tolde the thee trouthe of myn."

    Quod the geaunte, "Seist thow trouthe that thow art Arthur, the sone of

335 Uterpendragon, that slough Aungis before the Roche of Saisnes?" "Of the same, speke I withoute faile," quod Arthur. "I have made covenaunt," quod the geaunte, "that I shall telle thee myn name. I do thee to wite that I am the Kynge Rion of Iselonde and of alle the londes unto pastures and yef ferther, yef a man myght ferther passe. But oon may never passe till that the lawes be broken that Judas

340 Makabeus ther sette; and as olde auncient seyn that thei shall never be hadde awey till the aventures begynne in the reame of Logres of the Seynt Graal; and it behoveth hym to caste to the portes of the Goulf of Sathanye that it be never seyn after, for it is so of soche maner that so it moste be fallen. Now I have tolde thee

---

316 durste sue, dare to pursue. **318 Yeve**, Give. **319 quyte**, free. **321 dispite**, insult; **felly**, fiercely; **How wenest to**, Why do you. **322 recreaunt**, shamed. **324 outerly**, entirely; **thee assure but**, promise you [nothing] but. **325 lowgh**, laughed; **in traverse**, around. **326 what[1]**, who; **conjured**, urged; **creaunce**, faith. **330 all quyte**, entirely; **yove**, given; **me**, to me. **335 slough**, slew. **337 do thee to wite**, want you to know.

what I am. But I will never ete while I knowe thee on lyve, for by thee it is that I
345   am thus disconfited and chased from the felde; and therfore shall I avenge my
dooll yef I may."

"So helpe me God," quod Arthur, "than shalt thow longe be fastinge, for that
shall never falle that I shall be deed thourgh thee. And lo, here my swerde that thee
deffieth to the deth! And yef thow be so hardy, take now the vengaunce of hym
350   that thee diffieth to smyte of thyn heede."

And whan the geaunte herde Arthur thus speke, he was so wroth that nygh he
yede oute of his witte, and griped his shelde and com with his swerde in his honde
and lifte it high to smyte Arthur on the helme. But he caste the shelde ther agein
and lepte aside in the felde; and he smote so harde that a quarter fill to the erthe.
355   And Arthur stepped forth and yaf hym soche a stroke by the lifte yie and made
hym a grete wounde; and yef the swerde hadde not swarved, maymed hadde he
ben for ever. Whan the geaunte felt hym wounded and saugh the blode raile downe
by the lifte iye, he was nygh wode out of witte; and than he ran upon hym, for he
wende to take hym in his armes. But Arthur dide lepe aside, for abide that wolde
360   he not, and therwith raught hym a grete stroke; and ever he hym pursued with
swerde in honde, but atteyne hym myght he not.

And while thei demened hem in this manere, fill so that Nascien and Adragains
and Hervy de Rivell com upon hem, that chaced six Sarazins full fiercely, and alle
six were kynges; and that oon hight Cahainus, and that other Maltaillees, and the
365   thirde Fernicans, and the forth Heroars, and the fifth Branremes, and the sexthe
the stronge Kynge Mahidrap. These six kynges com down the rocher sore hem
diffendinge, and the swyfte horse com dryvinge like a tempest. And whan the
tweyne that foughten herde this noyse and brunt of hem that fledden, and behelde
and saugh the six kynges that the thre knyghtes chaced, the Kynge Rion was sore
370   adredde, for he knewe tho that ther com, for he wiste well thei were noble and
hardy; and yef he lenger ther abide, he knewe well that dye he moste.

Than he com to his horse and lept up lightly, and in the lepinge up Arthur hym

344 thee on lyve, you [are] alive. **345 disconfited**, defeated. **346 dooll yef**, sorrow if. **350
of**, off. **352 yede**, went. **354 fill**, fell. **355 yaf**, gave; **yie**, eye. **357 raile**, flow. **358 wode**,
mad. **359 wende**, hoped. **360 raught**, struck. **361 atteyne**, catch. **362 demened hem**,
conducted themselves. **364 oon hight**, one was named. **366 rocher sore hem**, field
vigorously themselves. **368 brunt**, tumult. **370 tho**, those.

smote so harde that he kutte awey a quarter of his helme that the mailes of the
hauberke apered all white, and astoned hym sore that he bowed on his horse
375 nekke; and yef he myght have recovered another stroke, he hadde fallen of his
horse to the erthe. But the horse was of grete force and aferde of the stroke, and
turned to flight with the kynge down the roche.

*[**Summary**. Arthur chases Rion but is overtaken by the six kings who attack him.
Arthur quickly hacks the arms off one of them and slices another clear down to his
teeth; then Nascien and Adrageins and Hervey rush to Arthur's aid. The battle rages
on, and a little later King Rion and Arthur once again confront each other. Fols.
120v (line 29)–122r (line 12).]*

Ther was slayin Mahidrap and Balfinnes and Gloriex and Mandones, wherefore the Kynge Rion was full wroth, for thei were his nygh kyn. And whan Kynge
380 Rion saugh this myschaunce turne upon hym so grete, he was so wroth that nygh
he was oute of his witte. And he helde his swerde naked and ran upon Arthur and
wende to smyte hym on the heede; but he glenched aside, for sore he dredde the
stroke of the geaunte. And he smote so harde in the shelde that he slitte it into the
myddell; and whan that he wende to pulle agein his swerde, the Kynge Arthur
385 smote hym on the arme that sore he hym hurte. And he lefte the swerde stykinge
in the shelde, that sore felt hym hurte and was wode for wrath. And Arthur caste
down the shelde with the swerde, for it dide hym but gref. And whan the geaunte
saugh that he hadde so loste his swerde, he was full of grete sorowe, and ran
upon Arthur with his horse and caught hym by the shuldres and wolde have hym
390 born with force, and so he sholde have don yef he hadde leiser, for he was of
grete strengthe.
    Whan Arthur felte the geaunte that so hym helde, he caste the swerde to the
erthe, for he was ferde leste he sholde have taken it from hym by force, and than
clippid his horse in bothe his armes aboute the nekke. And the geaunte pulled and
395 drough, but he myght hym not arace from the sadell. And the Kynge Ban behelde
and saugh the strif betwene the geaunte and Arthur, and anoon spored his horse

373 **kutte**, cut. 374 **astoned**, stunned; **bowed on**, slumped over. 375 **recovered**, received. 378 **slayin**, slain. 382 **glenched**, moved. 387 **dide hym but gref**, hindered him.
394 **clippid**, clasped. 395 **drough**, tugged; **arace**, remove.

that wey, for he hadde of hym grete drede. And [whan] the geaunte saugh hym come he lefte Arthur, for sore he douted the Kynge Ban, and ran upon hym with his handes that were grete and square. And the Kynge Ban hym smote with
400 Corsheuse, his goode swerde, that he rente his hauberke betwene his sholderes and wounde hym right depe.

And whan the Kynge Rion felt hym so sore wounded and saugh his felowes ly at erthe deed bledynge, he hadde grete drede, for he hadde nothinge hym to diffende, and turned the horse that was of gret bounté and wente fleynge as faste as he
405 myght renne. And thei lete hym passe, for it was nyght. And he wente so wroth that for litill he hadde gon oute of witte. And he cursed his feith and his creaunce, and seide he wolde never cesse in all his age till that he were avenged; and as soone as he com into his contré he wolde sende for his grete hoste so that no londe sholde agein hym endure till he hadde confounded all Bretaigne and all the
410 peple therynne, and take the Kynge Arthur and his helpers, and do hem be flayn all quyk. Thus wente Kynge Rion, makynge grete sorowe and weymentacion into his contrey.

Whan the Kynge Ban socoured the Kynge Arthur from the Kynge Rion that so wolde aborn hym awey, he com to Arthur and asked hym yef he hadde eny harme;
415 and he seide "Nay." Than seide Ban, "Where is youre swerde?" And Arthur seide it was at erthe, "For I caste it down as soone as the shrewe com rennynge on me to gripe me in his armes. And I have wonne the richest jewell, and that I love more than the richest citee that I have."

"What thinge is that?" seide the Kynge Ban. "That shall ye se anoon," quod
420 Arthur. Than he sette foot to grounde and yede firste to Calibourne and putte it in the skaberke, whan he hadde dried it clene, and than com to his shelde where-ynne stake the swerde of Kynge Rion. And he drough it oute and toke the shelde and com to his horse and lepte up, and than shewde the swerde to the Kynge Ban. And it shone so bright that Arthur hadde therof grete joye, and preide God sende
425 hym som aventure ther he myght it assay and prove yef it were so grete of bounté as it hadde bewtee.

And thei were ner the citee than thei wende; but er thei com ther hem fill soche

398 **douted**, feared. 406 **creaunce**, religion. 410 **do hem**, cause them. 410–11 **flayn all quyk**, skinned alive. 411 **weymentacion**, lamentation. 416 **shrewe**, wretch. 420 **yede**, went. 425 **ther**, where. 427 **ner**, nearer to; **wende**, thought.

aventure that ther was noon so wight ne hardy but he hadde inough to done. But now resteth a litell of hem and speke of the Kynge Leodogan.

[Summary. King Leodegan and his steward Cleodalis find themselves separated from the rest of their troops in the dark. The enemy attack them, killing Leodegan's horse; Cleodalis sets his lord on his own horse and urges him to ride to safety, but Leodegan will not go without him. By enchantment, Merlin raises a storm and confounds the enemy. Meanwhile Arthur fights well using Marmyadoise, the sword he captured from King Rion. Then Merlin urges Arthur and the others to ride to the rescue of Cleodalis and Leodegan; Arthur's troop arrives at midnight and saves them. After losing several of their leaders, the enemy forces flee. Arthur's forces rest and eat, and then Arthur dispenses riches among his men. Then they ride toward the city of Toraise. Fols. 122v (line 23)–127r (line 30).]

430   Whan the Kynge Arthur and his companye com to Toraise, thei were richely resceyved with grete honour. And ther thei sojourned two dayes. And the thridde day com the Kynge Leodogan to the Kynge Arthur and hym somowned to spousen his doughter Gonnore. And Merlin seide that he moste firste do another grete werke, and the kynge asked what. And Merlin seide that he moste firste passe into
435   the reame of Benoyk, and tolde hym for what nede; but that was in counseile, for he wolde not have the thinge knowen of no man that sholde go thider. And whan he herde the nede, he praide hym to repeire agein as sone as he myght. And Merlin seide he neded not nothinge therof hym to prayen, and bad make hem redy, "for tomorowe moste we remove." Quod Arthur, "Shall we not abide the Kynge
440   Bohors, that is at the Castell of Charroye?" Quod Merlin, "Ye shull abyde hym at Bredigan, youre castell." And Arthur seide that all sholde be at his wille.

       Than thei hem appareilleden, and on the morowe sette hem on here wey. And so departed the Kynge Leodogan and the Kynge Arthur, and kisten at the departynge. And Gonnore hym praide soone to come agein, "For never," quod
445   [she], "shall I be in ese of herte unto the tyme that I yow se agein." And the kynge seide that he wolde he were come agein oute of the contrey.

---

428 wight ne, able nor; **done**, do. **432 spousen**, marry. **435 counseile**, private. **437 repeire**, return. **441 at his wille**, i.e., as Merlin wished.

Arthur and Gonnore; and The Battle against King Rion

[**Summary**. Arthur, the Knights of the Round Table, and a force of 20,000 travel to Bredigan. In the meantime, King Ban and his brother Guynebans the Clerk have an adventure deep in a forest where they encounter an old knight, a lovely young woman, and carol dancers in a meadow. Guynebans is smitten by the woman's beauty; he tells her that if she will give him her love, he will make the dancers go on dancing until a knight comes who has never been false to his love, a knight who will be the best knight of his time. She agrees, and Guynebans begins his enchantments. He also makes a chessboard on which only a man who has never been false to his love can achieve checkmate. Ban then departs to rejoin Arthur; but Guynebans chooses to stay with the lady, and he remains with her for the rest of his life. Fols. 127v (line 12)–128v (line 12).]

[Arthur and Gawain]

[Summary. King Bors and his men, on their way to Bredigan to join Arthur and Ban, are threatened by King Amaunt, who tells Bors he must surrender Castle Charryoe, which Amaunt claims is his. Bors replies that Uterpendragon gave the castle to him, but he will relinguish it if Amaunt agrees to do homage to Arthur. Amaunt refuses, proposing instead that they settle the matter by single combat. They fight and Bors kills Amaunt. Amaunt's knights then do homage to Arthur, and both groups ride to Bredigan. Fols. 128v (line 12)–131r (line 10).]

Thus thei sojourned at Bredigan thre dayes full. And than sente the kynge to enquere for workemen and labourers with mattokkes and shoveles till he hadde well five hundred. Than thei wente to the tresour, as Merlin hem taught, in the foreste, and lete digge in the erthe and fonde the tresour that never er was seyn, and toke it oute of the erthe and charged cartes and chariettes in tonnes that thei hadde brought thider grete plenté. And whan thei hadde all the tresour charged, thei made it to be condited to Logres, whereas Arthurs nevewes dide abide. And Merlin made hem digge depe undir an oke till thei fonde a vessell of lether, and therin twelve the beste swerdes and the feirest that eny man nede to seche. These ledde the Kynge Arthur to Logres with his tresour, till that thei were come to court that thei sholde on be emploide.

And as soone as the children herde speke that the Kynge Arthur hir oncle was comynge, thei lepte on theire horse and rode agein hym alle togeder, that noon ne lefte but wente alle gladde and myrie that never peple myght make more joye. And whan thei com nygh, Merlin toke the Kynge Arthur apart and the two kynges and made hem alight under a feire tre for to abide the children that com; and [he]

---

2 enquere for, enlist. **5 charged**, filled; **charietts**, wagons; **tonnes**, barrels. **6 charged**, loaded. **7 condited**, taken; **whereas**, where. **8 oke**, oak; **fonde**, found. **10 ledde**, took; **till that**, so that when. **11 be emploide**, be put to good use. **12 children**, squires. **13–14 noon ne lefte**, no one stayed behind.

comaunded her hoste to ride all wey forth till that thei come to Logres, and take theire logginges and ese hem all by leiser.

And whan thei herde the comaundement of the kynge, thei passed forth withoute
20 more abidinge and mette with the cheldren that com with grete chyvachie. And whan thei mette the routes, thei asked where was the Kynge Arthur; and thei hem shewde the tre ther he was alight. And the childeren hem dressed that wey that moche hem dide haste. And Gawein wente before, that thei helde for maister and lorde, and thei hadde right, for he was the beste taught and the moste curteise that
25 ever was, and in whom was lefte vilonye, and the wisiste that myght be whan he com to chivalrie.

Whan thei com to the tree ther the kynge was alight, and these other two kynges with hym, and the Knyghtes of the Rounde Table. And as soone as the children hem saugh, thei alight afoote from theire horse and wente afoote theras these
30 knyghtes were sette upon the fresshe herbes in the shadowe of the foreste. And hem aventeed and keeled, for it hadde be hoote all the day, and thei hadde riden all the day armed for doute of the Saisnes that were in the londe; and it was aboute the ende of Maye.

Whan the Knyghtes of the Rounde Table saugh the children approche nygh,
35 that eche hadde take other hande in hande godely and alle were thei well clothed and richely araied and full of grete bewté, and semed well that thei were alle come of gode issue; and it becom hem well that thei com so entreprised, and thei helde it a grete debonerté that thei helde togeder so feire. And whan the knyghtes hem saugh come, thei roos ageins hem. And whan thei com nygh Gawein hem salued,
40 that was of the chief and the eldeste; and than he seide, "Feire lordinges, we seche the Kynge Arthur, wherefore we praye yow that ye will us shewen where he is, that we may hym knowen."

At this worde ansuerde Nascien and salued hym agein debonerly and seide, "My feire sones, lo, hym yonde, ther tho noble men ben sette, and he is also the

20 chyvachie, horsemanship. **21 routes,** companies of men. **22 dressed,** proceeded. **23 before,** ahead. **24 right,** good reason. **25 lefte,** absent. **26 chivalrie,** knighthood. **27 Whan,** Then; **ther,** where. **29 saugh,** saw; **theras,** where. **31 hem aventeed,** opened their helmet vents; **keeled,** cooled. **32 doute,** fear. **37 issue,** parentage; **entreprised,** well organized. **38 debonerté,** virtue. **39 ageins,** before; **salued,** greeted. **43 debonerly,** politely.

45   yongeste of alle," and shewde hym with his fynger. And whan Gawein hym saugh, he paste forth and seide, "Sir, gramercy," and com that wey ther the kynge was and his felowes. And thei stode upon foote as soone as thei saugh the children come.

    Whan Gawein saugh his oncle and his felowes, he and alle the children kneled
50   down and salued the kynge and his companye, for hym and his felowes that were with hym icomen. "Sir," quod Gawein, "I am come to yow, I and my brethern and my cosins, as to my liege lorde; and these other be come also for the goode that thei here speken of yow, and for to seche oure armes of yow, and that it plese yow for to make us knyghtes; and [we] shull gladly yow serve, as we owe
55   to do, yef oure servise may yow plese. And I sey not but that thei have yow served, for somme ther ben here that while ye have been oute of contrey have diffended youre londe as wele as it hadde ben theire owne agein alle youre enmyes, and have be in helpinge to alle hem that ye lefte it to kepe. And seth thei come have thei suffred many a grete travaile, and I will well that ye it wite, for to a
60   goode man ther sholde be reported honour and bounté whan he hath don; and of a shrewe oweth oon consele, for he hath no herte it to guerdone, ner the iyen power a gode man to beholde, ne to knowe the halvendell of the bounté that in hym is."

    Whan the kynge undirstode the childe that so wisely spake, he toke hym by the
65   hand and anoon comaunded hem alle to arise. And thei did his comaundement. And than the kynge aresond hem and asked of Gawein what thei were. "Sir," seide Gawein, "er ye knowe more by us wolde we wite youre volunté; and after that, demaunde us that yow plesith, and we shull telle yow gladly that we knowen."

    Whan the two kynges herde the wordes of the childe, thei helde hym right
70   wise, and seide to the Kynge Arthur that he seide right. And than spake the Kynge

46 gramercy, great thanks; **com,** went; **ther,** where. **50 salued,** greeted. **53 here speken,** hear spoken; **and²,** if. **54 owe,** ought. **55 yef,** if. **55–56 yow served,** you [already] served. **57 as it,** as if it; **agein,** against. **58 be in helpinge to,** assisted; **seth,** since. **59 travaile,** hardship; **will well,** much desire; **wite,** know. **61 shrewe,** wicked man; **oweth oon consele,** ought to keep silent; **it to guerdone,** [a worthy] person to reward; **ner,** nor; **iyen,** eyes. **62 halvendell,** extent; **bounté,** virtue. **65 anoon,** then; **hem,** them. **66 aresond hem,** spoke with them; **what,** who. **67 wolde we wite,** we would know; **volunté,** wishes. **68 demaunde,** ask; **that¹,** whatever; **that²,** what.

Arthur and seide, "Feire frendes, I will withholde yow with right gladde chere and will make yow knyghtes, bothe yow and youre companye, of myn owne, and ye be right welcome. And I will that fro hensforth that ye be my frendes and my felowes and of my privé counseile and lordes of my court." And whan the childeren

75 herde how the kynge spake, thei kneled and hym thonked; and the kynge toke hem by the hondes and seide to Gawein, "Feire frende, now telle me what ye be, and of youre felowes telle me the verité, for longe me thinketh it to wite."

"Sir," quod the childe, "men clepe me by my right name Gawein, the sone of Kynge Loot of Leoneys and of Orcanye. And these thre that I holde by the hondes

80 beth my brethern; and the name of that oon is Agravayn, and the tother is Gaheret, and the thridde Gaheryes. And oure moder hath do us to undirstonde that she is youre suster on hir moder side. And thise gentilmen ben oure cosins germain, as oure auntes sones. And the name of the lesse that is short and fatte is Galashin, and [he] is sone to Kynge Ventre. And this other that is longe and yonge is sone to

85 Kynge Urien, and his name is Ewein; and this gentilman is his brother on his fader side and is cleped also Ewein. And these tweyne other that ye se holde togeder, thei be gentilmen of high lynage, for this feire broun is sone to the Kynge Belinans of South Walis and is nygh cosin to Galashin; and these other tweyne be nevewes to the Kynge of Strangore and ben nygh sibbe to Galashin. And these other tweyne

90 ben nevewes also to the Kynge of Strangore, and the name of that oon is Kay Destranx and the tother Kehedin.

"And these other tweyne that ther stonde togeder aperteyne to the Kynge Loot, my fader, and be erles sones; and oon is cleped Ewein White Hande, and the tother Ewein Esclins, and the tother Ewein Cyvell, and the tother Ewein de Lyonell.

95 And this other gentilman that is of so grete bewté, that is so moche and semly and well shapen of body and of alle membres, is nevew to the emperour of Costantynnoble, and his name is Seigramor; and [he] is come with us be his debonerté and his fraunchise to take armes, and that ye hym make knyght. And he will yow gladly serve with gode will, and will that he and I be felowes in armes

71 withholde, support. **73 will,** wish. **76 what ye be,** who you are. **77 verité,** truth; **for . . . wite,** for I have long desired to know. **78 clepe,** call. **82 cosins germain,** first cousins. **83 lesse,** smaller one. **84 longe,** tall. **86 cleped,** called; **holde,** stand. **89 ben nygh sibbe,** are close kin. **92 aperteyne,** belong. **95 moche,** large; **semly,** handsome. **97 be,** by. **98 debonerté,** courtesy; **and²,** if. **99 will³,** desires.

100   while hym liketh to abide in this contrey. And these other gentilmen that ye seen
aboute us whereof be so grete plenté ben alle frendes and kynnesmen, and have
lefte her londes and hir honours for to come serve yow for the grete love that thei
have to yow."

Whan the Kynge Arthur hadde herde Gawein thus speke, he leide his arme
105   aboute his nekke and seide, "He is right wellcome [. . .]," and made of hem grete
joye; and than [to] his brethern and his cosins and to Segramor he made merveilouse
joye. And whan he hadde welcomed hem alle, than he seide to Gawein, "Gawein,
feire neveve, com hider, and that I yow enffeffe ye will take the constabilrie of
myn housolde and of all the lordship of my londe after me, and fro hensforth to be
110   lorde and comaunder of alle hem that ben in my londe, for I will it so be." And
Gawein kneled and seide, "Sir, gramercy." And the kynge hym feffed with his
right glove, and than he reised hym upon his feet. And than [thei] lept to theire
horse and rode forth to Logres.

And whan the kynge entred into the citee, his suster com agein hym, the wif of
115   Kynge Loot of Orcanye, and with hir com Morgne le Fee hir suster that was so
grete a clergesse. And whan the kynge hem knewe, he made of hem grete joye, for
longe tyme hadde he not hem sein; and thei kissed as brother and suster. And thus
thei come to the maister paleys that was hanged with clothes of silke and strowed
with fressh herbes softe and swote smellinge. And [thei] maden grete joye thourgh
120   the town all day on ende and all nyght, so that no man may reherse the joye and
the gladnesse of all the peple. The same nyght the kynge comaunded the children
to go wake in the cheiff mynster till on the morowe before messe, that no lenger
he wolde abide. And the storie seith this was the quynsyme after Pentecoste; and
ther was the Kynge Ban and the Kynge Bohors and the sixty-one Knyghtes of the
125   Rounde Table with these children all day, that hem in no wise wolde leven.

Whan it com before the tyme of high messe, Arthur toke Calibourne, his gode
swerde that he drough oute of the ston, and by the counseile of Merlin therwith he
girde Gawein his nevewe; and than he sette on the spore on the right hele and the
Kynge Ban upon the lifte hele; and after that the Kynge Arthur yaf hym the acolee

100 hym liketh, he chooses; **abide**, stay. **108 enffeffe**, request that; **constabilrie**, man-
agement. **110 will**, desire. **111 feffed**, i.e., struck lightly. **114 agein**, to. **116 clergesse**,
scholar. **118 strowed**, bestrewn. **122 wake**, keep vigil; **mynster**, cathedral. **123 quynsyme**,
the fifteenth day. **129 acolee**, accolade.

130   and bad God make hym a gode knyght. And after he adubbed his thre brethern also, and yaf eche of hem a suerde of tho that were founde in the tresour that Merlin taught; and than the tweye sones of Kynge Urien; and than Galashin, and Dodinell, and Kay, and Kehedin; and to everiche of these he yaf a swerde of the tresour.

135   And than the kynge adubbe Seigramor with soche garmentes as he hadde brought from Costantynnoble, for he was come well araide of alle thinges that behoveth to a newe knyght. And the kynge girde hym with a gode swerde that he hadde brought out of Costantynnoble that his graunsire the Kynge Adrian hadde hym yoven. And than he sette on his right spore and the Kynge Bohors his lifte spore;

140   and than the Kynge Arthur yaf hym the acolee. And than he dubbed the four cosins — Ewein White Honde and Ewein Esclyn and Ewein Cyvell and Ewein de Lyonell — and Alain and Acon; and to ech of these six he yaf a swerde of tho that were of the tresour. But the storie seith that Dodynell hadde noon, but he hadde the swerde that was the Kynges Amaunt; and the Kynge Bohors hym it yaf, for he

145   was somdell of hys kyn.

    Whan these children were thus adubbed, than eche of hem adubbed soche companye as thei wolde lede of soche as thei hadde brought with hem. And whan thei were alle redy, thei wente to high messe that the archebisshop sange; and whan messe was don, thei com agein to the paleise to mete. And ther helde Arthur

150   grete court and grete feste, and it nedith not to speke of the meesse ne the servise that thei hadde that day, for it were but losse of tyme. And after mete wolde these yonge bachelers have reised a quyntayn in the medowes, but the kynge hem diffended by the counseile of Merlin, for that the contrey was so trouble and full of werre, and the Cristin sore turmented with Saisnes that were entred in the londe.

155   Thus lefte the envysenx of these yonge bachillers and newe knyghtes at this tyme; and [thei] sojourned in the town three dayes. And the kynge departed grete richesse to yonge bachelers that he withheilde, that of alle parties were come grete plentee; for ther com so many of oon and other that thei were sixty thousande,

130 adubbed, knighted. **131 yaf eche**, gave each; **of tho**, from those. **132 taught**, had told them about. **133 everiche**, everyone. **136 behoveth**, pertains. **139 yoven**, given. **140 acolee**, accolade. **142 yaf**, gave. **145 somdell of hys kyn**, related to him. **149 mete**, dine. **151 mete**, dinner. **152 quyntayn**, tilting board. **152–53 hem diffended**, dissuaded them. **155 lefte**, ended; **envysenx**, sporting. **157 withheilde**, upheld.

160 what on horsebak and on foote, withoute hem that he hadde brought out of the reame of Tamelide.

And in the menewhile that thei sojourned in the town, Morgne le Fee aqueynted hir with Merlin and was with hym so privé; and so moche she was with hym that she knewe what he was. And many merveilles he hir taught of astronomye and of egramauncye; and she helde it right wele.

165 And on the thridde day spake Merlin to the kynge and badde hym appareile for to move, for Pounces and Antony and Frolle ben entred now into the reame of Benoyk; and also the peple of the Kynge of Gaule, and also Claudas the Kynge de la Desert. And Arthur seide he was redy to go whan hym liked, for he abode but his comaundement. Than seide Merlin, "Comaunde alle youre hoste to be redy

170 armed for to move at mydnyght, and take with yow of this londe twenty thousande, and twenty thousande of the reame of Tamelide; and twenty thousande ye shull leve in this town, for this reame may not be lefte withoute peple; and lete Doo of Cardoell of hem have the governaunce." And thus ended her counseile.

And than the kynge comaunded Gawein as Merlin hadde seide, and anoon

175 Gawein dide his comaundement and made hem redy appareilled. And hem departed and dissevered asonder, and hem he logged in the medowes of Logres, alle that sholde with hem go. And whan he hadde do thus, he com to the kynge and to Merlin that he saugh in counseile togeder and seide how all was redy. And whan Merlin hym saugh, he bad the kynge aske hym what was the knyght that ledde

180 hym to socour his moder in the medow of Glocedon. And he hym turned and seide, "Sir, how knowe ye this, and who hath this to yow itolde?"

"Certes," quod the kynge, "he that tolde me knoweth alle these thinges well inough." "So helpe me God, sir," seide Gawein, "I knowe not what he was, for I saugh hym never before ne after." "Now," quod Merlin, "aske hym yef he knewe

185 hym that brought hym the letter from his cosin Ewein, the sone of Kynge Urien." And whan Gawein saugh and behelde hym that satte by the kynge, he asked whi he made the kynge hym so demaunde. And than he bethought hym agein wisely and remembred the wordes that Doo of Cardoell hadde to hym seide. And the

159 withoute hem, excluding those. **162 so privé,** very privately. **164 egramauncye,** necromancy; **helde,** learned. **165 appareile,** prepare. **176 dissevered asonder,** separated; **logged,** stationed. **179 bad,** bade; **what,** who. **183 what,** who. **184 yef,** if. **187 demaunde,** question.

kynge asked yef he hym kenned. And he seide, "Nay; but oon dide me for to
190 undirstonde that it was Merlin; but trewly, I knowe hym not. And many other
bountees and servyses hath he me don; for Seigramor, the emperoures nevew, he
made me delyver from pereile of deth; and my moder and my cosin Ewein and
also oureself at the Castell of Arondell; and he is the man of the worlde that I
wolde faynest knowe this day."

195 "Ye shull knowe hym inough," quod Merlin, "whan hym liketh." Than began
the kynge to laugh right lowde and seide, "Gawein, feire nevew, sitte down here
by me, and I shall telle yow that I knowe." And he sette hym down be the kynge,
and ther were no mo but thei thre. Than seide the kynge to Gawein, "Feire nevew,
lo, here the gode man by whom ye wente to the Castell of Arondell, where that ye
200 fought with the Saisnes that day that Dodynell the Savage and Kay Destranx and
his neveu com oute of her contrey; and therfore, now thonke hym of the servises
that he hath yow don, and well ye owe so to do, and to love hym for his gode herte
that he hath to yow."

"Sir," seide Gawein, "I can not inowgh hym quyte as he is of worthynesse; but
205 thus moche I sey, that I am all his and at his comaundement; and he is so wise that
knowe I well that he knoweth all my corage that I have to hym." And he seide ye,
that he knewe well his herte, and that he wolde with hym ben aqueynted and be
oon of his privees; but he bad hym that he sholde not telle no creature of nothinge
that he seide to hym, were he never so pryvé ne frendly. "And ye shull se me,"
210 quod he, "in so many gises that I will not be knowe of no man, for moche is the
envye for covetyse in this worlde." And Gawein seide that never wolde he speke
therof to no creature of the erthe.

Thus was Merlin and Sir Gawein aqueynted before his oncle. And whan thei
hadde longe spoke togeder, than seide Merlin, "Feire frende, go take youre leve of
215 youre moder, and than goith to the hoste and make youre peple go to horsebak
anoon after mydnyght; and than goith forth youre wey towarde Dover to the portes.
And do appareille vesselles and assemble shippes at the ryvage, so that youre
uncle whan he cometh, and the two kynges in his companye that beth worthy

189 **yef**, if; **kenned**, knew; **oon dide**, one caused. 194 **faynest**, most happily. 197 **that**,
what; **be**, by. 198 **mo**, more. 201 **her**, their. 202 **owe**, ought. 204 **quyte**, repay. 206
corage, love; **ye**, yes. 208 **privees**, confidants. 209 **pryvé**, trustworthy. 217 **appareille**,
ready; **ryvage**, seacoast.

men, may enter withoute lenger lettinge. And for Godes sake, loke ye do hem
220　worship and honour, for though thei be the Kynge Arthurs men, yet ben thei
comen of higher lynage than is he. And loke ye lete no man knowe what wey that
ye shull go." And Gawein seide it sholde be don as he hadde devised.

Than departed Gawein and toke leve of his moder, that was right wise and
moche hym loved, and comaunded hym to God to diffende hym from evyll. And
225　he departed and com to the hoste, he and his brethern, and Sir Ewein his cosin that
moche hym loved, and Galashin, and Dodinell, and Seigramor, and Ewein
Avoutres, and the foure cosins that alle were cleped Ewein, and Kay Destranx,
and Kehedin his nevew; these ne departed gladly asonder; these hadde the hoste
in governaunce, as Sir Gawein hem assigned, so that alle were at the comaundement
230　of my lorde Sir Gawein.

And anoon after mydnyght, Gawein made trusse sommers and other cariage,
and made goode wacche aboute the hoste that ther ne ascaped noon aspie; and thei
hit kepten that the booke hath rehersed; and than thei rode forth a softe paas till
thei com to the port of Dover. And the Kynge Arthur abode at Logres, and Merlin,
235　and the Kynge Ban, and the Kynge Bohors, and the forty-one knyghtes that thei
ledde into Tamelide, and the Knyghtes of the Rounde Table.

And Sir Gawein made serche all the ryvages and take shippes and assembled a
grete navie. And whan Merlin knewe that all was redy, he sente to the kynge and
made hym move be nyght, and seide er thei moved that thei sholde aryve at the
240　Rochell, and badde hem do make her men rowe hem up thider. "And whan ye bith
arived, loke that ye move not till that ye se me agein." Quod the kynge, "Shull ye
not than come with us?" "No," quod Merlin, "but ye shull ly ther but oon nyght
whan ye shull se me with yow."

With that departed that oon from that other. And Merlin wente into
245　Northumbirlonde to Blase, his maister, that of hym was right gladde, for hertely
he hym loved, and asked hym how he hadde don seth he departed. And he hym

219 lettinge, delay. **224 comaunded**, commended. **228 ne departed gladly asonder**, were
happy not to be parted. **231 made trusse sommers**, readied the packhorses. **232 made
goode wacche**, posted guards; **ascaped noon aspie**, escaped any spy. **233 kepten**,
guarded; **softe paas**, easy pace. **237 serche**, searched; **ryvages**, coastal areas; **take**,
took. **239 be**, by; **er**, before. **240–41 bith arived**, have arrived. **242 ly**, wait. **246 seth**,
since.

tolde alle the thinges as thei were befallen, and Blase hem wrote in his booke. And whan Merlin com to that he behoved to telle, of the damsell that he loved par- amours. And Blase was therof right hevy, for he douted she wolde hym disseyve

250 and that she sholde lese his grete witte, and he gan hym to chastise. And he hym tolde soche prophesies as were for to come and of other that sholde falle in other londes, as ye shull here herafter. And alle Blase wrote in his boke; but now returne we to speke of the Kynge Arthur.

---

248 **whan**, then; **that**, what; **behoved**, was compelled. **248–49 paramours**, romantically. **249 hevy**, sad; **douted**, feared; **disseyve**, deceive. **250 lese**, cause him to lose; **he²**, i.e., Merlin. **251 falle**, occur.

[The Begetting of Lancelot; and Merlin and Nimiane]

[Summary. The story now concerns the war between King Ban and King Bors and their enemies — Claudas de la deserte and the King of Gaul, who are being aided by the Romans Pounce Antony and Frolle. Arthur and his men cross over to the conti-nent with the intention of helping Ban and Bors defend their kingdoms of Benoyk and Gannes. A great battle takes place before the city of Trebes, and in it many of Arthur's knights perform heroically. Gawain, in particular, displays his surpassing prowess as a knight; and Gaheris, Gawain's young brother, also emerges as one of the best knights after Gawain. Eventually the enemy forces suffer great losses and are forced to retreat to the "desert." Fols. 134r (line 19)–145v (line 16).]

Thus were the foure princes discounfited, as ye have herde, be the witte of Merlin. And whan thei hadde chaced hem to the nyght, thei returned with grete plenté of prisoners and com before the Castell of Trebes, where thei were loigged in tentes and pavilouns of thiers that were discounfited. And [thei] made grete
5   joye and feste all the nyght, for thei fonde the loigginges well stuffed of all that neded to man that nothinge failed. And whan thei were herberowed, that nyght wacched the hoste Pharien and Grascien that thei were not assailled of somme maner peple. And the Kynge Ban and the Kynge Bohors ledde the Kynge Arthur and Sir Gawein and the Knyghtes of the Rounde Table and the Forty Knyghtes
10   that ye have herde named and the Newe Knyghtes into the Castell of Trebes, where he made to hem grete joye and feste, and were well three hundred knyghtes of the contrey. And that nyght were thei well served of all that behoved.

But who that was gladde or noon, ther was noon like to the joye of the two queenes that were sustres, whan thei saugh theire two lordes that thei hadde so
15   longe desired for to seen. And thei were yonge ladyes and of grete bewté. And

---

1 discounfited, defeated; **be**, by. **2 to the**, until. **4 of thiers**, belonging to those. **6 herberowed**, lodged. **7 wacched**, guarded; **that**, so that. **11 were well**, there were at least. **12 behoved**, was fitting. **13 who that**, whoever; **noon**, not. **14 saugh**, saw. **15 seen**, see.

216

gretly thei hem peyned to honour the Kynge Arthur and alle his companye. Wherto sholde I tarie to reherse theire servise and the ese of softe beddes that thei hadde that nyght? For thei were served richely as worthi men. And after soper thei wente to reste, for therto hadde thei nede, for thei were wery for travaile that thei hadde that day suffred. And Arthur and Gawein and Segramor and Ewein and Dodinell and Kay and Antor lay in a feire chamber by hemself; and with hem was Merlin that from hem that nyght wolde not departe. And the Knyghtes of the Rounde Table and the Newe Knyghtes and the Forty Felowes layn in other chambers.

And whan the Kynge Ban and the Kynge Bohors hadde hem loigged at ese, thei wente to bedde with theire wiffes, and lefte grete torches brennynge before hem in chambres. That nyght shewed the two kynges grete love to theire wiffes. That nyght the Queene Heleyne conceyved a childe by her lorde the Kynge Ban. And whan thei were on slepe, the wiff of Kynge Ban fill into a merveilouse drem that longe endured that sore she was afeerde whan she dide awake. For she semed that she was on a high mountayn and saugh aboute her grete plenté of bestes of all maner kendes that were in a feire pasture of grene grasse. And whan thei hadde longe tyme fedde hem on the herbes, ther roos amonge hem a grete noyse that thei ronne that oon upon the tother to dryve oute of the pasture.

And thei turned into two pastures, and the two partes wente on oon side, and hem ledde a grete lyon full huge and merveillouse. And on that other side, whereas were not so many by the halvendell, was a grete crowned lyon maister leder; but he was not so grete as the tother. This lyon crowned hadde in his companye eighteen lyonsewes crowned, wherof eche of hem hadde lordship and domynacion over the tother bestes that were turned to the lyon crowned. And that other lyon that was not crowned hadde with hym thirty lyonsewes that alle were crowned, wherof eche of hem hadde domynacion of a parte of the bestes that were drawe toward the lyon that was uncrowned. And whan these beestes were thus dissev-

---

16 Wherto, Why. **19 travaile,** hardships. **21 hemself,** themselves. **29 on slepe,** asleep; **fill,** fell. **30 sore,** greatly; **afeerde,** afraid; **semed,** thought. **31 bestes,** beasts. **32 kendes,** kinds. **33 hem,** themselves; **roos,** arose. **34 ronne,** ran; **that oon,** one. **35 turned,** separated. **36 whereas,** where. **37 the halvendell,** half; **grete,** large. **39 lyonsewes,** young lions. **40 were turned to,** supported. **41 lyonsewes,** young lions.

ered and departed, she loked toward the crowned lyon and saugh four hundred
boles that alle were teyed be the nekkes before a grove, and ete at a rakke small
grasses and herbes that was newe mowen.

And for the lyon uncrowned semed thei hadde better pasture with the crowned
lyon than hadde he, he ran upon hym for envye for to bereve hym his pasture, and
toke a partie of his bestes that he made thre grete hepes, and thei lepe to fight with
the crowned lyon that hadde his bestes departed into eighteen mouncels; and in
eche mouncell was a lyonsewe that hadde lordshippe over hem to governe hem
and gide. And the four hundred boles that weren full fierce and full prowde and
the eighteen mouncels were with the crowned lyon. And [thei] smote betwene
hem the grettest bateile that she ever hadde seyn or herde speke. But in the fyn the
bestes with the crowned lyon behoved to turne bakke, and the crowned lyon was
sore adredde to lese his pasture.

And while these beestes fought thus as ye have herde, the lady semed that a
grete leopart full fierce and the moste prowde that ever was seyn com oute of hir
right thigh, and wente through a grete valey that was right depe; and whan he was
entred into the valey, the lady semed that a grete blaste toke awey her sight that
she wiste not where he was become. And whan she hadde hym loste, he turned
toward the beestes that yet were fightinge and saugh that the crowned lyon and
his bestes hadde moche the werse. And whan the leopart com oute of a grete
foreste that was savage, he behilde the bataile of the beestes full longe. And whan
he saugh the crowned lyon hadde the werse, he yede to helpe hym, and ran upon
the beestes of the lyon uncrowned that faught with hem so fiercely that he made
hem resorte bakke; and as longe as he was agein hem myght thei never have the
better of the bataile. And whan the lyon that was uncrowned saugh he myght not
have the better while he was agein hym, he made departe the bataile and aqueynte
hym with the leopart, till he drough hym on his partye and ledde hym with hym.

43–44 **dissevered**, separated. **45 boles**, bulls; **teyed be**, tied by; **ete**, ate; **rakke**, feeding
rack. **47 for**, because; **semed**, thought. **48 bereve hym**, take away. **49 hepes**, groups. **50
departed**, divided; **mouncels**, parts. **54 bateile**, battle; **herde speke**, heard spoken of;
fyn, end. **55 behoved**, were forced. **55–56 was sore adredde**, greatly feared. **56 lese**, lose.
57 semed, thought. **60 semed**, thought; **blaste**, storm. **61 wiste**, knew. **62 saugh**, saw. **63
hadde moche**, had it much. **64 behilde**, beheld. **65 yede**, went. **67 resorte**, turn. **69 made
departe**, left. **69–70 aqueynte hym**, spoke. **70 drough**, drew; **partye**, side.

And the thridde day began agein the bateile of the beestes as it hadde be byforn, and the leopart was with the lyon that was uncrowned. And the beestes fought so togeder that the crowned lyon turned to discounfiture, and he made signe to the lyon withoute crowne that he sholde go crye mercy. And so he dide, and so was made the pees betwene the two lyouns in soche maner that never after were in no wratthe togeder. And than the lady behilde the leopart to wite yef she cowde hym knowe be eny wey; and at the laste hir thought it was the same that com oute of hir thigh that was so woxen and amended. And hir thought that alle the beestes of the Bloy Breteyne to hym enclyned, and alle thei of Gannes and of Benyok. And whan he hadde alle the lordship of these beestes, she knewe not where he was becomen.

Thus she aboode all nyght in this avision till it was day; and than she awoke, all affraied of the merveile of hir dreme. And whan the Kynge Ban saugh hir so affraied, he asked hir what her eyled. And she tolde hym hir dreme as she hadde seyn in her slepe; and whan she hadde all tolde, the kynge seide therof sholde come but goode, with Goddes grace. Than thei aroos and wente to the firste masse, bothe the kynge and his wif, as erly as thei myght; but thei wolde not awake the Kynge Arthur so erly ne his companye that slepten savourly for the grete travaile that thei hadd the day before. And the Kynge Ban praied oure Lorde with goode herte that He wolde yeve hym the deth soche tyme as he wolde it aske. And this prayour made he many tymes, till on a nyght in his slepe a voyse seide that his prayour sholde be trewe and that he sholde have the deth as soone as he wolde it aske the same day. But ones before sholde he synne dedly in avoutré er he dyed, but therof not to be dismayed, for he sholde therof well acorde with oure Lord; and he was right a goode man in his feith and creaunce.

In this dreme that the Kynge Ban was, hym thought whan the voyse departed that it caste soche a crye as it hadde ben a thunder, the grettest and merveillouse that ever he hadde herde. And he sprange therwith so sore theras he hilde the

---

73 turned to discounfiture, was defeated. **74 go crye mercy**, beg for mercy. **76 behilde**, beheld; **wite**, discover; **yef**, if; **cowde**, could. **77 be**, by. **78 woxen and amended**, grown and changed. **79 enclyned**, bowed. **82 aboode**, lay sleeping. **83 affraied of**, frightened by. **84 her eyled**, ailed her. **85 seyn**, seen it. **88 savourly**, deeply. **90 yeve**, give. **93 avoutré**, adultery; **er**, before. **94 well acorde with**, be forgiven by. **95 creaunce**, belief. **97 as**, as if. **98 so sore theras**, so strongly that.

queene in his armes, that nere he hadde fallen oute of the bedde that was grete and
100 large. And the queene was therwith so affraied that she myght speke no worde in
a longe while, and the kynge hymself so that he wiste not where he was. And
whan the kynge was come agein into his memorie, he aroos and wente to cherche
and was shriven, and than herde the servyse of oure Lorde. And ever after, as
longe as he lyved, was he confessed every eight dayes and was hoseled with the
105 blissed sacrament; and so dide Kynge Bohors his brother that was a full goode
man and of holy lyvinge.

Thus was the Kynge Arthur in the reame of Benoyk, he and his men, a moneth.
And [thei] ronne every day into Claudas londes and wasted it, so that longe tyme
after myght he have no power to arise upon the Kynge Ban. But after, he aroos
110 ageins hym by the force of Pounce Antony and by the force of the Kynge of
Gaule, as ye shall heren hereafter, and turmented so these two brethern that he
lefte hem noo foote londe, that thei died in poverté upon the grounde, and theire
yonge wiffes lefte withoute comfort, that after were nonnes veilled in the abbey
of the royal mynster for drede of Claudas. Ne never after myght thei have socour
115 of the Kynge Arthur, for he hadde so moche to done in his contrey that he myght
not come at that tyme. And so the heires that thei begat were longe tyme after
disherited. But in the ende Kynge Arthur hem therto restored and drof Claudas
oute of the londe, and yaf hem the reame of Gaule, as the booke shall reherse. But
now we shall reste to speke these thinges till tyme com therto, and returne to telle
120 how Merlin departed from the Kynge Arthur and how he certified the Kynge Ban
and his wif of dyvers dremes that thei hadden mette.

Upon a day com the Kynge Ban to Merlin and seide, "Sir, I am gretly in dispeir
of avision that is befalle to me and to my wif, wherefore I have grete nede of
counseile. And ye be the wisest man that now liveth; and therfore, yef it plese
125 yow, telle me what it betokeneth." "Certes, sir," seid Merlin. "In these two avisions
ther is grete significacion, and it is no wonder though ye therof be dredfull."

99 **nere**, nearly. **101 wiste**, knew. **102 memorie**, senses. **103 shriven**, confessed; **than**,
then. **104 hoseled with**, received. **110 ageins**, against. **111 heren hereafter**, hear later
on. **112 noo foote londe**, not a foot of land. **113 that after were**, that later became;
nonnes, nuns. **114–15 socour of**, help from. **115 done**, do. **117 disherited**, disinherited.
118 yaf, gave. **119 reste to speke**, put off speaking. **121 dyvers dremes**, various dreams;
mette, dreamed.

The Begetting of Lancelot; and Merlin and Nimiane

Than asked the Kynge Arthur what avisiouns ben thei, and Merlin hym tolde even as the kynge hadde mette in his dreme, that the kynge hymself knewe well he seide trouthe. Whan the Kynge Arthur and the Kynge Bohors and Sir Gawein

130 herde the fierce wordes that Merlin hadde seide, thei merveiled sore what hit myght signyfie, and thoughten inough of many thinges. And than seide the Kynge Arthur, "Ye have tolde what were the dremes. Now, yef it plese yow, telle us the betokenynges, for it is a thinge that I wolde fayn knowe." "Sir," seide Merlin, "of all will I not to yow declare, ne I ought not to do. But I shall telle yow a partye that

135 to yow apendeth." And than he gan to sey:

"Kynge Ban," quod Merlin, "hit is trouthe that the lyon that is not crowned betokeneth a prince that is right riche and myghty of londes and of frendes, that shall conquere twenty-nine reames by force and make come in his companye alle these twenty-nine kynges crowned. And that other lyon that she saugh icrowned

140 that hadde the eighteen lyonsewes signyfieth a kinge that is right myghty that shall have eighteen kynges under hym that alle shull be his liege men. And the four hundred booles that she saugh betokeneth four hundred knyghtes that alle shull be assured that oon to the tother eche of hem to helpe, and not faile for no drede of deth, and alle shull thei be the kynges men. And this prince that I spake of firste

145 shall come upon this kynge for to conquere his londe. But he shall hym diffende as longe as he may.

"And whan this prince hath the better of this kynge, than shall come a knyght unknowen that longe hath be loste and helpe this kynge that the prince may not hym chase oute of the felde ne discounfite. And this leopart signyfieth this knyght,

150 for like as the leopart is fierce and prowde above alle other bestes, so shall he be the beste knyght that shall be in hys tyme. And by that knyght shall the pees be made betwene the prince and the kynge that so sore shull have foughten. Now," quod Merlin, "have ye herde youre avision and the tokenynge. And now I moste departe, for moche have I to do in other places."

155 And whan thei hadde iherde the merveile of the dreme that Merlin hadde tolde, thei were more abaisshed and more pensef than thei were before. And than Arthur

128 mette, dreamed; **that**, so that. **130 fierce**, wondrous. **133 fayn**, happily. **134 partye**, portion. **135 apendeth**, pertains. **139 saugh**, saw. **142 booles**, bulls. **143 assured**, pledged; **oon**, one. **151 pees**, peace. **152 sore**, greatly. **156 abaisshed**, astonished; **pensef**, pensive.

221

asked yef he wolde declare eny othir wise to theire understondinge, and he seide,
"Nay." With that departed Merlin oute of Kynge Bans house, whereas the Kynge
Arthur was with grete companye of knyghtes; and this was on the Feeste of Seynt
160 John.

And Merlin wente to his love that aboode hym at the welle, for to holde the
covenaunt that she hadde with hym imade. And whan she hym saugh she made to
hym grete chere, and ledde hym into the chambres so prively that he was not
aperceyved of no man. And she asked and enquered hym of many thinges, and he
165 her taught all her askynge for the grete love that he hadde to hir. And whan she
saugh he loved hir so wele, she asked hym how she myght make a frende for to
slepe and not to awake till that she wolde; and Merlin knewe well all hir thought;
and nevertheles he asked her whi she enquered, and yet he wiste it wele inough.
Quod she, "For I wolde make my fader aslepe alle the tymes that I wolde speke
170 with yow — whos name is Dionas — and my moder, that thei aparceyve never of
yow ne me, for witeth it well, thei wolden me sle yef thei parceyved of us two
ought."

These wordes seide the mayden ofte to Merlin. And it fill on a day that thei
were in a gardin by the fountayne hem to disporte, and were sette upon an ympe.
175 And the mayden made hym to slepe in hir lappe and hilde her so with hym that
Merlyn loved hir merveillously wele. Than the maiden required hym so that he
taught hir to make oon slepe, and he knewe hir menynge right wele; but nevertheles
he it hir taught, bothe that and many other thinges, for so wolde our Lorde. And
he taught hir thre names that she wrote for to helpe hirself at alle tymes whan she
180 sholde with hym ly that were full of grete force, for never as longe as thei were
upon hir ne myght never man touche her flessly.

And fro thensforth she tysed ever Merlin to come speke with hir, for he ne
hadde no power to dele with hir agein her will; and therfore it is seide that woman
hath an art more than the devell. Thus Merlin abode eight dayes full with the
185 damesell. But we fynde not in no writing that ever he required eny vylonye of hir

157 wise, wisdom. **161 aboode,** awaited. **163 ledde,** took; **prively,** secretly. **164
aperceyved of,** seen by; **no man,** anyone. **165 for,** because of. **167 till that,** until; **wolde,**
wished. **170 aparceyve,** know. **171 sle yef,** slay if. **173 fill,** befell. **174 sette,** seated;
ympe, tree. **176 required hym so,** urged him so much. **177 menynge,** intention. **180 ly,**
lie. **181 flessly,** physically. **182 tysed,** enticed. **183 dele with,** resist.

ne of noon other. But she it douted sore whan she knewe what he was, and therfore she garnysshed hire so agein hym. And in tho eight dayes he taught hir many wonderfull thinges that eny mortall herte cowde thinke — of thinges paste, and of thinges that were don and seide, and a partye of that was to come. And she putte hem in writinge.

190

And than Merlin departed from hire and com to Benoyk, where the Kynge Arthur rested, that gladde were whan thei saugh Merlin.

[Summary. Gawain and his knights make a pillaging expedition into the lands of Claudas de la deserte; and then at Merlin's direction, they go to Rochelle, cross the sea, and set out for Tamelide. Fols. 148r (line 12)–148v (line 11).]

186 douted sore, feared greatly. **187 garnysshed,** prepared; **tho,** those. **188 cowde,** could. **189 partye,** portion; **that,** what. **192 saugh,** saw.

[Merlin and Grisandolus]

As soone as Merlin was departed from Arthur, he wente into the forestes of
Rome that were thikke and depe. And in that tyme Julyus Cesar was emperour.
But it was not that Julyus Cesar that the deed knyght slough in his pavilion of
Perce, but it was that Julius that Gawein, the nevew of Kynge Arthur, slough in
5 bateile under Logres at the grete disconfiture that after was betwene hym and the
Kynge Arthur that hym diffied. And what the cause was that Merlin wente that
wey, it is reson it be declared.

This is the trouthe, that this Julyus Cezar hadde a wif that was of grete bewté.
And she hadde with hir twelve yonge men araied in gise of wymen with whom
10 she lay at alle tymes that the emperour was oute of hir companye, for she was the
moste lecherouse woman of all Rome. And for the drede that theire beerdes sholde
growe, she lete anoynte her chynnes with certeyn oynementes made for the nones.
And thei were clothed in longe traylinge robes, and theire heer longe waxen in
gise of maydenes and tressed at theire bakkes, that alle that hem saugh wende
15 wele thei were wymen. And longe thei endured with the empresse unknowen.

In this tyme that the emperesse ledde this lif, it fill that a mayden com to the
emperours court that was the doughter of a prince; and the name of this prince
was Matan, Duke of Almayne. This mayden com in semblaunce of a squyer. And
this Matan, the Duke Frolle hadde disherited and driven out of his londe. And she
20 com to serve the emperour, for she wiste not where her fader ne moder were
becomen. And she was moche and semly and well-shapen, and demened hir well
in all maners that a man ought, saf only eny vylonye; and never was she knowen
but for a man by no semblante. And so [she] aboode with the emperour and was
of grete prowesse, and peyned tendirly to serve well the emperour, and plesed

5 **disconfiture**, warfare. **11 for the drede**, for fear. **12 her**, their; **nones**, occasion. **14**
tressed, arranged. **21 moche**, large; **semly**, attractive; **demened**, conducted. **22 saf only**,
without.

25   hym so well that she was lorde and governnour of hym and his housolde. And the emperour hir loved so well that he made hir knyght atte a Feeste of Seint John with other yonge squyers, wherof were mo than two hundred, and after made hir stiward of all his londe.

    Than the newe knyghtes reised a quyntayne in the mede of Noiron and begonne
30   the bourdinge grete and huge. And many ther were that dide right wele, but noon so well as dide Grisandoll, for so she lete hir be cleped; but in bapteme her name was Avenable. This bourdinge endured all day on ende till evesonge that thei departed; and Grisandols bar awey the pris amonge alle other. And whan the emperour saugh Grisandoll of so grete prowesse, he made hym stiward of all his londe and
35   comaunder above alle that ther weren. And Grisandols was well beloved of riche and pore.

    And upon a nyght after, it fill that the emperour lay in his chamber with the emperesse. And whan he was aslepe, he hadde a vision that hym thought he saugh a sowe in his court that was right grete before his paleys; and he hadde never seyn
40   noon so grete ne so huge. And she hadde so grete bristelis on her bakke that it trayled on the grounde a fadome large, and hadde upon hir heed a cercle that semed of fyn golde. And whan the emperour avised hym wele, hym thought that he hadde seyn hir other tymes and that he hadde hir norisshed up; but he durste not sey of trouthe that she were hys. And while he entended to avise hym on this
45   thinge, he saugh come oute of his chamber twelve lyonsewes, and com into the courte to the sowe and assailed hir, oon after another.

    Whan the emperour saugh this merveile, he asked his barouns what should be do with this sowe by whom these lyonsewes hadde thus leyn. And thei seide she was not worthi to be conversaunt amonge peple, ne that no man sholde ete nothinge
50   that of hir come, and juged hir to be brente and also the lyonsewes togeder. And than awooke the emperour, sore affraied and pensif of this avision. Ne never to man ne to wif wolde he it telle, for he was full of grete wisdom.

    On the morowe as soone as he myght se the day, he aroos and yede to the mynster to here messe. And whan he was come agein, he fonde the barouns

29 quyntayne, tilting board; **mede**, meadow. **30 bourdinge**, games. **31 bapteme**, baptism. **33 bar awey the pris**, took first place. **41 a fadome large**, a fathom freely. **42 avised**, considered. **45 lyonsewes**, youthful lions. **48 do**, done. **49 conversaunt**, spoken of. **53 yede**, went.

55   assembled, and hadde herde messe at the mynster, and the mete was all redy. And whan thei hadde waisshen, thei satte to mete and were well served. Than fill that the emperour fill into a grete stodye, wherfore all the courte was pensif and stille. And ther was noon that durste sey a worde, for sore thei dredde for to wrathe the emperour. But now we moste turne a litill to Merlin, that was come into the

60   foreste of Romayne to certefie these thinges and these avisiouns.

    While that the emperour satte at his mete amonge his barouns thus pensif, Merlin come into the entré of Rome and caste an enchauntement merveilouse. For he becom an herte, the gretteste and the moste merveilouse that eny man hadde seyn, and hadde oon of his feet before white, and hadde five braunches in the top,

65   the grettest that ever hadde be seyn. And than he ran thourgh Rome so faste as all the worlde hadde hym chaced. And whan the peple saugh hym so renne and saugh how it was an herte, the noyse aroos and the cry on alle partyes, and ronne after grete and small with staves and axes and other wepen, and chaced hym thourgh the town. And he com to the maister yate of the paleys whereas the

70   emperour satte at his mete. And whan thei that served herde the noyse of the peple, thei ronne to the wyndowes to herkene what it myght be; and anoon thei saugh come rennynge the herte and all the peple after. And whan the herte com to the maister paleys, he drof in at the yate sodeynly, and than he ran thourgh the tables abandon, and tombled mete and drynke all on an hepe, and began therin a

75   grete trouble of pottis and disshes.

    And whan the herte hadde longe turned therynne, he com before the emperour and kneled and seide, "Julius Cezar, emperour of Rome, wheron thinkest thow? Lete be thi stodyinge, for it availeth nought; for never of thyne avision shalt thow not knowe the trouthe before that man that is savage thee certefie. And for nought

80   is it that thow stodyest theron eny more."

    Than the herte hym dressed, and saugh the yate of the paleyse cloos. And he caste his enchauntement that alle the dores and yates of the paleise opened so rudely that thei fly alle in peces. And the herte lept oute and fledde thourgh the town, and the chace began agein after hym longe, till that he com oute into the

85   playn feeldes. And than he dide vanysshe that noon cowde sey where he becom.

57 stodye, study. **60 certefie**, explain. **62 entré**, entry. **63 herte**, hart. **66 renne**, run. **67 partyes**, sides. **74 abandon**, unchecked; **began**, caused. **83 rudely**, suddenly. **85 sey**, saw.

And than thei returned agein.

And whan the emperour wiste the herte was ascaped, he was wroth, and lete crye thourgh the londe that who that myght brynge the savage man or the herte sholde have his feire doughter to wif, and half his reame, yef that he were gentill

90 of birthe, and after his deth have all. And lepe to horse many a valiaunt knyght and squyer of pris, and serched and sought thourgh many contrees. But all was for nought, for never cowde thei heere no tidinges of that thei sought. And whan thei myght no more do, thei returned agein.

But ever Grisandols serched thourgh the forestes, oon hour foreward, another

95 bakke, that so endured eight dayes full. And on a day as Grisandol was alight under an oke for to praye oure Lorde to helpe and to spede for to fynde that he sought. And as he was in his prayours, the herte that hadde ben at Rome com before hym and seide, "Avenable, thow chacest folye, for thow maist not spede of thy queste in no maner; but I shall telle thee what thow shalt do. Purchese

100 flessh newe and salt, and mylke and hony, and hoot breed newe bake, and bringe with thee foure felowes and a boy to turne the spite till it be inough rosted. And com into this foreste by the moste uncouthe weyes that thow canste fynde; and sette a table by the fier, and the breed and the mylke and the hony upon the table. And hide thee and thi companye a litill thens, and doute thee nought that the

105 savage man will come."

Than ran the herte a grete walope thourgh the foreste. And Grisandol lept to horse and thought well on that the herte hadde seide; and thought in his corage that it was some spirituell thinge that by hir right name hadde hir cleped; and thought well that of this thinge sholde come some merveile.

110 And Grisandol rode forth to a town nygh the forest seven myle, and toke ther that was myster, and com into the foreste theras he hadde spoke with the herte as soone as he myght, and roode into the deepe of the foreste whereas he fonde a grete oke full of leves; and the place semed delitable. And he alight and sette their horse fer thens, and made a grete fier and sette the flesshe to roste, and the

115 smoke and the savour spredde thourgh the foreste that oon myght fele the savour right fer, and than sette the table be the fier. And whan all was redy, thei hidde

89 gentill, noble. **96 spede**, aid. **100 flessh newe**, fresh meat. **102 uncouthe**, secret. **104 thens**, thence; **doute**, doubt. **106 walope**, gallop. **107 that**, what. **111 myster**, needed; **theras**, to where. **115 fele**, smell. **116 be**, by.

hem in a bussh.

    And Merlin, that all this knewe and that made all this to be don, covertly that he were not knowen drough that wey with a grete staffe in his hand, smytinge grete strokes from oke to oke. And [he] was blakke and rough forrympled, and longe berde, and barfoote, and clothed in a rough pilche. And so he com to the fier theras the flesshe was rosted. And whan the boy saugh hym come, he was so aferde that he fledde nygh oute of his witte. And he thus com to the fier and began to chacche and frote aboute the fier, and saugh the mete, and than loked all aboute hym, and began to rore lowde as a man wood oute of mynde, and than beheilde and saugh the cloth spredde and soche mete theron as ye have herde. And after he behielde towarde the fier and saugh the flesshe that the knave hadde rosted that was tho inough, and raced it of with his hondes madly, and rente it asonder in peces, and wette it in mylke and after in the hony, and ete as a wood man that nought ther lefte of the flessh. And than he eete of the hoot breed and hony that he was full and swollen grete. And somwhat was it colde, and he lay down by the fier and slepte.

    And whan Grisandol saugh he was onslepe, she and hir felowes com as softely as thei myght and stale awey his staffe. And than thei bounde hym with a cheyne of iren streytely aboute the flankes, and than delyvered hym to oon of the companye by the tother ende of the cheyne. And whan he was so well bounde, he awooke and lept up lightly and made semblaunt to take his staff as a wilde man. And Grisandolus griped hym in his armes right sore and hilde hym stille. And whan he saugh hym so bounde and taken, he hilde hym as shamefaste and mate. And than the horse were brought forth, and he was sette upon oon of hem and bounden to the sadell with two bondes. And a man sette behynde hym that was bounde to hym and enbraced hym by the myddill; and so thei rode forth her wey.

    And the savage man loked on Grisandolus that rode by hym, and began to laugh right harde. And whan Grisandolus saugh hym laughe, he approched ner and rode side by side and aqueynted with hym the beste that he myght, and enquered and asked many thinges; but he ne wolde nought ansuere. And Grisandol asked why

120

125

130

135

140

145

120 forrympled, rumpled. **121 pilche**, outer garment of furs. **124 chacche and frote**, scratch and poke. **125 rore**, roar; **wood**, insane. **128 tho inough**, i.e., cooked enough; **raced it of**, grabbed it off. **133 onslepe**, asleep. **135 streytely**, tightly. **138 right sore**, very tightly. **139 shamefaste**, ashamed; **mate**, confused. **140 horse**, horses.

he lough, but he wolde not telle saf that he seide, "Creature formed of Nature chaunged into other forme, fro hensforth begilynge alle thinges, venimouse as serpent, holde thi pees! For nought will I telle thee till that I com before the emperoure."

150

With that the savage man hilde his pees and spake no more and rode forth togeder. And Grisandolus of this that he hadde seide spake to his companye. And thei seide that he was wiser than he shewed and that som grete merveile sholde falle in the londe. Thus thei ride spekynge of many thinges till thei passede before an abbey, and saugh before the yate moche pore peple abidinge almesse; and than the savage man lowgh right lowde. And than Grisandol com toward hym and swetly praide hym to telle wherefore he lough. And he loked proudly on traverse and seide, "Ymage repaired and disnatured fro Kynde, holde thy pees! Ne enquere no mo thinges, for nought will I telle thee but before the emperour." And whan Grisandolus this undirstode, he lete hym be at that tyme, and no more thinge hym asked; and hereof spake thei in many maners.

155

160

Thus thei rode forth all day till nyght and on the morowe till the hour of prime. And fill that thei passed byfore a chapell where a preste was toward masse, and fonde a knyght and a squyer heringe the servyse. And whan Grisandolus saugh this, thei alight alle the companye, and entred in to here the masse. And whan the knyght that was in the chapell saugh the man bounde with chaynes, he hadde merveile what it myght be. And while the knyght beheilde the man that was savage, the squyer that was in an angle behynde the chapel dore com agein his lorde, and lifte up his hande and yaf hym soche a flap that alle thei in the chapell myght it here; and than returned thider as he com fro, all shamefaste of that he hadde don. And whan he was come in to his place, he ne rofte nothinge, for the shame lasted no lenger but while he was in returnynge. And whan the savage man saugh this, he began to laugh right harde. And the knyght that was so smyten was so abaisshed that he wiste not what to sey, but suffred. And Grisandolus and the other companye merveiled sore what it myght be.

165

170

175

Anoon after the squyer com agein to his lorde and yaf hym soche another

147 **saf**, save. 155 **moche**, many; **abidinge almesse**, waiting for alms. 157 **on traverse**, askance. 158 **repaired**, altered; **disnatured fro Kynde**, distorted from Nature. 163 **fill**, it befell; **toward**, beginning. 168 **agein**, to. 169 **flap**, blow. 170 **shamefaste**, ashamed. 171 **ne rofte nothinge**, cared not at all. 174 **abaisshed**, astonished.

229

stroke as he dide before, and wente agein in to his place. And the savage man hym behilde, and began to laughe right harde. And yef the knyght before were abaisshed, he was than moche more. And the squyer that hadde hym smyten returned sorowfull

180 and pensif to the place he com fro, and hilde hymself foule disceyved of that he hadde don. And whan he was in his place, he rought never. And Grisandolus and the companye merveiled right sore, and herden oute the servise be leyser. And in the menewhile that thei thoughten upon these thinges that thei hadde seyn, the squyer com the thridde tyme and smote his lorde sorer than he hadde don before.

185 And therat lowgh the wilde man sore.

And be that was the masse at an ende; and than Grisdandolus and alle wente oute of the chapell. And the squyer that hadde smyten his lorde com after and asked of Grisandolus what man it was that thei hadde so bounde. And thei seide that thei were with Julius Cezar, emperour of Rome, and ledde to hym that savage

190 man that thei hadde founden in the foreste for to certefie of a vision that was shewed hym slepinge.

"But sir," seide Grisandolus, "tell me wherefore hath this squyer yow smyten thre tymes, and ye ne spake no worde agein. Have ye soche a custome?" And the knyght ansuerde that he sholde it wite in tyme comynge. Than the knyght cleped

195 his squyer and asked hym before Grisandolus wherefore he hadde hym smyten. And he was shamefaste and seide he wiste never, but so it fill in his corage. And the knyght hym asked yef he hadde now eny talent hym for to smyte. And the squyer seide he hadde lever be deed. "But that," quod he, "it fill in my mynde that I myght not kepe me therfro." And Grisandolus lough of the merveile.

200 Than seide the knyght that he wolde go to court with hem for to here what the savage man wolde sey. And with that thei rode forth on her wey, and Grisandolus by the savage mannes side. And whan thei hadde a while riden, he asked the wilde man wherfore he lough so thre tymes whan the squyer smote his lorde. And he loked on hir a traverse and seide, "Ymage repeyred, semblaunce of creature wherby

205 men ben slayn and diffouled, rasour trenchaunt, fountayne coraunt that never is full of no springes, holde thy pees and nothinge of me enquere! But before the

178 **behilde**, watched. 182 **be leyser**, at their leisure. 183 **that[1]**, as. 186 **be that**, by then. 194 **wite in tyme comynge**, soon know. 196 **fill in**, came into; **corage**, heart. 198 **hadde lever be deed**, would rather be dead. 204 **a traverse**, askance. 205 **diffouled**, destroyed; **rasour**, razor; **fountayne coraunt**, flowing fountain. 206 **But**, Except.

emperour, for nought will I telle thee." And whan that Grisandolus undirstode the fell wordes that he spake, he was all abaisshed and pensef and durste not no more enquere; and rode forth till thei come to Rome.

210 And whan thei entred into the town and the peple hem parceyved, thei wente alle ageins hem for to se the man that was savage. And the noyse was grete of the peple that folowed and behilde his facion as longe as thei myght; and so thei conveyed hym to the paleise. And whan the emperour herde the tidinges, he com hem ageins, and mette with hem comynge upon the graces. And than com Grisandolus

215 before the emperour and seide, "Sir, have here the man that is savage that I to yow here yelde; and kepe ye hym fro hensforth, for moche peyne have I hadde with hym."

And the emperour seide he wolde hem well guerdon, and the man sholde be well kepte. And than he sente to seche a smyth to bynde hym in chaynes and feteres.

220 And the savage man badde hym therof not to entermete; "for wite it right well," quod he, "I will not go withoute youre leve." And the emperour hym asked how he therof sholde be sure; and he seide he wolde hym asure by his Cristyndome. Quod the emperour, "Art thow than Cristin?" And he seide, "Ye, withoute faile." "How were thow than baptized," seide the emperour, "whan thow art so wilde?" "That

225 shall I well telle you," quod he.

"This is the trouthe, that my moder on a day com from the market of a town. And it was late whan she entred into the Foreste of Brocheland, and wente oute her wey so fer that the same nyght behoved hir to lye in the foreste. And whan she saugh she was so alone be hirself, she was aferde, and lay down under an oke

230 and fill aslepe. And than com a savage man oute of the foreste and by hir lay because she was sool by hirself. Durste she not hym diffende, for a woman aloone is feerfull. And that nyght was I begeten on my moder. And whan she was repeired hom, she was full pensif longe tyme till that she knewe verily that she was with childe. And [she] bar me so till I was born into this worlde, and was baptised in a

235 fonte, and dide me norishe till I was grete. And as soone as I cowde lyve withouten hir, I wente into the grete forestes, for by the nature of my fader behoveth me thider to repeire; and for that he was savage, I am thus wilde. Now have ye herde

208 fell, fierce. **211 ageins**, toward. **212 facion**, appearance. **214 graces**, steps. **220 entermete**, bother. **222 Cristyndome**, Christian faith. **231 sool**, alone; **Durste**, Dared. **232 repeired**, returned.

what I am."

"So God me helpe," seide the emperour, "never for me shalt thow be putte in
240   feteres ne in irenes, seth thow wilt me graunte that thow will not go withoute my
leve."

Than tolde Grisandolus how he dide laugh before the abbey and in the chapell
for the squyer that hadde smyten his maister, and the dyverse wordes that he
hadde spoken whan he asked wherefore he dide laughe. "And he seide that never
245   wolde he nought sey till he com before yow, and now is he here; and therfore,
aske hym why he hath so often laughed by the wey." And than the emperour hym
asked; and he seide he sholde it knowe all in tyme. "But sendeth first for alle youre
barouns, and than shall I telle yow that and other thinges."

With that entred the emperour into his chamber and the savage man and his
250   privé counseile. And ther thei rested and disported and spake of many thinges.
And on the morowe the emperour sente to seche his barouns, hem that he sup-
posed sonest to fynde. And than thei come anoon, bothe oon and other, from alle
partyes.

On the fourthe day after, the savage man was comen where that the lordes
255   were assembled on the maister paleise. And the emperour [called] this savage
man and made hym to sitte down by hym. And whan the barouns hadde inough
hym beholden, thei asked why he hadde for hem sente. And he tolde hem for a
vision that hym befill in his slepynge, "for I will that it be expowned before yow."
And thei seide that the significacion wolde thei gladly heren.

260   Than the emperour comaunded this man to telle the cause why that he was
sought. And he ansuerde and seide that he wolde nothinge telle till that the
emperesse and hir twelve maydones were comen. And she com anoon with gladde
semblaunce, as she that yaf no force of nothinge that myght befalle. Whan the
emperesse and hir twelve maydones were come amonge the barouns, the lordes
265   aroos agein hir and dide hir reverence.

And as soone as the savage man hir saugh comynge, he turned his heed in
traverse and began to laughe as in scorne. And whan he hadde a while laughed, he
loked on the emperour stadfastly, and than on Grisandolus, and than on the
emperesse, and than on hir twelve maydenys that weren with hir. And than he

240 seth, since. **253 partyes**, sides. **263 yaf no force of nothinge**, had no concerns
about anything. **266–67 in traverse**, askance.

270   turned toward the barouns and began to laughe right lowde as it were in dispite. Whan the emperour saugh hym so laughe, he preied hym to telle that he hadde in covenaunt, and whi that he lough now and other tymes.

      With that he stode up and seide to the emperour so lowde that all myght it heren, "Sir, yef ye me graunte as trewe emperour before youre barouns that ben here that

275   I shall not be the werse ne no harme to me therfore shall come, and that ye will yeve me leve as soone as I have yow certefied of youre avision, I shall telle yow the trewe significacion."

      And the emperour hym ansuerde and graunted that noon harme ne annoye to hym sholde be don, ne that he sholde conne hym no magré, to telle hym that he

280   was so desirouse for to heren, and that he sholde have leve to go whan hym liste. "But I praye thee, telle me myn avision in audience of alle my barouns what it was, and than shall I thee better beleve the significacion, whan thow haste me tolde of that I never spake to no creature." And he ansuerde, as for that sholde hym not greve, and therfore wolde he not lette. And than he began the avision.

285   "Sir," seide the savage man to the emperour, "it fill on a nyght that ye lay by youre wif that is here. And whan ye were aslepe, ye thought ye saugh before yow a sowe that was feire and smothe; and the heer that she hadde on her bakke was so longe that it trailed to grounde more than a fadome; and on hir heed she hadde a cercle of goolde bright shynynge. And yow semed that ye hadde norisshed that

290   sowe in youre house, but ye cowde it not verily knowe; and therwith yow semed that ye hadde hir othir tymes sein. And whan ye hadde longe thought on this thinge, ye saugh come oute of youre chamber twelve lyonsewes full feire and smothe. And thei com by the halle thourgh the courte to the sowe, and lay by hir oon after another. And whan thei hadde do that thei wolde, thei wente agein into

295   youre chamber.

      "Than com ye to youre barouns and hem asked what sholde be do with this sowe that ye saugh thus demened. And the barouns and alle the peple seide she was nothinge trewe, and thei juged to be brent bothe the sowe and the twelve lyonsewes. And than was the fier made redy grete and merveillouse in this courte,

270 dispite, scorn. **276 yeve**, give; **certefied**, explicated. **279 conne**, do, cause; **magré**, grief. **287 heer**, hair. **288 fadome**, fathom. **289 semed**, believed. **291 sein**, seen. **292 lyonsewes**, young lions. **294 do that**, done what; **wolde**, wanted. **297 demened**, treated. **298 brent**, burned.

300 and therynne was the sowe brente and the twelve lyonsewes. Now have ye herde
youre swevene in the same forme as ye it saugh in youre slepinge. And yef ye se
that I have eny thinge mystaken, sey it before your barouns." And the emperour
seide he hadde of nothinge failed.

"Sir Emperour," seide the barouns, "seth that he hath seide what was youre
305 avision, hit is to beleve the significacion yef he will it telle; and it is a thinge that
[we] wolde gladly heren."

"Certes," seide the man, "I shall it declare to yow so openly that ye may it se
and knowe apertly that I yow shall sey. The grete sowe that ye saugh signifieth
my lady the emperesse, youre wif that is ther. And the longe heer that she hadde
310 on hir bakke betokeneth the longe robes that she is ynne iclothed. And the sercle
that ye saugh on her heed shynynge betokeneth the crowne of goolde that ye made
her with to be crowned. And yef it be youre plesier, I will no more sey at this
tyme."

"Certes," seide the emperour, "yow behoveth to sey all as it is, yef ye will be
315 quyte of youre promyse."

"Certes," seide the man, "than shall I telle yow. The twelve lyonsewes that ye
saugh come oute of a chamber betokeneth the twelve maydenes that be ther with
the emperesse. And knowe it for very trouthe that thei be no wymen, for it be
men; and therefore make hem be dispoiled and ye shull se the trouthe. And as ofte
320 as ye go oute of the town, she maketh hem serve in hir chamber and in hir bedde.
Now have ye herde youre avision and the significacion. And ye may se and knowe
yef that I have seide to yow the soth."

Whan the emperour understode the untrouthe that his wif hadde don, he was so
abaisshed that he spake no worde a longe while. And than he spake and seide that
325 that wolde he soone knowe. And than he cleped Grisandolus and seide, "Dispoile
mo tho dameseles, for I will that alle the barouns that be hereynne knowe the
trouthe." And anoon Grisandolus and other lept forth and dispoiled hem before the
emperour and his barouns, and fonde hem formed alle as other men weren. And
than the emperour was so wroth that he wiste not what to do.
330 Than he made his oth that anoon ther sholde be do justice soche as was right to

---

301 swevene, dream; **yef,** if; **se,** see. **302 sey,** say. **304 seth,** since. **307 se,** see. **308
apertly,** clearly. **309 heer,** hair. **314 behoveth,** need. **315 quyte,** free. **324 abaisshed,**
disturbed. **325–26 Dispoile mo tho,** Unclothe more those. **330 do,** done.

be awarded. And the barouns juged seth she hadde don hir lorde soche untrouthe, that she sholde be brente and the harlottes hanged; and some seide that thei sholde be flayn all quyk. But in the ende thei acorded that thei sholde be brente in a fier. And anoon as the emperour herde the jugement of the barouns, he comaunded to make the fier in the place, and anoon it was don. And thei were bounde hande and foot and made hem to be caste into the brynynge fier; and in short tyme thei were alle brent, for the fier was grete and huge. Thus toke [the] emperour vengaunce of his wif. And grete was the renomede that peple of hym spake whan that it was knowen.

Whan the emperesse was brente, and thei that she hadde made hir maydenes, the barouns returned agein to the emperour and seide oon to another that the savage man was right wise and avisee, for yet shall he sey some other thinges wherof shall come some grete merveile [to] us and to all the worlde. And the emperour hymself seide that he hadde seide his avision as it was in trouthe. Thus wiste the emperour the lyvinge of his wif. And than the emperour hym called and asked yef he wolde sey eny more. And he seide "Ye," yef he asked hym whereof.

"I wolde wite," quod he, "wherefore thow didst laughe whan thow were in the foreste and loked on Grisandolus; and also whan thow were ledde before an ab-bey; and in the chapell whan the squyer smote his lorde; and why thow seidest tho wordes to my stiwarde whan he asked why thow loughe; and after, telle me what betokeneth the laughter hereynne whan thow saugh the emperesse come."

"Sir," seide the savage man, "I shall telle yow inowgh. I do yow to wite that the firste laughter that I made was for that a woman hadde me taken by her engyn, that no man cowde not do. And wite ye well that Grisandolus is the beste maiden and the trewest withynne youre reame; and therefore was it that I lough. And the laughter that I made before the abbey was for ther is under erthe before the yate the grettest tresour hidde that eny man knoweth; and therfore I lough for that it was under feet of hem that aboode after the almesse. For more richesse is in that tresour than alle the monkes beth worth, and all the abbey, and all that therto belongeth. And the pore peple that theron stoden cowde it not take. And Avenable your stywarde, that Grisandolus doth her clepen, saugh that I lowgh and asked

335

340

345

350

355

360

331 seth, since. **333 flayn all quyk,** skinned alive. **338 of,** on; **renomede,** renown. **342 avisee,** informed. **349 tho,** those. **353 engyn,** subtlety. **358 aboode after,** waited for; **almesse,** alms. **361 her,** herself.

me wherefore. And the coverte wordes that I to hir spake was for that she was chaunged into the fourme of man, and hadde take anothir habite than hir owne. And alle the wordes that I spake thei ben trewe, for by woman is many a man

365 disceyved.

"And therefore I cleped hir disceyaunt, for by women ben many townes sonken and brent, and many a riche londe wasted and exiled, and moche peple slayn. But I sey it not for noon evell that is in hir. And thow thyself maist well perceyve that be women be many worthi men shamed and wratthed that longe have loved togeder,

370 yef it were not for debate of women. But now rech thee not for thy wif that thou haste distroied, for she hath it well deserved. And have therfore no mystrust to other, for as longe as the worlde endureth it doth but apeire. And all that cometh to hem be the grete synne of luxuré that in hem is closeth. For woman is of that nature and of that disire, that whan she hath the moste worthi man of the worlde

375 to hir lorde, she weneth she have the werste. And wite ye fro whens this cometh of the grete fragelité that is in hem, and the foule corage and the foule thought that thei have where thei may beste hir volunté acomplish. But therfore be not wroth, for ther ben in the worlde [many] that ben full trewe. And yef thow have be desceyved of thyn, yet shall thow have soche oon that is worthy to be emperesse

380 and to resceyve that high dignité. And yef thow wilt it beleve, thow shalt wynne theron more than thow shalt lese.

"But the prophesie seith that the grete dragon shall come fro Rome that wolde distroie the reame of the Grete Breteyne and put it in his subjeccion, and the fierce lyon crowned, maugré the diffence of the turtill that the dragon hath norisshed

385 under his wynges. And as soone as the grete dragon shall meve to go to the Grete Breteigne, the lyon crowned shall come hym ageins, and shull fight so togeder that a fierce bole that is prowde, whiche the lyon shall bringe with hym, shall smyte so the dragon with oon of his hornes that he shall falle down deed; and therby shall

362 **coverte**, veiled. 363 **habite**, appearance. 366 **hir**, i.e., woman (not Avenable); **disceyaunt**, deceitful; **sonken**, destroyed. 369 **be¹**, because of; **wratthed**, angered. 370 **debate of**, dispute over; **rech**, concern. 372 **apeire**, occur. 373 **luxuré**, lechery; **closeth**, enclosed. 375 **weneth**, thinks. 376 **fragelité**, frailty; **corage**, desire. 377 **volunté**, wishes. 379 **of thyn**, by yours. 380 **wynne**, win. 381 **lese**, lose. 384 **maugré the diffence**, despite the contrary advice. 387 **bole**, bull.

be delyvered the grete lyon. But I will not telle the significacion of these wordes,
390 for I owe it nought to do. But all this shall falle in thy tyme; and therfore, be well
ware of evell counseile, for grete part longeth to thee.

"The tother laughter that I made in the chapell was not for the buffetes that the
squyer yaf his lorde but for the betokenynges that therynne ben. In the same place
ther the squyer stode was entred, and yet ther is undir his feet a merveillouse
395 tresour. The firste buffet that the squyer yaf his lorde signifieth that for avoure
the worlde becometh so prowde that he douteth nother God ne his soule, no more
than the squyer douted to smyte his maister. But the riche wolde oppresse the
pore under theire feet; and that make these untrewe riche peple whan enythinge
cometh to hem be myschaunce, thei swere and stare and sey maugré have God
400 for His yeftes. And wite ye what maketh this? Nothinge but pride of richesse.

"The seconde buffet betokeneth the riche userer that deliteth in his richesse and
goth scornynge his pore nyghebours that be nedy whan thei come to hym ought
for to borough. And the userer so leneth hem litill and litill, that at laste thei moste
selle theire heritage to hym that so longe hath it coveyted.

405 "The thridde buffet signifieth these false pletours, men of lawe, that sellen and
apeire theire neyghbours behinde here bakke for covetise and envye of that thei se
hem thrive, and for thei be not in her daungier. For whan these laweers sen that
her neighbours don hem not grete reverence and servise, thei thenken and aspien
how thei may hem anoyen in eny wise, and to make hem lese that thei have. And
410 therfore men seyn an olde sawe: who hath a goode neighbour hath goode morowe.

"Now have ye herde the significaciouns why the buffetes were yoven. But the
squyer delited nothinge therynne whan that he smote his maister; but he wiste not
fro whens this corage to hym com. But God that is almyghty wolde have it to be
shewed in exsample that men sholde not be prowde for worldly richesse; for to
415 covetouse theire richesse doth hem but harme, that slepen in averice and foryete
God and don the werkes of the devell, that ledeth hem to everlastinge deth. And all
is for the grete delite that thei have in richesse.

390 **owe,** ought; **nought,** not; **falle,** befall. 391 **longeth,** pertains. 393 **betokenynges,**
meanings. 394 **ther¹,** where. 395 **avoure,** possessions. 396 **douteth,** fears; **nother,** neither. 399 **be myschaunce,** by misfortune; **sey maugré,** blame (?). 402 **ought,** anything.
403 **borough,** borrow. 405 **pletours,** pleaders. 406 **apeire,** abuse. 407 **daungier,** power.
410 **sawe,** saying. 411 **yoven,** given. 413 **corage,** desire.

"But now shall I telle you whi I lough today whan I saugh the emperesse comynge and hir lechours. I do yow to wite that it was but for dispite, for I saugh that she
420 was youre wif, and hadde oon of the worthiest men of the worlde that eny man knoweth of youre yowthe. And she hadde take these twelve harlottes and wende ever for to have ledde this foly all hir lif. And therfore hadde I grete dispite for the love of yow and of youre doughter, for she is youre doughter withoute doute, and draweth litill after hir moder. Now have ye herde alle the laughtres and wherefore
425 thei were. And therfore, may I go yef it be youre plesier?"

"Now abide a litill," seide the emperour, "and telle us the trouthe of Grisandolus. And also we shull sende to digge after the tresour, for I will wite yef it be trewe." And he therto dide assent. Than the emperour comaunded that Grisandolus were sought, and so she was founden, oon of the feirest maydenes that neded to enquere
430 in eny londe. And whan the emperour knewe that Grisandolus, his stiwarde that longe hadde hym served, was a woman, he blissed hym for the wonder that he ther-of hadde. Than he asked the savage man counseile what he sholde do of that he hadde promysed to yeve his doughter and half his reame, for loth he was to falsen his promyse of covenaunt.

435 "I shall telle yow," quod the man, "what ye shull do, yef ye will do my counseile. And wite it well, it is the beste that eny man can yeven." "Sey on, than," seide the emperour, "for what counseile that thow yevest, I shall it well beleve, for I have founde thy seyinge trewe."

Than seide the savage man, "Ye shall taken Avenable to be yowre wif. And wite
440 ye whos doughter she is? She is the doughter to the Duke Matan that the Duke Frolle hath disherited and driven oute of his londe for envye with grete wronge. And he and his wif be fledde, and his sone, that is a feire yonge squyer, into Province into a riche town that is called Monpellier. And sende to seche hem and yelde hem her heritage that thei have loste with wronge. And make the mariage of
445 youre doughter and Avenables brother that is so feire, and ye may her no better be setten."

And whan the barouns undirstode that the savage man seide, thei spoke moche amonge hem, and seiden in the ende that the emperour myght do no better, after

419 **dispite**, anger; **for**, because of. 424 **draweth**, follows. 425 **yef**, if. 429 **neded to enquere**, one could find. 433 **reame**, realm. 435 **do²**, follow. 443 **seche**, seek. 444 **yelde**, give. 447 **that**, what.

theire advis. And than the emperour asked his name, and what he was, and the
450   hert that so pertly spake unto hym. And than seide he, "Sir, of that enquere no
more, for it is a thinge the more ye desire to knowe, the lesse shull ye witen."
"For sothe," seide the emperour, "now suppose I well what it may be. But shull
ye telle us eny more?"

    "Ye," quod he. "I tolde yow right now of the lyon crowned and of the lyon
455   volage; but now shall I telle yow in other manere for that ye shull be better
remembred whan tyme cometh. emperour of Rome," quod he, "this is trewe
prophesie, that the grete boor of Rome, that is signified by the grete dragon, shall
go agein the lyon crowned of the Bloy Breteyne, agein the counseile of the turtell
that hath an heed of golde and longe hath ben his love. But the boor shall be so full
460   of pride that he will not hir beleve, but shall go with so grete pride with all his
generacion into the parties of Gaule to fight with the crowned lyon that shall
come ageins hym with alle his beestes.

    "Ther shall be grete slaughter of beestes on bothe sides. Than shall oon of the
fawnes of the lyon crowned sle the grete boor. And therfore I praye thee, yef
465   thow wilt ought do for me er I departe, that thow do nothinge agein the volunté of
thy wif after that day that thow haste her wedded. And wite well, yef thow do
thus, thow shalt have profite. And now I take my leve, for here have I no more to
do."

    And the emperour betaught hym to God, seth it myght no better be. And therwith
470   he wente on his wey. And whan he com to the halle dore, he wrote letteres on the
lyntell of the dore in Grewe that seide: "Be it knowe to alle tho that these letteres
reden, that the savage man that spake to the emperour and expounded his dreme,
hit was Merlin of Northumberlande, and the hert brancus with fifteen braunches
that spake to hym in his halle at mete amonge alle his knyghtes, and was chaced
475   thourgh the citee of Rome, that spake to Avenable in the foreste whan he tolde hir
how she sholde fynde the man savage. And lete the emperour well wite that
Merlin is maister counseller to Kynge Arthur of the Grete Breteyne." And than he
departed and spake no mo wordes.

    Whan this savage man was departed from the emperour, he sente into Province

454–55 lyon volage, zealous lions. **461 parties,** territories. **464 fawnes,** i.e., young
knights. **465 volunté,** wishes. **469 betaught,** consigned. **471 Grewe,** Greek; **tho,** those.
473 hert brancus, antlered hart. **476 wite,** know.

480   to seche the fader and the moder of Avenable and Patrik hir brother, in the town of Monpeller, whider as thei were fledde. And anoon thei com, gladde and joyful of the aventure that God hadde hem sente. And whan thei were comen, thei hadde grete joye of theire doughter that thei wende never to have seyn. Than thei abide with the emperour longe tyme, and the emperour restored hem to here herytage

485   that Frolle hadde hem berafte. But as Frolle myght, he it agein seide, for he was of grete power. And so endured the werre longe tyme; but in the ende the emperour made the pees. And than he maried his doughter to Patrik, and hymself toke Avenable to his wif. And grete was the joye and the feeste that the barouns maden, for moche was she beloved bothe of riche and pore.

490   And as the emperour was in joye and deduyt of his newe spouse, ther com a massage to hym oute of Greece for a discorde that was betwene the barouns of Greese and the Emperour Adrian that sholde hem justise, for the Emperour Adrian myght unethe ride for febilnesse of age. And whan the messager hadde spoke to the emperour and don all that he sholde, he toke his leve to go. And as he caste up

495   his yie upon the halle dore, he saugh the letteres that Merlin hadde writen in Grewe. And anoon he redde hem lightly, and than he gan to laughe right harde, and shewed hem to the emperour and seide, "Sir, is this trewe that these lettres seyn?"

"What sey thei?" quod the emperour. "Wote I never." Quod the massager, "Thei

500   seyn that he that tolde yow the untrouthe of youre wif, and youre dreme expowned, and spake to yow in the gise of an herte, that it was Merlin of Northumbirlande, the maister counseller of Kynge Arthur of Breteyne, by whos counseile ye have spoused youre wif Avenable."

And whan the emperour undirstode these wordes, he merveiled sore. And than

505   befill a grete merveile whereof alle that were therynne hadde wonder, and the emperour hymself. For as soone as the emperour herde what the letteres mente, anoon the letteres vanysshed so sodeynly that no man wiste how. And therof hadde thei grete wonder, and moche it was spoken of thourgh the contrey. But now cesseth the tale of the emperour of Rome that abode in his paleis gladde and

481 whider as, where. **482 aventure**, good fortune. **483 wende**, thought. **485 hem berafte**, from them taken; **agein seide**, opposed. **487 pees**, peace. **490 deduyt**, delight. **491 massage**, message. **493 unethe**, scarcely. **495 yie**, eyes. **496 Grewe**, Greek; **lightly**, easily.

510   myry with his wif Avenable, and ledde goode lif longe tyme. For bothe were thei
yonge peple, for the emperour was but twenty-eight yere of age at that hour, and
his wif was twenty-two. And yef thei ledde myri lif, yet Patrik and Foldate, the
doughter of the emperour, lyved in more delite. But now returneth the tale agein to
speke of Merlin.

[*Summary*. *The scene shifts to Britain where the rebel barons, having consolidated
their forces, directly confront the Saxon invaders. A terrible and chaotic battle takes
place in a rain storm; when the weather clears, the Saxons drive the Christians from
the field. That night the Christians mount yet another attack upon the Saxons, and
they slaughter a great many of them. But the Saxons regroup; and returning to the
battlefield, they thoroughly rout the Christians. The defeated barons now retreat to
their home cities, not wishing to do further battle with the Saxons. Fols. 155r (line
10)–158v (line 4).*]

[The Marriage of Arthur and Gonnore]

Now seith the storie that whan the Kynge Arthur and the barouns were assembled and entred into the shippes, thei sailed till thei come to the Bloy Breteyne.
And as soone as thei were arived, thei lepe upon horse and ryde so day and nyght
till thei come to Logres the thirde day. And ther were thei richly welcomed, and
5   the moste joye that myght be made to eny peple; and ther thei dide sojourne thre
dayes with grete feeste. And the fourthe day remeved the Kynge Arthur and Gawein
and his brethren and the Kynge Ban of Benoyk and the Kynge Bohors of Gannes,
with thre thousande men of armes without moo, and rode so by her journeyes that
thei come to the reame of Carmelide, a two myle from Toraise, where the Kynge
10   Leodogan sojourned.

And whan he herde tydinges that the Kynge Arthur com, he rode ageins hym,
he and his meyné, two myle or more. And whan thei were mette ther was made
grete joye and welcomynge betwene the two kynges that well loved; and so dide
alle the other barouns and lordes. And whan thei com into the town, thei fonde it
15   all hanged with riche clothes and strowed with fresh herbes and fonde ladyes and
maydenes carolinge and daunsinge and the moste revell and disport that myght be
made. And on that other side these yonge bachelers of pris brake speres in
bourdinge oon agein another; and thus thei conveyed hem unto the town whereas
Gonnore, the doughter of Kynge Leodogan, com hem for to meten.
20   But whoso made joye, she was gladdest of alle other; for as soone as she saugh
the Kynge Arthur, she ran to hym with armes spredde abrode, and seide he was
welcome and alle his companye. And she kiste his mouth tendirly, seynge hem
alle that wolde; and than eche toke other by the hande and wente up into the
paleise. And whan it was tyme of soper, thei ete and dranke grete plenté, for

6 **remeved**, departed. **8 moo**, more. **11 ageins**, toward. **12 meyné**, company. **14 fonde**,
found. **15 strowed**, bestrewn. **17 pris**, worth; **brake**, broke. **18 bourdinge**, sport; **whereas**,
where. **20 whoso**, whoever. **22–23 seynge hem alle**, in sight of them all.

25 inough thei have whereof. And whan thei hadde disported hem a longe while after
soper, they wente to bedde for to resten hem, for wery they were of traveile.

And on the morowe erly aroos the Kynge Arthur and the Kynge Bohors and
the Kynge Ban and Sir Gawein and Ewein, that gladly roos ever erly more than
eny other, and wente to the mynster to here messe. And than [thei] com agein into
30 the paleise above and fonde the Kynge Leodogan that hadde herde messe in his
chapell. And than thei asked horse and rode forth tho six withoute eny moo, and
yede to disporte hem and to se the medowes and the river. And than the Kynge
Leodogan aresoned the Kynge Arthur and asked hym whan he sholde spousen his
doughter, for he seide that it was tyme. And the Kynge Arthur ansuerde that
35 whiche hour that hym plesed, for he was therto redy. "But I moste abide the beste
frende that I have, for withoute hym will I do nothinge in no manere." And than
he asked whiche was that frende, and he tolde hem how it was Merlin, "Be whom
I have recovered londe and honour and all the goode that I have ellis." And whan
Sir Gawein undirstode tho wordes, he seide that he hadde grete reson for to love
40 hym well. "And eche oon of us oweth to desire his comynge; and wite it well, he
shall come er ought longe, seth that ye hit desire."

"Certes," seide the Kynge Arthur, "he tolde me that he sholde be here all in
tyme." "Than ther is no more," quod Gawein, "but lete us sette the day of
spousaile." And than toke thei day togeder the utas after, and com thus spekynge
45 into the halle, and fonde the clothes leyde and all thinge redy. And than thei waissh
as thei ought to do, and weren served as noble princes sholden be. And after mete
thei wente to disporte, thei that wolde; and thus thei sojourned alle the eight days
full. But now resteth a litill to speke of hem at this tyme, and returne to the twelve
princes that were disconfit before the town of Clarence.

*[Summary. The rebel barons learn that Arthur has knighted the Young Squires and
that King Lot's wife is safe and in Logres but will not be returned until Lot does*

25 whereof, thereof. **29 agein,** afterward. **30 fonde,** found. **31 tho,** those; **moo,** more. **32
yede,** went. **33 aresoned,** spoke to; **spousen,** wed. **35 whiche,** whatever; **abide,** wait for.
37 Be, By. **38 recovered,** received; **ellis,** also. **40 oweth,** ought; **wite,** know. **41 er ought,**
before; **seth,** since. **42 Certes,** Indeed. **44 spousaile,** the wedding; **toke thei day,** they
chose the day; **the utas after,** one week later. **45 clothes leyde,** tablecloths in place. **46
mete,** dinner.

homage to Arthur. The rebels also hear of Arthur's success against Claudas de la deserte, of his success against King Rion, and of his plan to marry the daughter of King Leodegan. Most of the rebels now regret ever opposing Arthur. Lot is relieved to learn his wife and baby son are safe but is angered by his sons' actions against him; he forms a plan to kidnap Gonnore when Arthur sends her to Logres. Meanwhile Merlin reports all that has been happening to Blase.

A second plot is being formed against Gonnore, this one involving Gonnore's half-sister, the false Gonnore, who is the illegitimate daughter of Leodegan and the wife of Cleodalis (Leodegan's seneschal). Because Leodegan has dishonored his seneschal by sleeping with his wife, he has many enemies among Cleodalis's friends and kin who are eager for a chance to get back at him. Unbeknownst to Cleodalis, a group of them plan to kidnap Gonnore and put the false Gonnore in her place. Fols. 159r (line 15)– 160r (line 21).]

50   But anoon as thei hadde this treson spoken, Merlin it wiste and tolde it to Ulfin and to Bretell, and toke hem aside in counseile alone by hymself, and tolde hem worde for worde all the untrouthe that thei purposed to don. And whan Ulfin and Bretell herde the treson that these wolde have don, thei hadde therof grete merveile; and than thei preied Merlin to telle how thei sholde spede of this thinge. "With
55   gode will," seide Merlin. "Tomorowe at even whan ye have souped, arme yow well undir youre robes and goth into the chamber next the gardin under the graces that is ther, for thei shull come alle unarmed saf hir swerdes and shull come though the gardin streight to the wiket, whereas thei shull bide till that that maistresse bringe hir to disporte. But loke anoon as thei have hir sesed that ye be
60   not feynte her to rescowe, for than anoon have ye her loste for ever yef thei may bringe hir to the shippe."

"Sir," seide these two goode men, "yef God will, we shull not her lese, seth we knowe so moche therof." "And loke also," quod Merlin, "that ye speke hereof no worde to no man of nothinge that I have to yow iseide, for than shall I never yow
65   love." "Certes," seide these two noble men, "we hadde lever be disherited and chaced oute of the londe."

50 **wiste**, knew. 52 **untrouthe**, deception. 53 **merveile**, wonder. 54 **preied**, asked; **spede of**, deal with. 54–55 **With gode will**, Gladly. 55 **at even**, in the evening; **souped**, supped. 56 **graces**, steps. 58 **wiket**, doorway; **whereas**, where. 59 **sesed**, seized. 60 **not feynte**, not afraid; **yef**, if. 62 **lese**, lose; **seth**, since. 65 **lever**, rather.

Tho dide departe these thre frendes and com into the halle and fonde that the knyghtes sholde departe and wente to theire loigginge till on the morowe that it was day. And than arise the barouns and the knyghtes and assembled faste in the mynster paleise. And the Kynge Leodogan appareiled his doughter so richely as that never quene ne myght be better araied. And she therto was so full of grete bewté that all the worlde was gladde hir to beholden. And whan she was all redy, the Kynge Ban toke hir on that oon side and the Kynge Bohors on that other side and ledde hir to the mynster of Seynt Stephene the Martir. Ther was many a baron hir to conveien, holdinge be the hondes two and two, and formest that wente was Kynge Arthur and Kynge Leodogan. And the other tweyne was nexte after was Gawein and Seigramour, and than Galashin and Agravain the Prowde, and than Dodinell and Gueheret, and than Ewein le Graunt and Gaheries, and after that Ewein Avoutres and Kay Destranx, and Kay the Stiward and Antor his fadir; and after hem com the maiden that the Kynge Ban and the Kynge Bohors ledden that was of so grete bewté. And she was discheveled and hadde the feirest heed that eny woman myght have, and hadde a sercle of goolde on hir heed full of preciouse stones, the feirest and the richest that eny man knewe, and was clothed in a riche robe that trayled to the grounde more than two fadome, that satte so well with hir bewté that all the worlde myght have joye her to beholden.

And after hir com the stepdoughter of Cleodalis that hight also Gonnore, whiche was right feire and avenaunt; and hir ledde Gifflet and Lucas the Boteller. And after com the newe dubbed knyghtes two and two; and after com the Knyghtes of the Rounde Table; and after that com the barouns of the reame of Carmelide and the knyghtes; and after the burgeys of the contrey; and than the ladyes of the contrey and maydenes. And so thei come to the mynster.

Whan thei come to the dore, thei fonde ther the goode archebisshop that ther hem abode, and Sir Amnistan, the chapeleyn of Kynge Leodogan, that was a gode man of lyvinge. And the archebisshop hem blessed; and before alle the peple wedded the Kynge Arthur and Gonnore togeder. And the goode archebisshop entred into the chirche and sange the high masse, and Sir Amnistan hym served; and ther was riche offringe of kynges and princes. And whan the servise was

67 **Tho**, Then. 68 **wente**, go. 69 **arise**, arose. 73 **oon**, side. 75 **conveien**, accompany; **be**, by. 80 **ledden**, led. 81 **discheveled**, bare-headed. 82 **sercle**, circlet. 86 **hight**, was named; **whiche**, who. 87 **avenaunt**, comely. 93 **abode**, awaited; **chapeleyn**, chaplain.

fynisshed, the Kynge Arthur and the barouns returned into the paleys whereas was grete plenté of mynstralles and jogelours and other. Whereto sholde I yow

100   devise the joye and the deduyt that thei hadden? For the fourthe part cowde I not telle.

Thus endured the joye and the melodye all the mete-while. And after mete, whan the boordes were uppe, than was arered a quyntayn, and thyder yede the newe adubbed knyghtes for to bourde with sheldes aboute theire nekkes; and the

105   Forty Knyghtes that com into Carmelide with the Kynge Arthur wente with hem, and also com thider the Knyghtes of the Rounde Table. And whan thei were comen, thei begonne to do maistries jolily and in myrthe, as thei that were worthy men and noble knyghtes; so that tidinges com to Sir Gawein that satte at mete amonge his fellowes that hadden served. And whan Gawein undirstode that his frendes

110   were oversette, he aroos up and asked his armes and horse and his shelde, and anoon it was brought. And so dide alle his felowes. And Gawein dide on an habergon of double maile under his robes, for that was ever more his custome ever as longe as he lyved — nought for that he thought to do eny vilonye ne treson, but for he douted ever that debate sholde arise amonge his felowes thourgh the dedes of

115   some musarde or eny treson, whereof ther were inowe in the londe.

But whan that Gawein and his felowes com into the medowes, whereas was the turnement well begonne. But the Newe Knyghtes were evell ledde, for the Knyghtes of the Rounde Table ledde hem at her volunté. And whan that Gawein saugh that thei were so at the werse, he was nothinge gladde. Than he and his

120   companye wenten in that were well foure score acounted; and anoon these yonge knyghtes come to Gawein and asked yef he wolde be with hem, and he seide "Ye,

99 jogelours, entertainers; **Whereto,** Why. **99–100 yow devise,** relate to you. **100 deduyt,** delight; **cowde,** could. **102 all the mete-while,** all through dinner. **103 boordes were uppe,** tables were removed; **arered,** raised; **quyntayn,** tilting board; **thyder yede,** thither went. **104 bourde,** sport. **107 maistries,** great deeds. **108 so that,** and so; **tidinges com,** messages were taken. **109 undirstode,** realized. **110 oversette,** defeated. **111 dide on,** put on; **habergon,** mail shirt. **113 nought for that,** not because; **thought to do,** expected to be done. **114 douted ever,** always suspected; **debate,** strife; **thourgh,** through. **115 musarde,** trouble-maker; **eny,** some. **116 whereas,** already. **117 evell ledde,** ill-treated. **118 volunté,** wishes. **120 wenten in,** charged in.

bothe now and also other tymes."

Whan the Forty Sowdiours herde that Sir Gawein wolde be with hem at that
same turnement, thei were wonder gladde and joyfull, and the tother were full
125   wroth. And than thei assured that never noon sholde faile other for deth ne for lif;
and no more thei diden, and that well shewed that day, for thei diden so well that
the Knyghtes of the Rounde Table therof hadde envye. For dere sholde be bought
the same turnement, in the turnement that was made at Logres, theras Gawein
was called lorde and maister for the wele doinge that he ther dide, as ye shull
130   heren hereafter, whan that he was become the Queenes Knyght. And whan that
Gawein hadde take the suerté of his felowes and of the Forty Knyghtes, of whiche
ye have herde, thei renged hem and araide hem and girde agein theire horse. And
Gawein sette hem in aray as he that was a wise knyght and withoute pride and the
moste curteise that was in the Bloy Breteyne and the beste taught in alle thinges
135   and ever trewe to God and to his lorde.

And whan that Gawein hadde ordeyned his felowes in aray, thei rode two and
two togeder eche after other; and tweyne the firste was Sir Gawein and Sir Ewein
le Graunt, the sone of Kynge Urien, that Gawein loved beste of alle other, for he
was the beste after Gaheries; and the nexte tweyne were Seigramour and Galashyn;
140   and than Gefflet and Lucas the Boteller for to assemble theire sheldes aboute her
nekkes and her speres streight in theire handes. And the Kynge Arthur and the
Kynge Ban and the Kynge Bohors and Merlin and Bretell and Ulfin and Antor
were lefte with the Kynge Leodogan in the paleise, and were comen up on high
for to se and beholde the bourdeyse. And with hem weren ladyes and maydenys
145   grete plenté, and saugh that thei were redy araide for to mete.

*[Summary. In the Tournament at Toraise, the 150 Knights of the Round Table chal-
lenge the New Knights who are led by Gawain. They agree to Gawain's suggestion
that a limited and equal number of knights should fight at one time, and they set the
number at forty vs. forty. In the mêlée, Gawain overcomes Nascien and urges him to
yield; when Nascien says he would rather die than yield, Gawain is so impressed by
Nascien's "high herte" that he offers to yield to Nascien; seeing Gawain's great
courtesy, Nascien yields to Gawain; and then the two knights embrace.*

123 Sowdiours, Soldiers. **124 tother,** other. **131 suerté,** pledges. **132 renged hem,**
ordered themselves; **araide hem,** readied themselves. **136 ordeyned,** ordered; **aray,**
formation. **144 bourdeyse,** jousting. **145 redy araide,** prepared; **mete,** meet each other.

As the fight continues, Gawain's knights overcome forty of the Round Table knights, who then send in a fresh group. Gawain overthrows many of them, and Ewain and Galashin and Dodinell also do well. The Knights of the Round Table are angry at being humilated by these young knights, and tempers begin to flare. Then Gawain sets aside his sword and enters the fray wielding a spar of oak, raging like a wild boar. Because the tournament has gotten out of hand, Merlin and the kings rush down to the field and separate the wrathful knights. Merlin and Arthur both tell Gawain that he has done enough and that the tournament is over. The Round Table knights are still resentful; but they praise Gawain and invite him to become one of them. Fols. 161v (line 9)–164r (line 25).]

With that were the tables leide and the knyghtes wash; and ther were thre halles full of knyghtes, and thei were well served and by leiser of alle thinges. And after soper, whan the clothes weren up, thei ennoysed the worthi knyghtes, and eche reported of other honour as was right. And than thei ronge to evesonge in the Mynster of Seynt Stephene, and thider thei wente to here the servise; and after was the bedde of Arthur blessed, as was right. And than departed the knyghtes and wente to theire hostelles for to slepe and resten.

And Gonnore belefte in the chamber, she and hir maistresse alone. And that day was purchesed the treson wherby she sholde be taken and traied of the parentes of Gonnore, the stepdoughter of Cleodales the stiwarde, for thei hadde yoven so moche to the olde maistresse of Arthurs wif that she graunted to do theire volunté. And [thei] tolde hir thei wolde abide in the gardin under the paleise, and thei sholde have the tother Gonnore in her companye. And all thus thei were acorded and wente into the gardin and hidde hem under the trees, ten of hem. But thei were not armed saf thei hadde eche of hem a suerde; and with hem was the false Gonnore. And ther thei abide so longe that the barouns were departed to her hostels.

And thei made dispoile the quene to go to hir bedde. And than the olde maistresse hir toke and ledde hir into the gardin for to pisse. And whan the ten traitoris that were quatte in the gardin under an ympe saugh her come, thei were stille and coy and drough towarde the wall litill and litill. And Bretell and Ulfin hadde not foryete

150

155

160

165

148 **ennoysed**, praised. 153 **belefte**, remained. 154 **purchesed**, done; **traied of**, betrayed by; **parentes**, i.e., relatives. 155 **yoven**, given. 156 **volunté**, wishes. 160 **saf**, except; **suerde**, sword. 162 **made dispoile**, prepared. 164 **quatte**, hidden; **ympe**, tree; **coy**, quiet. 165 **drough**, drew.

the wordes that Merlin hadde seide, but were well armed under her robes, and
weren quat under the steyres theras the queene sholde come down, and hilde hem
so stille that thei were not aparceyved of man ne woman, and herkened in this
manere longe while, and than thei saugh the queene that the maistresse brought by
170   the hande and wente that wey whereas the traitours hadde sette theire waicch.

And whan thei saugh that thei weren oute of the chambre, thei lepe up and sette
hande on hir and toke to the olde maistresse the tother false Gonnore. And anoon
as the queene hem saugh, she wiste well she was betraied and wolde crye as she
that was sore affraied. And thei seide that yef she spake eny worde she sholde
175   anon be slain; and therwith thei drough theire swerdes oute and wente toward the
river that ran under the gardin, where thei hadde a barge iteyed wherein thei were
come into the gardin. And the gardin was right high above the river, and noon
myght come therto but by a lane or by a barge. And the lane was full thikke and
comberouse to come up or down for the rokkes wherof was grete plenté. And yef
180   thei myght have brought hir into the barge, the queene hadde ben loste withoute
recover.

Whan Ulfin and Bretell saugh that thei hadde so longe awayted, thei lepte oute of
theire enbusshement and hem ascryed and cleped hem traitours and seide thei
sholde dye. And whan that the traitours saugh thei were but tweyne and dide hem
185   ascrye, thei preised hem at nought. Than five of hem toke the queene, and five
abode for to fight with the tweyne that com with swerdes drawen. And whan the
queene saugh hir ledde in soche manere, she hadde grete drede and fill to grounde
upon the grene; and thei lifte hir up and bare hir awey maugré hire. And whan she
saugh tweyne come hir to socour, she braied rudely oute of there handes and
190   [ronne] down the gardin till she com to an ympe and clippe it in hir armes full
hard. And thise com for to take hir awey, but they myght not hir remeve, and yet
thei pulde and drough, but more dide thei nought. And thei were nygh woode for

166 her, their. **167 quat**, hidden; **steyres**, stairs; **theras**, where. **168 aparceyved of**, seen
by. **173 wolde crye**, wanted to cry out. **174 sore affraied**, greatly frightened; **yef**, if. **176
wherein**, in which. **179 comberouse**, difficult; **yef**, if. **182 that**, that which. **183
enbusshement**, ambush; **ascryed**, rebuked; **cleped**, called. **184 and**, i.e., that. **185 ascrye**,
acost; **preised**, valued. **188 maugré hire**, despite her wishes. **189 braied rudely**, jerked
quickly. **190 ympe**, tree; **clippe**, clasped. **191 thise**, these men; **yet**, though. **192 woode**,
insane.

sorowe and angre that for a litill thei wolde hir have slayn.

And Ulfin and Bretell be come to these five that hem abide with swerdes drawen;
195   and Bretell smote so the firste that he mette that he slytte hym to the teth, and
Ulfin smote another that the heede fill to grounde. And the other thre smyte at hem
sore, but nought thei myght hem apeire, for thei were well armed. And thei wolde
have fledde, but thei kepte hem so shorte that alle thre there were deed. And thei
com to the tother fyve that peyned to lede awey the quene by force, but thei
200   myght not have hir awey from the ympe. And thei plukked at hir so sore that nygh
thei rente bothe armes from the body. And whan that Ulfin and Bretell saugh the
queene in soche turnement, thei ronne thider and hem ascried. And anoon thei
com hem ageins, and yaf togeder grete strokes with swerdes theras thei myght
atteyne, that thei slowgh tweyne of the five. And thei saugh thei were but thre,
205   and thei turned to flight down the lane towarde the barge.

And whan Ulfin and Bretell saugh hem fleen, thei sette no force hem to enchace
but com to the olde devell, the maistresse, and caught hir by the sholderes and
caste hir down the roche; and [she] rolled fro roche to roche till she com to the
river. And than thei caste in the bodyes of alle hem that thei hadde slayn. And
210   than thei toke the queene and ledde hir to hir chambre sore affraied, and thei
badde hir be nothinge dismayed. Than thei toke the false Gonnore and ledde hir to
theire hostell, for thei wolde that noon aparceyved her covyne.

Thus, as ye have herde, were the traitours demened by the counseile of Merlin,
and the Queene was socoured by these two worthi men. And as soone as thei were
215   gon, anoon Merlin it knewe well; and than he badde the kynge sende two maydenes
into the chamber to the queene for to bringe hir to bedde. And the kynge asked,
"Wherefore is ther not inowgh of the maistresse?" And Merlin tolde him the trouthe,
all as it was befallen. And whan the kynge it herde, he merveiled moche of this
thinge, and seide he sholde not be in ese till he hadde spoken with his doughter.

196 **heede,** head. 197 **apeire,** injure. 198 **kepte hem so shorte,** dealt with them so
quickly. 199 **peyned,** tried. 200 **sore,** strongly; **nygh,** nearly. 201 **rente,** tore. 202
turnement, torment; **ascried,** acosted. 203 **yaf,** gave; **theras,** where. 204 **atteyne,** reach;
slowgh, slew. 206 **sette no force,** made no attempt; **enchace,** chase. 212 **wolde,** wished;
noon aparceyved her covyne, no one knew where she was confined. 213 **demened,**
thwarted. 215 **the kynge,** i.e., Leodegan. 217 **Wherefore . . . maistresse,** Why is not
the mistress sufficient. 219 **in ese,** relieved.

220   And than departed the Kynge Leodogan and com into the chamber whereas
Gonnore his doughter was, and brought with hym two maydenes to helpe hir to
bedde. And whan she saugh hir fader, she began tenderly to wepe; and the kynge
toke hir by the hande and spake with hir sooll by hirself, and he badde hir not to be
dismayed, for she sholde no more have no drede. And she tolde hym all the aventure
225   that was befallen. And than the kynge comaunded the maydenes to make hir redy
and bringe hir to bedde, and thei anoon dide his comaundement. And the Kynge
Leodogan wolde never departe oute of the chambre till that he saugh the signe of
the crowne upon hire reynes; and than wiste he verily that it was his doughter
upon his wif, and than he covered hir agein and wente oute of the chambre and
230   spake no worde. And the dameseiles merveiled sore whi that he dide so.

And than com the Kynge Arthur and his companye from theire disporte. And
whan he com into the halle, the Kynge Leodogan and Merlin com hym ageins and
badde hym go to his wif to bedde, for it was reson and high tyme. And he seide he
wolde with goode will, and com into the chambre where the two maidenes weren
235   that hadde brought the queene to bedde. And as soone as he was in his bedde, thei
departed oute of the chambre and lefte no moo but hem two; and ther thei ledde
myri lif togeder as thei that well loved.

Thus sholde the queene have be disceyved be these traitours, and thorugh hem
afterward hadde she grete annoye that longe tyme endured, as the storye shall
240   declare, how that the kynge hir lefte thre yer, that she com never in his companye
but was with Galehaut, a riche prince in the reame of Sorloys, for the love of
Launcelot. And the Kynge Arthur hilde in avoutrye the false Gonnore till that a
maladie hir toke; and Bertelak a traitour that made he wolde hir not forsake for no
man till that she stanke and rotened above erthe. And the reame was therfore nygh
245   thre yere enderdited, and stode acursed that never manes body ne womans was
byried in noon halowed place, but acursed be the centense of Holy Cherche. And
all this trouble suffred oure Lorde hem for to have for hir synnes that were right
grete; and all this com thourgh a knyght that died after upon myschevouse deth,
as ye shull here declared in the seconde book of this storie, and it is reson to telle

223 sooll, alone. **228 reynes**, loins. **229 upon**, begotten upon. **232 hym ageins**, to him.
238 be², by. **239 annoye**, difficulties. **240 the kynge**, i.e., Arthur; **lefte**, abandoned; **yer**,
years. **242 hilde in avoutrye**, held in adultery. **243 toke**, took; **that made**, made it so
that. **245 enderdited**, under interdict. **246 centense**, sentence. **249 here**, hear.

250 what was the cause that it fill.

This was the trouthe, that the Kynge Leodogan was a noble knyght and kepte well justice and right. And he hadde with hym a wise knyght that hadde don hym goode servise; and he was come of high lynage and hadde be a goode knyght in his tyme and was cleped Bertelak. And he hated a knyght dedly for that he hadde

255 slayn his cosin germain for his wif that he loved. And whan Bertelak wiste that he hadde his cosin slain and his wif diffouled, he ne deyned not to make no playnt to the Kynge Leodogan but com to hym and hym diffied, and awaited hym after many a day and many a nyght.

And it fill that same even that Arthur hadde wedded his wif that the knyghtes

260 departeden fro the court and wente to theire hostels; and [it] happed that Bertelak mette that knyght and with hym two squyers; and anoon Bertelak ran upon hym and hym slowgh. And whan he hadde don, he wente to his hostell; and the two squyers that were with the knyght made a grete crie that the peple ronne oute on alle parties with lanternes and brondes of fire and torches brennynge, and fonde

265 the knyght slayn. And thei aske the two squyers that made so grete doell who hadde hym slain, and thei seide that Bertelak the Rede hadde it don. And whan the squyers hadde cried and braied for theire lord longe while, thei toke hym up and bar hym to theire hostell, and dide hym birie as oon sholde do a deed knyght, and dide the servise at cherche as therto belonged.

270 And on the morowe, Ulfin and Bretell sente after Cleodalis the Stiward for to come speke with hem in her hostell; and he com anoon with goode chere as fre and debonair. And anoon as he was comen, thei toke hym in counseile and tolde hym all the aventure as it was befallen how his doughter hadde wrought. And whan he hadde herde the untrouthe of hire, he seide his doughter was she not.

275 "For yef she hadde be my doughter, she hadde not don this for nothinge that is in the erthe." And as thei spake togeder amonge hem thre.

The Kynge Leodogan was arisen erly, for sore was he affraied of the merveiles that were befalle that nyght of his doughter. And Merlin was also arisen and seide,

255 cosin germain, first cousin; **wiste,** knew. **256 diffouled,** raped; **ne deyned not,** chose not; **no playnt,** a complaint. **257 diffied,** challenged; **awaited hym after,** watched for him. **261 anoon,** immediately. **262 slowgh,** slew. **264 parties,** sides; **brennynge,** burning. **267 braied,** wept. **268 birie,** bury. **271–72 fre and debonair,** [one] generous and courteous. **273 wrought,** acted. **275 yef,** if. **276 as,** thus.

"Sir, God yeve yow goode morowe." And whan the kynge hym saugh, he made
280   hym feire chere and bad God hym blisse. Than eche toke other be the hande and
wente spekynge of many thinges till thei com to the hostell of Ulfin and Bretell.
And thei entred in so stilliche that thei therof wiste no worde till thei were even
comen upon hem. And anoon as thei were of hem war, thei yede hem ageins as
thei that nothinge were abaisshed to worship eny worthi man. Than thei entred
285   into a chambre alle five, and Ulfin brought forth Gonnore and tolde how she and
the traitours hadde wrought, notwithstondinge thei knewe it alle wele, for Merlin
hadde it tolde the kynge all as it was.

Than spake the Kinge Leodogan to his stiwarde and seide, "Sir Senescall, I love
yow well, and fayn I wolde purchace youre worship for to encrece, and so I shall
290   do yef I may lyve, for full well ye have me served and trewly. And therfore wolde
I do nothinge that sholde yow turne to shame or reprof, and wite ye wherfore I it
sey. Se here youre doughter, that wele hath deserved that ther sholde be don on
hir justice. But ye have be so trewe to me that I ought it wele to pardon for the
love of yow, or a gretter thinge than is this. But for that me behoveth for to take
295   vengaunce in some manere, hit behoveth yow to bringe hir oute of this reame in
soche wise that never she be sein of man ne of woman that hir knowe; for so I will
that it be done."

And the stiwarde ansuerde and seide that his doughter ne was she never. But in
as moche as it was his wille and his comaundement, he wolde hit don. "For so
300   God helpe me," quod he, "I hadde lever she hadde be biried all quyk than this
hadde hir befallen. Ne to me she ne aperteyned nothinge never." "Now," quod the
kynge, "lete be all this matier and loke that it be don in soche maner that I never
here more speche of hir hereafter, and that ye take of myne what that is youre
plesier."

279 **yeve**, give. 282 **stilliche**, quietly; **wiste**, knew. 283 **anoon as**, as soon as; **war**,
aware; **yede hem ageins**, went to him. 284 **abaisshed**, hesitant. 286 **wrought**, done;
notwithstondinge, despite the fact. 289 **fayn I wolde purchace**, happily would I cause;
worship, honor; **encrece**, increase. 292 **Se**, See. 293 **be**, been. 294 **me behoveth for**, I am
required. 295 **hit behoveth**, it is right for. 296 **sein of**, seen by; **will**, wish. 298 **ne was**,
was. 299 **wolde hit don**, would it do. 300 **hadde lever**, would rather; **be biried all quyk**,
been buried alive. 301 **Ne**, Nor; **ne aperteyned nothinge**, means nothing at all. 303 **here**,
hear.

305 Thus was take the counseile of the barouns. And Cleodalis appareiled hym and his stepdoughter to go withouten lenger respite, and rode forth by theire journeyes till thei com oute of the reame of Carmelide into an abbey that stode in a full wilde place. And ther he hir lefte, as seith the storie, till that Bertelak the Reade hir fonde, whiche by his art and his engyn by hir lay longe tyme after. But of hir as

310 now speketh no more the tale, saf that Cleodalis lefte hir there and com agein to Toraise into the grete court of the Kynge Leodogan in Carmelide whereas was the Kynge Arthur.

---

305 take, taken; **appareiled hym**, prepared himself. **306 lenger respite**, further hesitation. **307 wilde**, desolate. **309 fonde**, found; **engyn**, devices; **as**, for. **310 saf**, except.

[The Banishment of Bertelak; and King Arthur and King Lot]

Whan the Kynge Leodogan hadde comaunded his stiwarde to bringe his stepdoughter oute of the reame, he and Merlin departed from Ulfin and Bretell and com into the halle hande in hande, where thei fonde the barouns alle redy. And oon hadde ronge to masse, and so thei wente to the mynster; and whan masse was seide, thei com agein into the halle.

And than com the kyn of the deed knyght that Bertelak hadde slain for to make theire complainte to the kynge. And the Kynge Leodogan sente for to seche hym at his hostell, and he com anoon withoute daunger, well armed undir his robes, and brought with hym grete plenté of knyghtes, for he was full of feire courtesie and a feire speker. And anoon the kynge hym asked why he hadde the knyght slain in treson. And he seide that of treson he sholde hym wele diffende agein alle tho that wolde hym apele. "And I sey no nay but that I slough the knyght; but firste I dide hym deffie; and it was not withoute grete cause, for moche peple knowe wele that he slough my cosin germain for his wif that he diffouled. And me semeth that in alle maners that oon may, oweth he to greve his mortall enmye after that he hath hym diffied."

And the kynge seide that that was not inough. "But yef ye hadde yow complayneth to me and I wolde not have it redressed, than myght ye have take vengaunce; but ye ne spake therof to me never worde." "Sir," quod he, "ye sey your volunté. But ageins yow mysdide I never, ne never ne shall, yef God will."

---

7 **seche**, seek. **11 of treson**, concerning treason; **agein**, against. **12 tho**, those; **apele**, accuse; **sey no nay but**, do not deny; **slough**, slew. **13 deffie**, challenge; **moche**, many. **14 cosin germain**, first cousin; **diffouled**, defiled. **14–15 me semeth**, I believe. **15 in alle maners that oon may**, in any way one can; **oweth he to greve**, he should injure. **16 diffied**, formally challenged. **18 take**, taken. **19–20 ye sey your volunté**, you may say what you wish. **20 ageins**, against; **mysdide I never**, I never did wrong; **ne¹**, nor.

255

Quod the kynge, "I will that right be hadde." "Sir," seide Bertelak le Rous, "I se well that I moste be at youre volunté." And than comaunded the Kynge Leodogan that jugement sholde be yoven be the rede of his barouns.

At this jugement was the Kynge Arthur and the Kynge Ban and the Kynge
25   Bohors and Sir Gawein and Sir Ewein and Galasshin and Nascien and Adragain and Hervy de Rivel and Guyomar. These ten were at the jugement, and spake togeder of oon thinge and other; and thei acorded in the ende that he sholde be disherited and voyde the londe of the Kynge Leodogan forever more. And the Kynge Ban, that was of feire eloquense, tolde the tale as he was charged; and he
30   spake so high that he myght wele be herde bothe of nygh and fer.

"Sirs," quod he, "these barouns that beth here awarded that Bertelais le Rous shall be disherited of all his londe that he holdeth in youre powere, and shall forswhere the contré forever more, for that he toke the justice upon hymself of the knyght that he slough, and namly by nyght, for the justice longed not to hym. And
35   on that other side, ye holde court open and myghty that oweth to condite alle saf goynge and saf comynge to alle tho that come at this high feste." And with that sat down the Kynge Ban that no more seide at that tyme.

And whan Bertelays saugh he was forjuged and that he ne myght noon otherwise do, he returned withoute moo wordes; for he durste not the jugement withsey,
40   for the highest lordes of the worlde and the moste puyssaunt hadde it don. But yef eny other hadde it don, anoon he wolde the jugement have falsed. And thus wente Bertelais le Rous; but many a knyght hadde he hym to conveye to whom he hadde yoven many feire yeftes, for he hadde be a noble knyght and a vigerouse.

And so he past forth on his journeyes that he com to the same abbey whereas
45   was the false Gonnore; and ther he abode and sojourned longe tyme, and was in grete thought as he that cowde moche evell, how that he myght be avenged of the Kynge Leodogan and the Kynge Arthur that hadde hym thus forejuged. And for

21 will, desire; **right be hadde,** justice is observed; **se,** see. **22 moste be at youre volunté,** must abide by your wishes. **23 yoven be,** given by; **rede,** advice. **28 voyde,** leave. **29 tale,** verdict. **30 high,** loudly. **31 awarded,** decided. **33 forswhere,** forswear. **34 longed,** belonged. **35 on that other side,** in addition to which; **holde,** held; **oweth,** ought to; **condite,** permit; **saf,** safe. **36 tho,** those. **38 saugh,** saw; **forjuged,** found guilty; **noon,** nothing. **39 moo,** more; **durste,** dared; **withsey,** oppose. **40 puyssaunt,** powerful. **41 have falsed,** challenged. **44 that,** until; **whereas,** where. **46 cowde,** knew. **47 forejuged,** condemned.

that fill to Arthur grete trouble and so grete discorde betwene hym and his wif that he lefte her longe tyme, as ye shull here in the seconde book of this processe, yef God will vouchsaf to graunte me so longe space to writen it. But now we must cesse of this mater and speke of the goode Kynge Arthur that is at Toraise in Carmelide with the Kynge Leodogan, and with the grete companye.

Full myry lif ledde the Kynge Arthur with his wif eight dayes. And the neynthe day after that he was spoused, he cleped his barouns and badde hem make hem redy to ride, for he was in talent for to repeire into the reame of Logres; and thei seide that thei were all redy to ride. And than the kynge toke Gawein in counseile and seide, "Feire nevew, take with yow as many of youre companye that ther leve here but five hundred, for I will come ride after stilleche and esely. And ye shall go to Logres, my chief citee, and ordeyne redy alle thinges that is nessessarie, and of vitaile and of deynteis as ye may, so that nothinge ne faute. And sendith fer and nygh that I will holde court this mydde August, the richest that I may." "Sir," seide Gawein, "I have drede lest ye be encombred be the wey of some maner peple." "Of that have ye no drede," quod the kynge, "but go ye in all haste."

Than departed Sir Gawein from his uncle and com to his felowes, and bad hem to make hem redy for to ride. And thei wente to theire hostelles and hem armed; but firste thei toke leve of the Kynge Leodogan and of the barouns of Carmelide; and thus departed Gawein fro the courte, he and his companye. And the Kynge Arthur abode with five hundred men, whereof two hundre and fifty were Knyghts of the Rounde Table.

And Gawein and his companye com to Logres. But Gawein was ever pensif for his uncle that he hadde lefte in Carmelide, that hym sholde eny thinge myshappe upon the wey, for he hadde fer contrey to ride that marched into his enmyes er he com into his londe in safté. And he hym hasted to do the kynges comaundement, and sente to alle hem that the kynge loved that thei sholde come to his court at the myddell of August. And eche made hym redy to come to court as strongely as thei

47–48 **for that fill to,** as a result it caused. **49 here,** hear; **yef,** if. **51 cesse,** cease. **53 myry,** merry. **55 was in talent,** desired. **57–58 that ther leve here,** so that is left here. **58 will come ride,** wish to ride; **stilleche,** slowly. **59 ordeyne redy,** prepare. **60 vitaile,** food; **deynteis,** delicacies; **ne faute,** is lacking. **62 encombred,** threatened; **be the wey,** along the way; **of,** by. **70 pensif,** concerned. **71 myshappe,** harm. **72 marched into,** bordered upon. **75 strongely,** quickly.

myght. And Gawein ordeyned that vitaile com on alle parties with cartes and
chariettis, that he stuffed so well the citee as longed to soche a feste, as he that full
well coude hym entermete that nothinge ne failed. For as the storye seith, he was
oon of the beste knyghtes and wiseste of the worlde, and therto the leste mys-
80 speker and noon avauntor, and the beste taught of alle thinges that longeth to
worship or curtesie. And whan he hadde made all redy, he toke his wey toward his
uncle, for grete drede he hadde of that he sholde be distrobeled on the wey of
some peple. But now we shull a while cesse of hym and his companye and speke
of the Kynge Arthur.

85 The thridde day after that Gawein was departed from the Kynge Arthur his
uncle, the kynge toke his wey towarde the Castell of Bredigan, he and his wif, and
in her companye was the Kynge Ban of Benoyk and the Kynge Bohors of Gannes
that was his brother and the beste knyght that eny man neded to seche; and so ther
were two hundred fifty Knyghtes of the Rounde Table that alle were feed men
90 with the Kynge Leodogan. And the queene hadde so praied Sir Amnistian, that
was chapelein with the Kynge Leodogan hir fader, that he com with hir and was
sithen hir chapelein longe tyme. And so ledde Gonnore hir cosin, that was feire
and debonaire and amyable to alle peple, and Sadoyne hir brother, that was elther
than she and castelein of Daneblaise the noble citee.

95 And as soone as the Kynge Arthur was departed oute of the reame of Carmelide,
the Kynge Loot hadde knowinge by his asspies. And he and his knyghtes rode
agein hym and hem enbusshed in the Foreste of Sapernye. And [he] seide that ther
sholde he abide the Kynge Arthur and take from hym his wif, yef he myght. But
of hym we shull now cesse, and speke of the Kynge Arthur that was departed oute
100 of Carmelide.

And the storie seith how the Kynge Leodogan conveyed hem thre dayes hole,
and the fourthe day he returned into his reame. And than com Merlin to the Kynge
Arthur and toke leve and seide that he sholde go to his maister Blaase, for longe

76 **parties**, sides. 77 **as longed to**, as was fitting for. 78 **coude**, could; **entermete**, conduct. 79–80 **leste mysspeker**, least speaker of ill. 80 **noon avauntor**, not a boaster; **longeth
to**, concerns. 81 **worship**, honor. 82 **of that**, that; **distrobeled**, set upon; **of**, by. 87 **her**,
their. 88 **seche**, seek; **so**, also. 89–90 **feed men with**, retainers of. 91 **com**, came. 92 **sithen**,
afterwards. 93 **elther**, older. 94 **castelein**, marshall. 96 **asspies**, spies. 97 **agein**, towards;
hem enbusshed, lay in wait for them. 101 **conveyed hem**, accompanied them.

hadde he hym not seyn; and the kynge hadde well spedde of that he hadde for to

105 done. Than seide the kynge, "Merlin, feire frende, shull ye not be at my court at Logres?" "Yesse," seide Merlin, "I shall be ther er it departe"; and therwith eche of hem comaunded other to God. But he was but litill wey thens whan no man wiste where that he was becomen.

And Merlin wente to Blaase the same nyght, and he hym resceyved with grete

110 joye whan that he hym saugh. And Merlin tolde hym alle the aventures that were falle seth that he departed; and he tolde hym how the Kynge Loot was enbusshed in the Foreste of Sapernye, and tolde hym other thinges inowghe that after befill in the reame of Logres. And Blaase hem wrote as he tolde, and by his booke have we the knowinge. But now cesseth to speke of Merlin and Blase, and speke of

115 Arthur.

Whan the Kynge Arthur was departed from the Kynge Leodogan, and Merlin also, as ye have herde, he rode with five hundre men of armes, and ledde with hym his wif Gonnore the queene. And he rode smale journeyes till he com into the Foreste of Sapernye, whereas the Kynge Loot was enbusshed with seven hundre

120 men of armes. And the gromes that ledde the somers wiste never worde till that thei were fallen even amonge hem. And as soone as thei saugh thei were men of armes, thei wiste well thei were not well come. Than thei abode and wente no ferther, and sente to the Kynge Arthur that thei hadde founde men iarmed. Whan the kynge saugh that he was aspied, he alight on foote and made his peple come

125 aboute hym and ordeyned for bataile; and comaunded forty knyghtes to kepe the queene and bad hem lede hir to garison yef thei saugh nede.

And than thei ride forth, her heedes bowed down undir theire helmes redy hem to diffende, yef thei founde eny peple to stoppe hem the wey. And so thei ride till thei dide falle upon the wacche; and the Kynge Arthur was before in the firste

130 frounte, and the Kynge Ban and the Kynge Bohors and the Knyghtes of the Rounde Table. And the Kynge Looth spronge oute with seven hundre men of armes and com hem ageins theire spers, agein the assels of the sadeles, and the sheldes before theire breste, as faste as horse myght renne. And hem ascride so high that all

104 well spedde of that, understood what. **106 departe**, concludes. **108 wiste**, knew. **111 seth that**, since. **120 gromes**, grooms; **somers**, pack horses; **wiste**, knew. **121 saugh**, saw. **126 hem**, them; **lede hir to garison**, lead her to safety. **129 dide falle upon**, encountered; **wacche**, scouts. **132 assels**, shoulders. **133 hem ascride so high**, they shouted so loudly.

135 the foreste resounded; and these other com upon hem boldely with sharpe trenchaunte speres, and mette togeder upon sheldes that many of hem perced and slitte. Many were throwe to grounde on bothe sides, and many ther were that brake theire speres and passed forth withoute fallinge. And whan the spers were spente, thei drowgh oute theire swerdes and begonne the bateile right grete, that never of so fewe peple ne saugh no man so fierce bateile, for thei were full noble

140 knyghtes upon bothe parties.

And so longe it lasted that the Kynge Arthur and the Kynge Looth mette togeder with speres in hande, and lett renne that oon agein that other so harde as horse myght renne, and mette so harde togeder with speres upon sheldes that the spere poyntes stynte at the hauberkes. And thei theron shof with all theire force, and the

145 Kynge Loot brake his spere, and the Kynge Arthur smote hym so harde that he bar hym to grounde over his horse croupe; but soone was he lepte upon foote as he that was of grete prowesse, and drowh his swerde and covered hym with his shelde and was so doelfull that nygh he yede oute of witte for that he was overthrowe be the myght of a knyght alone, for he was not acustomed for to falle

150 often.

And the Kynge Arthur hadde made his returne and com toward the Kynge Loot gripinge his spere, for he coveited to take hym quyk. And whan the Kynge Looth saugh hym come, he glenched aside and Arthur failed of hym and past forth; and in the passinge the Kynge Loot smote Arthurs horse in the bely thourgh the guttes.

155 And Arthur fill to grounde, and his horse upon his body that his thigh was betwene the horse and the grounde so that he myght not arise. And the Kynge Loot sterte to and caught hym by the helme and drough and pulled all that he myght, and sore hym peyned for to smyten of his heede. And soone ther sholde have be so grete damage that never myght it have be restored, but as the Kynge Ban and the Kynge

160 Bohors and the Knyghtes of the Rounde Table com fiercely upon the peple of Kynge Loot, and began sore bateile and harde so that ther was noon but that he hadde inough to done. And so thei peyned hem on both parties that the two kynges be remounted, and begonne the stour grete and merveillouse. But at grete myschef

142 **renne**, run. 144 **stynte**, stopped; **hauberkes**, mail shirts; **shof**, shoved. 146 **croupe**, cruppers. 147 **drowh**, drew. 148 **for that**, because. 149 **be**, by. 152 **coveited**, desired; **quyk**, alive. 153 **glenched**, moved. 156–57 **sterte to**, leaped to him. 158 **smyten of**, smite off. 159 **but as**, except that. 160 **com**, came. 163 **stour**, battle; **myschef**, danger.

were the peple of Kynge Arthur, for the Kynge Loot hadde two hundre knyghtes
165   moo than hadde Kynge Arthur.

With that com Sir Gawein with foure score felowes well armed, and Kay the
Stiwarde bar the baner. And Arthur behielde and saugh Gawein come and knewe
hym well by his armes, and also Kay the Stiwarde be the baner that he bar in his
handes that sore desired the assemble, as he that was hardy and enterpendaunt and
170   right sure, ne hadde ben oon tecche that he hadde, for that he was copiouse of
langage in his disporte for the jolynesse that was in hym and the myrthe; for he
was ever bourdinge and japinge in game, and was the beste felowe in companye
that eny man knewe. And for that ever he wolde of custome borde of the sothe,
hym hated many a knyght for the shame that thei hadde of his wordes; and therfore
175   he myshapped in many a place, for the knyghtes that he had scorned in myrthe
didde hym after grete annoye. But a trewe knyght was he ever agein his lorde, and
agein the queene, ever into the ende of his deth. Ne never in all his live dide he
treson saf oon, and that was of Lohoot, the sone of Kynge Arthur, that he slough
for envye in the Foreste Perilouse; and for that Percevale ly Galoys was accused
180   with grete wronge for the deth of the same Hoot, like as an ermyte hit tolde after,
that hadde seyn all the dede.

Whan the Kynge Arthur saugh Gawein his nevew come so fiercely, his herte
aroos for grete joye that he hadde. Than he com to the Kynge Ban and seide, "Sir,
se how riche socour to us cometh! Knowe ye not hym that rideth before upon the
185   blakke stede that gripeth the grete spere under the shelde of goolde and azur, therynne a lyon rampaunt?" And the Kynge Ban beheilde and seide, "Who is it? Telle
me, for I knowe hym not, saf that me semeth it sholde be Gawein youre nevew."
"Certes," quod Arthur, "he it is, and now may I me avaunten that in evell tyme
come these us for to assailen; for yef thei were yet as many moo, thei myght not

---

165 moo, more. **167 behielde**, looked. **168 be**, by. **169 sore desired the assemble**, greatly
wished to reach the assembly; **enterpendaunt**, enterprising. **170 right sure**, constant; **ne
hadde ben oon tecche**, if not for one trait. **170–71 copiouse of langage**, excessive in
speaking. **172 bourdinge**, playing; **japinge**, joking; **game**, fun. **173 for that**, because; **of
custome**, by habit; **borde of the sothe**, make fun of the truth. **175 myshapped**, was ill-
treated. **176 didde**, caused; **annoye**, harm; **agein**, to. **178 saf oon**, except one; **slough**,
slew. **180 ermyte**, hermit. **181 that**, who; **seyn**, seen; **dede**, deed. **188 avaunten**, declare.

190   agein us endure, yef God hym diffende from evell, he and his companye." "Trewly,"
seide the Kynge Ban, "thei be not wise yef thei hym abide till that he be amonge
hem medled."

And while thei spake thus togeder com Gawein all before gripinge his grete
spere. And whan he com nygh, he knewe well his uncle and saugh that he hadde
195   grete myster of socour; and than he spronge in amonge hem rudely as tempest of
thunder. And [it] fill that he mette with his fader the Kynge Loot that newliche
was sette on horse and heilde a stronge spere. And [he] com agein hym as moche
as the horse myght renne, and [thei] mette togeder upon the sheldes with all theire
forces. And the kynge brake his spere upon Gaweins shelde, and Gawein smote
200   hym agein so harde that he perced shelde and hauberke and wounded hym somwhat
in the lifte side that the blode folowed after. And the kynge fill so harde to grounde
that he wiste not wheder it was day or nyght. And Gawein paste forth rudely
withoute arestinge; and whan he was returned agein, he fonde his fader lyinge on
the erthe upright; and he rode over hym on horsebak thre or foure tymes, and
205   broused hym sore and foule that nygh he was therwith slayn.

And than Gawein alight and pight his spere in the grounde and drough oute
Calibourne his goode swerde that shone bright and clier. And [he] com to the
Kynge Loot that yet lay upright, and plukked hym by the helme and raced it of his
heede so harde that on his nose and his browes it was well seene, for he was hurte
210   right sore. And than he avaled the coyf of his hauberke benethe his shuldres, and
seide that he was but deed but yef he wolde yelde hym to prison. And he was so
anguysshous that litill he hym ansuerde; nevertheless, he dide hymself enforce so
that he seide with grete sorowe at his herte, "Ha, sir gentilman, ne sle me nought!
For never dide I forfet agein thee wherfore that thow sholdest me sleen." "Yesse,"
215   quod Gawein, "that haste thow, and alle thi companye that have assailed myn
uncle for to distrouble him his weye." "How so?" quod Kynge Loot. "Who be ye
that calle hym youre uncle?" "What is that to thee what I am? Me liste nothinge

190 yef, unless. **192 medled**, fighting. **195 myster**, need; **rudely**, strongly. **196 newliche**,
newly. **197 moche**, strongly. **201 lifte**, left. **205 broused**, bruised. **206 pight**, stuck; **drough**,
drew. **208 upright**, face up; **raced it of**, tore it off. **210 avaled**, opened. **211 but yef**,
unless. **211–12 so anguysshous**, in such anguish. **213 sle**, slay. **214 forfet agein thee**,
harm to you; **wherfore**, for which; **sleen**, slay. **216 distrouble**, disturb. **217 Me liste
nothinge**, I do not choose.

thee to telle. But do anoon that as I thee sey, or thow art deed. And alle these other
that ben in thi companye shull dye, and shull curse the tyme that ever thei were of
220   moder born."

"Telle me," quod the Kynge Loot, "who ye ben, for the love of that ye love
moste in this worlde." "But what art thow," quod Gawein, "that this doste me
demaunde?" Quod he, "Myn name is Looth, a caitife kynge of Orcanye and of
Leonoys, to whom nothinge doth falle but myschef, ne not hath don longe tyme.
225   Now telle me youre name what ye be." And whan Gawein undirstode verily that it
was his fader, anoon he nempned his name and seide his name was Gawein, the
nevew of Kynge Arthur. And whan the Kynge Loot herde that, anoon he lepte up
and wolde have clypt him in his armes and seide, "Feire sone, ye be welcome; and
I am the sorowfull caitif youre fader that ye have thus viliche overthrowen."

230   And Gawein bad hym drawe hym ferther arome, for his fader sholde he not be
ne his goode frende till that he were acorded with the kynge his uncle, and hadde
cried hym mercy for his forfet, and than do to hym homage seynge alle his barouns.
"For othirwise, loke never to truste in me, for elles shull ye leve noon other wedde
saf youre heed." And than the Kynge Looth sowowned and fill down to the grounde;
235   and whan he awoke of swownynge, he cride hym mercy and seide, "Feire sone, I
will do all that yow may plese; and holde here my swerde, for I yelde it to yow."
And Sir Gawein, that therof hadde grete pité, hit toke with gladde chere and myri,
and wepte right tendirly water with his iyen undir his helme, for sore he repente in
his herte of that he hadde so hurte his fader. But as moche as he myght, he kepte
240   hym so that he was not aperceyved.

Than thei com bothe to theire horse, and lept up and com to theire peple, and
hem departed. But fowlé were the Kynge Loothis men overleide, for the Knyghtes
of the Rounde Table and the Felowes of Sir Gawein hadde hem so evyll beseyn at
the first metynge that moo than forty thei hadde felde to grounde that thei hadde

218 **anoon,** now; **that as,** what; **thee sey,** tell you. 221 **that,** the one that. 223 **caitife,**
wretched. 224 **myschef,** misfortune; **ne not hath don,** nor has done for. 226 **nempned,**
spoke. 227 **nevew,** nephew. 228 **wolde have clypt,** desired to embrace. 229 **caitif,** wretch;
viliche, vilely. 230 **arome,** back. 232 **seynge,** in the sight of. 233 **for elles,** or else; **leve,**
leave; **wedde,** pledge. 234 **saf,** except for; **sowowned,** swooned. 238 **iyen,** eyes. 240
aperceyved, seen. 242 **hem departed,** separated them; **fowlé,** foully; **overleide,** treated.
243 **evyll beseyn,** harshly treated. 244 **moo,** more.

245   no power to remounte. And Sir Gawein com and hem departed; and than wente
Gawein to Arthur his uncle.

     And as soone as the kynge saugh hym come, he com hym ageins and seide,
"Feire nevew, ye be welcome. Wherefore be ye come into this parties? Wiste ye
eny thinge of this awayte?" And Gawein seide that he douted hit sore, "For I

250   myght never be in hertes ese till I hadde yow seyn; and oure Lorde God," quod he,
"now be thanked and honoured of this assemble; for it is the Kynge Looth my
fader with whom that ye were in medlé. And now hit is so befallen that he is come
to crye yow mercy as to his liege lorde erthly, for the trespasse that he hath done
agein yow. And therfore resceyveth his homage like as ye owe for to do, for he is

255   here all redy hit to performe and do."

     Whan the Kynge Arthur that herde, he joyned his handes toward hevene and
thanked God of the worship that He hadde hym shewed. And with that com the
Kynge Loot and his knyghtes down the medowes alle on foote, and hadde don of
theire helmes from theire heedes and valed theire coiffes of mayle upon theire

260   sholderes and com full symple. And whan Gawein saugh his fader come before,
he seide to his uncle, "Sir, lo here my fader cometh to yow for to do homage."
And anoon the Kynge Arthur sette foot to the grounde and alle the other barouns
after. And the Kynge Loot com before Arthur and sette hym on his knee, and
hielde his swerde be the poynte as he that hadde forfeted; and seide, "Sir, I yelde

265   me here to youre mercy as he that hath often agein yow forfeted, and dide yow
never but grevaunce and annoye. Now do yowre plesire of me and of my londe."
And ther becom the Kynge Loot liegeman to the Kynge Arthur before alle his
barouns; and assured his feith to do hym servyse whan that he hym comaunded.

     Than Arthur toke hym be the right hande and made hym to arise on his feet and

270   seide, "Sir, stondeth up, for longe inough have ye kneled, for I ought it yow to
pardon for that ye be so worthi a man. And a gretter forfet than this is, for thowgh
that I have hated yow never so dedly, ye have here soche children that have do me
soche servise that I may have no will to do yow noon evell. And therfore I offre

248 **Wherefore be**, Why have; **parties**, area; **Wiste**, Knew. 249 **awayte**, ambush; **douted**,
feared. 251 **of**, by. 252 **medlé**, battle. 254 **owe**, ought. 257 **worship**, honor; **hym shewed**,
given him. 258 **don of**, taken off. 259 **valed**, opened. 260 **saugh**, saw. 264 **be**, by. 265
forfeted, surrendered. 271 **for that**, because; **forfet**, victory.

275 here to yow all thinge that is myn at youre volunté, for the love of Gawein youre
sone that I love beste of eny knyght that is in the worlde. And ther be here two
knyghtes that I owe to love as wele, and bothe ben thei kynges that moche have
me socoured in grete nede." And he stode up and seide, "Sire, gramercy."

Thus was made pees betwene Kynge Loot and the Kynge Arthur. And than thei
lepe to theire horse gladde and joyfull of this aventure, and riden so by here
280 journeyes till thei com to Logres, where thei were resceyved with the grettest joye
of the worlde. And every day the peple dide encrese, for the dwellers of the contrey
com thider for drede of the Saisnes that hem distroyed and the londe. And ther
was so grete prees of peple that many behoved to loigge in the medowes. And
whan the Kynge Arthur saugh so grete plenté of peple, he was gladde and myry
285 and seide that he wolde holde court open and enforced, and sente by his messangers
that alle sholde come to his court roiall.

And on the morowe the Kynge Loot dide his homage to the Kynge Arthur, and
made his oth in the chief mynster, seinge alle the peple, that was right grete and
huge. And the Kynge Arthur refeffed hym agein in his londe that he hadde before,
290 to hym and to hys heires forever more; and who that dide hym eny wronge he
sholde hym supporte to his power. And [he] resceyved hym gladde and jocunde as
a noble man; and fro that day forth were thei goode frendes all her lif.

And whan the masse was seide, thei com agein to the paleyse and yede to mete;
and thei were well served and richely. And after mete wente the knyghtes to se the
295 medowes and the river and the tentes and the pavilouns that were pight withoute
the town, for ther were many full feire and riche. And [in] this disporte and solace
were thei eight dayes hool. And the peple dide sore encrece, for the kynge dide hit
comaunde for that he wolde holde court roiall and plentevouse, and bere crowne
he and his wif at the mydde of August. And whan it com to the evene that the
300 feeste sholde begynne on the morowe, Arthur yaf his yeftes soche as to hym
apertened, of horse and palfreyes and armour and money as golde and silver, for
he hadde plenté. And the queene yaf hem robes fressh and newe, as she that well

274 **volunté**, desire. 276 **owe**, ought. 278 **pees**, peace. 285 **enforced**, expanded. 287 **on**, in.
288 **seinge**, before. 289 **refeffed**, re-installed. 291 **jocunde**, happy. 293 **yede**, went. 295
pight withoute, pitched outside. 297 **hool**, altogether; **sore encrece**, greatly increase. 298
roiall and plentevouse, royally and generously. 300 **yaf**, gave; **yeftes**, gifts. 301 **apertened**,
belonged.

hadde therfore ordeyned and moche cowde of honour and all curteysie, that alle
peple hadde hir in so grete love that hem thought thei hadde recovered the lady of
305   alle ladyes. And yef the knyghtes hadde riche presentes, the ladyes and dameselles
hadden also, and maydenes bothe fer and nygh.

And so spradde the renoun thourgh every contrey of Arthur, that the princes
that weren with hym wroth wisten of the pees that the Kynge Loot hadde made
with the Kynge Arthur, and how he sholde holde his court roiall at the myddill of
310   August, and that alle peple were thider somowned. And some of hem seiden secretly to theire counseile that thei wolde gladly have spedde in the same manere
as the Kynge Loot hadde done. And some ther were of hem that thoughten in
theire hertis and praied to God that thei sholde never dye on no deth er thei were
acorded with the Kynge Arthur, "For all this trouble and myschef that is fallen
315   unto us is com thourgh the synne that we have don agein God and forfet to hym."
Thus seide oon to another.

And the Kynge Arthur was in his maister citee in joye and solace, as ye have
iherde. And whan it com to the day of the myddill August, thider com alle the
knyghtes to the courte clothed and araied in the richest robes that thei hadden.
320   And the queene was appareiled, she and hir ladyes and maidenys and dameseles,
richely as longeth to soche an high feeste. And whan thei hadde ronge to high
masse, thei wente alle to the mynster and herde the servise that the archebisshop
dide singe. And that day bar Arthur crowne, and the Queene Gonnore his wif.
And the Kynge Ban and the Kynge Bohors were crowned also for the love of hem.
325   And after masse thei com to the halle where the clothes were leyde; and the lordes
were sette thourgh the halle as thei owe for to be.

That day served Gawein at the high deyse theras the foure kynges seten. And
Kay the Stiward, and Lucas the Boteller, and Sir Ewein le Graunt the sone of
Kynge Urien, and Gifflet, and Ewein Avoutres, and Segramor, and Dodinell le
330   Savage, and Kay Destranx, and Kehedins ly Bens, and Kehedins le Petit, and
Ayglyns des Vaux that was his brother, and Galegantius the Walsh, and Blyoberis,
and Galescowde, and Colegrevaunt, and Lanval, and Aglovall, and Ewein Esclains,

303 cowde, knew; **that,** so that. **304 recovered,** found. **307 that,** so that. **308 wisten,**
knew; **pees,** peace. **310 somowned,** summoned. **311 spedde,** done. **313 er,** before. **315
forfet,** the damage; **hym,** i.e., Arthur. **321 longeth to,** is right for. **323 bar,** wore; **crowne,**
the crown. **326 owe for to,** should. **327 deyse,** dais; **theras,** where.

and Ewein de Lionell, and Ewein White Hande, and Guyomar, and Synados, and Gosevain Hardy Body, and Agravain the Prowde, and Gueheret, and Gaheries, and Acon de Bemonde — and alle these twenty-one served at the high deyse. And forty other yonge bachelers served at other tables therynne. And thei were so well served of alle maner thinges that never peple were better.

And whan alle the meesse were served in, than spake the Kynge Arthur so lowde that alle that were in the halle myght it heren, and he seide: "Now lordinges, alle ye that ben come here into my courte me for to gladen and counforte, I yelde yow graces and thonkinge for the honour and the joye that ye have me don, and that ye be come for to do. And I do yow to wite that I will stablissh to my courte alle the tymes that I shall bere crowne, that never from hensforth shall I not sitte to mete into the tyme that I here some straunge tydinge or elles some aventure, be soche forwarde, that yef it be myster, I shall do it to be redressed by the knyghtes of my court, whiche for prise and honour hiderto repeire, and ben my frendes and my felowes and my peres." And whan the Knyghtes of the Rounde Table herde this avow that the kynge hadde imade, thei spake togeder and seiden, "Seeth that the kynge hath made avow in his courte, hit behoveth that we make oure avow." And thei acorded alle to oon thinge, and therwith thei charged Nascien to reherse it before the kynge.

Than wente alle the Knyghtes of the Rounde Table; and Nascien began to speke before the kynge so high that thei alle myght here that were in the halle. "Sir," seide Nascien, "the Kynghtes of the Rounde Table be come here to God and in youre audyence and to alle the barouns that here ben. Inasmoche as ye have made avow, thei make here another that shall ever endure while her life lasteth, that yef eny maiden have eny nede, or come to youre courte for to seche helpe or socour by so that it may be acheved by the body of oon knyght agein another, thei will with goode will go into what contrey she will hem leden hir for to delyver, and make alle the wronges to be redressed that to hir hath be done." And whan the kynge this undirstode, he asked of the Knyghtes of the Rounde Table yef thei dide

335

340

345

350

355

360

338 meesse were served in, dinner had been served. **340 yelde,** give. **344 into,** until; **here,** hear; **be,** by. **345 forwarde,** promise; **yef it be myster,** if there is need; **do,** cause. **346 prise,** fame; **hiderto repeire,** hither are come. **347 peres,** peers. **348 Seeth,** Since. **350 acorded alle,** all agreed; **reherse,** say. **353 high,** loudly; **here,** hear. **354 to,** before. **356 yef,** if. **358 by so that,** of such a kind that.

graunte to that as Nascien hadde seide. And thei seiden, "Ye." And to this thei
wolde be sworn hit for to mayntene, and not to spare for lif ne for deth.

And than began the joye gretter than it hadde byfore. And whan Gawein
365 undirstode the joye that thei maden for the avowes that were ther istablisshed, he
seide to his felowes, as he that cowde all norture and curtesie, "Sirs," seide Gawein,
"yef eche of yow will acorde to that I shall seyn, I shall ofre soche avow wherof
shall come to yow and to me grete honour alle the dayes of oure lif." And thei
ansuerde and seide that thei wolde graunte and assente to alle that ever he wolde
370 speke with his mowthe. "Than," quod he, "assureth me youre feith to holde me
companye." And anoon thei hym assured, and were twenty-four be counte.

Whan that Sir Gawein hadde take the feith of his felowes, he come before the
Queene and seide: "Madame, I and my felowes be come to yow and praye yow
and requere that ye will withholde us to be youre knyghtes and youre meyné. That
375 whan thei come in eny strange contrey to seche loos and pris, yef eny man hem
aske with whom thei be and of what londe, than thei may seyn of the reame of
Logres and be the Knyghtes of Queene Gonnore, the wif of Kynge Arthur." Whan
the queene undirstode this, she dressed hir upstondinge and seide, "Feire nevew,
gramercy to yow and to hem alle, for I yow resceyve with gladde chere as lordes
380 and my frendes; and as ye offre yow to me, so I offre me to yow with trewe herte.
And I pray God, lete me so long lyve that I may yow guerdon of the worship and
the curtesie that ye promyse me for to do."

"Madame," seide Gawein, "we be alle youre knyghtes. And ye have us withholde,
God it yow quyte. Now shull we make avow: that what man or woman cometh to
385 yow for to seche socour or helpe ageyn the body of oon knyght, he shall not faile
to have oon of us to delyver hym body for body, and go with hem into what
contrey thei will us bringe. And whiche of us so it be that take eny soche journey
on hande, and hit happe that he come not agein withynne a moneth, eche oon of us
shall go for to seche hym sool by hymself a yere and a day withoute repeire to

362 **graunte to that as**, assent to what. 363 **ne**, nor. 364 **it hadde**, there had been. 366
cowde, knew; **norture**, manners. 367 **ofre**, offer. 371 **be**, by. 374 **withholde**, claim; **meyné**,
company. 375 **come in**, go into; **seche**, seek; **loos and pris**, fame and honor. 375–76 **eny
man hem aske**, anyone asks them. 378 **dressed hir upstondinge**, stood up. 381 **guerdon
of**, reward for. 383 **And**, And since; **withholde**, claimed. 384 **quyte**, reward. 389 **sool**,
alone; **repeire**, returning.

390   courte, but yef withynne that terme he can bringe trewe tydinges of his felowe. And whan thei be come to court, everyche shall telle his aventures that hym befalleth in the tyme, whatsoever thei be, gode or evell; and thei shull be sworn to sey the trouthe of all, bothe in the goynge and in the comynge."

Whan the queene undirstode the avow that Gawein hadde made, she was the
395   gladdest woman in the worlde, and the kynge was glader than eny other that was in the courte. And for the kynge wolde comforte the queene he seide, "Dame, seth God hath ordeyned yow this honour to have so feire a companye, some curtesie moste I do for the love of hem, and also for the love of youre self. And wite ye wherof I putte in youre governaunce my tresour in soche maner that ye be lady
400   and partyner of all at youre plesier." And whan the queene this herde, she kneled before the kynge and seide, "Sir, gramercy."

And than the queene called Sir Gawein and seide, "Feire nevew, I will that foure clerkes be stablisshed hereynne that shull do nothinge elles but write the aventures that falle to yow and youre felowes, so that after youre deth it may be
405   remembred the high prowesse of the worthi men hereynne." "Madame," seide Gawein, "I graunte." And than were ther chosen foure clerkes to write the aventures as thei fill into the courte fro thensforth. And than seide Gawein that he sholde not here speke of noon aventure but he sholde go to seche it; and he and his felowes sholde do so moche that thei sholde bringe therof trewe tidinges to courte. And so
410   seiden the Knyghtes of the Rounde Table in the same manere. And allwey fro thensforth was Sir Gawein and his felowes called the Queenes Knyghtes.

With that were the clothes taken up, and than began the joye right grete of oon and other therynne. But over alle other that were therynne was iherde Dagenet of Clarion, for he made gret myrthe amonge hem so that alle thei beheilde hym for
415   merveile. But a fooll he was of nature, and the moste coward pece of flessh that was in the worlde. This Dagenet began to trippe and daunce and cried so lowde with high voyse and seide, "Tomorow shall I so seche these aventures," and seide to Gawein, "Will ye come? And ye, Sir Ewein and Segramor, will ye come thider that be so feire and moche? And ye lordinges of the Rounde Table? Certes, I

390 but yef, unless. **391 everyche**, everyone. **396 wolde comforte**, wished to please; **seth**, since. **398 moste**, must; **wite**, know. **399 wherof**, therefore. **402 will**, wish. **412 With that**, Then; **clothes taken up**, tablecloths removed. **413 iherde**, heard. **415 fooll**, clown. **419 moche**, large.

420 trowe not that ye have the herte ne the hardynesse me for to sewen ther I shall go
tomorowe."

Thus seide Dagenet the Coward, and the knyghtes therat lowen and hadde grete
game. And withoute faile, he hym armed many tymes and wente into the forestes
and henge his shelde on an oke and smote it so that alle the colours were faded

425 and the shelde tohakked in many places. And than wolde he seyn that he hadde
slayn a knyght or tweyne; and whan he mette eny knyght armed, he turned to
flight as fer as he myght here hym speke at the leeste. And many tymes fill yef he
mette eny knyght erraunt that were pensif that spake no worde, he wolde take hym
by the bridell and lede hym forth as he hadde hym taken. Of soche maners was

430 Dagenet, and yet he was right a feire knyght and of high lynage, and yet it semed
not by his countenaunce that he was soche a fooll.

420 **sewen ther**, follow where. 422 **lowen**, laughed. 424 **henge**, hung. 425 **tohakked**,
hacked all to pieces; **seyn**, say. 427 **fill yef**, it happened if. 429 **as**, as if.

[The Tournament at Logres; King Lot and his Sons; and Morgan and Gyomar]

[**Summary**. *Still chaffing over their humiliation in the Tournament at Toraise, the Knights of the Round Table challenge the Queen's Knights to compete in a tournament at Logres. Arthur, fearing a repetition of the malice and rancor that surfaced previously, asks Gawain to promise that it will not occur this time, but Gawain refuses to do so. King Ban advises Arthur to arm another group and hold them in reserve in case trouble develops.*

The Knights of the Round Table take on a group of Gawain's young knights, who are assisted by King Lot's knights. When the Round Table Knights begin to get the upper hand, Gawain, Ewain, Sagremor, and Gifflet rush into the fray and drive their opponents back toward the river. Now greatly incensed, the Round Table Knights decide to arm themselves with "speres, grete and rude" — weapons whose use had been forbidden. Seeing what their foes are going to do, Gawain and his fellows decide to do likewise. Now the fighting becomes bitter and intense, with the two sides acting as if they are fighting a "mortal werre." Gawain unsheathes Calibourne and kills forty men himself. The Round Table Knights flee, with Gawain and his fellowship in pursuit. At this point Arthur and the three kings rush to the scene and intervene. Arthur rebukes Gawain, but Gawain insists that the real fault lies with the Round Table Knights. King Lot sternly berates his son, telling him to end his folly. At last Gawain begins to cool down.

The knights retire from the field, wash themselves, and then return to the court. The Knights of the Round Table agree to make amends, which pleases the king and queen. Gawain, however, remains hostilely silent. The king reproves Gawain for continuing in his anger. The queen, in a gentler fashion, urges Gawain to leave his anger and reminds him that all of Arthur's men should "love eche other and helpe agein alle peple; and yef youre enmyes come agein yow, to hem ye sholde be fierce, and not to hem that tomorowe shull put her bodyes in aventure of deth for my lorde." Gawain, moved by the queen's words, says he will do as she wishes. The Round Table Knights bow down to Gawain and ask him to pardon them. Gawain then joins their fellowship, and all of Arthur's knights agree never to tourney against each other again. The other Queen's Knights also become members of the Round Table, making a total of 90 Round Table Knights. Later, the author says, that number will become 400.

Tidings are brought to the people of Britain concerning the "Seint Graal," the holy

271

vessel in which Joseph of Arimathea collected the blood that flowed from Christ's wounded side. They learn that this holy vessel, along with the Holy Spear, have come from heaven to the City of Sarras, and from there out into the world. Now no one knows what has become of them. Indeed, they are told that these objects will never be found until the coming of the best knight of the world. After learning this, Arthur's knights invite all the best knights from other countries to join their knightly fellowship. Fols. 172v (line 28)– 179r (line 29).]

    Full gladde and jocounde were the companye of the Rounde Table for that thei were acorded with Sir Gawein. And full moche thei hym preised and comended for the grete prowesse that thei saugh hym do at this turnement, and seide amonge hem in counseile that ten the best knyghtes therynne sholde not agein hym en-

5   dure, body for body. Thus the knyghtes therynne seide theire volunté. But moche more spake the ladyes and the maydenes in the chambers. Than was water asked; and whan thei hadde waisshen, than sat every knyght as hym ought for to do. And the Quenes Knyghtes were sette by the Knyghtes of the Rounde Table. And the Kynge Arthur and the Kynge Ban and the Kynge Bohors and the Kynge Looth sat

10   at the high deyse as thei ought for to do, and mo sat ther not but thei foure. And that day served Gawein and Kay the Stiward and Lucas the Botiller and Gifflet and other aboute a forty.

    *[**Summary**. After dinner, the four kings retire to a chamber and discuss what they should do in regard to the Saxons. Lot believes that if all of the British barons would unite behind Arthur, they could drive the Saxons out; he suggests that they ask the Saxons for a year's truce. Ban urges Lot to take that message to the Saxons, and Lot agrees to do so. Fols. 179v (line 6)–180r (line 23).]*

    Whan the Kynge Looth saugh how thei acorded that he sholde go upon this nede, he knewe well how thei hadde reson. Than he seide he wolde go and have

15   with hym his foure sones. "Trewly," seide the Kynge Bohors, "yef thei bene with yow, than have ye no drede of no man of moder born." Whan [the Kynge Arthur] saugh that thei were to this acorded that the Kynge Looth sholde lede with hym his foure sones, he yaf a grete sigh, for he douted of Sir Gawein, in whom he

1 jocounde, cheerful; **for that,** because. **4 agein,** against. **6 asked,** called for. **10 deyse,** dais. **12 a forty,** forty more. **13 acorded,** agreed. **14 nede,** errand. **17 lede,** take. **18 douted of,** feared for.

20 hadde so tentefly sette his love, so that ther was nothinge in the worlde that he loved so moche. And the quene knewe a partie of his thought and seide to the kynge, "Sir, graunte the Kynge Looth to lede with hym his children hardely, for thei shull have no drede yef God will; for the more thei be youre frendes the better, and withe the more tendir herte shull thei do youre message as is nede, more than sholde another that therof sette no charge. And lever I hadde that my

25 frende counseiled with myn enmyes than another that were straunge."

"Dame," seide the Kynge Arthur, "I me acorde, seth the barouns have it ordeyned." And than he seide to the Kynge Looth and praide hym to appareile hym to go secretly that no man knewe whider he wolde go. With that was Gawein cleped and his brethren that were pleyinge in the halle. And whan thei come to the

30 quene, she aroos and wente hem ageins and seide thei were welcome. And thei dide yelde hir agein hir salew debonerly. Than Arthur tolde hem all as was devised, how thei moste go on the message, and why thei hadde it amonge hem purveyed. And than thei ansuerde and seide that it was goode for to be don.

After that seide the Kynge Looth to Sir Gawein, "Feire sone, goth forth and

35 appareile yow and youre brethern, that ye faile nought whan we shull go." "Sir," seide Gawein, "what arayment sholde we have eny more but oure armours and oure horse? We shull neither have somer ne male trussed, neither grete ne small, but goode stedes and swyft on the whiche we shull ride, that may bere us to garison yef myster be. Ne here behoveth noon abidinge, for yef ye do my counseile, we

40 shull meve yet this nyght at the first somme, and ride as grete journeyes as we may, for soche a nede as this is sholde not be put in no delay." "Trewly, nevew," seide Arthur, "ye sey soth. Now, go reste yow awhile and slepe."

Than Gawein turned hym to the quene and seide, "Madame, I prey that ye thinke on my felowes that leven here with yow, for the Knyghtes of the Rounde Table ne

19 tentefly, intensely. **21 hardely**, boldly. **22 no drede**, nothing to fear. **24 lever I hadde**, I would prefer. **25 counseiled**, negotiated. **26 me acorde**, concur; **seth**, since. **27 ordeyned**, proposed. **27–28 appareile hym**, arrange. **28 that¹**, so that; **whider**, where. **29 cleped**, summoned. **30 hem ageins**, to them. **31 yelde hir**, returned to her; **salew debonerly**, greeting politely. **32 moste**, must. **32–33 amonge hem purveyed**, to them assigned. **36 but**, besides. **37 somer ne male trussed**, pack horse nor bags packed. **38 garison**, safety. **39 yef myster**, if need; **behoveth**, profits us; **noon abidinge**, no waiting. **40 somme**, light. **43–44 thinke on**, care for. **44 leven**, remain.

45   love not hem wele in herte, but have to hem envye, as ye knowe well youreself.
And paraventure whan I and my brethern be gon, thei will make some bourde or
some turnement agein hem; wherefore I praye yow, as my goode lady, that ye
suffre hem to make no party." "And I yow graunte," seide the quene, "that ther ne
shall noon be; yef my lorde will leve my counseile, ther shall never be turnement
50   as longe as the Saisnes be in this londe." And than the kynge seide, "Be the feith
that I owe unto yow, no more ther sholde." With that thei departed and wente to
theire chambres for to slepe and to reste; and thei that were in the halle wente to
theire hostelles and departeden.

     But who that departed, Gyomar ne departed never but abode spekynge with
55   Morgain, the sustur of Kynge Arthur, in a wardrope under the paleys, where she
wrought with silke and golde, for she wolde make a coyf for hir suster, the wif of
Kynge Looth. This Morgain was a yonge damesell, fressh and jolye. But she was
somwhat brown of visage and sangwein colour, and nother to fatte ne to lene, but
was full apert, avenaunt, and comely, streight and right plesaunt, and well syngynge.
60   But she was the moste hotest woman of all Breteigne and moste luxuriouse; and
she was a noble clergesse, and of astronomye cowde she inough, for Merlin hadde
hir taught. And after he lerned hir inough, as ye shull heren afterward, and so
moche she sette theron hir entent and lerned so moche of egramauncye that the
peple cleped hir afterward Morgain le Fee, the suster of Kynge Arthur, for the
65   merveiles that she dide after in the contrey. And the beste workewoman she was
with hir handes that eny man knewe in eny londe; and therto she hadde oon of the
feirest heed and the feirest handes under hevene, and sholdres well shapen at devise. And she hadde feire eloquense, and tretable and full debonair she was, as
longe as she was in hir right witte; and whan she were wroth with eny man, she

46 **paraventure**, perhaps; **bourde**, game. 48 **suffre hem to make no party**, do not permit
them any such activity; **graunte**, promise. 50 **Saisnes**, Saxons; **Be**, By. 53 **departeden**,
separated. 54 **abode**, remained. 55 **wardrope**, small room. 56 **wrought**, worked; **coyf**,
scarf. 58 **brown of visage**, dark-complexioned; **sangwein colour**, ruddy; **nother**, neither;
to, too. 59 **apert**, lively; **avenaunt**, cheerful; **streight**, slender. 60 **moste hotest**, lustiest;
luxuriouse, lecherous. 61 **clergesse**, scholar; **cowde**, knew. 62 **and**, then. 63 **egramauncye**,
necromancy. 66 **therto**, also. 67 **feirest heed**, fairest heads; **sholdres**, shoulders. 67–68 **at
devise**, to see. 68 **tretable**, gracious; **debonair**, courteous. 69 **in hir right witte**, i.e.,
when calm; **and**, but.

70   was evell for to acorde. And that was well shewed afterward, for hir that she sholde moste have loved of all the world dide she after the moste shame, wherof it was after alle the dayes of hir lif; and that was the Quene Gonnore, as that ye shull it heren hereafter, and wherfore it was.

    Whan Guyomar entred into the chambre theras was Morgain the Fee, he hir
75   salued full swetly, and she hym salued agein curteisly. And he sette hym down by hir and helped to wynde the threde of golde, and asked hir what she sholde therwith make. And he was a feire knyght and comly, well shapen, and his visage well coloured, and his heer was crull and yelowe, and was feire and plesaunt of body and of chere laughinge. And he aresoned hir of many thinges, and she beheilde
80   hym gladly and was well plesed with all that he seide and dide. And so longe thei spake togeder that he praied hir of love; and the more that she hym behilde, the better she was with hym plesed, and that she gan love hym so well that she re-fused nothinge that he wolde hir require. And whan he aparceyved that she wolde suffre gladly his requeste, he began hir to enbrace, and she hym suffred; and he
85   began to kysse hir tendirly that bothe thei begonne to chauffe, as nature wolde, and fellen down on a grete bedde and pleyde the comen pley, as thei that gretly it desired. For yef he were desirouse, she was yet moche more, so that thei loved hertely togeder longe tyme that noon it wiste. But after it knewe the Quene Gonnore, as ye shull here telle, wherfore thei were departed; and therfor she hated the
90   quene and dide hir after gret annoye and of blames that she areised that ever en-dured while hir lif lasted. But now retourne we to Kynge Looth and his sones that be go to slepe.

    [**Summary**. *That night Lot and his sons set out. After riding for eight days they encoun-ter a large party of Saxons. Clarion, one of the Saxon leaders, rides upon a magnificent horse. Fol. 181r (line 32)–181v (line 23).]*

70 evell for to acorde, vile tempered. **73 wherfore**, why. **74 theras**, where. **75 salued**, greeted. **78 crull**, curly. **79 chere**, demeanor; **aresoned hir**, spoke to her; **beheilde**, con-sidered. **82 and that**, so that; **gan**, began to. **83 aparceyved**, saw. **85 bothe thei**, both of them; **begonne to chauffe**, became excited; **nature wolde**, was natural. **86 pleyde the comen pley**, i.e., made love. **87 yef**, if. **88 noon it wiste**, no one knew it; **after**, later. **89 departed**, separated. **90 annoye**, harm; **blames**, troubles; **areised**, caused. **92 be go**, have gone.

This Clarion rode on Gringalet, an horse that was so cleped so for the grete bounté that he hadde. For as the storye seith, for ten myle rennynge abated he never his corage ne hym neded no spore, ne no skyn of hym therfore ne sholde not swete. And whan the Saisnes hem saugh ridinge on her wey, thei knewe well by theire armes and hir conysshaunce that thei were noon of her companye; and thei hoved and abode. And whan Gawein saugh that, he hoved stille and bad his fader and his brethren to lepe upon theire horses, and so thei dide delyverly. And the gromes toke the palfreys and lepte up and rode into the foreste that wey streight as theire wey turned.

And thei com toward the Saisnes as the wey hem ledde, for thei deyned not to glenche. And mid-day was than passed and drough towarde noone. And so rode the Kynge Looth formest, and Gawein after, and his brethern hym beside a softe paas. And whan thei hadde so riden that thei began to come nygh, than seide Gawein to his fader that he ne sholde entende to noon other thinge ne coveite but to perce hem thourghout — and to his brethern he seide the same — till thei were come on that other side.

Than the Saisnes hem ascride and seide, "Ye knyghtes that come ther, yelde yow and telle us what ye be and what ye go sechinge." And the Kynge Looth ansuerde, "We ben fyve messagiers of the Kynge Arthur that go on his erunde ther he hath us sente; and more will we not sey." And thei seide, "Cesse and go no ferther; for we kepe the weyes in the name of Kynge Hardogabran and Orienx, the sone of Brangue of Saxoyne, and in the name of Margrat, to whom we lede this pray and these prisoners; and of yow also shull we make present." "Ye," quod the Kynge Looth, "whan ye may!"

---

93 so cleped so, so named. **95 corage,** strength; **ne,** nor; **no spore,** any spur. **95–96 ne no skyn . . . swete,** nor did he anywhere show sweat. **96 hem,** i.e., Lot and his sons. **97 conysshaunce,** heraldic emblems. **98 hoved and abode,** stopped and waited; **bad,** told. **99 delyverly,** swiftly. **100 gromes,** grooms. **103 glenche,** turn aside; **noone,** 3 p.m. **104–05 a softe paas,** an easy pace. **106 ne sholde . . . coveite but,** should desire nothing but. **107 perce hem thourghout,** ride right through them. **109 hem ascride,** shouted to them. **110 what,** who. **112 Cesse,** Stop. **113 kepe,** guard; **weyes,** roads. **114–15 this pray,** these livestock. **116 whan ye may,** i.e., if you can.

The Tournament at Logres; King Lot and his Sons; and Morgan and Gyomar

*[**Summary**. King Lot and his sons charge through the Saxons, who turn and pursue them. When Lot's horse is killed, he fights on foot. Using Calibourne, Gawain defends his father against forty Saxons. Then he brings the horse of a dead Saxon to his father while his three brothers inflict great harm to the other Saxons. Lot and his sons then make another attempt to escape. Fols. 182r (line 10)–182v (line 14).]*

And whan the thre kynges saugh hem departe, thei cried upon her men, "Now after hem, and lete not the traitours ascape." Than thei passed the forde and chaced hem harde. And the Kynge Clarion that satte upon the Gringalet chaced hem formest

120 the lengthe of an arblast. And Sir Gawein was behynde alle his felowes, his swerde in his hande all blody. And the sarazin that sore peyned hym to overtake ascried hym, "Wy, yelde thee, or thow art but deed!" And Gawein loked and saugh the horse so swyftly renne that he gate grounde sore after hym; and gretly he hym coveited in his herte, and seide yef he myght gete soche an horse, he wolde not

125 yeve it for the beste citee that Kynge Arthur hadde. And than he gan to ride a softer paas and rode walopinge; and Clarion hym enchased faste after.

And whan Gawein saugh he was come so nygh, he turned his shelde, and Clarion smote so harde hym upon the shelde that the spere fly on peces. And Gawein hym hitte upon the helme that he slytte thourgh the coyf of mayle and the flessh to the

130 harde boon, that he was so astoned that he fill in swowne to the grounde out of his sadill. And Gawein caught Gringalet be the bridell and ledde hym to a grove ther faste by of half a myle. And his fader rode alwey forth before and his thre sones, and entended to nought elles but to go theire wey, and wende thei hadde alle foure be by hym. And the duste and the powder was so thikke that oon myght not se fer

135 from hym; and so thei hadde lefte Gawein behynde the space of half a myle.

And whan Gawein was come into the grove, he sawgh the five gromes come oute of the foreste that rode on the five palfreyes, and than was he gladde and preised hem moche for that thei hadde peyned hem sore hem for to sewe. Than he alight of his horse and lepte on the Gringalet, and toke his horse to oon of the

---

117 her, their. **120 arblast**, bow shot. **121 sore peyned**, tried hard. **121–22 ascried hym**, shouted at him. **122 Wy**, Man (Wight). **123 gate**, gained; **sore**, quickly. **125 yeve**, i.e., trade. **126 walopinge**, galloping. **130 swowne**, a swoon. **133 entended**, attended; **nought elles**, nothing else; **wende**, thought. **134 se fer**, see far. **138 peyned hem sore hem for to sewe**, taken great pains them to follow.

140 gromes for to lede, and comaunded hem to go after his fader and his brethern that
were gon before, and bidde hem spede hem faste on hir journey. "And I shall
folowe anoon after, but I will se where these peple will be come." But he abode
for nought, for thei chaced no ferther after thei fonde the Kynge Clarion lyinge,
but stode abowte hym and wende well he hadde ben deed, and made gret doel that

145 Sir Gawein myght here the crye ther he was.

> [**Summary**. *Lot and his sons, discovering that Gawain is not with them, mourn his
demise. But then the grooms arrive with the palfreys and tell them that Gawain is safe.
Meanwhile, Gawain sets upon the Saxons, who chase him but are not able to catch the
fleet-footed Gringolet. Then Lot and his sons ride to Gawain's aid, slaying many of the
Saxons. The remaining Saxons ride back to Clarion; Lot and his sons ride on their way
until evening. Fols. 183r (line 6)–184v (line 15).]*

And the Kynge Loot and his sones saugh it drough to nyght and rode forth
theire wey, but who hadde sein theire armours, he myght have seide thei hadde
not ben at sojourne, for theire sheldes were slitte and theire helmes tohewen and
theire armours all torente and theire horse all blode and brayn; and it semed that

150 out of stronge stour thei were departed, with that thei be come to the grove ther
the gromes hem abiden. And thei alight of theire horse and lepe on the palfreyes.
And the gromes ledde theire horse and bare theire speres and theire sheldes and
theire helmes, and rode thourgh the wode that was grete till it was fer in the nyght.
And the mone shone right clier till that thei come to a forester, that was a goode

155 man and hadde foure sones that were feire yonge bachelers and hadde a wif that
was a goode lady.

This foresters place was stronge and well closed with depe diches full of water,
and was environed with grete okes; and therto it was so thikke of busshes and of
thornes and breres that noon wolde have wende that ther hadde be eny habitacion.

160 Thider com the Kynge Loot and his foure sones at the first cok crowinge, and

142 **anoon**, soon. 142–43 **abode for nought**, waited in vain. 144 **wende**, thought; **that**, so
that. 145 **ther**, where. 147 **who**, whoever. 148 **at sojourne**, idle. 150 **stronge stour**, fierce
battle; **with that**, when; **ther**, where. 151 **gromes**, grooms; **of**, off. 153 **grete**, large. 154
that², who. 157 **closed**, enclosed. 158 **environed**, surrounded by; **therto**, near. 159 **breres**,
briars; **noon wolde have wende**, no one would have thought.

happed that her wey hem ledde to a posterne wherby men entred into the place, and made oon of theire gromes to crie and knokke till the yate was opened. And oon of the foresteres sones hem asked what thei were; and thei seide thei were five erraunt knyghtes that wente upon theire grete nede. "Sirs," seide the yonge
165 man, "ye be welcome," and ledde hem into the middill of the court, and thei alight of theire horse. And ther were inowe that ledde hem to stable and yaf hem hay and otes, for the place was well stuffed.

And a squyer hem ledde into a feire halle be the grounde, hem for to unarme. And the vavasour and his wif and his foure sones that he hadde and his tweyne
170 doughtres dide arise and light up torches and other lightes therynne, and sette water to the fier and waisshed theire visages and theire handes, and after hem dried on feire toweiles and white, and than brought eche of hem a mantell. And the vavasour made cover the tables and sette on brede and wyne grete foyson, and venyson and salt flessh grete plenté. And the knyghtes sat down and ete and dranke
175 as thei that therto have grete nede. The vavasours two doughtres behilde Sir Gawein tenderly and his brethern, and sore thei merveiled what thei myght be. And the foresters foure sones served before the knyghtes, and the maidenes served of wyn. And the lady satte before Sir Gawein, and the hoste before Agravain and Gueheret and Gaheries togeder; and the Kynge Loot satte even beside his hoste a litill above.
180 And thei were well served as aboute soche hour, for it was full nygh mydnyght.

[*Summary*. *When King Lot discovers that the forester is the liegeman of King Clarion of Northumberland and that his wife is related to several of Arthur's knights, he tells the forester that all of the barons are to assemble at a certain place in Scotland on St. Bartholomew's Day; the forester agrees to take that message to Clarion. The story then turns to King Pelles of Lystenoys, the brother of King Pellynor. King Pelles's son wishes to go to Arthur's court and receive his arms from Gawain, who he says is the best knight of the world. The youth sets out, accompanied by one squire, but they soon encounter the Saxons, who chase them. With the Lord's help, they defend themselves from the Saxons, killing several of them. Fols. 184v (line 12)–187v (line 4).*]

161 **her**, their; **posterne**, back gate. 162 **crie**, shout. 163 **what**, who. 167 **otes**, oats; **stuffed**, supplied. 168 **be the grounde**, through the grounds. 169 **vavasour**, landholder. 173 **foyson**, quantity. 174 **salt flessh**, salted meat. 175 **behilde**, looked at. 176 **merveiled**, wondered; **what**, who. 180 **as aboute soche**, for such.

Whan the Kynge Looth and his foure sones were departed from the forester, thei rode thourgh the foreste that was grete and high and delitable in for to traveile. And it was feire weder and stille, and that nyght hadde ben a grete dewe; and the briddes songen for swetnesse of the myry seson, and thei songe so myrily and so

185 high in theire langage that all the wode ronge. And the kynge hem herkened, and his foure sones that were yonge and lusty, and remembred hem on theire newe loves. And so thei ride a two myle, thinkinge on the briddes songe. And Gaheries, that was amourouse, began for to singe a newe made songe; and he songe right wele and merily and well entuned. And whan the sonne was up and he saugh his

190 brethern were somwhat fer behynde hym, he turned beside the wey to make his horse stale till thei were come to hym, for thei herkened hym gladly. And Gaheries com to Agravain and to Geheret and seide, "Let us singe"; and than thei begonne to singe alle thre.

And than seide Gaheries to Agravain and to Gueheret, "Now telle me by the

195 feith that ye owe to the Kynge Looth my fader and yours, yef ye hadde the two doughtres of oure hoste that was this nyght and thei were now here, telle me, what wolde ye do?" "So God me helpe," seide Agravain, "I sholde have my wille." "So helpe me God," seide Gaheries, "so wolde not I do, but I wolde bringe hem to saftee. And ye, Gueheret, what wolde ye do?" Quod Gueheret, "I sholde make hir

200 my love, yef I myght therto hir entrete; but be force wolde I nothinge do, for than were the game nought but yef it plesed hir as well as me."

While thei seide these wordes, overtoke hem the Kynge Looth and Gawein that wele hadde herde that thei hadde seide. And thei lough alle togeder. And than thei asked whiche hadde seide beste. "Of that," quod the kynge, "shall Gawein youre

205 brother by juge." "And I shall soone have seide," quod Gawein. "Gaheries hath seide beste and Agravain werste, for Agravain sholde se that noon dide hem noon harme but sholde helpe to diffende hem at his power; but me semeth ther were no

---

182 delitable, delightful. **184 briddes songen**, birds sung. **185 high**, loudly; **wode ronge**, woods rang; **hem herkened**, listened to them. **186 remembred hem on**, thought about. **187 thinkinge on**, listening to. **188 that**, who; **amourouse**, in love; **newe**, newly. **191 stale**, wait. **192 begonne**, began. **195 yef**, if. **197 wille**, desires. **200 be**, by. **201 nought**, worth nothing; **but yef**, unless. **202 that**, what. **203 lough**, laughed. **205 by**, be. **206–07 se that noon dide hem noon harme**, see that no one harmed them.

werse enmy than he. And Geheret hath yet seide better than he, for he seith he wolde nothinge do be force; and that he seith so cometh hym but of love and
210 curtesie. And Gaheries hath seide as a goode man, for so as he seith wolde I do the same, yef it were for me to do."

And than thei lough and japed with Agravain, and the kynge hymself more than eny other, and rode to Agravain and seide, "What, Agravain, hadde ye the doughter of youre hoste for youre foule delite, a feire rewarde yelde ye for the feire servise
215 and the goode chere that she hath yow don, for trewly, she hath it evill besette." "Sir," seide Agravain, "thei sholde not therfore have no mayme of hande ne foote." "No, " quod the kynge, "but thei shull lese all worship." "I cannot sey," quod Agravain, "of eny man that wolde hem spare, yef he hadde hem alone by hymself, for after that he lete her passe, she sholde hym never love." "But he sholde kepe
220 and save his honour," seide the kynge. "Certes," seide Agravain, "never after he hadde lefte hir, she wolde but skorne and preyse hym the lesse." Quod the kynge, "I wolde not sette at a boton what oon seide, so that my worship were saved, so that I hadde no vylonye ne reprof." "Ya, ther is no more of," quod Agravain, "but we shull us yelden into soche place ther we shull se no women." "Ha, Agravain,"
225 quod the Kynge Looth, "yef ye yow thus demene as ye sey, wite ye well ye shull myscheve, and that shull ye well se."

And even as the kynge seide, so hym befill after that he langwissid longe above the erthe for the vilonye that he dide to a mayden that rode with hir frende with whom he faught till that he hadde hym discounfited and maymed of oon of his
230 armes. And after wolde [he] have leyen by his love, and fonde hir roynouse of oon of hir thighes; and [he] seide hir soche vilonye that she after hurte his oo thigh and his arme so that it sholde never be made hooll, but yef it were be tweyne of the best knyghtes of the worlde, to whom she sette terme of garison. And the booke

---

208 seide, said; **seith**, says. **212 japed**, joked. **214 yelde**, yield. **215 evill besette**, evilly received. **216 no mayme of hande ne foote**, i.e., any physical harm. **217 lese all worship**, i.e., be disgraced. **222 sette at a boton**, set at the value of a button. **224 yelden into**, go to; **ther**, where. **225 demene**, believe. **226 myscheve**, have trouble. **227 hym befill after**, it befell him later; **langwissid**, suffered. **230 roynouse**, ruinous (diseased). **231 seide hir soche vilonye**, said such mean things; **oo**, one. **232 hooll**, whole; **but yef**, unless; **be tweyne of the**, by one of the two. **233 terme of garison**, condition of relief.

shall yow devyse hereafter how that it was warisshed by Gawein his brother and
235   by Launcelot de Lak that was so noble a knyght. But of this mater speketh no
more at this tyme, but returneth how the Kynge Looth speketh to his sone Agravain
that was prowde and fell. And thus thei rode in the foreste till it was paste pryme.

*[**Summary**. Lot and his sons meet the squire of King Pelles's son, who has become
separated from him. Then, seeing King Pelles's son being chased by Saxons, they ride to
his aid and fight the Saxons. It is a difficult fight in which Gawain performs great deeds.
At one point Gaheris rescues his father. The Saxons finally retreat, and Lot and the others
escape into the forest. Fols. 188r (line 22)–190v (line 29).]*

Whan the Saisnes were discounfited in the Valey of Rorestok, the Kynge Looth
was gladde for the squyer that thei hadde rescowed. And than thei wente to the
240   somers that the Saisnes sholde have ledde to the siege before Clarence, and gadered
hem togeder and behelde hem gretly. And than seide Gaheries a worde that was
well herde. "Lord God!" quod he, "why be ther so many pore bachelers in the
contrey whan thei myght thus wynne inough? Certes, thei lose nothinge but for
slouthe and cowardise, for thei ne sholde not slepe in no bedde but wayte aboute
245   on the marches." "Feire sone," seide the kynge, "so myght thei have evell suerté,
for who that soche thinge will undirtake, yef oon tyme hym happe wele, hit falleth
hym foure tymes evell."

And than seide Gaheries to his fader, "Sir, aske Agravain my brother yef he
have eny talent now to rage within these maydenes, yef he hadde hem here on this
250   playn." And Agravain loked on hym a traverse full proudly and seide to hym in
reprof, "Gaheries, it is not longe tyme past that ye hadde no talent to jape whan
the Saisne smote yow down of youre horse with his axe; and ne hadde be Gawein,
ye hadde mette with hym in evell tyme." "Though I fell," quod Gaheries, "I may
no more do therto. But I was not at so grete myschef, but I me diffended so as it
255   myght be. And of that ye myght wele have holde youre pees, for I saugh yow

234 **warisshed**, accomplished. 237 **fell**, cruel; **pryme**, 9 a.m. 238 **discounfited**, defeated.
240 **somers**, pack horses. 245 **evell suerté**, certain misfortune. 246 **happe wele**, succeeds.
247 **evell**, badly. 249 **talent**, desire; **rage within**, flirt with; **maydenes**, maidens. 250 **a
traverse**, a glance. 251 **talent**, desire. 252 **Saisne**, Saxon; **ne hadde be**, if not for. 253–54
may no more do therto, i.e., do not deny it. 254 **myschef**, danger. 255 **pees**, peace.

today at soche pointe that though the feirest lady of the worlde hadde preide yow of love, ye wolde not have ansuered hir a worde, for a maiden of five yere of age myght have take from yow youre breche!"

And whan Agravain undirstode this, he was wroth and angry and for that he cleped hym recreaunt. Wax he rody for shame and loked on hym with maltalent; and yef thei hadden be alone, he wolde with hym have foughten. But the kynge turned the wordes into other maner, for he wolde not have in no wise distrif betwene hem two. And than he asked what sholde be do with the somers. "Sir," quod Gaheries, "asketh of Agravain." And than began Agravain sore to wrathe and seide he sholde it abeyen, and hilde a tronchon of a spere in his honde and smote Gaheries on the helme that it fly all to peces; and Gaheries remeved not but suffred. And Agravain recovered and smote twys or thries so that nought of the tronchon lefte in his handes. And his brother Gueheret ne hys fader cowde hem not so departe, but ever he ran upon hym as he myght from hem ascape.

Than com Gawain from the chace, and asked what aray that was. And the kynge tolde hym all, worde for worde. And Gawein com to Agravain and blamed hym sore for that he hadde so idon. And Agravain swor all that he myght swere that never he wolde it hym foryeve. And whan Gawein undirstode the grete felonye, he seide he sholde abye on his body but yef he wolde be ruled. "Fy," quod Agravain, "in dispite of the devell this were of the newe that I sholde lette for yow to do ought!" "Now shall it be sene," quod Gawein, "what thow wilt do." Than Agravain smote the horse with the spores and ran to Gaheries with swerde drawen, and smote hym on the helme that the fire sparcled oute. Ne Gaheries ne remeved litill ne moche, for nothinge that he dide. And whan Gawein saugh his, he drough oute Calibourne and swor by his fader sowle that in evell tyme he hadde it begonne.

And whan the fader behilde all this he seide, "Now upon hym, feire sone! And

256 at soche pointe, i.e., so scared. **258 breche**, breeches. **259 and for that**, because. **260 recreaunt**, coward; **maltalent**, malice. **262 distrif**, strife. **263 do**, done; **somers**, pack horses. **265 it abeyen**, pay for it; **tronchon**, shaft. **268 lefte**, remained; **ne**, nor; **cowde**, could. **270 what aray that was**, i.e., what was going on. **273 felonye**, wrong. **274 abye**, pay; **be ruled**, be controlled. **275 of the newe**, something new. **275–76 lette for yow to do ought**, stop because you might do something. **278–79 Ne Gaheries . . . litill ne moche**, i.e., Gaheris remained still. **281 it**, i.e., this strife.

go sle this harlot, for he is fell and proude!" And Gawein thought well what he
wolde do, and com to Agravain and smote hym with the pomell of his swerde
285 under the temple that he fill from his horse to the erthe so astoned that he wiste not
where he was. And Gaheries seide to Gawein, "Sir, be not wroth for nothinge that
he doth to me, for he is fell and proude; and therfore taketh nothinge to herte that
he doth to me ne seith." "Fle from hens," quod Gawein, "mysproude lurdeyn!
Never shall I love thee, whan thou wilt not spare for my lorde my fader, ne for
290 noon of us." "Sir," seide Gaheries, "he is myn elther brother, and it sitteth me to
do hym honour and reverence; ne for nothinge that I dide ne seide to him, ne dide
I but jape."

"He is a fole and prowde," quod Gueheret, "but all that hast thow meved, and
therfore have thow evell happe." And Gaheries hym ansuerde, "Full evell sholde I
295 pleye with a straunger whan I may not pley nother with yow ne with hym. And
wyte ye well," quod he, "this is the firste tyme and the laste that ever I shall pleye
or jape with hym or with yow; and yef it were not for because that we be comen
oute togeder, I wolde returne anoon right that no more companye sholde I yow
holde." And Geheret seide agein, "Evell happe have Agravain but he quyte yow
300 this dere for this acolee that he hath hadde for yow."

"So God me helpe," quod Gawein, "yef owther of yow do enything othirwise
than ye owe to do, I shall sette yow in soche place where ye shull not se nother
hande ne foote this seven monethes. And therfore I diffende yow as dere as ye
have youre owne bodyes that ye loke ye do hym noon evell." "Sir," seide Gueheret,
305 "we shull kepe us therfro right wele, seth ye it comaunde; for agein youre
comaundement ne may we not do, ne we will not, but it hevyeth me whan ye will
medle yow agein us for hym, and that ye have Agravain thus diffouled for nought."
"For nought is it not," quod Gawein, "whan agein my deffence he ran upon hym in
dispite of me, in my fader sight and myn. Ne never Gaheries ne wrathed for buffet

---

283 harlot, rascal; **fell,** mean. **285 astoned,** stunned. **288 mysproude lurdeyn,** prideful
villain. **290 elther,** older; **sitteth me,** is right for me. **293 fole,** fool; **meved,** i.e., started.
294 evell happe, misfortune. **298 anoon right,** right now. **299 but,** unless; **quyte,** repay.
300 acolee, blow. **301 yef,** if; **owther,** either. **302 owe,** ought. **303 diffende,** charge; **dere,**
dearly. **304 have,** hold; **noon evell,** no harm. **306 hevyeth,** grieves. **307 medle yow,** turn
yourself; **diffouled,** injured; **nought,** no reason. **308 agein,** against; **deffence,** command.
308–09 in dispite of, as an insult to. **309 wrathed,** got angry; **buffet,** blow.

310   that he hym yaf. In dispite of the devell sholde he be so proude, for his pride shall greve bothe thee and hym."

"So helpe me God," quod the Kynge Looth, "For litill I shall take awey all the armes that thow haste, and of Agravain also, and leve yow in myddell of the felde like lurdeynes." "Sir, " seide Gueheret, "ye speke not of this of youre owen mouthe

315   but of others; for of this that ye sey ye have no talent for to do ne power, yef other ne were." "Ha, boyes!" quod the kynge, "thow art fell and forswollen. Verilé art thow his brother, for ye bothe be contrariouse. And I comaunde my sone Gawein that yef thow or Agravain do ought to my sone Gaheries that he do upon yow as grete reddure as upon harlottes or ribaudes."

320   Whan the squyer saugh that Gawein hadde smyte down Agravain that he bledde bothe at mouthe and nose, he ran to take his horse and brought hym by the bridill and made hym for to lepen up. And Gawein com to hym and seide, "Harlot, fle from hens! For with thee have I nought to do. And loke that I se thee never more in my companye! And go where thow wilt, for with me shalt thow come no more.

325   And go ye alle forth with hym that love hym better than me, and with me that love my companye."

*[**Summary**. The young squire who is son of King Pelles now reveals his name; he is called Elizer; he says he has come to be knighted by Gawain. That night they lodge with a hermit. Hearing cries for help, Gawain and Elizer ride to the aid of a woman and a knight. Gawain rescues the lady from six attackers, while Elizer rescues the knight; they take them to the Castle of Roestok. In the morning Lot's party rides on to Cambenyk, where Duke Escam is being besieged by the Saxons. They tell the duke of the meeting of all the barons to be held in Scotland; then follows a great battle with the Saxons. Duke Escam sends messengers to the other barons, informing them of the meeting to be held on the Nativity of the Virgin. Lot and his sons proceed to the meeting place, and the barons arrive there also. Fols. 192r (line 2)–199r (line 19.]*

And whan thei were alle assembled, the Kynge Looth seide that on the morowe he wolde telle wherefore he hadde made hem to assemble. And this was on Seint

310 In dispite of, To shame. **312 litill,** a little. **313 haste,** have. **314 lurdeynes,** felons. **315 talent,** desire. **316 boyes,** uncouth youths; **fell,** cruel; **forswollen,** enraged; **Verilé,** Truly. **319 reddure,** punishment; **harlottes,** rascals; **ribaudes,** thieves. **322 Harlot,** Villain. **328 wherefore,** why.

Marie Even in Septembre. And eche of hem made to other grete joye and myrthe,
330   and rested ther all that nyght.

And on the morowe, thei assembled togeder all the prevy counseile and Sir
Gawein and his thre bretheren. And whan thei weren all sette upon a cloth of silke
that was leide upon the grene grasse, than aroos Gawein by the comaundement of
his fader the Kynge Looth, and seide: "Feire lordes, we be come hider for to speke
335   with yow in the name of the Kynge Arthur with whom we be. And my lorde yow
sendeth and prayeth as to hem that he wolde gladly have to his frendes yef it
myght be, that ye sholde yeve hym trewys saf to come and saf to go by feith and
suerté betwene this and Yole. And ye also to go and come thourgh his power
suerly, and he in yours at youre plesier. For yef it plese yow that we go alle togeder
340   and fight with the Saisnes that be come into this contrey till that we have hem oute
chaced, and yef God will ordeyne, that thei be discounfited, than acorde yow
togeder yef ye may be, and the pardon is yoven and graunted to alle tho that will
go fight with the Saisnes, that thei shull be clene quyte of alle ther synnes as thei
were the day of theire birthe."

345   Whan the princes herde the request of Sir Gawein of that he dide hem amonesté,
thei asked the Kynge Looth his advise. And he seide it was the grettest bounté that
ever was seide or don. "And I do yow to wite I sey it nothinge for that I am his
sworn man, but I sey as longe as ye have ben ageins hym ye have myshapped, for
as I trowe this peple hadde never entred into this londe yef we hadde holden togeder,
350   and knowe it verily that it cometh thourgh oure synnes."

"What!" seide the Kynge Urien. "Have ye don hym homage? Ye have nothinge
do as a trewe knyght, and I will telle yow whi, for yef it fill so that we yede upon
hym, hit behoveth us to go agein yow." "That were right," seide the Kynge Looth,
"withoute faile; and wite ye well, whoso hath werre agein hym hath werre agein
355   me." "For sothe," seide the Kynge Urien, "that is untrewly don, for ye be oon of
us, and ye sholde not us so leven." "Sir," seide the Kynge Looth, " I dide it magré
myn and agein my will, for I do yow to wite that day that I wende hym moste to

---

335 we be, we are allied. **337 trewys,** truce. **338 this,** now; **Yole,** Yuletide. **339 suerly,**
safely. **343 clene quyte,** entirely acquited; **synnes,** wrongs. **345 dide,** offered; **amonesté,**
amnesty. **348 myshapped,** had misfortune. **349 trowe,** believe; **this peple,** i.e., the Saxons. **351–52 nothinge do,** not behaved. **352 yede upon,** went against. **354 faile,** a doubt.
356 leven, desert. **356–57 magré myn,** against my wishes. **357 wende,** intended.

greve or anoyen, I dide hym homage, and all this made me Gawein for to do, that
ye here se."

360   Than he tolde hem alle worde for worde how the cas was befallen. And whan
the other princes herde this, thei seide he myght noon other do, seith it was so he
was not moche to blame. And some of hem that were there wolde right gladly that
thei hadde happed in the same maner. Thei spake of oo thinge and of other, that
thei accorded to holde the trewis. And therto thei it assured in Sir Gaweins honde
365   hit trewly to holde, and sette hem a day that eche of hem sholde be with all his
power on the playn of Salisbery with all his peple as eche of hem myght bringe.
But thei seide well that whan the Saisnes were driven oute of the londe, that thei
dide the kynge to wite that he diffende hym from theym. And Sir Gawein hem
tolde that whan it were come therto that yef thei wolde hym ought mysdon, thei
370   sholde fynde that thei sholde have bothe theire armes wery and overcharged.

    Whan the princes undirstode the wordes of Sir Gawein, ther were some that
lough and some frowned with the heede. And the Kynge de Cent Chivaliers, that
liste not hym to avaunte ne noon other to manace, seide he wolde be ther at
Halowmesse, yef God hym sende lif, in the playn of Salisbery. And so seid eche
375   of hem for his partye.

357–58 to greve, injure. **358 anoyen**, harm; **made**, made. **360 cas was befallen**, adventure occurred. **361 seith**, since; **so**, thus. **362 wolde**, wished. **363 happed**, acted; **that**, and. **372 lough**, laughed. **373 avaunte ne noon other to manace**, boast or anyone to threaten.

[King Arthur vs. King Rion]

[*Summary*. Merlin goes to Blase and reports all that has happened. Then he goes to Brittany to summon their armies to Salisbury for the great battle against the Saxons; he also makes a brief visit to Nimiane before returning to Logres. Sagremor, Galashin, and Dodinell ride off together seeking adventures, and three Round Table knights ride after them, hoping to provoke a confrontation; but Ewain, Kay, and Gifflet prevent that and bring the six knights back to court.

The Saxons, learning that Arthur is assembling a great force at Salisbury, also prepare for battle. Merlin tells Arthur that as long as he trusts in God, he will have the victory over his enemies. Arthur assures Merlin that he does. Merlin also predicts that never again will so many good knights be assembled in one place until "*the fader shall sle the sone and the sone the fader, and that shall be in this same place.*" Arthur asks Merlin to explain this cryptic remark, but Merlin prefers not to.

Arthur thanks all the barons for coming together with him, but several respond that they have come out of their love of God and Holy Church, not their love of Arthur. King Lot urges the barons to make peace with Arthur, but Uriens and Ventres respond angrily. King Pelles's son Elizer comes to Gawain and requests to be made a knight. Gawain, assisted by Gaheris, soon obliges. Meanwhile, the Saxon army is on the move. At King Ventres's fortress of Garlot they kill the steward and capture King Ventres's wife. Gawain and Elizer lead a party to the rescue; they attack the Saxons and retrieve the queen; then Gawain presents her to her husband King Ventres, who is overjoyed.

The battle between the Saxons and Christians commences, with both sides inflicting great slaughter. Eventually the Saxons give ground. Sensing defeat, they flee toward their ships with the Christians in pursuit. The Saxons clamber aboard their ships and hoist the sails, though many of them drown in the process. At last all of the barons do homage to Arthur. Then they ride together to the city of Clarence where they force the Saxons besieging the city to flee. These Saxons also sail for Saxony, finally freeing Britain from all Saxon invaders.

Arthur and his barons give thanks to God, and then Arthur and his closest companions return to Camelot. Merlin advises King Ban and King Bors to return to their country and protect it from Claudas de la deserte. Enroute, King Ban has an adventure at the castle of Adravadain where, through Merlin's enchantment, he begets a son (Estor de Maris) on]

King Arthur vs. King Rion

Adravadain's daughter. Ban and Bors then go on to Benoyk, and Merlin makes a brief visit to Nimiane, before reporting everything to Blase. Fols. 199v (line 27)–217v (line 16).]

Whan the Kynge Ban and the Kynge Bohors and Merlin were departed from the Kynge Arthur for to go into theire owne contrey, the kynge abode stille at Cameloth, gladde and myri with the Quene Gonnore that moche hym loved, and he hir; and so thei abide in joye and myrthe longe tyme till it drough nygh the myddill of

5 Auguste. And than seide the kynge to Sir Gawein his nevew that at the Feste of Assumpcion he wolde holde court roiall, and that alle sholde be sent fore that were of hym holdinge londe or feo. For he seide he saugh never his hool power togeder at no feeste that he hadde holden before. "And therfore," quod he, "I will that alle be sent fore, bothe fer and nygh, bothe privé and straunge; and also I will

10 that eche bringe with hym his wif or his love that my court may be the more honoured." And Sir Gawein seide that he hadde well devised and that of gentell herte meved this purpos. "And therfore I beseke yow that this be so don that it be to youre honour." And the kynge seide, "Certes, feire nevew, I desire to do so that I have therof honour and that all the worlde therof may speke."

15 Than Sir Gawein lete write lettres and writtes and sente hem to the barouns and to knyghtes of the londe and comaunded hem alle, as dere as thei hym loved, that thei be on the Assumpcion Even at Cameloth, for than wolde he holden court grete and roiall, and every man to bringe with hym his wif or his love. And the messagers wente to the princes and barouns and shewed hem theire lettres and

20 dide theire message thourgh the contrey. And the princes and the barouns made hem redy in the moste roiall wise and com to the court as the kynge hadde comaunded. And every man brought with hym his wif, and he that hadde no wif brought with hym his love. And than ther com thider so many that merveile it was to beholde the nombre, for ther ne myght not the tenthe part into the citee of

25 Cameloth, but loigged withoute in the feire medowes in tentes and in pavelouns.

And the kynge hem resceived with grete joye and grete honour. And the Quene Gonnore, that was the wisest lady of the worlde, resceyved the quenes and the ladyes and the maydenes and damesels with grete honour, everiche of hem by

7 feo, rents; **hool**, whole. **8 will**, desire. **9 fer and nygh**, far and near; **privé and straunge**, intimate friends and strangers. **16 dere**, dearly. **17 Even**, Eve. **28 everiche**, every one.

30 hemself, as she that hadde more witte and curtesie than eny lady in hir dayes, and
yaf to hem riche yeftes of golde and silver and clothes of silke, everiche after
theire astate. And she demened hir so well that thei seide ther was not soche
another lady in all the worlde as was she. And the kynge departed to knyghtes
robes and armes and horse, and dide hem so moche worship that day and curtesie
that thei loved hym the better as longe as theire lif endured. And that shewed well
35 after in many a stour and in many a nede, as ye shull heren herafter.

Grete was the feeste that the kynge hilde on the Even of the Assumpcion to the
riche baronye that to hym were come. Whan the kynge and the barouns hadde
herde evesonge at the Mynster of Seint Stephene, the tables were sette in teintes
and pavelons, for thei myght not alle into the town. And on that othir side was the
40 Quene Gonnore and the ladyes and damesels, with soche joye that merveile it
were to reherse; for in all the londe of Breteigne ne in all the power of Kynge
Arthur, ne lefte mynstrall ne jogelour ne oon ne other, but alle were come to that
feeste. And at that soper were thei served so well as was convenient to so myghty
a prince as was the Kynge Arthur. And thus endured thei in joye and myrthe till
45 tyme was to go to reste till on the morowe.

And on the morowe aroos the Kynge Arthur and the riche barouns and the
quene and wente to hire masse at the Mynster of Seint Stephene, and the servise
was honorably seide in the worship and reverence of that high feste, and grete and
riche was the offrande. And the Kynge Arthur and alle other kynges and quenes
50 that day bar crownes in worship of the day; and so ther were sixty crownes, what
of kynges and quenes. And whan the masse was seide and the servise ended, the
Kynge Arthur lepe on his palfrey, and alle the other kynges after hym icrowned,
and so dide the Quene Gonnore and alle the other quenes, and everyche of hem a
crowne of golde on theire heedes. And the Kinge Arthur satte at the high deyse
55 and made alle the twelve kynges sitte at his table downwarde a renge. And also in
honour of the high feste of Oure Lady, he made the Quene Gonnore sitte by hym
crowned, and so dide alle the other twelve quenes byfore theire lordes. And at

30 yeftes, gifts. **30–31 after theire astate**, according to rank. **31 demened**, conducted. **32
departed**, gave. **35 stour**, battle; **nede**, need. **41 ne**, nor; **power**, i.e., realm. **42 ne lefte**,
was overlooked; **jogeloure**, entertainer; **ne oon ne other**, i.e., of this kind or that. **43
convenient to**, fitting for. **49 offrande**, offering. **50 bar**, wear. **54 deyse**, dais. **55 a renge**,
in a row. **56 feste**, feast.

other tables satte other princes, dukes, and erles, and othir knyghtes were sette richely thourgh the medowes in tentes and pavelouns, with grete joy and melodye
60   that never was seyn gretter in no court.

   And as thei were in this joye and in this feste, and Kay the Stiward that brought the firste mese before the kynge, ther com in the feirest forme of man that ever hadde thei seyn before; and he was clothed in samyte and girte with a bawdrike of silke harnysshed with golde and preciouse stones, that all the paleys flamed of
65   the light. And the heir of his hede was yelowe and crispe with a crowne of golde theron as he hadde ben a kynge; and his hosen of fin scarlet and his shone of white cordewan orfraied, and bokeled with fin golde. And [he] hadde an harpe abowte his nekke of silver richely wrought, and the stringes were of fin golde wire, and the harpe was sette with preciouse stones. And the man that it bar was
70   so feire of body and of visage that never hadde thei sein noon so feire a creature. But this apeired moche his bewté and his visage for that he was blinde; and yet were the iyen in his heed feire and clier.

   And he hadde a litill cheyne of silver tacched to his arme, and to that cheyne a litill spayne was bounde as white as snowe, and a litill coler aboute his nekke of
75   silke harneysed with golde. And this spaynell ledde hym streght before the Kynge Arthur, and he harped a lay of Breteigne full swetely that wonder was to here. And the refraite of his laye salewed the Kynge Arthur and the Quene Gonnore and alle the other after. And Kay the Stiward that brought the firste cours taried a while in the settinge down to beholde the harpur ententifly. Bot now we moste
80   cesse of hem a while and speke of the Kynge Rion.

*[**Summary**. King Rion, smarting from his earlier humilation by Arthur, assembles a huge force and marches against the city of Toraise in Tamelide; and he sends a messenger to Camelot with a letter for Arthur. Fol. 218v (line 18)–219v (line 26).]*

62 mese, course; **feirest forme of**, handsomest. **63 samyte**, silk; **girte**, girded; **bawdrike**, baldric. **64 harnysshed**, adorned. **65 crispe**, straight. **66 shone**, shoes. **67 orfraied**, gold-adorned. **71 apeired**, impaired. **72 iyen**, eyes. **73 cheyne**, chain; **tacched**, attached. **74 spayne**, spaniel; **bounde**, tied; **coler**, collar. **75 harneysed**, decorated. **77 refraite**, refrain; **salewed**, addressed.

Whan this messager was departed from his lorde, he and his squyer rode forth
till thei com to Cameloth on the Day of the Assumpcion, and alight down of his
horse and com into the halle as Kay hadde sette the firste cours before the Kynge
Arthur. This knyght saugh these kynges and these quenes that satte at the high
85 deyse alle crowned for the high feeste and saugh the harpour crowned with golde,
[and] he was all astonyed and for the dogge that hym ledde thourgh the paleis.
And he asked of Kay that served whiche was the Kynge Arthur; and Kay hym
shewed anoon right. And the knyght, that was wise and well cowde speke, com
before the kynge and seide so lowde that alle myght it undirstonde, "Kynge Arthur,
90 I grete thee nought, for I am not therto comaunded by hym that hath me to thee
isente. But I shall do thee to undirstande what he doth to the sende. And whan
thow hast herde his comaundement, do as thow art avised. And yef thow do his
will, thow shalt finde therin profite; and yef thow wilt it nought do, thee byhoveth
to forsake thi londe and fle in exile." And whan the kynge this herde, he began to
95 smyle and seide full sobirly, "Avise thee of thi message; for of all that thow art
comaunded, thou mayst say boldly all thy will withoute eny encombraunce of me
or of eny other."

  And than he seide: "Kynge Arthur, to thee sente me the kynge of alle Cristin
that is the Kynge Rion of the Yles, whiche is at sege before Toraise in Carmelide.
100 And with hym nine kynges that alle ben his liege men and holde of hym theire
londes and their fees in honour, for he hath made hem alle enclyne to hym by his
prowesse. And of alle the kynges that he hath conquered wherof ther be nine, he
hath flayn of theire beerdes. Now my lorde sendeth the comaundement that thou
become his man; and that shall be to the grete honour to become liege man to so
105 puyssaunt a kynge as is my lorde, for he is lorde from the east into the west of all
the londe."

  And whan the knyght hadde thus seide, he drough oute the letter of Kynge
Rion that was seled with ten seles roiall and seide to the Kynge Arthur, "Sir, do

---

84 saugh, saw. **86 astonyed**, amazed; **and for**, because. **90 grete thee nought**, do not
greet you. **91 do thee to undirstande**, let you know. **92 avised**, advised. **93 thee byhoveth**,
it would behove you. **95 Avise thee**, i.e., Proceed in delivering. **96 encombraunce of**,
trouble from. **98 Cristin**, the Christians. **99 whiche**, who; **sege**, siege. **101 fees**, rents;
enclyne, do homage. **103 flayn of**, cut off; **beerdes**, beards. **105 puyssaunt**, myghty.

110　rede this letter that my lorde hath thee sente, and than shalt thou heren his wille
and his corage." And therwith he delyvered hym the letter. And the kynge hit
toke to the archebisshop that was come thider to undirstonde the massage. And
he it unfolded and began to rede alowde that thei myght it wele undirstonde that
were in the halle.

115　　"I, the Kynge Rion, that am lorde of all the west, do hem alle to wite that these
letteres shull seen, that I am at sege before Toraise in Carmelide, and with me be
nine kynges of my meyné and alle theire peple of theire londes that armes may
bere. And of alle the kynges that I conquere, I have theire suerdes be my prowesse;
and also I have made a mantell of reade samyte furred with the beerdes of these
kynges. And this mantell is nygh all redy of all that therto longeth saf only tasselles;

120　and for the tassels faile, I have herde tidinges of thy grete renoun that is spredde
thourgh the worlde, I will that it be honoured more than eny of the other kinges;
and therfore I comaunde thee that thow sende me thy beerde with all the skynne;
and I shall hit sette on the tassels of my mantell for the love of thee, for never
before this mantell be tasselled shall it not hange aboute my nekke. Ne I will of

125　noon other have it made but of thy beerde, for aboute the handes and the nekke
ought every prince sette the moste honorable thinges. And for thow art the moste
puyssaunt kynge as the renoun of thee recordeth, I will that thow sende me thy
beerde by oon or tweyne of thy frendes; and after, come thou to me and become
my liege man and holde of me thy londes in goode pees. And yef thou wilt nought

130　thus don, I comaunde thee that thou go exiled and forsake thi londe; for as soone
as I have conquered the Kynge Leodogan, I shall come upon thee with all myn
hoste and make thy beerde be flayn and drawe from thy chyn boustously; and that
thou shalt knowe verily."

　　　Whan the archebisshop hadde redde this letter before the Kynge Arthur and
135　before alle the barouns, he delyvered the letter agein to the kynge that was full
wroth and angry with this comaundement. And the messager seide, "Kynge Arthur,

---

108–09 do rede, read. **110 corage**, desire. **111 undirstonde**, translate. **116 meyné**, liegemen.
117 suerdes, swords. **118 reade samyte**, red silk. **119 nygh all**, nearly; **therto longeth**,
i.e., is needed. **120 faile**, that are lacking. **121 will**, desire. **123–24 never before**, not until.
124–25 Ne I will of noon other, Nor will I of any other. **127 puyssaunt**, mighty. **129 pees**,
peace; **nought**, not. **130 don**, do. **132 boustously**, vigorously.

do that my lorde thee comaundeth that I may returne." And the kynge seide he
myght wele returne whansoever he wolde, and telle his lorde that his beerd sholde
he never have while he myght it diffende. And the knyght departed and com to his
140   horse and rode forth, he and his squyer, till thei come to Toraise in Carmelide,
where he fonde the Kynge Rion that assailede the castell full fiercely.

And thei withynne diffended hem full harde, that thei withoute loste moche of
theire peple; and therfore was the Kynge Rion full wroth. And whan the knyght
was come before the Kynge Rion and tolde his ansuere from the Kynge Arthur, he
145   seide he sholde not so soone have take the Kynge Leodogan, but anoon he wolde
come upon hym with so grete power that he sholde not hem sustene ne endure.
And now shull we speke of the Kynge Arthur and of his barouns.

Whan the knyght that hadde brought this message from the Kynge Rion was
departed, the Kynge Arthur lefte stille, sitting at mete in myrthe and in joye. And
150   the harpour wente from oon place to another and harped myrily, so that thei behilde
hym for a merveile, bothe oon and other; and hem liked more the melodye of this
harpour than eny thinge that this other mynstralles diden. And the Kynge Arthur
hadde grete merveile fro whens this man myght come, and yet he ought hym well
to knowe, for many tymes hadde he hym seyn in other maner and in other
155   semblaunces.

And whan thei hadde eten and the clothes were taken up, the harpour com before the kynge and seide, "Sir, yef it plese yow, graunte me reward for my servise."
"Certes, frende," seide the kynge, "it is reson, and ye shull it have with goode
will; and therfore sey youre will, for ye shull not faile yef it be soche thinge as I
160   may yeve, savinge myn honour and my reame." "Sir," seide the harpour, "ye shull
never have therin but honour, yef God will." "Than sey youre volunté," seide the
kynge boldely. Than seide the harpour, "I aske yow and require to bere youre
chief baner in the firste bataile that ye shall go to." "Feire frende," seide the kynge,
"sholde that be worship to me and my reame? Oure Lorde hath sette yow in His
165   prison. How myght ye youreself guyde, that may nought se, to bere a baner in
bateile of a kynge that ought to be refute and counfort to alle the hoste?" "Haa,

137 **that**[1], what; **that**[2], so that. 142 **thei withynne**, those inside; **moche**, many. 145 **anoon**,
now. 146 **sustene**, protect. 149 **lefte**, remained. 152 **this**, these. 154 **maner**, forms. 155
semblaunces, guises. 158 **Certes**, Surely; **reson**, right. 160 **reame**, realm. 161 **but**, only;
volunté, desires. 165 **that**, who; **nought se**, nothing se. 166 **refute**, refuge.

sir," quod the harpour, "God, that is the very guyde, me shall condite and lede that in many perilouse places me hath ledde; and wite ye well, it shall be for youre prowe." And whan the barouns it undirstode, thei hadde merveile.

170   Than behilde hym the Kynge Ban and remembred hym of Merlin that in the Castell of the Marasse hym served in disgise of a yonge knyght of fifteen yere age, and thought it sholde ben he. And [he] seide anoon to the kynge, "Sir, graunte hym his request, for he semeth to be soche a man that his desire ne ought not to be refusid." "Why," seide Arthur, "trowe ye it sholde be to oure profite and oure

175 honour that a mynstrall sholde bere oure baner in bateile, whiche may not lede hymself? Though I hit withsey, I do nothinge agein right; for it is a thinge that I sholde not graunte lightly but I knewe right well the persone that it sholde bere."

And anoon as this worde was seide, the harpour vanysshed amonge hem that noon wiste where he be com. Than Arthur bethought hym on Merlin, and was

180 sory and wroth that he ne hadde it hym graunted. And alle that were therynne were abaisshed for that he was loste so sodeinly. And the Kynge Ban of Benoyk, that well aparceived it was Merlin, seide to the Kynge Arthur, "Certes, sir," quod he, "ye ought hym wele for to knowen." "Trewly," seide Arthur, "ye sey full trewe, but for that he hath made a whelpe hym for to lede that hath take awey fro

185 me the knowinge." "Sir," seide Gawein, "what is he, than?" "Nevew," quod the kynge, "it is Merlin oure frende." "Yee," seide Gawein, "so helpe me God, I trowe yow wele that it be he, for often hath he be disgised before youre baronye; and this hath he don to make yow solas and counfort."

And as thei stode spekinge hereof, in the halle com in a litill childe that semed

190 of eight yere of age. And he was all naked and brecheles, and bar a staf in his honde, and com before the kynge and seide, "Sir, appareile yow for to go agein the Kynge Rion in bateile, and delyver me youre baner for to bere." And whan thei that were in the paleys saugh hym in that aray, thei begonne to laugh harde. And the kynge ansuerde all in laughinge, as he that soposed well it was Merlin,

---

167 **very guyde**, true guide; **condite**, conduct. 169 **prowe**, profit. 170 **behilde**, looked at. 174 **trowe ye**, think you. 175 **whiche**, who. 176 **hit withsey**, oppose it; **agein right**, unreasonable. 177 **but**, unless. 179 **wiste**, knew. 181 **abaisshed**, astonished; **for that**, because. 182 **aparceived**, realized. 184 **whelpe**, puppy. 185 **what**, who; **than**, then. 188 **solas**, solace. 190 **brecheles**, pants-less. 191 **appareile**, prepare. 193 **paleys**, palace.

195 "So helpe me God, ye owe it well to bere, and I it yow graunte." "Gramercy, sir,"
seide the childe, "for in me it shall be wele employde." And with that he comaunded
hem alle to God and wente oute of the paleis. And than anoon he toke his owne
semblaunce soche as he was wonte to have, and seide to hymself that now hym
behoveth to somown the kynges hoste.

200   And [Merlin] wente toward the see and passed over and com to Gannes, to
Pharien and to Leonces of Paierne, and badde hem to assemble theire power of all
that thei myght bring oute of the londe and come to Cameloth. And thei seide thei
wolde do hys comaundement. And Merlin com to the see and passed over and
wente to the londe of Kynge Urien and by the londe of Kynge Looth and seid to
205   the barouns and to othir princes that thei be withynne fifteen dayes afte Oure
Lady Day the Nativité in Septembre before Cameloth; and thei hym grauntede alle.
And than he departed from them and com agein to the court er evesonge were alle
seide, upon the same day of the Assumpcion. And the kinge of hym made grete
joye and asked why he hadde hym so kept oute of sight. And he ansuerde that he
210   ought hym wele to knowen. "Ye, certes," seide the kynge, "yef in me were eny
witte." Thus thei abide in feeste and joye all that day.

On the morowe the kynge made alle his princes to assemble in his paleis and
ther also was Merlin. And the Kynge Arthur seide how hem behoveth to somowne
all the power that thei myght assemble, for he wolde socour the Kynge Leodogan
215   that was fader to the Queene Gonnore. And Merlin seide how thei were alle
somowned bothe at Gannes and at Benoyk and thourgh alle the londes of the other
barouns. And the Kynge Arthur hym asked whan that was don, and he seide,
"Seth yesterday after mete." And whan the kynge and the other princes this
undirstode that he hadde this don, thei hadde grete wonder, and were ther in joye
220   and in feste till all here peple was assembled. And than meved the Kynge Arthur
and his baronye and rode towarde the reame of Carmelide. And the kynge graunted
his baner to Merlin, as he hadde promysed before. And [thei] sped theire journyes
till thei come a litill journey fro Toraise, where the Kynge Rion had besege the
Kynge Leodogan.

225   And whan thei were nygh the hoste, Merlin seide to Gawein and to Sir Ewein
and to Segramor, "Loke ye be ever nygh aboute me"; and thei seide thei wolde

195 owe, ought. **207 er**, before. **214 socour**, aid. **218 Seth**, Since.

don his pleisir. "Now than," quod Merlin, "sueth after me softely, and alle thei of the hoste, till we be in bateile; and ye shull smyte upon hem of that other partye withoute rennynge of youre bateile; and thinke ever to come nygh after my baner,

230   what wey that ever ye se me turne." And thei ansuerde that so thei wolde with goode will; and so he seide to Arthur and to alle the other princes. And [thei] wente forth till thei com into the hoste of Kynge Rion, and Merlin before hem alle so harde as his horse myght renne, with the dragon in his hande that caste thourgh his mouthe fire and flame, that alle thei therof were abaisshed. And Gawein, that

235   folowed hym next, mette with the Kynge Pharaon that with all his bateile com hym ageins. And as soone as he saugh hem approche, Sir Gawein hym smote so that shelde ne hauberk myght hym warante, but bar hym thourgh the body deed to the erthe. And than he seide in game, "He this is sworn to pees, for by hym shall never the Kynge Arthur lese acre of his londe ne his beerd be flayn from his

240   chyn."

   With that assembled bothe hostes, that oon agein that other. And grete was the noyse and the fray of the peple of Kynge Rion and of the peple of Kynge Arthur. And ther dide Gawein and Ewein and Segramor and Gaheries and the Knyghtes of the Rounde Table merveiles with theire handes. For whan bothe hostes were

245   mette, ye myght have sein many oon leide to grounde of oo party and of other, for thei were bold and hardy on bothe seides. And Merlin, that bar the dragon, drof into the prees, and Sir Gawein and his companye after, and smote hem so harde that thei metten that thei neded no salve; and the speres fly in peces.

   And that was a thinge that discounforted the Kynge Rion and his peple, for thei

250   wende verily that fendes were fallen amonge the hoste. But thei were so bolde and so chivalrouse that therfore thei wolde not be discounfited but hilde bateile grete and merveilouse agein the peple of Kynge Arthur, and made hem resorte bakke at hir first comyng. And therfore was Sir Gawein and his companye full of dolour. And Merlin, that rode before hem, cried, "What, lordinges, what shall this bemene?

255   Be ye now arested? Sueth me, yef ye will youre loos encrese and your pris." Than

227 sueth, follow; **softely**, slowly. **229 nygh after**, close behind. **232 into**, near. **233 renne**, run. **234 abaisshed**, frightened. **237 warante**, protect. **238 game**, jest; **pees**, peace. **239 lese**, lose. **248 metten**, met. **250 wende verily**, truly believed; **fendes**, fiends. **251 discounfited**, defeated. **253 dolour**, sadness. **254 bemene**, mean. **255 Be ye now arested**, Are you resting; **Sueth**, Follow; **loos**, worship; **pris**, fame.

these felowes smyten in amonge hem of Irelonde, that well hem resceyved with trenchaunt wepenes. But Sir Gawein and his companye dide so well in armes that thei pressed thourgh the peple of Kynge Rion, but first was ther many a hevy stroke yoven and resceived, and many a knyght straught deed to the erthe.

260   And the Kynge Arthur and the Kynge Looth of Orcanye and the Kynge Ban and the Kynge Bohors were smyte into the bateile on another side where thei dide merveiles amonge theire enmyes, for agein theire strokes endured noon armure. But the peple of Kynge Rion mette hem so fiercely that thei smote down the Kynge Looth and the Kynge Bohors from theire horse amydde the presse; and so thei

265   myght soone have hadde grete damage ne hadde ben the grete prowesse that was in hem bothe. For thei lept on foote full vigerousely with theire swerdes drawen, and begonne to smyte down horse and men so crewelly that ther ne was noon that hem saugh but he hilde it for a merveile. And the Kynge Arthur and the Kynge Ban pressed that wey hem to remounte. And Merlin com drivinge with the baner

270   in his hande that thourgh his throte caste fire and flame, and smote into the grettest presse. And whan the peple of Kynge Rion saugh the grete merveile of the dragon that so caste fire, thei hadden grete drede and forsoke place and the two kynges on whom they dide abide. And Merlin com to them and delyvered to everiche of theym a good horse and a swifte, for inowe ther were astray thourgh the felde.

275   And thei anoon lept upon horse and rode into the bateile and begonne to do so well in armes, and so dide alle theire companye.

But the force of Kynge Rion was so grete that thei of the reame of Grete Breteigne myght it not endure, but sholde alle have be discounfited, as to my felinge, ne hadde be the prowesse of Sir Gawein and his companye and the Knyghtes of the

280   Rounde Table, for these shewed merveiles wher thei com, for thei smyte down men and horse bothe that alle that hem withstode semed it were feendes.

On another side of the bateile was the Kynge Ventres and the Kynge Tradilyvans and the Kynge Urien and the Kynge de Cent Chivalers, that full fiercely faught agein the peple of the Yles that kept hem short, for of the Yles was many a valiaunt

285   knyght and bolde in armes. And [oon] hadde smyte down the Kynge Tradilyvans

---

259 yoven, given; **straught deed**, struck dead. **261 were smyte**, had charged. **267 begonne**, began. **273 dide abide**, i.e., were attacking. **274 inowe**, enough. **278–79 ne hadde be**, if not for. **281 bothe**, so; **semed it**, they thought; **feendes**, fiends. **284 hem short**, hemmed them in.

of North Wales and hilde hym by the helme. And Merlin com to Gawein and seide, "Now lete se what ye will do, for we have loste the Kynge Tradilyvans but he hastely [have] socour. Sewe me!" Than wente Merlin that wey and Sir Gawein and his felowes folowinge, till thei com to the Kynge Tradilyvans that was in

290   grete aventure of deth. And than begonne thei so harde bateile that wonder was to beholde, so that thei that hilde the Kynge Tradilyvans, that were bolde and hardy and durable in bateile, were alle abaisshed; but yet dide thei grete peyne hym to withholde. And thei of the Rounde Table have hym rescowed and sette on horse, and were full wroth and angry and begonne agein the bateile and the medlé, that

295   hidiouse was to have seyn; for oon fill deed upon another so that ther were grete mountayns of deed cors thourgh the feelde theras the bateile was. For Sir Gawein hadde so many slain with his swerde that bothe swerde and arme were all besoiled with blode and brayn.

Than the Kynge Leodogan saugh the bateile so crewell and so fell theras he

300   stode lenynge out at a wyndowe, and saugh the dragon that Merlin bar that caste fier thourgh his mouthe so that the heyr was all reade. And he knewe it wele, for he hadde it sein before tymes, and knew well it was the signe of Kynge Arthur. And than he called upon his knyghtes and cried, "As armes, for my sone the Kynge Arthur fighteth with oure enmyes, and is come me for to socour, God

305   quyte hym!" And whan thei this undirstode, thei ronne alle to armes thourgh the castell and com oute at the yate iarmed ten thousand and moo of bolde men and hardy, and smyten into the hoste of the kynges of the Yles full fiercely, and thei hem resceived, for thei were of grete hardynesse. And Cleodalis the Stiward and Hervy de Rivell and her other felowes begonne to do merveiles of armes. And the

310   bateile was so grete and so thikke on alle sides of the hoste of Kynge Rion that it was merveile so many ther were deed of oo parte and of other.

And whan the Kynge Rion saugh the grete mortalité and slaughtur of his peple, and also of the peple of Kynge Arthur, his herte wax tender and hadde therof pitee, and seide to hymself that that mortalité wolde he no lenger suffre. And than

286 hilde, held. **287 but,** unless. **288 Sewe,** Follow. **290 aventure,** danger. **292 abaisshed,** frightened. **294 medlé,** melee. **295 fill deed,** fell dead. **296 deed cors,** dead bodies; **theras,** where. **299 fell,** fierce; **theras,** where. **300 lenynge,** leaning. **301 heyr,** air; **reade,** red. **303 As,** To. **305 quyte,** reward. **306 yate,** gate; **moo,** more. **311 oo parte,** one side. **312 saugh,** saw. **313 wax,** grew. **314 suffre,** permit.

315 he toke a braunche of sicamor in his hande and wente before the hoste to dissever
the bateiles, and wente forth till he fonde the Kynge Arthur, and spake so high
that he myght wele ben herde. "Kynge Arthur, wherfore doost thow suffre thi
peple to be slayn and distroied, and also myn? Do thow now well, yef ther be so
moche worthinesse in thee as the worlde recorded. Delyver thy peple fro deth,
320 and I shall deliver also tho of myn, and we shull make oure peple withdrawe on
bothe parties a rowme. And thow and I shull fight togeder body for body, by
soche covenaunt that yef thow may me conquere, I shall returne to my contrey
with the peple that is me beleft on lyve; and yef I may thee conquere, thow shalt
holde thi londe of me and be my soget, as ben these other kynges that I have
325 conquered. And I shall have thy berde with all the skyn to make the tasselles of
my mantell."

 "In the name of God," quod the Kynge Arthur, "thow sholdest so have the
better part of the pley whan thow sholdest repeire into thy contrey all hooll yef I
thee conquered, and ne sholdest not become my man. And thow desirest that I
330 sholde be thy man yef thow myght me conquere! But I will fight with thee in this
maner as thow hast seide, that yef I thee conquere thow shall be my liege man;
and in the same wise I graunte it thee yef thow me conquere." "Sir," seide the
Kynge Rion — that was so stronge that he douted no man body for body, and he
hadde conquered so nine kynges that alle were his liege men — "and I it yow
335 graunte, like as ye have seide."

 Than thei sured theire feithes betwene hem two to holde these covenauntes, and
made departe the bateiles that were so horible. And the barouns drough aside that
were wroth and angry with these covenauntes. And Sir Gawein, that was wrother
than eny other, com to the kynge his uncle and seide, "Sir, yef it plese yow, graunte
340 me this bateile." "Now therof require ye no more," quod the Kynge Arthur, "nother
ye, ne noon other. For noon other than I shall sette therto noon hande, for I shall
do the bateile with the helpe of God, seith he hath me therto requireth."

315 **sicamor**, sycamore; **dissever**, separate. 316 **bateiles**, armies. 318 **yef**, if. 319 **recorded**,
i.e., believes; **Delyver**, Save. 320 **tho**, those. 321 **rowme**, distance. 322 **covenaunt**, agreement. 323 **is me beleft on lyve**, to me remain alive. 324 **of**, from; **soget**, subject. 328 **all
hooll**, i.e., alive; **yef**, if. 333 **douted**, feared. 336 **sured**, swore; **feithes**, oaths. 337 **departe**,
withdraw; **bateiles**, armies; **drough**, drew. 338 **wrother**, angrier. 340 **require**, ask; **nother**,
neither. 341 **ne noon**, nor any. 342 **seith**, since.

King Arthur vs. King Rion

Than bothe hostes were drawen aside on that oon part and on that other, and the two kynges were armed full richely all that nedeth to a noble prince. And eche of

345 hem toke a spere stronge and rude, and than rode eche of hem from other more than two but lengthe, and than smote the horse with spores and mette togeder as tempest, for well ran bothe horse and were of grete force. And the two kynges were fierce and hardy and mette with so grete raundon with speres that were grete and shorte and the heedes sharp igrounden, upon the sheldes that thei perced; but

350 the hauberkes were so harde that thei fauced no mayle; and the horse were of grete force and the knyghtes of grete prowesse that the speres splindered in splyntes.

And than thei leide hande to theire swerdes that weren of grete bounté, and smyten grete strokes upon helmes that thei breke the serkeles of golde and stones

355 whiche weren of grete vertu, and tohewen the sheldes and hauberkes, and in the flessh so depe that the blood stremed after. And in short tyme eche of hem so araied other that ther ne was nother of hem but he hadde nede of a leche. And theire sheldes weren slitte and hewen that ther was left of theym [not] so moche that thei myght with hem cover. And than thei caste the remenaunt to grounde and

360 caught the swerdes in bothe hondes, and smyte pesaunt strokes at discovert so that thei toslitte helmes and torente hauberkes, so that the flessh shewed all bare. And ther ne was noon of hem bothe but he was wery for traveile of yevinge of strokes and receivinge. And that was oon thinge that lengest hem hilde, for yef thei hadde ben fressh and newe to that thei weren withouten sheldes and theire

365 hauberkes torente and theire helmes toquasshed, thei myght not have endured. Nevertheles, ther ne was noon of hem bothe but he was sore hurt and wounded.

Whan the Kynge Rion, that was bolde and hardy above alle thoo of the londe, saugh the Kynge Arthur hym contene ageins hym, he hadde therof grete merveile, for he wende that he sholde not agein hym have endured, and seide to hymself

370 that never beforn hadde he seyn so goode a knyght. And than he douted hym sore and seide, "Kynge Arthur, hit is grete harme of thee, for thow art the beste knyght

346 **but**, butts (archery targets). **348 raundon**, force. **350 fauced**, pierced. **353 leide**, laid. **354 serkeles**, circles. **355 vertu**, value. **357 araied**, dealt with; **nother**, neither; **leche**, doctor. **360 pesaunt**, strong, heavy; **discovert**, unprotected places. **362 traveile**, the efforts; **yevinge**, giving. **363 hilde**, saved. **364 to that**, when. **365 toquasshed**, smashed. **368 hym contene**, himself defend. **369 wende**, thought. **370 douted**, feared.

that I faught with ever beforn; and I se well and knowe verily that thy grete herte
that thow hast shall make thee to dye, for it will not suffre thee to come to my
mercy; and I knowe well that thow haddest lever dye than be conquered, and that
375   is grete damage. And therfore, I wolde pray thee and requyre for the grete prowesse
that is in thee, that thou have pitee on thyself and yelde thee for outraied, for to
save thi lif thourgh the covenauntes that ben betwene us, so that my mantell were
parformed in my live. For better I love thi lif than thi deth, and thow art come to
thi fin — that knowest thow well, and so don alle these barouns here aboute that
380   here ben."

Whan the Kynge Arthur undirstode the wordes of the Kynge Rion, he hadde
grete shame, for so many a valiante prince hadde it undirstonde. And than he ran
upon hym with his swerde in bothe handes as he that was full wroth and full of
maltalente, and wende to smyte hym on the helme. But the Kynge Rion blenched
385   that saugh the stroke comynge with so grete ravyne; and nevertheles, he araught
hym upon the helme and kutte of the nasell; and the stroke descended and smote
the stedes nekke asounder, and the Kynge Rion fill to the erthe.

And as he wende to have rise, Arthur smote hym on the lifte shuldre into the
flesshe two large ynche, and the Kynge Rion stombeled therwith and fill agein to
390   the erthe. And whan the Kynge Arthur saugh the Kynge Rion falle agein to grounde,
anoon he alight to grounde and ran to hym lightly and caught hym by the helme
and drough it to hym with so grete force that the laces brast asonder; and he it
raced from his heed, and than lifte up the swerde and seide he was but deed but he
wolde yelde hym outerly. And he seide that wolde he never, for he hadde lever
395   dye than live recreaunt. And whan Arthur saugh that he myght hym not therto
bringe to holde hym for outraied, he smote of the heed in sight of alle that were in
the feelde.

And than ronne to [hym] the princes on alle parties and made grete joye and
sette hym on a horse, and brought hym into the Castell of Toraise and hym un-
400   armed and serched his woundes. And the baronye of Kynge Rion com to hym and

---

374 lever, rather. **375 damage**, shame. **376 for outraied**, as defeated. **378 parformed**,
completed; **live**, lifetime. **379 fin**, end. **384 maltalente**, malice; **blenched**, turned aside.
385 ravyne, force; **araught**, struck. **386 kutte of**, cut off; **nasell**, nose piece. **387 fill**, fell.
388 wende, i.e., tried; **lifte**, left. **392 brast**, burst. **393 raced**, pulled. **394 outerly**, utterly.
394–95 lever dye, rather die. **395 recreaunt**, shamed. **396 outraied**, defeated; **of**, off.

resceived of hym theire londes and theire fees and dide hym homage, and than returned into theire contrey, and with hem bar the body of Kynge Rion, and it biried with grete lamentacion and wepinge.

And the Kynge Arthur was at Toraise, gladde and joyfull of the victorie that
405   God hym hadde yoven; and sojourned in the castell till he was warisshed of his woundes that he hadde in the bateile. And whan he was all hool, he departed fro Toraise with grete joye and feste; and the Kynge Leodogan conveyed hym on his wey and after returned. And the Kynge Arthur and his companye ride till thei come to Cameloth whereas the Quene Gonnore and the other quenes were abidinge,
410   that of theire comynge made grete joye. And ther sojourned the princes four dayes, and on the fifte day thei departed; and every man repeired to his owne contrey and ledde with hem theire wyves, thei that eny hadden.

And the Kynge Arthur com agein into the citee of Logres and sojourned ther longe tyme with the quene, and with hym was Sir Gawein and the Companye of
415   the Rounde Table and Merlin, that dide hem grete solas and grete companye. And he com to Kynge Arthur and seide that from hensforth he myght hym wele forberen, for he hadde somdell apesed his londe and sette it in reste. And therfore he wolde go take his disporte where hym liked.

Whan the kynge this undirstode, he was pensif and sory, for he loved hym
420   entirly and fain wolde he that he abood stille, yef it myght be. And whan he saugh he myght hym not withholde, he praied hym dierly that he wolde come to hym agein in short tyme; and Merlin seide he sholde come agein all be tyme er he hadde nede. "Certes," seide the kynge, "every day and every hour have I to yow nede and myster, for withoute yow I can nought; and therfore I wolde we sholde
425   never departe companye." And Merlin seide, "I shall come another tyme to youre nede, and I shall not faile day ne hour."

And the kynge was stille a longe while and began to stodie sore. And whan he hadde be longe in this thought, he seide all sighinge, "Ha, Merlin, feire swete frende, in what nede shull ye me helpe? I pray yow telle me, to sette myn herte in
430   more ese." "Sir," seide Merlin, "and I shall yow telle, and after I shall go my way.

405 yoven, given; **warisshed of,** recovered from. **406 hool,** whole. **416 forberen,** not see. **417 somdell apesed,** somewhat pacified. **418 disporte,** enjoyment. **419 pensif,** sad. **421 praied,** requested; **dierly,** sincerely. **422 all be tyme,** eventually. **423 Certes,** Indeed. **424 myster,** urgent want; **wolde,** would wish. **427 stodie sore,** reflect seriously.

The lyon that is the sone of the bere and was begeten of a leopart shall renne by the reame of the Grete Breteigne; and that is the nede that ye shall have." With that Merlin departed and the kynge belefte in grete myssese and sore abaisshed of this thinge, for he knewe not to what it myght turne. But therof shull we cesse at this tyme and returne to speke of Merlin.

435

431 bere, bear. **433 belefte**, left; **myssese**, uneasiness; **abaisshed**, concerned. **434 cesse**, cease.

304

[Merlin and Nimiane; and Arthur and the Giant of St. Michael's Mount]

[**Summary**. *Merlin leaves Logres and goes to Jerusalem where King Flualis, the powerful saracen ruler, has had an engimatic dream. When Flualis's wisemen cannot explain the dream, Merlin proceeds to do so. The dream signifies the coming of the Christians and the defeat of the saracens. Fols. 224r (line 13)–225r (line 5)*].

And Merlin wente a grete spede that never he stinte till he com to the reame of Benoyk, and yede to Nimiane his love that sore desired hym for to seen, for yet cowde not she of his art of that she desired for to knowe. And she made hym the grettest joye that she myght; and [thei] ete and dranke and lay in oon bedde. But so moche cowde she of his connynge that whan he hadde will to ly with hire, she hadde enchaunted and conjured a pelow that she kepte in his armes; and than fill Merlin aslepe. And the storie maketh no mencion that ever Merlin hadde flesshly to do with no woman. And yet loved he nothinge in this worlde so wele as woman; and that shewed well, for so moche he taught hir oo tyme and other that at laste he myght holde hymself a fooll; and thus dide he sojourney with his love longe tyme. And ever she enquired of his connynge and of his maistries ech thinge by hitself. And he lete her all knowe; and she wrote all that he seide, as she that was well lerned in clergie, and lerned it lightly all that Merlin hir taught. And whan he hadde sojourned with hir longe tyme, he toke his leve and seide that he sholde come agein at the yeres ende; and so eche of theym comaunded other to God full tendirly.

And than com Merlin to Blase his maister, that gladde was of his comynge and sore he longed hym for to se, and he hym also. And Merlin tolde hym alle the aventures that were befalle seth he fro hym departed, and how he hadde be with

1 stinte, stopped. **2 yede**, went; **sore**, greatly. **3 cowde**, knew; **of that**, what. **5 connynge**, skill; **will**, desire; **ly**, lie. **6 pelow**, pillow. **9 oo**, one. **13 clergie**, knowledge; **lightly**, quickly. **15 comaunded**, commended. **19 seth**, since.

20   Nimiane his love, and how he hadde hir taught of his enchauntmentz. And Blase wrote all in his boke.

[**Summary**. *Merlin rejoins Arthur at Logres. As the court is assembled in the great hall, a beautiful damsel enters accompanied by an ugly dwarf; she asks the king for a boon; Arthur agrees, as long as her request is honorable. To the amusement of the court, she asks Arthur to make the dwarf a knight; she claims he is actually a lord of noble birth. Kay makes jokes at the dwarf's expense, but Arthur agrees to her request. Then two squires appear at court bearing knightly equipment, and the damsel herself produces a pair of golden spurs. Kay asks for the honor of knighting the dwarf, but the damsel refuses him. Arthur knights the dwarf; then the damsel and the dwarf ride on their way.*

Shortly thereafter a group of twelve messengers arrive at the court bearing a letter from Lucius, the emperor of Rome. Arthur is accused of having taken lands and rents away from the emperor; and he is ordered to appear before the emperor in Rome to make amends. Arthur and his privy council consider the matter; they decide that rather than Rome having a claim on Britain, Britain has firm historical precedents for making a claim on Rome. Thus Arthur gives the messengers gifts and then sends them back to the emperor with his negative reply. Angered, the emperor assembles his forces. Arthur does likewise; and then he and his army sail to Brittany. There Arthur has a vision in which he sees a great bear on a mountain attacked by a fiery dragon. Merlin interprets the dream, saying that the bear is a giant and Arthur is the dragon. Fols. 225r (line 20)–228v (line 12).]

    With that thei trussed tentes and pavilons and ride forth on theire wey. But thei hadde not longe gon when tidinges com to the Kynge Arthur of the geaunte that distroied the londe and the contrey so that therynne duelled nother man ne woman
25   but fledde thourgh the feldes as bestes disolate for drede of the geaunte. And [he] hadde born by force a mayden of the contrey that was nyece to a lorde of the contrey that was a grete gentilman. And he hadde born hir with hym up to a mounteigne whereas he repeired, that was all closed with the see. And that mounteign is yet cleped the Mounte Seint Michel, but at that tyme ther was nother
30   mynster ne chapell; ne ther was no man so hardy ne so myghty that durst fight with the geaunte. And whan the peple of the contrey dide hym assaile, thei myght not agein hym endure neither on londe ne on se, for he slough hem with the roches

22 trussed, packed. **23 geaunte**, giant. **25 disolate**, frightened. **26 born**, taken. **28 whereas**, where; **repeired**, dwelled; **closed with**, surrounded by; **see**, sea. **29 yet cleped**, still called; **nother**, neither. **30 ne**, nor; **durst**, dared. **32 slough**, slew; **roches**, rocks.

and made theire shippes to sinke. And the peple of the contrey fledde thourgh the wodes and forestes and mounteynes with theire children in theire armes; and so
35 thei lefte theire londes and theire richesses.

Whan Arthur herde how the geaunte distroied so the londe, he cleped Kay the Stiward and Bedyver and badde hem make hem redy-armed aboute mydnyght; and thei dide his comaundement and com togeder, thei thre and two squyres only and no mo, and rode till thei come upon the mounte and saugh a grete fire bright
40 shynynge on that o side. And on that othir side was another mounte that was not so grete as that, and theron was a fire merveilouse grete; and thei wiste not to whiche thei sholde gon. Than he cleped Bediver and bade hym go loke on whiche mounte the geaunte was. Than Bediver wente into a bote that was full of the flos of the see. And whan he was come to the next monteyn, he wente up hastily on the
45 roche and herde grete wepinge. And whan he that herde he hadde doute, for he wende the geaunte hadde be there. But he toke upon hym hardynesse and drough his swerde, and wente forth and hoped for to fight with hym, as he that for no drede of deth ne wolde be founde no cowarde; and in this thought he clymbed upon the mountein.
50 And whan he was come up, he saugh the fier that was clier brennynge and saugh a tombe faste by that was newly made; and beside that tombe satte an olde woman discheveled and all torente hir heir, and wepte and sighed full sore. And whan she saugh the knyght she seide, "Haa! Gentilman, what art thow? What dolour hath brought thee into this place? For with grete dolour thou shalt ende thy
55 lif, yef the geaunte thee finde. Fle hens hastely as faste as thow maist, for thou art to unhappy yef thow abide till that this devell come that hath no pité of nothinge! Fle hens as fer as thou maist, yef thow wilt thy lif save!"

Whan Bediver saugh the woman so wepe and so pitously regrated Helayn sighinge, and bad hym to fle but yef he wolde dye. And he seide, "Good woman,
60 lete be thy wepinge, and telle me what thou art and why thou makest so grete

36 **cleped**, summoned. 40 **o**, one. 43 **bote**, boat; **flos**, tide. 44 **see**, sea. 45 **doute**, fear. 46 **wende**, thought; **be**, been; **hardynesse**, courage; **drough**, drew. 47 **hoped for**, expected. 50 **saugh**, saw; **clier brennynge**, brightly burning. 52 **torente**, torn. 53 **what**, who. 54 **dolour**[1], grief; **dolour**[2], sorrow. 55 **yef**, if; **Fle hens hastely**, Flee from here quickly; **maist**, may. 56 **unhappy**, misfortunate. 58 **Whan**, Then; **regrated**, sorrowed for. 59 **but yef**, unless. 60 **what**, who.

sorowe and why thou art upon this mounte by this tombe. And telle me all the occasion of thy sorowe, and who lith here in this sepulture."

"I am," quod she, "a dolerouse caitif that wepe and make waymentacion for a mayden that was nyece to Hoell of Nauntes, that I norished and yaf souke with my

65   mylk; and she lieth under this tombe, and it was me comaunded hir to norish and to kepe. Now is ther a devell that hir hath taken awey and brought hider her and me, and wolde have leyn by the childe that [was] yonge and tender. But she myght hym not suffre ne endure, for he was moche and hidiouse and lothly. And so he made the soule departe from the body, and thus he berafte my doughter, falsly and

70   be treson. And ther I have hir biried, and for hir wepe bothe day and nyght."

"And wherfore," quod Bediver, "gost thou not hens, seth thou art left here alone and hast hir loste seth that ther is noon recover?" "Sir," quod she, "I knowe well ther is no recover; but for that I se ye be a gentilman and therto so curteise, I will kepe nothinge from youre knowinge but I will telle yow the trouthe. Whan that

75   my dere doughter was entered, for whos love I wende wele have loste my witte and dyed for doel, the geaunte made me to abide stille to have his foule lecherouse lust upon me. And he hath me diffouled by his strengthe that I moste suffre his wille whedir I wolde or noon, for I have no myght agein hym. And I take oure Lorde God to recorde it was never my will, and ner therwith he hadde me slain;

80   for with hym have I suffred grete peyne and gret anguysh, for he is unmesurable grete; and he cometh hider to fulfille his lecherie upon me. And thou art but deed and maist in no maner ascape, for he cometh anoon right; for he is ther above in that mountayn where thou seist that fier. And therfore I pray thee go hens thy wey, and lef me here to compleyne and make my mone for my doughter."

85   Grete pité hadde Bediver of the woman, and moche he hir counforted. And seth he com agein to the kynge and tolde that he hadde sein, and seide how the geaunte

---

62 lith, lies. **63 dolerouse caitif**, pitiful wretch; **waymentacion**, lamentation. **64 that**, who; **yaf souke**, gave suck. **65 it was me comaunded**, I was ordered; **norish**, nurture. **66 kepe**, protect. **67 leyn**, lain. **68 suffre**, permit; **moche**, huge. **69 berafte**, murdered; **falsly**, wickedly. **70 be**, by; **biried**, buried. **71 wherfore**, why; **hens**, away; **seth**, since. **73 for that**, because; **se**, see. **75 entered**, interred; **wende wele have**, nearly. **76 abide**, stay. **77 that**, so that; **moste**, must. **78 whedir I wolde or noon**, whether I wished to or not. **79 ner**, nearly. **82 maist**, may; **maner**, way; **ascape**, escape; **anoon right**, right now; **in**, on. **84 lef**, leave. **85 seth**, then. **86 that**, what.

was upon the high hill ther he saugh the grete fier and smoke. Than the kynge made his felowes go with hym upon the mounteyne, and thei were come upon the hill. Than the kynge comaunded his felowes to abide and seide that hymself alone
90 wolde go fight with the geaunte. "Nevertheles," seide the kynge, "loke that ye waite well upon me; and yef it be myster, cometh me to helpe." And thei seide thei wolde with good will, and thei abide.

And the kynge wente toward the geaunte that satte before the fire and rosted flessh on a spite, and kut of the side that [was] most inough and ete it. And the
95 kynge wente toward hym with swerde in honde drawen a softe pas gripinge his shelde, for he wende hym to have supprised. But the geaunte, that was full false and maliciouse, behelde and saugh the kynge come and lept up, for the kynge hadde his swerde in his hande. And the geaunte stert to a grete clobbe that stode by hym, that was grete and hidiouse of a plante of an oke, that was a grete birthon
100 for a myghty man; and caught it from the fire, and leide it on his nekke and com fiercely agein the kynge as he that was of a grete force, and seide to the kynge that a grete fooll was he to come ther, and reised the batte for to smyte the kynge on the heed. But he was wight and delyver, and lept aside so that he of hym failed; and therwith the kynge smote at hym and wende to smyte hym on the heed. But
105 the geaunte, that was bolde and hardy, kept it on his clobbe or elles hadde he be deed. Nevertheles, somdel he touched hym with Marmyadoise, his good swerde that he conquered of the Kynge Rion, and touched hym betwene the two browes that he wax all blinde for the blode that ran over his yen. And that was a thinge that sore hym greved, for he myght not se where to smyte, and began to scarmyshe
110 and to grope aboute hym with his staffe as a wood devell and sore abaisshed. And the kynge hasted hym full harde but areche hym myght not, for the geaunte caste about hym grete strokes that yef he hadde hym smyten he hadde ben all tobrosed.

And thus thei foughten longe that the oon ne touched not that other, and therfore

87 ther, where. **91 yef it be myster**, if there is need. **92 abide**, waited. **94 kut of**, cut off; **[was] most inough**, was well cooked. **95 a softe pas**, i.e., moving silently. **96 wende**, hoped. **98 stert to**, reached for. **99 plante**, branch; **oke**, oak; **birthon**, burdon. **100 leide**, placed; **nekke**, shoulder. **103 he**, i.e., Arthur; **wight**, agile; **delyver**, quick. **104 wende**, hoped. **105 kept it on**, blocked it with. **106 somdel**, somewhat; **touched**, hit. **107 conquered of**, had captured from. **108 yen**, eyes. **109 scarmyshe**, flail about. **110 wood**, mad. **111 areche**, reach. **112 tobrosed**, battered. **113 that[1]**, while.

115 thei were sore anoyed. And than the geaunte wente tastinge here and there that he
sesed the kynge by the arme. And whan he hadde hym caught he was gladde and
joyfull, for anoon he wende hym to have threst to deth. And so he hadde, but that
the kynge was wight and delyver and wrast out of his gripinge with grete peyne.
And than he ran upon hym with his swerde and smote hym on the heed and on the
lifte sholdre that all the arme fremysshed. And so harde was the hide of the ser-
120 pent that in the flessh myght it not atame. And the geaunte myght hym not se, for
his iyen were all covered with blode; and than he saugh the shadowe of the kynge,
and than he ran that wey. But the kynge, that wiste he was of grete force, durste
not come in his handes.

And so hath he gon up and down that he stombeled on his clubbe; and it sesed
125 and ran theras he wende to finde the kynge. But the kynge blenched so that he
myght hym not areche, and therfore hadde he grete sorow in herte. And than he
caste awey his clubbe and tasted to chacche the kynge in his armes. And so he
wente gropinge and frotinge his iyen till he saugh the light and the shadowe of the
kynge. And than he spronge to hym and caught hym by the flankes with bothe his
130 armes that nygh he hadde with his gripes brosten his chyne. And than he began to
craspe after his arme for to take from hym his swerde out of his honde. But the
kynge it well perceyved and threwe down the swerde, that in the fallinge he myght
here it ringe cler. And than he griped the kynge with that oon hande and stouped
down to take the swerde with that other hande; and in the stoupinge, the kynge
135 smote hym with his kne that he fill in swowne. And than he lept to the swerde and
hente it up, and stert to the geaunte ther he lay and lifte up the serpentes skyn and
rof hym thourgh the body with the swerde. And so was the geaunte slain.

And Kay the Stiwarde and Bediver made grete joye of the kynge, and behelde
the geaunte that so grete [was] that wonder was to beholden, and thanked oure

---

114 **tastinge**, searching; **that**, until. 115 **sesed**, seized. 116 **anoon**, now; **wende**, expected;
threst, stabbed; **he hadde**, he would have. 117 **wight**, agile; **delyver**, quick; **wrast**, twisted;
peyne, effort. 119 **fremysshed**, shook. 120 **atame**, penetrate. 122 **wiste**, knew; **durste**,
dared. 124 **it sesed**, he halted. 125 **theras**, where; **wende**, hoped; **blenched**, moved back.
126 **areche**, reach. 127 **tasted**, tried; **chacche**, catch. 128 **frotinge**, rubbing; **iyen**, eyes.
130 **gripes**, grip; **brosten**, broken; **chyne**, spine. 131 **craspe**, reach. 133 **here**, hear. 135
kne, knee; **swowne**, swooning. 136 **hente**, grabbed; **ther**, where. 137 **rof**, stabbed. 138
grete, huge.

140   Lorde of the honour and the victorie that he hadde yove the kynge, for never hadde thei seyn so grete a feende. And the kynge bad Bediver smyte of the heed that it myght be born into the hoste to se the grete merveile of the gretnesse of hym. And he dide his comaundement; and than [thei] com down of the mounteyn and lepe on their horse. And the flode was come agein that gretly hem disesed.

145   And with grete peyne thei passed the greves and com agein to the hoste. And the barouns were sore abaisshed for the taryinge of the kynge, for that thei wiste not whider he was wente; and thei were meved hym for to seche in diverse parties, ne hadde ben Merlin that bad hem be nothinge dismayed, for he sholde come hastely.

While the princes and the barouns were in this afray for the Kynge Arthur, he
150   and the stiwarde and Bediver com down into his teinte, and hadde the heed of the geaunte trussed at Bedivers sadell by the heir. And thider com alle the barouns whan he was alight, and asked fro whens he com, for he hadde put hem in grete afray. And he seide he com fro thens ther he hadde foughten withe the geaunte that distroied so the londe and the contrey theraboute, and how he hadde hym
155   slayn thourgh the grace of oure Lorde. And than he shewed hem the heed that Bediver hadde trussed. And whan the barons it saugh, thei blessed hem for the wonder therof, and seide that never in all theire lif had thei not seyn so grete an heed. And alle that were in the hoste preised God for the kynges victorie. And than thei dide unarme the kynge with grete joye and gladnesse.

140 yove, given. **141 of**, off. **142 of**, from. **144 flode**, tide; **disesed**, bothered. **145 peyne**, effort; **passed the greves**, crossed the sands. **146 sore abaisshed**, greatly concerned; **wiste**, knew. **147 whider**, where; **meved**, inclined. **147–48 ne hadde ben**, if not for. **148 hastely**, soon. **149 afray**, fear. **150 teinte**, tent. **151 trussed at**, tied to. **153 afray**, fright; **ther**, where. **156 trussed**, brought.

[The Defeat of Lucius; and Arthur and the Devil Cat]

[*Summary*. *Arthur's forces proceed against the Romans. Gawain leads an envoy to the Roman camp, telling the Romans they must leave Arthur's lands. The emperor is angered by this demand; and when a young man sitting beside him says the Briton's words are greater than his deeds, Gawain immediately cuts off his head. The messengers leap to their horses, with the Romans in pursuit. Arthur's men ride to the rescue, and the Britons slaughter many Romans. The entire Roman force enters the fray, causing the Britons to lose many knights; the Britons are forced to retreat. Before the great battle is about to commence, the emperor gives his troops a stirring talk; then they prepare to attack. The battle ensues, with both sides using their full forces. The Britons do many great deeds, yet 2,000 of them are slain. Gawain advances on the emperor, and they fight; using Calibourne, Gawain succeeds in killing Lucius. The enraged Romans fight on, but the Britons prove too much for them, and the surviving Romans are forced to flee. Fols. 230r (line 28)–235r (line 9).*]

Full gladde was the Kynge Arthur of the discounfiture of the Romains and of the victorie that God hadde hym yoven. And than [thei] com into the feelde ther the bateile hadde be and biryed the deed bodies in chirches and abbeyes of the contrey, and the wounded lete hem be ledde to townes and serched theire sores.

5 And after, [the Kynge Arthur] made take the body of the emperour and sente it to Rome on a beere and sente worde to the Romains that it was the trewage of Bretaigne that he sent to Rome; and yef thei wolde aske eny more, he wolde hem sende soche another in the same wise. And whan he hadde don thus, he toke counseile wheder he sholde holde forth his wey or turne agein into Gaule; and the

10 princes seide he sholde take counseile of Merlin.

Than the kynge called Merlin and seide, "Dere frende, how pleseth it you that I shall do?" "Sir," seide Merlin, "ye shull not come at Rome ne ye shull not yet

---

1 discounfiture, defeat. **2 yoven**, given; **ther**, where. **4 serched**, attended to; **sores**, wounds. **6 beere**, bier; **trewage**, tribute. **9 agein into**, back toward. **12 at**, to; **ne**, nor.

returne, but holde forth youre wey, for ther be peple that have grete nede of youre helpe." "How so?" seide the kynge. "Is ther werre in this contrey?" "Sir," seide

15 Merlin, "ye, beyonde the Lak de Losane, for ther repeireth a devell, an enmy so that ther dar nother abide man ne woman, for he distroieth the contrey and sleth all that he may gete." "How so?" seide the kynge. "May ther no man hym endure, than is he no man as other ben?" "No," quod Merlin, "it is a catte full of the devell that is so grete and ougly that it is an horible sight on to loke." "Jhesu mercy!"

20 seide the kynge to Merlin, "whens myght soche a beeste come?" "Sir," seide Merlin, "that can I welle telle you.

"Hit befill at the Assencion hens a foure yere that a fissher of the contrey com to the Lak de Losane with his nettes and his engynes. And whan he was redy to caste his nette into the water, he promysed to oure Lorde the firste fissh that he

25 sholde take. And whan he drough up his nette, he toke a fissh that was worth thirty shillings. And whan he saugh the fissh so feire and grete, he seide to hymself softly betwene his teth, "God shall not have this, but He shall have the next that I take." Than he threwe his nett agein into the water and toke another fissh that was better than the firste. And whan he saugh it was so good and so feire, he seide that

30 yet oure Lorde God myght wele abide of this, but the thridde sholde He have, withoute eny doute. And than he caste his nett into the water and drough oute a litill kyton as blakke as eny cool. And whan the fissher it saugh, he seide that he hadde nede therof in his house for rattes and mees. And he it norisshed and kept up in his house till it strangeled hym and his wif and his children, and after fledde

35 into a mountayn that is beyonde the lak that I have to you of spoken. And [he] hath be ther into this tyme, and distroieth and sleth all that he may se and areche. And he is grete and horible that it is merveile hym to se; and we shull go that wey, for it is the right wey toward Rome. And yef God will, ye shull sette the peple in reste that be fledde into straunge londes."

40 Whan the barons undirstode these wordes, thei gonne to blesse hem for the

14 werre, war. **15 repeireth**, dwells; **an enmy so**, such an enemy. **16 dar nother**, dares neither; **sleth**, slays. **17 May ther no man hym endure**, If no man can survive him. **18 than**, then; **catte**, cat. **19 ougly**, ugly. **20 whens**, from whence. **22 hens a foure yere**, four years ago; **fissher**, fisherman. **23 engynes**, equipment. **32 kyton**, kitten; **cool**, coal. **33 mees**, mice. **36 into**, until; **se**, see; **areche**, reach. **38 sette**, restore. **38–39 in reste**, to comfort. **40 gonne**, began.

grete merveile that thei hadden, and seiden that it was vengeaunce of oure Lorde, and a tokne that he was wroth for the synne that the fissher hadde broken his promys. And therfore thei trowed oure Lorde were wroth with hym for that he hadde falsed his covenaunt. Than the kynge comaunded to trusse and to make

45 hem redy to ride. And thei dide his comaundement and toke theire wey toward the Lak de Losane, and fonde the contrei wasted and voide of peple that nother man ne woman durste therynne enhabite.

And thei laboured so till that thei com under the mounte whereas this devell dide abide, and loiged hem in a valey a myle fro the mountein. And the Kynge

50 Looth toke his armes, and Sir Gawein and Gaheries and the Kynge Ban and Merlin for to go withe the Kynge Arthur, and seide thei wolde go se this feende that so grete damage and harme hadde don in the contrey. And thei clymbe upon the mountein as Merlin hem ledde that well knewe the wey for the grete witte that was in hym.

55 And whan thei were come up, than seide Merlin to Arthur, "Sir, in that roche ther is the catte," and shewed hym a grete cave in a medowe that was right large and depe. "And how shall the catte come oute?" seide the kynge. "That shull ye se hastely," quod Merlin. "But loke ye be redy you to diffende, for anoon he will yow assaile." "Than drawe yow alle abakke," seide the Kynge Arthur, "for I will

60 preve his power." And thei dide his comaundement; and anoon as thei were withdrawen, Merlin whistelid lowde. And whan the catte that herde, anoon he lept oute of the cave, for he wende that it had be som wilde beste, and he was hungry and fastinge and ran woodly astraye toward the Kynge Arthur.

And as soone as the kynge saugh hym comynge, he bar agein hym a short spere

65 and wende to smyte hym thourgh the body. But the feend caught the steill heed in his teth so harde that he made it bende; and in the turnynge that the kynge made, the shaft tobrake faste by the heed that was in [the] cattes mowthe. And he began to make a grym noyse as he were wood. And the kynge caste down the tronchon of the spere and drough his suerde and caste his shelde hym before. And the catte

70 lepte to hym anoon, and wende to sese hym by the throte; and the kynge lifte the

42 **tokne**, sign. 43 **trowed**, believe. 44 **falsed**, broken; **covenaunt**, promise. 46 **contrei**, country. 51 **se**, see. 55 **roche**, rock. 57–58 **se hastely**, soon see. 60 **preve**, test 61 **lowde**, loudly. 62 **wende**, hoped. 65 **wende**, thought. 68 **wood**, mad; **tronchon**, shaft. 70 **wende**, hoped; **sese**, seize.

shelde agein hym so fiercely that the catte fill to grounde. But soone he lepte upon his feet and ran upon the kynge full fiercely, and the kynge lifte up the suerde and smote the catte on the heed that he cutte the skyn. But the heed was so harde that he myght not entre; and nevertheles, he was so astonyed that he fill to the erthe

75 upright. But er the kynge myght his shelde recover, the catte sesed hym at discovert be the sholdres so harde that his clawes griped thourgh his hauberke into the flesshe, and plukked so hard that he brast moo than four hundred mayles that the reade blode folowed his clawes. And ther failed but litill that the kynge hadde falle to the erthe.

80 And whan the kynge saugh his blode, he was wonder wroth. Than he caste his shelde before his breste and hilde his swerde in his right hande and ran to the catte vigerously, that likked his clawes that were weet of blode. And whan he saugh the kynge come toward hym, he lepe hym ageins and wende to sese hym as he hadde do beforn. But the kynge launched his shelde hym before, and the catte smote

85 therin his two feet before with so grete fiersnesse thourgh the shelde, and breied so harde that the kynge enclyned to the erthe so that the gige of the shelde fly from his nekke. But he griped the shelde so faste by the enarmynge that the catte myght it not hym bereve ne pulle oute his clawes, but henge in the shelde be the two feet before.

90 And whan the kynge saugh this, he griped faste the shelde and smote hym with his swerde upon bothe legges that he cutte hem asonder by the knees, and the catte fill to grounde. And the kynge caste awey his shelde and ran to hym with swerde drawen; and the catte sterte upon the hynder feet and grenned with his teth and coveited the throte of the kynge. And the kynge launched at hym and wende

95 to smyte hym on the heed. And therwith the catte strayned hys hynder feet and lept in his visage and griped hym with her hynder feet and with hir teth into the flesshe, that the blode stremed out in many places of breste and sholdres on high. And whan the kynge felte hym holde so harde, he sette the point of his swerde to the bely for to launche hym thourgh; and whan the catte felte the suerde, she lefte

74 astoyned. stunned. **75 upright,** face-up. **75–76 at discovert,** unprotected. **76 be,** by. **77 brast,** burst. **78 reade blode,** red blood. **82 likked,** licked. **84 do,** done; **launched,** raised. **85 breied,** pounced. **86 gige,** strap. **87 enarmynge,** handle. **88 bereve,** release; **henge in,** hung on; **be,** by. **93 sterte,** leaped; **grenned,** grinned. **94 coveited,** desired; **launched,** lunged; **wende,** hoped. **95 therwith,** then. **97 that,** so that. **98 holde,** held.

100 hir bitinge and wolde have falle to grounde. But the two hynder feet were so depe ficched in the hauberke that the heed of the catte hanged downwarde; and than the kynge smote asonder the two hynder feet, and the body fill to grounde.

  And as soone as the catte was fallen, she began to whowle and to braye so lowde that it was herde thourgh the hoste. And whan she hadde caste this cry, she
105 began to crepe faste down the foreste by the grete strengthe that was in hir, and drough toward the cave whereas she com oute. But the kynge wente betwene hir and the cave and ran upon the catte; and the catte launched toward hym and wende to cacche hym with hir teth. But in the launchinge, the kynge smote of hir two legges before.

110 And than Merlin and the other ronne to hym and asked how it was with hym. "Well," seide the kynge, "blessed be oure Lorde, for I have slain this devell that grete harm hath don in this contrey. And wite it verily that I hadde never so grete doute of mysilf as I hadde now agein this catte, saf only of the geaunte that I slough this other day on the mounten; and therfore I thanke oure Lorde."

115 "Sir," seide the barouns, "ye have grete cause." Than thei loked on the feet that were lefte in the shelde and in the hauberk, and thei seide that never soche feet hadde thei sein before. And Gaheries toke the shelde and wente to the host makinge grete joye. And whan the princes saugh the feet and the clawes that were so longe, thei were abaisshed, and ledde the kynge to his tente and unarmed hym, and loked
120 on the cracchinges and the bitinge of the catte. And the leches waisshed softly his woundes and leide therto salve and oynementes to clense the venym, and dight hym in soche maner that he letted nothinge to ride.

  And that day thei sojourned till on the morowe that thei returned toward Gaule. And the kynge lete bere the shelde with the cattes feet; and the feet that were in
125 the hauberk lete put in a cofer and comaunded to be well kept. And the kynge asked Merlin how this mountein was cleped; and Merlin seide that peple of the contrey cleped it the Mountein de Lak, for the lak that was in the valey. "Certes," seide the kynge, "I will that this name be taken awey; and I will it be cleped the

100–01 depe ficched, deeply embedded. **103 whowle**, howl; **braye**, cry. **106 whereas**, from which. **107 launched**, leaped; **wende**, hoped. **108 of**, off. **112 wite**, know. **113 doute of**, fear for. **119 abaisshed**, astonished. **120 cracchinges**, scratches; **leches**, doctors. **121 dight**, readied. **122 letted nothinge**, was able. **124 lete bere**, carried. **125 cofer**, chest. **127 lak**, lake. **128 will**, wish.

Mountein of the Catte, for the catte hadde ther his repeire and was ther slain."
130   And after that the name of that hill never chaunged, ne never shall while the worlde
dureth. And now awhile cesseth the tale and returneth to hem that ledde the prisoners.

130 ne, nor. **131 dureth**, endures.

[Merlin's Imprisonment; and Gawain and the Dwarf Knight]

[**Summary**. As Arthur's forces are returning through France, they are set upon by men loyal to Claudas de la deserte, King Ban and King Bors's old enemy. Many men are killed in the fighting before Claudas's men finally flee. Then Arthur's army proceeds on to Benoyk. Meanwhile, a rich lord comes to Agravadain at the Castle of the Marasse and asks for his daughter in marriage. When Agradavain's daughter privately tells her father she is carrying King Ban's child, he is angry, but he agrees to ask the rich lord to postpone the marriage for two years. Angered by being put off, the rich lord besieges the castle. Agradavain successively fights the best knights in the besieging army, defeating them all; his daughter has her baby, naming him Estor.

In Jerusalem, all that Merlin had predicted now comes about. The saracen ruler Flualis is overcome by the Christians and his children are slain. He and his wife convert to Christianity, being baptized and changing their names. They have four daughters who marry four Christian princes and have fifty-four children. Those children prove to be good knights who claim pagan lands for the Christian faith; some of them go to Logres to serve King Arthur.

In Benoyk, tidings are brought to Arthur that King Leodegan of Tamelide has died. Arthur immediately prepares to depart for Britain. He says his final farewells to King Ban and King Bors, and after that time he never sees them again. Fols. 236v (line 15)–239v (line 12).]

Whan the Kynge Arthur was departed fro the two kynges that were brethern that so moche honour hadde hym don, he traveiled so by his journeyes that he com to the see and entred into shippes and passed over and landed at the port of Dover. And [they] lepe on theire horse and ride forth to Logres, and ther thei
5   fonde the Quene Gonnore that hem resceived with grete joye. And [she] tolde how hir fader was passed oute of this worlde, and he hir counforted in the beste wise he myght. And after, the kynge departed his peple, and thei yode hom into theire contreyes. And the Kynge Arthur aboode at Logres, and Sir Gawein and the Knyghtes of the Rounde Table and Merlin sojourned ther longe tyme.

7 departed, dismissed; **yode**, went; **into**, unto.

10　　Than he hadde grete talent for to se Blase his maister for to telle hym of all that
was befallen seth he fro hym departed; and fro thens he wolde go to Nimiane his
love, for the terme drough faste on that was sette. And he wente to the kynge and
seide that hym behoved to go. And the kynge and the quene prayed hym right
entierly soone for to come agein, for he dide hem grete solas and counfort of his
15　　companye, for the kynge hym loved feithfully, for in many a nede he hadde hym
socoured and holpen, for by hym and by his counseile was he kynge. And he
seide to hym right tenderly, "Dere frende Merlin, seth ye will go, I dar yow not
withholde agein youre wille and volunté. But I shall never be in hertes ese till that
I may se yow; and therfore, I praye you for the love of oure Lorde, haste you
20　　soone to come agein."

"Sir," seide Merlin, "this is the laste tyme; and therfore, to God I you comaunde."
Whan the kynge herde how he seide it was the laste tyme that he sholde hym se,
he was sore abaisshed. And Merlin departed withoute moo wordes sore wepinge,
and travailed till he com to Blase his maister that grete chere hym made, and
25　　asked how he hadde sped sethen; and he seide "Wele."

And than he tolde him alle thinges as thei were befalle of the Kynge Arthur and
of the geaunte that he hadde slayn; and of the bateile of the Romains; and how he
had slain the cat; and tolde hym also of the litill duerfe how the damesell hadde
hym brought to court, and how the kynge hadde made hym knyght. "But thus
30　　moche," seide Merlin, "I shall telle yow; he is a grete gentilman and is no duerf
by nature; but thus hath a damesell hym myshapen whan he was thirteen yere of
age for that he wolde not graunte hir his love. And he was than the feirest creature
of the worlde; and for the sorowe that the damesell hadde, araied she hym in
soche wise that now is the lothliest creature and of moste dispite. And fro hens
35　　nine wikes shall cesse the terme that the damesell sette, and [he] shall come into
the age that he ought for to be, for at that day shall he be twenty-two yere olde."

Whan Merlin hadde alle thinges rehersed and Blase hadde hem alle writen oon
after another in ordre, and by his boke have we the knowinge therof. And when

10 **he**, i.e., Merlin; **talent**, desire. 11 **seth**, since. 12 **drough**, drew; **faste on**, near; **sette**,
agreed upon. 13 **behoved**, needed. 14 **entierly**, earnestly. 17 **seth**, since. 18 **agein**, against;
volunté, desire. 23 **sore abaisshed**, greatly upset. 25 **sped**, fared; **sethen**, since [last time].
27 **of**, with. 28 **duerfe**, dwarf. 32 **for that**, because. 33 **araied she**, she transformed him.
34 **dispite**, shame. 35 **wikes**, weeks; **cesse**, end.

Merlin hadde be ther eight dayes, he toke leve of Blase and seide, "This is the
laste tyme that I shall speke with yow eny more, for fro hensforth I shall sojourne
with my love, ne never shall I have power hir for to leve ne to come ne go."

Whan Blase undirstode Merlin, he was full of sorowe and seide, "Dere frende,
seth it is so that ye may not departe, cometh not ther." "Me behoveth for to go,"
quod Merlin, "for so have I made hir covenaunt; and also, I am so supprised with
hir love that I may me not withdrawen. And I have her taught and lerned all the
witte and connynge that she can, and yet shall she lerne more, for I may not hir
withsein ne it disturve."

Than departed Merlin from Blase, and in litill space come to his love that grete
joye of hym made, and he of hir, and dwelled togeder longe tyme. And ever she
enquered of his craftes, and he hir taught and lerned so moche that after he was
holden a fooll, and yet is. And she hem well undirstode and put hem in writinge as
she that was well expert in the Seven Artes.

Whan that he hadde hir taught all that she cowde aske, she bethought hir how
she myght hym withholde forever more. Than began she to glose Merlin more
than ever she hadde do even beforn and seide, "Sir, yet can I not oon thing that I
wolde fain lerne, and therfore I pray you that ye wolde me enforme." And Merlin,
that well knewe her entent seid, "Madame, what thinge is that?" "Sir," quod she,
"I wolde fain lerne how I myght oon shet in a tour withouten walles or withoute
eny closure be enchauntement, so that never he sholden go oute withouten my
licence." And whan Merlin it herde, he bowed down the heed and began to sigh;
and [whan] she it aparceived, she asked whi he sighed.

"Madame," seide Merlin, "I shall telle yow. I knowe well what ye thinke, and
that ye will me withholde; and I am so supprised with love that me behoveth to do
youre plesier." And than she caste hir armes aboute his nekke and hym kiste, and
seide that wele he ought to be hirs seth that she was all his. "Ye knowe wele that
the grete love that I have to you hath made me forsake alle other for to have yow
in myn armes nyght and day; and ye be my thought and my desire, for withoute

41 **ne**[1], and; **ne**[2], nor; **ne**[3], or. 43 **seth**, since. 44 **hir covenaunt**, her a promise; **supprised
with**, overcome by. 46–47 **hir withsein**, from her withhold. 47 **ne it disturve**, nor it prevent. 50 **after**, later. 51 **holden**, considered. 53 **cowde**, did. 54 **withholde**, possess; **glose**,
flatter. 55 **can**, know. 58 **shet**, shut; **tour**, tower. 59 **be**, by. 63 **withholde**, imprison;
supprised, overwhelmed.

yow have I neither joye ne welthe. In you have I sette all my hope, and I abide noon other joye but of yow; and seth that I love you and also ye love me, is [it] not

70   right than that ye do my volunté and I yours?"

"Certes, yesse," seide Merlin. "Now sey than what ye will." "I will," quod she, "ye teche me a place feire and covenable that I myght enclose by art in soche wise that never myght be undon; and we shull be ther, ye and I, in joye and disporte whan that yow liketh." "Madame," seide Merlin, "that shall I well do." "Sir,"

75   quod she, "I will not that ye it make, but lerne it to me that I may it do, and I shall make it than more at my volunté." "Well," seide Merlin, "I will do youre plesire."

Than he began to devise the crafte unto hir, and she it wrote all that he seide; and whan [he] hadde alle devised, the damesell hadde grete joye in herte. And he hir loved more and more, and she shewed hym feirer chere than beforn. And so

80   thei sojourned togeder longe tyme till it fill on a day that thei wente thourgh the foreste hande in hande, devisinge and disportinge, and this was in the Foreste of Brochelonde, and fonde a bush that was feire and high of white hawthorne full of floures; and ther thei satte in the shadowe. And Merlin leide his heed in the damesels lappe, and she began to taste softly till he fill on slepe. And whan she felt that he

85   was on slepe, she aroos softly and made a cerne with hir wymple all aboute the bussh and all aboute Merlin, and began hir enchauntementez soche as Merlin hadde hir taught, made the cerne nine tymes and nine tymes hir enchauntementes. And after that she wente and satte down by hym and leide his heed in hir lappe and hilde hym ther till he dide awake. And than he loked aboute hym, and hym semed

90   he was in the feirest tour of the worlde and the moste stronge, and fonde hym leide in the feirest place that ever he lay beforn.

And than he seide to the damesell, "Lady, thou hast me disceived but yef ye will abide with me, for noon but ye may undo this enchauntementes." And she seide, "Feire swete frende, I shall often tymes go oute, and ye shull have me in

95   youre armes, and I yow. And fro hensforth shull ye do all youre plesier." And she hym hilde wele covenaunt, for fewe hours ther were of the nyght ne of the day but

69 seth that, since. **70 volunté**, wishes. **71 will**, desire. **72 teche**, to show; **convenable**, private. **76 volunté**, desire. **77 devise**, teach; **crafte unto**, skill to. **83 shadowe**, shade. **84 taste**, touch him. **85 cerne**, circle; **wymple**, scarf. **87 cerne**, circle. **89 hilde**, held; **hym semed**, thought. **90 tour**, tour. **92 but yef**, unless. **93 abide**, stay. **96 hym hilde wele covenaunt**, kept her promise to him.

she was with hym. Ne never after com Merlin oute of that fortresse that she hadde hym in sette, but she wente in and oute whan she wolde. But now moste we reste a while of Merlin and of his love and speke of the Kynge Arthur.

100   The same hour that Merlin was departed fro the Kynge Arthur and that he hadde seide how it was the laste tyme that he sholde hym se, the kynge aboode sore abaisshed and full pensif of that worde. And in soche maner he aboode after Merlin seven wikes and more. But whan he saugh that he com nought, he was full pensif and full of hevynesse. And on a day, Sir Gawein asked what hym eiled.

105   "Certes, nevew," seide the kynge, "I thinke on that I trowe I have loste Merlin, and that he will never more come to me; for now hath he abiden lenger than he was wonte. And gretly I am dismayed of the worde that he seide whan he fro me departed, for he seide this is the laste tyme; therfore I am in doute that he sey soth, for he ne made never lesinge of nothinge that he seide. For so helpe me God, I

110   hadde lever lese the cité of Logres than hym. And therfore, fain wolde I wite yef eny myght hym finde fer or nygh; and therfore I praye you as derely as ye me love that ye hym seche till ye knowe the verité."

"Sir," seide Gawein, "I am all redy to do youre volunté, and anoon ye shull se me meve fordwarde. And I suere to you be the oth that I made to you whan ye

115   made me knyght that I shall seche hym a yere and a day, but withynne that space I may knowe trewe tidinges." In this same wise swor Sir Ewein and Segramor and Agravain and Geheret and Gaheries and twenty-five of her felowes.

[*Summary. The knights set out on the quest to find Merlin. In the meantime, the lady and the dwarf-knight that Arthur had knighted have a series of adventures. The dwarf defeats a knight in single combat and requires him to go to Arthur's court where he tells of his defeat by the dwarf. Ewain and his companions encounter this same lady, who now rides mourning for her love (who is called Avadain the Dwarf), for she believes he is about to be killed by five knights. Ewain rides to help the dwarf-knight; when he gets*

97 **Ne,** But. **98 wolde,** wished; **moste,** must. **101–02 sore abaisshed,** greatly troubled. **102 aboode after,** waited for. **103 wikes,** weeks. **104 hevynesse,** sadness; **eiled,** ailed. **105 trowe,** believe. **106 abiden,** stayed away. **108 in doute,** fearful; **sey soth,** spoke the truth. **109 lesinge,** a falsehood. **110 lever,** rather; **wite,** know. **112 seche,** seek; **verité,** truth. **113 volunté,** wishes. **114 meve fordwarde,** make a promise; **suere,** swear; **be,** by. **115 but,** unless. **117 her,** their.

there, the dwarf has already defeated several of his foes. Ewain unhorses one of the attacking knights. When the dwarf-knight attempts to kill the knight, Ewain stays his hand, telling him he has done enough. The defeated knight thanks Ewain for saving his life, and yields his sword to the dwarf. Ewain and his companions ride on their way; and at the end of the year, they return to court, not having found Merlin. The story now returns to Gawain. Fol. 241r (line 3)–243r (line 22).]

    Whan that Sir Gawein was departed fro his felowes, he rode forth thourgh the foreste, he and five knyghtes of his companye; and ther thei departed and eche

120   wente his wey, for he wolde ride sooll by hymself. And in this wise thei departed so that eche of hem toke his wey. And Sir Gawein rode so alone serchinge grete part of the londe till it fill on a day that he rode pensif and hevy for that he myght not finde Merlin. And in this stody he entred into a foreste; and he hadde riden aboute two Walsh myle, ther com a damesell hym agein that rode on the feirest

125   palfrey of the worlde. And [it] was all blak, and the sadell and the stiropes were all of golde, and the cloth of scarlet trailinge to the erthe, and the bridill of golde. And she was clothed in white samyte and hir kirchires of silke and richely atired, and com ridinge before Sir Gawein, as he was in this pensifnesse, that he dide her not salue.

130   And whan he was passed the damesell, she reyned hir bridill and turned the heed of hir palfrey and seide, "Gawein, Gawein, hit is not trewe the renomee that renneth of thee thourgh the reame of Logres; for it is seide of thee that thou art the best knyght of the worlde; and of that thei sey [not the] trouthe. Also it is seide that thou art the gentilest and the moste curteise knyght; but in that faileth the

135   renoon, for thou art the moste vileyn knyght that ever I mette in my lif, that in this forest so fer fro peple haste me imet alone; and so grete felonye in the is roted that thow deynest not me ones to salue ne to speke a worde; and knowe thow verily, thow shalt it repente of that thow hast don in so moche that thou shalt wissh thou haddest it not don for all the reame of Logres."

140   And whan Sir Gawein undirstode the damesell, he was sore ashamed and turned

---

118 departed, separated. **120 sooll,** alone. **124 Walsh myle,** Welsh miles; **hym agein,** towards him. **127 samyte,** silk; **kirchires,** scarfs. **129 salue,** greet. **130 was,** had. **131 renomee,** fame. **132 renneth of thee,** circulates about you. **135 renoon,** renown; **that²,** who. **136 haste,** have; **felonye,** crime; **roted,** rooted. **137 ones,** once; **salue ne,** greet nor.

agein hir his bridell of Gringalet, and seide all shamefast as ye shull heren. "Damesell," quod Sir Gawein, "so help me God, I thought upon a thinge that I go sechinge; and therfore I pray yow that ye foryeve it me that I have mysdon." "So helpe me God," quod the damesell, "rather shalt thou abye it full dere, for inough
145   thou shalt have of shame and lothlynesse; and therfore, remembre another tyme whan thou metest with eny lady or damesell that thou hir salue for curtesie. But I sey not that it shall thee ever endure; ne of that thou goist sechinge, shalt thou finde noon in the reame of Logres that thee can telle no tidinge, but in the Litill Breteigne maist thou here som maner tidinges. And I will go now theras I have to
150   don; and thou shalt go seche that thou art moved fore. And the firste man that thou metest with mote thou be like, till thou se me eftsones."

    Than departed Sir Gawein and the damesell. But he hadde not riden fully half a Walissh myle thourgh the foreste that he mette with the duerf knyght and the damesell that on the even before were departed fro Sir Ewein and hadde sent the
155   foure knyghtes in Arthurs prison; and it was on Trinité Sonday aboute mydday. And than he remembred hym on the damesell that he hadde mette before, and lefte his pensifnesse and seide to the damesell, "God yeve you good day and moche joye of hir companye." And the damesell and the duerf hym ansuerde that God yeve hym good aventure. And so thei past a litill asonder, Sir Gawein on that oon
160   part and thei on that other. And whan thei were departed a litill thens, the duerf knyght becom agein into his bewté as he hadde be at the first tyme, and was in the age of twenty-two yere, right wele furnysshed and wonderly well shapen of large stature; and therfore hym behoved to do awey his armes, for thei were to hym nothinge meete. And whan the damesell saugh hir love come agein into so grete
165   bewté, she hadde so grete joye that no tonge myght it telle; and caste hir armes aboute his nekke and hym kiste an hundred tymes. And [they] ride forth that oon by that other, gladde and joyfull in grete solas, and thanked oure Lorde of the honour that he hadde hem don, and praied oure Lorde to sende Sir Gawein good

141 agein, towards. **143 sechinge,** seeking. **144 abye,** pay for; **dere,** dearly. **146 salue,** greet. **147 ne of that thou goist sechinge,** as to what you are seeking. **148 noon,** it not. **149 theras,** where. **150 that[1],** what; **moved fore,** looking for. **151 mote,** must; **se,** see; **eftsones,** later on. **153 Walissh,** Welsh; **duerf,** dwarf. **154 even,** evening. **159 yeve,** give; **aventure,** fortune. **161 bewté,** handsomeness; **be,** been. **163 hym behoved,** he needed; **do awey,** discard. **164 nothinge meete,** unsuitable.

aventure that hadde seide that God yeve hem joye. And so hadde he done, and
170 thus thei ride forth theire journey. But now shull we speke of Gawein.

Whan that Sir Gawein was passed the duerf knyght and the damesell wele a
two bowe draught, anoon he felte that the sleves of his hauberk passed fer of
lengthe over his hondes, and also the lengthe of his hauberk henge down benethe
his feet, and his legges were waxen so short that thei passed not the skirtes of the
175 sadill. And [he] behilde and saugh how his hosen of stiell resten in the stiropes,
and saugh how his shelde henge toward the erthe, and aperceyved wele that he
was become a duerf; and seide to hymself that it was that the damesell hadde hym
promysed. And therwith he wax so wroth that for a litill he hadde gon oute of his
witte; and rode forth so in that wrathe and in that anguyssh in the foreste till he
180 fonde a crosse and a ston therby. And thider he rode and alight upon the ston and
toke his stiropes and made hem shorter and his hosen of stiell and the renges of
his swerde and the gige of his shilde and the sleves of his hauberk with thonges of
lether upon his shuldres, and araied hym in the beste wise he myght, so wroth and
angry that he hadde lever to be deed than on lyve.

185 And after that he lepte up and rode forth his wey, and cursed the day and the
hour that ever he entred into that quest, for shamed he was and dishonoured. And
so hath he gon in this maner that never he lefte castell ne towne ne burgh but that
he asked tidinges of Merlin of alle the men and women that he mette; and many
oon he mette that grete shame and grete reproves hym seiden. And nevertheles he
190 dide many prowesses, for though he were a duerf and mysshapen, he hadde not
loste his strengthe netthir his hardinesse, and many a knyght he conquered. And
whan he hadde serched the reame of Logres up and down and saugh that he cowde
not finde Merlin, he thought to passe the see and go into the Litill Breteigne. And
so he dide, and serched it fer and nygh, but never cowde he here no tidinge of
195 Merlin. And so it drough nygh the terme that he hadde promysed to returne.

And than he seide to hymself, "Allas, what shall I now do, for the terme aproched
that I muste returne, by the oth that I have sworn to myn oncle to repeire. Returne
moste I nede, for elles sholde I be forsworne and untrewe, and that will I not in no

172 **two bowe draught,** two bow shots. **175 behilde,** looked. **177 that²,** what. **181 renges,**
belt. **182 gige,** strap. **184 lever to,** rather. **189 reproves hym seiden,** insults said to him
190 prowesses, fine deeds. **191 netthir,** nor. **192 cowde,** could. **194 here,** hear. **195 drough
nygh,** drew near.

maner, for the oth was soche that yef I were in my delyver powsté, and in my
powsté am I nought, for I am foulé disfigured and a thinge of grete dispite and I
have nought of myself; and therfore may I wele abide of goinge to court. Certes,
now have I evell seide, for never will I be forsworne for to go ne to come, what
persone that ever I be; and for that I am not shet in prison, I may go at my wille.
And I may not abide but I be forsworne; and therfore me behoveth to go, for
untrouthe will I never do. But I pray to God to have of me mercy and pité, for my
body is shamefully and lothly arayed."

In these complayntes that Sir Gawein ther made, he returned bak for to come to
courte; and fill as he rode thourgh the Foreste of Brocheliande and wolde turne
for to come to the see. And ever as he rode he made grete moone; and as he made
this weymentacion, he herde a voice a litill upon the right side above. And he
turned that wey where he hadde herde the voice, and loked up and downe and
nothinge he saugh but as it hadde ben a smoke of myste in the eyre that myght not
passe oute. Than he herde a voice that seide, "Sir Gawein, disconfort you nothinge,
for all shall falle as it behoveth to falle."

Whan Sir Gawein herde the voyce that hadde hym cleped by his right name, he
ansuerde and seide, "Who is that, in the name of God, that to me doth speke?"
"How is that?" quod the voice. "Ne knowe ye me nought? Ye were wonte to
knowe me right wele, but so goth the worlde; and trewe is the proverbe that the
wise man seith, that 'Who is fer from his iye is soone foryeten'; and so fareth it be
me. For while that I haunted the courte and served the Kynge Arthur and his
barouns, I was wele beknowen of yow and of many other. And for that I have left
court, I am unknowen; and that ought I not to be, yef feith and trouthe regned
thourgh the worlde."

Whan Sir Gawein herde the voice thus speke, he thought anoon it was Merlin,
and ansuerde anoon. "Certes, it is trouthe I ought you wele for to knowe, for many

200

205

210

215

220

225

---

199 yef, if; **delyver powsté,** normal condition. **200 nought,** not; **dispite,** ridicule. **201
abide,** delay; **of goinge,** returning; **Certes,** To be sure. **202 evell seide,** evilly said. **203 for
that,** because. **204 abide but,** delay unless. **207 In,** After. **208 fill as,** it happened that. **209
moone,** moan. **210 weymentacion,** lamentation. **212 eyre,** air. **214 behoveth,** needs. **215
cleped,** called. **217 Ne knowe ye me nought,** Do not you know me; **were wonte to,** used
to. **219 iye,** eye; **foryeten,** forgotten; **be,** with. **221 for that,** because. **222 yef,** if.

tyme have I herde youre speche; and therfore I pray you that ye will apere to me so that I may yow se." "My lorde Sir Gawein," quod Merlin, "me shull ye never se; and that hevieth me sore that I may do noon other. And whan ye be departed fro hens, I shall never speke with yow no more, ne with noon other saf only with

230   my leef. For never man shall have power hider for to come for nothinge that may befalle. Ne fro hens may I not come oute, ne never I shall come oute, for in all the worlde is not so stronge a clos as in this whereas I am. And it is nother of iren ne stiell ne tymbir ne of ston, but it is of the aire withoute eny othir thinge by enchauntemente so stronge that it may never be undon while the worlde endureth.

235   Ne I may not come oute ne noon may entre, saf she that me here hath enclosed, that bereth me companye whan hir liked, and goth hens whan hir liste."

"How is that, swete frende," quod Gawein, "that ye be in this maner withholden, that noon may you delyver by no force that may be do, ne ye may not you shewe to me, that be the wisest man of the worlde?" "Nay, but the moste fole," quod

240   Merlin, "for I wiste wele that sholde befalle; and I am soche a fole that I love another better than myself, and have hir lerned so moche wherethourgh I am thus beclosed and shette in prison, ne noon may me oute bringe." "Certes," seide Sir Gawein, "that me hevieth sore, and so [it] will the Kynge Arthur myn uncle whan he it knoweth, as he that maketh yow to be sought thourgh alle londes."

245   "Now he moste it suffre," quod Merlin, "for he shall me se never more, ne I hym, for thus is it befalle. Ne never shall no man speke with me after you. Therfore for nought meveth eny man me for to seche. For youreself, anoon as ye be turned fro hens, ye shull never here me speke. And therfore, now returne and grete wele the Kynge Arthur and my lady the quene and alle the barouns, and telle hem how

250   it is with me; and ye shull fynde the kynge at Cardoell in Wales. And whan ye come thider, ye shull finde alle youre felowes ther that fro you were departed. And discounforte yow not of that is yow befalle, for ye shall fynde the damesell

---

226 apere, appear. **228 hevieth**, grieves. **229 saf**, save. **230 leef**, love. **231 Ne fro hens,** Nor from here. **232 a clos**, an enclosure; **whereas**, where. **235 ne noon**, nor none. **238 do,** done. **238–39 ne ye may not . . . me**, can you not show me. **239 that be,** [you] who are; **moste fole**, greatest fool. **241 lerned**, taught. **244 as**, for. **245 suffre**, endure. **247 meveth,** attempts; **seche**, seek. **248 grete**, greet. **252 discounforte . . . befalle**, do not be discouraged by what has befallen you.

that so hath yow mysshapen in the foreste whereas ye hir mette. But foryete not hir to salue, for it were folye." "Sir," seide Gawein, "ne nought I shall, yef God 255 will." "Now," quod Merlin, "I beteche yow to God that kepe the Kynge Arthur and the reame of Logres as for the best peple of the worlde."

Than departed Sir Gawein gladde and sorowful — gladde for that Merlin hadde hym assured to be releveth from his lothlynesse, and sory for that he hadde Merlin thus loste. And [he] rode so forth till he com to the see, and passed over hastely 260 inough, and than toke his wey to ride to Cardoell in Walis. And [it] fill that he mette the damesell that [he] hadde passed by withoute saluynge in the foreste. And than he remembred of that Merlin hadde hym seide that he sholde not foryete hir to salue whan he hir mette. And he hadde grete feer and douted lesse she passed er he myght hir salewe; and [he] dide of his helme of his heed for to se hir 265 more clerly, and began to beholde before and behynde and on alle sides, till that he com in the same place where he mette the damesell. And than he loked betwene two busshes, for the forest was somdell depe and thikke, and saugh two knyghtes that were armed at alle poyntes, saf of theire sheldes and helmes that thei hadde don of, and hadde theire horse reyned to theire speres that were pight in the grounde, 270 and hilde a damesell betwene hem two and made semblaunce hir to enforce, and yet therto hadde thei no talent, for the damesell made hem it for to do for to assaye the will and the corage of Sir Gawein; and she made countenaunce like as thei hadde constreyned hir be force.

And whan Sir Gawein saugh this, he wax wroth and rode thider gripinge his 275 spere, and seide to the knyghtes that thei were but deed for that thei dide force the damesell withynne the lordship of Kynge Arthur. "For ye knowe wele," quod he, "that thei sholde go sure." And whan the damesell hym saugh, she hym ascried and seide, "Gawein, now shall it be sene yef ther be soche prowesse in you that ye may me delyver from this shame." "Damesell," seide Gawein, "so God be my

---

253 **whereas**, where. 254 **salue**, greet; **ne nought I shall**, I shall not. 255 **beteche**, commend; **kepe**, protects. 258 **releveth**, relieved. 260 **Walis**, Wales. 261 **saluynge**, greeting. 262 **of that**, what. 263 **douted**, worry. 264 **er**, before; **dide of**, took off. 267 **somdell**, somewhat. 269 **don of**, taken off; **pight**, stuck. 270 **hilde**, held; **enforce**, rape. 271 **therto**, to do that; **talent**, desire; **assaye**, test. 275 **deed**, dead; **for that**, because. 276 **lordship**, realm. 277 **sure**, safely; **saugh**, saw; **ascried**, called out.

280 socour, as ye shull have no shame theras I may you diffende, for owther I shall
dye or I shall you delyver." And whan the knyghtes this undirstode, thei hadde
therof grete disdeyne and dispite; and lepte on foote and laced theire helmes, for
yet thei douted of hym, and nevertheles the damesell hadde hem assured that of
hym sholde thei have noon harme, and hadde hem so enchaunted by hir art that no
285 man myght hem anoye; and therfore thei were the more sure at that tyme. And
whan theire helmes were laced, thei henge theire sheldes aboute theire nekkes and
seide to Sir Gawein, "So helpe me God, false duerf countirfeted, thou art but
deed; and nevertheless shame us semeth to dele with soche a wrecche as thou art."

And whan Sir Gawein herde hymself cleped duerf and so dispised, he hadde
290 grete sorowe in herte and seide, "As lothly a wrecche as I am, in evell tyme I am
come to youre behof. But lepe upon youre horse, for vilonye me semeth to requere
you on horsebak while ye be on foote." "Trustest so moche in thyself," seide the
knyghtes, "that thou wilt abide till we be horsed?" "I trust so moche in God,"
quod Gawein, "that whan ye departe fro me ye shull never forfete to lady ne
295 damesell in the londe of Kynge Arthur."

Than thei lepe to theire horse and hente theire speres and seide to Sir Gawein
that he was but deed; and drough hem to the wey that was moste playne and
withdrough that oon fro that other. And than thei bothe lete renne agein Sir Gawein
and he agein hem. And thei smote bothe upon his shelde so harde that theire speres
300 braste asonder, but thei hym meved not from his sadill. And he smote so that oon
that he bar hym to the erthe upright, and the spere brake in peces, and he rode over
hym that was fallen and unhorsed so that he brosed hym sore. Than he drough his
suerde and rode toward that other and wolde smyte hym upon the helme. And
than the damesell cried, "Inough, Sir Gawein, ne do no more!" "Damesell," seide
305 Gawein, "will ye that it so be?" And she seide, "Ye." "And I will suffre than for
youre sake, that God yeve you than good aventure and to alle the damesels of the
worlde. And wite ye well, ne were it for youre prayer, thei sholde be slayn; for

280 theras, where; **owther,** either. **283 douted of,** feared; **and nevertheles,** even though.
285 anoye, harm. **287 duerf,** dwarf; **countirfeted,** ill-shaped. **288 dele,** deal. **291 behof,**
need; **me semeth,** it seems to me; **requere,** fight. **294 forfete,** do harm; **ne,** nor. **296 hente,**
took. **297 wey,** path; **playne,** open. **298 withdrough,** withdrew; **agein,** toward. **300 braste,**
burst; **hym meved not,** did not budge him. **301 upright,** on his back. **302 brosed,** bruised.
306 yeve, give; **aventure,** fortune. **307 ne were it,** if not.

thei have don you to grete shame and anoye, and to me seide vilonye, that "countirfet
duerf" have me called. And yet therof thei seide soth, for I am the moste lothly
310 creature of dispite that is in the worlde, and in this foreste it me befill eight monethes
passed."

And whan the damesell and the knyghtes hym undirstode, thei begonne to laugh;
and than seide the damesell, "What wolde ye yeve hir that of that wolde warisshen?"
"Certes," seide Gawein, "yef it myght be that it were warisshed, I wolde yeve
315 mysilf firste and formest, and after, all that I myght raunsome in all the worlde."
"It shall not nede you yeve so moche," seide the damesell, "but ye shull make to
me an oth soche as I shall you devise." "Lady," seide Gawein, "I will do all youre
volunté." Quod she, "Ye shull to me swere be the oth that ye made to the Kynge
Arthur youre uncle that never ye shull faile lady ne maiden ne damesell, ne never
320 mete lady ne damesell but ye shull hir salue er she salue you, yef ye may." "Lady,"
quod Gawein, "this I graunte as I am trewe knyght." "And I take the oth in this
maner that yef ye breke youre oth that ye become into the same poynte that ye be
now." "Lady," quod he, "to this I assent, with that the quarell be trewe of hir that
of helpe me requereth, for untrouthe will I not do in no maner wise, nother for lif
325 ne for deth." "Thus I you graunte," quod the damesell, "for I will that ye be soche
as ye were before."

Anoon brake the layners that he had bounden up his hosen of stiell, for his
membres that were strecched oute and com agein anoon in his owne semblaunce.
And whan he felte that he was come agein into his power, he kneled before the
330 damesell and seide that he was hir knyght for ever more. And the damesell hym
thanked and raught hym up be the honde. Than toke the damesell leve of Sir Gawein
and departed, and hir two knyghtes with hir, and comaunded eche other to God.

And Sir Gawein abood there and lengthed his hauberke and appareiled his shelde
and his armes full richely, and lepte upon the Gringalet with his shelde aboute his
335 nekke and his spere in hande, and rode forth toward Cardoell so fro day to day till
that he com thider at the terme devised. And the same day that Sir Ewein and

___

308 **you to,** to you; **anoye,** harm; **countirfet,** ill-shaped. 310 **dispite,** ridicule. 313
warisshen, correct. 318 **volunté,** desires. 320 **salue er,** greet before. 322 **poynte,** condition. 323 **with,** so. 327 **brake,** broke; **layners,** thongs. 328 **membres,** limbs. 331 **raught,**
caught.

Merlin's Imprisonment; and Gawain and the Dwarf Knight

Segramor and her felowes were comen; and eche of hem hadde seide his aventure of that was hem befallen in [this quest].

[Here the Middle English text breaks off.]

*[**Summary**. Everyone marvels at Gawain's adventures, but Arthur grieves for Merlin. While the court is celebrating Gawain's return, a handsome young man enters accompanied by a damsel. He informs the king he is the dwarf that Arthur had knighted earlier, and he explains how he came to regain his real shape. Arthur invites this handsome knight, whose name is Evadem, to join the Round Table.*

The story turns to events in Benoye, where King Ban and King Bors are living joyfully with their wives. King Ban's wife gives birth to a son who is baptised Gallead and is surnamed Lancelot; King Bors's wife gives birth to a son named Lyonel and a year later to a son named Bohort. These three sons will achieve great renown in the land of Logres later on. But now the fortunes of King Ban and King Bors take a turn for the worse, for King Bors is stricken by a terrible sickness, and their old enemy Claudas de la deserte begins to mount a new military campaign against the land of Benoye. King Ban has too few people to repel Claudas's attack; and when King Ban is betrayed by his own seneschal, the Castle of Trebes falls to his enemy, as the story will later describe.]

337 her, their.

Commentary

The Birth of Merlin

[Fols. 1r–8r (line 10)]

Geoffrey of Monmouth is the first medieval writer to provide an account of Merlin's conception and birth. In *The History of the Kings of Britain* Geoffrey offers a relatively brief recounting of the impregnation of Merlin's virtuous human mother by an invisible incubus demon (Thorpe, pp. 167–68). Wace, in his *Roman de Brut*, adds little to Geoffrey's narrative. "The Birth of Merlin," however, follows the French Vulgate version by developing this basic story much further and providing a specific rationale for the begetting of Merlin that is absent from Geoffrey's work. The motif of a great consultation among the fiends occurs in several places in medieval and Renaissance literature, the most famous of which is in Book II of John Milton's *Paradise Lost*; in ME literature there is the poem "The Devils' Parliament," which depicts the devils' consternation over the Virgin Birth. Here the fiends have been thrown into confusion by Christ's recent Harrowing of Hell, during which he releases the Old Testament patriarchs from Satan's bondage. Plotting revenge, the devils decide to father a fiendish child — a kind of antichrist — by producing a "virgin birth" of their own. The result of their plan is the boy Merlin. But the devils' revenge goes awry, due to the basic goodness of Merlin's mother and the timely advice of a holy hermit named Blase.

2   *Adam and Eve and other*. A reference to the Harrowing of Hell, in which Christ, following the Crucifixion, descended into Hell and released the Old Testament patriarchs from Satan's hellish prison. Although this event is not described in the New Testament, it was well-known in the Middle Ages, principally from the account in the apocryphal Gospel of Nicodemus (See M. R. James, *The Apocryphal New Testament: A Collection of Apocryphal Christian Literature in an English Translation* [Oxford: Clarendon Press, 1993]). Plays

333

on the liberation of the patriarchs are prominent in the English mystery cycles, and references to the Harrowing of Hell are common in English medieval literature — compare the lyric "Adam lay i-bounden" — and it is described in some detail in works such as in *Piers Plowman* (B.18 and C.20) and *Death and Liffe* (lines 388–430).

4–17   The *he* here clearly refers to God, but I have left it without capital because the devil, in his confusion, has no idea of who the intruder might be.

10   *the prophetes*. The speaker is referring to the Old Testament prophets whose messianic prophecies foretold the birth of Christ, e.g., Isaiah 11:10 and Jeremiah 23:5–6.

11–12   *the synners of Adam and Eve*. The descendants of Adam and Eve, who have been born in sin.

18   *waisshen in a water*. The speaker is referring to baptism, one of the most important of the seven sacraments for medieval Christians.

25   *we yede and assaied Hym*. A reference to the tempting of Christ in the wilderness, depicted in Matthew 4:1–11 and Luke 4:1–13.

Summary   For the text of the summary, see *EETS* 10, pp. 3–7.

60   *a comyn woman*. A prostitute. The plight of the two sisters may seem somewhat curious, since the one guilty of fornication is executed while the one who turns to prostitution is spared. But this accords with medieval law, which often condoned open prostitution but condemned women caught out in covert acts of immorality, which might endanger purity of lineage and inheritance.

73   *grete ire or wrath*. As the holy man points out, people who succumb to the sin of wrath offer the devil an easy avenue into their hearts. In Chaucer's The Parson's Tale, for example, wrath is said to chase the Holy Spirit out of a person's soul and to put in its place the likeness of the devil (*CT* X.543–45).

Indeed, as the passage in The Parson's Tale indicates, "Ire is a ful greet pleasaunce to the devel." The second part of the holy man's advice — that she always sleep in the presence of a light — proves to be just as crucial as his advice to avoid anger, for the devil loves darkness.

112–13   *grete sorowe and grete ire at hir herte.* This phrase suggests that she is about to fall into the sin of despair, which the fiend believes will place her *owte of Goddes grace* (line 114).

234   *knewe of soche mysteré.* These knowledgeable women, presumably, are especially skilled as midwives.

261   *cristened Merlyn.* The suggestion that Merlin was given the name of his grandfather, his mother's father, is also found in some of the OF MSS and in Lovelich's *Merlin*; but it is not commonplace in later Arthurian tradition.

Summary   Based on *EETS* 10, pp. 18–21.

367   *Than [Merlin] toke the juge apart.* This little episode offers the first demonstration of Merlin's remarkable knowledge and prophetic powers.

421   *Joseph Abaramathie.* Joseph of Arimathea, from Matthew 27:57, one of Jesus's dedicated followers, and a figure who became especially important in medieval works focusing on the Grail Legend. As will be seen below, Joseph was the first "Grail Keeper" in a long line of men entrusted with this most holy object.

422   *Pieron, and of othir felowes.* This refers to the earliest group of men who were closely associated with the Grail in the segment of the story known as The History of the Grail. Pieron is probably Petrus (not St. Peter, Jesus's Disciple), and the *othir felowes* might include men such as Alain le Gros and Bron.

443   *Maister Martyn.* The alleged translator of a book from Latin into the vernacular, describing the early kings of the Britons. He is referred to in only a few of the OF MSS; in Lovelich's *Merlin* (lines 1667–74) he is called "Martyn de Bewre," and he is said to have translated "the Story of Brwttes book" (i.e.,

335

Brutus's book) "From latyn into Romaunce" (i.e., French). Both the book and its translator are obscure.

Vortiger's Tower

[Fols. 8r (line 11)–13v (line 33)].

For the events surrounding Vortiger's rise to power and his ill-fated attempt to build an impregnable citadel, the author of the *PM* adapts materials from several earlier sources, sometimes altering them in significant ways. His handling of the story of King Constantine and his three sons appears somewhat muddled, at least in comparison with the accounts found in Geoffrey of Monmouth (Thorpe, pp. 150–69) and Wace (lines 7491–7710), where the three sons are named Constans, Aurelius Ambrosius, and Uterpendragon. In the *PM* King Constantine is called Constans, and his sons are identified as Moyne, Pendragon, and Uter. Later on in the *PM* an explanation is offered for the conflation of the names Uter and Pendragon.

The story of Vortiger's tower is found in Nennius's *Historia Brittonum* (sections 40, 42, 47, 48). Nennius's account includes the wisemen's suggestion that the foundation of the tower will not hold unless it is sprinkled with the blood of a fatherless boy; and it also describes the pair of dragons whose struggles prevent the tower from standing. In Nennius, however, the fatherless boy is not specifically identified as being Merlin. The versions of the story contained in Geoffrey and Wace more closely parallel the one in the *PM*, but major differences remain.

Summary Based on *EETS* 10, pp. 23–30.

67   *this werke that I have begonne.* Blase is referring to the book that Merlin has commissioned him to write, in which he will record all the things that Merlin periodically tells him, events that will lead up to and include the Grail story. It should be noted that neither Geoffrey nor Wace includes the figure of the holy Hermit named Blase (or Blaise or Blasy). References to a hermit that Merlin occasionally visits do occur in Layamon's *Brut*, but the author of the *PM* appears not to have known Layamon's work.

101–02   *a carl that hadde bought a payre of stronge shone.* Two minor incidents of a prophetic kind occur on the road as Merlin and his companions make their way to Vortiger. In the first incident Merlin laughs when he sees a man with a new pair of shoes, for he knows the man will die before he can wear them. In the second, Merlin laughs when he sees a priest chanting before a funeral procession, because he knows the dead child is the priest's own son, though the weeping husband does not know it. Somewhat analogous incidents occur in Geoffrey of Monmouth's *Vita Merlini* (lines 490–532), a work which the author of the *Prose Merlin* probably did not know. It is more likely that he was familiar with stories of this kind from popular oral tradition.

208   *two dragons.* The fighting dragons, one red and one white, originate in Nennius and occur also in Geoffrey of Monmouth and Wace. It should also be noted that the pseudo-historical tale from the *Mabinogion,* "Lludd and Llevelys," provides an explanation of how the dragons came to be buried in the ground in the place where Vortiger wishes to build his tower. The relationship between the tale in the *Mabinogion* and the accounts in Geoffrey of Monmouth and Wace is unclear.

280–81   *swere never to entermete of that arte.* Geoffrey of Monmouth and Wace have nothing to say concerning the fate of Vortiger's wisemen, whose flawed acts of divination had placed Merlin's life in jeopardy. But here Merlin has them renounce their practicing of the black arts, confess themselves, and receive penance. Thus Merlin is presented as being compassionate towards the very ones who had plotted his death.

285–86   *the significaunce of the two dragons.* The meaning attributed to the two dragons here departs significantly from that proposed by Geoffrey of Monmouth (Wace omitted any interpretation). Whereas Geoffrey has the red dragon representing the British nation and the white dragon representing the Saxons, here the red dragon betokens Vortiger and the white dragon stands for the surviving sons of Constans.

Vortiger's Demise; The Battle of Salisbury; and The Death of Pendragon

[Fols. 13v (line 34)–20r (line 14)]

This section of the *PM* depicts several important events that are also found in Geoffrey of Monmouth (Thorpe, pp. 186–204) — the burning of Vortiger's tower, the battle against the Saxon invaders, the death of Pendragon (called Aurelius by Geoffrey), and Merlin's marvelous feat of moving and erecting the stones of Stonehenge. However, the two works differ considerably in their treatment of these events.

Summary Based on *EETS* 10, pp. 41–54.

<table>
<tbody>
<tr>
<td>1</td>
<td>the Boke of Prophesyes. Incorporated into Geoffrey of Monmouth's The History of the Kings of Britain is a section devoted exclusively to the prophecies of Merlin (Thorpe, pp. 170–85). It was originally written as a separate work, and the reference here is undoubtedly to a work of this kind.</td>
</tr>
<tr>
<td>3</td>
<td>the sarazins. Throughout the PM the Saxon invaders of Britain are frequently referred to as the sarazins, occasionally as the Danes, and sometimes simply as the "heathen people."</td>
</tr>
<tr>
<td>19</td>
<td>yef ye will do my counseile. This is the first time in the work that Merlin serves as a military strategist. Later on he fills this role frequently, for King Arthur and for others.</td>
</tr>
<tr>
<td>44</td>
<td>Tamyse. The Thames River does not pass very close to the area in which this battle is supposed to occur, the Salisbury Plain. But the geography of Arthurian literature often bears only a faint resemblance to actual fact.</td>
</tr>
<tr>
<td>55–56</td>
<td>go betwene hem and the aryvage. Merlin's strategy is to cut off the Danes' escape route by positioning half the British army between the Danes and their ships.</td>
</tr>
<tr>
<td>58</td>
<td>a dragon all reade fleynge up in the ayre. The red dragon that Merlin says will appear in the sky is apparently a peculiar astrological or meteorological phe-</td>
</tr>
</tbody>
</table>

nomenon (a comet, perhaps?). It is not clear whether Merlin causes it to happen or if he simply knows that it will happen. In any case, it provides a connection between the red dragon of Vortiger's tower and the golden dragon image that Uther (and later Arthur) will employ as their battle standard.

89   *Logres.* In general in the *PM*, *Logres* refers to a city, and very likely to London. More commonly in Arthurian literature, however, *Logres* refers to the geographical area roughly equivalent to modern-day England. According to Geoffrey of Monmouth, this name derives from Locrinus, the eldest son of Brutus, who was the legendary founder of Britain. Brutus gave Locrinus that portion of the island; he gave Kamber, his second son, the area of Wales (Kambria); and he gave Albanactus, his youngest son, Scotland (Albany).

104   *Sende after the grete stones.* Merlin's bringing the stones of Stonehenge from Ireland is described at much greater length by Geoffrey of Monmouth and Wace, and in those earlier works the stones are brought for a different purpose. Indeed in Geoffrey, Aurelius is still alive at the time that Merlin performs this feat. In the *PM*, in contrast to the earlier accounts, there is no mention of the fact that the stones were believed to have medicinal properties.

119–20   *they sholde be dressed upright.* Merlin is credited not only with the feat of moving the stones of Stonehenge but also with devising and implementing their final architectural design. The fact that Merlin believes they will *seme feyrer* (look more attractive) if they are standing upright brings to mind the important Neolithic stone circle at Arbor Low in Derbyshire, where the stones in the stone circle lie flat on the ground.

143   *this knyght whiche hadde taken oure Lorde down.* The "knight" is Joseph of Arimathea, and he is being introduced here as the first of the Grail knights, a line of knights entrusted with the keeping of the Holy Grail. The episode briefly described here is a section from the larger narrative that recounts the history of the Holy Grail.

148 *make a table.* The author is intent on establishing a parallel between this table and the one used by Jesus and his Disciples at the Last Supper. The building of this second table by Joseph of Arimathea anticipates the creation of yet a third table, the famous Arthurian Round Table. These three tables replicate each other, and, taken together, they reflect the concept of the Holy Trinity.

173 *Cardoll, in Walys.* The city of *Cardoll* in Wales, though one of the most famous cities in Arthurian literature, cannot be finally identified. It might be logically associated with Cardiff, but it is more likely that it corresponds to the ancient Roman fortress of Caerleon, a "city" that Geoffrey of Monmouth describes in *The History of the Kings of Britain* at great length (Thorpe, pp. 226–27).

175 *I shall go before and make the table.* There is great variation in medieval accounts concerning the origin of the Round Table. The Round Table is completely absent from Geoffrey of Monmouth, making its first appearance in Wace's *Roman de Brut* (lines 9,994–10,005), where it was established by Arthur, not Uther. In Layamon's *Brut*, following an unruly upheaval at court, the Round Table was fashioned by a Cornish carpenter at Arthur's request. Here, Merlin creates the Round Table for Uterpendragon, and the table is explicitly linked to the story of the Grail. In later versions of the story, including Malory's, the table was passed from Uther to King Leodegan, Guenevere's father, and then passed back again to Arthur as a part of Guenevere's dowry.

Uther and Ygerne

[Fols. 20r (line 15)–31v (line 13)]

The story of Uther's great desire for the wife of the Duke of Cornwall and the subsequent begetting of Arthur is one of the most important episodes in Arthurian literature. It first occurs in Geoffrey of Monmouth's *The History of the Kings of Britain* (Thorpe, pp. 204–08), and treatments of it remain relatively consistent throughout the Middle Ages — compare Geoffrey's account, for example, with the version of the story with which Thomas Malory begins his *Morte D'Arthur*. The version in the *PM*, while somewhat fuller than most of the treatments of this episode and also somewhat richer in characterization, preserves all the essential narrative features.

2–3   *Pentecoste* and *Witsontyde*. The Feast of Pentecost is one of the most impor-
        tant religious holidays of the Middle Ages, and it is also one of the most impor-
        tant time periods in Arthurian literature, for more of the central events in the
        Arthur Story occur around this date than around any other. Pentecost is a
        moveable feast, with its date determined by the date of Easter. Pentecost oc-
        curs on the seventh Sunday after Easter and celebrates the descent of the Holy
        Spirit upon the Disciples. Whitsunday is another name for Pentecost, and
        Whitsuntide is the period of several days immediately following Pentecost.
        Also important during this holy time is the first Sunday after Pentecost, which
        is Trinity Sunday, and the first Thursday after Trinity Sunday, which is Cor-
        pus Christi, a festival celebrating the Eucharist.

7   *fyfty*. It appears that Merlin's Round Table is designed to seat a total of fifty-
        one, if the fifty knights that Merlin is going to select occupy every seat except
        for the one that remains empty. In comparison with other medieval romances,
        this is a smaller number of seats than is usual. In Malory, for example, the
        number of seats is 150. On the other hand, the number of seats at the table
        used for the Last Supper was merely thirteen.

10   *the voyde place*. The empty place at the table, as will soon be explained, is
        reserved for a person of unusual merit. Anyone else attempting to sit in this
        seat will suffer dire consequences. In Malory and other accounts the empty
        seat is called the *Siege Perelous*.

20–21   *we be entred as brethern*. The fifty knights, by virtue of sitting together at the
        Round Table, have formed a special bond of brotherhood which they are now
        loath to break. The suggestion seems to be that this is the initial formation of a
        fellowship of knights who will be known as the Knights of the Round Table.

26   *who shall fulfille the place that is voyde*. In response to the king's question,
        Merlin explains that the empty seat will not be filled until some time well in the
        future. Merlin also points out that the person who will do this will also sit in

341

the empty seat at the table of Joseph of Arimathea, providing another link between the two tables. The knight who will accomplish these deeds will be the pre-eminent Grail knight, Sir Galahad.

32   *hensforth that ye hoilde alle youre grete festes in this town.* Thus Cardoell is established as Uther's principal city and the place where the Round Table resides permanently.

85   *hem that wolden begile.* The belief that a "beguiler will himself be beguiled" was a common medieval proverb. Chaucer's Reeve quotes a version of it near the end of his tale when he says, *A gylour shal hymself bigyled bi* (*CT* I.4321).

101   *the Duke of Tintagel.* Throughout this section of the *PM* Ygerne's husband is always called the Duke of Tintagel; he is never referred to as the Duke of Cornwall, nor is he named Gorlois, as he is in most accounts.

105   *she was right a gode lady.* Ygerne's moral rectitude is emphasized here, as it is throughout Arthurian tradition. She makes every effort to thwart Uther's desires and to remain a virtuous wife. Malory, similarly, refers to her as "a passyng good woman" (Vinaver, p. 3).

145–46 *ete ne slepe . . . ne ride.* Uther, in his inability to eat, sleep, or ride, exhibits traits shared by many a medieval lover.

167   *alle the londe of Logres.* Here *Logres* refers to a large geographical area, whereas earlier (and more commonly in the *PM*) it refers to a city.

266–67 *sende, . . . forty dayes before.* The king is advised by his council to give the duke forty days in which to respond to the king's challenge. If the duke fails to do the king's bidding by the end of that time, then the king may launch his assault.

278   *another castell.* The other castle is not named in the *PM*. Geoffrey of Monmouth calls it Dimilioc, and Malory identifies it as Castel Terrabyl.

324–25   *he mette with a man that he nothinge kenned.* Merlin's shape-shifting abilities are fully displayed in this episode, as Merlin appears to Ulfin first in the guise of an old man and then as a cripple. This anticipates the more remarkable shape-shifting that Merlin will soon engage in involving Ulfin, the king, and Merlin himself.

451   *he toke an herbe.* Here Merlin, Ulfin, and the king achieve the likenesses of the duke and his men by rubbing an herb on their skin. In Geoffrey of Monmouth they drink a concoction that Merlin has devised. Malory offers no explanation as to how their physical transformations were brought about.

Arthur and the Sword in the Stone

[Fols. 31v (line 14)–35v (line 26)]

The "sword in the stone" episode became a integral part of the Arthurian story during the thirteenth century; its origin, however, is obscure. The episode is not found or even alluded to in the works of Geoffrey of Monmouth, Wace, Layamon, or Chrétien de Troyes, but it does occur in the OF Vulgate. Perhaps a parallel to it occurs in the *Volsunga Saga* (ch. 3), in an episode in which Sigmund succeeds in pulling a sword out of the Branstock after others have failed — a sword that was divinely sent from the wizard-god Odin, whom some have seen as a forerunner of Merlin. Rough similarities may also be seen in the story of Theseus and his father Aegeus in Greek myth. Theseus is fathered out of wedlock by Aegeus, who leaves a pair of shoes and a sword under a huge stone; later, Thesues proves himself by having the strength to raise the stone and retrieve the shoes and the sword. A stone playing a vital role in the selection of the king is also encountered in Celtic tradition in the magical stone called Lia Fail, or Stone of Destiny, which gave a shriek when the rightful king stood upon it. That tradition may still be reflected in the British custom of a monarch being crowned while seated upon the Stone of Scone. None-theless, medieval romance literature contains many episodes in which only one person can accomplish a particular deed — several such episodes occur in Malory alone.

What is especially significant about this episode is that the sword provides proof that Arthur, despite the questions surrounding his birth, is king by divine election. It is also significant that Merlin bows out of the proceeding, turning it over to the archbishop, the highest official of the church. The *PM* does not identify the archbishop, who in Geoffrey and Wace is said to be the Archbishop Dubricius. It is likely that he is the same clergyman who is called Bishop Brice in several other Arthurian stories.

Malory's rendition of this episode, while somewhat briefer, contains most of the basic narrative elements found here in the *PM*. In the *PM*, however, the tactics of the feet-dragging barons are drawn in much greater detail. In both versions Arthur's foster father (here named Antor, in Malory named Ector) does not know the real identity of the child he has raised as his own son, and in both versions the scene in which Arthur learns that Antor/Ector is not his father possesses considerable dramatic power.

13   *Martinmasse*. The Feast of St. Martin, which celebrates St. Martin of Tours, occurs on November 11.

33   *I shall not be ther*. Merlin's decision to be absent during the episode in which Arthur proves himself to be Uther's rightful successor probably has to do with Merlin's fiendish origins. Because Merlin is the son of a devil, and because Arthur is being chosen according to the Divine Will, it might be inappropriate for Merlin to have any direct involvement with Arthur's election.

42   *Halowmasse*. Allhallows, or All Saints' Day, a church festival honoring all the saints; it is November 1.

47–48   *thei ledde . . . Yoole Even*. Christmas Eve, which was the feast of Adam and Eve, was a day of partial fasting.

84   *Te Deum Laudamus*. "We praise thee, O Lord" — a famous Latin hymn, frequently used for official celebrations, from funerals to coronations.

112–13 *justice in erthe . . . in the swerde*. The archbishop observes that the sword represents the king's responsibility to uphold justice for all people, to defend the church, and to maintain righteousness. He also seems to suggest that the sword symbolizes the nobility, while the anvil symbolizes the commoners.

133   *the eight dayes*. This is the octave of Christmas, which extends from Christmas Day through New Year's Day.

141–42   *the knyghtes to boorde.* The knights customarily hold a great tournament on New Year's Day following Mass.

200   *that for no forfet.* Antor's main request of Arthur is that he assign the high office of King's Steward to Sir Kay, Arthur's foster brother. In addition, Antor (Ector) wants Arthur to overlook any future offences that Kay may commit, anticipating Kay's later rude behavior, and helping to explain why Arthur is so tolerant of Kay's frequent lack of civility.

235   *Candelmesse.* Candlemas, observed on February 2, is an important feast day celebrating the Presentation of the baby Jesus in the Temple (Luke 2:22–39), as well as the Purification of the Virgin Mary.

245   *every man do . . . .* I.e., "In that case, it is every man for himself," meaning that all agreements are canceled. The barons are trying to have things all their own way, and the archbishop, in order to preserve the peace, tolerates their delaying tactics.

317   *Alle that nyght.* On the Eve of Pentecost, Arthur keeps an all-night vigil in the minster; he is preparing himself spiritually for his coronation on the following day.

The Barons' Revolt

[Fols. 35v (line 27)–40r (line 17)]

The barons' refusal to accept Arthur's kingship and their rebellion against him is one of the major narrative strands of the *PM*, and it is woven throughout the greater part of the work. There is nothing comparable to this rebellion in the writings of Geoffrey of Monmouth or Wace, but the initial events in the barons' revolt have a close parallel in Malory's *Morte D'Arthur* (Vinaver, pp. 11–13), though Malory's rendition is much briefer, as is usually the case.

It is at this point in the OF Vulgate *Merlin* that the sequel section to Robert de Boron's

Merlin commences. In the ME text, the only indication of this is a large capital letter on fol. 35v that is similar to the one with which the text began.

Summary Based on *EETS* 10, pp. 107–13.

31   *This is in the reame of Kynge Leodegan of Tamalide.* Although the text is not very explicit about this, it becomes clear that the Knights of the Round Table have left the realm of Logres to help King Leodegan defend his kingdom against his enemy King Rion. Leodegan's kingdom is sometimes called Tamelide and sometimes Carmelide. This confusion probably results from the fact that the capital letters C and T are often difficult to distinguish in many scribal hands.

39   *he hath taken alle their berdes.* As the text indicates, King Rion trims his mantle with the beards of defeated kings. Later in the *PM*, as well as in Malory (Vinaver, p. 36), King Rion sends a messenger to Arthur requesting Arthur's beard, which is the final beard he needs to complete his mantle. Arthur points out that his beard is still rather meager because of his youth. In the Balin section in Malory, Balin and his brother capture King Rion and present him to Arthur (Vinaver, pp. 46–47). Geoffrey of Monmouth noted that Arthur had once killed a giant named Retho who made a fur cloak from the beards of kings he had slain (Thorpe, p. 240); there appears to be a connection between Geoffrey's Retho and King Rion in the *PM*, who also hails from a land of giants.

44   *yef he lese his londe, thow shalt lese thyn after.* If King Rion is able to capture Tamelide, Merlin suggests, then Arthur's kingdom of Logres will soon be overcome also — a medieval variation on the domino theory.

48   *he shall yeve thee his doughter to be thy wif.* Here Merlin predicts that Arthur will wed Gonnore, King Leodegan's daughter. It is important to note that throughout the *PM* Merlin always speaks favorably of Gonnore, and he fully endorses Arthur's marriage to her. His attitude stands in sharp contrast to that of Malory's Merlin, who warns Arthur that she will not be wholesome for him (Vinaver, p. 59).

54–55   *archebisshop shall a-curse*. As Merlin here indicates, the archbishop will soon set his curse upon the rebel kings. In all probability, by cursing them the archbishop is placing them under interdict rather than the more serious curse of excommunication. Interdict would mean that all church services were forbidden except for baptism and last rites. Early in the thirteenth century Pope Innocent III had placed just such an interdiction on King John's England.

66   *Merlin made to Kynge Arthur a baner*. This is the famous dragon banner which is similar to that which Merlin had fashioned earlier for King Uterpendragon. Kay, Arthur's foster brother and steward, is chosen to bear the standard for Logres.

118   *cosin germains*. This phrase means that they are first cousins, which is one of the most important relationships in Arthurian romances; at times first cousins share an even stronger bond of loyalty and friendship than brothers do.

132   *he drowgh his swerde oute of skabrek*. This passage has a close parallel in Malory: "thenne he drewe his swerd Excalibur, but it was so bryght in his enemyes eyen that if gaf light lyke thirty torchys . . ." (Vinaver, p. 12). Here Arthur's famous sword is called *Escaliboure*, but later it is called *Calibourne*, and the two names are used indiscriminately. These and other variations on the name of Arthur's sword occur throughout Arthurian literature. Geoffrey of Monmouth called it Caliburn, and noted that the sword was forged in the Isle of Avalon. In the story of "Culhwch and Olwen" from the *Mabinogion* Arthur's sword is named *Caledywlch* (Gantz, p. 140). In "The Dream of Rhonabwy" from the *Mabinogion* it is described as having two serpents on its golden hilt, and when it is unsheathed, "What was seen from the mouths of the serpents was like two flames of fire, so dreadful that it was not easy for anyone to look upon" (Gantz, p. 184). In Malory the sword which Arthur receives from the Lady of the Lake is also called *Excalibir*, which is said to have the meaning "Kutte Stele" (Vinaver, p. 40). The suggestion that the name originates in Hebrew occurs in the OF Vulgate.

147   *the seven kynges*. In the *PM* it is repeatedly stated that there are seven kings who oppose Arthur, but only six are clearly identified: Lot of Orcanye, Uriens of Gorre, Ventres of Garlot, Carados of Strangore, Aguysas of Scotlonde, and Ydiers. The seventh may be Briadas, who is said to have married one of Ygerne's daughters. At this point in Malory there are only six rebel kings: Lott, Uryens, Nayntres, Cardos, the Kynge of Scotland, and the Kyng with the Honderd Knyghtes (Vinaver, p. 11).

The Grand Tournament at Logres

[Fols. 40r (line 18)–47v (line 20)]

In this section Arthur's two most crucial allies, King Ban and King Bors, come from their kingdoms of Benoyk and Gannes in Brittany to help him to quell the barons' rebellion. Later on in the larger Arthurian narrative the sons of these two men become central figures in Arthur's knightly fellowship, with Lancelot, the son of King Ban, emerging as Arthur's pre-eminent knight. Other important relationships are established in this section also, in particular the close bond formed by Kay and Lucas the boteler and Lucas's cousin Gifflet.

Summary Based on *EETS* 10, p. 120 to *EETS* 21, p. 132.

    In lines 5 ff. of the summary reference is made to *Ygerne's daughters and their husbands*. Although the *PM* is not consistent on the matter of Ygerne's daughters, here it is stated that she and the Duke of Tintagel had five daughters, in addition to two other daughters from an earlier marriage. In addition, the writer claims that Ygerne's youngest daughter, Morgan, was illegitimate. Each of Igerne's daughters, including Morgan, becomes the wife of one of Britain's lesser kings.

    In lines 6 ff. we learn that *Arthur himself fathered the last one*. The story of Arthur's involvement with Blasine, the wife of King Lot, which is mentioned in passing here by Merlin, will soon be related in full by the narrator in the form of a flashback. Merlin mentions it here to make Arthur aware of the fact that Mordred is his illegitimate son.

Commentary

5   *as aboute August.* Although the weather resembles that of August, the time is actually late October and hence a kind of Indian summer.

12   *coriouse ordenaunce.* For descriptions of the devices that made up components of the *coriouse ordenaunce* of splendid feasts see "The Manner of Serving a Knight, Squire, or Gentleman" in *Hugh Rhodes's Boke of Nurture,* or the receipts for serving wine, meats, fish, and grand feasts with several courses in John Russell's *The Book of Nurture* (from Harlin MS 4011) in *The Babees Book, The Bokes of Nurture of Hugh Rhodes and John Russell, etc.,* ed. Frederick J. Furnivall *EETS* o.s. 32 (London: N. Trübner & Co., 1868; rpt. New York: Greenwood Press, 1969), especially pp. 66–68 and 139–75.

16   *Lucas the Boteler.* This significant character — who is usually named Lucan, not Lucas — holds the important position of King's Butler, making him one of the highest-ranking officials in the royal court. Normally a "butler" was responsible for overseeing the provisioning of a nobleman's hall.

20   *the yonge bachelers.* "Bachelors" are young noblemen training for knighthood. Chaucer's Squire in the *Canterbury Tales*, the son of the pilgrim Knight, is similarly described as a "lusty bacheler" (*CT* I.80).

82–83   *felisship of the table of Logres.* This refers to the best of Arthur's knights, who are taking a brief respite from the tournament. The use of the word "table" may simply be a mistake — since these are clearly not the Knights of the Round Table, who at this time are with King Leodegan in Tamelide — or it may just imply that these knights are bound together in knightly fellowship.

93   *This tecche . . . . he dide of sowke.* Kay's habit of "evil speech" stems from the fact that he was taken away from his mother and nursed by a woman of low birth, so that Arthur could be nursed by Kay's mother. This is part of the debt that Arthur owes to Kay and his family.

106–07   *cride "Clarence," the signe of Kynge Arthur.* "Clarence" is Arthur's battle cry, used to spur on his troops in the heat of battle. In some medieval accounts of

349

the Arthur Story, however, "Clarence" is said to be the name of another of
Arthur's swords; see *The Alliterative Morte Arthure*, lines 4193–4205.

170   *the wordes that Merlin hadde hym tolde.* Merlin, apparently, has already informed Arthur about the difficulties that Ulfin and Bretell experienced in delivering Arthur's message to King Ban and King Bors.

The Battle of Bredigan Forest

[Fols. 47v (line 21)–58r (line 27)]

The Battle of Bredigan Forest and its immediate aftermath is also described at length in
Malory's *Morte D'Arthur* (Vinaver, pp. 16–26). It is one of Arthur's most decisive victo-
ries against the rebel barons, and it depicts great feats of arms by Arthur, Ban, Bors, and
several other prominent knights. It also presents Merlin in several distinctive roles — as
magician, military strategist, moral conscience, and shape-shifting prankster. Near the
end of this episode Arthur has a sexual encounter with a young woman named Lysanor;
Arthur's illegitimate son Hoot results from that union.

Summary Based on *EETS* 21, pp. 140–52.

3   *the eleven kynges.* Earlier there were six (or seven) lesser kings opposing
Arthur; now they have been joined by five more, thus increasing the forces
against Arthur.

Summary Based on *EETS* 21, pp. 155–59.

Summary Based on *EETS* 21, pp. 160–64.

124   *And than com Merlin and seide.* Merlin checks Arthur's pursuit of his enemies
at this point and directs him to return home, thus bringing the battle to an end.
There may be a hint of disapproval in Merlin's words to Arthur, but if so, it is
not nearly so explicit as the direct rebuke that occurs in Malory, where Merlin
says: "'Hast thou nat done inow? Of three score thousande thys day hast thou

leffte on lyve but fyftene thousand! Therefore hit ys tyme to sey, "Who!" for God ys wroth with the for thou woll never have done'" (Vinaver, p. 24).

132   *Blase seide he dide but foly.* Apparently Blase has misgivings about the extent to which Merlin has become involved in Arthur's activities. There is no hint of this in Malory.

159–60   *sente agein alle knyghtes and squyres . . . saf forty.* At this point Arthur dismisses his army, keeping only a core group of forty knights with him. This group of forty, along with Arthur and Merlin, become Arthur's famous "Forty-two" who perform impressive deeds subsequently at Tamelide.

193   *Who hath tolde this cherll?* The kings are astonished to discover that this rustic figure knows about the treasure that is hidden in the earth, and they wonder who could have told him.

249–50   *he is dowted of many a man.* Merlin's supernatural powers, such as the shape-shifting abilities he demonstrates in this episode, cause many people to fear him; and as this passage goes on to indicate, there are many people who would like to see Merlin dead.

261   *Arthur aqueynted hym with a mayden.* Arthur's brief affair with Lysanor (in Malory she is named *Lyonors*) results in the begetting of Hoot (in Malory named *Borre*, and elsewhere named *Loholt* or *Lohoot*), who later becomes a good knight of the Round Table. This is presumably the same man mentioned by Malory in the healing of Sir Urry episode called "sir Boarte le Cure Hardy that was kynge Arthurs son" (Vinaver, p. 667). It is notable that Merlin assists Arthur in his affair with Lysanor and that there is no suggestion of moral disapproval.

The Young Squires

[Fols. 58r (line 28)–65r (line 34)]

The Young Squires introduced in this section of the *PM* are the sons or close relatives of the rebelling barons; but unlike their fathers or uncles, they take up arms in support of Arthur, not against him. Hoping to be knighted by Arthur, they set off to find him and offer their support. The author emphasizes the noble lineage of these young men and describes the circumstances that prompt them to set off in search of Arthur. The Young Squires' brave deeds against the Saxon invaders are depicted in the sections that follow.

Also occurring in this section is the important episode concerning the begetting of Mordred; he is the fifth son of King Lot's wife but is fathered by Arthur. This event is told as a flashback, and the author's intention is to suggest that both Arthur and King Lot's wife are essentially blameless. Arthur is portrayed as an exuberant, lusty youth, while Lot's wife does not realize she has slept with someone other than her husband until Arthur confesses it to her later.

9   *Bandemagu.* This character is more commonly known in Arthurian works as Bagdemagus or Baugdemagus. Early in Malory he is called Sir Bagdemagus and later Kynge Bagdemagus. In Chrétien's *Lancelot*, as in Malory, he is the father of Meleagant (Mellyagaunce in Malory), the evil knight who abducts Queen Guenevere.

Summary Based on *EETS* 21, pp. 172–77.

22–23   *Basyne, the wif of Kynge Ventres.* In Malory, the woman who marries King Ventres of the land of Garlot is named Elaine; in both the *PM* and Malory she is said to be Arthur's half-sister and one of the daughters of Ygerne and the Duke of Tintagel.

24–25   *two hundred fifty Knyghtes of the Rounde Table.* The number of Round Table knights varies from work to work, and here the author suggests the number was 250. Malory states the number was 150, not 250.

43–44   *I have herde my moder sey.* This description of Ygerne's great sorrow at the loss of her son is a poignant humanizing detail; it does not occur in Malory.

Commentary

82–88   *Kynge Loot . . . frely yaf hem all . . . were come of.* The writer praises King Lot's noble qualities and emphasizes the fact that his sons inherit their noble qualities from their father. Malory is far less charitable in his characterization of King Lot; he never portrays Lot as coming to see the error of his ways, nor does he describe any reconciliation between Lot and Arthur. In Malory, Lot lives and dies a villain.

93–94   *Mordred . . . that the Kynge Arthur begat.* The author of the *PM* offers a very different account of the begetting of Mordred from the one given by Malory. As he says, "moche peple it preyse the lesse that knowe not the trouthe" (lines 96–97) and his clear intention in this little digression is to set the record straight and to do all he can to exculpate both parties from harsh moral judgments. Malory has no such intention; indeed, Malory suggests that Arthur's adulterous and incestous act will have dramatic and disastrous consequences.

98   *Hit befill in the tyme that.* In the *PM* the begetting of Mordred occurs before Arthur has even become a knight; in Malory it occurs after Arthur has become king, after his liaison with Lyonors, and after he has seen and fallen in love with Guenevere. In neither work, though, does Arthur know that Lot's wife is also his own half-sister.

154–55   *of hym deviseth no more here saf only of a tecche that he hadde.* Gawain's waxing and waning strength, one of his most famous attributes in medieval Arthurian literature, is here detailed. Although the *PM* author's account is a little confusing, it appears that Gawain's great strength doubles once by the time it is fully *prime* (the period from 6 to 9 a.m.); doubles again by the completion of *tierce* (the period from 9 to 12 a.m.); and doubles yet again by *mydday* (the period from 12 a.m. to 3 p.m.), when the sun has reached its zenith. Then his strength decreases by the similar amounts at similar intervals. Here the term *noone* seems to refer to the period extending from 3 p.m. until 6 p.m. Some scholars interpret this linking of Gawain's strength to the strength of the sun as suggesting that Gawain was originally a solar deity.

      In Malory the first mention of Gawain's waxing and waning strength occurs in his fight against the Irish knight Sir Marhaus: "But sir Gawayne, fro hit was nine of the clok, wexed ever strenger and strenger, for by than hit cam to the howre of noone he had three tymes his myght encresed. And all this aspyed sir Marhaus and had grete wondir how his myght encreced. And so they wounded eyther other passyng sore. So whan hit was past noone, and whan it drew toward evynsonge, sir Gawayns strenght fyebled and woxe passyng faynte, that unnethe he myght dure no lenger, and sir Marhaus was bygger and bygger" (Vinaver, p. 96). Late in Malory's *Morte D'Arthur*, Lancelot will perceive the variability of Gawain's strength and will use this to his own advantage in his fights against Gawain.

200–01   *by I ones oute of my fader house, I will.* Gawain here swears an oath that he will not return until he has brought peace between his father (King Lot) and his uncle (King Arthur); later in the *PM* he makes good on this vow.

206   *And than seide Agravain.* From the outset Agravain is characterized as a brash and outspoken young man. In this instance, his chiding of Gawain stems from noble instincts, but later on his outspokenness causes trouble. Malory charges Agravain with being "ever opynne-mowthed" (Vinaver, p. 612) and considers him one of the parties most responsible for the downfall of Arthurian society (Vinaver, p. 669).

Summary Based on *EETS* 21, pp. 184–86.

239–40   *Renomee, . . . so that every contrey spake of the Kynge Arthur.* The spread of Arthur's fame, and the attraction that Arthur's court held to noble young men everywhere, was first suggested by Geoffrey of Monmouth in *The History of the Kings of Britain*: "Arthur then began to increase his personal entourage by inviting very distinguished men from far-distant kingdoms to join it. In this way he developed such a code of courtliness in his household that he inspired peoples living far away to imitate him" (Thorpe, p. 222).

Summary Based on *EETS* 21, pp. 187–88.

Summary Based on *EETS* 21, pp. 189–91.

Commentary

The Deeds of the Young Squires

[Fols. 65r (line 35)–69r (line 30)]

In an episode unique to the *PM*, the Young Squires hold the Saxon invaders at bay while Arthur is absent from Logres. Nothing of this kind occurs in the Geoffrey of Monmouth or in the other chronicle accounts, nor does it occur in later renditions such as Malory's. Here these yet-to-be knighted youths prove themselves deserving of knighthood, and their noble actions also lay the groundwork for the later reconciliation between Arthur and the rebel barons. Especially emphasized are the great deeds of Gawain, who proves himself a warrior of superior prowess. Here Gawain's great love for his brothers is also depicted, especially for Gaheris, who corresponds to Malory's Gareth. Besides describing the heroic deeds of the Squires, this section of the *PM* offers a realistic portrayal of the devastation that could be visited on the land by a foraging, pillaging army.

1   *aboute the entré of May.* This passage depicting the season of May, while highly conventional, reflects the joy at the coming of spring so often expressed in medieval literature, especially in lyric poetry. It brings to mind the opening verses of Chaucer's *Canterbury Tales* as well as Malory's famous passages on the merry month of May (Vinaver, pp. 648–49; 673).

14–15   *wherof was grete pité . . . for myslyvinge.* This is one of the few places in the *PM* where the writer suggests that the Saxons are a divine scourge sent to punish the British for their sins. This remark is reminiscent of the attitude toward his fellow countrymen expressed by the sixth-century British monk Gildas, who bitterly denounced the sinfulness of the British in *De Excidio Britonum* (The Ruin of Britain).

66   *neded hym no salve.* This is ironic understatement, of course, for it would take more than salve to help anyone who had been on the receiving end of a direct blow from Gawain's ax.

83   *that ther were dwellynge.* The reference is to the local British inhabitants whom the Young Squires have enlisted to take the baggage train, now recaptured from the Saxons, back to the city.

355

99–100   *he was of merveilouse prowesse . . . to Gawein his brother.* Gaheris (Malory's
Gareth) is usually the youngest of King Lot's sons, while Gawain is the oldest.
It is pointed out here that in time Gaheris will prove himself to be Gawain's
equal in prowess. Indeed, in Malory Gareth reaches the point where he surpasses his older brother, not only in physical prowess but in chivalric virtue.

131–32   *Seinte Marie Virgin . . . ne suffre not that I lese my brother.* The fact that
Gawain offers a prayer to the Virgin may simply be what any medieval Christian would do in similar circumstances. However, in some other Arthurian
works, particularly *Sir Gawain and the Green Knight*, Gawain is shown to
have a special association with Mary and is even described as being Mary's
knight. In any case, Gawain is especially distraught here because it is Gaheris,
the brother he loves most, who is in danger of being killed. When Gareth is
killed in the final section of Malory's *Morte D'Arthur*, Gawain is inconsolable.

167   *two Scottissh myle.* According to the OED, the Scottish mile was somewhat
longer than the English mile. It is now obsolete as a measure of distance,
unlike the Irish mile (also different from the English mile) which still survives.
In "Merlin's Imprisonment" the *PM* writer uses the phrases *two Walsh myle*
(line 124) and *half a Walissh myle* (lines 152–53) .

231   *ye shall se my strokes and my prowesse double.* It is not clear whether Gawain
means that he intends to double his efforts, or if he is actually referring to the
fact that his strength increases during the day as the heat of the sun increases.

Arthur at Tamelide

[Fols. 69r (line 31)–90r (line 11)]

The mission of "the Forty-two Soldiers" (Arthur, Merlin, and the Forty Companions) to
assist King Leodegan in his war against King Rion is yet another section of the narrative
that is largely unique to the *PM*. One of its central purposes is to introduce Arthur to his
future wife Gonnore, the daughter of King Leodegan. Geoffrey of Monmouth, one of the
first writers to mention Arthur's wife, offered little information about her except to say

that she was descended from a noble Roman family and was the most beautiful woman in Britain (Thorpe, p. 221); but the author of the *PM* tells us a great deal about Gonnore's parents and about the night when she and her notorious half-sister, known as the "False Gonnore," were begotten by Leodegan. Malory, on the other hand, reduces all of the material in this section to a mere ten lines, and one has the impression that he prefers to avoid the attractive and appealing descriptions provided by this author of Arthur and Gonnore falling in love. Malory simply says, "And there had Arthure the firste syght of queene Gwenyvere, the kyngis doughter of the londe of Camylarde, and ever afftir he loved hir" (Vinaver, p. 26).

21–22   *alle yonge bacheleres at pryme barbe.* Arthur and his companions (other than Ban, Bors, and Merlin) are all in the first stage of young adulthood; they are youthful knights proudly sporting their first beards (their *pryme barbe*).

30   *not to knowe oure names.* Knights choosing to conceal their identities until after they have proved themselves is a narrative device that occurs often in medieval romances. One of the most famous examples is in Malory's "Tale of Gareth."

73   *at the Ascencion.* Ascension Day, commemorating Christ's Ascension into heaven, is the fortieth day after Easter (see Acts 1:9).

81–82   *in tho dayes fyve hundred was cleped a thousande.* The writer may be uneasy about the extremely large numbers of warriors involved in these battles; this appears to be an attempt to preserve credibility.

104–06   *a smal ganfanon . . . crownes of golde.* Both the smaller standard that Cleodalis bears and the larger one that Hervy bears display typical medieval heraldic devices. The smaller banner has two red diamond-shapes ("losenges") displayed on a field of gold, along with two blue crowns; the description of the great banner is less specific, but it seems to have four diamond-shapes (also on a field of gold?) with gold crowns inside the losenges.

285   *to reherse the names of tho worthi men.* Long catalogs listing the names of knights are common in Arthurian literature. Chrétien, for example, provided catalogs in *Erec* of the best of Arthur's knights and of the people attending Erec's wedding. Perhaps the most famous catalog of knights is Malory's listing of the knights who attempt to heal Sir Urry (Vinaver pp. 665–67). There is no group of knights in Malory corresponding to the Forty-two Soldiers of the *PM*, but during the Battle of Bredigan Forest Malory does list twenty-one knights who performed well there, and most of them are included in this list of the Forty-two.

321–22   *a Feste of Seint John.* This would probably be the Feast of John the Baptist, celebrated on June 24, rather than December 27, the saint's day commemorating St. John the Divine (Christ's disciple).

326   *that was cleped Gonnore.* The name of Leodegan's daughter, the woman who will become Arthur's wife, occurs in a variety of forms in medieval literature. In the early Welsh legends she is called Gwenhwyvar; in Geoffrey of Monmouth she is Guanhumora; in Malory her name is Gwenyvere. But the form used in the *PM*, Gonnore, is one of the more common forms of her name in medieval Arthurian works.

329–30   *to sey Matyns and to heere all servyse to messe.* Leodegan's wife is a very devout woman whose custom is to attend all the religious services of the day, beginning with matins (the earliest service, often sung at 2 a.m.) and on until Mass when the Eucharist is celebrated.

337   *and than he . . . bad hir be stille.* Although medieval rulers often took great liberties with their subjects, Leodegan's behavior here is deplorable. And, as often happens in medieval and Renaissance stories, the child conceived in such a circumstance — in this case "the False Gonnore" — will turn out to be morally corrupt, as in the famous instances of Mordred and the bastard Edmund in Shakespeare's *King Lear*.

342–43   *upon the childes reynes a litill crosse like a crowne for a kynge.* The true Gonnore possesses a tiny birthmark, the only physical difference between these virtually identical half-sisters; later on, of course, Gonnore's birthmark will provide the means by which the sisters are distinguished.

Summary Based on *EETS* 21, pp. 214–24.

453–54   *be ye not abaisshed at youre sopere.* Gonnore's remark is said in the spirit of light-hearted banter — "you should not be frightened by your supper, a man like you who today showed no fear of the Saxons."

506–07   *saf only Helayn that was withouten pere.* Gonnore, the writer claims, surpasses all the women of Britain in beauty and virtue except for one — Elaine, the daughter of King Pelles, the niece of the Fisher King and the Maimed King, and the mother of Sir Galahad.

508–09   *the Kynge Pesceor and of the seke kynges wounded.* King Pesceor is the Fisher King, and the "sick wounded king" is his brother Alain, also known as the Maimed King.

510   *the spere vengeresse.* This is the weapon by which Alain is wounded through both thighs; Malory calls the event in which this wounding takes place the striking of the "dolorouse stroke" (Vinaver, pp. 53–54).

Summary Based on *EETS* 21, pp. 229–57.

Merlin and the Young Squires

[Fols. 90r (line 12)–103v (line 29)]

Making considerable use of his shape-shifting abilities, Merlin tests the mettle of the Young Squires; Gawain, in particular, proves himself up to the challenge. Here Sir Sagremor, who has come all the way from Constantinople to be knighted by Arthur, establishes himself as one of the best young knights within the group also.

359

87–88   *lefte theire palfreyes and lepe upon stedes.* Here the young knights exchange
their riding horses (their palfreys) for their warhorses (their steeds).

Summary Based on *EETS* 21, pp. 271–95.

Gawain's Rescue of his Mother

[Fols. 103v (line 29)–106v (line 15)]

In this brief but dramatic episode, King Lot and his wife and their baby son Mordred
flirt with disaster when they leave the safety of the city in an attempt to escape the
Saxons. Gawain, prodded by Merlin who appears in yet another of his guises, performs a
daring rescue of his mother, who has been captured and vilely mistreated by a Saxon
named Taurus. What is perhaps most significant about this section is the way it reveals the
powerful bond of kinship that exists among the members of Gawain's family. By the end
of this section, Gawain is determined to use those powerful feelings as leverage in bringing about a reconciliation between his father King Lot and his uncle King Arthur.

9–10   *But he desired it not gretly . . . distroied all environ.* Prior to besieging the city,
the Saxon King Arans accompanies his troops as they lay waste to the surrounding countryside. Realizing this, King Lot and his group decide to make a
run for it before the siege commences.

30   *Than the squyer fledde.* This is the squire who is carrying Mordred in his
cradle. The squire's quick response prevents Mordred from falling into the
Saxons' hands.

34   *a knyght right well armed.* It comes as no surprise when we learn later that this
"knight" is Merlin.

105–06   *Seint Marie, . . . helpe me and socour!* Prayers to the Virgin to aid one in their
hour of need are very common and reflect the important role of Mary as Inter-
cessor. Compare Gawain's prayer to the Virgin in *Sir Gawain and the Green
Knight* (lines 736–39), when he prays to find lodging on Christmas Eve.

136–37   *for it was not inough to hem . . . smale peces.* After Gawain has killed Taurus, his brothers vent their anger by mutilating the body of the man who had abused their mother. Whether or not this gruesome scene foreshadows what Malory calls their "vengeable" natures (Vinaver, p. 224), it certainly attests to their powerful emotions.

139   *Gawein slough so many . . . blode and brayn.* This description of Gawain covered with blood and gore has a close parallel in Malory in his description of Arthur during the Battle at Bredigan Forest: "And kynge Arthure was so blody that by hys shylde there myght no man know hym, for all was blode and brayne that stake on his swerd and on hys shylde" (Vinaver, p. 22).

185–86   *And the foure bretheren swore . . . theire uncle.* Here Gawain and his brothers hit upon the plan to use their mother as a bargaining chip in securing the peace between King Lot and King Arthur.

Merlin and Nimiane

[Fols. 106v (line 16)–109v (line 22)]

In this section Merlin has his initial encounter with the young woman who will prove his undoing. The author of the *PM* provides far more information about the developing relationship between Merlin and Nimiane than does Malory, surrounds it with greater moral complexity, and brings the two together under very different circumstances. In Malory, the young woman named Nenyve, who is said to be one of the damsels of the Lady of the Lake (Vinaver, p. 76), is first brought to Arthur's court by Pellynore; and Malory treats Merlin's fatal attraction to her, and her attempts to avoid his designs on her, in less than two pages. In the *PM*, Merlin goes to Brittany to seek her out, after first informing Blase that in that land is "the wolf" (Nimiane) who will bind "the leopard" (Merlin).

16   *the two remes of Benoyk and Gannes.* Benoyk and Gannes are the two small kingdoms in Brittany ruled by King Ban and King Bors. They are vulnerable because Ban and Bors are in Britain helping Arthur deal with the rebellious

barons. (Later on in the story King Ban fathers Lancelot and his half-brother Estor, and King Bors fathers Bors, Lionel, Blamour, and Bleoberis.)

27–31   *"And yet," quod Merlin . . . he shall not meve.* Here Merlin obliquely foretells his own demise at the hands of Nimiane, who will bind him in "circles" made of no earthly material. The closest parallel to this prediction in Malory occurs when Merlin informs Arthur that Arthur will die a worshipful death, but Merlin will "dye a shamefull dethe, to be putte in the erthe quycke" (Vinaver, p. 29). In both cases the clear suggestion is that despite his foreknowing, there is nothing Merlin can do to avoid his fate.

42–48   *the merveillouse leopart . . . ordenaunce of God.* Here Merlin predicts the coming of Lancelot (the leopard), who will father the greatest of the Grail Knights, Galahad (the lion). Merlin knows that his responsibilities, which require him to go to Brittany, will also lead to his downfall; indeed, if he were not obligated to fulfill God's "ordenaunce," Merlin would prefer not to go there at all.

Summary   Based on *EETS* 21, pp. 305–07

61–62   *Diane . . . the goddesse.* There is a curious, though not unusual, blending of mythologies here. It is not made clear why Dionas is the goddess Diana's godson, but it *is* clear that Diana has plans of her own for Dionas's daughter. Since Diana is the moon goddess — i.e., "The White Goddess" — Nimiane's abilities and designs may be informed by paganism.

76   *the deduyt of the wode and the river.* Dionas's love of hunting and hawking (which often occurred along the edge of a river) identifies him as a young nobleman of aristocratic tastes, as does his building of a manor house in the forest to which he can "repair."

85   *[and] hym served with nine knyghtes.* Dionas appears to be one of ten knights who are most esteemed by King Ban; for his service in the war against Claudas de la deserte, Dionas is richly rewarded by both King Ban and King Bors.

96   *And this turned upon Merlin.* Nimiane's name — which means "I shall not lie" — is rather ironic, since she "turns" Merlin's infatuation to her own advantage and to Merlin's considerable disadvantage.

104–06   *and thought . . . God to lese and displese.* As this passage reveals, Merlin is fully aware of the danger in allowing his reason to be seduced by his sensuality. He knows it is sinful; he knows he will shame himself; he knows he will displease God — yet he is unable to stop himself from proceeding.

108   *That lorde that alle thoughtes knoweth.* In her welcoming remarks to Merlin, Nimiane suggests that she is aware of the powers he possesses, and hints at her willingness to grant him what she knows he desires.

127   *by covenaunt that . . . youre love.* Here Nimiane states her intentions quite clearly, although promising to be his love does not necessarily imply her willingness to give him her physical love; Merlin is quick to accept her offer.

131   *that noon evell ne thought.* The text is ambiguous in regard to which of them expected no harm to come from it, and it might be argued that young Nimiane is the naive one. But in the larger context of this passage, it seems fairly clear that it is Merlin who is being led down the garden path by the young woman rather than the other way round.

145–46   *Vraiement . . . dolours.* In a piece of ironic foreshadowing, the singers Merlin has conjured up provide a perfect description of what will occur in Merlin's affair with Nimiane in the refrain of their song.

187–88   *and ye also for to do my plesier of what I will.* Now Merlin asks that she be willing to give him *whatever* he wishes, a more explicit indication of his desire for her physical love. After a moment's thought Nimiane assents, on the condition that she will be able to perform herself all the things that she asks him to teach her. Falling into her trap, Merlin readily agrees.

Prose Merlin

Arthur and Gonnore; and The Battle against King Rion

[Fols. 109v (line 23)–128v (line 12)]

The author of the *PM* treats the initial phase of the Arthur-Gonnore relationship at great length and with great tenderness, in contrast to Malory, who describes it in just two sentences — "And there had Arthure the firste sighte of queene Gwenyvere, the kyngis doughter of the londe of Camylarde, and ever aftir he love hir. And aftir they were wedded, as hit tellith in the booke" (Vinaver, p. 26). Especially important in this section is Gonnore's desire to attend upon Arthur as he is armed for battle; and as Merlin insists, Arthur's arming is not completed until he has been armed with Gonnore's kiss.

The battle with King Rion is also treated at great length in the *PM*, although we have summarized much of it here. One especially notable aspect of the battle concerns King Rion's weapons. While it is mentioned at one point that he carries a huge ax, King Rion's preferred weapon is his *betill* of brass, a mighty hammer or club. Only after Arthur has destroyed the club does Rion resort to using his famous sword "Marmyadoise," about which the author provides a detailed background account. After King Rion loses his acclaimed sword to Arthur, Arthur delights in using it himself.

Summary Based on *EETS* 21, pp. 312–17.

102   *the dragon.* This is the same fire-breathing battle standard that Merlin had used so effectively in earlier battles.

112–16 *Ydiers . . . yow declare hereafter.* Here the writer alludes to a marvelous deed that Ydiers will perform at a later time, when he will be able to do what no one else in Arthur's court can do — remove five rings from a dead man's hand. Ydiers's deed is similar to other one-of-a-kind deeds in Arthurian literature such as Balyn's extracting the sword from the sheath and Lancelot's healing of Sir Urry.

131   *the two Gonnores.* As will be explained more fully later, Gonnore has a half-sister (also named Gonnore) who is practically her twin. They differ only slightly in physical appearance, but the real Gonnore surpasses her sister in virtue and

courteous speaking. One physical difference not noted here is Gonnore's birth-mark, which will serve as an important recognition token later on.

147 *Bertelaux the traitour*. The initial phase of the Bertelaux (or Bertelak) story will soon be related in the *PM*. The later phase of his story, in which he commits his acts of treachery, occurs when he seeks revenge on Arthur for the harsh punishment he received for his alleged crime. It is probable that this figure is connected in some way to Bertilak de Hautdesert in *Sir Gawain and the Green Knight*.

Summary Based on *EETS* 21, pp. 326–38.

296–97 *it was som tyme Hercules*. King Rion's sword "Marmyadoise" had once belonged to Hercules, who is also King Rion's distant ancestor. This sword is a weapon of great distinction; it was originally made by Vulcan and subsequently owned by many men of great renown.

339–43 *oon may never passe . . . it moste be fallen*. This obscure passage seems to suggest that no one will be able to pass beyond King Rion's realm — i.e., Iceland — until the laws established by Judas Maccabeus (hero of 1 and 2 Maccabees in the Old Testament, and one of the Nine Worthies) are nullified by a Grail Knight (presumably Galahad), who will succeed in passing through the gates of the Gulf of Satan.

Summary Based on *EETS* 21, pp. 342–46.

Summary Based on *EETS* 21, pp. 347–59.

Summary Based on *EETS* 21, pp. 360–63.

Prose Merlin

Arthur and Gawain

[Fols. 128v (line 12)–134r (line 18)]

In this section of the *PM* Arthur and Gawain finally meet. Arthur is so impressed by his nephew that he formally invests him as the king's constable, a position of great honor as well as of great authority. In addition, what the Young Squires have so fervently desired — to be knighted by Arthur — finally occurs. In formal knighting ceremonies each of them receives a new sword and his spurs (the symbol of knighthood), which are ceremoniously attached to his feet by the attending kings. Gawain has the supreme honor of being given Arthur's sword Calibourne.

Once again there is little here that has a direct counterpart in Malory's *Morte D'Arthur*. In Malory, Gawain requests that Arthur make him a knight on the same day that Arthur weds the queen (Vinaver, p. 60); but when the king knights Sir Pellinor's son Torre ahead of Gawain, Gawain feels slighted and insulted. No others are knighted at this time in Malory; indeed, Gawain's younger brothers are yet to figure in the story at all.

Summary Based on *EETS* 21, pp. 363–70.

3   *the tresour.* This refers to the buried treasure that Merlin had revealed to Arthur and Ban and Bors earlier.

59–63   *for to a goode man . . . in hym is.* Gawain seems to be saying that it is right to report honorable and virtuous deeds to a good man (one such as Arthur); but it is better not to do so to a wicked leader, for he will be unappreciative and will fail to reward such deeds appropriately.

83   *the name of the lesse that is short and fatte.* In the description of the Young Squires, the author (in Gawain's words) makes some attempt to individualize the young men on the basis of their physical appearance. Thus one is said to be short, another tall, another darker complexioned, and so on. Sagremor is singled out particularly for his "great beauty" and well-shaped body.

105   *right wellcome [. . .].* About three words at the end of Arthur's speech are indecipherable in the MS.

107–08   *"Gawein, feire nevewe . . . I yow enffeffe."* Here, in formal feudalistic terms (*"I yow enffeffe"*), Arthur bestows upon Gawain the constableship of his household and the lordship of his lands. Gawain is thus established as one of Arthur's most important liegemen.

121   *The same nyght.* An important part of the spiritual preparation for knighthood is the vigil that young knights-to-be must observe on the night prior to their knighting. The knighting ceremony itself occurs the next morning and is followed by a high Mass.

126   *Arthur toke Calibourne.* During the knighting ceremony a young knight is given his sword and his spurs. Here Arthur bestows a very special honor on Gawain by giving him his own sword Calibourne. Arthur then attaches Gawain's right spur, and King Ban attaches the left one. Finally, Arthur gives Gawain the "acolee," an embrace signifying his entry into the chivalric brotherhood of knights. The other knights are given swords from the treasure that Merlin had directed them to, with the exception of Sagremor, who has brought a special family heirloom from Constantinople for this purpose.

The Begetting of Lancelot; and Merlin and Nimiane

[Fols. 134r (line 19)–158v (line 4)]

After Arthur and his men help to repulse the attack on Benoyk and Gannes mounted by the several enemies of King Ban and King Bors, Merlin is called upon to interpret a pair of prophetic dreams, one experienced by Ban's wife Heleyne, and one by Ban himself. Although the dreams are enigmatic and Merlin refrains from explicating them fully, it is clear that the leopard in the queen's dream represents Lancelot, who has been conceived on that very night. King Ban's dream is not as fully related as the queen's, but the voice he hears is apparently providing an affirmative answer to what he had prayed for earlier, that he be allowed to die on the day that he desires it.

This episode does not occur in *Morte D'Arthur*, although Malory does briefly describe a visit Merlin makes to Benwyke in which he meets King Ban's wife and has his first sight of Lancelot as a young boy: "And there Merlion spake with kyng Bayans wyff, a fayre lady and a good; and hir name was Elayne. And there he saw yonge Launcelot. And there the queene made grete sorowe for the mortal werre that kynge Claudas made on hir lord and on hir londis" (Vinaver, p. 76).

Near the end of this section, Merlin goes once more to visit Nimiane, who now asks him to teach her how to accomplish some very particular things. Merlin knows very well why she wants to learn those things; he teaches her anyway, because he also knows he can deny her nothing.

Summary Based on *EETS* 36, pp. 379–411.

10   *the Newe Knyghtes*. This phrase is used to refer to the young men previously called the Young Squires. Now the New Knights, and the Knights of the Round Table (Uther's knights who had been with Leodegan), and the Forty Fellows (or Forty Soldiers or Forty Companions, Arthur's original core of knights) are the three main groups within Arthur's forces.

28   *Queene Heleyne conceyved a childe . . . Kynge Ban*. The child she conceives is Lancelot; and in her dream that follows, he is represented by the leopard who becomes involved in the struggle between the crowned lion and the uncrowned lion.

44–45   *four hundred boles*. The 400 bulls represent Arthur's knights. In a very different context, Arthur's knights are also represented by bulls in Gawain's dream during the Grail section in Malory. In his vision in *Morte D'Arthur*, Gawain sees 150 bulls, almost all of which are black. He also sees three white bulls, representing the three successful Grail Knights (Vinaver, pp. 558–59).

93   *he synne dedly in avoutré*. King Ban learns in his dream that on one occasion he will succumb to the sin of adultery. This event is subsequently described in the *PM* when, by means of Merlin's enchantment, Ban sleeps with the daughter of Agravadain ly Noir, who then conceives Estor (Ector de Maris), Lancelot's half-brother. Because Ban was not personally responsible for his sinning, God forgives him.

Commentary

127–28 *Merlin hym tolde even as the kynge hadde mette.* Merlin has the ability to relate both the queen's and king's dreams, even though no one has told them to him.

174 *sette upon an ympe.* This may mean that Merlin and Nimiane are sitting on the branch of a tree, but more likely they are sitting beneath the tree.

175 *the mayden made hym to slepe in hir lappe.* Perhaps Nimiane has simply lulled Merlin to sleep with his head in her lap; or perhaps she is trying out her newly-acquired ability to cause a person to sleep. There is nothing overtly sexual in the phrase "to slepe in hir lappe," and as we discover below, the author asserts that Merlin never required any sexual favors from Nimiane.

179 *he taught hir thre names.* Merlin gives Nimiane three magic names, or perhaps phrases, to protect her from being harmed sexually. It is likely that she believes she needs them in order to protect herself from Merlin.

185 *we fynde not . . . eny vylonye of hir.* The author of the *PM* declares there is no evidence in any written work to suggest that Merlin ever desired Nimiane (or any other woman) to engage in sex with him. But it is also clear that Nimiane suspected that that is precisely what he desired from her. Malory, on the other hand, offers a very different view of Merlin's intentions, stating of Merlin that "allwayes he lay aboute to have hir maydynhode . . . " (Vinaver, p. 77).

188 *of thinges paste.* In his mentoring of Nimiane, Merlin teaches her about things that have happened, about things that are happening, and about things that will happen in the future.

Summary Based on *EETS* 36, pp. 419–20.

Merlin and Grisandolus

[Fols. 148v (line 12)–158v (line 4)]

This largely self-contained episode allows Merlin to showcase his multifarious talents as prankster, shape-shifter, prophet, philosopher, and moral counselor; and it also provides some important information concerning the conflict that will develop before much longer between Britain and Rome. But the most intriguing aspect of this episode, in all likelihood, is the daring young woman named Avenable. Having been separated from her family, she turns up in Rome disguised as a young man named Grisandolus. By virtue of her abilities Grisandolus becomes knighted, and shortly thereafter he/she is appointed by the emperor to be the steward of Rome. By the time the events in this episode reach a conclusion, her true identity and her true sex have been revealed; and in the end, Avenable/ Grisandolus marries the emperor of Rome — all of which may seem reminiscent of Shakespearean comedies, such as *Twelfth Night*.

4   *it was that Julius.* Arthur's later victory over the Romans is here foreshadowed, although the Roman leader that Gawain will kill is Lucius, not Julius.

18   *This mayden com in semblaunce of a squyer.* There are a great many stories and episodes in medieval and Renaissance literature involving cross-dressing, particularly ones in which a young woman is disguised as a man; but this story, which probably derives from an independent source, is one of the few to find its way into Arthurian narrative.

64   *five braunches.* The hart that Merlin has transformed himself into has a very impressive rack of antlers.

108   *that by . . . hir cleped.* The hart has addressed the steward by her true name — Avenable — rather than as Grisandolus, the name by which she is known in Rome.

226–38   *This is the trouthe . . . what I am.* The savage man's account of his begetting, birth, and Christian baptism provides a rough analogue to — or perhaps a kind of allegorical version of — his actual birth as it was told in the initial section of the *PM*.

227   *Foreste of Brocheland*. This is the famous Forest of Broceliande, a place of wondrous and mysterious occurrences throughout Arthurian literature.

353   *that a woman hadde*. Merlin is saying that only a woman — not a man — could possess the crafty subtlety of mind needed to ensnare him. This remark anticipates his lecture on the nature of women that soon follows; and it may also provide an oblique comment on Merlin's relationship with Nimiane.

357   *the grettest tresour hidde*. This is the second time in the *PM* that Merlin serves as a kind of divining rod for buried treasure.

382   *But the prophesie seith*. This somewhat misplaced paragraph provides the first installment of Merlin's prophecies concerning the war that will occur between Britain and Rome.

401   *the riche userer*. Following his general comments on the sin of avarice, Merlin offers a more specific commentary on the sin of usury — lending money at exorbitant rates. Medieval texts frequently contain satire against usurers and usury, and also against lawyers, the next group that Merlin will comment on.

410   *who hath a goode neighbour hath goode morowe*. This is the first recorded example of this proverbial saying in English (see Whiting N77); and see its opposite: "Evil neighbor makes evil morn" (Whiting N75). The gist of the proverb is that if you have a good neighbor, you can wake up in the morning knowing that he has not stolen from you during the night.

443   *Province . . . Monpellier*. Montpellier is located in Provence, in southeastern France.

454–55   *the lyon crowned . . . the lyon volage*. Arthur is the crowned lion; and Gawain, presumably, is the *lyon volage* – the youthful (or perhaps over-eager) lion.

454–64   *I tolde yow . . . sle the grete boor.* Merlin now elaborates upon the prophecy he had mentioned earlier concerning the coming warfare between Britain and Rome. In his allegorical depiction of it, the dragon is the Emperor Julius, the turtle is Avenable, and the boar is Lucius; the lion is Arthur, and the fawn that will kill the boar is Gawain. In his earlier comment Merlin had called Gawain a *bole* (bull), not a fawn.

Summary From *EETS* 36, pp. 437–47.

The Marriage of Arthur and Gonnore

[Fols. 158v (line 5)–166v (line 12)]

The *PM*, in contrast to Malory's *Morte D'Arthur*, offers an extensive account of the events surrounding the wedding of Arthur and Gonnore. Included among these events is the Tournament at Toraise, in which feelings of rivalry and jealousy are revealed among the major groups of Arthur's knights. Also described here is the plot to abduct Gonnore and replace her with her half-sister, the False Gonnore. This abduction attempt is foiled through the wits of Merlin and the brave efforts of Sir Ulfin and Sir Bretell. Also introduced here is the figure of Bertelak (who has been alluded to earlier), a man whose cause is just but who makes the grave mistake of taking the law into his own hands and pays a heavy penalty for so doing.

Summary Based on *EETS* 36, pp. 449–52.

127–29   *For dere sholde be bought . . . he ther dide.* As this line suggests, the resentment and envy the Knights of the Round Table harbor toward Gawain and the other young knights will come to a head in the Tournament at Logres, which is described in the next section of the *PM*. In that tournament the rancor reaches such a high level that a great many knights are killed.

Summary Based on *EETS* 36, pp. 455–62.

150–51   *after was the bedde of Arthur blessed.* The final event in the celebration of the nuptials of Arthur and Gonnore, as was often customary for medieval marriages, is the priest's blessing of their wedding bed.

227–28   *the signe of the crowne upon hire reynes.* Gonnore and her half-sister look so much alike that the only sure way to tell them apart is by the crown-shaped birthmark that Gonnore has on her *reynes*. The word "reynes" is the common term for the kidneys, or the seat of emotions, and thus, by metaphoric extension, the loins, where the kidneys (and the passions) find egress.

238–45   *Thus sholde the queene . . . and stode acursed.* The *PM* contains several references to the treachery that will occur later on, when the spiteful Bertelak tricks Arthur into abandoning Gonnore in favor of her sister, the False Gonnore. But the text of the *PM* ends before these events actually occur.

The Banishment of Bertelak; and King Arthur and King Lot

[Fols. 166v (line 13)–172r (line 27)]

Arthur's strife against the rebel barons now nears its end, as King Lot agrees to do homage to Arthur and the two become reconciled. This section is important also for establishing the foundations for a code of knightly conduct, for depicting the ways in which Arthur wishes to conduct his court, and for introducing several of the specific customs of the court. For example, it is here for the first time that Arthur declares he will not eat when he is holding court until he has heard some strange tiding. Here, too, is established the tradition of Arthur's knights returning to the court no later than a year and a day from the time they set out and openly reporting their adventures to the court.

This section of the *PM* begins, however, with the trial of Bertelak le Rous, who was mentioned earlier as a great traitor to Arthur. Bertelak's most serious crime is not that he has killed the man who raped his cousin's wife, but stems from the fact that by taking the law into his own hands he has violated the safe-conduct the king had established during the time surrounding his daughter's wedding. Thus, despite his many good qualities as a knight, he is judged quite harshly by the king's council of barons (which includes Arthur and Gawain), who recommend that he be stripped of his land and banished. As he embarks on his exile, Bertelak arrives by chance at the same abbey where the False Gonnore had taken shelter earlier; and now having been thrown together by chance, the pair of outcasts begin plotting revenge.

12–13   *but firste I dide hym deffie.* Bertelak is saying that he announced his hostile intentions to his enemy in an open and formal manner. Normally, serving such notice to one's enemy in this fashion is the honorable way for a knight to act.

21   *Bertelak le Rous.* Bertelak le Rous, or Bertelak the Rede, may have some relationship to the figure of Bertilak de Hautdesert in *Sir Gawain and the Green Knight.* The two men possess similar knightly attributes; each lives far off in a wild country; each is associated with a wily, attractive temptress; and each becomes involved in a plot to challenge the supremacy of Arthur's court. Bertilak de Hautdesert's "beaver-hued" beard (*Sir Gawain and the Green Knight*, line 845) may even relate to Bertelak's epithet — "le Rous" or "the Red."

35–36   *ye holde court open . . . this high feste.* In addition to taking justice into his own hands, Bertelak has also violated the general safe-conduct that King Leodegan had ordered for the period of time surrounding the royal wedding.

47–50   *And for that fill to Arthur . . . to writen it.* Once again the author alludes to the great difficulties Bertelak will create for Arthur later on; however, the ME version of the *PM* breaks off before reaching this section of the story.

170–76   *for that he was copiouse of langage . . . grete annoye.* The author is very understanding of Kay's joking and jesting nature, as is Arthur; but as the author points out, many of Kay's fellow knights were not so forgiving or understanding, and as a result, they often treated him with malice.

176–81   *But a trewe knyght was he . . . all the dede.* The author suggests that in his lifetime Kay was only guilty of one real act of treachery — the killing of Loholt (or Hoot), the son Arthur had begotten on Lysanor. While this act of treachery is only alluded to in the *PM*, it is actually described in the OF *Perlesvaus.*

185   *the shelde of goolde and azur.* The heraldic device on Gawain's shield is a "lyon rampaunt" (a lion standing upright on its hind legs) in "azur" (blue), displayed on a field of gold. The device on Gawain's famous shield in *Sir Gawain and the Green Knight* is a golden pentangle (five-pointed star) displayed on a field of "gules" (red).

292   *and fro that day forth . . . all her lif.* This reconciliation and newly established friendship between King Lot and King Arthur stands in stark contrast to what occurs in Malory's *Morte D'Arthur*, where King Lot remains Arthur's bitter enemy until he is killed in battle (Vinaver, p. 48).

342–43   *I will stablissh to my courte alle the tymes.* Arthur is declaring that he will hold his high court (those special occasions when he "shall bere crowne") at regular times throughout the year — e.g., at the high feasts of Christmas, Easter, Pentecost, and so on. He also announces that on such occasions he will not sit down to eat until after something unusual has occurred. This famous custom turns up frequently in medieval Arthurian works — e.g., in Chrétien's *Perceval*, in *Sir Gawain and the Green Knight*, and in both the "Gareth" and "Grail" sections in Malory.

356–57   *yef eny maiden have eny nede.* This vow that all of the Knights of the Round Table swear — that they will aid any maiden who comes to the court and requests assistance — becomes one of the fundamental tenets of the Chivalric Code.

377   *the Knyghtes of Queene Gonnore.* Gawain and his fellows wish to establish a special bond of "fealty" with the queen, and the queen is pleased to grant their request. Thus comes into being "The Queen's Knights," an important subgroup within the larger knightly fellowship. In Malory's *Morte D'Arthur* ten of these knights accompany the queen when she goes a-Maying at the beginning of "The Knight of the Cart" episode: "And that tyme was such a custom that the quene rode never wythoute a grete felshyp of men of armys aboute her.

And they were many good knyghtes, and the moste party were yonge men that wolde have worshyp, and they were called the Quenys Knyghtes" (Vinaver, p. 650).

387–93   *And whiche of us so it be . . . in the comynge.* Here Gawain sets guidelines for how his knights will conduct themselves in their individual adventures: they must endeavor to complete their tasks and return to the court within a year and a day, if not sooner; and they must swear that upon their return they will report truthfully all that has happened to them.

399–400   *I putte in youre governance . . . at youre plesier.* This is a remarkable gesture of love and trust on Arthur's part.

413–14   *Dagenet of Clarion.* In Malory, Dagonet appears only in the "Tristrem" section, where he is portrayed as being little more than the court fool. So too in Tennyson's "The Last Tournament."

The Tournament at Logres; King Lot and his Sons; and Morgan and Gyomar

[Fols. 172r (line 28)–199v (line 27)]

This section of the *PM* is unusually rich in characterization, offering glimpses into the individual personalities of Gawain's brothers, in particular Gaheris and Agravain, as well as a glimpse into the character of Arthur's half-sister Morgan le Fay. The brief episode involving Morgan not only reflects her intensely amorous nature, but it also establishes the fact that she can be powerfully vindictive. Indeed, this episode provides an explanation for the great antagonism that develops later between Morgan and Gonnore.

The rancorous dispute that occurs in this section between Gawain's younger brothers serves to do two things — it creates sharp distinctions amongst them, separating them into a highly virtuous pair (Gawain and Gaheris) and a much-less-virtuous pair (Agravain and Gueheret); and it also allows for the introduction of a discussion of proper attitudes and behavior towards women, as Agravain's extremely unchivalrous attitude is played off against Gaheris's more idealistic one. This section is notable, too, for containing the brief episode in which Gawain wins the magnificent horse Gringolet away from one of his Saxon foes.

Summary Based on *EETS* 36, pp. 483–503.

Summary Based on *EETS* 36, pp. 504–06.

88   *But after it knewe the Quene Gonnore.* This later episode occurs in the Vulgate *Lancelot* (Sommer, vol. 4, p. 121). When Gonnore learns of the love affair between Morgan and Gyomar (who is Gonnore's cousin), the queen insists upon breaking it up and forcing the lovers to go their separate ways. As a result, Morgan develops an intense hatred for Gonnore. It should be noted that in Chrétien's *Erec* there is a reference to a man named Guingamar, who is said to be "the friend of Morgan le Fay." It seems probable the figures of Gyomar and Guingamar are closely related.

Summary Based on *EETS* 36, pp. 509–10.

99   *to lepe upon theire horses.* That is, Gawain directs them to shift from their riding horses (their palfreys) to their warhorses. The grooms then take the palfreys into the forest for safekeeping.

Summary Based on *EETS* 36, pp. 510–12.

Summary Based on *EETS* 36, pp. 513–16.

Summary Based on *EETS* 36, pp. 518–25.
      After line 182. *St. Bartholomew's Day.* The Feast of St. Bartholomew (who was one of the twelve Disciples) is celebrated on August 24. In fact, though, the meeting with the barons actually takes place on the Feast of the Nativity of the Virgin Mary, which is September 8.

Summary Based on *EETS* 36, pp. 528–35.

205–06   *Gaheries hath seide beste*. Gawain's judgment on the views of his three broth-
         ers establishes a basic tenet of the knightly code of conduct — that a knight
         should never take a woman by force; for as Gawain says, "ther were no werse
         enmy than he" (lines 208–09). This provision of the Arthurian code of ethics is
         made very explicit in Malory's *Morte D'Arthur*: "Allwayes to do ladyes, dam-
         sels, and jantilwomen and wydowes [socour:] strengthe hem in hir ryghtes,
         and never to enforce them, uppon payne of dethe" (Vinaver, p. 75).

Summary Based on *EETS* 36, pp. 528–35.

263–64   *"Sir," quod Gaheries*. Gaheris's remark is nothing more than a wisecrack in
         which he implies that Agravain is a know-it-all. As this scene makes clear,
         Gaheris has a talent for getting under Agravain's skin.

266–67   *Gaheries remeved not but suffred*. Gaheris stands stock still and suffers the
         blows that Agravain inflicts upon him; and he also refrains from retaliating —
         noble behavior, to be sure, but undoubtely infuriating to his attacker.

Summary Based on *EETS* 36, pp. 538–58.

328–29   *Seint Marie Even*. The Eve of the Feast of the Nativity of the Virgin Mary,
         September 7.

350   *knowe it verily that it cometh thourgh oure synnes*. Beginning with Gildas in the
         sixth century, Arthurian writers frequently suggested that the Saxon invasion
         was visited upon Britain because of the sinful behavior of the British people,
         particularly their leaders. Here it is also suggested that if the barons had only
         accepted Arthur at the outset as God's duly appointed king, they would not
         have had such great difficulties dealing with the Saxons. Hence, they have
         brought their troubles upon themselves.

Commentary

King Arthur vs. King Rion

[Fols. 199v (line 27)–224r (line 12)]

This section contains the grand climax of the *PM*. Now, with the rebellious barons finally pacified and the Saxons invaders finally expelled, the last remaining threat to Britain is posed by King Rion of the Western Isles (Ireland and the other islands west of Britain such as the Isle of Man). It is here that King Rion makes his demand for Arthur's beard, which he needs to complete his mantle that is trimmed with the beards of vanquished kings. This section culminates with King Arthur and King Rion confronting each other in single combat.

Near the close of this section Merlin tells Arthur that he will now be pursuing his own interests, since peace and order have been established in Arthur's kingdom. But Merlin assures a concerned Arthur that he will return to assist him when the lion that is the son of the bear shall run through Great Britain — a prophecy alluding to the later treachery of Arthur's son Mordred.

Summary Based on *EETS* 36, pp. 559–612.

5–6   *the Feste of Assumpcion.* The Feast of the Assumption of the Virgin Mary is celebrated on August 15.

22–23   *And every man brought with hym his wif . . . his love.* It is customary when Arthur holds high court that every man must be accompanied by a woman, whether his wife or his love. One of the earliest occurrences of this practice is found in the twelfth-century Anglo-Norman tale "The Lay of the Horn," attributed to Robert Biket.

56–57   *he made the Quene Gonnore sitte by hym crowned.* Normally at major celebrations the women would not be seated with the men. In Geoffrey of Monmouth's description of Arthur's coronation, for example, the women feast quite separately: "the king went off with the men to feast in his own palace and the queen retired with the married women to feast in hers; for the Britons still observed the ancient custom of Troy, the men celebrating festive occasions with their fellow-men and the women eating separately with the other women" (Thorpe,

p. 229). But because this particular feast is in honor of the Blessed Virgin Mary, Arthur insists on having the women seated on equal terms with the men.

Summary Based on *EETS* 36, pp. 615–18.

89–90   *Kynge Arthur, I grete thee nought.* The messenger has been instructed not to give Arthur a proper salutation, thus emphasizing the insulting nature of the message he brings.

105   *he is lorde from the east into the west.* In keeping with the general vagueness of Arthurian geography, it is never made entirely clear what lands King Rion controls, though it appears to be all the islands in the sea to the west of Britain, the chief of which would be Ireland. It is clear, however, that King Rion, in contrast to Arthur's Saxon foes, is a Christian and rules over a Christian people. He also abides by a more chivalric code of behavior than do the pagan Saxons.

110–11   *And the kynge hit toke to the archebisshop.* It is not clear whether the letter is given to the archbishop as a matter of ceremonial responsibility, or because Arthur lacks the ability to read it himself. It is true, however, that during the earlier Middle Ages many European monarchs were not highly literate.

118–19   *I have made a mantell of reade samyte furred with the beerdes of these kynges.* Beginning with Geoffrey of Monmouth, many Arthurian writers describe the request of an arch foe for Arthur's beard, which they wish to use in the trimming of a cloak or mantle. In Geoffrey of Monmouth, it is a giant called Retho who makes this request and who challenges Arthur to a duel. In the duel Arthur kills the giant and takes *his* beard (Thorpe, p. 240).

144–45   *he seide he sholde not so soone have take the Kynge Leodogan.* King Rion was planning to take his time during the siege of Toraise; now that Arthur has insulted him, he intends to take the city more quickly so that he can get on to the matter of dealing with Arthur.

164–65   *Oure Lorde hath sette yow in His prison.* The prison Arthur is referring to is the harper's "prison" of blindness.

200–01   *to Pharien and to Leonces.* These are the chief lieutenants of King Ban and King Bors who have been minding things in Benoyk and Gannes in the absence of their lords. King Ban and King Bors, of course, are currently fighting at Arthur's side.

248   *that thei neded no salve.* They needed no salve because they are dead — an example of ironic understatement.

345–46   *more than two but lengthe.* That is, they moved apart more than the distance between two archery targets — two "butts."

431–32   *The lyon that is the sone of the bere . . . ye shall have.* Merlin is here foretelling the final confrontation that will occur much later between Arthur and his son Mordred. (Arthur's epithet as "the bear of Britain" appears to have a very early origin; there is a marginal note in one of the "Nennius" MSS indicating that the name Arthur means "the dreadful bear.") One peculiarity of Merlin's prediction is his suggestion that he will return to assist Arthur in his great need against Mordred. In the traditional accounts, however, Merlin plays no role in the final battle between Arthur and Mordred.

Merlin and Nimiane; and Arthur and the Giant of St. Michael's Mount

[Fols. 224r (line 13)–230r (line 28)]

Surprisingly, Arthur's European campaign against the Romans takes up relatively little space in the *PM*. This portion of the Arthurian story originates with Geoffrey of Monmouth's *The History of the Kings of Britain*, comprising more than half of the narrative material concerning Arthur in that work. It is also the central focus in the ME *Alliterative Morte Arthure*; but by the time of Malory's *Morte D'Arthur*, its centrality to Arthur's story was considerably diminished. Arthur's great personal combat against the Giant of St. Michael's Mount also has it origin in Geoffrey of Monmouth's *The History of the Kings of Britain*, and it remains a basic component of the Arthurian narrative in many later medieval accounts. Perhaps the most stirring rendition of this episode is found in the ME

Alliterative Morte Arthure (lines 900–1221), which is also the direct source for Malory's version of the episode in *Morte D'Arthur* (Vinaver, pp. 119–23).

Summary Based on *EETS* 36, pp. 631–34.

Summary Based on *EETS* 36, pp. 635–45.

      In line 9, the arrival of *a group of twelve messengers* provokes Arthur's compaign against the Romans as they demand his allegedly unpaid tribute to the Roman Emperor Lucius. Arthur treats the messengers who bring this demand hospitably, but he sends them back to Rome bearing a strongly hostile reply. In line 13, Britain's claim on Rome is based on *historical precedents*, that is, the exploits of earlier British heroes whose European campaigns are described by Geoffrey of Monmouth — first Belinus and Brennius, and later, Maximianus.

29   *Mounte Seint Michel.* This is the famous Mont Saint Michel, located on the seacoast of Normandy close to the border with Brittany.

58   *Helayn.* The name of the young woman for whom the old woman is grieving is Elaine or Helena; she is the niece of Hoell of Nantes, the Duke of Brittany.

119–20   *the hide of the serpent.* The giant is protected by the skin of a serpent (perhaps a dragon's hide); when Arthur finally kills the giant, he has to lift the skin and stab the giant beneath it.

The Defeat of Lucius; and Arthur and the Devil Cat

[Fols. 230r (line 28)–236v (line 14)

    Stories about monstrous cats or devil cats are common in European folklore and were especially prevalent in medieval France, where the story of the monster cat "Le Capalu" first became associated with the story of Arthur. In early Celtic literature cats were often depicted as possessing dark and demonic powers, and perhaps the most famous of these Celtic cats is the monstrous "Cath Palug." In the *PM*, the story of the murderous monster cat is for all intents and purposes little more than a moral fable about keeping one's promises to God. When the fisherman's selfishness causes him to break his promise to God, he pays a great price personally, and he unleashes this terrible monster on the world.

Summary   Based on *EETS* 36, pp. 650–64.

In line 4, Gawain's impulsive act of cutting off his head, first described by Geoffrey of Monmouth who depicts Gawain as a rash and impassioned youth, jeopardizes the mission and precipitates a great battle. In lines 10–11, the drama of Gawain's killing of Lucius using Calibourn is at odds with most other medieval accounts. Geoffrey of Monmouth states that Lucius was felled by an unknown hand; and Malory, following the account in the ME *Alliterative Morte Arthure*, has Arthur being the one to inflict the fatal wound.

22   *the Assencion*. The Feast of the Ascension of the Virgin, which is celebrated on August 15.

26   *thirty shillings*. Perhaps the amount is intended to suggest a parallel with the pieces of silver Judas received for his betrayal of Christ.

Merlin's Imprisonment; and Gawain and the Dwarf Knight

[Fols. 236v (line 15)–245v (line 33)]

The final section of the *PM* focuses on Merlin's departure from Arthurian society. After saying his personal farewells to Arthur and Blase, his two dearest friends, Merlin proceeds to his fateful rendezvous with Nimiane, knowing that it will result in his permanent imprisonment. Overlapping with this poignant account of Merlin's fated demise is the strange episode of the handsome knight who has been transformed into a dwarf by a woman to whom he denied his love. That enchantment is subsequently shifted from the knight to Gawain, who has gone in search of Merlin. It is while Gawain is still in this dwarfish form that he has his final encounter with Merlin, or rather with the voice of Merlin, for all Gawain is able to see is a misty cloud. After Merlin details his plight to Gawain, Gawain carries the story back to Arthur and the court.

This episode also provides an explanation for Gawain's great courtesy toward women;

for it is when Gawain inadvertently fails to accord proper respect to a woman that the enchantment is cast upon him that transforms him into a dwarf. This explanation for Gawain's kindness toward women is strikingly different from the one provided in Malory's *Morte D'Arthur*; there, the act for which Gawain must atone is the beheading of an innocent lady.

Summary *Based on EETS 36, pp. 669–78.*

Estor (line 9), who is the son of King Ban, is also Lancelot's brother; the usual form of his name is Ector de Maris.

52   *the Seven Artes.* These are Seven Liberal Arts of the Trivium and the Quadrivium. The Trivium, the three verbal arts, are grammar, rhetoric, and logic (or dialectic); the Quadrivium, the four mathematical arts, are arithmetic, geometry, astronomy, and music.

94–95   *Feire swete frende . . . do all youre plesier.* Here Nimiane indicates that she will spend much time with Merlin as his companion in his captivity, and her attitude toward Merlin is clearly benign. But this is not at all the case in Malory's *Morte D'Arthur*, where she desires to be rid of his unwanted attentions. See E. A. Robinson's *Merlin* (1917), which likewise presents an eroticized version of Merlin and Nimiane's happy love of each other in Broceliande.

Summary *Based on EETS 36, pp. 682–89.*

155   *Trinité Sonday.* Trinity Sunday is the Sunday following Pentecost; it usually falls on the first or second Sunday of June, depending on the date of Easter.

210   *he herde a voice a litill upon the right side above.* Gawain hears Merlin's voice coming out of a smoky-mist in the air above him, which is quite a different concept from that suggested in Malory, where Merlin is trapped in the ground beneath a huge rock. In *Morte D'Arthur* it is Bagdemagus, not Gawain, who hears Merlin's voice (Vinaver, p. 81).

318–20   *Ye shull to me swere be the oth . . . er she salue you.* Gawain's oath to never fail lady, maiden, or damsel serves the practical end of undoing the enchantment that has been placed upon him, but it also explains his great courtesy toward women. In Malory, the queen and the ladies of the court force Gawain to swear a similar oath, after he explained why he returned to court with a lady's head hanging from a rope around his neck (Vinaver, p. 67).

Summary Based upon the OF text found in BL Additional MS 10292, from fol. 216r, col. 3, I.14 to its end on fol. 216v, where the OF text concludes with the rubric: "Explicit lenserrement de merlin; / dieux tous a boine fin" [Here ends the imprisonment of Merlin; / May God bring us all to a good end].

Textual Notes

The Birth of Merlin

26   *[assaied]*. MS is illegible.

        [synne]. MS is illegible.

28   *[wolde]*. MS is illegible.

36   *rather.* MS: *raher.*

        [But]. MS is illegible.

38   *[maystrie]*. MS is illegible.

121   *[thi dere]*. MS is illegible.

122   *[aros, and sought aboute]*. MS is illegible.

123   *[therynne, and she ran to the]*. MS is illegible.

125   *[chamber]*. MS is illegible.

135   *[eny]*. MS is illegible.

141   *[on her]*. MS is illegible.

142   *[sorowe made hir]*. MS is illegible.

145   *[thynge myght]*. MS is illegible.

        [this]. MS is illegible.

163   *performe.* MS: *perfome.*

168   *creature.* MS: *crature.*

184   *and* deleted between MS: *frendes axeden.*

214   *anon.* MS: *anono.*

231   *and yef* written twice.

252   *Thus.* MS: *This.*

261   *and so it was* written twice.

262 *the¹* written twice.

263 *it¹* written above line.

264 *And* written twice.

274 *that* written twice.

276 *chelde.* MS: *chede.*

290 *creature.* MS: first *e* written above line.

291 *ye* written above line.

340 *armes.* MS: *pud* (?).

   to written twice.

341 *not.* MS: *no.*

344 *Friende.* MS: *Reinde.*

367 *[Merlin].* MS: *he.*

426 *and¹* written above line.

443 *resteth.* MS: *rested.*

Vortiger's Tower

58 *hymself.* MS: *hymslef.*

71 First letter in *sef* is illegible.

105 *he²* written above line.

113 *quod.* MS: *quo.*

117 *knowes.* MS: *knowe.*

149 *that* repeated in MS.

182 *ther* written twice.

231 *significacion.* MS: *singnificacion.*

278 *sholde be.* MS: *sholbe.*

316 *brethern.* MS: *bethern.*

Vortiger's Demise; The Battle of Salisbury; and The Death of Pendragon

12 *We* written above line.

35	*ther.* MS: *thet.*
40	*brethern.* MS: *bethern.*
43	*weke.* MS: *woke.*
66	*tolde* written twice.
103	*worldes.* MS: *worles.*
122	*covenaunt.* MS: *comenaunt.*
131	*above that* deleted between *hath* and *yove.*

Uther and Ygerne

151–52	*and juwels* are the first words on fol. 23; fols. 22 and 23 have been transposed in the MS.
156	*to* written above line.
220	*yowr.* MS: *yow.*
276	*he²* written above line.
316	*was* written above line.
340	*messager.* MS: *message.*
358	*and seide* deleted after *lawghynge.*
393	*he.* MS: *ye.*
396	*performe.* MS: *perfome.*
412	*as.* MS: *a.*
439	*I* written above line.
445	*a* in *shall* added above line.
466	*thought.* MS: *dought.*
482	*seynynge.* MS: *seynge.*
484	*it.* MS: *is.*
486	*I.* MS: *ye* written above line.
493	*so* written above line.

Arthur and the Sword in the Stone

8   *acordeth*. MS: *acorded*.

20   *thourgh*. MS: *though*.

27   *but* written above line.

29   *cherches*: MS: *cherche*.

41   *never*. MS: *ver* with *ne* inserted above line.

59   *amonge*. MS: *amonges*.

88–89 *that noon*. MS: *that god noon*.

98   *that* written above line.

112   *he* struck through before *oure*.

194   *yow* written above line.

200   *not* written above line.

205   *turnement*. MS: *turment*.

252   *the archebisshop*. MS: *tharchebisshop*.

302   *were*. MS: *we*.

303   *thought*. MS: *dought*.

325   *ther* in *therwith* written above line.

The Barons' Revolt

12   *Arthur*. MS: *archebisshop* with *Arthur* written above line.

87   *thought*. MS: dought.

90 .   *and¹*. MS: an.

97   *part* written above line.

196   *two pence*. MS: *ijd*.

The Grand Tournament at Logres

15   *two*. MS: *tw*.

77   *Savage*. MS: *sauge*.

80   *hem.* MS: *he.*

133   *delyvred.* MS: *delyued.*

169   *[King Arthur].* MS: *he.*

235   *hem.* MS: *he.*

267   *it* written above line.

The Battle of Bredigan Forest

5   *for* deleted before *thei.*

90   *and.* MS: *an.*

144   *the* written above line.

147   *Leonces.* MS: *Leone.*

158   *and².* MS: *a.*

166   *Kynge.* MS: *ky.*

189   *yeve* written twice.

        Following *yeve* in the MS is a misplaced line that reads: *Sir quod Ulfin and this is not the firste tyme.*

229   *hym.* MS: *hem.*

249   *ye* written above line.

The Young Squires

15   *never.* MS: *ever.*

19   *[Kynge Ventres].* MS: *he.*

65   *resteth.* MS: *rested.*

74   *and.* MS: *a.*

92   *com* written above line.

134   *ne* written above line.

181   *bretheren.* MS: *betheren.*

        for. MS: *fo.*

234   *at* written above the line.

247   *evry*. MS: *euy*.

The Deeds of the Young Squires

61   *as*. MS: *at*.

83   *ther*. MS: *the*.

93   *his²* written twice.

103   *brotheres*. MS: *brother*.

176   *thei*. MS: *the*.

205   *and* deleted before *heilde*.

244   *heed* written above line.

259   *a* deleted after *as*.

272   *a* written above line.

Arthur at Tamelide

3–4   *Tamelide* and *Toraise* are transposed in the MS.

41   *worthynesse*. MS: *wordynesse*.

120   *of* written twice.

130   *he*. MS: *it*.

188   *that*. MS: *than*.

292   *Blois*. MS: *Blios*.

302   *Amadius*. MS: *anmadius*.

411   *plesynge*. MS: *pelesynge*.

453   *displese*. MS: *dispelse*.

Merlin and the Young Squires

4   *served*. MS: *serneved*.

69   *sones*. MS: *sone*.

81	*mysbelevinge.* MS: *mybelevinge.*
97	*sholdered.* MS: *sholderes.*
162	*felowes.* MS: *felowles.*
163	*sone as* written above live.
218	*so* written above line.
234	*lothly.* MS: *lotly.*
236	*taken.* MS: *tken.*
276	*troubled.* MS: *trouble.*
359	*while.* MS: *wihile.*
367	*wend.* MS: *we.*
382	*the²* written above line.
392	*and.* MS: *a.*

Gawain's Rescue of his Mother

16	*men.* MS: *man.*
23	*than.* MS: *tha.*
	Taurus. MS: *Teucus.*
88	*shull* deleted between *ne* and *may.*
114	*smote.* MS: *somte.*
170	*it* between *lady* and *understode* is struck through in the MS.

Merlin and Nimiane

35	*thus* written above the line.
53	*speke.* MS: *seyde.*
82	*whan it* written twice.
175	*and³* written twice.
197	*it* canceled between *bringe* and *to ende.*

Arthur and Gonnore; and The Battle against King Rion

15   *thei.* MS: *the.*

87   *the³* written twice.

168   Three words struck through between *armes* and *and.*

269   *malentelent.* MS: *mantelent.*

318   *thyn.* MS: *thym.*

327   *that he wolde telle hym* deleted between *covenaunt* and *what.*

408   *com* written in margin.

428   *ne* written above line.

Arthur and Gawain

31   *thei.* MS: *the.*

58   *in* written above line.

105   Three words expunged between *wellcome* and *and.*

124   *Knyghtes* written above line.

223   *and.* MS: *a*

The Begetting of Lancelot; and Merlin and Nimiane

46   Final *s* in *grasses* inserted above line.

50   *in* written above line.

94   *not.* MS: *no.*

168   *yet.* MS: *ye.*

Merlin and Grisandolus

6   *that Merlin* written twice

8   *is.* MS: *it.*

        the trouthe. MS: *throuthe.*

32   *Avenable.* MS: *Auable.*

90   *valiaunt.* MS: *vailaunt.*

119   An extra *that he were not knowen* deleted between *wey* and *with.*

       hand. MS: *nekke.*

154   *Thus.* MS: *this.*

155   *an* added above line.

162   *rode.* MS: *rde.*

211   *hem.* MS: *hym.*

273   *with.* MS: *wt.*

301   *se* added above line.

348   *foreste.* MS: *freste.*

362   *spake.* MS: *sapake.*

378   *be* added above line.

396   *douteth.* MS: *doutheth.*

402   *scornynge.* MS: *sornynge.*

426   *the* added above line.

460   *not hir.* MS: *nothir.*

487   *to* written twice.

493   *messager.* MS: *messagers.*

495   *he.* MS: *and.*

499   *I.* MS: *ye.*

The Marriage of Arthur and Gonnore

13   *the* written twice.

58   *bide* written above line.

60   *not.* MS: *no.*

107   *men.* MS: *me.*

185   *thei.* MS: *and.*

196   *that the slytte hym to the teth, and Ulfin smote another* deleted between *another* and *that.*

211   *be* deleted between *nothinge* and *dismayed.*

223   *he.* MS: *the.*

229   *and².* MS: *a.*

The Banishment of Bertelak; and King Arthur and King Lot

73   *in-* in *into* added above line.

76   *that vitaile* written twice.

367   *to* written above line.

The Tournament at Logres; King Lot and his Sons; and Morgan and Gyomar

16   *no* written above line.

       [the Kynge Arthur]. MS: *he.*

59   First *g* in *syngynge* added above line.

65   Second *wo-* in *workewoman* added above line.

124   *his.* MS: *hir.*

208   *than.* MS: *that.*

233   *And.* MS: *As.*

363   *Thei* written twice.

King Arthur vs. King Rion

117   First *e* in *theire* added above line.

120   *the* written above line.

200   *[Merlin].* MS: *he.*

215   *fader.* MS: *fade.*

284   *valiaunt.* MS: *vailaunt.*

359   *hem.* MS: *he.*

       remenaunt. MS: *renenaunt.*

382   *valiante.* MS: *vailante.*

Textual Notes

389   *and².* MS: *a.*

Merlin and Nimiane; and Arthur and the Giant of St. Michael's Mount

22   *thei.* MS: *the.*

The Defeat of Lucius; and Arthur and the Devil Cat

5   *[the Kynge Arthur].* MS: *he.*

26   *thirty shillings.* MS: *xxxs.*

83   *hym.* MS: *hy.*

125   *kynge* written above line.

Merlin's Imprisonment; and Gawain and the Dwarf Knight

15   *loved.* MS: *love.*

19   *and.* MS: *a.*

118   *thourgh* written above line.

142   *God.* MS: *go.*

284   *so.* MS: *se.*

318   *ye* written above line.

330   *ever.* MS: *evever.*

Volumes in the Middle English Texts Series

The Floure and the Leafe, The Assemblie of Ladies, and *The Isle of Ladies*, ed. Derek Pearsall (1990)

Three Middle English Charlemagne Romances, ed. Alan Lupack (1990)

Six Ecclesiastical Satires, ed. James M. Dean (1991)

Heroic Women from the Old Testament in Middle English Verse, ed. Russell A. Peck (1991)

The Canterbury Tales: Fifteenth-Century Continuations and Additions, ed. John M. Bowers (1992)

Gavin Douglas, *The Palis of Honoure*, ed. David J. Parkinson (1992)

Wynnere and Wastoure and The Parlement of the Thre Ages, ed. Warren Ginsberg (1992)

The Shewings of Julian of Norwich, ed. Georgia Ronan Crampton (1993)

King Arthur's Death: The Middle English Stanzaic Morte Arthur and Alliterative Morte Arthure, ed. Larry D. Benson and Edward E. Foster (1994)

Lancelot of the Laik and Sir Tristrem, ed. Alan Lupack (1994)

Sir Gawain: Eleven Romances and Tales, ed. Thomas Hahn (1995)

The Middle English Breton Lays, ed. Anne Laskaya and Eve Salisbury (1995)

Sir Perceval of Galles and Ywain and Gawain, ed. Mary Flowers Braswell (1995)

Four Middle English Romances: Sir Isumbras, Octavian, Sir Eglamour of Artois, Sir Tryamour, ed. Harriet Hudson (1996)

The Poems of Laurence Minot (1333–1352), ed. Richard H. Osberg (1996)

Medieval English Political Writings, ed. James M. Dean (1996)

The Book of Margery Kempe, ed. Lynn Staley (1996)

Amis and Amiloun, Robert of Ciseyle, and Sir Amadace, ed. Edward E. Foster (1997)

The Cloud of Unknowing, ed. Patrick Gallacher (1997)

Robin Hood and Other Outlaw Tales, ed. Stephen Knight and Thomas H. Ohlgren (1997)

The Poems of Robert Henryson, ed. Robert Kindrick (1997)

Moral Love Songs and Laments, ed. Susanna Greer Fein (1998)

John Lydgate, *Troy Book: Selections*, ed. Robert R. Edwards (1998)

Thomas Usk, *The Testament of Love*, ed. R. Allen Shoaf (1998)

Prose Merlin, ed. John Conlee (1998)

Middle English Marian Lyrics, ed. Karen Saupe (1998)

Four Romances of England: King Horn, Havelok the Dane, Bevis of Hampton, Athelston, ed. Ronald B. Herzman, Graham Drake, and Eve Salisbury (1998)

Other TEAMS Publications

Documents of Practice Series:

Love and Marriage in Late Medieval London, by Shannon McSheffrey (1995)

A Slice of Life: Selected Documents of Medieval English Peasant Experience, edited, translated, and with an introduction by Edwin Brezette DeWindt (1996)

Sources for the History of Medicine in Late Medieval London, by Carole Rawcliffe (1996)

Regular Life: Monastic, Canonical, and Mendicant Rules, selected with an introduction by Douglas J. McMillan and Kathryn Smith Fladenmuller (1997)

Commentary Series:

Commentary on the Book of Jonah, by Haimo of Auxere, translated with an introduction by Deborah Everhart (1993)

Medieval Exegesis in Translation: Commentaries on the Book of Ruth, translated with an introduction by Lesley Smith (1996)

Nicholas of Lyra's Apocalypse Commentary, translated with an introduction and notes by Philip D. W. Krey (1997)

Rabbi Ezra Ben Solomon of Gerona: Commentary on the Song of Songs and Other Kabbalistic Commentaries, selected, translated, and annotated by Seth Brody (1998)

To order please contact:

MEDIEVAL INSTITUTE PUBLICATIONS
Western Michigan University
Kalamazoo, MI 49008–3801
Phone (616) 387–8755
FAX (616) 387–8750

http://www.wmich.edu/medieval/mip/mipubshome/html